Welcome to

McGraw-Hill Education

ASVAB

Congratulations! You've chosen *McGraw-Hill Education: ASVAB.* You probably know McGraw-Hill Education from many of the textbooks you used in school or college. Now we're ready to help you reach your next goal—an exciting career in the U.S. Armed Forces.

This book gives you everything you need to succeed on the ASVAB. You'll get in-depth instruction and review of every topic tested, tips and strategies for every question type, and plenty of practice exams to boost your test-taking confidence. You'll also get answers to your questions about enlistment and jobs in today's military. Additionally, in the following pages you'll find:

- **How to Get the Most Out of This Book:** A map of what you can find in this book.

- **What It Takes to Achieve Enlistment:** Learn the difference between selection and classification and how the military uses your ASVAB scores.

- **Your ASVAB Preparation Program:** Figure out what you know and don't know and decide on a study strategy.

- **Your ASVAB Study Schedule:** Be focused with your study time.

- **Test-Time Advice:** Follow this good advice.

- **Other Criteria for Enlistment:** Keep these factors in mind as you apply for the military.

ABOUT McGRAW-HILL EDUCATION

This book has been created by a unit of McGraw-Hill Education. McGraw-Hill Education is a leading global provider of instructional assessment, and reference materials in both print and digital form. McGraw-Hill Education has offices in 33 countries and publishes in more than 65 languages. With a broad range of products and services—from traditional textbooks to the latest in online and multimedia learning—we engage, stimulate, and empower students and professionals of all ages, helping them meet the increasing challenges of the 21st-century knowledge economy.

Mc
Graw
Hill
Education

Learn more. **Do more.**

How to Get the Most Out of This Book

This book provides all the material you need to score well on the ASVAB. It will teach you the knowledge that is required for this difficult exam, including information about every type of question the test includes. It also provides ample practice for you to refine the skills you are learning and then test yourself with full-length practice tests. To make the best use of this book, follow the following suggestions. Then develop your own personalized ASVAB study plan (see Chapter 6).

1 **If you are not sure which branch of the military interests you:**
- Read Chapter 1: "Deciding on Military Service."
- Go to Part 5 and learn about various military occupations.

2 **If you want to know about the ASVAB and why scoring high matters to you:**
- Read Chapter 2: "Introducing the ASVAB."
- Read Chapter 3: "ASVAB Scores and Score Reports."
- Read Chapter 4: "The ASVAB, the AFQT, and Military Entrance."
- Read Chapter 5: "Taking the CAT-ASVAB."

3 **If you want general study tips and guidelines for planning your study:**
- Review Chapter 6: "Follow These Suggestions to Ace the ASVAB."

4 **If you want to find out how well you might do right now on the real ASVAB:**
- Take the ASVAB Diagnostic Test Form in Part 2 and use it to identify your strengths and weaknesses.

5 **If you want to refresh your knowledge of the ASVAB subject areas:**
- Go to Part 3 of this book, which provides a complete review of every topic tested.

6 **If you want to practice taking the ASVAB test:**
- Go to Part 4 of this book and take the ASVAB Practice Test Forms 1 through 3 under actual test conditions.

7 **If you want to know about how high you have to score for specific jobs and training programs in the military:**
- Go to Part 5 of this book.

What It Takes to Achieve Enlistment

You can think of military enlistment as a two-step process: first selection and then classification. To be initially "selected" to enter the military at all, you need to do well on the ASVAB, in particular on four of the eight tests that make up the Armed Forces Qualifying Test (AFQT). So it is important to focus on those four tests: Arithmetic Reasoning, Word Knowledge, Paragraph Comprehension, and Mathematics Knowledge. You need to score well on those four tests in order to reach the minimum AFQT score to even be considered for enlistment. You should aim for higher than the minimum; the higher your score, the more job and training options you have.

Once you meet the selection criteria, the second step is classification. That means a review of your scores in various combinations, called line scores, to see which jobs/training program you are eligible for. Many of the line scores include one or more of the initial AFQT scores, so, again, concentrating on the four AFQT tests is very important.

ASVAB Factoids

The ASVAB is the most widely-used multiple aptitude test in the world.

The ASVAB was introduced in 1968. Over 40 million examinees have taken various updated forms of the ASVAB since then.

The ASVAB is administered via both computer and paper and pencil. Roughly 70 percent of military applicants take the test via computer.

The CAT-ASVAB was implemented after 20 years of extensive research and evaluation. It was the first large-scale adaptive test battery to be administered in a high-stakes setting.

On average, the CAT-ASVAB takes about half the time of the paper-and-pencil ASVAB.

The Assembling Objects test is taken by all military applicants, but only used by the Navy.

Women compose about 16 percent of enlisted personnel in the military.

Your ASVAB Preparation Program

Take the Diagnostic Test

Start your ASVAB preparation program by taking the Diagnostic Test in Part 2 of this book. The steps outlined as follows will help you figure out what you know and don't know. Be sure to read the directions for each test and work as fast as you can while being very careful with your answers.

Starting on page 116, you can begin to score each of the tests. Depending on how well you do, you may be happy with the results or realize that you need to buckle down and start to study hard. Here is an example of how to interpret your scores:

Part 4. Paragraph Comprehension

Item Number	Correct Answer	Mark X if You Picked the Correct Answer
1	A	X
2	B	
3	C	X
4	A	
5	D	X
6	B	
7	A	X
8	B	X
9	C	
10	A	X
11	C	X
12	A	
13	B	X
14	C	
15	D	X
Total Correct		**9**

Score Interpretation–Total Correct

15 14	This is pretty good work. Review the explanations of the answers you got incorrect. This test is a part of the AFQT, and you must do well.
13 12	You are doing pretty well. Review the explanations for the items you got incorrect. This test is a part of the AFQT, and you must do well.
11 10 9 8 7 6 5 4 3 2 1 0	You need to keep studying. Pay close attention to the explanations for each item, even for the ones you got correct. This will help you understand why the answer is correct. Spend time reviewing the Paragraph Comprehension and Word Knowledge reviews in Part 3 of this book. Keep reading books and newspapers.

If you scored 11 or lower on this test (the dark gray area for any of the tests in this book), you need to put some skin in the game and start studying. Fortunately, your ASVAB book shows you how to do better in two ways. First, for the Diagnostic Test and the other three full ASVAB tests, this ASVAB book gives you the explanation for the correct answers. For example, for the Paragraph Comprehension test, pages 132 and 133 give you an explanation of why each correct answer is correct. This type of information is provided for the Diagnostic Test and the other three practice tests. Be sure to read the explanations because they will help you do better on the real ASVAB.

Second, for the Paragraph Comprehension test, there is an entire review section that helps to build your skills in this important ASVAB area. The review information for Paragraph Comprehension starts on page 227. This type of information is provided for each of the content areas as described in the next section.

If you faithfully follow this advice, you will know which tests you need to focus on with more time and energy. That's where you should put in more study time.

Review ASVAB Test Content

Starting on page 141, you will find an extensive review of all the ASVAB test topics starting with the General Science test. Each content area is thoroughly covered and contains an end-of-section quiz that will help you figure out if you learned the material in the review section. Where you answered incorrectly, go back to the section and study the material until you are sure you understand it.

This book provides almost 200 pages of content review, because you can't predict specifically what information will be asked on the ASVAB. Part 3 covers all ASVAB test topics and gives you the tools you need to answer ASVAB questions. For example, you will learn how to figure out vocabulary words, how to set up math problems to get the right answer, how to answer geometry items, how to decipher levers and pulleys, how to figure out electrical circuits, how to conquer angles and geometric shapes, how to answer auto and shop questions, and hundreds of other topics that you could be tested on.

Memorizing *isn't* always the best way to score high on the ASVAB. Be sure that you *understand* the concepts behind each question. For example, you could memorize the answer to a math question, but on the real ASVAB you probably won't find that same question. You will need to understand the steps in solving the problem, regardless of the numbers involved.

Take the Practice Tests

Once you have taken the Diagnostic Test, reviewed the test content that you needed to study, and taken the end-of-section quizzes, you are now ready to test yourself again. Go to page 337 to start the first test form in the book. Sit in a quiet location and prepare to spend about 2 to 2½ hours taking this test. Make sure you have a few pencils and a clock to show the time.

Carefully tear out page 339 and use it as your answer sheet. When you are ready to begin, read the instructions for each section and answer the questions to the best of your ability. When you have finished, go to pages 388 to 396 and compare your answers with the correct answers. Check the score interpretation chart for each subject test. If your number of correct answers is in the dark gray area, you need to review that test content in depth to raise your score. You will probably find some areas where you can improve. Go back to Part 3 of this book and spend some quality time studying. If your number of correct answers is in the light gray area, you're doing better, but you should still spend some time studying that content area to improve your score.

Here are some tips to help you prioritize your study time:

● If your scores are in the dark gray area on the AFQT tests—Arithmetic Reasoning, Word Knowledge, Paragraph Comprehension, or Mathematics Knowledge—you should spend most of your time on the AFQT subjects.

● If your scores on the AFQT tests are in the light gray areas but you have other scores in the dark gray areas, go back and review the content for tests where your scores were lowest.

● If all of your scores are in the light gray areas, focus again on the four AFQT tests.

● If it takes you more than 2½ hours to complete each test form, try to speed up your pace. This is particularly important on the four AFQT tests.

Plan Your Study Time

Let's be realistic. Maybe you were a whiz kid in high school and just need to brush up your knowledge and skills. Perhaps you totally blew off high school and just got your diploma by the skin of your teeth, or perhaps you have been away from school activities for a few years.

Regardless of your situation, the advice in the previous section on how to use this book is right on target. The difference may be in the amount of time you need to spend on getting yourself up to speed on the content of a particular test.

If you just need a refresher, you should probably spend about one to two hours per day for two weeks in focused study. If you really need to improve after starting from a low point, you should plan on one to three months of work, at least 8 to 10 hours per week.

Set up your study schedule accordingly. Use the chart in Figure 6.3 to see an example of what you might do, and then you can construct your own schedule with the chart in Figure 6.4.

Don't be a couch potato. Add some exercise into your schedule as it will keep your brain clear and your stress level down. This will also help you in the enlistment process, as you will need a decent level of fitness to be accepted into the military and to do well in your basic training. Keep in mind that many military applicants are rejected because they are not in shape!

Study Tips

Dos:

- Find a quiet place to study. Quiet means no TV, texting, phone, or other distractions.

- Take notes and summarize what you have learned as you move through the material.

- Highlight special facts or concepts you want to remember.

- Take a break every 30 to 45 minutes.

- Think about the kinds of test questions you might be asked as you study the content review sections of this book.

- Eat healthy foods and eliminate fatty foods and alcohol.

- Stick to your study schedule but be sure to also include a decent amount of sleep each night.

Don'ts:

- Pretend you are studying, when you are actually daydreaming or multitasking. You are just wasting your time if you are not focused.

- Study with others unless they are very serious about studying for the ASVAB or they are serious about helping you study.

- Wait until the last few days before the real test to start studying.

- Get stressed out. Know and believe that if you study the material you will do well on the ASVAB.

Test-Time Advice

The Day Before the Test

- It's too late to cram now. You have followed a good study schedule and have prioritized your studies. Be proud of your hard work. It will pay off.

- Put this book down and just use the day to get some fresh air. Go for a run or a long walk, or relax with your favorite hobby.

- Eat light, healthy meals and go to sleep a little earlier than usual. No alcohol, please. Try for a good eight hours of shut-eye.

The Day of the Test

- Get up early and take a short walk or run. A half-hour of exercise will do you wonders. It will clear the cobwebs from your brain and help you relax.

- Spend a few minutes skimming any important notes you may have taken—no more than a half-hour, though.

- Have a decent breakfast, but no sticky buns or heavy, fatty food. Think cereal, yogurt, fruit, eggs, veggies, milk, and coffee. You won't feel your best if you overload on goopy food.

- Do some deep-breathing exercises to relieve any stress.

- Get to the testing room with time to spare. No sense in adding more pressure on yourself by running late.

- Adjust your attitude upward. You have worked hard, you know the material, and you will do well. Be confident in your ability. Turn your knowledge into a powerhouse of confidence.

During the Test

- Show your stuff. If you have followed the study and review suggestions in this book, you will be able to go into the real test with a positive attitude. Feel confident that you've got the right stuff to succeed in the military.

- Breathe. Take a few moments to breathe deeply and relax if you get stressed during the test. You will feel better.

- Pace yourself. Budget enough time for each question so that you won't have to rush at the end of the section.

- Stay focused. Ignore the things going on around you that you cannot control.

- Use what you know. When you don't know the answer and need to guess, try to make an educated guess by eliminating answer choices that you know are wrong. The more you can eliminate, the better your chance of getting the answer right.

Other Criteria for Enlistment

Education

Success in any branch of the military depends on a good education, and a high school diploma is most desirable. Candidates with a GED can enlist, but some services may limit opportunities. It is very difficult to be considered a serious candidate without either a high school diploma or accepted alternative credential. Your minimum score on the AFQT will change depending on whether or not you have a regular high school diploma. In any case, staying in school is important for entering the military.

Physical Requirements

Because of the varying physical demands on service members in each branch, physical requirements vary greatly. These differences can vary even within each branch of the service. Generally speaking, potential service members should be in good physical condition, of appropriate weight, and be able to pass a standard physical screening prior to entry. Certain physical conditions can disqualify you, but talking with a recruiter will help you understand the specifics.

Behavior and Moral Character

The services do not want to enlist troublemakers or persons with serious offenses. Each service takes a different approach to evaluating the severity and number of offenses on a candidate's record. The results of this evaluation may—or may not—disqualify candidates. A review is done on a case-by-case basis.

A word of caution: The military looks down on persons who lie about their record. The military conducts background checks; if you've provided false information, you'll be exposed as a liar and receive the appropriate punishment.

Age Requirements

Take a look at the following chart to see the age requirements for each of the services and the Coast Guard.

	Army	Marine Corps	Navy	Air Force	Coast Guard
Active Duty	17–35	17–29	17–34	17–39	17–27
Reserve	17–35	17–29	18–39	17–38	17–39
Guard	17–35	N/A	N/A	17–39	N/A
Service Academies	17–22	17–22	17–22	17–22	17–22

Gender

Both men and women are eligible to enlist in the military. As of January 2016, all jobs in the military are open to women. The percentage of women serving on active duty in the military has doubled since 1978. Clearly, women play a very important role in today's military. Each service has physical requirements specific to female enlistees.

Citizenship

Noncitizens may enlist. However, each service has its own enlistment requirements for noncitizens. You should contact a recruiter for details about a specific situation. For enlistment purposes, the United States includes Guam, Puerto Rico, the U.S. Virgin Islands, the Northern Marianas Islands, American Samoa, the Federated States of Micronesia, the Marshall Islands, and Palau. There are some special programs for certain ethic and cultural groups who may want to enlist.

NOW GO ACE THE ASVAB! YOU CAN DO IT!
BEST WISHES FOR A SUCCESSFUL MILITARY CAREER

McGRAW-HILL
EDUCATION
ASVAB

McGRAW-HILL
EDUCATION
ASVAB

Armed Services
Vocational Aptitude Battery

Fourth Edition

Dr. Janet E. Wall

Former Manager
ASVAB Career Exploration Program
Department of Defense

New York Chicago San Francisco Athens London Madrid
Mexico City Milan New Delhi Singapore Sydney Toronto

1 2 3 4 5 6 7 8 9   LHS   21 20 19 18 17 16 (book alone)
1 2 3 4 5 6 7 8 9   LHS   21 20 19 18 17 16 (book for set)

ISBN 978-1-259-83700-5 (book alone)
MHID   1-259-83700-9

ISBN 978-1-259-83705-0 (book and disk set)
MHID   1-259-83705-X

ISBN 978-1-259-83702-9 (book for set)
MHID   1-259-83702-5

e-ISBN 978-1-259-83701-2 (e-book alone)
e-MHID   1-259-83701-7

e-ISBN 978-1-259-83704-3 (e-book and disk set)
e-MHID   1-259-83704-1

McGraw-Hill Education books are available at special quantity discounts to use as premiums and sales promotions, or for use in corporate training programs. To contact a representative please visit the Contact Us pages at www.mhprofessional.com.

The views expressed in this book are those of the author and do not reflect the official position of the Department of Defense or any other agency of the U.S. Government.

ASVAB is a registered trademark of the United States Department of Defense, which was not involved in the production of, and does not endorse, this product.

The Electronics Information, Auto and Shop Information, and Mechanical Comprehension portions of this book were contributed by David Tenenbaum.

CONTENTS

Foreword

If you are interested in joining the U.S. Army, Navy, Marine Corps, Air Force, or Coast Guard, you should understand the importance of the Armed Services Vocational Aptitude Battery, or ASVAB, and prepare yourself to achieve the highest possible score on it when you take the test.

The strength of the Armed Forces of the United States is based on intelligent service members who can exercise initiative, effectively operate the highly technical equipment that provides us a competitive advantage over potential enemies, and think quickly and logically.

That is why the ASVAB, a battery of tests that measure aptitude in a wide variety of skills, is administered to everyone who wants to enlist in the American military services. Applicants must attain at least a minimum score to be accepted. The higher the score you achieve, the more military occupational specialties will be made available to you from which to choose.

McGraw-Hill Education ASVAB provides information and practice tests on the various areas measured by the ASVAB. A systematic study of this book will help you not only to increase your relevant knowledge of essential information, but also to familiarize yourself with the test to increase your confidence when you take it. Use this book to score high on the ASVAB so you will have more opportunities in the military.

The author of this book, Dr. Janet E. Wall, is a uniquely qualified expert on the ASVAB. Her educational and professional accomplishments in career development and assessment are nationally recognized. As manager of the ASVAB Career Exploration Program, she has been a leader in the design of, and provided content to, the ASVAB program for several years as an official in the Department of Defense.

Good luck on the ASVAB, and thank you for considering service to our country.

Lieutenant General (U.S. Army, Retired) Robert G. Gard, Jr., PhD
Former Director, Human Resources Development, U.S. Army
Former President, National Defense University

Introduction

If you are considering buying this book or have already done so, you must be interested in the Armed Services Vocational Aptitude Battery—the ASVAB. Without a doubt, this book is for you. It is packed with information and advice to help you do your best on the test. If you pay close attention to the advice you'll find here, you can get a much better ASVAB score.

Why should you pay attention to the advice? If you are interested in learning about careers and career planning, the ASVAB can help you know about yourself and how well you are suited for various occupations so that you can make better decisions. If your goal is to enter the military, you will want to perform your best on the ASVAB so that your options for military training programs and careers are the very best possible. In either case, this book will help you reach your goals. In either case, you need this book.

The contents of this book are based on the very latest reports and documents provided and sponsored by the U.S. Department of Defense (DoD) as of this writing. On occasion, DoD may make some small changes that are not reflected here.

Part 1 of this book will help you learn about the various branches of the military so that you can determine which opportunities are best for you. This information comes directly from the Services. It will show you how and why your ASVAB results matter to the military and matter to you. You will also learn about the differences between the paper-and-pencil ASVAB and the computer versions.

This section will also provide you with successful study skills and "blue-ribbon" test-taking strategies that you can use to reach your goals. These strategies are some of the most powerful and effective ones known today. By using the information in this section, you will learn how to plan your studying activities to fit your schedule.

Part 2 contains a full-length simulated ASVAB form that is just like the real thing! By taking this Diagnostic Test Form, you will find out exactly what to expect on the ASVAB. You will also learn which kinds of test questions you can answer with confidence, and which kinds give you difficulty. By pinpointing your ASVAB strengths and weaknesses, you will be able to focus your preparation on the test topics that you need to study most. This section will also provide you with the exact directions that you will hear from your test administrator and see in your test booklet if you are taking the paper-and-pencil version of the test. No other test preparation book has this information. You'll also find an exact replica of the actual answer sheet you will use with the paper-and-pencil version. At the end of the test, you will be able to see the answers to the items and explanations that will help you understand why the correct answer is correct and why the other answers are wrong. The information in these explanations can help you prepare for the real ASVAB.

Part 3 of this book will give you the most comprehensive review of the ASVAB test topics you are likely to encounter. No other book on the market and no existing website will provide you with as complete a content review as this book does. These topic reviews are keyed to the ASVAB and can definitely help you improve your ASVAB scores, but they can also help you score high on other tests such as the SAT and ACT. You'll also find topic-based quizzes that can help you know your strengths and weaknesses.

Part 4 contains three additional full-length model ASVAB forms. Each one gives you the opportunity to practice taking a test that is just like the real ASVAB. Use these Practice Test Forms to strengthen your test-taking skills. Take each one under actual test conditions. Use a timer to help you keep track of the time limit for each section. Keep a record of your results and note the improvements you see from one test to the next in your scores and in the number of questions you are able to answer in the time allowed, Practice is the key to higher ASVAB scores! In addition, read the answer explanations that follow each test form. These explanations offer you even more information about the tested area beyond the review sections. Between the subject area reviews and these explanations, you will certainly be in a position to score at the upper end of the ASVAB.

Part 5 gives you information on military occupations, including a description of the occupation, what people in the occupation do, helpful attributes, training provided, physical demands, work environment, civilian counterparts, opportunities, and services that offer that occupation.

HOW TO USE THIS BOOK

If you are not sure which branch of the military interests you:

- Read Chapter 1: "Deciding on Military Service."
- Go to Part 5 and learn about various military occupations.

If you want to know about the ASVAB and why it is important to the military:

- Read Chapter 2: "Introducing to the ASVAB."
- Read Chapter 3: "ASVAB Scores and Score Reports."
- Read Chapter 4: "The ASVAB, the AFQT, and Military Entrance."
- Read Chapter 5: "Taking the CAT-ASVAB."

If you want general study tips and guidelines for planning your study:

- Review Chapter 6: "Follow These Suggestions to Ace the ASVAB."

If you want to find out how well you might do right now on the real ASVAB:

- Take the ASVAB Diagnostic Test Form in Part 2 and use it to identify your strengths and weaknesses.

If you want to refresh your knowledge of the ASVAB test areas:

- Go to Part 3 of this book, which provides a complete review of every topic tested.

If you want to practice taking the ASVAB test:

- Go to Part 4 of this book and take ASVAB Practice Test Forms 1 through 3 under actual test conditions.

If you want to know about how high you have to score for specific jobs and training programs in the military:

- Go to Part 5 of this book.

This book contains information that was current and accurate at the time of writing. On occasion the branches of the military change policies and requirements, so checking with a military recruiter will give you the most current data.

This book does not guarantee that it contains the actual ASVAB test questions. There are several forms of the paper-and-pencil version of the ASVAB and many hundreds of items on the computerized version of the test. This book, if you use it as we recommend, will certainly give you a major advantage in scoring high on the ASVAB. This will give you increased job and training opportunities that will help you in your military career and in civilian jobs.

Good luck in your efforts!

Part 1

ALL
ABOUT
THE
ASVAB

Chapter 1

Deciding on Military Service

YOUR GOALS FOR THIS CHAPTER:

- **Find out about opportunities in the armed services.**
- **Learn about enlistment, training, advancement, and education programs in each service branch.**
- **Get information about military pay and benefits.**

Your choice to join the military is a personal one. You may wish to join because it is an honorable family tradition. You may wish to join because the military offers you the best training and education opportunities available to you or anyone. You may wish to join because the military is the largest employer of young people just starting their careers. You may wish to join because you have a deep desire to give back to your country what it has given you, your family, and your friends.

Regardless of your motivation, the decision to join the military is a serious and important one that will influence your life in many ways.

One of your first decisions will be to identify the branch of the armed services you wish to join. Your decision will determine what you do, where you live, what training you will receive, and your future opportunities.

The following pages give you an overview of the four branches of military service and the Coast Guard, and the benefits you can obtain by joining.

OPPORTUNITIES IN THE ARMY

Today's "Army of Excellence" is a modern and powerful military force composed of about 81,968 officers, 15,853 warrant officers, and 463,886 enlisted soldiers. Army men and women work in many types of jobs, ranging from general administration to the operation and maintenance of the Army's many

thousands of weapons, vehicles, aircraft, and highly technical electronic systems. Soldiers, working as a team, perform the Army's mission of protecting the security of the United States and its vital resources. The Army stands constantly ready to defend American interests and the interests of our allies through land-based operations anywhere in the world. The Army needs 77,900 new enlistees (62,500 regular, 15,400 reserve) and 6,170 new officers (5,350 ROTC, 820 Officer Candidate School) each year. Those who enlist in the Army will find hundreds of challenging career opportunities that can offer a lifetime of security and excitement to them and their families.

Enlistment

You can enlist in the Army for three, four, five, or six years. You must be between 17 and 35 years old, an American citizen or registered alien, and in good health and physical condition. To determine what careers you are best suited for, you must take the Armed Services Vocational Aptitude Battery (ASVAB). The ASVAB is offered at most high schools and at military enlistment processing sites.

In most cases, qualified applicants can be guaranteed their choice of training or duty assignment. There are often combinations of guarantees that are particularly attractive to those who are qualified. For those who wish to be guaranteed a specific school, a particular area of assignment, or both, the Army offers the Future Soldier Training Program (FSTP). An applicant for the FSTP can reserve a school or an assignment choice as much as one year in advance of entry into active duty. Other enlistment programs include the Army Civilian Acquired Skills Program, which gives recognition to those skills acquired through civilian training or experience. This program allows enlisted members with previously acquired training to be promoted more quickly than they ordinarily would be. In some cases, the Army also offers enlistment bonuses.

Enlistment programs and options vary from time to time. Local Army recruiters always have the latest information and are ready to answer inquiries without obligation.

Training

Initial Army training is provided in two phases: basic training and advanced individual training (job training).

Basic Training Basic training is a rigorous 10-week orientation for men and women entering the Army. Basic training transforms new enlistees from civilians into soldiers. During basic training, new soldiers gain the discipline, spirit, pride, knowledge, and physical conditioning necessary to perform Army duties. Army basic training is given in four locations throughout the country, including training centers in South Carolina, Georgia, Oklahoma, and Missouri.

Upon reporting for basic training, new soldiers are assigned to a training company and are issued uniforms and equipment. They are introduced to their training leaders, otherwise known as drill sergeants. Drill sergeants are experienced noncommissioned officers who direct soldiers' training to ensure that they are successful.

Army basic training stresses teamwork. Soldiers are trained in groups known as squads or platoons. These groups range from 9 to approximately 80 soldiers; they are small enough that individual soldiers can be recognized for their special abilities. Such groups tend to become closely knit teams and develop group pride and camaraderie during the 10 weeks of rigorous training they experience together.

Basic training is conducted on a demanding schedule, but individual soldiers progress at the rate they can handle best. Soldiers attend a variety of classes that include first aid, CPR, land navigation, physical fitness, self-defense, and military drills. All training emphasizes teamwork and Army values and,

therefore, includes classes in human relations. These classes help trainees from different backgrounds learn to work closely together. Only limited personal time is available during basic training, but there is plenty of time for receiving and answering mail, for personal care, and for attending religious services.

Advanced Individual Training After basic training, Army soldiers go directly to advanced individual training in the occupational field that they have chosen and qualified for, where they learn a specific Army job. Advanced individual training schools are located at many Army bases throughout the country.

The Army offers skills training in a wide range of career fields, including programs maintenance, administration, electronics, healthcare, construction, and combat specialty occupations, to name a few.

Advanced individual training students generally attend traditional classes very similar to those in a high school or college. These classes are supplemented with demonstrations by highly qualified instructors and by practical exercises that use hands-on training, Army equipment, or Army procedures in a way that prepares students for their jobs. Many soldiers also receive on-the-job training, learning job skills by working at a job with other soldiers under the guidance of qualified instructors.

All advance individual training courses are reviewed by the American Council on Education (ACE) for recognizing military educational experiences in terms of civilian academic credit. The majority of colleges and universities recognize these ACE reviews. Additionally, some advanced individual training courses are registered with the U.S. Department of Labor as certified apprenticeship training programs. Generally, this training qualifies participants for both federal and state apprenticeship programs and helps them secure future civilian employment in their chosen trade.

Advancement

Every job in the Army has a career path leading to increased pay and responsibility with well-defined promotion criteria. After six months of service, new soldiers advance to Private (E-2). The next step in the promotion ladder is Private First Class (E-3), which occurs after the twelfth month. Promotion to Corporal or Specialist (E-4) occurs after established time-in-grade and time-in-service requirements are met. These times vary, but soldiers can ordinarily expect to reach the level of corporal within their first three years of service.

Starting with grade E-5, promotions to Sergeant through Sergeant Major are made on a competitive basis. At each grade, there are minimum periods of time in service and time in grade that must be met before a soldier can be considered for promotion. In some cases, there also are educational requirements that must be met for promotion.

The Army offers a number of ways to advance beyond enlisted status as either a warrant officer or a commissioned officer. These programs usually are reserved for the best-qualified soldiers. Warrant officers perform duties similar to those of commissioned Army officers. Many warrant officers are directly appointed from the enlisted grades as vacancies occur. These opportunities usually exist in the technical fields, especially those involving maintenance of equipment. Other opportunities are available in Army administration, intelligence, and law enforcement.

Unique among the armed forces is the Army's Warrant Officer Aviator Program. Qualified personnel may enlist for Warrant Officer Candidate School and, upon completion, receive flight training and appointment as Army Warrant Officer Aviators. Enlisted soldiers may also compete for a limited number of selections to attend Officer Candidate School (OCS) or the U.S. Military Academy. Upon graduating from OCS or the academy, soldiers receive officer commissions.

Education Programs

For enlisted personnel, the Army has a well-defined system for progressive service school training. Soldiers are often able to volunteer for this schooling; in some cases, they are selected on a competitive basis.

As a soldier progresses in his or her career, advanced technical training opportunities are offered. These courses include, but are not limited to, advanced noncommissioned officer courses at the E-6 grade level, senior leadership at the E-7 grade, and the Sergeants Major Academy at the E-8 and E-9 levels.

Civilian education is stressed as a means to improve both the soldier's work performance and his or her preparedness for life in a technical and competitive society.

The Army Continuing Education System provides assistance with tuition, counseling, academic services, and vocational-technical services at no cost. The Tuition Assistance (TA) program provides financial assistance for voluntary off-duty education programs in support of a soldier's professional and personal self-development goals. TA is available for courses that are offered in the classroom or by distance learning and are part of an approved academic degree or certificate program. In a few cases, the Army sends its soldiers to college, but generally they are encouraged to pursue college training during their off-duty time. Army personnel are also eligible to participate in educational assistance programs with the government, such as the Post-9/11 GI Bill, which comprises multiple payments. All tuition and fees are paid directly to any in-state public school, and includes a yearly $1,000 stipend for books and supplies. Additionally, a monthly housing allowance is also provided, whose amount varies according to where you live.

OPPORTUNITIES IN THE NAVY

The Navy plays an important role in helping to maintain the freedom of the seas. It defends the right of our country and its allies to travel and trade freely on the world's oceans, and helps protect our country and national interests overseas during times of international conflict through power projection ashore. Navy sea and air power make it possible for our country to use the oceans when and where our national interests require it.

The Navy is a large and diverse organization. It is made up of about 326,000 officers and enlisted personnel. Navy personnel operate and repair almost 450 ships and over 3,700 aircraft. They serve in over 60 ratings in career fields ranging from administration to aviation to cryptology and intelligence, or medical/dental or construction (Seabee) plus security and special warfare/special operations to submarines, or supply and surface engineering communities. Navy personnel serve on ships at sea, on submarines under the sea, in aviation positions on land and sea, and at shore bases around the world. The Navy recruits a total of more than 40,000 officers and enlisted personnel each year to fill openings in Navy career fields.

Enlistment

To qualify for enlistment in Navy programs, men and women must be between the ages of 17 and 34. Parental consent is required for all 17-year-olds. In the nuclear field, the maximum enlistment age is 23 (up to age 25 with an administrative waiver) because of the extensive training requirements. Because most Navy programs require enlistees to be high school graduates, future sailors are allowed to choose a career and select a shipping date while completing their senior year in high school.

To enlist, you must be a citizen of the United States or a resident alien with immigration and naturalization papers. A physical examination and the Armed Services Vocational Aptitude Battery (ASVAB) must be completed.

Initial enlistment in the Navy usually is for four years. However, five- and six-year enlistments are also available for men and women, depending on the programs they select.

After Navy people go through the enlistment process at a Military Entrance Processing Station, they are placed in the Delayed Entry Program (DEP) for a minimum of 90 days. While in DEP, recruits work on their Personal Qualification Standards (PQS) while they await their shipping date. DEP allows enlistees to finish high school or college, take care of personal business, or just relax before reporting for duty.

There is even an opportunity to earn advancement while in DEP, which translates into a higher pay grade when entering basic training. There is extra pay in the Navy for sea duty, submarine duty, demolition duty, diving duty, work as a crew member of an aviation team, and other jobs that require special training. Signing bonuses are available for those who enter the nuclear field or other highly technical fields. Because the nuclear field is such a critical and unique area of the Navy, quicker promotions are earned and bonuses are available when the training in this field is completed and also when sailors with nuclear training reenlist.

Training

The Navy is known for the excellent training it provides. The Navy provides both recruit training and job training. The first assignment for every Navy enlistee is recruit training. It is a challenging eight-week period of transition from civilian to Navy life. It provides the discipline, knowledge, and physical conditioning necessary to continue serving in the Navy.

The Navy's recruit training command, or "boot camp," is located in Great Lakes, Illinois. After reporting, recruits are placed in training divisions, issued uniforms and equipment, and assigned living quarters. The recruit's day starts at 0600 (6 a.m.). Taps (lights out) is at 2200 (10 p.m.). During weekdays, the daily schedule varies and includes periods of physical fitness, classroom training, and hands-on instruction.

Physical fitness training includes push-ups, sit-ups, distance running, water survival, and swimming instruction. Recruits are tested for physical fitness at the beginning and end of recruit training. The test requirements differ slightly for men and women.

Recruits are given classroom training covering more than 30 subjects, including aircraft and ship familiarization, career incentives, decision making, time management, military drill, Navy mission and organization, military customs and courtesies, and the chain of command. Recruits are also given hands-on training including basic deck seamanship, firefighting, firearms familiarization, and damage control.

The final test before graduating from boot camp is Battle Stations 21 (BST-21), a 12-hour test of a recruit's skills in several shipboard scenarios, including firefighting, combating flooding, and transporting casualties. The test is held on board a 210-foot-long Arleigh Burke-class destroyer replica, the USS Trayer, the Navy's largest simulator.

After graduation from boot camp, many new sailors go directly to the technical school ("A" school) they signed up for at the Military Entrance Processing Station. The Navy has more than 72 from which enlistees may choose. Navy "A" schools are located on military bases throughout the United States, including Great Lakes, Illinois; San Diego, California; Newport, Rhode Island; and Pensacola, Florida.

Training programs range in length from a few weeks to many months, depending on the complexity of the subject. Those who complete recruit training and are still undecided about what career path they want to take in the Navy can begin an on-the-job apprenticeship training program. This training is part of the Seaman-Airman-Fireman pipeline. When apprentices finish on-the-job training, they should have an idea of what type of job (rating) they want to pursue during the rest of their Navy service.

Advanced training in most job fields ("C" school) is available later in a Navy person's career. The Office of Education Credit of the American Council on Education regularly reviews and evaluates Navy training and experience. It has recommended that colleges and universities award credits for nearly all Navy courses. Those recommendations, from the American Council on Education, are formalized and available for the service member and colleges or universities on a Sailor/Marine American Council on Education Registry Transcript (SMART).

Advancement

Like other branches of the armed services, the Navy has nine enlisted pay grades, from E-1 to E-9. A new enlistee entering the Navy is an E-1 (Seaman deciding on military service recruit). After nine months in the Navy, the E-1 normally is eligible for advancement to E-2 (Seaman Apprentice).

Navy promotions are based on (1) job performance, (2) competitive examination grades, (3) recommendations of supervisors, (4) length of service, and (5) time in present level of work. It is impossible to predict exactly when promotions will occur; however, every job in the Navy has a defined career path leading to supervisory positions.

People with highly developed skills in certain critical occupations may enter the Navy at advanced pay grades. Some people qualify for one of the specialized technical training programs in the electronics, computer, or nuclear field, where advancement is often rapid.

Enlisted petty officer ratings (E-4 through E-9) are not to be confused with Navy commissioned officer rankings. More and more Navy enlisted personnel enter with some college courses or degrees. Most Navy commissioned officers have college degrees.

The Navy offers several programs that allow enlisted personnel to advance to officer status. These programs include Limited Duty Officer (LDO), Warrant Officer (WO), Seaman to Admiral (STA-21), Officer Candidate School (OCS), Medical Enlisted Commissioning Program (MECP), and Nurse Corps Program (NCP), all of which permit enlisted Navy personnel to advance to commissioned officer status. Enlisted Navy people interested in officer commissions through these programs should start planning for them early in their careers. These commissions are available to successful career petty officers. The competition is keen, and the standards are high.

Education Programs

The Navy believes that the more education people receive, the better equipped they are to perform their jobs and fulfill personal goals. Navy College Offices (NCOs) are available worldwide and assist in providing opportunities for enlisted members to continue college or technical classes throughout their Navy careers. Through Navy College, enlisted members can pursue all levels of education and training, from high school equivalency to vocational certificate to college degree(s), regardless of their location and duty station. Navy College offers on-duty and off-duty study to provide a complete package of educational benefits to Navy people. Enlisted members can enroll in any combination of Navy College programs and keep adding credits toward a civilian college degree or vocational certificate of their choice.

Officer preparatory programs for enlisted personnel are available through the Naval Academy Preparatory School and the Navy's "STA-21," which includes 21 different paths and programs. The U.S. Naval Academy offers a fully subsidized four-year college education—plus a monthly salary. About 1,300 people are selected for the Naval Academy each year from nominations by senators, representatives, the president and vice president of the United States, and the secretary of the Navy. Candidates must be U.S. citizens, aged 17 to 22, and single with no children.

Enlisted Navy sailors applying to the academy must have served at least one year of active duty by the date of entrance. Graduates receive a Bachelor of Science degree and a commission. The NROTC program offers a fully subsidized tuition scholarship plus a monthly stipend. Approximately 1,100 people are selected for the NROTC program each year.

OPPORTUNITIES IN THE AIR FORCE

The mission of the Air Force is to defend the United States through control and exploitation of air and space. The Air Force flies and maintains aircraft, such as long-range bombers, supersonic fighters, Airborne Warning and Control System (AWACS) aircraft, and many others, whenever and wherever necessary, to protect the interests of America and American allies. Almost 320,000 highly trained officers and airmen make up today's Air Force. Some pilot aircraft—everything from helicopters to the space shuttle. Many others do the jobs that support the Air Force's flying mission; they may work as firefighters, aircraft mechanics, security police, or air traffic controllers, or in many other Air Force career fields. The Air Force currently recruits about 24,000 to 31,000 men and women each year to fill openings in hundreds of challenging Air Force careers.

Enlistment

Applicants for enlistment in the Air Force must be in good health, possess good moral character, and make the minimum scores on the Armed Services Vocational Aptitude Battery (ASVAB) required for Air Force enlistment. They must also be at least 18 years of age. (Individuals who are 17 years of age may enlist if they are married, have parental consent to enlist, or have been emancipated by the courts.)

Prior to taking the oath of enlistment, qualified applicants may be guaranteed either to receive training in a specific skill or to be assigned within a selected aptitude area. The Guaranteed Training Enlistment Program guarantees training and initial assignment in a specific job skill. The Aptitude Area Program guarantees classification into one of four aptitude areas (mechanical, administrative, general, or electronic); specific skills within these aptitude areas are selected during basic training.

After choosing one of these programs, applicants will enter the Delayed Entry Program (DEP). DEP enlistees become members of the Air Force Inactive Reserve with a delayed date for active-duty enlistment. They do not participate in any military activities or earn pay or benefits while in the DEP. The individual agrees to enter active duty on a certain date, and the Air Force agrees to accept the individual (if still qualified) and provide training and initial assignment in the aptitude area or job specified.

Training

The Air Force provides two kinds of training to all enlistees: basic training and job training. Selected candidates can also pursue a management training program, explained later in this section.

Basic Training   All Air Force basic military training (BMT) is conducted at Joint Base San Antonio–Lackland, Texas. BMT teaches enlistees how to adjust to military life, both physically and mentally, and promotes pride in being a member of the Air Force. It lasts approximately seven and one-half weeks and consists of academic instruction, confidence courses, physical conditioning, and marksmanship training. This is followed by a one-week course known as "Airman's Week." Trainees who enlist with an aptitude-area guarantee receive orientation and individual counseling to help them choose a job specialty that is compatible with Air Force needs and with their aptitudes, education, civilian experience, and desires. After graduation from BMT, recruits receive job training in their assigned specialty.

Job Training All BMT graduates go directly to one of the Technical Training Centers (DoD or another service) for formal, in-residence training. In-residence job training is conducted at Keesler AFB, Biloxi, Mississippi; Joint Base San Antonio–Lackland, San Antonio, Texas; Sheppard AFB, Wichita Falls, Texas; Goodfellow AFB, San Angelo, Texas; and several other locations nationwide. In formal classes and practice sessions, airmen learn the basic skills needed for the first assignment in their specialty.

Air Force training does not end with graduation from basic training and technical training school. After three months at their first permanent duty station, airmen begin on-the-job training (OJT). OJT is a two-part program consisting of self-study and supervised job performance. Airmen enroll in skill-related correspondence courses to gain broad knowledge of their Air Force job, and they study technical orders and directives to learn the specific tasks they must perform. They also work daily with their trainers and supervisors, who coach them during hands-on task performance. Through OJT, they develop the job skills needed to progress from apprentice airmen to skilled noncommissioned officers (NCOs). Airmen also complete advanced training and supplemental formal courses throughout their careers to increase their skills in using specific equipment or techniques.

Management Training In addition to becoming skilled in their specialties, Air Force airmen and NCOs are also leaders and supervisors. Schools in the professional military education (PME) system teach airmen and NCOs to be more effective in the operation of the Air Force. PME is a progressive system consisting of leadership schools for airmen, NCO academies for intermediate NCOs, and the Senior NCO Academy for selected master sergeants and senior master sergeants. Through PME, airmen and NCOs develop management abilities that are valuable in any career, military or civilian.

Advancement

Typically, Airman Basic (pay grade E-1) is the initial enlisted grade. However, there are several programs available that may qualify individuals for enlistment at a higher initial grade. These programs include successful completion of a Civil Air Patrol program and receipt of the Billy Mitchell, Amelia Earhart, or Carl Spaatz Award; successful completion of at least three years of a Junior Reserve Officer Training Corps (JROTC) program (any service); receipt of a Boy Scout Eagle Scout or Girl Scout Gold Award; or completion of certain levels of course work at accredited colleges or universities.

Every job in the Air Force has a defined career path leading to supervisory positions. Airman Basic enlistees are normally promoted to Airman (E-2) upon completion of six months of service and to Airman First Class (E-3) after 16 months of service. Promotion to Senior Airman (E-4) usually occurs at the three-year point. However, some airmen qualify for accelerated promotion. Local Air Force recruiters have all the details on qualifications for accelerated promotions and advanced enlistment grades.

Promotions to the higher enlisted grades of Staff Sergeant (E-5), Technical Sergeant (E-6), Master Sergeant (E-7), and Senior and Chief Master Sergeant (E-8 and E-9) are competitive. Eligible airmen compete with others worldwide in the same grade and skill, based on test scores, performance ratings, decorations, and time in service and grade. All airmen receive a promotion score that shows how they stand in relation to others in their specialty and where improvement may be needed. Additionally, E-7, E-8, and E-9 candidates are reviewed by an evaluation board.

Chief master sergeants occupy the top enlisted grade, and they have great responsibility and prestige in the Air Force. They have the management ability to head several enlisted specialties related to their own skill, or they may be the top enlisted expert in a highly technical field.

Normally, enlisted airmen and commissioned officers advance along separate career paths. However, the Air Force offers three programs through which airmen can receive commissions: the Air Force ROTC Scholarship Commissioning Program, the Airman Education and Commissioning Program, and the Air Force Academy. The Air Force ROTC Scholarship Commissioning Program allows airmen to complete their college degrees and earn officer commissions through Air Force ROTC scholarships. If selected for the program, the individual is transferred from active duty into the Air Force Reserve, then attends college (at the same time enrolling in the college's Air Force ROTC program) for completion of degree requirements. This highly competitive program pays tuition, fees, and a monthly allowance.

Airmen can also apply for a commission as an Air Force officer under the Airman Education and Commissioning Program (AECP) or by acceptance to the U.S. Air Force Academy. Under AECP, enlisted personnel attend school full time and draw full pay and allowances. Enlisted personnel who have bachelor's degrees or who complete their degree requirements under AECP in areas of critical need may be accepted into the Officer Training School. They are commissioned upon graduation.

Each year, airmen on active duty and airmen serving in the Air Force Reserve and Air National Guard receive appointments to the Air Force Academy. There are 85 appointments available for active-duty airmen and another 85 for those in the Air Force Reserve or Air National Guard. All candidates are considered for admission on a competitive basis. Examination results and previous performance determine selection. Graduates from the Air Force Academy receive Bachelor of Science degrees and are commissioned as second lieutenants in the active-duty Air Force.

Education Programs

The Air Force has many education programs to help men and women pursue their educational goals while serving in the Air Force that can now award bachelor's degrees. These programs are in addition to veterans' educational benefits set up by the federal government for members of all services. All Air Force bases have education service centers, where trained counselors help airmen decide on a program or combination of programs and help them enroll. Here are some of these programs.

Community College of the Air Force The Community College of the Air Force (CCAF) offers education programs directly related to Air Force specialties; graduates are awarded an associate degree. The college works with Air Force training schools, regional accrediting agencies, and hundreds of cooperating civilian colleges and universities. Since the technical nature of most Air Force courses places them on a level with college study, airmen earn fully recognized college credits for most of what they learn in job training and on-the-job training. They can combine those credits with attendance at off-duty courses from civilian colleges to earn a two-year accredited associate degree in applied sciences from CCAF. The college offers more than 80 fields of study, ranging from police science to environmental services technology. Registration is free, and CCAF establishes a special study program for each student. Professional, industrial, and government organizations that issue licenses and certifications and set standards for civilian work recognize Air Force training and education through CCAF. CCAF now also offers a BA program of study.

College Level Examination Program (CLEP) This program allows airmen to receive credit for selected college courses by examination. The program is free, and education service centers maintain a current list of college tests available.

Extension Course Institute The Extension Course Institute (ECI) is the Air Force's correspondence school. It offers, free of charge, nearly 400 courses to some 250,000 students who register for ECI each year. These courses include everything from fundamentals of solid-state devices to apprentice carpentry. Air Force personnel may voluntarily enroll in courses such as auto mechanics, plumbing, carpentry, or electric wiring simply for background knowledge.

Tuition Assistance The Air Force will pay up to 100 percent of the tuition costs of most college courses. College programs are offered on all Air Force bases, with local college professors coming to the base at most installations. Tuition assistance is also available for online classes.

OPPORTUNITIES IN THE MARINE CORPS

The U.S. Marine Corps was created November 10, 1775, by a resolution of the Continental Congress. Since then, the Marine corps has grown to be one of the most elite fighting forces in the world. To perform the many duties of the Marine Corps, approximately 170,000 officers and enlisted Marines fly planes and helicopters; operate radar equipment; drive armored vehicles; gather intelligence; survey and map territory; maintain and repair radios, computers, jeeps, trucks, tanks, and aircraft; and perform duties in 42 occupational fields with more than 220 different Military Occupational Specialties (MOS) open to entry-level Marines. Each year, the Marine Corps recruits more than 39,000 men and women to fill openings in its career fields. The Marine Corps training programs offer practical, challenging, and progressive skill development. The Marine Corps stresses professional education for all ranks and emphasizes the development of mental strength as well as traditional physical prowess. In this way, the Marine Corps provides the nation with a modern, well-armed force that is both tough and smart.

Enlistment

Marine Corps active duty enlistment terms are for four, five, or six years, depending on the type of enlistment program. Men and women enlisting in the Marine Corps must meet exacting physical, mental, and moral standards. Applicants must be between ages 17 and 28, American citizens or registered aliens, and in good health to ensure they can meet the rigorous physical training demands.

The ASVAB, described in this guide, is used by the Marine Corps to assess each person's vocational aptitudes and academic abilities. Some applicants for enlistment may have taken the ASVAB while in high school. For those applicants who have not recently taken the ASVAB, a Marine recruiter can arrange for them to do so. Applicants for enlistment can be guaranteed training and duty assignment with a wide variety of options, depending on their level of education and the qualifications they possess. All occupational fields are open to men and women. In addition to regular enlistment, the Marine Corps offers special enlistment programs.

Delayed Entry Program Enlistment in the Marine Corps Delayed Entry Program (DEP) allows applicants to postpose their initial active duty training for up to a full year. Enlisting in the DEP has two principal

benefits. First, highly desirable enlistment programs available in limited numbers, such as computer and aviation specialties, can be reserved while the enlistee completes high school, a college semester, or other obligation. Secondly, DEP members meet regularly with recruiters and peers to mentally and physically prepare them for recruit training.

Musician Enlistment Option Program The Musician Enlistment Option Program gives graduates with musical talent an opportunity to serve in Marine Corps bands or the Marine Corps Drum and Bugle Corps. The program's incentives include formal school training, accelerated promotions, and duty station choices.

Enlistment Options Program The Enlistment Options Program guarantees well-qualified applicants, before they enlist, assignment to their chosen occupational fields. The occupational fields comprise every job available in the Marine Corps, ranging from combat arms to motor transport to highly technical avionics, electronics, and computer science. Some enlistment options feature cash bonuses as well as formal training programs.

Quality Enlistment Program The Quality Enlistment Program is for highly qualified young men and women for enlistment and assignment primarily to technical occupational fields. The program provides incentives, including choice of geographic assignment, to those who qualify.

Training

Marine Corps training occurs in three sections: recruit training, combat training, and job training.

Recruit Training Upon completing the enlistment process, all applicants enter Marine Corps recruit training. Men attend either at Parris Island, South Carolina, or San Diego, California. All women attend recruit training at Parris Island. Recruit training is rigorous, demanding, and challenging. The overall goal of recruit training is to instill in recruits the military skills, knowledge, discipline, teamwork, pride, and self-confidence necessary to perform as United States Marines.

In the first several days at the recruit depot, a recruit is assigned to a platoon, receives a basic issue of uniforms and equipment, and is given a physical. Each platoon is led by a team of three or more drill instructors. A typical training day for recruits begins with reveille at 0500 (5 a.m.), continues with close order drill, physical training, and classes, then ends with taps at 2100 (9 p.m.).

Combat and Job Training Upon graduation from recruit training, each Marine takes a short vacation, then reports to combat training. Marines in combat arms job fields attend the School of Infantry, while Marines in other career fields attend the shorter Marine Combat Training. Upon graduation, Marines report to Military Occupational Specialty (MOS) training at their formal schools or to their unit for on-the-job training. The Marine Corps sends students to more than 200 basic formal schools and more than 300 advanced formal schools. The length of formal school training varies from a few weeks to more than a year, depending on the level of technical expertise and knowledge required to become proficient in a particular job skill. Marines assigned to combat arms specialties receive much of their training outdoors. Marines assigned to highly technical specialties receive the majority of their training in a classroom. Emphasis is placed on practical application of newly acquired skills, and many times as soon as classroom instruction is complete, students are placed in an actual work environment to obtain experience and develop confidence.

After completion of entry-level MOS training, most Marines receive orders to operational units of the Fleet Marine Force. Marines assigned to more technical MOSs may require more advanced training and attend follow-on schools before their first assignments. After attaining some fleet experience, additional training in advanced or specialized subjects is available to Marines in many MOSs. Job performance requirements in many MOSs are comparable to requirements needed to earn a Certificate of Apprenticeship through the United States Department of Labor, and some Marines earn their certificates before completing their Marine Corps service.

Advancement

Advancement is directly linked to an individual's development as a Marine, of which performance in the Marine's MOS is one factor among many.

Each Marine is evaluated based on a "whole-Marine" concept. Physical fitness, rifle qualification, military and civilian education, work performance, time in grade and service, and other factors all contribute an individual's promotion prospects. Marines are in competition with peers of the same rank and MOS, ensuring the best and brightest rise to the top. Promotion becomes increasingly competitive as Marines advance in rank. In addition to minimum time-in-grade requirements, educational and other prerequisites factor into the promotion system. For example, to be selected for promotion to sergeant, a corporal must first have attended a formal Corporals' Course; for promotion to staff sergeant, a sergeant must have attended a Sergeants' Course, etc. Unit leaders ensure their Marines have opportunities to attend appropriate formal Primary Military Education courses. Promotions to the Staff Noncommissioned Officer (SNCO) ranks are determined by promotion boards.

The Meritorious Promotion System is used to recognize Marines who demonstrate outstanding performance and professional development. Marines recommended for meritorious promotion are carefully screened for accelerated advancement before their peers. Qualified enlisted Marines can also compete for and be accepted into the officer corps through several different programs. Competition is keen, and only the best-qualified Marines are accepted.

Marine Enlisted Commissioning Education Program MECEP provides exceptional selected enlisted Marines who have little college experience the opportunity to earn baccalaureate degrees by attending college or university as full-time students while maintaining active duty status and pay. Marines in this program who earn their degrees and complete officer candidate training are commissioned as second lieutenants.

Enlisted Commissioning Program ECP provides an opportunity for enlisted Marines who have a four-year degree to apply for assignment to the Officer Candidate School and subsequent appointment as unrestricted commissioned officers.

Education Programs

All Marines on active duty are encouraged to continue their education by taking advantage of service schools and Marine Corps–funded off-duty courses at civilian colleges. The Marine Corps has developed an extensive professional military education program to provide Marine leaders with the skill, knowledge, understanding, and confidence that will better enable them to make sound military decisions. Several educational assistance programs are available to enlisted Marines.

Tuition Assistance Program The Marine Corps Tuition Assistance Program provides Marines up to 100 percent of financial tuition assistance to pursue educational programs at civilian secondary and postsecondary institutions during their off-duty time. Tuition assistance may be used only to fund courses at a higher academic level than the degree or diploma currently held by the Marine.

Servicemembers Opportunity Colleges The Servicemembers Opportunity Colleges (SOC) is a consortium of colleges and universities that have agreed to help military personnel gain access to higher education by minimizing residency requirements, recognizing nontraditional education attainment, such as the College Level Examination Program (CLEP) tests, easing the transfer of college credit from similarly accredited institutions, and granting credit for formal military training.

Deployed Education Programs Marines deployed around the globe can still pursue higher education by taking classes facilitated by accredited institutions with which the Marine Corps has established a memorandum of understanding. Credit for the courses is in most cases transferrable via the Marine's SOC agreement.

Marine Library Program The Marine Corps General Library Program assembles, organizes, and makes easily and freely available balanced and unbiased collections of library materials and accompanying library services to support professional, educational, recreational, and lifelong learning pursuits. These include research databases, encyclopedias, foreign language lessons, continuing education classes, e-books, digital magazines, and other materials and services.

Joint Service Transcripts Joint Service Transcripts include all military and civilian training and education with the American Council on Education's recommendations for equivalency credit hours for courses they have reviewed.

College After the Corps Marines are also eligible to participate in educational assistance programs with the government, such as the Montgomery GI Bill or the Post-9/11 GI Bill, which can cover up to the full tuition at public and some private universities and colleges, and the Marine Corps College Fund.

OPPORTUNITIES IN THE COAST GUARD

Although it is organizationally under the Department of Homeland Security, the Coast Guard is one of the nation's five military services. It exists to defend and preserve the United States. Its goal is to protect the personal safety and security of our people, the marine transportation system and infrastructure, our natural and economic resources, and the territorial integrity of our nation—from both internal and external threats, natural and man-made. Guard members protect these interests in U.S. ports and inland waterways, along the coasts, and on international waters.

The Coast Guard is a unique branch of the military responsible for an array of maritime duties, from ensuring safe and lawful commerce to performing rescue missions in severe conditions. Nearly 42,000 men and women are actively serving in the Coast Guard to defend America's borders and protect the maritime environment.

The Coast Guard is a military, multimission, maritime force offering a unique blend of military, law enforcement, humanitarian, regulatory, and diplomatic capabilities. These capabilities underpin its three broad roles: maritime safety, maritime security, and maritime stewardship. There are 11 missions that are interwoven within these roles.

Missions

The Coast Guard is assigned 11 official missions, including:

Port & Waterway Security Along with search and rescue, port and waterway security is the Coast Guard's primary homeland security mission. Coast Guard members protect marine resources and maritime commerce, as well as those who live, work, or recreate on the water.

Port and waterway security also involves prevention of terrorist attacks and response when terrorist acts do occur. Counterterrorism preparedness and response operations all fall within the scope of port and waterway security.

Drug Interdiction The Coast Guard is the nation's first line of defense against drug smugglers seeking to bring illegal substances into the United States. The Coast Guard coordinates closely with other federal agencies and countries within a vast six-million-square-mile region to disrupt and deter the flow of illegal drugs. Coast Guard drug interdiction accounts for more than half of all U.S. government seizures of cocaine each year.

Aids to Navigation One important mission entrusted to the Coast Guard is the care and maintenance of maritime aids to navigation. Much like drivers need stoplights, street signs, and universally accepted driving rules, boaters also need equivalent nautical "rules of the road."

The Coast Guard is responsible for ensuring this network of signs, symbols, buoys, markers, lighthouses, and regulations is up to date and functioning properly so recreational and commercial boaters can safely navigate the maritime environment.

Search & Rescue Search and rescue (SAR) is one of the Coast Guard's oldest missions. Warding off the loss of life, personal injury, and property damage by helping boaters in distress has always been a top Coast Guard priority. Coast Guard SAR response involves multimission stations, cutters, aircraft, and boats linked by communications networks.

Living Marine Resources The nation's waterways and marine ecosystems are vital to the country's economy and health. Ensuring America enjoys a rich, diverse, and sustainable ocean environment is an important Coast Guard mission. This includes ensuring the country's protected marine species are provided the protection necessary to help their populations recover to healthy, sustainable levels.

Marine Safety While search and rescue is one of the Coast Guard's most well-known missions, crews do much more than save mariners in peril.

Promoting safe boating practices is a key objective to help prevent an incident at sea. The Coast Guard investigates maritime accidents, merchant vessels,

offshore drilling units, and marine facilities. Additionally, the Coast Guard is responsible for licensing mariners, documenting U.S. flagged vessels, and implementing a variety of safety programs.

Despite best efforts, mariners sometimes find themselves in harm's way. When they do, the Coast Guard has a proud tradition of immediate response to save lives and property in peril. To be part of its search and rescue team takes more than physical ability; it also requires that special desire and bravery with which heroes are born.

Defense Readiness In our post-9/11 society, national security interests can no longer be defined solely in terms of direct military threats to America and its allies. The Coast Guard's role in national defense and antiterrorism is a cornerstone of homeland security efforts to protect the country from the ever-present threat of terrorism.

The Coast Guard has four major national defense missions: maritime intercept operations, deployed port operations/security and defense, peacetime engagement, and environmental defense operations. These missions are essential military tasks assigned to the Coast Guard as a component of joint and combined forces in peacetime, crisis, and war.

Migrant Interdiction Thousands of people try to enter this country illegally every year by sea, many via highly dangerous and illegal smuggling operations. Intercepting these offenders at sea means they can be safely returned to their country of origin without the costly processes required if they had successfully entered the United States.

As the United States' primary maritime law enforcement agency, the Coast Guard enforces immigration laws at sea. The Coast Guard conducts patrols and coordinates with federal agencies and foreign countries to detain undocumented migrants at sea and prohibit entry via maritime routes to the United States and its territories.

Marine Environmental Protection Protecting the delicate ecosystem of our oceans is a vital Coast Guard mission. The Coast Guard works with a variety of groups and organizations to ensure the livelihood of endangered marine species.

Through the Marine Environmental Protection program, the Coast Guard develops and enforces regulations to avert the introduction of invasive species into the maritime environment, stop unauthorized ocean dumping, and prevent oil and chemical spills.

Ice Operations Frigid, subzero temperatures heighten the dangers for any operation. Adding hazardous icy waters and icebergs makes for treacherous conditions for maritime commerce. To facilitate safe maritime commerce in icy waters and to protect communities in emergency situations, the Coast Guard conducts ice breaking operations in the Great Lakes and Northeast regions.

Law Enforcement Preventing illegal foreign fishing vessels from encroaching on the Exclusive Economic Zone (EEZ) is a priority for the Coast Guard. Protecting the integrity of the nation's maritime borders and ensuring the health of U.S. fisheries is a vital part of the Coast Guard mission.

The Coast Guard also enforces international agreements to suppress illegal, unreported, and unregulated fishing activity in international waters.

Training

As with any military service, the journey begins at basic training.

Basic training is tough. Recruits are challenged every day, both mentally and physically. They are pushed, tested, and worked harder than they ever thought possible, but they graduate confident and proud.

Recruits arrive at Sexton Hall in Cape May, New Jersey, and the first days of basic training are spent getting oriented, receiving uniforms, getting haircuts (women may pin their hair up within regulation standards), and filling out entry forms.

Here, they meet their company commander (CC)—their mentor, instructor, leader, coach, and guide through basic training. The company commander's job is to motivate, teach self-discipline, and teach how to obey orders. From the CC, recruits learn commitment and service as a productive Coast Guard member.

Academic Training In addition to being subject to physical demands, recruits are challenged in the classroom. The intense academic program at basic training is designed to provide them with entry-level skills and knowledge needed to succeed in the junior member field. In class, they receive training in everything from military justice, customs, and ethics to Coast Guard history.

Moreover, many classes are hands-on. During training, they participate in a variety of practical instruction, including small arms training, seamanship, firefighting, and damage control. They fire at the basic pistol course, learn how to handle lines, practice helm commands, and participate in safety and rescue training. Additionally, all throughout basic training, they are coached through a myriad of team-building training exercises.

Around the fourth week of training, recruits are asked to request a geographic location for their first assignment and the type of unit they wish to serve, whether ashore or afloat. They receive their first assignment orders about a week later.

After graduation from basic training, recruits are ready to serve.

Advancement

The Coast Guard is the smallest of all the military services. At any given time, there are about 46,000 men and women in service. That means two things: every job an individual does is important and everything an individual does gets noticed. Those who excel are rewarded with better pay, more responsibility, and more diverse missions.

Upon completing eight weeks of basic training, recruits are promoted to seaman or fireman (E-2). Normally, they then proceed to their first unit and learn the skills needed to move up to seaman or fireman (E-3). While at their first unit, they are exposed to many of the different ratings available in the Coast Guard and can narrow down the career path they want to pursue. For aviation-specific rates, the USCG Aviation Technical Training Center in Elizabeth City, North Carolina, incorporated the airmen training program into the "A" school curriculum.

Recruits who already know what they want to do in the Coast Guard can ask their recruiter about the guaranteed "A" school program. With guaranteed "A" school, they can go directly from basic training to their rating's training program. However, not all ratings participate in this program. Coast Guard training provides members with the highest level of readiness because lives and mission success depend on how the Corps performs its duties.

Enlisted personnel continue to receive higher-level training in their field, which leads to more responsibility, potentially a higher ranking, and greater pay.

To become a petty officer in the Coast Guard, individuals must either graduate from "A" school or complete the corresponding "striker" program (on-the-job training). Not all ratings have striker programs.

By demonstrating practical skills on the job, recruits can advance within their rating. They also have to successfully complete leadership training, pass the appropriate end-of-course test, and compete in a national service-wide exam.

The highest rank an enlisted member can attain is Master Chief Petty Officer (E-9). If they want to keep going, as a four-year enlistee in the Coast Guard, if they obtain the rank of E-5 or higher and have a minimum of 30 college credits, they can apply for Officer Candidate School. To get in, applicants compete against civilians who have a four-year college degree and other members of the Coast Guard in their position.

It is also possible to move up the enlisted ladder to warrant officer and later compete in the Warrant-to-Lieutenant program.

Those who join as officers participate in a different training program.

MILITARY PAY AND BENEFITS

The most important components of compensation in the military are pay and allowances. There are various types of pay. *Basic pay* is received by all and is the main component of an individual's salary. Basic pay increases about 2 to 3 percent each year.

There are other compensations for specific qualifications or events. For example, there are *special pays* for aviators and parachutists; special pays are also paid for dangerous or hardship duties.

Allowances are the second most important element of military pay. Allowances are monies provided for specific needs, such as food or housing. Monetary allowances are provided when the government does not provide for that specific need.

For example, not all military members and their families live in housing provided by the government. Those who live in government housing do not receive full housing allowances. Those who do not live in government housing receive allowances to assist them in obtaining commercial housing.

The most common allowances are the Basic Allowance for Subsistence (BAS) and Basic Allowance for Housing (BAH). A majority of the force receives both of these allowances, and, in many cases, these allowances are a significant portion of the member's total pay.

Most allowances are not taxable, which is an additional benefit to military personnel. The charts on page XXX show the most recent pay for enlisted military members. To access the most recent information visit http://www.dfas.mil/militarymembers/payentitlements/military-pay-charts.html.

MILITARY MYTHS AND REALITIES

There are many myths about joining the military. Here are some of the realities.

Myths	Realities
The Military is a roadblock to a higher education.	• Qualified servicemembers can receive more than thousands of dollars in tuition benefits. • The Military operates over 300 schools, teaching more than 10,000 courses. • The Military offers retired personnel up to $100/month reimbursement for tutorial assistance. • The new GI Bill improves those benefits.
People in the Military are not compensated as well as private-sector workers.	• Military pay is comparable to, and in some cases better than, its civilian counterpart. • The services offer significant signing bonuses. • After 20 years of service, retired personnel can potentially receive military retirement pay for life.
You don't need to finish high school to join the Military.	• You must have a high school diploma or equivalent to enlist. • A GED may be accepted with special approval.
Military training and jobs have little relation to the civilian world.	• 95% of military jobs have direct civilian counterparts. • Veterans of the U.S. Armed Forces are less likely to be unemployed than nonveterans.
Women have a hard time achieving success in the Military.	• All jobs in the Military are open to women. • Women account for around 18% of the U.S. Military.

Women in the Military

As of January 2016, all military occupations and positions are open to women, without exception. Although women have served in combat prior to this date, about 10 percent of military jobs were closed to females. These included infantry, armor, reconnaissance, and some special operations units. Now more than 220,000 new jobs are available to women.

According to the Secretary of Defense, "They'll be allowed to drive tanks, fire mortars, and lead infantry soldiers into combat. They'll be able to serve as Army Rangers and Green Berets, Navy SEALs, Marine Corps infantry, Air Force parajumpers, and everything else that was previously open only to men."

About 16 percent of the military enlisted personnel are women. Part of the challenge is that, on average, men are physically stronger than women and many jobs in the military require strength. That said, there are women who are stronger than some men. The services have been looking at the physical requirements of military jobs to determine what is necessary to successfully accomplish these tasks.

If you are a female military applicant, you need to know that you will be assigned to positions based on ability, not gender, but that does not mean that there will be equal participation by men and women in each occupation. For jobs that require a certain level of physical strength, you will have to meet the requirement.

Some cultures do not understand why women should take on military roles at all. It may take some time to fully integrate women into various positions previously closed to them. As in the civilian world, attitudes and perspectives may need to change.

For more information, visit these recruiting websites:

- www.goarmy.com
- www.navy.com
- www.airforce.com
- www.marines.com
- www.uscg.mil

What If the Recruiter Won't Send Me to Take the ASVAB?

A recruiter's primary job is to ensure that applicants meet all necessary qualifications. Before an applicant is allowed to test, the recruiter will conduct an interview looking for disqualifying factors such as too young or old, too many dependents, a medical problem, drug usage, or criminal history. If a recruiter has determined that you are not qualified to enlist, he or she will not send you to be tested. Sometimes, recruiters have applicants take a short pre-screening test to get an estimate of how they would perform on the AFQT portion of the ASVAB. Based on these results, the recruiter may choose not to spend time and resources to send you for full ASVAB testing. The only way to know for sure is to ask your recruiter.

Estimated Pay Effective 2016					
Enlisted Monthly Pay Chart for Years of Service Ranging from Less than 2 to over 6					
	Less than 2	Over 2	Over 3	Over 4	Over 6
E-9					
E-8					
E-7	2,816.10	3,073.50	3,191.40	3,347.10	3,468.90
E-6	2,435.70	2,680.20	2,798.40	2,913.60	3,033.60
E-5	2,231.40	2,381.40	2,496.60	2,614.20	2,797.80
E-4	2,046.00	2,150.40	2,267.10	2,382.00	2,483.40
E-3	1,847.10	1,963.20	2,082.00	2,082.00	2,082.00
E-2	1,756.50	1,756.50	1,756.50	1,756.50	1,756.50
E-1	1,566.90				

Enlisted Monthly Pay Chart for Years of Service Ranging from 8 to over 16					
	Over 8	Over 10	Over 12	Over 14	Over 16
E-9		4,948.80	5,060.70	5,202.30	5,368.20
E-8	4,050.90	4,230.00	4,341.00	4,473.90	4,618.20
E-7	3,678.00	3,795.60	4,004.70	4,178.70	4,297.50
E-6	3,303.30	3,408.60	3,612.30	3,674.40	3,719.70
E-5	2,989.80	3,147.60	3,166.20	3,166.20	3,166.20
E-4	2,483.40	2,483.40	2,483.40	2,483.40	2,483.40
E-3	2,082.00	2,082.00	2,082.00	2,082.00	2,082.00
E-2	1,756.50	1,756.50	1,756.50	1,756.50	1,756.50
E-1					

Enlisted Monthly Pay Chart for Years of Service Ranging from 18 to over 26					
	Over 18	Over 20	Over 22	Over 24	Over 26
E-9	5,536.20	5,804.70	6,032.10	6,270.90	6,636.90
E-8	4,878.00	5,009.40	5,233.80	5,358.00	5,664.00
E-7	4,423.80	4,472.70	4,637.10	4,725.30	5,061.30
E-6	3,772.50	3,772.50	3,772.50	3,772.50	3,772.50
E-5	3,166.20	3,166.20	3,166.20	3,166.20	3,166.20
E-4	2,483.40	2,483.40	2,483.40	2,483.40	2,483.40
E-3	2,082.00	2,082.00	2,082.00	2,082.00	2,082.00
E-2	1,756.50	1,756.50	1,756.50	1,756.50	1,756.50
E-1					

Chapter 2

Introducing the ASVAB

YOUR GOALS FOR THIS CHAPTER:

• Identify the two major formats of the ASVAB.

• Find out what areas the ASVAB tests.

• Get important information about where you can take the ASVAB.

• Learn what you must do if you want to retake the test.

WHAT IS THE ASVAB?

You learned in the preceding chapter that everyone seeking to enlist in any branch of the U.S. Armed Forces must take the Armed Services Vocational Aptitude Battery (ASVAB). The education level of military personnel is a major concern, and the military does not take just anyone who wants to join. The ASVAB is one tool that the military uses to measure the abilities of potential recruits. The ASVAB is also given to high school students to help them explore their aptitudes and interests for different careers. Results from the high school assessment can be used for military entrance.

The ASVAB is actually a group of individual aptitude tests. The tests are listed in the following charts. Each test measures something that is important for military entrance or for acceptance into training programs for certain military jobs.

Once you are accepted into the military, your ASVAB scores are used to qualify you for various military occupations. The higher your scores, the more choices you will have for training in different occupations.

Different Formats of the ASVAB

The ASVAB comes in two formats. Persons who take the ASVAB in schools and in certain other locations in the country are given a paper-and-pencil test battery. This format of the test has 225 items. Testing time, including administration time and instructions,

is three to four hours. The test taker reads the questions in a test booklet and answers them by filling in bubbles on a machine-readable answer sheet. The sheets are taken to a scoring location, and the results are returned to the school and to recruiters. There are four separate forms of the paper-and-pencil version of the test. The chart on page 20 shows the subtests that make up the paper-and-pencil ASVAB.

In recent years, the Department of Defense has implemented a computer format of the test. Individuals who take this form of the ASVAB sit in a room with computers and answer the questions using the keyboard. One of the special characteristics of the computer format is that the test is adapted to the ability level of each individual. The feature is called computer adaptive testing (CAT), so this version of the ASVAB is called CAT-ASVAB.

The CAT-ASVAB uses fewer items than the paper-and-pencil version and takes less time. Because the items are tailored to your ability level, you will

The Paper-and-Pencil ASVAB

Subtest	Minutes	Questions	Description
General Science	11	25	Measures knowledge of physical, earth and space, and biological sciences
Arithmetic Reasoning	36	30	Measures ability to solve basic arithmetic word problems
Word Knowledge	11	35	Measures ability to select the correct meaning of words presented through synonyms
Paragraph Comprehension	13	15	Measures ability to obtain information from written material
Mathematics Knowledge	24	25	Measures knowledge of high school mathematics concepts and applications
Electronics Information	9	20	Tests knowledge of electrical current, circuits, devices, and electronic systems
Auto and Shop Information	11	25	Measures knowledge of automotive maintenance and repair and wood and metal shop practices
Mechanical Comprehension	19	25	Measures knowledge of the principles of mechanical of mechanical devices, structural support, and properties of materials
Assembling Objects	15	25	Measures ability to comprehend the sizes and shapes of different objects shown in a series of pictures

not receive many easy items or many items that are way too difficult for you. Items are selected based on whether or not you got the previous answers correct. The items that are given to you are drawn from a very large pool of items, and no two people get the exact same test. The chart at the top of page 21 shows the subtests that make up the CAT-ASVAB.

It doesn't matter which format of the ASVAB you take because you will end up with the same military enlistment score.

WHO TAKES THE ASVAB?

About 1.3 million people take the ASVAB each year, making it the most popular aptitude test in this country. The ASVAB can be taken by students in grades 10, 11, and 12 and those in postsecondary schools. It is used in about 14,000 schools across the country. Many students take the ASVAB in order to help them identify their strengths and weakness and to help them seek out and explore careers and jobs.

Scores of students in grade 11 and beyond can be used for enlistment purposes. Also, if you have never taken the ASVAB in school, you can contact a recruiter or visit a local recruiting station to request the test.

Scores are acceptable for use in the military enlistment process if the scores are no more than two years old. If you took the ASVAB more than two years ago, you must take the test again for purposes of enlisting in the military.

Hundreds of thousands of people take the ASVAB at government locations for the purpose of enlisting in the military. If you take the ASVAB at a government location, you must be 17 years of age or older for your scores to count for enlistment purposes.

WHERE CAN YOU TAKE THE ASVAB?

There are several places where you can take the ASVAB: at your school, at a Military Entrance Processing Station (MEPS), or at a mobile examining team site (MET). Since its inception, more than 40 Million people have taken the ASVAB.

Your School

About 800,000 students take the ASVAB at their school every year. If you are a student at a high school or postsecondary school, it is very likely that the ASVAB is offered at your school at least once a year. It is offered at more than 14,000 schools across the United States. There is no charge to students for taking the ASVAB.

Watch for school announcements that mention testing dates and times. Keep your eyes open for announcements on the bulletin board. Visit your career center and ask about the ASVAB testing dates

THE CAT-ASVAB

Subtest	Minutes	Questions	Description
General Science	8	16	Measures knowledge of physical, earth and space, and biological sciences
Arithmetic Reasoning	39	16	Measures ability to solve basic arithmetic word problems
Word Knowledge	8	16	Measures ability to select the correct meaning of words presented through synonyms
Paragraph Comprehension	22	11	Measures ability to obtain information from written material
Mathematics Knowledge	20	16	Measures knowledge of high school mathematics concepts and applications
Electronics Information	8	16	Tests knowledge of electrical current, circuit, devices, and electronic systems
Auto Information	7	11	Measures knowledge of automotive maintenance and repair
Shop Information	6	11	Measures knowledge of wood and metal shop practices
Mechanical Comprehension	20	16	Measures knowledge of the principles of mechanical devices, structural support, and properties of materials
Assembling Objects	16	16	Measures the ability to interpret diagrams showing special relationships and how objects are related and connected

scheduled for your school. Ask your school counselor when the ASVAB will be offered at your school or a nearby school. Your school counselor has received information about the ASVAB from a local representative and should be able to tell you where and when the ASVAB will be offered. If the ASVAB is not offered at your school, your counselor can arrange to include you in a testing session at a nearby school.

Unlike taking the SAT and ACT, taking the ASVAB at your school does not cost you anything except your time and effort.

The ASVAB can be taken by students in grades 10 through 12 and also by students at the post-secondary level. Scores at the tenth-grade level cannot be used for military entrance, but taking the test then is a good idea because it can give you an idea of how you will do on an ASVAB test that counts for military enlistment. It is good practice for other tests that you will take during your lifetime as well.

Scores from ASVAB tests at grades 11 and 12 and the postsecondary level can be used for military entrance for up to two years. If you took the test in eleventh or twelfth grade and you think that you could score higher, you may wish to retake the ASVAB at a MEPS to see if you can exceed your high school scores. Following the advice in this book will help you score higher.

If you take the ASVAB at a school, you will probably take it with a group of students. The administration procedures should be professionally delivered by competent government test administrators. This is important because you need to perform your very best on this test and any other test you may take.

The MEPS

You can take the ASVAB test at a local Military Entrance Processing Station (MEPS). There are 65 MEPS located all across the United States. (See the list of MEPS in this chapter.) At the MEPS, you will take a computer version of the test. This test will seem different from the paper-and-pencil version, as it will have fewer items, but those items will be tailored by the computer to your level of ability. This ASVAB test is called CAT-ASVAB. CAT means computer adaptive test. The word *adaptive* means that the test is tailored to or adapts to your particular ability level.

Don't worry about taking the CAT-ASVAB, as it will give you the same scores as the paper-and-pencil version.

Later on in this book, you will learn more about how the CAT-ASVAB works and what you should expect.

MET Sites

There are approximately 500 mobile examining team (MET) sites across the country. They have been set up to qualify military applicants at locations that may be remote or distant from MEPS. If you live a long way away from the nearest MEPS, you can take the ASVAB at a MET site. That way, you and the recruiter can determine whether you are qualified by aptitude to enter the military without spending the time and money it would take you to travel to a MEPS.

At a MET site you will receive the paper pencil version of the ASVAB or the iCAT which is delivered via the Internet.

WHO ADMINISTERS THE ASVAB?

The answer to this question depends on where you take the test battery. If you take the ASVAB at a school or at a MET site, you will have a trained civilian test administrator from the Department of Defense or other agencies. These are individuals who are contracted by the federal government to adhere to the strict timing and directions of ASVAB administration.

If you take the ASVAB at a MEPS, you will have a military administrator who will help you get started on the CAT-ASVAB. The directions will be self-explanatory, and you will determine the pace of the test. It is likely that you will finish the CAT-ASVAB in less time than it would take you to finish the paper-and-pencil instrument.

CONTACT INFORMATION FOR THE MILITARY ENTRANCE PROCESSING STATIONS

ALABAMA
Montgomery
Maxwell Air Force Base—Gunter Annex
705 McDonald Street
Building 1512
Montgomery, AL 36114-3110

Phone: (334) 416-7863
Fax: (334) 416-5034
www.mepcom.army.mil/Units/Eastern-Sector/
    8th-Battalion/Montgomery

ALASKA
Anchorage
1717 "C" Street
Anchorage, AK 99501

Phone: (907) 274-9142
Fax: (907) 274-7268
www.mepcom.army.mil/Units/Western-Sector/
    5th-Battalion/Anchorage

ARIZONA
Phoenix
2800 N. Central Ave
Suite 400
Phoenix, AZ 85004-1007

Phone: (602) 258-1703
Fax: (602) 258-8206
www.mepcom.army.mil/Units/Western-Sector/
    7th-Battalion/Phoenix

ARKANSAS
Little Rock
1520 Riverfront Drive
Little Rock, AR 72202-1724

Phone: (501) 666-6377
Fax: (501) 663-5863
www.mepcom.army.mil/Units/Western-Sector/
    11th-Battalion/Little-Rock

CALIFORNIA
Los Angeles
1776 Grand Ave
El Segundo, CA 90245

Phone: (310) 640-6050, ext. 221
Fax: (310) 640-9754
www.mepcom.army.mil/Units/Western-Sector/
    7th-Battalion/Los-Angeles

Sacramento
1651 Alhambra Blvd.
Suite 100
Sacramento, CA 95816

Phone: (916) 455-9000
Fax: (916) 455-9012
www.mepcom.army.mil/Units/Western-Sector/
    7th-Battalion/Sacramento

San Diego
4181 Ruffin Rd
Suite B
San Diego, CA 92123

PHONE: (858) 874-2400, ext. 241
FAX: (858) 874-0415
www.mepcom.army.mil/Units/Western-Sector/
7th-Battalion/San-Diego

San Jose
546 Vernon Avenue
Mountain View, CA 94043

PHONE: (650) 603-8201
FAX: (650) 603-8225
www.mepcom.army.mil/Units/Western-Sector/
7th-Battalion/San-Jose

COLORADO
Denver
721 19th Street
Suite 275
Denver, CO 80202

PHONE: (303) 623-1020, ext. 234
FAX: (303) 623-2210
www.mepcom.army.mil/Units/Western-Sector/
3rd-Battalion/Denver

FLORIDA
Jacksonville
7178 Baymeadows Way
Jacksonville, FL 32256

PHONE: (904) 737-5220
FAX: (904) 737-5339
www.mepcom.army.mil/Units/Eastern-Sector/
10th-Battalion/Jacksonville

Miami
7789 NW 48th Street
Suite 150
Miami, FL 33166

PHONE: (305) 463-0891, ext. 248
FAX: (305) 629-8923
www.mepcom.army.mil/Units/Eastern-Sector/
10th-Battalion/Miami

Tampa
3520 West Waters Avenue
Tampa, FL 33614-2716

PHONE: (813) 932-0079, ext. 1105
FAX: (813) 932-8763
www.mepcom.army.mil/Units/Eastern-Sector/
10th-Battalion/Tampa

GEORGIA
Atlanta
1500 Hood Avenue, Building 720
Forest Park, GA 30297-5000

PHONE: (404) 469-3090
FAX: (404) 469-5367
www.mepcom.army.mil/Units/Eastern-Sector/
10th-Battalion/Atlanta

HAWAII
Honolulu
490 Central Avenue
Pearl Harbor, HI 96860

PHONE: (808) 471-8725
FAX: (808) 471-2888
www.mepcom.army.mil/Units/Western-Sector/
5th-Battalion/Honolulu

IDAHO
Boise
550 West Fort Street
MSC 044
Boise, ID 83724-0101

PHONE: (208) 334-1450, ext. 202
FAX: (208) 334-1580
www.mepcom.army.mil/Units/Western-Sector/
3rd-Battalion/Boise

ILLINOIS
Chicago
8700 W. Bryn Mawr Ave
Suite 200
Chicago, IL 60631

PHONE: (773) 714-3008
FAX: (773) 714-8150
www.mepcom.army.mil/Units/Eastern-Sector/
6th-Battalion/Chicago

INDIANA
Indianapolis
5541 Herbert Lord Drive
Indianapolis, IN 46216

Phone: (317) 554-0531, ext. 201
Fax: (317) 554-0541
www.mepcom.army.mil/Units/Eastern-Sector/
  6th-Battalion/Indianapolis

IOWA
Des Moines
7105 NW 70th Avenue
Building S-71
Johnston, IA 50131

Phone: (515) 224-0125, ext. 312
Fax: (515) 224-4906
www.mepcom.army.mil/Units/Western-Sector/
  1st-Battalion/Des-Moines

KENTUCKY
Louisville
600 Dr. Martin Luther King, Jr. Place
Room 477
Louisville, KY 40202

Phone: (502) 582-5921, ext. 2222
Fax: (502) 582-6566
www.mepcom.army.mil/Units/Eastern-Sector/
  8th-Battalion/Louisville

LOUISIANA
New Orleans
Belle Chasse Naval Air Station
400 Russell Avenue
New Orleans, LA 70143-5077

Phone: (504) 678-3535
Fax: (504) 678-8925
www.mepcom.army.mil/Units/Western-Sector/
  11th-Battalion/New-Orleans

Shreveport
2715 Alkay Drive
Shreveport, LA 71118-2509

Phone: (318) 671-6080, ext. 203
Fax: (318) 671-6097
www.mepcom.army.mil/Units/Western-Sector/
  11th-Battalion/Shreveport

MAINE
Portland
510 Congress Street
3rd Floor
Portland, ME 04101-3403

Phone: (207) 775-0910
Fax: (207) 775-2947
www.mepcom.army.mil/Units/Eastern-Sector/
  2nd-Battalion/Portland-ME

MARYLAND
Baltimore
850 Chisholm Avenue
Fort Meade, MD 20755

Phone: (301) 677-0010
Fax: (301) 677-0440
www.mepcom.army.mil/Units/Eastern-Sector/
  12th-Battalion/Baltimore

MASSACHUSETTS
Boston
Barnes Building
495 Summer Street
4th Floor
Boston, MA 02210

Phone: (617) 753-3100
Fax: (617) 753-3997
www.mepcom.army.mil/Units/Eastern-Sector/
  2nd-Battalion/Boston

Springfield
551 Airlift Drive
Westover JARB
Springfield, MA 01022-1519

Phone: (413) 593-9543, ext. 200
Fax: (413) 593-9485
www.mepcom.army.mil/Units/Eastern-Sector/
  2nd-Battalion/Springfield

MICHIGAN
Detroit
1172 Kirts Blvd.
Troy, MI 48084-4846

Phone: (248) 244-8534
Fax: (248) 244-9352
www.mepcom.army.mil/Units/Eastern-Sector/
  6th-Battalion/Detroit

Lansing
120 East Jolly Road
Lansing, MI 48910

PHONE: (517) 887-1714
FAX: (517) 877-9160
www.mepcom.army.mil/Units/Eastern-Sector/
6th-Battalion/Lansing

MINNESOTA
Minneapolis
1 Federal Drive
Suite 3201
Fort Snelling, MN 55111

PHONE: (612) 725-1757
FAX: (612) 725-1749
www.mepcom.army.mil/Units/Western-Sector/
1st-Battalion/Minneapolis

MISSISSIPPI
Jackson
664 South State Street
Jackson, MS 39201

PHONE: (601) 355-3835, ext. 203
FAX: (601) 352-5708
www.mepcom.army.mil/Units/Eastern-Sector/
8th-Battalion/Jackson

MISSOURI
Kansas City
10316 NW Prairie View Road
Kansas City, MO 64153-1350

PHONE: (816) 891-9490
FAX: (816) 891-8258
www.mepcom.army.mil/Units/Western-Sector/
11th-Battalion/Kansas-City

St. Louis
Robert A. Young Federal Building
1222 Spruce Street
St. Louis, MO 63103-2816

PHONE: (314) 331-4040
FAX: (314) 331-5699
www.mepcom.army.mil/Units/Western-Sector/
11th-Battalion/St-Louis

MONTANA
Butte
22 West Park Street
Butte, MT 59701

PHONE: (406) 723-8883, ext. 222
FAX: (406) 782-7797
www.mepcom.army.mil/Units/Western-Sector/
3rd-Battalion/Butte

NEBRASKA
Omaha
4245 S. 121 St. Plaza
Omaha, NE 68137

PHONE: (402) 733-7474
FAX: (402) 733-7660
www.mepcom.army.mil/Units/Western-Sector/
1st-Battalion/Omaha

NEW JERSEY
Fort Dix
Building 5645 Texas Avenue
Fort Dix, NJ 08640

PHONE: (609) 562-6050, ext. 2306
FAX: (609) 562-5207
www.mepcom.army.mil/Units/Eastern-Sector/
2nd-Battalion/Fort-Dix

NEW MEXICO
Albuquerque
10500 Copper Ave. NE
Suite J
Albuquerque, NM 87123

PHONE: (505) 246-8020
FAX: (505) 246-8861
www.mepcom.army.mil/Units/Western-Sector/
3rd-Battalion/Albuquerque

NEW YORK
Albany
Leo W. O'Brien Federal Building
North Pearl Street & Clinton Avenue
Albany, NY 12207

PHONE: (518) 320-9860
FAX: (518) 320-9869
http://www.mepcom.army.mil/Units/
Eastern-Sector/4th-Battalion/Albany/

Buffalo

2024 Entrance Ave

Building 799

Niagara Falls ARS, NY 14304-5000

PHONE: (716) 501-9012

FAX: (716) 501-9027

www.mepcom.army.mil/Units/Eastern-Sector/
    4th-Battalion/Buffalo

New York

Fort Hamilton Military Community

116 White Avenue

Brooklyn, NY 11252-4705

PHONE: (718) 630-4646

FAX: (718) 765-7338

www.mepcom.army.mil/Units/Eastern-Sector/
    2nd-Battalion/New-York

Syracuse

6001 East Malloy Road

Building 710

Syracuse, NY 13211-2100

PHONE: (315) 455-3012

FAX: (315) 455-7807

www.mepcom.army.mil/Units/Eastern-Sector/
    4th-Battalion/Syracuse

NORTH CAROLINA

Charlotte

3545 Whitehall Park

Suite 200

Charlotte, NC 28273

PHONE: (704) 504-2498

FAX: (704) 504-1335

www.mepcom.army.mil/Units/Eastern-Sector/
    12th-Battalion/Charlotte

Raleigh

2625 Appliance Court

Raleigh, NC 27604

PHONE: (919) 834-7787

FAX: (919) 755-1303

www.mepcom.army.mil/Units/Eastern-Sector/
    12th-Battalion/Raleigh

NORTH DAKOTA

Fargo

225 Fourth Avenue North

Fargo, ND 58102

PHONE: (701) 234-0473

FAX: (701) 234-0597

www.mepcom.army.mil/Units/Western-Sector/
    1st-Battalion/Fargo

OHIO

Cleveland

20637 Emerald Parkway Drive

Cleveland, Ohio 44135-6023

PHONE: (216) 267-1286, ext. 201

FAX: (216) 522-9860

www.mepcom.army.mil/Units/Eastern-Sector/
    4th-Battalion/Cleveland

Columbus

775 Taylor Road

Gahanna, OH 43230

PHONE: (614) 868-8430, ext. 220

FAX: (614) 856-9065

www.mepcom.army.mil/Units/Eastern-Sector/
    6th-Battalion/Columbus

OKLAHOMA

Oklahoma City

301 Northwest 6th Street

Suite 150

Oklahoma City, OK 73102

PHONE: (405) 609-8700

FAX: (405) 609-8639

www.mepcom.army.mil/Units/Western-Sector/
    11th-Battalion/Oklahoma-City

OREGON

Portland

7545 NE Ambassador Place

Portland, OR 97220-1367

PHONE: (503) 528-1630

FAX: (503) 528-1640

www.mepcom.army.mil/Units/Western-Sector/
    5th-Battalion/Portland-OR

PENNSYLVANIA
Harrisburg
4641 Westport Drive
Mechanicsburg, PA 17055

PHONE: (717) 691-6180, ext. 221
FAX: (717) 691-8039
www.mepcom.army.mil/Units/Eastern-Sector/
    4th-Battalion/Harrisburg

Pittsburgh
William S. Moorehead Federal Building
1000 Liberty Avenue
Suite 1917
Pittsburgh, PA 15222-4101

PHONE: (412) 395-5873
FAX: (412) 281-5464
www.mepcom.army.mil/Units/Eastern-Sector/
    4th-Battalion/Pittsburgh

PUERTO RICO
San Juan
Millennium Park Plaza
15 Second St., Suite 310
Guaynabo, PR 00968-1741

PHONE: (787) 277-7500
FAX: (787) 277-7507
www.mepcom.army.mil/Units/Eastern-Sector/
    10th-Battalion/San-Juan

SOUTH CAROLINA
Fort Jackson
2435 Marion Avenue
Fort Jackson, SC 29207

PHONE: (803) 751-6522
FAX: (803) 751-5744
www.mepcom.army.mil/Units/Eastern-Sector/
    12th-Battalion/Fort-Jackson

SOUTH DAKOTA
Sioux Falls
2801 South Kiwanis Avenue
Suite 200
Sioux Falls, SD 57105

PHONE: (605) 334-0280
FAX: (605) 332-8412
www.mepcom.army.mil/Units/Western-Sector/
    1st-Battalion/Sioux-Falls

TENNESSEE
Knoxville
710 Locust St.
Room 600
Knoxville, TN 37902

PHONE: (865) 531-8221
FAX: (865) 531-8741
www.mepcom.army.mil/Units/Eastern-Sector/
    8th-Battalion/Knoxville

Memphis
1980 Nonconnah Blvd. 3rd Floor
Memphis, TN 38132

PHONE: (901) 526-2100
FAX: (901) 527-7832
www.mepcom.army.mil/Units/Eastern-Sector/
    8th-Battalion/Memphis

Nashville
20 Bridgestone Park
Nashville, TN 37214-2428

PHONE: (615) 833-1347, ext. 111
FAX: (615) 833-2570
www.mepcom.army.mil/Units/Eastern-Sector/
    8th-Battalion/Nashville

TEXAS
Amarillo
1100 South Fillmore
Suite 100
Amarillo, TX 79101

PHONE: (806) 379-9037
FAX: (806) 374-9332
www.mepcom.army.mil/Units/Western-Sector/
    9th-Battalion/Amarillo

Dallas
Federal Building
207 South Houston Street
Suite 400
Dallas, TX 75202

PHONE: (214) 655-3200
FAX: (214) 655-3213
www.mepcom.army.mil/Units/Western-Sector/
    9th-Battalion/Dallas

El Paso

6380 Morgan Avenue
Suite E
El Paso TX 79906-4611

PHONE: (915) 568-3505
FAX: (915) 568-4477
www.mepcom.army.mil/Units/Western-Sector/
9th-Battalion/El-Paso

Houston

701 San Jacinto Street
P.O. Box 52309
Houston, TX 77052-2309

PHONE: (713) 718-4229
FAX: (713) 718-4228
www.mepcom.army.mil/Units/Western-Sector/
9th-Battalion/Houston

San Antonio

1950 Stanley Road
Suite 103
Fort Sam Houston, TX 78234-2712

PHONE: (210) 295-9045
FAX: (210) 295-9151
www.mepcom.army.mil/Units/Western-Sector/
9th-Battalion/San-Antonio

UTAH

Salt Lake City

546 West Amelia Earhart Drive
Suite 130
Salt Lake City, UT 84116

PHONE: (801) 975-3701
FAX: (801) 975-3715
www.mepcom.army.mil/Units/Western-Sector/
3rd-Battalion/Salt-Lake-City

VIRGINIA

Fort Lee

2011 Mahone Avenue
Ft. Lee, VA 23801-1707

PHONE: (804) 765-4000
FAX: (804) 765-4190
www.mepcom.army.mil/Units/Eastern-Sector/
12th-Battalion/Fort-Lee

WASHINGTON

Seattle

4735 East Marginal Way South
Suite 161, Box 16
Seattle, WA 98134-2388

PHONE: (206) 766-6400, ext. 7525
FAX: (206) 766-6430
www.mepcom.army.mil/Units/Western-Sector/
5th-Battalion/Seattle

Spokane

8570 West Highway 2
Spokane, WA 99224

PHONE: (509) 456-4641
FAX: (509) 747-1988
www.mepcom.army.mil/Units/Western-Sector/
5th-Battalion/Spokane

WEST VIRGINIA

Beckley

409 Wood Mountain Road
Glen Jean, WV 25846

PHONE: (304) 465-0208
FAX: (304) 465-3194
www.mepcom.army.mil/Units/Eastern-Sector/
12th-Battalion/Beckley

WISCONSIN

Milwaukee

11050 West Liberty Drive
Milwaukee, WI 53224

PHONE: (414) 359-1315
FAX: (414) 359-1390
www.mepcom.army.mil/Units/Eastern-Sector/
6th-Battalion/Milwaukee

CAN YOU RETAKE THE ASVAB?

If you have taken the ASVAB within the past two years, you can retake the test as long as you follow certain rules. If you are taking the ASVAB for enlistment purposes, your most recent valid score is the one that will be considered.

The rules about retaking the ASVAB are as follows. First, you must take the entire test battery—that is, all subtests, not just one. Military applicants who have taken an initial ASVAB—student or enlistment—can retest after one calendar month has elapsed. For example, if you first took the test on February 3, the earliest you could retake it would be March 3. If you wished to retake the test a second time, you would have to wait until April 3. After that, you would need to wait at least six months before you could take the test again. In other words, if you first took the test on February 3, took a retest on March 3, and took a second retest on April 3, you would have to wait until October 3 before you could take a third retest (see Sample Retesting Schedule chart below).

Retesting with the same version of the ASVAB that was used on any previous test is strictly prohibited for at least six months. If an applicant is retested with the same test version within a six-month period, the retest score will be invalidated and the previous valid test score will stand as the score of record. However, if the condition is the result of a MEPS or OPM test administrator procedural or administrative error, the MEPS commander may authorize an immediate retest using a different ASVAB version. This is not such an issue with the CAT-ASVAB.

Applicants who are dismissed for cheating or disruptive behavior will have their test invalidated, and are not permitted to retest for six months from the date of the invalid test.

If you are taking the ASVAB in order to enlist in the military and your Armed Forces Qualification Test (AFQT) score (see Chapter 4) on your most recent test is 20 points or more higher than your score on an ASVAB you took less than six months previously, you may be required to complete a confirmation test.

Retaking the ASVAB for Enlistment If You Took It in High School

If you took the test in high school, should you take it again if you want to join the military? Remember that you can retake the test every six months and that your most recent valid score will be the one used for military enlistment purposes. That being the case, it is a good idea to take the test again if you think you can get a better score. Use the information in this book to help you score higher.

Retaking the ASVAB If You Are on Active Duty

Low ASVAB scores on initial tests do not have to be permanent, barring access to certain schools and other opportunities. Active-duty military personnel whose original ASVAB scores were low can retest to raise their scores and improve their eligibility for some programs. Higher ASVAB scores can help active-duty personnel change to more technical ratings and can improve eligibility for a class A school.

However, enlisted personnel are allowed to retake the ASVAB only once, and that test score becomes permanent, even if it is lower than the original score. As a result, if you are already in the military and wish to retake the ASVAB, you must be certain that you have made the improvements necessary to raise your score. If you want to retake the test, you must prove that you have improved your abilities enough—through training, practical experience, and schools—to expect a higher ASVAB score. See the review sections in this book to increase your score.

Improvements may be gained in a number of ways: functional skills training, completing study at public or private institutions, participation in training courses, study at academic skills learning centers, or using this test preparation book. Other proven ways to achieve higher ASVAB scores include command programs to enhance basic academic skills, attending boot camp, military experience, and increased maturity.

Sample Retesting Schedule

3 Feb.	3 Mar.	3 Apr.	3 May	3 June	3 July	3 Aug.	3 Sept.	3 Oct.
Initial test	First retest	Second retest						Third retest

ASVAB Scores and Score Reports

Once you take the ASVAB, the score report you will receive depends on where you took the test. The amount of information you will receive also depends on whether you took the paper-and-pencil version or the computer-adaptive version of the ASVAB.

IF YOU TAKE THE ASVAB AT A SCHOOL

If you take the ASVAB at a school, a score report will be sent to your school within 14 days after the test. Your score report will include a number of different scores.

The Department of Defense it piloting and rolling out a computer adaptive version of the ASVAB program. It is being used in certain selected schools, but will be available more broadly as time goes on as improvements are made. Results on your test will be almost immediate.

Subtest Scores and Career Exploration Scores

Your score report will include scores for each of the subtests in the test battery. These are General Science, Arithmetic Reasoning, Word Knowledge, Paragraph Comprehension, Mathematics Knowledge, Electronics Information, Auto and Shop Information, Mechanical Comprehension, and Assembling Objects.

Your score report will also show three Career Exploration Scores: Verbal Skills, Math Skills, and Science and Technical Skills. These are composite scores combining your scores on several ASVAB subtests. The ASVAB Career Exploration Scores are a good indicator of the kinds of tasks that test takers do well and the kinds of tasks that they may find difficult.

- *Verbal Skills* is a general measure of the vocabulary and reading skills covered in the Word Knowledge and Paragraph Comprehension tests. People with high scores tend to do well in tasks that require good vocabulary or reading skills, while people with low scores have more difficulty with such tasks.

- *Math Skills* is a general measure of the mathematics skills covered in the Mathematics Knowledge and Arithmetic Reasoning tests. People with high scores tend to do well in tasks that require knowledge of mathematics, while people with low scores have more difficulty with these kinds of tasks.

- *Science and Technical Skills* is a general measure of science and technical skills, which are covered in the General Science, Electronics Information, and Mechanical Comprehension tests. People with high scores tend to do well in tasks that require scientific thinking or technical skills, while people with low scores have more difficulty with such tasks.

Standard Scores and Percentile Scores

Each of the scores just listed is reported in two ways: as standard scores and as percentile scores. Each standard score is calculated by applying statistical methods to the student's raw score. This method produces a numerical score with a short range of possible statistical error above and below it. Most student ASVAB takers achieve standard scores between 30 and 70. This means that a standard score of 50 is an average score and a score of 60 is an above-average score. The score report shows the numerical standard scores, which are estimates of your true skill level in that area. According to the report, if you took the test again, your new score would probably be similar to, but not necessarily exactly like your initial score.

The percentile scores on the ASVAB score report indicate how well the you did in relation to others in the same grade. For each ASVAB test and composite (called a Career Exploration Score), students receive a same grade/same sex, same grade/opposite sex, and same grade/combined sex percentile score. For example, if you are a female eleventh grader, you would get percentile scores showing how well you did compared to other females in the eleventh grade, males in the eleventh grade, and all eleventh graders. For example, if you scored a percentile of 65 on Math Skills, that means you scored as well as or better than 65 out of 100 eleventh-grade females in Math Skills. When compared to males and all eleventh grade students, your percentile score may be different.

Because the experiences of males and females differ, they can perform somewhat differently on tests. On the more technically oriented tests, such as Electronics Information, the mean performance of males is higher than that of females. This does not mean that women cannot learn this information or that they should be discouraged from considering occupations in related areas. Typically, this difference occurs because more males than females have had exposure to electronics principles. As a result, it is fairer to report how students do compared to members of their own sex, but also to let them know how they compare to members of the opposite sex on tests that might be important to them. For example, a female student might be interested in a career in mechanics, surveying, or civil engineering. Knowing how she scores relative to both her own sex and the opposite sex is useful information. In the past, these career fields have traditionally been dominated by males. Since she will be competing with males, it is important for her to know how she stands relative to males. The same is true for males interested in occupations traditionally dominated by females.

The AFQT is a general measure of trainabi-lity and a predictor of on-the-job performance. Chapter 4 explains how the AFQT is used in military recruiting.

Figure 3.1 shows a sample score report from an ASVAB test taken at a school.

IF YOU TAKE THE PAPER-AND-PENCIL ASVAB AT A MILITARY FACILITY

If you take the ASVAB at a military facility called a MET site, you may be given a paper-and-pencil version of the test. You won't receive as much information about your results as those who take the ASVAB at a high school or postsecondary school. At at MET site you also may be given an Internet delivered version of the CATASVAB, the iCAT.

Figure 3.2 shows the only information you will receive: the AFQT percentile. This is an unofficial score calculated by the local test administrator.

IF YOU TAKE THE CAT-ASVAB AT A MEPS

If you take the CAT-ASVAB at a MEPS, you will receive more scoring information than if you took the test at a MET site, but less than if you took the ASVAB at a high school. The CAT-ASVAB report provides your scores on every subtest of the ASVAB, your AFQT, and your general scores for qualifying for services occupations. (See Part 5 for how your scores qualify you for various jobs in each of the services.) The score report in Figure 3.3 is a sample of the CAT-ASVAB score report.

ASVAB SUMMARY RESULTS

Student
12th Gr Female (Form: 23G)
SSN: XXX-XX-9999
Test Date: Jul 11, 2005
Old Dominion Hs
Hometown DC

ASVAB Results

	Percentile Scores			12th Grade Standard Scores
	12th Grade Females	12th Grade Males	12th Grade Students	12th Grade Standard Scores
Career Exploration Scores				
Verbal Skills	97	95	96	65
Math Skills	22	17	19	42
Science and Technical Skills	81	48	64	53
ASVAB Tests				
General Science	91	81	86	61
Arithmetic Reasoning	43	30	37	47
Word Knowledge	98	95	96	66
Paragraph Comprehension	92	91	91	62
Mathematics Knowledge	14	12	13	37
Electronics Informations	13	10	11	38
Auto and Shop Information	53	21	37	45
Mechanical Comprehension	95	76	85	59

Military Entrance Score (AFQT) 57

EXPLANATION OF YOUR ASVAB PERCENTILE SCORES

Your ASVAB results are reported as percentile scores in the three highlighted columns to the left of the graph. Percentile scores show how you compare to other students - males and females, and for all students - in your grade. For example, a percentile score of 65 for an 11th grade female would mean she scored the same or better than 65 out of every 100 females in the 11th grade.

For purposes of career planning, knowing your relative standing in these comparison groups is important. Being male or female does not limit your career or educational choices. There are noticeable differences in how men and women score in some areas. Viewing your scores in light of your relative standing both to men and women may encourage you to explore areas that you might otherwise overlook.

You can use the **Career Exploration Scores** to evaluate your knowledge and skills in three general areas (Verbal, Math, and Science and Technical Skills). You can use the **ASVAB Test Scores** to gather information on specific skill areas. *Together, these scores provide a snapshot of your current knowledge and skills.* This information will help you develop and review your career goals and plans.

EXPLANATION OF YOUR ASVAB STANDARD SCORES

Your ASVAB results are reported as standard scores in the above graph. Your score on each test is identified by the "X" in the corresponding bar graph. You should view these scores as *estimates* of your true skill level in that area. If you took the test again, you probably would receive a somewhat different score. Many things, such as how you were feeling during testing, contribute to this difference. This difference is shown with gray score bands in the graph of your results. Your standard scores are based on the ASVAB tests and composites based on your grade level.

The score bands provide a way to identify some of your strengths. Overlapping score bands mean your true skill level is similar in both areas, so the real difference between specific scores might not be meaningful. If the score bands do not overlap, you probably are stronger in the area that has the higher score band.

The ASVAB is an aptitude test. It is neither an absolute measure of your skills and abilities nor a perfect predictor of your success or failure. A high score does not guarantee success, and a low score does not guarantee failure, in a future educational program or occupation. For example, if you have never worked with shop equipment or cars, you may not be familiar with the terms and concepts

assessed by the Auto and Shop Information test. Taking a course or obtaining a part-time job in this area would increase your knowledge and improve your score if you were to take it again.

USING ASVAB RESULTS IN CAREER EXPLORATION

Your career and educational plans may change over time as you gain more experience and learn more about your interests. *Exploring Careers: The ASVAB Career Exploration Guide* can help you learn more about yourself and the world of work, to identify and explore potential goals, and develop an effective strategy to realize your goals. The *Guide* will help you identify occupations in line with your interests and skills. As you explore potentially satisfying careers, you will develop your career exploration and planning skills.

Meanwhile, your ASVAB results can help you in making well-informed choices about future high school courses.

We encourage you to discuss your ASVAB results with a teacher, counselor, parent, family member or other interested adult. These individuals can help you to view your ASVAB results in light of other important information, such as your interests, school grades, motivation, and personal goals.

USE OF INFORMATION

Personal identity information (name, social security number, street address, and telephone number) and test scores will not be released to any agency outside of the Department of Defense (DoD), the Armed Forces, the Coast Guard, and your school. Your school or local school system can determine any further release of information. The DoD will use your scores for recruiting and research purposes for up to two years. After that the information will be used by the DoD for research purposes only.

MILITARY ENTRANCE SCORES

The **Military Entrance Score** (also called AFQT, which stands for the Armed Forces Qualification Test) is the score used to determine your qualifications for entry into any branch of the United States Armed Forces or the Coast Guard. The Military Entrance Score predicts in a general way how well you might do in training and on the job in military occupations. Your score reflects your standing compared to American men and women 18 to 23 years of age.

Use Access Code: 123456789X
(for online Occu-find and FYI)
Access Code expires: Jul 15, 2007

Explore career possibilities by using your Access Code at

www.asvabprogram.com

SEE YOUR COUNSELOR FOR FURTHER INFORMATION

DD FORM 1304-5(S)

Figure 3.1. Sample score report from an ASVAB taken at a school

ASVAB SCORE AND TEST DESCRIPTIONS

Verbal Skills is a general measure of language and reading skills which combines the Word Knowledge and Paragraph Comprehension tests. People with high scores tend to do well in tasks that require good language or reading skills, while people with low scores have more difficulty with such tasks.

Math Skills is a general measure of mathematics skills which combines the Mathematics Knowledge and Arithmetic Reasoning tests. People with high scores tend to do well in tasks that require a knowledge of mathematics, while people with low scores have more difficulty with these kinds of tasks.

Science and Technical Skills is a general measure of science and technical skills which combines the General Science, Electronics Information, and Mechanical Comprehension tests. People with high scores tend to do well in tasks that require scientific thinking or technical skills, while people with low scores have more difficulty with such tasks.

General Science (GS) tests the ability to answer questions on a variety of science topics drawn from courses taught in most high schools. The life science items cover botany, zoology, anatomy and physiology, and ecology. The earth and space science items are based on astronomy, geology, meteorology, and oceanography. The physical science items measure force and motion mechanics, energy, fluids, atomic structure, and chemistry.

Arithmetic Reasoning (AR) tests the ability to solve basic arithmetic problems one encounters in everyday life. One-step and multi-step word problems require addition, subtraction, multiplication, and division, and choosing the correct order of operations when more than one step is necessary. The items include operations with whole numbers, operations with rational numbers, ratio and proportion, interest and percentage, and measurement. Arithmetic reasoning is one factor that helps characterize mathematics comprehension and it also assesses logical thinking.

Word Knowledge (WK) tests the ability to understand the meaning of words through synonyms – words having the same or nearly the same meaning as other words. The test is a measure of one component of reading comprehension since vocabulary is one of many factors that characterize reading comprehension.

Paragraph Comprehension (PC) tests the ability to obtain information from written material. Students read different types of passages of varying lengths and respond to questions based on information presented in each passage. Concepts include identifying stated and reworded facts, determining a sequence of events, drawing conclusions, identifying main ideas, determining the author's purpose and tone, and identifying style and technique.

Mathematics Knowledge (MK) tests the ability to solve problems by applying knowledge of mathematical concepts and applications. The problems focus on concepts and algorithms and involve number theory, numeration, algebraic operations and equations, geometry and measurement, and probability. Mathematics knowledge is one factor that characterizes mathematics comprehension; it also assesses logical thinking.

Electronics Information (EI) tests understanding of electrical current, circuits, devices, and systems. Electronics information topics include electrical circuits, electrical and electronic systems, electrical currents, electrical tools, symbols, devices, and materials.

Auto and Shop Information (AS) tests aptitude for automotive maintenance and repair and wood and metal shop practices. The test covers several areas commonly included in most high school auto and shop courses such as automotive components, automotive systems, automotive tools, troubleshooting and repair, shop tools, building materials, and building and construction procedures.

Mechanical Comprehension (MC) tests comprehension of the principles of mechanical devices and properties of materials. Mechanical comprehension topics include simple machines, compound machines, mechanical motion, fluid dynamics, properties of materials, and structural support.

Military Entrance Score (AFQT) is the score used if an individual decides to enter any of the armed services. See your local recruiter for details.

UNVERIFIED TEST SCORES (SINGLE APPLICANT)
For use of this form, see USMEPCOM Reg 611-1

FOR OFFICIAL USE ONLY

FOR TA USE ONLY

Name		SSN	
Date of Test 5-2A-0A	Test Version 26a		MET Site 4321
Service AR NA (AF)	MC CG	Component (Active) Reserves National Guard

Enter the percentile score:

39

AFQT Percentile

USMEPCOM Form 611-1-2-R-E, NOV 01   Replaces USMEPCOM Form 611-1-2-R-E, 1 MAR 0C, which is obsolete.

34813(11-01)

©

Figure 3.2. Sample score report from an ASVAB taken at a MET site. This is an unofficial score calculated by the local test administrator

```
                    FOR OFFICIAL USE ONLY

            UNVERIFIED WINDOWS CAT-ASVAB TEST SCORE REPORT

Testing Site ID:      987654                Service:  DNR

Testing Session:   Date 2005/09/24      Starting Time: 05:00

Applicant:      Name:  Jay Jones        SSN:  123-45-6789

Test Form:            04D                Test Type:  Initial
```

	GS	AR	WK	PC	MK	EI	AS	MC	AO	VE
Standard Scores:	56	57	56	35	46	37	37	48	40	50

COMPOSITE SCORE:

Army:	GT	CL	CO	EL	FA	GM	MM	OF	SC	ST
	108	101	092	092	-94	091	085	093	093	097

Air Force:	M	A	G	E
	38	40	59	47

Navy/CG:	GT	EL	BEE	ENG	MEC	MEC2	NUC	OPS	HM	ADM
	107	196	205	083	142	145	201	193	152	096

Marine:	MM	GT	EL	CL
	088	104	098	096

AFQT Percentile Score: 49

Figure 3.3. Sample CAT-ASVAB score report

Chapter 4

The ASVAB, the AFQT, and Military Entrance

YOUR GOALS FOR THIS CHAPTER:

• Learn how ASVAB AFQT scores are used to determine eligibility for enlistment.

• Find out about other educational requirements for military recruits.

• Learn what happens during the rest of the military entrance process.

When you take the ASVAB in order to enlist in the U.S. Armed Forces, your ASVAB scores will be used in several ways. In the previous chapter, you learned about an ASVAB score called the Military Entrance Score (AFQT). You will need to achieve a certain AFQT score in order to be eligible for initial enlistment. Later, your ASVAB scores will be used to qualify you for various occupations in the military. The higher your scores, the more choices you will have for training in various occupations. So you want to do your best on the ASVAB so that you will have the widest choice of training programs and job responsibilities.

AFQT SCORES AND ELIGIBILITY FOR ENLISTMENT

The Military Entrance Score or AFQT is a composite of your scores on four ASVAB tests that make up what is called the Armed Forces Qualification Test. The AFQT is the primary score that indicates the training potential of persons who wish to enlist in the military. Your AFQT score determines your eligibility for military service. It also is able to predict how well you will perform on the job.

AFQT scores are reported as percentile scores. The percentile shows how your score compares to the scores of other test takers, and it also determines where you fit into what are called AFQT categories. The services use these categories to set

recruiting goals. Recruiters prefer recruiting people in the highest categories because they are generally smarter and easier to train in the various occupations needed by the military. It is also more economical for the Department of Defense to recruit smarter individuals because they learn what is needed much more quickly and they perform better on the job.

Persons in categories I and II are above average in trainability. Category III recruits tend to be average in trainability, and category IV recruits are below average in trainability. Applicants scoring in category V are forbidden by law to be accepted into the military. In addition, military applicants in category IV who do not have a high school diploma are generally forbidden to enter the military.

Armed Forces Qualification Test (AFQT) Categories and Corresponding Percentile Score Ranges

AFQT Category	Percentile Score Range
I	93–99
II	65–92
IIIA	50–64
IIIB	31–49
IV	10–30
V	1–9

The services are required to enlist at least 60 percent of recruits from AFQT categories I through IIIA, and no more than 4 percent of the recruits can come from category IV. To give you an idea of the percentages of recruits in each AFQT category, look at Table 4.1. You can see that very few recruits come from category IV and none come from category V.

ADDITIONAL EDUCATIONAL REQUIREMENTS

The amount of education you have obtained also matters in your eligibility to enter military service. The Department of Defense uses a three-tier classification of educational credentials. The three tiers are:

Tier 1. Regular high school graduates, adult diploma holders, and nongraduates with at least 15 hours of college credit.

Tier 2. Alternative credential holders, including those with a General Education Development (GED) certificate of high school equivalency.

Tier 3. Those with no educational credentials.

The reason for this classification system is that there is a strong relationship between educational credentials and successful completion of the first term of military service. That is, if you have a good AFQT and good educational credentials, you are likely to complete your required service and not drop out partway through (an outcome that would waste the taxpayer dollars spent to train you).

Table 4.1. Non-Prior Service (NPS) Active Component Enlisted Accessions, FY11: by Armed Forces Qualification Test (AFQT) Category, Service, and Gender with Civilian Comparision Group

Gender	AFQT Category[1]					
	I	II	IIIA	IIIB	IV	Total
Army						
Males	3,898	17,819	11,811	18,155	147	51,830
Females	367	2,665	2,308	4,720	52	10,112
Total	**4,265**	**20,484**	**14,119**	**22,875**	**199**	**61,942**
Navy						
Males	3,000	12,620	7,561	2,438	0	25,622
Females	413	3,199	2,839	1,282	0	7,734
Total	**3,413**	**15,819**	**10,400**	**3,720**	**0**	**33,356**
Marine Corps						
Males	1,463	11,042	7,895	6,842	10	29,077
Females	91	848	806	751	3	2,285
Total	**1,554**	**11,890**	**8,701**	**7,593**	**13**	**31,362**
Air Force						
Males	2,324	12,933	7,429	312	0	22,998
Females	302	2,657	2,221	87	0	5,267
Total	**2,626**	**15,590**	**9,650**	**399**	**0**	**28,265**
Total DoD						
Males	10,685	54,414	34,696	27,747	157	127,702
Females	1,173	9,369	8,174	6,840	55	25,612
Total	**11,858**	**63,783**	**42,870**	**34,587**	**212**	**153,314**

Coast Guard

	I	II	IIIA	IIIB	IV	Total
Males	288	1,594	624	131	0	2,656
Females	59	365	219	27	0	676
Total	**347**	**1,959**	**843**	**158**	**0**	**3,332**

The services are required to ensure that at least 90 percent of first-time recruits are high school graduates. Services often set even higher educational standards, sometimes requiring nearly 100 percent of the recruits in their enlistment pool to be high school graduates. If you don't have a high school diploma, you will need a very high AFQT score.

There are different AFQT scoring standards for individuals in each tier. Generally, tier 3 applicants must have higher AFQT test scores than tier 2 applicants, who must have higher test scores than tier 1 individuals. The Air Force and Marine Corps follow these differential standards, requiring different minimum test scores for each tier. The Army and Navy require applicants with alternative credentials (tier 2) and those with no credentials (tier 3) to meet the same AFQT standards, which are more stringent than those for high school graduates (tier 1).

So if you want to enlist in the military, your chances are much better if you have graduated from high school with a traditional diploma and score high on the AFQT.

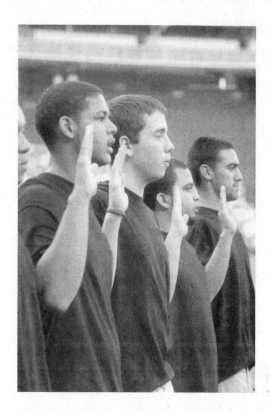

BEYOND THE ASVAB

Physical Condition and Moral Character Requirements

If you achieve a satisfactory ASVAB score and continue the application process, you will be scheduled for a physical examination and background review at one of the 65 Military Entrance Processing Stations (MEPS). The examination determines your fitness for military service. It includes measurement of blood pressure, pulse, visual acuity, and hearing; blood testing and urinalysis; drug and HIV testing; medical history; and possibly tests of strength and endurance. If you have a fixable or temporary medical problem, you may be required to get treatment before proceeding. It is possible but very difficult to obtain a waiver of certain disqualifying medical conditions and be allowed to enlist.

> Obesity is the leading medical reason for not qualifying for the military.

To enter one of the services, you must meet rigorous moral character standards. You will be screened by the recruiter and will undergo an interview covering your background. You may undergo a financial credit check; a computerized search for a criminal record may also be conducted. Some types of criminal activity are clearly disqualifying; other cases require a waiver. The service to which you applied will examine your circumstances and make an individual determination of qualification. Since it has been shown that applicants with existing financial problems generally do not overcome those problems on junior enlisted pay, a credit history may be part of the decision to allow you to enlist or not.

Military Occupational Counseling

If your ASVAB scores, educational credentials, physical fitness, and moral character qualify you for entry and you wish to proceed with the process, you will meet with a service classification counselor at the MEPS to discuss options for enlistment. The counselor has the record of your qualifications and computerized information on available service training/skill openings, schedules, and enlistment incentives.

A recruit can sign up for a specific skill or for a broad occupational area (such as the mechanical or electronics area). In the Army, most recruits (95 percent) enter for specific skill training; the others are placed in a military occupational specialty during basic training. Approximately 70 percent of

Air Force recruits enter for a specific skill, while the rest sign up for an occupational area and are classified into a specific skill while in basic training. In the Navy, approximately 79 percent of recruits enlist for a specific skill, while the rest go directly to the fleet after basic training, classified into airman, fireman, or seaman programs. Approximately 86 percent of Marine Corps enlistees enter with a guaranteed occupational area and are assigned a specific skill within that area after recruit training; the rest enlist with either a specific job guarantee or assignment to a job after recruit training.

Your counselor will discuss your interests with you and will explain what the service has to offer. Typically, the counselor will describe a number of different occupations to you. In general, the higher your test scores, the more choices you will have. The counselor may suggest incentives to encourage you to choose hard-to-fill occupational specialties. You are free to accept or reject these offers. Many applicants do not decide immediately, but take time to discuss options with their family and friends; others decide not to enlist. The services do not discriminate based on race, religion, or gender. In fact, about 16 percent of active duty and reserves are female.

What Happens Next?

When you accept an offer and sign a contract, you will need to choose between two options. One option is to proceed directly to a recruit training center within a month of signing the contract. However, very few people select this option. Most people choose the second option, which is to enter the Delayed Entry Program (DEP). This allows you up to a year before you need to report for duty. During this time, you can continue your education, obtain your high school diploma, take advantage of a supervised exercise program, and in general become acclimated to the military. The length of time in the DEP depends on the training opportunities for the occupation you have selected.

If you are selected, you will be one of the nearly 400,000 individuals who have elected to serve and protect their country by joining the Armed Forces of the United States.

Women in the Military

As of January 2016, all military occupations and positions are open to women, without exception. Although women have served in combat prior to this date, about 10 percent of military jobs were closed

---

MEPS Visit Reminders

1. Discuss any childhood medical problems with your parents and bring documentation with you.
2. Bring your Social Security card, birth certificate, and driver's license.
3. Remove all piercings.
4. Profanity and offensive wording or pictures on clothing are not tolerated.
5. Hats are not permitted inside the MEPS.
6. If you wear either eyeglasses or contacts, bring them along with your prescription and lens case.
7. Bathe or shower the night before your examination.
8. Wear underclothes.
9. Get a good night's sleep before taking the ASVAB.
10. Wear neat, moderate, comfortable clothing.
11. Don't bring stereo headphones, watches, jewelry, excessive cash, or any other valuables.
12. Ask your recruiter for a list of recommended personal items to bring to basic training.
13. Processing starts early at the MEPS—You must report on time.

to females. These included infantry, armor, reconnaissance, and some special operations units. Now more than 220,000 new jobs are available to women.

According to the Secretary of Defense, "They'll be allowed to drive tanks, fire mortars, and lead infantry soldiers into combat. They'll be able to serve as Army Rangers and Green Berets, Navy SEALs, Marine Corps infantry, Air Force parajumpers, and everything else that was previously open only to men."

About 16–18 percent of the military enlisted personnel are women. Part of the challenge is that, on average, men are physically stronger than women and many jobs in the military require strength. That said, there are women who are stronger than some men. The services have been looking at the physical requirements of military jobs to determine what is necessary to successfully accomplish these tasks.

If you are a female military applicant, you need to know that you will be assigned to positions based on ability, not gender, but that does not mean that there will be equal participation by men and women in each occupation. For jobs that require a certain level of physical strength, you will have to meet the requirement.

Some cultures do not understand why women should take on military roles at all. It may take some time to fully integrate women into various positions previously closed to them. As in the civilian world, attitudes and perspectives may need to change.

Taking the CAT-ASVAB

YOUR GOALS FOR THIS CHAPTER:

- **Find out the pros and cons of taking the CAT-ASVAB.**
- **Preview the directions for the computer-based test.**
- **Find out strategies that can raise your CAT-ASVAB score.**

HOW THE CAT-ASVAB WORKS

The CAT-ASVAB is the computer-based version of the test that is offered to potential recruits at the military facilities called MEPS. The CAT-ASVAB subtests measure the same abilities as the paper-and-pencil (P&P) ASVAB subtests. One difference is that the paper-and-pencil ASVAB's Automotive and Shop Information subtest is broken into two separate subtests in CAT-ASVAB. In addition, the tests are adaptive.

With a group-administered paper-and-pencil test, all examinees answer the same questions in the same order. An adaptive test automatically tailors questions to the ability level of the individual examinee. All examinees start with a question of medium difficulty. If you answer the question correctly, you are given a question that is more difficult. If you answer the question incorrectly, you are given a question that is easier. This pattern continues until the test is complete. Therefore, you only answer questions that are appropriate for your ability level, not wasting time answering questions that are too easy or too difficult.

If you take this version of the test, you will be seated in front of a computer and monitor in a room with others. The test comes up on the screen. As you answer the test questions, the program records your answer, scores it, and then calculates your ability level. Based on that information, the next item is selected. After you have completed the test, the AFQT and composite scores will be calculated.

The chart below shows the general idea of how the items are selected for you.

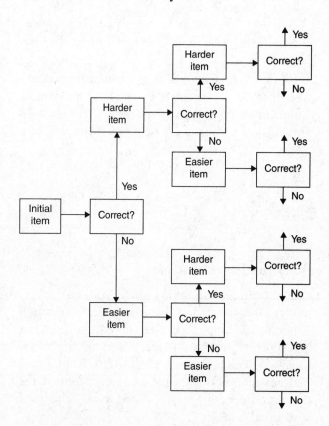

So you can see that the CAT-ASVAB is tailored to you and your ability level. The items come from a huge pool of items that range in difficulty from very easy to very hard. After each item is administered, information is collected and evaluated, and the item best suited to you is selected to be administered next. This selection process provides a more accurate score with fewer items than the paper-and-pencil version. On the whole, the CAT-ASVAB takes less time than the paper-and-pencil version.

The adaptive item selection process of the CAT-ASVAB results in higher levels of test-score precision and shorter test lengths than the paper-and-pencil ASVAB. The figure below illustrates that shorter test lengths can be achieved on the CAT-ASVAB by tailoring the test to the ability level of each examinee.

Test Type	Examinee Ability	Item Difficulty			Test Length
		Easy	Medium Hard	Hard	
P&P	All				30
CAT	Low				15
	Medium				15
	High				15

It is important for you to know that no two test takers get the same items, so you need a good background in the areas tested to do well. Chapters 7–18 in this book will certainly help you achieve a high score.

> See Chapter 3 for a sample CAT-ASVAB score report.

Possible Advantages

One advantage of taking the CAT-ASVAB is that it takes less time than the paper-and-pencil version. Also, the test can be scored immediately, and scoring errors are reduced because of the automation. The test can be administered with minimal advance notice, while administration of the paper-and-pencil ASVAB needs to be scheduled well in advance.

Unlike scores on the paper-and-pencil ASVAB, the CAT-ASVAB score you get is not based solely on the number of items you answered correctly. Some people have claimed that the CAT-ASVAB is easier and can give you better scores because you get more "points" for answering more difficult items.

Possible Disadvantages

Unlike the paper-and-pencil ASVAB, the CAT-ASVAB does not give you an opportunity to go back to questions you previously answered to change your answer or think about the question again. You also cannot skip questions and go on to other questions that you might know. If you get items wrong, the computer will give you easier items, but your score will be lower than if you answered a few difficult items.

CAT-ASVAB Directions

When you arrive to take the CAT-ASVAB, you will be escorted to a waiting room. You will complete various forms, if you haven't already done so. Your Social Security number will be verified. There you will get a briefing similar to the one that follows.

Briefing

[*Your test administrator will read aloud to you directions similar to the following.*]

Welcome, I am [administrator's name], and I will be administering your test today. First of all, has anyone here taken the Armed Services Vocational Aptitude Battery at any time in the past, either in a high school or at another testing site, and not indicated this on the USMEPCOM Form 680-3AE you provided? It is extremely important to identify this because your test will be checked against a nationwide computer file for armed forces applicants. If it is discovered that you were previously tested, but did not tell us, the results from today's test may not be valid for enlistment.

[*If anyone raises his or her hand, the administrator will check that person's USMEPCOM Form 680-3AE to ensure that he or she has marked the retest box and entered the previous forms.*]

It is important that you are physically fit to take this test. Is there anybody here who doesn't feel well enough to take the examination?

[*If anyone says that he or she doesn't feel well, the administrator will remove that person from the session group, inform the service (if available), and indicate the reason for removal on USMEPCOM Form 680-3AE.*]

The test you are about to take is administered by computer. Instructions for taking the test are on the computer, and the guidelines are very easy to follow. If you need assistance during any part of the test, press the red HELP key, raise your hand, and I'll assist you.

The use of calculators, crib sheets, or other devices designed to assist in testing is not permitted. No talking is allowed while in the testing room. Use the scratch paper and pencil on the side of your computer for any figuring you need to do while taking the test. If you need more paper or another pencil, press the red HELP key and then raise your hand.

Do not touch any keys except for the letter choices, the red HELP key, and the ENTER bar. Be careful not to kick the computer under the table.

After completing the examination, give your scratch paper to me, and then you will be released. If you are staying at the hotel, wait at the front desk for transportation.

Does anyone have any questions?

What Happens Next?

After the briefing by the test administrator, you will be brought into the testing room and assigned a seat.

The CAT-ASVAB is designed so that individuals with very little or no computer experience can take the exam. It is recommended that you practice using a computer before taking the CAT-ASVAB. A recruiter may be able to give you some of this practice. The bottom line is to be prepared—well prepared.

The keyboard has been modified to make it easy for you to find the keys. The computer program will give you directions on how to answer the items. It will also tell you about time limits and give you the chance to do some practice items to be sure that you know how to navigate the keyboard.

The directions are quite simple. If you need help during the session, you need only press the HELP key. The administrator will come by to assist you. You should do this only if you are experiencing technical problems with the test, or if you are in need of more scratch paper or another pencil to use for your calculation. When you press the HELP key, the clock on the test will stop. It will restart when you restart the test.

You will answer each item by pressing the key that represents your answer. To register your response, hit the ENTER key, which is the space bar. The next item will then be presented to you.

Recent Changes

Recently, the Department of Defense began a rollout of a new Windows-based version of the CAT-ASVAB. It has a Windows look and feel, and you can use a mouse instead of the keyboard to record your answers. The modified keyboard described earlier can be used as well if that is more comfortable for you.

Changes have been made in the look of the on-screen items, and the graphics have been improved. You can mark buttons for the various answer choices, or you can type the letter of the response.

This new system should be in place before you take the CAT-ASVAB.

No electronic devices are allowed in the testing room. It is best not to take cell phones into the MEPS because the phones will not be secured while you are testing. In addition, coats, jackets, and bags will be left in the CAT-ASVAB waiting room.

Recently the DoD has been implementing the i-CAT a CAT ASVAB that is delivered via the Internet. Using the i-CAT will be similar to the computer version and will get you the same score. Recently the DoD has been implementing the i-CAT a CAT ASVAB that is delivered via the Internet. Using the i-CAT will be similar to the computer version and will get you the same score.

SPECIAL STRATEGIES FOR TAKING THE CAT-ASVAB

Except where noted, the strategies for taking the CAT-ASVAB are the same as for the paper-and-pencil test. Here are some special things to keep in mind.

- To raise your scores, try your very best to answer every item correctly. Take your time, especially with the early items in each test. If you get the early items correct, the computer will give you more difficult questions, and these carry more value. If you get the early items wrong, the computer will give you easier items, and even if you answer these correctly, your score will be lower than if you answered the same number of difficult items. Unlike on the paper-and-pencil tests, guessing is not necessarily a good strategy.

- Focus hard and give the test your full attention.

- Pay attention to the directions. Directions will not be given to you verbally. They will only be on the computer screen to be read.

- Try hard to finish all the items. For every item you do not finish, there is a penalty. The more

---

CAT-ASVAB Myths

Myth: The CAT-ASVAB is harder than the paper-and-pencil ASVAB.

Reality: The CAT-ASVAB may seem harder to many people because the items are selected based on a person's previous answers. For example, a person with high ability will be able to skip over the easier questions that would be found on the paper-and-pencil version of the test.

A lot of research has been done to ensure that the score you would get on the paper-and-pencil or computer adaptive versions will be the same.

Myth: The paper-and-pencil ASVAB is easier than the CAT-ASVAB.

Reality: For persons of lower ability, the paper-and-pencil version may seem easier because the questions are generally arranged from easy to hard within each subtest. As a result, you will receive many easier items to answer before you are challenged with the more difficult ones.

On the CAT-ASVAB, once your general ability level is determined, you will be getting more difficult items to answer to see how well you do. The easier items are skipped.

---

unfinished items, the higher the penalty. Also, the penalty is high if you answer the last few items on each test incorrectly.

THE PiCAT

Applicants who hope to join the military can now take the Armed Services Vocational Aptitude Battery pretest from any computer with Internet access. It is called the PiCAT, which stands for the Pre-screening, internet-delivered, Computer Adaptive Test. The PiCAT is an unproctored version of the full ASVAB that provides recruiters with the ability to determine whether you are qualified before sending applicants to a MEPS or MET site for additional testing.

In order to take the PiCAT, you need an authorization code from a recruiter, which will provide you with access to the test. At this time, about 1,100 recruiters have the ability to give you a unique access code. This number is increasing.

You must start the test within 72 hours of receiving the code and will have 24 hours to complete the test once you have started. The recruiter will have immediate access to your scores once the test has been completed. The test can only be taken once and will not be given to anyone who has previously taken the ASVAB or Student ASVAB.

You need to achieve a minimum AFQT on the first five sections in order to complete the test. If you do not achieve the minimum AFQT score, you will not be permitted to proceed to a proctored verification test and will have to take the full ASVAB to enlist.

Once you complete the PiCAT, you will have 30 days to take a short verification test at the MEPS. This test confirms that you took the PiCAT without assistance and validates the PiCAT score for use as the official test score of record. If confirmed, you will enlist under that PiCAT score. If not confirmed, you will have to take a full-length ASVAB. Current retest rules will apply. Over the next months, the verification test may not be given to everyone, but just to randomly selected individuals.

You cannot use any resources such as books, the Internet, or people when taking the PiCAT. The test shows the recruiter your ability to pass the real ASVAB. If your PiCAT scores differ greatly from a real ASVAB, there may be a strong suspicion that you did not take the test as directed. To say the least, cheating is not tolerated by the military and consequences will be swift.

PiCAT can count as the official ASVAB. You can retest after a verified PiCAT is given; however, retest rules will apply, meaning applicants need to wait 30 days after completing the verification test to retest. You could be randomly chosen to take the ASVAB, even if you passed the PiCAT.

It is a good idea for you to take the PiCAT because you will gain familiarity with the ASVAB test and the types of questions that will be asked. For a lot of people who experience test anxiety, an added benefit is that the PiCAT is not timed.

Chapter 6

Follow These Suggestions to Ace the ASVAB

YOUR GOALS FOR THIS CHAPTER:

- **Create your own ASVAB study plan.**

- **Learn effective study techniques.**

- **Find out ways to reduce test anxiety.**

- **Learn test-taking pointers that can raise your score.**

SEVEN STEPS TO ACING THE ASVAB

There are several steps you can take to give yourself a leading edge on acing the ASVAB. If you follow these simple rules and stick to them during the time leading up to the ASVAB, you will do well. You need to be disciplined and persistent. Merely hoping that you will do well won't cut it. Merely flipping through this book won't do it. You need to work hard, stay consistent, and focus like a laser to achieve your goal.

1. Be Prepared

Don't count on luck, your good looks, or your charming personality to get you high scores on the ASVAB. The best way to do well on the ASVAB is to study hard and do well in your courses at school. Even if you did well in school, focusing on the contents of this book will help you perform better on the ASVAB. Since the main criterion for military entrance is the AFQT, you need to do especially well on the math and verbal tests. Reviewing the contents of this book should help boost your score in those areas.

The other ASVAB tests are used for entry into certain occupational fields and training programs. Doing well on these tests gives you a better chance of getting into the career field of your choice.

You may or may not have taken courses in these other areas. For example, not everyone takes automotive courses or shop courses in school, so it will be very helpful to review the material in this book and take the practice exams. Not everyone has had formal training in the skills of mechanical comprehension. Spending time on learning the content of these areas is well worth your while in getting good jobs in the military.

2. Set Up a Study Plan and Don't Procrastinate

Give yourself three to five months of study and review before taking the ASVAB. You may need to spend more or less time studying, depending on how strong your abilities are in each content area. For example, maybe your math skills are just fine, but your knowledge of auto and shop concepts or general science needs a lot of work. Adjust the schedule to meet your own needs.

A sample 20-week study plan is shown in Figure 6.1. It is followed by Figure 6.2, a blank study plan for your own use.

Tasks begun well, likely have good finishes.

SOPHOCLES
496–406 BC

Figure 6.1   Sample study plan

Week 1	Select a place to study and gather all necessary books and materials. Develop a weekly study plan.
Week 2	Take the diagnostic test in this book and identify your strengths and weaknesses. Determine which areas need the most work.
Week 3	Review the math skills section in this ASVAB book.
Week 4	Review math skills and take the ASVAB math tests in Practice Test 1 in this book.
Week 5	Review the vocabulary lists and meanings in this book and take the Word Knowledge test in Practice Test 1 in this book.
Week 6	Read some books and magazines. Identify the main characters and the main idea, and make inferences about what would happen next for 50 different paragraphs. Take the Paragraph Comprehension test in Practice Test 1 in this book.
Week 7	Review science concepts and take the General Science test in Practice Test 1 in this book.
Week 8	Continue to review math and science concepts.
Week 9	Work on review sections in this ASVAB book for Auto and Shop, Electrical Information, Mechanical Comprehension, and Assembling Objects.
Week 10	Work on review sections in this ASVAB book for Auto and Shop, Electrical Information, Mechanical Comprehension, and Assembling Objects. Take the Auto and Shop, Electrical Information, Mechanical Comprehension, and Assembling Objects tests in Practice Test 1 in this book.
Week 11	Go back and review the math and verbal concepts.
Week 12	Take Practice Test 2 and identify your strengths and weaknesses.
Week 13	Review all concepts.
Week 14	Review all concepts.
Week 15	Take Practice Test 3. Decide in what areas you need to continue your study efforts.
Week 16	Keep reviewing the content, focusing on your weakest areas. Concentrate on the AFQT tests.
Week 17	Review notes.
Week 18	Review subject reviews in this ASVAB book.
Week 19	Review.
Week 20	Review.

Figure 6.2   Study plan—blank

Week 1	
Week 2	
Week 3	
Week 4	
Week 5	
Week 6	
Week 7	
Week 8	
Week 9	
Week 10	
Week 11	
Week 12	
Week 13	
Week 14	
Week 15	
Week 16	
Week 17	
Week 18	
Week 20	

3. Set Up a Weekly Study Schedule

If you want to do well on the ASVAB, it is very important that you make studying for it a priority in your life. You should spend six to eight hours per week on your studies for this test. Setting up a weekly schedule and sticking to it is very important.

In Figure 6.3 you'll see a sample weekly study schedule. It is followed by Figure 6.4, a blank form that you can use to make your own schedule.

- *When can you study?* Before completing the plan, you need to review your typical week to determine when you can make time to study. If you go to school or have a job, your time for study may be limited to evenings and weekends.

- *What time of day is best?* Do you work better in the mornings, afternoons, or evenings? Schedule your study time when you are most likely to be efficient in your study. Use the chart at the bottom of this page to determine if you are a morning or an evening person.

- *How long can you study?* You know yourself better than anyone. Are you able to study well for short or long periods of time? Can you focus for one hour and then get restless, or can you work undistracted and focused for several hours? Block out the times that seem ideal for you. Adjust the time as you learn what's best for you.

- *It's not just the clock time.* Don't fool yourself into thinking that just because the clock has indicated that three hours have passed, you have spent three hours studying. Make sure that you are spending quality time on your studies.

- *Make room for exercise.* It's very important that you schedule in some exercise, as that will help reduce the stress associated with working hard to achieve a goal. It will also keep you healthier so that your study schedule is not interrupted by illness.

- *Write down your study schedule and stick to it.* Posting your schedule for your friends and family to see can help them understand that you need to use your time for study. This could help eliminate distractions. If you are really serious about doing well on the ASVAB, you may need to give up some nonessential activities, like dates, movies, and hanging out with your friends.

Be realistic. Don't plan study periods during the week if it is unlikely that you will follow through. In the beginning you may schedule one or two study periods and then increase your commitment to study as you get focused and organized. Your success depends on you.

Tips for Managing Your Time

- State your goals.
- Make up a weekly list of things to accomplish.
- Make up a "to-do" list for tomorrow and set priorities.
- Keep track on paper of time spent studying and what you accomplished.
- Reward yourself for finishing items on your "to-do" list.

Are You a Morning or Evening Person?

Morning Person	Evening Person
I often wake up before the alarm in the mornings.	When I hear the alarm, I feel awful and hit the snooze button.
When I wake up, I am ready to go.	When it's 10 a.m., I am just starting to feel awake.
In the mornings, my mind is clear and alert.	I'm still a little groggy into the afternoon.
The best time to talk with me is in the mornings.	Don't talk to me in the morning, I only feel human in the evenings.
I fade about 10 or 11 p.m.	I'm starting to feel sharp at about 8 p.m.

Figure 6.3 Sample weekly planning schedule

	Monday	Tuesday	Wednesday	Thursday	Friday	Saturday	Sunday
8–9 a.m.	School/Work	School/Work	School/Work	School/Work	School/Work	Errands	Personal Time
9–10 a.m.							
10–11 a.m.							ASVAB study
11 a.m.–12 p.m.	↓	↓	↓	↓	↓	↓	↓
12–1 p.m.	Lunch	Lunch	Lunch	Lunch	Lunch		Lunch
1–2 p.m.	School/Work	School/Work	School/Work	School/Work	School/Work	Lunch	
2–3 p.m.						ASVAB study	Fitness activity
3–4 p.m.						↓	↓
4–5 p.m.	↓	↓	↓	↓	↓		
5–6 p.m.	Fitness activity	ASVAB study	Fitness activity	ASVAB study	TGIF		
6–7 p.m.	↓	↓	↓	↓		Movie and Dinner	
7–8 p.m.	Dinner	Dinner	Dinner	Dinner	Dinner		Dinner
8–9 p.m.							

Figure 6.4 Blank weekly planning schedule

	Monday	Tuesday	Wednesday	Thursday	Friday	Saturday	Sunday
8–9 a.m.							
9–10 a.m.							
10–11 a.m.							
11 a.m.–12 p.m.							
12–1 p.m.							
1–2 p.m.							
2–3 p.m.							
3–4 p.m.							
4–5 p.m.							
5–6 p.m.							
6–7 p.m.							
7–8 p.m.							
8–9 p.m.							

4. Pick a Location Where You Study Best

Some people work best in a quiet room with the door closed and no distractions. Others prefer to flop on the couch, have music playing in the background, put their feet up, and hit the books. Think hard about what works best for you. Some people think they are studying just because they have a book in their hands, but they aren't working effectively because they are really listening to the music, texting, or paying attention to what's on the TV. Be honest and smart about where you study. Your best bet is to find a quiet place that is well lit and has no distractions. Get real about what's best for you.

Best Study Setting	
Quiet	At a desk
Good lighting	No distractions
No phones	No excuses
No TV or music	

Check out your local library. Many people live in busy and active households, making it very difficult to find a quiet place to focus on their studies. Maybe your local library is the best place if you can't find a quiet place at home, school, or work. The library is well lit, and it should reduce any eyestrain, making it easier for you to concentrate on your studies and allowing you to study longer without tiring.

5. Get Support from Friends and Family

Tell your family and friends about your goals and your study schedule. This will show them that you are serious about your plan, and they will be more likely to give you the support and space that you need. It is important to have some cheerleaders to help you stay on your course. Post your schedule where your family can see it so that they can be supportive.

You may want to engage your family and friends in helping you. They can use flash cards to test you on what you know, and can talk through some challenging concepts until you have those ideas down cold.

Since you will be spending a lot of time studying, ask your family if they would be willing to take on some of your household chores to give you more time to accomplish your goals. Do what you can to make your fair contribution, though.

When you have finished your study schedule, be sure to thank everyone who helped you achieve your goals. They probably had to make some sacrifices when you were studying.

Caution: Studying with Others
If you are taking the ASVAB with a friend or friends, it could be useful to study together. Friends may be able to help you with certain subject areas, and you may be able to help them with others. Be careful, though, because you might end up spending more time socializing than studying.

6. Know the Test

Good test preparation includes knowing what to expect on the test. What kinds of questions will you get? What test question format should you anticipate? Reviewing this book will go a long way toward helping you become comfortable with the types of test questions you will be seeing on the ASVAB.

7. Work at It

Everyone needs to work on succeeding and performing well. You are not alone. The smartest and most successful people that you know or have heard about haven't come by their successes easily. Everyone has to work at being successful. You can be successful as well, if you work at it. The great thing is that it is your choice. You can create your own destiny.

Steps to Acing the ASVAB!

1. Be prepared.
2. Set up a study plan and don't procrastinate.
3. Set up a weekly study schedule.
4. Pick a location where you study best.
5. Get support from family and friends.
6. Know the test.
7. Work at it—work hard.

TAKING CARE OF YOUR BODY AS WELL AS YOUR BRAIN

There are three areas that you need to attend to while you are studying: your stress level, exercise, and what you eat. Concentrating on these areas will help to facilitate the learning that you will undertake over the next several weeks.

Reduce Stress

When you are working toward an important goal, there is a certain level of stress that comes with the territory. If there is enough stress for a sustained period of time, eventually this can hurt your ability to focus and may even damage your health. You need to implement some stress-reducing actions on a regular basis.

It may sound silly, but staying quiet and doing some deep breathing exercises have been shown to reduce stress. If you have scheduled a two- to three-hour block of study time, do this every hour or so.

Also, try visualizing some wonderful, idyllic places that are particularly soothing to you, like waves on a beach, a gentle spring shower, or a snow-capped mountain range, as you breathe deeply. This should help to relax you.

If you are trying to sleep and are too wound up from working and studying, and you are in bed and the room is dark, start to breath deeply while relaxing your toes, then moving to your calves, your thighs, your hips, your shoulders, your arms, your jaw, your head, and so on. See the suggestions for the relaxation exercise.

Relaxation Exercise

While in bed or in a dark, quiet place, lie still with your eyes closed. Let your body and mind slow down for a few moments. Stay still and quiet. Breathe deeply. Be aware of your breathing.

As you stay still and quiet, focus on your toes. Clench them and then let them relax. Do this two or three times. As you relax your toes, think about how they would feel if they turned into liquid. Let your toes turn to liquid. Release the tension. Then do this same exercise with your ankles, your calves, your knees, your thighs, your buttocks, your stomach, your chest, your back, your hands, your forearms, your biceps, your shoulders, your neck, your jaw, your cheeks, your eyes, and your forehead. Let them all turn to liquid as you move from your toes to your head.

Once your muscles are relaxed, let your mind float and dissolve. Let your thoughts flow away. Breathe deeply as you reduce your stress.

Exercises like those mentioned should help to reduce your stress level and should help you get to sleep faster and sleep better. With a good sleep, you will be more enthusiastic and better able to face the challenges of the next day and the next ASVAB study schedule. It will also help you retain more of what you study. Seven to nine hours of sleep is generally recommended.

Get Physical Exercise

Be sure to incorporate some vigorous physical exercise into your weekly routine. Doing some sort of aerobic activity, like running, power walking, or cycling, will help reduce your stress level and will also keep you physically stronger to contend with your study schedule. Don't skip your weight-training exercises, either. Physical activity has been shown to reduce stress and keep you healthier.

Plus, if you are really interested in joining and performing well in the military, you need to be physically fit, so why not start now to incorporate exercise into your weekly schedule? Start transforming that body fat into muscle. Do you need to lose extra pounds? Drop them now.

Eat and Act Right

It's very important for your heath that you maintain a good weight and eat well. Eating low-fat, healthy meals will keep your weight down, which will, in turn, help you feel more energetic, healthy, and focused on your task.

Abusing your body in any way will only hurt your efforts, as it will make you less alert and less focused. Clearly, if you are abusing drugs or alcohol, your entrance into the military will be problematic, at best. Get a grip on those behaviors, as they are likely to reduce your chances of qualifying for military enlistment. Shed those bad habits now!

Although you won't be disqualified from the military for smoking, it is a bad habit that damages your body and brain functioning. Smoking also reduces your athletic ability, a very important aspect of being successful in the military. Offload the smoking problem now, and if you haven't succumbed, don't start.

HOW TO STUDY

There are several ways that you can approach studying. The methods you select depend on how you have studied in the past and what feels most comfortable and productive to you. You may find many of the techniques listed here to be useful as you work on your preparation for the ASVAB.

Prioritize

Start with the most difficult subjects first. That way, you will give your freshest and most focused attention to the subject areas that are hardest for you.

Use Dead Time

Any time there is some space in your schedule, review your notes or lists.

Highlight Important Sections

In the reviews in this book or any textbook that you use, it is helpful to use a highlighter to focus on important concepts. Another good strategy is to take notes on the concepts that seem important to understand and remember.

Create Concept Maps

Concept maps are somewhat like a visual outline. They help you keep things straight and show the relationships between and among various ideas.

The concept map at the bottom of this page begins to describe the various types of rocks on the Earth.

Read and Summarize

As you read a section of material, stop and think about what you read for a moment. In a notebook, write down what you read in your own words. Do this for each section. The more active and interactive you are with the subject material, the more you will remember.

Develop Flash Cards

For things that you just need to memorize, develop flash cards with the question on one side and the answer on the other. Using flash cards, you can study while waiting for the bus, or your family and friends can test you. Just writing things down on the flash cards will help you retain the information.

Use the PQRST Method

Preview, question, read, summarize, and test yourself.

Preview. Skim the material to see what it generally contains.

Question. As you work through a section of material, think about what types of questions could be asked on a test. Write down the questions and the answers.

Read. Read sections of material carefully and actively.

Summarize. Summarize what you've read. Jot down notes, diagrams, key words, and processes.

Test. Recite and review what you have read and written down in your notes immediately after you have read and summarized.

THE DAY BEFORE THE TEST
Don't Cram

It's too late anyway. Studying for the ASVAB is not something you do the day before the test. At this point, it's too late to stuff information into your mind. If you paid attention to the advice in this book, you have undertaken a steady pace of study that is directed toward success on the test.

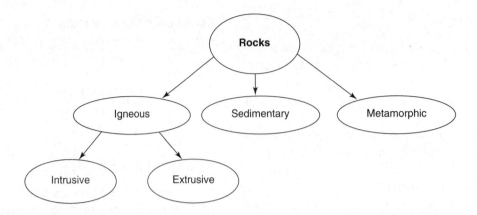

Exercise Your Body

If you have studied hard and followed your study plan, you should take the day before the test to pay attention to your personal well-being. Take a run or a long walk, play tennis or basketball, go rock climbing, or have a picnic. Do whatever physical activity gives you joy. Relax and feel good. Drink a good amount of water.

Revel in the fact that you have worked hard and will have the opportunity to show what you know tomorrow. Be excited that your hard work will finally have a payoff as you take the ASVAB. You've worked hard, and now you will obtain your reward.

Have a Healthy Dinner

Eat a decent, low-fat meal. Chicken or fish and a good supply of vegetables would be appropriate. Don't drink any alcoholic beverages or high-sugar or caffeine drinks.

Sleep Well

You have worked hard for the past several months. If you have followed the advice in this book, you should go to bed feeling confident and relaxed, and with a smile on your face. Go to sleep early and set your alarm well in advance of the time you need to be at the testing center. Setting a backup alarm is a good idea. If you have trouble sleeping, do some relaxation exercises.

THE DAY OF THE TEST

Eat a Good Breakfast

Have a modest breakfast, but lay off the butter, sausage, bacon, and syrup. Eat lightly, choosing foods that will give you energy and focus. Cereal and milk with some fruit would be good, as would oatmeal. A cup of coffee might sharpen your edge. Eating too much or eating foods that are too fatty can make you feel, think, and act sluggish, and you may not perform your best. Your best bet is to be eating healthy meals all along. One morning of eating right won't help you much. By all means, don't go to the test with an empty stomach.

Don't Drink a Lot of Fluid

Certainly don't go into the test dehydrated, but drinking lots of coffee and water before the test may cause you to be uncomfortable. This could distract you from performing your best.

Be Early

If you are taking the test at school, you probably need to arrive at your usual time. If you are taking the test at a MEPS or a MET site, it's a good idea to arrive a little early and get comfortable with the testing room.

Relax and Glance at Your Notes

A little stress before you start the test is a good thing, as it will help you stay mentally sharp. An excess of stress can cause test anxiety, a condition that is not helpful to your performance. You have studied hard and done all you can do to prepare, so be confident in yourself and relax. If you feel you need to keep reviewing, scan your notes one more time, but then set them aside. If you follow the advice in this book, you will approach the test as an opportunity to show them what you know. Take a deep breath and begin.

Reducing Test Anxiety

1. Be prepared. If you have studied hard, there is no reason that you can't show what you know.
2. Banish all your excuses for not studying.
3. Don't procrastinate.
4. Stay with an organized study routine that sets aside time each week to study.
5. Reduce as much stress from other aspects of your life as possible.
6. Stay in good physical condition by exercising and eating right.
7. Visualize your success. Imagine yourself receiving great ASVAB scores.

Read or Listen to the Directions

The ASVAB has very specific directions for each test within the test battery. Read the directions carefully and listen intently as the directions are read to you by the test administrator or provided to you on the computer screen. The directions will tell you what you need to do and how you need to approach the test items. You will be given a specified amount of time for each subtest. Pay attention to the time schedule, especially for the paper-and-pencil version of the ASVAB. There will probably be a clock in the room, but bring a watch so that you can manage your time.

The directions that you will be given for both the paper-and-pencil version and the computer version are provided elsewhere in this book, so you should have little in the way of surprises.

Before each test, you will be given some practice items. Be sure to pay attention to those items and the directions. If there is something you don't understand, ask for clarification.

Test Administration (Paper-and-Pencil ASVAB)

The Room You will probably be tested in a room that has a desk or a table that you can use to open the test booklet and record your answers on the answer sheet. There will be a clock visible to you to help you with the timing of the test. The test administrator will indicate the time the test will end on a sign or on the board. The room should be free from noise and visual distractions. The lighting should be sufficient for you to see the questions easily. An audible electronic timer will be used for timing the various subtests to let you know when to stop answering questions.

There will be a test administrator for every 25 persons. If there are more than 25 people, there should be one proctor for every 25 people.

The test directions will be read to you verbatim and in English. You will be given scratch paper to work with.

Cheating—Don't Even Think About It If you are taking the paper-and-pencil version along with other people, individuals will be given one of several versions of the ASVAB. So copying from others is likely to give you the wrong answers. You will also be seated in such a way that you cannot readily observe another person's answer sheet, and if you can see the answer sheet, the test version and thus the answers are going to be different.

Use of unauthorized assistance such as calculators, slide rules, other mechanical devices, or crib sheets and going forward or backward to other subtests are considered cheating. If you are caught cheating, your test results will be invalidated and you will not be able to retake the ASVAB for six months.

Given that moral character is important for the military, starting off your career with cheating is, well, *not your best decision, to say the least.*

TEST-TAKING POINTERS

The review sections of this book have some test-taking pointers that are specific to the subject matter. There are also some general test-taking strategies for multiple-choice questions that are good to keep in mind.

- Read each question carefully, then try to answer it without looking at the possible answers given. If you find your answer among those provided, you probably have a correct answer.

- Read all the answers before deciding on the correct answer. In many instances there could be more than one correct answer, but there will be one that is clearly the best.

- If there are two answers that are opposites, it is likely that one of them will be the correct answer.

- Try to eliminate answers that are clearly wrong and think through the possible remaining answers.

- Carefully consider answers that have qualifiers (*usually, mostly, most often, generally*). These tend to be correct.

- Pay attention to words like *always, never, all, none,* and *only*. They mean what they say.

- If you skip a question or want to go back and revisit it if you have time, jot the item number down on the scratch paper that you have been given. (This applies only to the paper-and-pencil version of the ASVAB.)

- If you have time, go back and review your answers, but remember that your first answer is usually correct. Change the answer only if you are very sure that it is wrong.

- Answer every item. On the paper-and-pencil version there is no penalty for guessing. On the CAT-ASVAB, try to answer every question correctly. Your score is higher if you answer harder questions.

> *Perhaps the most valuable result of all education is the ability to make yourself do the things that you have to do, when it ought to be done, whether you like it or not.*
> —THOMAS HUXLEY

Part 2

ASVAB
DIAGNOSTIC
TEST
FORM

ASVAB Diagnostic Test Form

Now that you have learned all about the ASVAB and the important role it can play in your future, it is time to try out your test-taking skills. The following pages present a full-length practice ASVAB that will give you a very good idea of what the actual test is like. You will see samples of every type of ASVAB question, and you will get to know all the different topics that the real test covers. You will also read the actual test directions that you will hear on test day, and you will mark your answers on a copy of the actual ASVAB answer sheet used by the Department of Defense.

Try to take this diagnostic test under actual test conditions. Find a quiet place to work, and set aside a period of approximately $2\frac{1}{2}$ hours when you will not be disturbed. Work on only one section at a time, and use your watch or a timer to keep track of the time limits for each section. Mark your answers on the answer sheet, just as you will when you take the real exam.

At the end of the test, you'll find an answer key and explanations for every question. After you check your answers against the key, you can complete a chart that will show you how you did on the test and what test topics you might need to study more. Then review the explanations, paying particular attention to the ones for the questions that you answered incorrectly.

Once you have worked your way through this diagnostic test, you will know how ready you are right now for the actual ASVAB. You will find out which test subjects and which types of question are easy for you, and which ones give you trouble. You will also find out whether you are able to work fast enough to finish each section within the time allowed, or whether you need to improve your test-taking speed. With the knowledge you gain, you'll be able to plan an ASVAB preparation program that fits your needs. Later on, when you read through the ASVAB subject reviews in Part 3 of this book, you'll know which topics and question types to focus on in order to get your best score.

TEST DIRECTIONS

IF YOU ARE TAKING THE PAPER-AND-PENCIL VERSION OF THE ASVAB, THE TEST ADMINISTRATOR WILL READ THE FOLLOWING ALOUD TO YOU.

I am [Administrator's name], your test administrator for today. I am here to administer the Armed Services Vocational Aptitude Test Battery, also known as the ASVAB. This is a battery of tests designed to assess various aspects of school and career aptitudes. The scores you obtain will be provided to your school guidance counselor to help you formulate your future plans. The scores can be useful to you only if they accurately reflect your abilities; therefore, it is important for you to do your best on these tests. Your score will have no effect on your school grades. If you are ill or too tired to take the test, please raise your hand at this time.

At this time, please clear your desk. Each of you will be given a test booklet, an answer sheet, scratch paper, and two pencils. Unauthorized assistance, such as calculators, slide rules, other electronic or mechanical devices, crib sheets, or talking during the test, is not permitted. Examinees who do not abide by these requirements will be dismissed from the test session, and their tests will be invalidated. *Do not open* your test booklet until told to do so.

Now turn off any electronic devices you might have with you (i.e., cellular phones, pagers, watch alarms, etc.). This will prevent disturbing other examinees in the room.

No breaks are permitted during the test. If it is necessary to use the rest room, please raise your hand. I will collect your test materials and will give them back to you when you return. You may not work on the same portion of the test once you return. Only one male and one female student may be out of the room at the same time.

You should now have in front of you a test booklet, answer sheet, scratch paper, and two pencils. If you are missing one of these items, please raise your hand now. Again, I must remind you, do not open your test booklet until told to do so.

In marking your answer sheet, use only the pencils that have been provided to you. If both your pencils break, please hold one up over your head and a replacement will be brought to you. Do not make any stray marks on the answer sheet; do not fold, crease, or tear it. Damaged answer sheets cannot be automatically scored. Please listen carefully to all directions. You will perform better if you understand what you are doing. If the directions are not perfectly clear, raise your hand.

Please take your scratch paper and print your name and today's date in the upper right-hand corner.

You should have a three-page answer sheet that is fastened together. (See the example on pages 67, 68, and 69.) Do not separate them. With the fastened edge on your left, you will see that on the upper center portion of the answer sheet there is a black printed seven-digit sequence number. Find that number now. That same number should also be printed in the upper center portion of pages 2 and 3. Check now to make sure that the sequence number is identical on all pages of the answer sheet. Also check to see that page 2 has a "Signature" block and that page 3 has parts 1 through 9. If you find anything different from that, please raise your hand and you will be provided with another answer sheet.

Turn to page 2 of the answer sheet. Essentially, the statement you are about to read tells you what purposes your scores will serve: counseling, research, military recruiting activities, etc. *If you fail to sign this statement acknowledging the intended uses and release of the test scores, your test will not be processed and no score will be available for your use.* Read the statement now. When you have finished reading the statement, please sign it and record today's date. A copy of this statement is available to you after the test session if you so desire.

Return to page 1 and turn your answer sheet sideways so you can read the section labeled "Student Name" at the upper left side. Please print your last name, one letter per box, starting with the first box on the left. Skip a box and print your first name, then skip another box and print your middle initial if you have one. It is all right if you run out of space; just print as much of your first name as possible. Below the boxes in which you printed your name are columns of letters. In each column, completely blacken the space corresponding to the same letter that you printed in the name boxes.

In block 2, titled "Home Mailing Address," enter as much of your street address as will fit in the boxes provided. If your mailing address is general delivery, enter "GENDEL." If you receive mail on a mail route, enter "ROUTE," skip a box, and enter your route number, letter, or name. If you have a post office box, enter "BOX," skip a space, and enter the box number. Then, as before, completely blacken in the appropriate spaces corresponding to the letters or numbers below the letters or numbers you have printed.

In block 3, titled "Home City," print the name of the city in which you live. Completely blacken in the corresponding spaces below.

In block 4, titled "ST" for state, print the two-letter abbreviation for your state, which is _____, and completely blacken in the corresponding spaces below.

In block 5, titled "Zip Code," enter the first five numbers of your home address zip code and completely blacken in the corresponding spaces below.

In block 6, titled "Area Code/Phone Number," enter the three-digit area code, then your seven-digit phone number and completely blacken in the corresponding spaces below. If you do not have a phone, leave this block blank.

In block 7, titled "School Code," enter the nine-digit number _____ and completely blacken in the corresponding paces below.

In block 8, print the name of this school.

In block 9, titled "Education Level," completely blacken in the space that corresponds to your present school grade. For example, if you are a senior, blacken in the circle next to 12. If you are a junior, blacken in the circle next to 11. Scores cannot be provided for you if you leave this block blank.

In block 10, titled "Sex," indicate your gender by completely blackening in the space next to "Male" or "Female."

In block 11, titled "Intentions," completely blacken in the space corresponding to your plans after completing high school. If you are not sure of your plans at this time, completely blacken in the space next to "Undecided."

In block 12, titled "Test Version," enter the test version number corresponding to the test version number printed on the front of your test booklet and completely blacken in the spaces below. The version number should either be 23A, 23B, 24A, or 24B. If you are unsure of your test version, please raise your hand now and someone will assist you.

Please leave block 13, titled "SS ASVAB," blank.

Are there any questions on filling out any of the blocks on page 1?

Now turn to page 2. On the line provided in the upper left-hand corner, print your last name, first name, and middle initial. Also enter your social security number on the line indicated as SSN.

In block 14, titled "Social Security Number," this is no longer required.

Please leave block 15, titled "TA IA Number," blank.

In block 16, titled "Code," place your school's distribution code and completely blacken in the corresponding spaces below the boxes.

In block 17, titled "Date of Birth," enter the year and date of your birth.

Leave block 18, titled "SP Studies," blank.

In block 19, titled "Test Booklet Number," enter the seven-digit number printed on the upper left corner of the cover of your test booklet. Completely blacken the corresponding spaces below. If your test booklet number has six digits, place a zero in the first box.

In block 20, titled "Racial Category," please blacken any of the appropriate responses to indicate the racial category or categories of which you consider yourself a member. If you do not wish to respond, please leave block 20 blank.

In block 21, titled "Ethnic Category," please blacken the appropriate response to indicate the ethnic category of which you consider yourself a member. If you do not wish to respond, please leave block 21 blank.

At this time, remove page 3 of the answer sheet. Pages 1 and 2 will now be collected from you.

On page 3, on the line provided in the upper left-hand corner, print your last name, first name, and middle initial. Also, enter your social security number on the line indicated as SSN.

Please open your test booklet to page 1 and read the instructions silently while I read them aloud.

GENERAL DIRECTIONS

DO NOT WRITE YOUR NAME OR MAKE ANY MARKS in this booklet. Mark your answers on the separate answer sheet. Use the scratch paper which was given to you for any figuring you need to do. Return this scratch paper with your other papers when you finish the test.

If you need another pencil while taking this test, hold your pencil above your head. A proctor will bring you another one.

This booklet contains 9 tests. Each test has its own instructions and time limit. When you finish a test you may check your work in that test ONLY. Do not go on to the next test until the examiner tells you to do so. Do not turn back to a previous test at any time.

For each question, be sure to pick the BEST ONE of the possible answers listed. When you have decided which one of the choices given is the best answer to the question, blacken the space on your answer sheet that has the same number and letter as your choice. Mark only in the answer space. BE CAREFUL NOT TO MAKE ANY STRAY MARKS ON YOUR ANSWER SHEET. Each test has a separate section on the answer sheet. Be sure you mark your answers for each test in the section that belongs to that test.

Here is an example of correct marking on an answer sheet.

S1 A triangle has

    A. 2 sides
    B. 3 sides
    C. 4 sides
    D. 5 sides

PRACTICE

S1 Ⓐ ● Ⓒ Ⓓ
S2 Ⓐ Ⓑ Ⓒ Ⓓ
S3 Ⓐ Ⓑ Ⓒ Ⓓ

The correct answer to Sample Question S1 is B.

Next to the item, note how space B opposite number S1 has been blackened. Your marks should look just like this and be placed in the space with the same number and letter as the correct answer to the question. Remember, there is only ONE BEST ANSWER for each question. If you are not sure of the answer, make the BEST GUESS you can. If you want to change your answer, COMPLETELY ERASE your first answer mark.

Answer as many questions as possible. Do not spend too much time on any one question. Work QUICKLY, but work ACCURATELY. DO NOT TURN THE PAGE UNTIL TOLD TO DO SO. Are there any questions?

ASVAB DIAGNOSTIC TEST FORM

ANSWER SHEET

ANSWER SHEET   PAGE 1
ARMED SERVICES VOCATIONAL
APTITUDE BATTERY

ASVAB DIAGNOSTIC TEST FORM

ANSWER SHEET

ANSWER SHEET   PAGE 2
ARMED SERVICES VOCATIONAL
APTITUDE BATTERY

16. CODE

15. TA ID NUMBER

14. SOCIAL SECURITY NO.

19. TEST BOOKLET NUMBER

18. SP STUDIES

17. DATE OF BIRTH

YEAR   MO   DAY

21. ETHNIC CATEGORY
- HISPANIC OR LATINO
- NOT HISPANIC OR LATINO

20. RACIAL CATEGORY
- AMERICAN INDIAN / ALASKA NATIVE
- ASIAN
- BLACK / AFRICAN AMERICAN
- NATIVE HAWAIIAN / OTHER PACIFIC ISLANDER
- WHITE

SSN

LAST   FIRST   MI

STUDENT TESTING PROGRAM
PRIVACY ACT STATEMENT
Armed Forces Vocational Aptitude Battery

1. **AUTHORITY:** 10 USC 133 and 3013; and E.O. 9397

2. **PRINCIPAL PURPOSE(S):** To compute and furnish test score products for career/vocational guidance and group assessment of aptitude test performance; for up to 2 years, to establish eligibility for enlistment (only for students at the eleventh grade or higher and only with the expressed permission of the school); for marketing evaluation, assessment of manpower trends and characteristics; and for related statistical studies and reports.

3. **ROUTINE USE(S):** None

4. **DISCLOSURE:** Voluntary. However, if you do not provide the requested information, your test will not be scored or otherwise processed.

SIGNATURE

DATE

ASVAB DIAGNOSTIC TEST FORM

ANSWER SHEET

ANSWER SHEET   PAGE 3
ARMED SERVICES VOCATIONAL
APTITUDE BATTERY

PART 1. GENERAL SCIENCE

THE TEST ADMINISTRATOR WILL READ THE FOLLOWING ALOUD TO YOU.

Turn to Part 1 and read the directions for General Science silently while I read them aloud. This test has questions about science. Pick the BEST answer for each question and then blacken the space on your separate answer sheet that has the same number and letter as your choice. Here are three practice questions.

S1. A rose is a kind of
    A. animal.
    B. bird.
    C. flower.
    D. fish.

S2. A cat is a
    A. plant.
    B. mammal.
    C. reptile.
    D. mineral.

S3. The earth revolves around the
    A. sun.
    B. moon.
    C. meteorite.
    D. Mars.

Now look at the section of your answer sheet labeled "PRACTICE." Notice that answer space C has been marked for question S1. Now do practice questions S2 and S3 by yourself. Find the correct answer to the question, then mark the space on your answer sheet that has the same letter as the answer you picked. Do this now.

You should have marked B for question S2 and A for question S3. If you make any mistakes, erase your mark carefully and blacken the correct answer space. Do this now.

Your score on this test will be based on the number of questions you answer correctly. You should try to answer every question. If you finish before time is called, go back and check your work in this part ONLY. Now find the section of your answer sheet that is marked PART 1. When you are told to begin, start with question number 1 in Part 1 of your test booklet and answer space number 1 in Part 1 on your separate answer sheet. DO NOT TURN THE PAGE UNTIL TOLD TO DO SO. This part has 25 questions in it. You will have 11 minutes to complete it. Most of you should finish in this amount of time. Are there any questions?

Turn the page and begin.

1. The basic unit of life is
   A. the cell.
   B. nucleus.
   C. the carbon molecule.
   D. oxygen.

2. When a plant undergoes photosynthesis, one of the by-products is
   A. carbon dioxide.
   B. light.
   C. ozone.
   D. oxygen.

3. Why is the nucleus so important to a living cell?
   A. It controls the production and elimination of cell waste.
   B. It controls most of the activities of the cell.
   C. It controls photosynthesis.
   D. It uses oxygen to make carbon dioxide.

4. Which of the following do not have organelles?
   A. Muscle cells
   B. Protozoa
   C. Nerve cells
   D. Bacteria

5. Plants bend toward a source of light on account of
   A. geotropism.
   B. thigmotropism.
   C. chemotropism.
   D. phototropism.

6. Which of the following terms can be used to describe a bird?
   A. Invertebrate, omnivore
   B. Vertebrate, warm-blooded
   C. Endoskeleton, cold-blooded
   D. Crustacean, endoskeleton

7. Why are decomposers important to an ecosystem?
   A. They make nutrients available for plants to use.
   B. They create soil for farming.
   C. They stabilize the soil.
   D. They enhance the habitat with specialized particles important to life.

8. Which of the following is the part of the skeletal system that protects the spinal cord?
   A. Marrow
   B. Cartilage
   C. Ligaments
   D. Vertebrae

9. A bruise on your skin is the result of which of the following?
   A. Excess strain on the muscle
   B. Broken capillaries
   C. Overactive sweat glands
   D. Swelling

10. The function that moves food from one part of the digestive system to another is called
    A. respiration.
    B. digestion.
    C. mechanical decomposition.
    D. peristalsis.

11. Which of the following words are all associated with the nervous system?
    A. Nephrons, urethra, bladder
    B. Antigens, T cells, cilia
    C. Hypothalamus, pons, cortex
    D. Lymph nodes, spleen, tonsils

12. Which of the following is the name for the space between two nerve cells where an electric charge transmits information?
    A. Nerve cell gap
    B. Synapse
    C. Axon
    D. Dendrite

13. Which of the following states is likely to have the greatest biodiversity?
    A. North Dakota
    B. Illinois
    C. Nebraska
    D. Florida

14. Which of the following best represents what happens to ultraviolet radiation from the sun when it reaches Earth's atmosphere?
    A. It changes into chlorofluorocarbons.
    B. Some of it is absorbed by the ozone layer.
    C. All of it reaches Earth's surface.
    D. It is deflected back into space.

15. Which of the following properties of a sound wave affects how loud or soft the sound is?
    A. Crest
    B. Trough
    C. Frequency
    D. Amplitude

16. The major force causing sea-floor spreading, continental drift, and the collision of continental plates is
    A. subduction of Earth's core.
    B. creation of oceanic ridges.
    C. compression of continents.
    D. convection currents in the mantle.

17. When two tectonic plates converge and one rises above the other, which of the following are likely to form?
    A. Volcanoes
    B. Hot spots
    C. Tsunamis
    D. Rifts

18. Breaking waves or breakers that occur near the shoreline are caused by which of the following conditions?
    A. Earthquakes that occur far out in the ocean
    B. Friction between the wave trough and the ocean bottom
    C. The expansion of the wavelength of the wave
    D. Increasing tidal forces

19. How long does it take for Earth to make one revolution around the sun?
    A. 1 year
    B. 1 month
    C. 1 week
    D. 1 day

20. An eclipse of the sun occurs under which of the following conditions?
    A. Earth is between the sun and the moon.
    B. Earth is rotating faster than the moon.
    C. Earth, the sun, and the moon are perpendicular to each other.
    D. The moon is between the sun and Earth.

21. Earth's greenhouse effect is caused by which of the following conditions?
    A. Changing rainfall patterns from global warming
    B. Heat from the sun that is trapped by atmospheric gases
    C. The increase in the thickness of the ozone layer
    D. The number of plants in tropical rainforests trapping CO_2

22. Which of the following can hold the most moisture?
    A. Cold air
    B. Moving air
    C. Stable air
    D. Warm air

23. When a prevailing wind reaches a mountain range, what happens to the air?
    A. It is blocked and starts to move backward.
    B. It rises and cools, causing condensation.
    C. It expands and heats, resulting in rain.
    D. It expands and heats, resulting in a dry, desert-like area.

24. The process of erosion is linked to the formation of which of the following types of rocks?
    A. Igneous
    B. Extrusive
    C. Sedimentary
    D. Metamorphic

25. Scientists believe that the universe is expanding because of which of the following indicators?
    A. The difference in time it takes for light from various stars to reach us
    B. The red shift in the spectra of stars
    C. The difference in chemical composition of various stars
    D. The explosion of supernovas

STOP! DO NOT TURN THIS PAGE UNTIL TIME IS UP FOR THIS TEST. IF YOU FINISH BEFORE TIME IS UP, CHECK OVER YOUR WORK ON THIS TEST ONLY.

PART 2. ARITHMETIC REASONING

THE TEST ADMINISTRATOR WILL READ THE FOLLOWING ALOUD TO YOU.

Turn to Part 2 and read the directions for Arithmetic Reasoning silently while I read them aloud.

This is a test of arithmetic word problems. Each question is followed by four possible answers. Decide which answer is CORRECT, and then blacken the space on your answer sheet that has the same number and letter as your choice. Use your scratch paper for any figuring you wish to do.

Here is a sample question. DO NOT MARK your answer sheet for this or any further sample questions.

S1 A student buys a sandwich for 80 cents, milk for 20 cents, and pie for 30 cents. How much did the meal cost?

　A. $1.00
　B. $1.20
　C. $1.30
　D. $1.40

The total cost is $1.30; therefore, C is the right answer. Your score on this test will be based on the number of questions you answer correctly. You should try to answer every question. DO NOT SPEND TOO MUCH TIME on any one question. If you finish before time is called, go back and check your work in this part ONLY.

Now find the section of your answer sheet that is marked PART 2. When you are told to begin, start with question number 1 in Part 2 of your test booklet and answer space number 1 in Part 2 on your separate answer sheet.

DO NOT TURN THIS PAGE UNTIL TOLD TO DO SO. You will have 36 minutes for the 30 questions. Are there any questions?

Begin.

1. Lisa went to the grocery store and bought a package of hot dogs for $3.54, a package of buns for $1.79, a container of mustard for $2.10, a jar of relish for $2.16, and a bag of charcoal for $5.15. What was her total bill?
   A. $12.64
   B. $14.74
   C. $16.15
   D. $16.74

2. Kim bought a blouse for $17.16, a skirt for $38.19, and a purse for $35.14. If she hands the clerk a $100 bill, what is her change?
   A. $1.53
   B. $9.51
   C. $10.67
   D. $14.15

3. Cassidy answered 38 questions correctly on a test with 45 items. To the nearest percent, what percent did she answer correctly?
   A. 72%
   B. 78%
   C. 84%
   D. 89%

4. Susan's test scores for Social Studies are 81, 76, 91, 73, and 79. What is her average score?
   A. 80
   B. 87
   C. 91
   D. 93

5. A box of chocolates has 45 pieces. If 9 pieces have nuts in them, what percentage are without nuts?
   A. 20%
   B. 45%
   C. 79%
   D. 80%

6. In the Metro Bicycle Club, 6 of 48 members are females. What is the ratio of females to all club members?
   A. $\dfrac{3}{16}$
   B. $\dfrac{1}{15}$
   C. $\dfrac{1}{4}$
   D. $\dfrac{1}{8}$

7. A teacher has assigned 192 pages of reading. If Vanessa starts reading on Monday and reads 48 pages each day, on what day will she complete the assignment?
   A. Wednesday
   B. Thursday
   C. Friday
   D. Saturday

8. Samuel is saving coins in a jar so that he can purchase a software program. He has saved 94 nickels, 44 quarters, and 112 dimes. If he reaches into the jar to pick one coin at random, what is the probability that he will pick a dime?
   A. $\dfrac{1}{2}$
   B. $\dfrac{2}{3}$
   C. $\dfrac{56}{125}$
   D. $\dfrac{112}{138}$

9. Rene deposits $4,000 in a savings account that earns 4% simple interest per year. How much interest will she earn after 3 years?
   A. $112
   B. $350
   C. $380
   D. $480

10. Leah flies 5,200 miles in 11 hours. What is the average speed of her airplane?
    A. 472.73 miles/hour
    B. 499.17 miles/hour
    C. 512.33 miles/hour
    D. 587.43 miles/hour

11. The Kent High School Booster's Club has 250 members. In 90 days it hopes to have a membership of 376 by initiating a Web-based membership campaign. On average, how many new members does it need to sign up each day to reach that goal?
    A. 1
    B. 1.4
    C. 1.5
    D. 2.2

12. Max has a rectangular garden that is 3 feet by 7 feet. If he needs 2 ounces of fertilizer per square foot for the garden to flourish, how many ounces must he use?
    A. 21 oz
    B. 42 oz
    C. 44 oz
    D. 56 oz

13. The local electronics store is holding a 20%-off sale on all its products. Marla selects 2 CDs at the original price of $16.99 each. What is the price of the two CDs after the 20% discount?
    A. $15.99
    B. $22.50
    C. $25.78
    D. $27.18

14. The Berkeley Department Store is running a special back-to-school sale on shoes in September. A pair of shoes costs $67.50. In October the price increases to $87.75. What percent increase is the price in October?
    A. 15%
    B. 20%
    C. 24%
    D. 30%

15. Two numbers together add to 300. One number is twice the size of the other. What are the two numbers?
    A. 25; 50
    B. 50; 100
    C. 75; 150
    D. 100; 200

16. Hugo is making a picture frame for a photo of his family. The photo is 8 inches by 10 inches. If the wood for the frame costs 50 cents an inch, how much will the wood for the frame cost?
    A. $9.00
    B. $12.00
    C. $15.00
    D. $18.00

17. The distance across the circular mouth of a volcano running through its center is 75 yards. What is the distance around its mouth?
    A. 145.5 yd
    B. 215.5 yd
    C. 235.5 yd
    D. 315.5 yd

18. Sue spent one-third of her life in Kansas. If Sue is 39, how many years did she spend in Kansas?
    A. 9
    B. 12
    C. 13
    D. 15

19. Brian shoots hoops with Dave, who is two years younger than Brian. If Brian is 17, how old is Dave?
    A. 15
    B. 17
    C. 19
    D. 21

20. Al has three times as much money as Bill. Bill has two times as much money as Charlie. If Charlie has $5.89, how much money does Al have?
    A. $11.78
    B. $19.79
    C. $29.24
    D. $35.34

21. The car owned by Marisa gets an average of 16 miles per gallon of gas on the highway. If she recently took a trip of 1,344 miles, how many gallons of gas did she use?
    A. 34 gallons
    B. 57 gallons
    C. 78 gallons
    D. 84 gallons

22. A rectangular swimming pool is 6 feet deep, 28 feet long, and 12 feet wide. What is the volume of the pool?
    A. 1,655 ft^3
    B. 1,799 ft^3
    C. 2,016 ft^3
    D. 2,546 ft^3

23. Josh wants to put a fence around his rectangular garden. The garden is 6 feet by 15 feet. How much fencing must he purchase?
    A. 30 feet
    B. 35 feet
    C. 42 feet
    D. 47 feet

24. In a recent election, Joe received 32% of the votes, Samantha received 14% of the votes, Sally received 42% of the votes, and Cal received 12% of the votes. If 5,000 votes were cast, how many votes did Samantha receive?
    A. 300
    B. 450
    C. 535
    D. 700

25. A circular pool is 3.5 meters deep and has a radius of 9 meters. What is the volume?
    A. 450.2 m^3
    B. 575.9 m^3
    C. 890.2 m^3
    D. 974.4 m^3

26. The diameter of a planet is 8,000 miles. What is its circumference?
    A. 19,412 miles
    B. 20,889 miles
    C. 25,120 miles
    D. 28,475 miles

27. Will has $4,355.19 in his checking account. He writes checks for $1,204.90 and $890.99. How much is left in Will's account?
    A. $1,189.65
    B. $2,259.30
    C. $2,867.30
    D. $2,989.50

28. A club collected $585.00. If 75% of that came from membership dues, how much money came from the dues?
    A. $413.15
    B. $438.75
    C. $465.75
    D. $525.05

29. Danny buys a computer originally priced at $750.00, software programs originally priced at $398.75, a printer originally priced at $149.98, and a case of paper originally priced at $24.99. All items are on sale for 20% off. How much will Danny save because of the sale?
    A. $124.94
    B. $196.74
    C. $236.24
    D. $264.74

30. A ladder is placed against a building. If the ladder makes a 55° angle with the ground, what is the measure of the angle that the ladder makes with the building?
    A. 35°
    B. 40°
    C. 55°
    D. 90°

STOP! DO NOT TURN THIS PAGE UNTIL TIME IS UP FOR THIS TEST. IF YOU FINISH BEFORE TIME IS UP, CHECK OVER YOUR WORK ON THIS TEST ONLY.

PART 3. WORD KNOWLEDGE

THE TEST ADMINISTRATOR WILL READ THE FOLLOWING ALOUD TO YOU.

Now turn to Part 3 and read the directions for Word Knowledge silently while I read them aloud.

This is a test of your knowledge of work meanings. These questions consist of a sentence or phrase with a word or phrase underlined. From the four choices given, you are to decide which one MEANS THE SAME OR MOST NEARLY THE SAME as the underlined word or phrase. Once you have made your choice, mark the space on your answer sheet that has the same number and letter as your choice.

Look at the sample question.

S1 The weather in this geographic area tends to be <u>moderate</u>.

    A. Severe
    B. Warm
    C. Mild
    D. Windy

The correct answer is "mild," which is choice C. Therefore, you would have blackened in space C on your answer sheet.

Your score on this test will be based on the number of questions you answer correctly. You should try to answer every question. DO NOT SPEND TOO MUCH TIME on any one question. If you finish before time is called, go back and check your work in this part <u>ONLY</u>.

Now find the section of your answer sheet that is marked PART 3. When you are told to begin, start with question number 1 in Part 3 of your test booklet and answer space number 1 in Part 3 on your separate answer sheet.

DO NOT TURN THE PAGE UNTIL TOLD TO DO SO. You will have 11 minutes to complete the 35 questions in this part. Are there any questions?

Begin.

1. <u>Exempt</u> most nearly means
   A. empty.
   B. exit.
   C. excuse.
   D. anoint.

2. <u>Recruit</u> most nearly means
   A. react.
   B. enlist.
   C. permit.
   D. recur.

3. The decision was <u>unanimous</u>.
   A. Questioned
   B. Undisputed
   C. Selective
   D. Trivial

4. <u>Temperamental</u> most nearly means
   A. benevolent.
   B. lazy.
   C. volatile.
   D. demure.

5. He chose the <u>economical</u> solution.
   A. Costly
   B. Logical
   C. Comical
   D. Thrifty

6. The <u>promotion</u> made Darrell happy.
   A. Notice
   B. Gift
   C. Elevation
   D. Letter

7. Her behavior was <u>unpredictable</u>.
   A. Consistent
   B. Random
   C. Dependable
   D. Regular

8. <u>Deny</u> most nearly means
   A. state.
   B. avoid.
   C. refuse.
   D. open.

9. Making that decision at that time was <u>irresponsible</u>.
   A. Hapless
   B. Giddy
   C. Easy
   D. Reckless

10. <u>Persistent</u> most nearly means
    A. gentle.
    B. unrelenting.
    C. resigned.
    D. manageable.

11. The opponent was more <u>dominant</u>.
    A. Helpful
    B. Overriding
    C. Understanding
    D. Joyous

12. Mark was more <u>conscientious</u> than his friend.
    A. Painstaking
    B. Popular
    C. Friendly
    D. Handsome

13. <u>Diversion</u> most nearly means
    A. distraction.
    B. containment.
    C. pressure.
    D. supply.

14. The <u>assumption</u> was that she was correct.
    A. Belief
    B. Decision
    C. Rumor
    D. Guess

15. <u>Profess</u> most nearly means
    A. work.
    B. claim.
    C. disguise.
    D. accuse.

16. The substance of their argument was <u>trivial</u>.
    A. Sinister
    B. Inconsequential
    C. Sad
    D. Demanding

17. His attitude was <u>optimistic</u>.
    A. Grouchy
    B. Angry
    C. Unusual
    D. Positive

18. <u>Variable</u> most nearly means
    A. different.
    B. gloomy.
    C. changeable.
    D. bifurcate.

19. His words needed <u>clarification</u>.
    A. Expansion
    B. Explanation
    C. Elimination
    D. Recognition

20. The view was <u>panoramic</u>.
    A. Beautiful
    B. Unrealistic
    C. Stylistic
    D. Expansive

21. <u>Compassionate</u> most nearly means
    A. unwieldy.
    B. modern.
    C. concerned.
    D. restrictive.

22. <u>Contingent</u> most nearly means
    A. rapid.
    B. dependent.
    C. difficult.
    D. mysterious.

23. <u>Velocity</u> most nearly means
    A. variety.
    B. veracity.
    C. swiftness.
    D. overflow.

24. Her house was <u>immaculate</u>.
    A. Cleaned
    B. Spotless
    C. Large
    D. Fancy

25. The <u>visibility</u> that day was very poor.
    A. Clarity
    B. Test
    C. Observation
    D. Dichotomy

26. The wind was so strong that the boat <u>capsized</u>.
    A. Overturned
    B. Accelerated
    C. Tilted
    D. Docked

27. The elected official <u>abdicated</u> responsibility for the situation.
    A. Welcomed
    B. Cheered
    C. Transitioned
    D. Abandoned

28. Her skills made her <u>eligible</u> for the position.
    A. Qualified
    B. Eager
    C. Adequate
    D. Thankful

29. <u>Buoyant</u> most nearly means
    A. floating.
    B. happy.
    C. significant.
    D. acrobatic.

30. The pond was <u>teeming</u> with fish.
    A. Empty
    B. Opaque
    C. Crowded
    D. Vigorous

31. <u>Bestow</u> most nearly means
    A. remove.
    B. have.
    C. give.
    D. question.

32. <u>Meander</u> most nearly means
    A. twist.
    B. reverse.
    C. exceed.
    D. renew.

33. <u>Infiltrate</u> most nearly means
    A. interfere.
    B. seek.
    C. enter.
    D. penetrate.

34. His science grade <u>plummeted</u> after that difficult exam.
    A. Soared
    B. Plunged
    C. Increased
    D. Failed

35. The monument was <u>defiled</u> by the visitors.
    A. Honored
    B. Desecrated
    C. Cleaned
    D. Respected

STOP! DO NOT TURN THIS PAGE UNTIL TIME IS UP FOR THIS TEST. IF YOU FINISH BEFORE TIME IS UP, CHECK OVER YOUR WORK ON THIS TEST ONLY.

PART 4. PARAGRAPH COMPREHENSION

THE TEST ADMINISTRATOR WILL READ THE FOLLOWING ALOUD TO YOU.

Turn to Part 4 and read the directions for Paragraph Comprehension silently while I read them aloud.

This is a test of your ability to understand what you read. In this section you will find one or more paragraphs of reading material followed by incomplete statements or questions. You are to read the paragraph and select one of four lettered choices which BEST completes the statement or answers the question. When you have selected your answer, blacken the space on your answer sheet that has the same number and letter as your answer.

Your score on this test will be based on the number of questions you answer correctly. You should try to answer every question. DO NOT SPEND TOO MUCH TIME on any one question. If you finish before time is called, go back and check your work in this part ONLY.

Now find the section of your answer sheet that is marked PART 4. When you are told to begin, start with question number 1 in Part 4 of your test booklet and answer space number 1 in Part 4 on your separate answer sheet.

DO NOT TURN THE PAGE UNTIL TOLD TO DO SO. You will have 13 minutes to complete the 15 questions in this part. Are there any questions?

Begin.

The evidence is growing and is more convincing than ever! People of all ages who are generally inactive can improve their health and well-being by becoming active at a moderate intensity on a regular basis.

Regular physical activity substantially reduces the risk of dying of coronary heart disease, the nation's leading cause of death, and decreases the risk of stroke, colon cancer, diabetes, and high blood pressure. It also helps to control weight; contributes to healthy bones, muscles, and joints; reduces falls among older adults; helps to relieve the pain of arthritis; reduces symptoms of anxiety and depression; and is associated with fewer hospitalizations, physician visits, and medications. Moreover, physical activity need not be strenuous to be beneficial; people of all ages benefit from participating in regular, moderate-intensity physical activity, such as 30 minutes of brisk walking five or more times a week.

Despite the proven benefits of physical activity, more than 50 percent of American adults do not get enough physical activity to provide health benefits. Twenty-five percent of adults are not active at all in their leisure time. Activity decreases with age and is less common among women than men and among those with lower income and less education. Furthermore, there are racial and ethnic differences in physical activity rates, particularly among women. Insufficient physical activity is not limited to adults. More than a third of young people in grades 9–12 do not regularly engage in vigorous-intensity physical activity. Daily participation in high school physical education classes dropped from 42 percent in 1991 to 32 percent in 2001.

Physical activity can bring you many health benefits. People who enjoy participating in moderate-intensity or vigorous-intensity physical activity on a regular basis benefit by lowering their risk of developing coronary heart disease, stroke, non-insulin-dependent (type 2) diabetes mellitus, high blood pressure, and colon cancer by 30–50 percent. Additionally, active people have lower premature death rates than people who are the least active.

1. Which of the following best represents the main idea of this passage?
   A. Even a moderate amount of exercise has health benefits.
   B. People who do not exercise need to be convinced to do so.
   C. Exercises cures heart disease and decreases stroke.
   D. Strenuous exercise is better than moderate exercise.

2. Which of the following can be inferred from this passage?
   A. More exercise is better.
   B. If you exercise, you are likely to improve your health.
   C. Exercise eliminates heart disease and strokes.
   D. People who exercise have no weight problems.

3. According to the passage, which of the following is <u>not</u> a benefit of regular exercise?
   A. Lowering blood pressure
   B. Reducing colon cancer
   C. Reducing fatty acids
   D. Reducing coronary heart disease

4. According to the passage, which of the following is true?
   A. Twenty-five percent of adults do no exercise at all in their leisure time.
   B. People are living longer because of exercise.
   C. Older people tend to exercise more than younger people.
   D. People who have been hospitalized tend not to exercise.

5. About what percent of Americans do not get enough exercise to obtain health benefits?
   A. 25 percent
   B. 32 percent
   C. 42 percent
   D. 50 percent

During the first decade of the nineteenth century, the geographic image of western North America began to change dramatically. Based on the observations of the explorers Meriwether Lewis and George Rogers Clark, information gathered from native people, and Clark's own cartographic imagination, this image evolved from an almost empty interior with a hypothetical single mountain range serving as a western continental divide to an intricate one showing a labyrinth of mountains and rivers. A continent that had once seemed empty and simple was now becoming full and complex.

The Lewis and Clark expedition established the precedent for army exploration in the West. Major Stephen H. Long's Scientific Expedition (1819–1820) advanced that tradition, this time centering attention on the central and southern Great Plains and the Front Range of the Rockies. For the first time, an American exploring party included professional scientists (a zoologist and a botanist) and two skilled artists. While not every future American expedition took along such skilled observers, the pattern was set for increasingly scientific exploration.

It would take another 50 years after Lewis and Clark to complete the cartographic image of the West we know today. Other explorers and mapmakers followed, each revealing new geographic and scientific details about specific parts of the western landscape. But this revealing process was not a simple one. New knowledge did not automatically replace old ideas; some old notions—especially about river passages across the West—persisted well into the nineteenth century. In the decades after Lewis and Clark, the company of western explorers expanded to include fur traders, missionaries, and government topographers, culminating in the 1850s with the Army's Corps of Topographical Engineers surveying the southwestern and northwestern boundaries of the United States as well as the potential routes for a transcontinental railroad. By the time of the Civil War, an ocean-to-ocean American empire with borders clearly defined was a fact of continental life.

6. Which of the following best summarizes the passage?
   A. Western North America has a single mountain range that was unknown before the early nineteenth century.
   B. Nineteenth-century explorers found western North America to be geographically more complex than they had originally thought.
   C. Western North America was barren and mostly empty before the early nineteenth century.
   D. Lewis and Clark discovered many rivers in western North America.

7. In the passage the word *labyrinth* most nearly means
   A. jumble.
   B. line.
   C. concentration.
   D. beautiful design.

8. According to the passage, which event set the pattern for scientific exploration in the West?
    A. The exploration of the Army's Corps of Topographical Engineers
    B. Long's Scientific Expedition
    C. The exploration of Lewis and Clark
    D. The discovery of a major mountain range in the West

9. According to the passage, which of the following is true?
    A. Lewis and Clark explored the Front Range of the Rockies, helping the fur traders to expand their business in that area.
    B. Fur traders boosted the economy of what is now the western part of the United States.
    C. Native people provided Lewis and Clark with information about the topography of what is now the western part of the United States.
    D. Mapmakers helped plot the route for the transcontinental railroad.

10. According to the passage, what group of people were most instrumental in setting the pattern for more scientifically oriented exploration of the West?
    A. The military
    B. Fur traders
    C. Mapmakers
    D. Missionaries

Heroes were an important part of Greek mythology, but the characteristics that Greeks admired in a hero are not necessarily identical to those we admire today. Greek heroes are not always what modern readers might think of as "good role models." Their actions may strike us as morally dubious.

For example, consider the encounter between the legendary Greek hero Odysseus and the Cyclops. The Cyclops was one of a race of giants who lived by themselves on a remote, rarely visited island. The name Cyclops means "round eye," because these giants had only one eye in the middle of their forehead. They lived in caves, tended flocks of sheep, and ate the produce of their fields; they were shepherds.

Odysseus visited the island as part of his exploration to look for supplies. He brought with him a flask of wine. Although he was regarded as an intruder by the Cyclops, he helped himself to the giant's supplies without permission. The Cyclops became very angry. To ease the anger, Odysseus served him some wine. The Cyclops enjoyed the wine and asked for more. Later, when the Cyclops was in a wine-induced stupor, Odysseus attacked him in the eye. Later Odysseus bragged to his comrades about blinding the one-eyed creature.

This does not mean the Greeks admired thievery and bragging, however. What they admired about Odysseus, in this instance, was his capacity for quick thinking. Odysseus was also known for pulling off great feats with panache and self-confidence.

Not all Greek heroes were admired for the same reasons. Some, such as Odysseus, were admired for their resourcefulness and intelligence, whereas others, such as Herakles, were known for their strength and courage. Some were not particularly resourceful but depended on help to accomplish their tasks.

Whether or not a given action or quality was admired depended upon its ultimate results. Being headstrong might succeed in one instance but lead to failure in another. The Greeks held the characters in their legends accountable for their actions, and a hero might be punished as well as rewarded.

11. In this passage, what is the meaning of the word *dubious*?
    A. Crass
    B. Wrong
    C. Doubtful
    D. On the high ground

12. Based on this passage, why did the Greeks admire Odysseus?
    A. He could react quickly to a situation.
    B. He was a good role model.
    C. He attacked when the Cyclops was incapacitated.
    D. He was a hero in Greek mythology.

13. According to the passage, what was Herakles known for?
    A. Kindness
    B. Bravery
    C. Resourcefulness
    D. Failure

14. What is the major idea in this passage?
    A. Odysseus was a murderer.
    B. Odysseus was a thief.
    C. The Greeks judged their legendary heroes by the results they achieved.
    D. The Greeks admired each of their legendary heroes for the same reasons.

15. What was the major occupation of the Cyclops?
    A. Sailor
    B. Farmer
    C. Weaver
    D. Shepherd

STOP! DO NOT TURN THIS PAGE UNTIL TIME IS UP FOR THIS TEST. IF YOU FINISH BEFORE TIME IS UP, CHECK OVER YOUR WORK ON THIS TEST ONLY.

PART 5. MATHEMATICS KNOWLEDGE

THE TEST ADMINISTRATOR WILL READ THE FOLLOWING ALOUD TO YOU.

Now turn to Part 5 and read the directions for Mathematics Knowledge silently while I read them aloud.

This is a test of your ability to solve general mathematics problems. You are to select the correct response from the choices given. Then mark the space on your answer sheet that has the same number and letter as your choice. Use your scratch paper to do any figuring you wish to do.

Your score on this test will be based on the number of questions you answer correctly. You should try to answer every question. DO NOT SPEND TOO MUCH TIME on any one question. If you finish before time is called, go back and check your work in this part ONLY.

Now find the section of your answer sheet that is marked PART 5. When you are told to begin, start with question number 1 in Part 5 of your test booklet and answer space number 1 in Part 5 on your separate answer sheet.

DO NOT TURN THE PAGE UNTIL TOLD TO DO SO. You will have 24 minutes to complete the 25 questions in this part. Are there any questions?

Begin.

1. $x + 9 = 13$

   $x = ?$

   A. 3

   B. 4

   C. 5

   D. 13

2. $3^2 + 4(5 - 2) =$

   A. 21

   B. 36

   C. 39

   D. 40

3. $1\frac{1}{4} \times 2\frac{1}{2} =$

   A. 2

   B. $2\frac{1}{2}$

   C. $2\frac{3}{4}$

   D. $3\frac{1}{8}$

4. The square root of $64 =$

   A. 4

   B. −8

   C. 9

   D. −9

5. What is the value of the following expression if $x = 2$ and $y = 4$?

   $2x^3y^2$

   A. 52

   B. 106

   C. 256

   D. 512

6. Add:

   $3x^2 + 3xy + 4y + 2y^2$
   $3x^2 + xy + 9y + y^2$
   $-5x^2 - 2xy - 13y + y^2$
   $-3x^2 + 3xy + y - 4y^2$

   A. $2x^2 + 4xy + y + y^2$

   B. $-2x^2 + 4xy + y + y^2$

   C. $2x^2 + 5xy + 2y + 2y^2$

   D. $-2x^2 + 5xy + y$

7. Factor the following expression: $y^2 - 16y + 48$

   A. $(y - 1)(y + 48)$

   B. $(y - 4)(y - 12)$

   C. $(y - 4)(y + 4)$

   D. $(y + 1)(y - 16)$

8. Solve for x.

   $12x + 6 = 8x + 10$

   A. $x = 1$

   B. $x = 2$

   C. $x = 4$

   D. $x = 6$

9. Solve for the two unknowns.

   $3y + 3x = 24$
   $6y + 3x = 39$

   A. $y = 3; x = 5$

   B. $y = 4; x = 6$

   C. $y = 5; x = 3$

   D. $y = 6; x = 2$

10. $\dfrac{x^{12}}{x^4} =$

    A. x^{-8}

    B. x^8

    C. x^{18}

    D. x^{-16}

11. Solve for y.

    $y^2 + 7y = -10$

    A. $y = -5; y = -2$

    B. $y = 1; y = -10$

    C. $y = -2; y = 6$

    D. $y = 5; y = -1$

12. Multiply:

$$\frac{6y}{11} \times \frac{2}{5x} =$$

A. $6y + 5x = 22$

B. $12y + 55$

C. $\dfrac{12y}{55x}$

D. $\dfrac{30xy}{22}$

13. Divide:

$$\frac{6x}{11} \div \frac{2}{5y}$$

A. $\dfrac{12x}{55y}$

B. $\dfrac{15xy}{11}$

C. $\dfrac{12}{55xy}$

D. $30 \ xy$

14. $\sqrt[3]{27} =$

A. 3

B. 4

C. 5

D. 2.25

15. Solve for g.

$$\frac{g}{h} = a$$

A. $\dfrac{ga}{h}$

B. $g = \dfrac{a}{h}$

C. $g = ah$

D. $g = a \div h$

16. Which of the following is an equilateral triangle?

A.

B.

C.

D.

17. What is the perimeter of the following rectangle?

9 m

3 m

A. 12 m

B. 18 m

C. 24 m

D. 12 m^2

18. What is the circumference of the following circle?

4 m

A. 6.56 m

B. 12.56 m

C. 25.12 m

D. 35.12 m

19. In the following equilateral triangle, what is the measure of ∠1?

  A. 30°
  B. 45°
  C. 60°
  D. 90°

20. If ∠1 is 34°, what is the measure of ∠2?

  A. 56°
  B. 110°
  C. 146°
  D. 180°

21. In the following right triangle, what is the length of side *AB*?

  A. 3 m
  B. 5 m
  C. 7 m
  D. 12 m

22. What is the area of the following triangle?

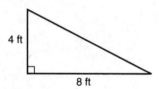

  A. 8 ft²
  B. 12 ft²
  C. 15 ft²
  D. 16 ft²

23. What is the diameter of the following circle?

  A. 40 cm
  B. 80 cm
  C. 160 cm
  D. 640 cm

24. If lines *A* and *B* are parallel and are intersected by line *C* and ∠2 is 30°, what is the measure of ∠7?

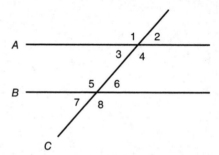

  A. 30°
  B. 50°
  C. 112°
  D. 130°

25. What is the volume of a cylinder with a height of 15 m and a radius of 5 m?
  A. 235.50 m³
  B. 1,177.50 m³
  C. 1,280.25 m³
  D. 1,340.25 m³

STOP! DO NOT TURN THIS PAGE UNTIL TIME IS UP FOR THIS TEST. IF YOU FINISH BEFORE TIME IS UP, CHECK OVER YOUR WORK ON THIS TEST ONLY.

PART 6. ELECTRONICS INFORMATION

THE TEST ADMINISTRATOR WILL READ THE FOLLOWING ALOUD TO YOU.

Now turn to Part 6 of your test booklet and read the directions for Electronics Information silently while I read them aloud.

This is a test of your knowledge of electrical, radio, and electronics information. You are to select the correct response from the choices given and then mark the space on your answer sheet that has the same number and letter as your choice.

Your score on this test will be based on the number of questions you answer correctly. You should try to answer every question. DO NOT SPEND TOO MUCH TIME on any one question. If you finish before time is called, go back and check your work in this part ONLY.

Now find the section of your answer sheet that is marked PART 6. When you are told to begin, start with question number 1 in Part 6 of your test booklet and answer space number 1 in Part 6 on your separate answer sheet.

DO NOT TURN THE PAGE UNTIL TOLD TO DO SO. You will have 9 minutes to complete the 20 questions in this part. Are there any questions?

Begin.

1. One hertz is defined as
   A. one ampere per second.
   B. one cycle per second.
   C. one volt per second.
   D. one coulomb per second.

2. One advantage of alternating current is that it is easy to
   A. store.
   B. convert into chemical energy.
   C. transport through wire.
   D. transmit through air.

3. Electric current can travel only through a
   A. wire.
   B. circuit.
   C. battery.
   D. load.

4. Copper is used in most electric wires because it is
   A. a semiconductor.
   B. not likely to heat up during normal usage.
   C. a good resistor and inexpensive.
   D. a good conductor and inexpensive.

5. Amperes are a measure of
   A. the number of electrons moving through a conductor.
   B. electrical pressure.
   C. a material's ability to store electric current.
   D. the total resistance of a series circuit.

6. Ohms are a measure of
   A. capacitance.
   B. resistance.
   C. current.
   D. cycles per second.

7. If amperes = volts/ohms, then volts =
   A. 1/(amperes × ohms).
   B. ohms/amperes.
   C. amperes/ohms.
   D. amperes × ohms.

8. A circuit with 20 amperes has a load of 12 ohms. What is the voltage?
   A. 60
   B. 120
   C. 240
   D. 24

9. If the resistance of a circuit is 0, the circuit is
   A. an open circuit.
   B. a short circuit.
   C. a superconductor circuit.
   D. a semiconductor circuit.

10. If a transformer raises the voltage, it will
    A. raise the resistance.
    B. reduce the resistance.
    C. raise the amperage.
    D. reduce the amperage.

11. Which of these devices depends on the close relationship between electricity and magnetism?
    A. Transformer
    B. Electromagnet
    C. Electric motor
    D. All of the above

12. If you are soldering two wires, you need solder,
    A. heat, and flux.
    B. and heat.
    C. and flux.
    D. flux, and electrical tape.

13. When connecting wires in the house, the bare copper wire is sometimes replaced by the
    A. the black wire.
    B. the white wire.
    C. the hot wire.
    D. conduit.

14. To hook up an electric heater, you need
    A. three supply wires.
    B. four supply wires.
    C. heavy supply wires.
    D. no supply wires.

15. In most home wiring, the hot wire is
    A. black.
    B. orange.
    C. green.
    D. white.

16. To control a light from each end of a hallway, you would install
    A. two single-pole switches.
    B. one four-way switch.
    C. one three-way switch.
    D. two three-way switches.

17. At 120 volts, a 15-ampere circuit will carry _____ power than a 20-ampere circuit.
    A. more
    B. less
    C. first less, then more
    D. first more, then less

18. To connect a battery properly, you must
    A. observe proper polarity.
    B. get the right voltage.
    C. both A and B.
    D. be certain the battery is chemical-free.

19. When you are making an electrical connection to a large battery,
    A. never tighten the terminal.
    B. tighten the terminal, then back off one turn.
    C. use salt water to prevent corrosion.
    D. tighten the terminal securely.

20. If you need to reduce the voltage in a certain part of a circuit, you could use a
    A. capacitor.
    B. transistor.
    C. resistor.
    D. inductor.

STOP! DO NOT TURN THIS PAGE UNTIL TIME IS UP FOR THIS TEST. IF YOU FINISH BEFORE TIME IS UP, CHECK OVER YOUR WORK ON THIS TEST ONLY.

PART 7. AUTO AND SHOP INFORMATION

THE TEST ADMINISTRATOR WILL READ THE FOLLOWING ALOUD TO YOU.

Now turn to Part 7 and read the directions for Auto and Shop Information silently while I read them aloud.

This test has questions about automobiles, shop practices, and the use of tools. Pick the BEST answer for each question and then mark the space on your answer sheet that has the same number and letter as your choice.

Your score on this test will be based on the number of questions you answer correctly. You should try to answer every question. DO NOT SPEND TOO MUCH TIME on any one question. If you finish before time is called, go back and check your work in this part ONLY.

Now find the section of your answer sheet that is marked PART 7. When you are told to begin, start with question number 1 in Part 7 of your test booklet and answer space number 1 in Part 7 on your separate answer sheet.

DO NOT TURN THE PAGE UNTIL TOLD TO DO SO. You will have 11 minutes to complete the 25 questions in this part. Are there any questions?

Begin.

1. If you hear a loud clanking noise from the rear of a rear-wheel-drive, front-engine car, you should look for trouble at
   A. the differential or driveshaft.
   B. the transmission.
   C. the engine.
   D. the clutch.

2. If one engine cylinder does not work right, you should check for problems in the
   A. drive train.
   B. pollution controls.
   C. ignition or fuel system.
   D. clutch.

3. If tire pressure gets low, what will happen?
   A. The tire will lose its shape and create extra friction, reducing gas mileage and possibly overheating the tire.
   B. The tire will not absorb energy from the engine.
   C. Vehicle weight will be reduced.
   D. The tire will get better traction on the highway.

4. If an engine with conventional ignition runs rough, what might you adjust on the breaker points, shown as part B of this diagram?
   A. The gap
   B. The timing
   C. Composition
   D. Lubrication

5. One important difference between front-wheel drive and rear-wheel drive is that in front-wheel drive,
   A. the layshaft moves the driveshaft.
   B. the engine must be rotated 180° from normal position.
   C. the driving wheels also steer.
   D. the rear wheels must also drive.

6. Which is the correct sequence in a four-cycle internal-combustion engine?
   A. Intake, compression, power, rest
   B. Reduction, power, compression, exhaust
   C. Intake, compression, power, exhaust
   D. Exhaust, compression, intake, power

7. If you suspect that not enough gasoline is entering the engine, what might you check first?
   A. Fuel system
   B. Ignition system
   C. Timing belt
   D. Engine control module

8. When a manual transmission is in a "direct-drive" gear, one revolution of the engine produces
   A. two revolutions of the driveshaft.
   B. one revolution of the driveshaft.
   C. one-half revolution of the driveshaft.
   D. two revolutions of the clutch.

9. In the diagram above, the arrows indicate
   A. viscosity.
   B. brake fluid.
   C. filters.
   D. temperature.

10. What must happen before the starter motor is engaged?
    A. The brakes must be adjusted.
    B. The starter relay must be closed.
    C. The gas tank must be full.
    D. The oil pump must be automatically primed.

11. If the exhaust valve does not open,
    A. the fuel-air mix cannot enter the engine.
    B. the car will not pollute.
    C. the engine will run a bit rough.
    D. burned gas cannot leave the cylinder, and the engine will not run.

12. If the differential ratio is 3 to 1,
    A. one turn of the driveshaft produces three turns of the wheels.
    B. three turns of the jack shaft produce one turn of the wheels.
    C. the ring gear is probably disengaged.
    D. three turns of the driveshaft produce one turn of the wheels.

13. When choosing a slot screwdriver,
    A. use a blade that slips easily into the slot.
    B. make the blade as wide as the screw head.
    C. always use the shortest possible handle.
    D. file out the screw to fit the screwdriver.

14. The tool shown above is a(n)
    A. locking pliers (Vise Grips).
    B. arc-joint pliers (Channel Locks).
    C. monkey wrench.
    D. side-cutting electrician's pliers.

15. A plywood-cutting blade for a circular saw
    A. has a few big teeth because plywood is so much harder than regular wood.
    B. cannot be used with particle board.
    C. must not be too sharp or else it will burn the wood.
    D. has many small teeth, to reduce splintering.

16. Which of the following is a poor use for a claw hammer?
    A. Pulling nails
    B. Hammering nails
    C. Driving screws
    D. Driving wood chisels

17. The tool shown above is used for
    A. clamping parts for gluing.
    B. tightening large pipe fittings.
    C. pressing a drill into the chuck.
    D. pressing glass into a window sash.

18. It helps to hit a larger chisel with a larger hammer because the hammer is
    A. heavier.
    B. more massive.
    C. bigger, and therefore less likely to miss the chisel.
    D. slower-moving.

19. Plywood is better than regular wood for a sub-floor mainly because
    A. it is more weatherproof.
    B. it is lighter.
    C. it is thinner.
    D. it is stronger.

20. Which tool might replace a hacksaw for some jobs?
    A. A circular saw with a carbide blade
    B. A keyhole saw
    C. A coping saw
    D. An oxyacetylene cutting torch

21. The tool shown above is a
    A. tin snip.
    B. magna-shear.
    C. bolt cutter.
    D. duckbill wrench.

22. Which of these tools does not start to clamp until you turn it?
    A. Screwdriver
    B. Locking pliers
    C. Pipe wrench
    D. Vise

23. What is not an advantage of a sharp drill bit?
    A. It creates a smaller amount of chips.
    B. It cuts with less pressure.
    C. It cuts cooler.
    D. It cuts faster.

24. Which of the following would not loosen a frozen nut?
    A. Heating it with a torch
    B. Pounding it with a hammer
    C. Soaking it in penetrating oil
    D. Dousing it in ice water

25. A plumb line makes what kind of angle where it intersects a level line?
    A. Acute
    B. Obtuse
    C. Square
    D. Straight

STOP! DO NOT TURN THIS PAGE UNTIL TIME IS UP FOR THIS TEST. IF YOU FINISH BEFORE TIME IS UP, CHECK OVER YOUR WORK ON THIS TEST ONLY.

PART 8. MECHANICAL COMPREHENSION

THE TEST ADMINISTRATOR WILL READ THE FOLLOWING ALOUD TO YOU.

Now turn to Part 8 and read the directions for Mechanical Comprehension silently while I read them aloud.

This test has questions about mechanical and physical principles. Study the picture and decide which answer is CORRECT and then mark the space on your separate answer sheet that has the same number and letter as your choice.

Your score on this test will be based on the number of questions you answer correctly. You should try to answer every question. DO NOT SPEND TOO MUCH TIME on any one question. If you finish before time is called, go back and check your work in this part ONLY.

Now find the section of your answer sheet that is marked PART 8. When you are told to begin, start with question number 1 in Part 8 of your test booklet and answer space number 1 in Part 8 on your separate answer sheet.

DO NOT TURN THE PAGE UNTIL TOLD TO DO SO. You will have 19 minutes to complete the 25 questions in this part. Are there any questions?

Begin.

1. The diagram shows five gears. If gear B turns as shown, then the gears turning in the same direction are
   A. A and C.
   B. A and D.
   C. C and D.
   D. D and E.

2. What is the theoretical mechanical advantage in using this lever?
   A. 1
   B. 2
   C. 3
   D. 4

3. A wrench is used to turn a bolt that has 20 threads per inch. After 15 complete turns of the wrench, the bolt will have moved
   A. ¼ inch.
   B. ½ inch.
   C. ¾ inch.
   D. 1 inch.

4. A gear and pinion have a ratio of 5 to 1. If the gear is rotating at a speed of 150 revolutions per minute (rpm), the speed of the pinion is most nearly
   A. 750 rpm.
   B. 300 rpm.
   C. 150 rpm.
   D. 30 rpm.

5. In the diagram, water is flowing from left to right. What is true of the water after it enters the 3-inch pipe?
   A. Its pressure decreases, but its speed increases.
   B. Its pressure and speed both decrease.
   C. Its pressure and speed both increase.
   D. Its pressure increases, but its speed decreases.

6. What is the force *F* needed to balance this lever?
   A. 20 kg
   B. 22 kg
   C. 25 kg
   D. 30 kg

7. Gear A, with 48 teeth, meshes with gear B, with 12 teeth. For every rotation that gear A makes, how many rotations does gear B make?
   A. 1
   B. 2
   C. 4
   D. 8

8. Pushing a heavy concrete block up an inclined plane will be easier if you
   A. raise the angle of the plane.
   B. turn the block upside down.
   C. heat the block with an electric coil.
   D. put the block on a wheelbarrow.

9. These pipes and cylinders are part of a hydraulic mechanism. If the piston in cylinder A moves,
   A. the piston in cylinder B will move.
   B. the fluid in cylinder A will not move.
   C. the piston in cylinder B will not move.
   D. the fluid in cylinder A will move, but the fluid in cylinder B will not move.

10. A 3 ft × 6 ft tank is filled with 3,600 lb of water. What is the pressure on the bottom, in lb/ft²?
    A. 100
    B. 200
    C. 400
    D. 800

11. Which cannot bend without breaking?

    A.

    B.

    C.

    D.

12. A knife blade is an example of which kind of simple machine?
    A. Pulley
    B. Wheel and axle
    C. Wedge
    D. Gear

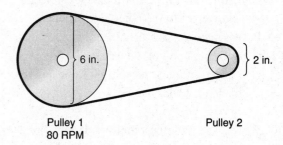

Pulley 1
80 RPM

Pulley 2

13. In the pulley (sheave) system shown, pulley 1 is rotating at 80 rpm. How fast is pulley 2 rotating?
    A. 180 rpm
    B. 240 rpm
    C. 300 rpm
    D. 360 rpm

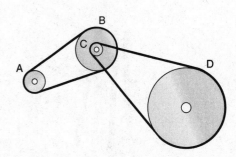

14. In the pulley system shown, which pulley is rotating the slowest?
    A. A
    B. B
    C. C
    D. D

15. Operating this car jack will take less effort if you
    A. add weight to the other side of the car.
    B. get a longer jack handle.
    C. open the hood of the car.
    D. replace the jack handle with one just like it made of wood.

16. Which material is best for the floor of a fireplace?
    A. Wood
    B. Plastic
    C. Stone
    D. Glass

100 lb

17. What effort is required to lift the load?
    A. 40 lb
    B. 50 lb
    C. 100 lb
    D. 200 lb

18. What makes the water flow out of the tank and through the siphon hose into the bucket?
    A. Air pressure
    B. Water pressure
    C. The weight of the water
    D. Magnetism

19. In the diagram, gear B is an idler gear. If gear B is rotating clockwise,
    A. gear A is rotating clockwise, but gear C is rotating counterclockwise.
    B. gear A and gear C are rotating clockwise.
    C. gear A and gear C are rotating counterclockwise.
    D. gear A is rotating counterclockwise, but gear C is rotating clockwise.

20. A wrench uses which simple machine to turn a bolt?
    A. Lever
    B. Inclined plane
    C. Pulley
    D. Wheel and axle

Books

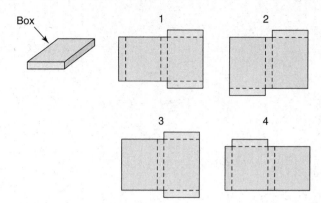

Box

1   2

3   4

21. The diagram shows a box of books on a shelf supported by two posts. Which post bears the greater part of the weight?
A. Post A.
B. Post B.
C. Each post bears the same amount of weight.
D. The shelf distributes the weight equally.

24. Which flat cardboard pattern can be folded along the dotted lines to form the complete, totally enclosed box shown?
A. 1
B. 2
C. 3
D. 4

22. Water is flowing into the tank from the upper faucet at the rate of 240 gallons per hour and draining out of the tank through the lower faucet at a rate of 1 gallon per minute. How many more gallons of water will be in the tank after 6 minutes?
A. 14
B. 16
C. 18
D. 22

B

A

25. After the crank (A) rotates 9.5 times, where will the piston (B) be?
A. In the same place as shown
B. At the top of the cylinder
C. At the bottom of the cylinder
D. B or C

23. The diagram at the right shows a rotating disk. When the disk rotates, which point travels farthest?
A. Point A.
B. Point B.
C. Point C.
D. Points B and C both travel the same distance.

STOP! DO NOT TURN THIS PAGE UNTIL TIME IS UP FOR THIS TEST. IF YOU FINISH BEFORE TIME IS UP, CHECK OVER YOUR WORK ON THIS TEST ONLY.

PART 9. ASSEMBLING OBJECTS

THE TEST ADMINISTRATOR WILL READ THE FOLLOWING ALOUD TO YOU.

Now turn to Part 9 and read the directions for Assembling Objects silently while I read them aloud.

This test has questions that will measure your spatial ability. Study the diagram, decide which answer is CORRECT, and then mark the space on your separate answer sheet that has the same number and letter as your choice.

Your score on this test will be based on the number of questions you answer correctly. You should try to answer every question. DO NOT SPEND TOO MUCH TIME on any one question. If you finish before time is called, go back and check your work in this part ONLY.

Now find the section of your answer sheet that is marked PART 9. When you are told to begin, start with question 1 in Part 9 of your test booklet and answer space number 1 in Part 9 on your separate answer sheet.

DO NOT TURN THE PAGE UNTIL TOLD TO DO SO. You will have 15 minutes to complete the 25 questions in this part. Are there any questions?

Begin.

For Questions 1–18, which figure best shows how the objects in the left box will appear if they are fit together?

15.

16.

17.

18.

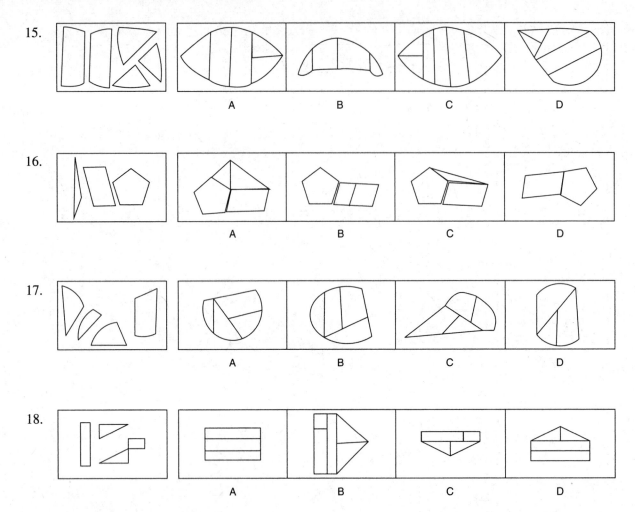

For Questions 19-25, which figure best shows how the objects in the left box will touch if the letters for each object are matched?

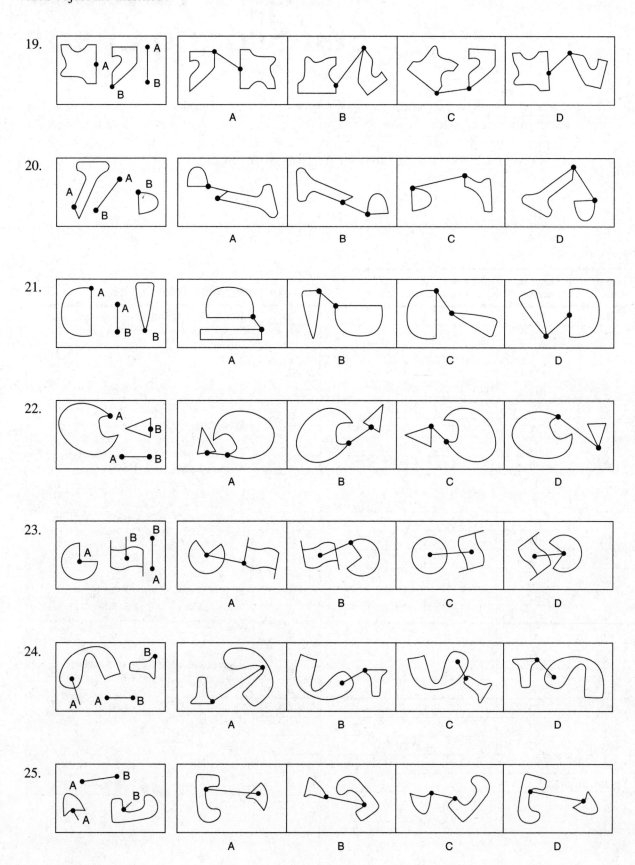

Answer Keys and Self-Scoring Charts

The following answer keys show the correct answers for each part of the diagnostic test that you just took. For each question, compare your answer to the correct answer. Mark an X in the column to the right if you got the item correct. Then total the number correct for each part of the test. Find that number in the corresponding chart to the right of the answer key. See the suggestions listed for your performance.

Part 1. General Science

Item Number	Correct Answer	Mark X if You Picked the Correct Answer
1	A	
2	D	
3	B	
4	D	
5	D	
6	B	
7	A	
8	D	
9	B	
10	D	
11	C	
12	B	
13	D	
14	B	
15	D	
16	D	
17	A	
18	B	
19	A	
20	D	
21	B	
22	D	
23	B	
24	C	
25	B	
Total Correct		

Score Interpretation—Total Correct

Score	Interpretation
25	This is pretty good work. Review the explanations of the answers you got incorrect.
24	
23	
22	
21	
20	You are doing pretty well. Review the explanations for the items you answered incorrectly. If you have time, review the other explanations and you will learn even more.
19	
18	
17	
16	
15	You need to keep studying. Pay close attention to the explanations for each item, even for the ones you got correct.
14	
13	
12	
11	
10	Spend time working on the General Science review in Part 3 of this book.
9	
8	
7	
6	If you have copies of your school science textbooks, it would be a good idea to study those.
5	
4	
3	
2	
1	
0	

Part 2. Arithmetic Reasoning

Item Number	Correct Answer	Mark X if You Picked the Correct Answer
1	B	
2	B	
3	C	
4	A	
5	D	
6	D	
7	B	
8	C	
9	D	
10	A	
11	B	
12	B	
13	D	
14	D	
15	D	
16	D	
17	C	
18	C	
19	A	
20	D	
21	D	
22	C	
23	C	
24	D	
25	C	
26	C	
27	B	
28	B	
29	D	
30	A	
Total Correct		

Score Interpretation–Total Correct

30	This is pretty good work. Review the explanations of the answers you got incorrect. This test is a part of the AFQT, and you must do well.
29	
28	
27	
26	
25	You are doing pretty well. Review the explanations for the items you answered incorrectly. If you have time, review the other explanations and you will learn even more.
24	
23	
22	
21	
20	You need to keep studying. Pay close attention to the explanations for each item, even for the ones you got correct.
19	
18	
17	
16	
15	Spend time working on the Arithmetic Reasoning review in Part 3 of this book.
14	
13	
12	
11	Keep working and reworking problems until you are comfortable with the processes.
10	
9	
8	
7	
6	
5	
4	
3	
2	
1	
0	

Part 3. Word Knowledge

Item Number	Correct Answer	Mark X if You Picked the Correct Answer
1	C	
2	B	
3	B	
4	C	
5	D	
6	C	
7	B	
8	C	
9	D	
10	B	
11	B	
12	A	
13	A	
14	A	
15	B	
16	B	
17	D	
18	C	
19	B	
20	D	
21	C	
22	B	
23	C	
24	B	
25	A	
26	A	
27	D	
28	A	
29	A	
30	C	
31	C	
32	A	
33	D	
34	B	
35	B	
Total Correct		

Score Interpretation–Total Correct

Score	Interpretation
35	This is pretty good work. Review the explanations of the answers you got incorrect. This is an important test that contributes to your AFQT.
34	
33	
32	
31	
30	You are doing pretty well. Review the explanations for the items you answered incorrectly. If you have time, review the other explanations and you will learn even more.
29	
28	
27	
26	
25	You need to keep studying. Pay close attention to the explanations for each item, even for the ones you got correct.
24	
23	
22	
21	
20	Spend time working on the Word Knowledge review in Part 3 of this book.
19	
18	
17	
16	Keep reading and identifying words you don't know.
15	
14	
13	
12	
11	
10	
9	
8	
7	
6	
5	
4	
3	
2	
1	
0	

Part 4. Paragraph Comprehension

Item Number	Correct Answer	Mark X if You Picked the Correct Answer
1	A	
2	B	
3	C	
4	A	
5	D	
6	B	
7	A	
8	B	
9	C	
10	A	
11	C	
12	A	
13	B	
14	C	
15	D	
Total Correct		

Score Interpretation–Total Correct

Score	Interpretation
15	This is pretty good work. Review the explanations of the answers you got incorrect. This test is a part of the AFQT, and you must do well.
14	
13	You are doing pretty well. Review the explanations for the items you got incorrect. This test is a part of the AFQT, and you must do well.
12	
11	You need to keep studying. Pay close attention to the explanations for each item, even for the ones you got correct. This will help you understand why the answer is correct.
10	
9	
8	
7	
6	Spend time reviewing the Paragraph Comprehension and Word Knowledge reviews in Part 3 of this book. Keep reading books and newspapers.
5	
4	
3	
2	
1	
0	

Part 5. Mathematics Knowledge

Item Number	Correct Answer	Mark X if You Picked the Correct Answer
1	B	
2	A	
3	D	
4	B	
5	C	
6	D	
7	B	
8	A	
9	C	
10	B	
11	A	
12	C	
13	B	
14	A	
15	C	
16	D	
17	C	
18	C	
19	C	
20	C	
21	B	
22	D	
23	C	
24	A	
25	B	
Total Correct		

Score Interpretation–Total Correct

25, 24, 23	This is pretty good work. Review the explanations of the answers you got incorrect.
22, 21, 20	You are doing pretty well. Review the explanations for the items you answered incorrectly. If you have time, review the other explanations and you will learn even more.
19, 18	This test is part of the AFQT. You must perform well on this test.
17, 16, 15, 14	You need to keep studying. Pay close attention to the explanations for each item, even for the ones you got correct.
13, 12, 11, 10, 9, 8, 7, 6, 5, 4, 3, 2, 1, 0	Spend time working on the Mathematics Knowledge reviews in Part 3 of this book, and work and rework the problems until you fully understand the processes.

Part 6. Electronics Information

Item Number	Correct Answer	Mark X if You Picked the Correct Answer
1	B	
2	C	
3	B	
4	D	
5	A	
6	B	
7	D	
8	C	
9	B	
10	D	
11	D	
12	A	
13	D	
14	C	
15	A	
16	D	
17	B	
18	C	
19	D	
20	C	
Total Correct		

Score Interpretation–Total Correct

20	This is pretty good work. Review the explanations of the answers you got incorrect.
19	
18	
17	You are doing pretty well. Review the explanations for the items you answered incorrectly. If you have time, review the other explanations and you will learn even more.
16	
15	
14	
13	
12	You need to keep studying. Pay close attention to the explanations for each item, even for the ones you got correct.
11	
10	
9	
8	Spend time working on the Electronics Information review in Part 3 of this book.
7	
6	
5	Your school electronics or physics books may have some helpful information as well.
4	
3	
2	
1	
0	

Part 7. Auto and Shop Information

Item Number	Correct Answer	Mark X if You Picked the Correct Answer
1	A	
2	C	
3	A	
4	A	
5	C	
6	C	
7	A	
8	B	
9	B	
10	B	
11	D	
12	D	
13	B	
14	B	
15	D	
16	C	
17	A	
18	B	
19	D	
20	D	
21	A	
22	C	
23	A	
24	D	
25	C	
Total Correct		

Score Interpretation–Total Correct

Score	Interpretation
25	This is pretty good work. Review the explanations of the answers you got incorrect.
24	
23	
22	
21	
20	You are doing pretty well. Review the explanations for the items you answered incorrectly. If you have time, review the other explanations and you will learn even more.
19	
18	
17	
16	
15	
14	You need to keep studying. Pay close attention to the explanations for each item, even for the ones you got correct.
13	
12	
11	
10	Spend time working on the Auto and Shop Information review in Part 3 of this book.
9	
8	
7	
6	
5	
4	
3	
2	
1	
0	

Part 8. Mechanical Comprehension

Item Number	Correct Answer	Mark X if You Picked the Correct Answer
1	D	
2	C	
3	C	
4	A	
5	D	
6	B	
7	C	
8	D	
9	A	
10	B	
11	A	
12	C	
13	B	
14	D	
15	B	
16	C	
17	B	
18	A	
19	C	
20	D	
21	B	
22	C	
23	B	
24	A	
25	A	
Total Correct		

Score Interpretation–Total Correct

Score	Interpretation
25	This is pretty good work. Review the explanations of the answers you got incorrect.
24	
23	
22	
21	
20	You are doing pretty well. Review the explanations for the items you answered incorrectly. If you have time, review the other explanations and you will learn even more.
19	
18	
17	
16	
15	You need to keep studying. Pay close attention to the explanations for each item, even for the ones you got correct.
14	
13	
12	
11	Spend time working on the Mechanical Comprehension review in Part 3 of this book
10	
9	
8	
7	
6	
5	
4	
3	
2	
1	
0	

Part 9. Assembling Objects

Item Number	Correct Answer	Mark X if You Picked the Correct Answer
1	C	
2	B	
3	D	
4	B	
5	A	
6	D	
7	A	
8	D	
9	C	
10	B	
11	A	
12	D	
13	C	
14	B	
15	A	
16	C	
17	B	
18	A	
19	C	
20	D	
21	B	
22	C	
23	A	
24	D	
25	D	
Total Correct		

Score Interpretation–Total Correct

25	This is pretty good work. Review the explanations of the answers you got incorrect.
24	
23	
22	
21	
20	You are doing pretty well. Review the explanations for the items you answered incorrectly. If you have time, review the other explanations and you will learn even more.
19	
18	
17	
16	
15	Keep studying. Pay close attention to the explanations for each item, even for the ones you got correct.
14	
13	
12	
11	Spend time working on the Assembling Objects review in Part 3 of this book.
10	
9	
8	
7	
6	
5	
4	
3	
2	
1	
0	

Answers and Explanations

PART 1. GENERAL SCIENCE

1. **A.** The nucleus is an important part of the cell. Although carbon and oxygen are important to life, the basic unit of life is the cell. Choice A is the correct answer.

2. **D.** During the process of photosynthesis, a plant uses carbon dioxide and water. Through the interaction of chlorophyll and light, glucose (a sugar) and oxygen are created. Carbon dioxide (choice A) is not a by-product of photosynthesis, but rather the raw material used by the plant, and light (choice B) acts to initiate the process of photosynthesis as it interacts with chlorophyll. Ozone is found high in the atmosphere and is not created by plants. Choice D, oxygen, is the correct answer.

3. **B.** The nucleus is important because it controls most of the activities of the cell. Choice B is the correct answer.

4. **D.** Muscle cells (choice A) and nerve cells (choice C) all have organelles. Protozoa (choice B), which are one-celled organisms, also have organelles. Bacteria (choice D) do not. Choice D is the correct answer.

5. **D.** Geotropism refers to plant growth responding to the force of gravity. Thigmotropism is when a plant moves or grows in response to touch or contact. Chemotropism is when a plant responds to chemicals. Phototropism is when a plant responds to light. D is the correct answer.

6. **B.** Birds are vertebrates that are warm-blooded. Choice B is the correct answer.

7. **A.** Decomposers break down tissue and release nutrients and carbon dioxide into the ecosystem. Choice A is the correct answer.

8. **D.** Marrow (choice A) is the soft tissue within the bone and does not protect the spinal cord. Cartilage (choice B) is a smooth, slippery covering on the ends of bones that acts as a shock absorber. Its purpose is not to protect the spinal cord. Ligaments (choice C) are one of the ways in which bones are joined and move together. They do not protect the spinal cord. The vertebrae, found in your back, do indeed protect the spinal cord. Choice D is the correct answer.

9. **B.** A bruise on your skin may cause a bit of swelling (choice D), but the bruise is not related to your sweat glands (choice C). Excess strain on your muscles (choice A) may cause some discomfort, but that is not likely to break your capillaries. Bruising is caused by some traumatic event that breaks the capillaries. Choice B is the correct answer.

10. **D.** Peristalsis is the muscular contraction of the digestive system that moves food from one part of the system to the next. For example, peristalsis is responsible for moving food from the stomach to the large intestine.

11. **C.** The hypothalamus, pons, and cortex (choice C) are all parts of the brain and thus of the nervous system. Nephrons, urethra, and bladder (choice A) are part of the excretory system. Antigens, T cells, and cilia (choice B) are all part of the immune system. Lymph nodes, spleen, and tonsils (choice D) are part of the lymphatic system. Choice C is the correct answer.

12. **B.** Dendrites (choice D) and axons (choice C) are parts of the nerve cell. The nerve cell gap (choice A) is not the correct answer because it is not related to the nervous system. The space between two nerve cells where an electric charge transmits information is called a synapse. Choice B is the correct answer.

13. **D.** Biodiversity tends to increase with warmer climate. Florida is the warmest state of those listed, so choice D is the correct answer.

14. **B.** Ultraviolet light is absorbed, at least in part, by the ozone layer in the atmosphere. Some of it passes through to Earth's surface. With the thinning of the ozone layer as a result of the introduction of chlorofluorocarbons into the atmosphere, more ultraviolet light is reaching Earth's surface, with possibly damaging effects on humans. Choice B is the correct answer.

15. **D.** The amplitude of a sound wave is responsible for the loudness of the sound. Choice D is the correct answer.

16. **D.** All the alternatives have something to do with sea-floor spreading, but only one is the cause. Subduction (choice A) is a downward force or movement that is a result of sea-floor spreading, not the cause. The same can be said for creation of the ridges (choice B) and for the compression of continents (choice C). They are both results, not causes. All these features are produced by the convection currents in the mantle, which cause the uprising and subduction of the crust. Choice D is the correct answer.

17. **A.** A rift (choice D) is a valley in the ocean floor formed by tectonic plates that are separating. A tsunami (choice C) is a wall of water that can overwhelm a shoreline. It is created when an earthquake creates an ocean wave. Hot spots (choice B) are undersea fissures that are spouting magma from the sea floor. The Hawaiian Islands have been and continue to be created from hot spots. When two tectonic plates converge and one rises above the other, it is common to find areas that experience earthquakes and volcanic activity. Choice A, volcanoes, is the correct answer.

18. **B.** When a wave is created in the ocean by persistent surface winds, the wave moves in the direction of the winds. When that wave approaches land, it moves through shallow water and the trough (bottom) of the wave starts to scrape the ocean

bottom. The scraping causes friction, and that makes the trough of the wave move more slowly than the crest (top) of the wave. Eventually the crest just topples over, creating a breaker. Choice B is the correct answer.

19. **A.** The definition of a year is the time it takes for Earth to make one revolution around the sun. Choice A, 1 year, is the correct answer.

20. **D.** A solar eclipse is created when the moon blocks the light from the sun from reaching Earth by casting a shadow on Earth's surface. The shadow covers only a very small area, so a total solar eclipse is visible only on a limited part of Earth's surface at any one time. The shadow has two parts, a darker part called the umbra, where a total eclipse occurs, and a lighter part called the penumbra, where a partial eclipse can be seen. In order for a solar eclipse to occur, the moon has to be between the sun and Earth. Choice D is the correct answer.

21. **B.** When solar radiation reaches Earth's atmosphere, the radiation is either reflected, absorbed by Earth's atmosphere, or trapped by Earth's atmosphere. When it is trapped by the atmosphere, it causes the atmosphere and Earth's surface to heat up. Choice B is the correct answer.

22. **D.** Warm air can hold more moisture than cold air. Air masses formed over the tropical oceans can hold significant amounts of moisture, while air masses formed over cold oceans or land masses are generally drier. Whether the air is moving or stable does not much affect the humidity in the air. Choice D, warm air, is the correct answer.

23. **B.** When a prevailing wind containing moisture reaches a mountain range, it rises and cools, causing condensation in the form of rain or snow. The side of the mountain range on which this happens is called the windward side. Much of the moisture in the air is deposited on the windward side of a mountain range. When the air reaches the tops of the mountains, it starts to spill down the other side. As it descends, it heats up. The side of the mountain range on which this happens is called

the leeward side. Often you will find deserts on the leeward side of a mountain range. The climate is definitely drier on the leeward side. Choice B is the correct answer.

24. **C.** Igneous rocks (choice A) are formed from molten material that eventually cools. Extrusive rocks (choice B) are igneous rocks that have formed on or above Earth's surface. Metamorphic rocks (choice D) are created by high temperature and pressure. Sedimentary rocks (choice C) are formed by rock that has been broken up into pieces and cemented together. The pieces can be somewhat large, as in a conglomerate, or small, such as in shale or limestone. Choice C is the correct answer.

25. **B.** When objects move away from a viewer, the light waves they produce lengthen, shifting toward the red end of the spectrum. Scientists have observed that light from distant stars shifts toward the red end of the spectrum. This supports the conclusion that the universe is expanding. Choice B is the correct answer.

PART 2. ARITHMETIC REASONING

1. **B.** This is a simple addition problem. Add the amounts to get the total of $14.74.

2. **B.** This problem has two steps. First you need to add the amount spent. Then you need to subtract that amount from the $100 bill. The total amount spent is $90.49, so, subtracting that from $100, the change is $9.51.

3. **C.** In order to calculate the percent, you need to divide the total number of items into the number answered correctly. In this case, you would divide 45 into 38 and get 0.8444. To change that to a percent, move the decimal point two places to the right and add the percent sign to get 84.44%. Since the question asks for the nearest percent, the answer would be 84%.

4. **A.** To find the average, add up the numbers and divide by the number of numbers. In this problem,

the numbers add to 400. Dividing that by 5 gives the correct result of 80 as the average.

5. **D.** This problem needs to be completed in two steps. First, you need to determine what percent of chocolates have nuts, then you subtract that from 100% to determine what percent do not have nuts. So, dividing 9 by 45 results in the percent that have nuts, which is 20%. Subtracting that number from 100% gives the correct answer: 80% of the chocolates do not have nuts.

6. **D.** To find the ratio of one number to another, create a fraction to show the relationship. In this problem, there are 6 female club members out of a total of 48 members. So the fraction that shows the relationship is $\frac{6}{48}$. This fraction needs to be simplified to $\frac{1}{8}$, the correct answer. You might see a ratio written as 1:8 on the ASVAB test. $\frac{1}{8}$ and 1:8 mean the same thing.

7. **B.** If Vanessa has 192 pages of reading and reads 48 pages each day, on Monday she has read 48 pages, on Tuesday she has read 2(48) or 96 pages, on Wednesday she has ready 3(48) or 144 pages, and on Thursday she has read 4(48) or 192 pages. Thursday is the correct answer. Another way to do this is to divide 192 by 48 to get 4. If Monday is 1, Tuesday is 2, Wednesday is 3, and Thursday is 4. Again, Thursday is the correct answer.

8. **C.** Probability = number of favorable outcomes/ number of possible outcomes. In this problem, a favorable outcome would be selecting a dime. There are 112 dimes or favorable outcomes. The number of possible outcomes is the sum of all the coins, or $94 + 44 + 112 = 250$. So Probability = $\frac{112}{250}$. Simplified, this is $\frac{56}{125}$.

9. **D.** Simple interest problems use the formula $I = prt$, where I is the amount of interest, p is the principal or the amount saved or invested, r is the rate of interest, and t is the amount of time that the interest is accruing. In this problem, you are asked to find the interest, given that the principal is $4,000, the rate of interest is 4%, and

the amount of time is 3 years. Substituting this information into the formula, you get

$$I = 4,000(0.04)(3) = \$480 \text{ of interest}$$

10. **A.** Set this up as a proportion.

$$\frac{5,200 \text{ miles}}{11 \text{ hours}} = \frac{x \text{ miles}}{1 \text{ hour}}$$

Cross-multiply to get

$$11x = 5,200$$
$$x = 472.73 \text{ miles per hour}$$

11. **B.** The Booster's Club has 250 members and wants to reach 376 members in 90 days. Subtracting 250 from 376, the club needs to attract 126 new members. To do this in 90 days, the club must attract $126 \div 90 =$ an average of 1.4 members each day.

12. **B.** Here you need to calculate the number of square feet in the garden and then determine how many ounces of fertilizer are needed. The area of a rectangular garden is calculated by multiplying the length × the width. So in this problem the area is 21 ft². If you need 2 oz of fertilizer for every square foot, then you need to multiply 2 by the number of square feet.

$$21 \times 2 = 42 \text{ oz}$$

13. **D.** Calculate the cost of the two CDs:

$$\$16.99 \times 2 = \$33.98$$

Reduce that amount by 20% by multiplying the total cost by 0.20:

$$0.20 \times 33.98 = \$6.80$$

Subtract $6.80 from the original cost:

$$\$33.98 - \$6.80 = \$27.18$$

A faster way to do this (and speed is important on the ASVAB) is to multiply the original cost by 80% or 0.80 because that is the cost of the items after the discount.

$$0.80 \times \$33.98 = \$27.18$$

14. **D.** Use the following formula:

$$\text{Percent of change} = \frac{\text{amount of change}}{\text{starting point}}$$

In this problem, the starting point is $67.50. The amount of change is the difference between the starting price and the ending price of $87.75.

$$\$87.75 - \$67.50 = \$20.25$$

Substitute the information into the formula:

$$\text{Percent of change} = \frac{\$20.25}{\$67.50} = 0.3$$

Change that number to a percent by moving the decimal place two places to the right and adding the percent sign.

$$0.3 = 30\%$$

15. **D.** Set this up as an equation. A number plus 2 times that number is 300.

$$x + 2x = 300$$

Solve for x.

$$3x = 300$$
$$x = 100$$

So one number is 100 and the other is twice that, or 200.

16. **D.** To answer this question, you need to know the perimeter of the frame. For a rectangle, the perimeter is $2l + 2w$. If $w = 8$ and $l = 10$, then the perimeter = 2(8) + 2(10) = 36 inches. At $0.50 per inch, multiply 36 × $0.50 to get the price of the wood.

$$36 \times \$0.50 = \$18.00$$

17. **C.** To find the circumference of a circle, use the formula $C = 2\pi r$. In this problem, you are given the diameter. You need to use the radius, which is $\frac{1}{2}d$, or 37.5 yards. Substitute the information into the formula.

$$C = 2\pi(37.5)$$
$$C = 2(3.14)(37.5) = 235.5 \text{ yd}$$

Note that you can skip a step if you remember the formula $C = \pi d$. Substitute the information you have.

$$C = \pi(75) = 235.5 \text{ yd}$$

18. **C.** In this problem, you need to find 1/3 of 39. Dividing 39 by 3 gives you 13.

19. **A.** Create an equation to solve this problem.

$$\text{Dave} = \text{Brian} - 2.$$

You are told that Brian is 17. Substitute that information into the formula.

$$\text{Dave} = 17 - 2$$
$$\text{Dave} = 15$$

20. **D.** Create equations to solve this problem.

$$\text{Al} = 3(\text{Bill})$$
$$\text{Bill} = 2(\text{Charlie})$$
$$\text{Charlie} = \$5.89$$

Solve for Al. Substitute what you know into the formulas.

$$\text{Bill} = 2(\$5.89)$$
$$\text{Bill} = \$11.78$$

To find Al, substitute what you know about Bill.

$$\text{Al} = 3(\$11.78)$$
$$\text{Al} = \$35.34$$

21. **D.** In this problem, you need to calculate the number of 16-mpg units there are in 1,344. Do this by dividing 1,344 by 16.

$$1,344 \div 16 = 84 \text{ gallons}$$

22. **C.** To solve this problem, use the formula $V = lwh$. You have been given the dimensions of $l = 28$ ft, $w = 12$ ft, and $h = 6$ ft. Substitute that information into the formula.

$$V = (28)(12)(6)$$
$$V = 2016 \text{ ft}^3$$

23. **C.** You need to calculate the perimeter of the garden. The perimeter is the sum of all the sides,

or use the formula $P = 2l + 2w$. You are given the dimensions of 6 feet and 15 feet. Substitute that information into the formula.

$$P = 2(6) + 2(15)$$
$$P = 42 \text{ ft}$$

24. **D.** To calculate 14% of 5,000, multiply 5,000 by 0.14.

$$5,000(0.14) = 700 \text{ votes}$$

25. **C.** To calculate the volume of a cylinder, use the formula $V = \pi r^2 h$. In this problem, the radius is 9 m. The height is given as 3.5 m. Substitute that information into the formula.

$$V = (3.14)(9^2)(3.5)$$
$$V = (3.14)(81)(3.5)$$
$$V = 890.19 \text{ or } 890.2 \text{ m}^3$$

26. **C.** Use the formula $C = 2\pi r$ or $C = \pi d$. You are given a diameter of 8,000 miles. Substitute that into the formula.

$$C = \pi(8,000)$$
$$C = 3.14(8,000)$$
$$C = 25,120 \text{ mi}$$

27. **B.** To calculate the answer to this question, add up the amount of the checks and subtract that from the current amount in the checking account.

$$\$4,355.19 - (\$1,204.90 + \$890.99)$$
$$= \$2,259.30$$

28. **B.** Multiply $585.00 by 0.75 to get $438.75.

29. **D.** Calculate the total cost of the items and then multiply by 20% to determine how much Danny will save.

$$\$750 + \$398.75 + \$149.98 + \$24.99$$
$$= \$1,323.72$$
$$\$1,323.72 \times 0.20$$
$$= \$264.74 \text{ savings from the sale}$$

30. **A.** In this problem, you know two of the three angles, one measuring 55° and the other measuring 90°. Together those two angles measure 145°. Since a triangle has a total of 180°, the third angle must measure $180° - 145° = 35°$.

PART 3. WORD KNOWLEDGE

1. **C.** The word *exempt* means "to free someone from a rule or requirement." The words *empty*, *exit*, and *anoint* do not seem related to the definition. The only word that comes close to this is C, *excuse*.

2. **B.** To *recruit* means "to take on, sign up, or enlist members into an organization or club." The words *react*, *permit*, and *recur* do not relate to the definition. So B, *enlist*, is the correct answer.

3. **B.** *Unanimous* uses the prefix "uni-," or "one," as in *unity* or *unify*. The only word that relates to the concept of one or unity is *undisputed*, suggesting that everyone is in agreement. Choice B is the correct answer. The words *questioned*, *selective*, and *trivial* do not relate to the definition.

4. **C.** *Temperamental* most nearly means "volatile." Think of temperament or having a temper. Choice C is the correct answer.

5. **D.** *Economical* has to do with finances or the economy. The words *logical* and *comical* have no relation to finances, so they can be eliminated as possibilities. This leaves *costly* and *thrifty* as the two possible answers. Since being economical means to not waste money, time, or other resources, choice D, *thrifty*, is the correct answer.

6. **C.** The prefix *pro-* means "forward." *Motion* has to do with moving. Combining the two gives you "moving forward." The only word that relates to this is *elevation*, meaning "to move forward or higher up in the ranks." Choice C is the correct answer

7. **B.** The prefix *un-* means "not." So the word means "not predictable." If something cannot be predicted, it is not *consistent*, *dependable*, or *regular*, as these words are somewhat the opposite of the definition. So the correct answer has to be choice B, *random*.

8. **C.** To *deny* means "to refuse to accept as correct or to not grant or give something." *State*, *avoid*, and *open* do not relate to the definition. *Refuse*

is the closest word to that meaning, so choice C is the correct answer.

9. **D.** The prefix *ir-* means "not." *Irresponsible*, then, means "not responsible." *Hapless*, *giddy*, and *easy* do not relate to the definition. *Reckless* is the only word that reflects the correct meaning, so choice D is the correct answer.

10. **B.** *Persistent* means "refusing to give up." *Gentle*, *resigned*, and *manageable* do not relate to this idea. *Unrelenting*, choice B, is the correct answer.

11. **B.** *Dominant* means "being overpowering or prevailing" or "ruling by superior power." The words *joyous*, *understanding*, and *helpful* do not seem to match the definition. The word that most closely relates to the definition is *overriding*, so choice B is the correct answer.

12. **A.** *Conscientious* has to do with doing what is right and correct. By knowing that, you can eliminate the words *popular*, *friendly*, and *handsome*. The word *painstaking* is most closely related to the meaning of *conscientious*, so choice A is the correct answer.

13. **A.** A *diversion* is something that makes you turn aside or distracts your attention. The words *containment*, *pressure*, and *supply* do not match the definition. So, *distraction*, choice A, is the correct answer.

14. **A.** To *assume* means "to take for granted or to presume that something is true." So *assumption* has to do with taking something to be true or correct. The words *decision*, *rumor*, and *guess* do not match the definition. The word *belief* most closely relates to this idea. The correct answer is choice A.

15. **B.** To *profess* means "to proclaim, state, or declare." The words *work*, *disguise*, and *accuse* do not match the definition. The word that most nearly resembles this idea is *claim*, so choice B is the correct answer.

16. **B.** *Trivial* means "unimportant or insignificant." The words *sinister*, *sad*, and *demanding* do not match the definition. *Inconsequential*, choice B, is the correct answer.

17. **D.** *Optimistic* means "having a hopeful view of the world," so the words *grouchy*, *angry*, and *unusual* can be eliminated. *Positive*, choice D, is the correct answer.

18. **C.** To *vary* means "to change," so *variable* means *changeable*. Choice C is the correct answer.

19. **B.** A *clarification* is something that makes information clearer or more explicit, so the words *elimination* and *recognition* are clearly wrong. The word *expansion* could have to do with providing more information to clarify something, but *explanation*, choice B, is the best answer.

20. **D.** *Panoramic* means "providing a wide view." So *beautiful*, *unrealistic*, and *stylistic* are not related to the word. The best answer is choice D, *expansive*.

21. **C.** The prefix *com-* means "to bring together." *Passionate* has to do with strong, caring feelings. Combining those ideas suggests that *compassionate* has to do with bringing strong or deep feelings together. The words *unwieldy*, *modern*, and *restrictive* do not match the definition. The only word that deals with feelings is *concerned*. Choice C is the correct answer.

22. **B.** One event is *contingent* upon another if it will happen only if the second event occurs. The best synonym is choice B, *dependent*.

23. **C.** *Velocity* has to do with quickness or speediness. The words *variety*, *veracity*, and *overflow* do not match the definition. So *swiftness*, choice C, is the correct answer.

24. **B.** *Immaculate* means "without flaws or errors." The words *large* and *fancy* do not match the definition. A house that has been *cleaned* may be immaculate, but *spotless* is the closest word to "without flaws or errors." Choice B is the best answer.

25. **A.** *Visible* relates to "being able to see something" or "vision," so *visibility* must have to do with being able to see. *Test* and *dichotomy* do not match the definition. A view may be an *observation*, but that is not the best answer. *Clarity* is the only word that relates to the definition of "being able to see." Choice A is the best answer.

26. **A.** *Capsized* means "turned over." The words *accelerated*, *tilted*, and *docked* do not match the definition. Choice A, *overturned*, is the correct answer.

27. **D.** *Abdicated* means "gave up or surrendered." *Welcomed*, *cheered*, and *transitioned* are unrelated to this concept. *Abandoned* is most closely related to the word *abdicated*. Choice D is the correct answer.

28. **A.** *Eligible* means "fit to be chosen." The words *eager*, *adequate*, and *thankful* are unrelated to this concept. Choice A, *qualified*, fits most closely and is the best answer.

29. **A.** To be *buoyant* means "to be able to float." The words *happy*, *significant*, and *acrobatic* do not match the definition. Choice A, *floating*, is the correct answer. You can remember this by thinking of a buoy, which floats in the water.

30. **C.** *Teeming* means "swarming, abounding, or being full." *Empty* is the opposite of this concept. *Opaque* means "dense or thick," and *vigorous* means "energetic, strong, or active." These words don't relate to being full or swarming, but *crowded* does. Choice C is the correct answer.

31. **C.** *Bestow* means "to give," as in giving a gift or an award. The words *remove*, *have*, and *question* do not match the definition. *Give*, choice C, is the correct answer.

32. **A.** A river that *meanders* is one that winds and turns as it flows. The best synonym is choice A, *twist*.

33. **D.** *Infiltrate* means "to pass into" or "to seize control from within." The words *interfere* and *seek* are not related to the definition. *Enter* is similar in meaning, but the word *penetrate* is the closest to the stated meaning. Choice D is the correct answer

34. **B.** *Plummeted* means "fell." *Soared* has somewhat the opposite meaning. The words *increased* and *failed* are not related. Choice B, *plunged*, is the correct answer.

35. **B.** *Defiled* means "contaminated or dishonored." *Honored* is the opposite of this idea. The words *cleaned* and *respected* are not related. *Desecrated*, choice B, is the correct answer.

PART 4. PARAGRAPH COMPREHENSION

1. **A.** There is nothing in the passage indicating that people need to be convinced to exercise (choice B), so that is not a correct option. The same can be said for strenuous versus moderate exercise (choice D), as no such comparisons are made in the passage. It is true that exercise is good for preventing heart disease and for preventing stroke, but the passage does not indicate that exercise cures anything (choice C). The main thrust of the passage is that moderate exercise has many positive benefits. Choice A is the correct answer.

2. **B.** The passage does not indicate that people who exercise don't have weight problems, so choice D is clearly wrong. The passage also does not address the amount of exercise, so choice A cannot be correct. There is no mention of exercise eliminating any health problems, so choice C cannot be correct. That leaves choice B, which is implied fairly directly in the passage. Choice B is the correct answer.

3. **C.** The passage does not mention anything about fatty acids. Choice C is the correct answer.

4. **A.** In the third paragraph, the passage clearly states that 25 percent of adults do not exercise in their leisure time. Choice A is the correct answer.

5. **D.** The passage states that more than 50 percent of American adults do not get enough physical activity to provide health benefits. Choice D is the correct answer.

6. **B.** You need to read the passage carefully because it is somewhat complex. The passage indicates that the thought or perception or understanding at the time was that the West was geographically somewhat simple, that it was empty, and that it had only a single mountain range (choices A and C), but those ideas were proven incorrect. There is no information on discovering rivers (choice D). The passage states that what Lewis and Clark discovered was a far more complicated geographic landscape than they had originally thought. Choice B is the correct answer.

7. **A.** A labyrinth is a structure with winding passages; it is a maze. The only word that conveys that message is *jumble*.

8. **B.** The passage indicates that Major Stephen H. Long's Scientific Expedition (1819–1820) was the first military expedition to take along scientists and artists. The passage indicates that this set the pattern for increasingly scientific exploration of the West. Choice B is the correct answer.

9. **C.** There is no indication that Lewis and Clark's actions did anything to help the fur traders (choice A) or that the fur traders boosted the economy of the United States (choice B). The passage also does not give credit to the mapmakers for scouting out the route for the railroad. The only option that is true is choice C, that Lewis and Clark used information provided by native people.

10. **A.** The passage clearly indicates that the military had much to do with the scientific exploration of what is now the western part of the United States.

11. **C.** The word *dubious* means "skeptical or questionable." Choice C, *doubtful*, is the correct answer.

12. **A.** The passage explains that the Greeks admired Odysseus because of his quick thinking. Choice A is the correct answer.

13. **B.** Herakles may have been kind (choice A) and resourceful (choice C), but the passage does not

indicate that. It also does not indicate that he was a failure (choice D). The passage does indicate that Herakles was known for his strength and courage. So choice B, bravery, is the correct answer.

14. **C.** The passage indicates that it is not true that all Greek heroes were admired for the same reasons, so choice D cannot be correct. Although Odysseus was indeed a murderer (choice A) and a thief (choice B), the best answer is choice C, that the Greeks judged their heroes by their results.

15. **D.** The passage says that the Cyclops were shepherds. Choice D is the correct answer.

PART 5. MATHEMATICS KNOWLEDGE

1. **B.** Isolate the unknown on one side. Subtract 9 from each side

$$x = 13 - 9$$
$$x = 4$$

2. **A.** Perform operations in parentheses first, then exponents, and then the remaining operations.

$$9 + 4(3) =$$
$$9 + 12 = 21$$

3. **D.** Change the mixed numbers to improper fractions. Carry out the operation by multiplying the two numerators and the two denominators.

$$\frac{5}{4} \times \frac{5}{2} = \frac{1}{8}$$
$$\frac{25}{8} = 3\frac{1}{8}$$

4. **B.** $-8 \times -8 = 64$

5. **C.** Substitute 2 for x and 4 for y into the expression. Multiply out the exponents.

$$2(2)^3 (4)^2 = 2(8)(16)$$
$$16 \times 16 = 256$$

6. **D.** When adding such expressions, place all similar terms under each other. Then perform the necessary operations. For this particular problem, place all the x^2 under each other and add the numbers, giving $-2x^2$. Then go to the next terms (xy) and add those. Adding these terms gives you $5xy$. Next, add the y terms. Adding these terms results in $1y$ or y. Next, add the y^2 terms. Notice that adding these terms leaves you with zero y^2, so this term drops out of the final answer. The answer is $-2x^2 + 5xy + y$. In this instance, you could have worked from right to left to notice that the y^2 term drops out of the result and that D is the only answer with that term missing. Doing this would have saved you a little time, but not all problems like this have that type of clue.

7. **B.** Note the minus sign in the middle term and the plus sign in the third term. This should tell you that the factors will contain a minus sign in each term. In this problem, the fact that the two terms will have a minus sign should lead you to the correct answer, as only one answer has a minus sign in each term. However, not all questions of this type will have that kind of clue. Note that the first term in each factor will be y. Now you need to find two numbers that multiply to 48 and add to 16. Those numbers are 4 and 12. This gives the factors $(y - 4)(y - 12)$.

8. **A.** To solve such problems, move all the terms with an unknown to one side of the equal sign and the numbers to the other. In this problem, subtract 6 from both sides to move the numbers to the right side, giving you $12x = 8x + 10 - 6$. Next, work on the $8x$ term by subtracting $8x$ from both sides, giving $12x - 8x = 10 - 6$. Combine the terms, resulting in $4x = 4$. Solve for x: $x = 1$.

9. **C.** Set each equation equal to zero. Next, arrange one of the equations so that when it is subtracted from or added to the other equation, one of the terms becomes zero and drops out of the equation. Next, solve for the remaining unknown.

In this problem:

$$3y + 3x = 24$$
$$6y + 3x = 39$$

Set each equation to zero:

$$3y + 3x - 24 = 0$$
$$6y + 3x - 39 = 0$$

Note that each equation contains the term $3x$. If you subtract the second equation from the first, the x term will drop out, leaving

$$3y + 3x - 24 = 0$$
$$-6y - 3x + 39 = 0$$

Subtracting the terms results in $-3y + 15 = 0$. Solve for y:

$$-3y = -15; \; y = 5.$$

To solve for x, take that result and substitute it into one of the original equations.

$$3(5) + 3x - 24 = 0$$
$$15 + 3x - 24 = 0$$
$$3x = 24 - 15$$
$$3x = 9$$
$$x = 3$$

The answer to the problem is $x = 3$; $y = 5$

10. **B.** To divide numbers with exponents, subtract the exponents. In this problem, subtract the 4 from the 12, leaving x^8 as the correct answer.

11. **A.** Set the equation to equal zero:

$$y^2 + 7y + 10 = 0$$

Factor the equation.

$$(y + 5)(y + 2) = 0$$

Solve for y by setting each factor equal to 0:

$$y + 5 = 0; \; y = -5$$
$$y + 2 = 0; \; y = -2$$

The correct answer is $y = -5$, $y = -2$.

12. **C.** To multiply fractions, multiply the numerators and denominators. Simplify where possible.

$$\frac{6y}{11} \times \frac{2}{5x} = \frac{12y}{55x}$$

This cannot be simplified any further, so it is the final answer.

13. **B.** To divide fractions, invert the second term and multiply. Simplify where possible.

$$\frac{6x}{11} \div \frac{2}{5y} \quad \text{Invert and multiply.}$$
$$\frac{6x}{11} \times \frac{5y}{2}$$
$$\frac{3x}{11} \times \frac{5y}{1} \quad \text{Simplify.}$$
$$\frac{15xy}{11}$$

14. **A.** The cube root is the number that, when multiplied by itself three times, results in the answer. In this instance, $3 \times 3 \times 3 = 27$, so the cube root of $27 = 3$.

> To answer most questions of this type on the ASVAB, you just need to memorize some basic cubes. It would be wise to memorize all the cubes from 2 to 10, just to prepare for ASVAB test item possibilities.

15. **C.** Isolate the variable of interest on one side of the equation. In this problem, you must multiply each side by h, leaving g on the left side of the equation and h on the right side. Therefore, the answer is $g = ah$.

16. **D.** An equilateral triangle has three equal sides and angles, so D is the correct answer.

17. **C.** To find the perimeter of a quadrilateral, add the lengths of the four sides. In this instance, 9 meters + 9 meters + 3 meters + 3 meters = 24 meters, the correct answer.

18. **C.** The formula for the circumference of a circle is πd. The figure gives the radius, which is one-half the length of the diameter. To find the diameter, multiply the radius by 2. In this problem, the diameter is 8 meters. Multiplying 8 by π gives the correct answer of 25.12 meters.

19. **C.** An equilateral triangle has three equal angles. A triangle has a total of 180°, so each angle must be 60°.

20. **C.** A straight line or straight angle is 180°. So if $\angle 1$ is 34°, $\angle 2$ is the difference between 180° and 34°, or 146°.

21. **B.** $\angle C$ is a right angle, so you can employ the Pythagorean Theorem, $a^2 + b^2 = c^2$, to get your answer. $3^2 + 4^2 = c^2$. So $9 + 16 = 25$. $c^2 = 25$ and $c = 5$.

22. **D.** This is a right triangle, so 4 ft is the height of the triangle and 8 ft is the base. The formula for the area of a triangle is $\frac{1}{2}bh$. Substituting the information into the formula gives $\frac{1}{2}(8)(4)$, making the correct answer 16 ft².

23. **C.** The diameter is $2r$. $r = 80$ cm, so the diameter is 160 cm.

24. **A.** $\angle 2$ and $\angle 7$ are alternate exterior angles and therefore are equal in measure. So both $\angle 2$ and $\angle 7$ are 30°.

25. **B.** The formula for finding the volume of a cylinder is $V = \pi r^2 h$. In this problem, the cylinder has a height of 15 meters and a radius of 5 meters. Substituting that information into the formula gives $\pi(5)^2(15)$, making the correct answer 1,177.50 m².

PART 6. ELECTRONICS INFORMATION

1. **B.** 1 hertz is defined as 1 cycle per second. A 60-hertz electric current oscillates at 60 cycles per second.

2. **C.** Alternating current travels much further through wire than direct current.

3. **B.** Without a circuit, electrons cannot travel, so there is no electric current.

4. **D.** Copper is a good conductor and inexpensive. Choice B, while true, is not the whole answer, as it also applies, for example, to gold.

5. **A.** Amperes measure the number of electrons moving through a conductor.

6. **B.** Ohms are a measure of resistance.

7. **D.** Using algebra, multiply both sides by ohms. You should get volts = amperes × ohms.

8. **C.** Volts = amperes × ohms = 20 × 12 = 240.

9. **B.** This circuit will have a dangerously high current and may burn up or cause a fire. It should trip a circuit breaker or blow a fuse before too much damage occurs.

10. **D.** The overall amount of power does not change. Power = amperes × volts. So if voltage rises, amperage must fall.

11. **D.** In a transformer, electricity is converted into magnetism and back into electricity. In an electromagnet, electricity is converted into magnetism. In an electric motor, electromagnets create a repulsive force that causes the rotor to spin.

12. **A.** Heat alone will not do the job, because the wires will start to corrode when you heat them. Solder does not adhere to corrosion.

13. **D.** Conduit (either flexible or rigid) provides a safe return path for electricity in many wiring systems.

14. **C.** Heaters use high current, which demands heavy wires.

15. **A.** Black is the most common color for hot wires, although red and blue are sometimes used.

16. **D.** Three-way switches are used in pairs to control one light from two locations.

17. **B.** Amperes × volts = power. Voltage does not change, so fewer amperes will carry less power.

18. **C.** Both the polarity and the voltage must be correct for a battery to work right.

19. **D.** Loose electrical connections can cause fire or equipment damage. Choice C, salt water, is wrong because it will cause corrosion, reducing conductivity across the connection.

20. **C.** A resistor reduces voltage.

PART 7. AUTO AND SHOP INFORMATION

1. **A.** The differential and driveshaft are the big moving parts at the rear of a rear-wheel-drive car that has the engine in front.

2. **C.** Either the spark plug is not working right or there is a problem with the incoming fuel-air mix.

3. **A.** Air pressure inside the tire pushes evenly against the entire inside of the tire, allowing it to hold its shape and to respond to unevenness in the road. Low tire pressure reduces efficiency, and engine power is converted into heat, which warms the tire.

4. **A.** Breaker points send quick jolts of electricity to the coil, which acts as a transformer to raise the voltage enough to spark a spark plug. The gap must be adjusted during a tune-up, and should be inspected whenever the engine runs rough.

5. **C.** Front-wheel-drive mechanisms are complicated because they both drive and steer.

6. **C.** Intake: The piston moves down, creating a partial vacuum that draws air (and sometimes fuel) into the cylinder. Compression: The piston moves up with both valves closed, compressing the air-fuel mixture. Power: The fuel explodes, creating heat and kinetic energy, pushing the piston down. Exhaust: The piston moves up, pushing burned gases from the cylinder through the exhaust valve. Choice A is tempting, but there is no "rest" cycle in a four-cycle engine. The cylinder is always working.

7. **A.** The fuel system must deliver enough fuel for combustion inside the engine. Choice D, the engine control module, is the second-best answer. Although it could cause the problem, the fuel system is the first thing to check.

8. **B.** Manual transmissions usually have one "direct-drive" gear, where the input speed is the same as the output speed. The drive shaft rotates along with the transmission's output shaft. Choice D is incorrect because the clutch moves at the same speed as the engine.

9. **C.** Because the pistons in the wheel cylinders are the only movable objects in the system, when you move the master cylinder, hydraulic fluid forces the pistons in the wheel cylinders to move.

10. **B.** The starter relay is a big switch located between the battery and the starter motor. Starter motors demand a huge current, which would require an expensive and clumsy cable from the battery to the ignition switch and the starter motor. Instead, the ignition switch activates the starter relay, which temporarily connects the battery to the starter motor.

11. **D.** After the power stroke, there is nothing left to burn inside the cylinder. The exhaust stroke clears the cylinder out through the exhaust valve, making room for a fresh fuel-air mixture. The engine will not run at all unless the exhaust valve opens.

12. **D.** The differential has reduction gears so that the engine can turn fast enough to make power. A 3-to-1 ratio means that 3 turns of the driveshaft produce 1 turn of the wheels. Why are the other answers incorrect? Choice A: The engine would run too slowly to make power. Choice B: Cars do not have a jack shaft. Choice C: The ring gear in a differential cannot be disengaged.

13. **B.** A blade that is as wide as the screw head will put maximum turning power on the screw.

14. **B.** Arc-joint pliers, commonly called Channel Locks, can adjust to grip a wide variety of objects.

15. **D.** Plywood splinters easily, and each small tooth takes a smaller "bite," reducing splintering. Why are the other answers incorrect? Choice A: Big teeth cause more splintering. Choice B: A plywood blade is fine for particle board. Choice C is dead wrong. In saw blades, sharper is better!

16. **C.** Choice D is tempting, but a claw hammer can drive some wood chisels without damage.

17. **A.** Bar clamps are also handy for holding parts for sawing or drilling, but not for the other three purposes listed.

18. **B.** Impact equals mass times velocity, so for any given hammer speed, a more massive hammer makes more impact. Why are the other answers incorrect? Choice A: Mass, not weight, determines the intensity of impact. Choice C: Size alone does not make the hammer more effective. Choice D: A slower-moving hammer will be less effective at driving the chisel.

19. **D.** Plywood is stronger than regular wood because the grain is crisscrossed, preventing splitting and reducing weakness at knots. Why are the other answers incorrect? Choice A: Plywood may be weatherproof, but subfloors don't face the weather. Choices B and C: Plywood may be lighter and thinner, but that's not as important as strength in a subfloor.

20. **D.** An oxyacetylene cutting torch is made for cutting metal. Why are the other answers incorrect? All the saws mentioned are designed to cut wood.

21. **A.** Tin snips act like big scissors to shear sheet metal.

22. **C.** A pipe wrench fits loosely on the pipe; turning activates the grabbing action. The other tools all must be tightened before use.

23. **A.** A sharp drill bit cuts faster, cooler, and with less pressure on the drill, but it makes the same amount of chips.

24. **D.** Cold water will cause the nut to contract and grab tighter on the bolt. A frozen (rusted) nut can be loosened with heat, which causes it to expand, by pounding, which creates vibration, or by penetrating oil, which softens rust.

25. **C.** A plumb line is vertical and a level line is horizontal, so the angle between them is square, or 90°.

PART 8. MECHANICAL COMPREHENSION

1. **D.** In this gear system, gear B is turning clockwise. That means that gears A and C are turning counterclockwise. Since gear C is turning counterclockwise, gears D and E are turning clockwise, the same direction as gear B.

2. **C.** For a class 1 lever, mechanical advantage is calculated as follows: MA = effort distance/load distance. In this case, MA = 18/6 = 3.

3. **C.** If the bolt has 20 threads per inch, each time the wrench makes one complete turn, the bolt will move 1/20 inch. So if the wrench makes 15 complete turns, the bolt will move $1/20 \times 15 = 15/20 = $ ¾ inch.

4. **A.** The gear is rotating at a speed of 150 rpm. At a ratio of 5:1, the pinion makes 5 revolutions for each revolution of the gear. So the speed of the pinion is $150 \times 5 = 750$ rpm.

5. **D.** Total flow through the pipe must be the same everywhere, so water must flow faster in the 1-inch section. When a fluid moves faster, its pressure drops. Therefore, pressure is lower in the 1-inch pipe and rises as the water enters the 3-inch pipe.

6. **B.** To balance the lever, sum the moments of force around the fulcrum:

$$(5 \times 10 \text{ kg}) + (3 \times 20 \text{ kg}) = 5F$$
$$50 + 60 = 5F$$
$$110 = 5F$$
$$F = 22$$

7. **C.** Gear A, with 48 teeth, meshes with gear B, with 12 teeth. So for every complete rotation of gear A, gear B makes $48/12 = 4$ complete rotations.

8. **D.** Of the choices, the only one that will make the job easier is to put the block on a wheelbarrow. The wheels will reduce friction and make it easier to move the block. Choice A, raising the angle of the plane, will decrease, not increase, the mechanical advantage. Choices B and C will have no effect.

9. **A.** Choice A is correct because the hydraulic system transfers movement between the cylinders. The cylinders are directly linked and contain an incompressible fluid.

10. **B.** The tank has an area of 18 square feet. Pressure = force/area. If the total weight of the water = 3,600 lb, weight per square foot = $3600/18 = 200$ lb/ft^2.

11. **A.** Of the choices, only the teacup cannot bend without breaking. The spoon, nail, and automobile tire are all made of materials that can bend without breaking.

12. **C.** A knife blade is an example of a wedge.

13. **B.** The ratio of diameters determines the ratio of sheave speed. $6/2 = 3/1$, so the driven sheave will rotate three times as fast as the drive sheave. $3 \times 80 = 240$.

14. **D.** The pulley with the greatest diameter is pulley D. Therefore, it is the one that is rotating the slowest.

15. **B.** The car jack is a lever. Of the choices, the only one that will make the job easier is choice B, getting a longer jack handle. This will increase the effort distance in the lever and thereby increase the mechanical advantage.

16. **C.** The floor of a fireplace must be made of a material that will not ignite or melt with the heat of the fire. Of the choices, the one that is best is stone.

17. **B.** Because the pulley has two supporting strands, it has a mechanical advantage of 2. Therefore, each pound of pull will produce 2 pounds of lift.

18. **A.** Air pressure is what makes a siphon function. The weight of the air on the surface of the water in the tank forces water through the hose and into the bucket.

19. **C.** To make two gears turn in the same direction, an idler gear is required between them. The idler gear turns in the opposite direction from the two gears on either side of it. If idler gear B is rotating clockwise, gears A and C are both rotating counterclockwise.

20. **D.** A wrench uses a wheel-and-axle effect to move a bolt or nut.

21. **B.** The post nearer to the load bears the greater part of the weight. In the diagram, post B is the one nearer to the weight of the box of books.

22. **C.** Water is flowing into the tank at the rate of 240 gallons per hour, or $240/60 = 4$ gallons per minute. Water is flowing out at the rate of 1 gallon per minute, so the net gain per minute is 3 gallons. In 6 minutes, the tank will gain $6 \times 3 = 18$ gallons of water.

23. **B.** A point on the circumference must travel a longer distance than a point closer to the center.

24. **A.** Of the choices, the only one that will form the complete, totally enclosed box shown is pattern 1.

25. **A.** Ignore the full turns, because after any number of full turns, the shaft will return to the starting position. After a half turn, the shaft will be 180° degrees from the position shown, but the piston will be where it is shown.

PART 9. ASSEMBLING OBJECTS

1. **C.** The original figure has three objects. Choice A has four, so eliminate it. The most distinctive object is the one that looks like a rectangle with a tail, so look for it first. Choice D does not have that shape, and choice B has a rectangle without the tail part. Choice C is the correct answer.

2. **B.** The original figure has three objects, while choice D has four. None of the objects are very distinctive, so just choose one—perhaps the square. Choice C has a rectangle rather than a square. Now look for the two identical domes. Choice A shows semicircles rather than the domelike shapes in the original. Choice B is the correct answer.

3. **D.** The original figure has six objects, while choice B has five and choice C has four. Look for the object at the bottom right. It is not present in choice A. Choice D is the correct answer.

4. **B.** The original figure has three objects, while choice D has four. Look for the object at the bottom that is NOT a circle. Choice A does not have it. Look for the tiny circle. Choice C does not have it. Choice B is the correct answer.

5. **A.** The original figure has four objects. Look for the wavy figure. The wavy figure in choice D does not have flat ends as it does in the original. Look for the triangle. It is not present in choice B. Look for the oval. It is not present in choice C. Choice A is the correct answer.

6. **D.** The original figure has four objects, while choice B has five. None of the objects are distinctive, so just choose one to look for. Look for the two triangles. Choice A has only one triangle. Look for the two quadrilaterals. Choice C has a square instead of an irregular quadrilateral. Choice D is the correct answer.

7. **A.** There are four objects in the original and choice C has three, so you can eliminate C. Since all of the objects are rectangles, look for the largest one first. Choices B and D do not have it. Choice A is the correct answer.

8. **D.** The original figure has three objects. Choice C has two, so eliminate it. The most distinctive object is the one that looks like a flag. Choice B does not have it. Look for the triangle. Choice A has a right triangle instead of an isosceles triangle. Choice D is the correct answer.

9. **C.** The original figure has four objects, while choice A has five. Look for one object at a time, perhaps beginning with the rhombus. Only choice C appears to have the same rhombus. Choice C is the correct answer.

10. **B.** The original figure has three objects, while choice C has four and choice D has only two. Look for the L-shaped object at the left. Choice A does not have it. Choice B is the correct answer.

11. **A.** All the options have three objects, so look for a distinctive object such as the chord of a circle. Choice D does not have this object and choice B has two of them. Look for the two identical triangles. Choice C has only one. Choice A is the correct answer.

12. **D.** There are four objects in the original and choice B has five objects, so eliminate B. Look for the only triangle. Choices A and C each have two triangles. Choice D is the correct answer.

13. **C.** There are five objects in the original and six in choice D, so eliminate D. The hexagon is a distinctive object, so look for that. Choice B does not have it. Look for the rectangle. The rectangle in choice A is too short. Choice C is the correct answer.

14. **B.** There are four objects in the original and only three in choice A. Look for the long parallelogram. The long object in choice C is not a parallelogram. Look for the triangle. The triangle in choice D is too small. Choice B is the correct answer.

15. **A.** There are five objects in the original and only four in choice B. Eliminate B. Choice C has six objects, so eliminate it as well. Look for the large three-sided object at the upper right. Choice D does not have it. Choice A is the correct answer.

16. **C.** There are three objects in the original. Choice A has four and choice D has two, so eliminate both A and D. Look for the triangle. Choice B does not have it. Choice C is the correct answer.

17. **A.** There are four objects in the original and only three in choice D. Look for the object at the left of the box that looks like a long triangle but with a curved end. Choices B and C do not have this same shape. Choice A is the correct answer.

18. **C.** There are four objects in the original and three in choice A and five in choice B, so eliminate A and B. There is one small rectangle, so look for that in the remaining choices. Choice D does not have it. Choice C is the correct answer.

19. **D.** Point A is marked at the center of the flat side of the first object. Choices B and C do not have the first object joined at the center of the flat side. Point B is at the tip of the longest side of the second object. Choice A does not join the second object at that point. Choice D is the correct answer.

20. **B.** If you picture the slanted object standing on its flat base, then point A is marked at the shorter (right) top corner. Choice D has the point joined at the longer (left) corner. In choice C, the object is not the right shape at all. If you picture the semicircle lying on its flat side, point B is marked at the left corner. Choice A has the point at the right corner. Choice B is the correct answer.

21. **C.** Choice A has a rectangle instead of a wedge. If you picture the semicircle lying on its flat side, point A is marked at the right corner. Choice D has the point in the middle. The thin wedge has point B marked at the pointed tip. Choice B has the point marked at a rounded edge. Choice C is the correct answer.

22. **A.** If you picture the rounded object with the cutout at the bottom, point A is on the right corner of the cutout. Choice B has the point on the left side of the cutout. The triangle has point B in the center of the base. Choice C has the point on a corner of the triangle. Choice D has the point on the apex of the triangle. Choice A is the correct answer.

23. **D.** Point A is at the center of a ¾ circle. Choice B has point A at the edge of the ¾ circle. Choice C shows an entire circle. Point B is at the center of the second object. Choice A connects at the wrong point on the second object. Choice D is the correct answer.

24. **B.** Point A lies at the center of the rounded end of the curvy object. Choice A has this point in the wrong spot. If you picture the other object lying on the wider base, then Point B is at the lower right corner. Choice C has the point in the middle of the narrower base, and choice D has it at the lower left corner. Choice B is the correct answer.

25. **D.** Point A is in the indentation of the left figure. Only choice D connects at that point. Choice D is the correct answer.

Part 3

REVIEW OF ALL ASVAB TEST TOPICS

Chapter 7

General Science

YOUR GOALS FOR THIS CHAPTER:

- Find out what science topics you need to know for the ASVAB.

- Review the basics of general science.

- Study and memorize important science terms and definitions.

INTRODUCTION: ASVAB GENERAL SCIENCE QUESTIONS

The ASVAB General Science test measures your knowledge of the life sciences (biology, human physiology, ecology), the Earth and space sciences (geology, meteorology, oceanography, astronomy), and the physical sciences (physics and chemistry). You will not need to be a scientist to answer these questions. You will just need to know some very basic information in the major science areas. This section will help to refresh your memory about the science information you will need to know to do well on the General Science test.

ASVAB General Science Test
Number of questions:
• Paper-and-pencil ASVAB: 25
• CAT-ASVAB: 16
Time limit:
• Paper-and-pencil ASVAB: 11 minutes
• CAT-ASVAB: 8 minutes

The following pages offer a concise, systematic review of the general science topics you need to know in order to score well on the ASVAB. Make sure that you carefully review every topic covered in this section. Pay particular attention to scientific terms and their definitions. Also, look carefully at the diagrams and other illustrations. In many cases, they contain important information that you should know.

GENERAL SCIENCE REVIEW

Topics
Biology
Cells
Viruses
Classification of living things
Plants
Animals
Ecology, habitats, and biodiversity
Human Physiology
Cells, tissues, organs, and organ systems
Muscular system
Skeletal system
Integumentary system
Respiratory system
Digestive system
Circulatory system
Lymphatic system
Immune system
Excretory system
Nervous system
Endocrine system
Reproductive system
The senses
Genetics
Nutrition
Chemistry
Elements
Compounds
Mixtures
Physical Sciences
The laws of motion
Work, energy, and power

Waves
Heat
Magnetism

Geology
Earth's history
Earth's structure
Categories of rocks
Weathering and erosion
Plate tectonics and continental drift

The Atmosphere
Composition and structure
Winds and storms
Climate

Oceanography and Water
Tides
The hydrologic cycle

Astronomy
The solar system
Motion of the earth
Sun and stars

BIOLOGY

Cells

The *cell* is the basic unit of life. The average human body contains over 75 trillion cells, but many life forms exist as single cells that perform all the functions necessary for independent existence. There are two types of cells, one that has no membrane-bound structures inside the cell (*prokaryotic*), and one that does have a membrane-bound structure inside the cell (*eukaryotic*). The following table illustrates the difference.

	Prokaryotic	Eukaryotic
Cell structure	No internal membrane to contain structures	Internal membrane contains internal structures
Examples	Bacteria	Protists, fungi, plants, and animals

Cells are the basic building blocks of all organisms. Plants and animals are made up of one or more cells. Some organisms, such as *bacteria*, are made up of a single cell. Other organisms are far more complex, such as your pet dog or even you.

Cells are so small that you need magnification to see them. Microscopes are generally used to observe and study cells. Using a powerful microscope, you would be able to see that cells are made up of parts that have special functions.

Cells are made up of several different parts, including an *outer membrane* (sometimes called the *plasma membrane* or *cell membrane*), *organelles*, and a large amount of mass called *cytoplasm*. The *cell membrane* is the dictator of the cell. It determines what goes into or out of the cell. Cytoplasm is a gelatin-like material that fills the cell. Cell functions are accomplished by structures called *organelles*. Organelles are specialized parts that move around the cell and perform functions that are necessary for life. Examples of organelles are the cell *nucleus*, *vacuoles*, and *mitochondria*.

The *nucleus* is a membrane that contains the cell's hereditary information and controls the cell's growth and reproduction. It is generally the most prominent organelle in the cell. The nucleus contains *chromosomes* that are made up of *DNA*. DNA determines the characteristics and traits of the organism, such as the color of your hair, the shape of a leaf, and so on.

Vacuoles are the storage containers of the cell. They may store waste until it is eliminated or food until it is needed. In plant cells, there are large vacuoles that hold water.

Energy for the cell is produced by *mitochondria* through a process called *respiration*. Respiration is a series of chemical reactions that combine food and oxygen to create energy and a waste by-product, carbon dioxide.

Plant cells have some additional components. They have a *cell wall* that gives the cell a firmer shape and support. The cell wall is made up of cellulose, which is not digestible by humans, but provides fiber for our good health. Plant cells also have organelles called *chloroplasts*; these contain *chlorophyll*, which uses the process of *photosynthesis* to make food for the plant cells. The chloroplasts are green; they are what give plants their green color. During photosynthesis, chloroplasts interact with light energy, combining carbon dioxide from the air with water to make food. With light, the green parts of plants produce a sugar called glucose ($C_6H_{12}O_6$) and oxygen (O_2) from carbon dioxide (CO_2) and water (H_2O).

Light
Carbon dioxide + water → glucose + oxygen
Chlorophyll

The basic difference between plant and animal cells is that plant cells have cell walls and chloroplasts, and animal cells do not.

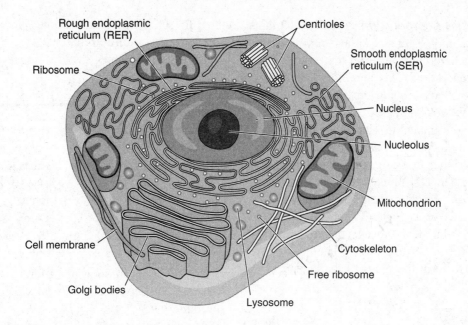

Rough endoplasmic reticulum (RER)

Ribosome

Centrioles

Smooth endoplasmic reticulum (SER)

Nucleus

Nucleolus

Mitochondrion

Cytoskeleton

Free ribosome

Cell membrane

Golgi bodies

Lysosome

Animal Cell

Lysosome

Central vacuole

Chloroplast

Free ribosome

Cell wall of adjacent cell

Smooth endoplasmic reticulum (SER)

Nucleus

Nucleolus

Ribosome

Rough endoplasmic reticulum (RER)

Golgi bodies

Mitochondrion

Cell wall

Cell membrane

Plant Cell

Cell and Species Reproduction Species of plants and animals cannot continue without reproduction. All cells have hereditary material that is passed on to the next generation. This hereditary material is called *DNA*, or deoxyribonucleic acid. DNA determines how one looks and how one functions. DNA is the instruction manual or blueprint for life.

The DNA molecule consists of two long strands that form a double helix. It spirals around like a twisted ladder. The DNA molecule has a sugar component, a phosphate component, and four different *bases—adenine* (A), *thymine* (T), *cytosine* (C), and *guanine* (G). Adenine is always paired with thymine, and cytosine with guanine. These pairs are held together to form the rungs of the ladder.

Adenine
Thymine
Cytosine
Guanine

Phosphate

Deoxyribose sugar

If a cell has a nucleus, the DNA is found in *chromosomes*. Chromosomes are duplicated before cell division takes place. The DNA unzips and separates. New bases are formed, and they link up in the proper order to form two new DNA helixes that are exactly alike. The instructions for the appearance and function of the new organism are contained in units called *genes*, which are parts of the DNA.

There are two reasons for cell division. One is to replace old or worn-out cells, and the other is for sexual reproduction. The process of *mitosis* takes place when cells are replacing themselves because they are old or worn out. The process called *meiosis* takes place with sex cell formation. In sex cell formation, cells with only 23 chromosomes are formed so that when an egg and a sperm join up, they have the full set of 46 chromosomes and possess the genetic makeup of both parents.

The chart indicates the difference between the processes.

Mitosis	Meiosis
For cell division	For sex cell formation
Nucleus divides once	Nucleus divides twice
Number of cells formed = 2	Number of cells formed = 4
Chromosomes in each new cell = 46	Chromosomes in each new cell = 23

Organisms reproduce in different ways: *sexual reproduction* between a sperm and an egg or *asexual reproduction*.

Some plants and animals reproduce asexually. Some examples are bacteria, the hydra, and the eye of a potato, which can grow new potatoes.

Some plants reproduce sexually. Examples are flowers, which have male and female parts. When the sperm and egg join, they produce seeds, which, when planted, reproduce the species.

Viruses

Viruses are not alive in the strict sense of the word, but they reproduce and have a close relationship with all living organisms. Viruses are not plants, animals, or bacteria, although they may seem to be. A virus is basically a piece of hereditary material surrounded by a protein coating. Viruses do not have a nucleus or other organelles.

Viruses need a host cell in order to reproduce and function. They cannot generate or store energy, but take their energy from the host cell. They also take basic building materials from the host. All viruses contain nucleic acid, either DNA or RNA (but not both), and a protein coat, which encases the nucleic acid. Since viruses cannot penetrate plant cell walls, nearly all plant viruses are transmitted by insects or other organisms that feed on plants.

Viruses cause such conditions as the flu, the common cold, cold sores, measles, chicken pox, and AIDS.

Classification of Living Things

Scientists use an ordered taxonomy (classification system) to classify living things. The levels within this system are called, in descending order, *kingdom*, *phylum/division*, *class*, *order*, *family*, *genus*, and *species*.

All life is categorized into five kingdoms.

Kingdom	Description/Example
Monera	One-celled or a colony of cells, decomposers and parasites, move in water, and both producers and consumers. *Examples*: bacteria, blue-green algae
Protista	One-celled or multicelled, absorb food, move with flagella, both asexual and sexual reproduction, producers and consumers. *Examples*: plankton, algae, amoeba, protozoans
Fungi	One-celled or multicelled, decomposers, parasites, absorb food, asexual reproduction and budding, consumers. *Examples*: mushrooms, molds, mildew, yeast, fungi
Plantae	Multicelled, photosynthesis, mostly producers. *Examples*: angiosperms, gymnosperms, mosses, ferns
Animalia	Multicelled, parasites, prey, both asexual and sexual reproduction, consumers. *Examples*: sponges, worms, insects, starfish, mammals, fish, amphibians, reptiles, birds, gorillas, humans

Human beings can be categorized according to the taxonomy in this way:

Kingdom	Animalia
Phylum	Chordates
Class	Mammals
Order	Primates
Family	Hominidae
Genus	Homo
Species	Sapiens
Scientific Name	Homo sapiens

Within each kingdom, there are various *phyla* (the plural of *phylum*) for animals and divisions for plants.

How Organisms Obtain Energy There are many ways to classify living things. One way is to divide them into consumers and producers. Producers use an outside energy source, such as sunlight, to produce energy. Most producers have chlorophyll, and most, but not all, are plants. Consumers cannot make their own energy; to live, they need to eat other organisms. Consumers may eat only plants, only animals, or both. (See the classification of animals for more information.)

Plants

Botany is the scientific study of plants. Many people consider everything from bacteria to the giant sequoia trees to be plants. That would include algae, fungi, lichens, mosses, ferns, conifers, and flowering plants. Today, scientists believe that bacteria, algae, and fungi have their own distinct kingdoms. The kingdom *Plantae* includes 250,000 species of mosses, liverworts, ferns, flowers, bushes, vines, trees, and other plants. Aquatic (water) and terrestrial (land) plants are the basis of all food webs. They emit into the atmosphere the oxygen that is needed by animals for survival.

Categorizing Plants Plants are categorized according to the structure by which the plant absorbs water. Plants are either *vascular* or *nonvascular*. Vascular plants transport water from the roots to the stems and to the leaves by means of tubelike structures. Nonvascular plants absorb water only through their surfaces.

Another way to categorize plants is according to how they reproduce. Some plants reproduce by producing *seeds*. Others produce *spores*. Yet another way to categorize plants is by whether they produce flowers (*angiosperms*, such as roses or apple trees) or don't produce flowers (*gymnosperms*, such as pine trees). Seeds store food for the growing plant; the part of the seed that stores the food is called the *cotyledon*. Some seeds have one cotyledon and are called *monocots*. Others have two and are called *dicots*.

Plants can also be classified by their life cycle. *Annuals* go through their entire life cycle, from germination through seed production to death, in one growing season. Corn, zinnias, beans, marigolds, and mums all have to be planted each year. *Biennials* have a two-year growing cycle. In year one, the seed germinates, produces leaves and roots, and forms a compact stem for food storage. In year two, the plant forms an elongated stem, produces flowers and fruits, and then ends with seed production. After seed production, the plant dies. Examples are onions, parsley, hollyhocks, and carrots.

Perennials live for many years. Parts of the plant may die back during the winter, but the plant will grow back in the spring.

Plants can also be categorized by their behavior in winter. *Deciduous* plants, including shrubs and trees, lose their leaves in the winter. Maple and oak trees are examples. *Evergreen* plants keep their leaves or needles throughout the year, sometimes shedding only old leaves or needles that are more than two years old. Pine and spruce trees are examples of evergreen trees.

Major Parts of a Plant Plants are made up of a number of different parts, including roots, stems, leaves, flowers, and fruits.

Roots Roots have several functions: absorbing nutrients and water, anchoring the plant into the soil, holding up the stem and leaves, and storing food. They are usually below ground and do not have chloroplasts (see the section on plant cells).

There are basically two types of root systems, a taproot system and a fibrous root system. A taproot system has one fat or sturdy main root, with just a few branching roots. Carrots, radishes, and parsnips are good examples of a taproot. A fibrous root system has many branched roots. Examples of plants with fibrous roots are most grasses.

Roots have tiny root hairs. Roots can have a very large number of root hairs, increasing the capability of the root to absorb water and food.

Stems The stem is the main trunk of a plant. Leaves, flowers, and fruits get support from the stem. Stems also carry nutrients and water. Some stems store food. Stems are generally above ground and vertical. Some stems grow below ground (bulbs) or fasten themselves to the ground. The strawberry plant is an example of a plant with a stem that hugs the ground.

Nodes are places on the stem where buds form. Spaces between the nodes are called *internodes*.

One of the major functions of the stem is to move water, nutrients, and food through the plant. The system that does this is called the *vascular system* and is similar to the circulatory system in humans. *Phloem tubes* move food from the roots through the stem to the leaves. *Xylem tubes* move minerals and water. These tubes are surrounded by the main tissue in the stem, the *cambium*.

Leaves Leaves grow out from the stem. The leaves' major job is to make food for the plant. For the most part, leaves are flat, broad, and green. The flat surface maximizes their ability to absorb light and transform it into food. There is a protective layer on leaves called the *cuticle* that reduces the evaporation of water from the plant and helps to protect the plant from disease-causing organisms. Leaves have tiny openings called *stomata* that enable the plant to take in carbon dioxide and release oxygen into the atmosphere. *Guard cells* cover the stomata openings and regulate the exchange of water vapor, oxygen, and carbon dioxide into and out of the stoma.

Flowers The main job of flowers is sexual reproduction or seed production. Various parts of the flower are involved in sexual reproduction. The *pistil* is the female portion of the flower. It includes the *stigma*, the surface that captures and holds *pollen*, and the *style*, the area between the stigma and the *ovaries*. The *stamen* is the male portion of the flower. It includes the *filament* that holds the *anther*. The anther is where the pollen is formed and released.

Some plants have flowers with both male and female parts, and others make flowers with only male or only female parts. Corn is an example of a plant that has both male and female flowers on one plant. The tassel is the male flower, and the ear is the female flower. The holly is an example of a plant that has either a male or a female flower. Plants of both sexes need to be planted close together so that

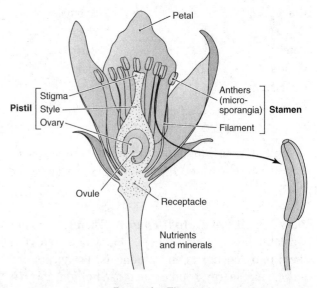

Parts of a Flower

the seeds (berries) can form on the female plant. Other parts of a flower are *sepals*, which enclose the various flower parts, and *petals*, the bright-colored parts like the petals of a rose or daisy.

Any edible part of a plant that is not a flower is considered to be a *vegetable*.

Fruits A fruit is a ripened ovary or group of ovaries containing the seeds. When the ovary is fertilized, the seeds develop and the ovary enlarges, forming the fruit. Examples of fruits are peanuts, sunflower seeds, barley, walnuts, tomatoes, grapes, oranges, apples, raspberries, cucumbers, squash, corn, eggplants, and strawberries.

How Plants Make Food The process is called *photosynthesis*. Photosynthesis is a process that converts the energy in sunlight into chemical forms of energy that can be used by biological systems. Green plants are the only organisms that make their own food. Photosynthesis begins when light strikes a plant's leaves. Cells in the leaves, called *chloroplasts*, contain a green pigment called *chlorophyll*. Chlorophyll interacts with sunlight to split the water in the plant into its basic components.

Carbon dioxide enters the leaf through the stomata and combines with the stored energy in the chloroplasts through a chemical reaction to produce a simple sugar. This sugar is then transported through tubes in the leaf to the roots, stems, and fruits of the plants. Some of the sugar is used immediately by the plant for energy; some is stored as starch; and some is built into a more complex substance, like plant tissue or cellulose. Some of the sugar is stored for future use or for use by us when we eat the plants. During the process, oxygen is released into the atmosphere.

Plant Responses Plants respond either positively or negatively to various stimuli. These responses are called *tropisms*. For example, the roots of plants respond positively to gravity, while the stem responds negatively (moving against gravity). Response to gravity is called *gravitropism*. Also, plants respond to light, growing toward it. This is called *phototropism*. Plants also respond to touch *thigmotropism*.

Animals

Categorizing Animals Animals are generally categorized in terms of whether or not they have a *backbone*. Animals that have a backbone are called *vertebrates*. Animals that do not have a backbone are called *invertebrates*.

All invertebrates lack backbones, but their other physical characteristics are varied. About 95 percent of all animals are invertebrates. Some invertebrates, like worms, have soft bodies with no bones. Other invertebrates, like snails, have soft bodies, but have developed a hard shell for protection. These types of invertebrates are called *mollusks*. Mollusks can live in water or on land. Some examples are snails, clams, mussels, and squid.

Some other invertebrates have tough coatings made of chitin on the outside of their bodies, called *exoskeletons*. They also have jointed legs and a segmented body. This group is known as the *arthropods* and includes spiders (*arachnids*), centipedes and millipedes, and *insects*, such as beetles and butterflies. In addition, *crustaceans*, such as shrimp, lobsters, and crabs, are also arthropods. There are more insects—over 900,000 species—than any other kind of animal, vertebrate or invertebrate.

All vertebrates have a backbone. Despite that common characteristic, vertebrates vary widely in appearance. One way to categorize vertebrates is according to their diet. Animals that primarily eat plants are known as *herbivores*. Animals that feed mostly on meat are known as *carnivores*. Some animals, like humans, eat both plants and meat and are called *omnivores.*

Meat eaters have jaws and teeth that are designed for tearing and crushing. The *canine* teeth are sharp, and the *molars* have a flattened surface for grinding. The digestive system is adapted for handling the quick digestion of meat. Plant eaters usually have large incisors for cutting plants. Their large molars are designed for grinding tough plant fibers. Their digestive system has a long intestine adapted for the slow digestion of plant fibers.

Vertebrates can also be classified according to their body temperature. All vertebrates are either *cold-blooded* or *warm-blooded.* An animal is called cold-blooded if its body temperature follows or matches the external temperature around it. Fish, amphibians, and reptiles are examples of cold-blooded animals. Warm-blooded animals can control their body temperature. Their internal body temperature remains the same no matter what the temperature is outside. Only birds and mammals (like people, cats, cows, and the like) are warm-blooded. Birds rely on their feathers to help them adapt to temperature changes.

Mammals use their hair, skin, or fur to adapt to temperature changes. Another differentiating characteristic of mammals is that the female produces milk to feed her offspring. Whales, which are mammals that live in the sea, must deal with changing water temperatures. Wolves and bears that live in mountainous areas or in polar regions must adapt to cold temperatures. Warm-blooded animals try to avoid or find ways to cope with temperature extremes in order to survive.

Ecology, Habitats, and Biodiversity

The sum of all the places on Earth where life can exist is called the *biosphere.* An *ecosystem* is the collection of all the living creatures and nonliving features or conditions in a particular environment. For example, a rainforest has certain creatures living in it. The amount of rainfall, the temperature, the soil conditions, the air, and the contour of the land are some of the nonliving features of the ecosystem. The study of ecosystems—the interactions between and among these living creatures and nonliving features—is called *ecology.*

The many thousands of species of plants and animals that live on the planet contribute to *biodiversity.* Biodiversity is the variety of life forms that exist. Scientists believe that a rich biodiversity creates a condition in which plants and animals are more likely to recover from stresses caused by nature and people. Biodiversity tends to increase as one approaches the equator. Warmer weather tends to support biodiversity.

Life forms live in what is called a *habitat,* a geographic area with conditions that support the continued reproduction of the species. Some habitats may be small, such as the dark corners of an underground cave or a hot thermal pool where only a few creatures live. Other habitats may be large, such as the thousands of square miles of prairie land that support certain grasses.

There are many threats to biodiversity. One is the reduction or destruction of habitat. Habitats can be destroyed by natural causes, such as volcanic eruptions or changes in climate like those that occurred during the Ice Ages. People have contributed to the loss of habitat and the destruction of species by actions such as building roads, cutting down forests, sending pesticides or other chemicals into the water, and sending pollutants from factories and cars into the atmosphere.

Global warming resulting from sending carbon dioxide into the atmosphere can raise temperatures and affect biodiversity. The thinning of the *ozone layer* in the atmosphere can increase the amount of ultraviolet radiation (UV) that reaches Earth's surface, resulting in harm to living organisms.

HUMAN PHYSIOLOGY

Physiology is the branch of biology that deals with the parts of the body, their functions, and the various bodily processes. Human physiology deals with the human body.

Cells, Tissues, Organs, and Organ Systems

In the human body, there are many different kinds of cells. Each kind is specialized for the primary function it performs. Examples are fat cells, skin cells, muscle cells, bone cells, and nerve cells. Groups of cells arrange themselves into *tissues,* and various tissues work together to form *organs,* such as the skin, liver, heart, gallbladder, and intestines. Organs work together to form *organ systems.* Organ systems include the muscular system, skeletal system, skin or integumentary system, respiratory system, digestive system, circulatory system, lymphatic system, immune system, excretory system, nervous system, endocrine system, and reproductive system.

Muscular System

The *muscular system* allows movement and locomotion. The muscular system helps you make body movements and supports the body in its activities. Muscles are involved in breathing, your heart beating, and the working of your digestive system.

Some actions are controlled by *voluntary* muscles, such as making a face, showing your biceps, or walking. Other muscle systems are *involuntary*, such as those that control breathing, your heart beating, and your digestive process.

Skeletal muscles help move the bones. They are attached to the bone by bands of tissue called *tendons*. Skeletal muscles work in pairs; when one muscle of the pair contracts, the other muscle relaxes. *Cardiac muscle* is found in the heart. *Smooth muscles* are found in some of your internal organs, such as your intestines and bladder.

Skeletal System

The skeletal system is a living system that provides shape and support to your body. It is built to protect your inner organs and to provide attachment points for muscles. The skeletal system provides a rigid framework for movement. It supports and protects the body and body parts, produces blood cells, and stores minerals. In lower animals, such as a grasshopper, the skeleton might be on the outside. This is called an *exoskeleton*.

Vertebrates have developed an internal mineralized *endoskeleton*. The endoskeleton is made up of *bone* and *cartilage*. Muscles are on the outside of the endoskeleton. Although our endoskeleton is mostly bone, some parts of our body are made of cartilage, such as the trachea, nose, and ears. The skeleton and muscles function together as the *musculoskeletal* system. Calcium and phosphorus are important components of bone; these elements make bone hard. *Osteoblasts* are bone-forming cells.

Places where your bones come together are called *joints*. Joints are held together by bands of tissue

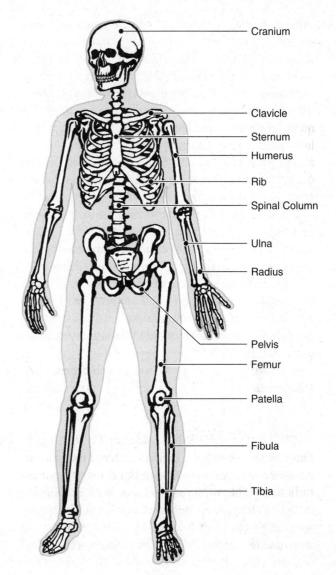

Skeletal System

called *ligaments*. Bones move at the joints. There are three major types of joints: *ball and socket joints*, like the shoulder and hip; *pivot joints*, like the elbow; and *hinge joints*, like the knee. These joints, working with the muscles and tendons, allow the body to move in certain ways.

Integumentary System

Skin or *integument* is your outermost protective layer. The skin is the largest organ in your body. It protects you from losing water and from the invasion of foreign organisms and viruses. Special nerve cells in the skin help send information to the brain, helping you to feel hot and cold, texture, softness, and pain. Your skin has hair, oil glands, and sweat glands.

Skin helps to regulate your body temperature by expanding or constricting blood vessels and through the operation of the *sweat glands*. The sweat glands move perspiration or sweat onto the skin, where evaporation takes place and cools the skin.

The skin has three layers. The *epidermis* is the outer, thinner layer of skin. Underneath the epidermis, skin cells are continually being produced. The next layer is the *dermis*, containing blood vessels, nerves, muscles, and oil and sweat glands. Underneath the dermis is a layer of *fat*. This is where a lot of fat is stored as you gain weight.

Skin gets its color from *melanin*. People with different color skin have different amounts of melanin. The darker the skin, the more melanin the skin has. Skin also helps produce vitamin D when it is exposed to ultraviolet light.

Skin bruises when tiny blood vessels beneath the skin burst.

Respiratory System

The respiratory system takes in oxygen and moves out waste material of carbon dioxide. Our lungs perform this job by breathing in and out (gills do this in fish). This system includes the lungs, pathways connecting them to the outside environment, and structures in the chest involved with moving air in and out of the lungs.

The Respiratory System

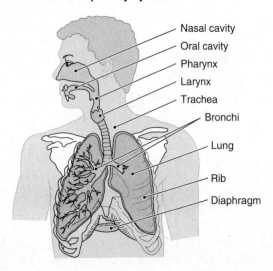

Nasal cavity
Oral cavity
Pharynx
Larynx
Trachea
Bronchi
Lung
Rib
Diaphragm

When we breathe in, air enters the body through the nose, where it is warmed, filtered, and passed through the *nasal cavity*. Air passes the *pharynx* (which has the *epiglottis* that prevents food from entering the *trachea*). The upper part of the trachea contains the *larynx*. After passing the larynx, the air moves into the *bronchi*, which carry air in and out of the lungs.

The bronchi are lined with *epithelium* and mucus-producing cells. The bronchi branch into smaller and smaller tubes known as *bronchioles*. The bronchioles terminate in little sacks known as *alveoli*. Alveoli are surrounded by a network of thin-walled *capillaries*. The exchange of oxygen takes place there, between the alveoli and the capillaries. The capillaries take in the oxygen. The hemoglobin in the blood picks up the oxygen and carries it off to various parts of the body. At the same time, waste material is transferred to the alveoli and eventually out of our bodies during exhalation.

It is important to note that breathing is different from respiration. Breathing is the physical action of moving the *diaphragm* up and down, which allows air to enter our lungs. Respiration is how our bodies use the oxygen from the air we inhale and eliminate the carbon dioxide when we exhale.

Digestive System

Digestion is accomplished by *mechanical* and *chemical* means, breaking food into particles small enough to pass into the bloodstream. The digestive process begins as soon as you put food into your mouth. Mechanical breakdown begins in the mouth by chewing (teeth) and moving the food around with your tongue. The food interacts with your *saliva* to begin a chemical breakdown. This mixture of food and saliva is then pushed into the *pharynx* and *esophagus* when you swallow. The esophagus is a long tube with muscles that contract and move the food to the *stomach*. The stomach is a sack or bag. It breaks down the food by both mechanical and chemical means. The stomach mixes the food by a process called *peristalsis*. Peristalsis is merely waves of muscle contractions. The stomach releases *enzymes* and *hydrochloric acid* to break down the food even further. Eventually the food moves to your *small intestine*.

The small intestine is narrow in diameter but very long in length. The upper part of the small intestine is the *duodenum*. This is where most digestion takes place. *Bile* is introduced from your *liver*. Bile breaks up the fat particles. Next comes the *pancreas*, which introduces pancreatic fluid. This fluid promotes the chemical digestion of carbohydrates, proteins, and fats. The fluid also neutralizes the stomach acid and releases insulin. Absorption of the food takes place in the small intestine.

Food that is not digested continues to move through your system into the *large intestine* by means of peristalsis. The large intestine absorbs water, making the contents more solid. Eventually the *rectum* and *anus* control the release of the semi-solid waste called *feces*.

The Digestive System

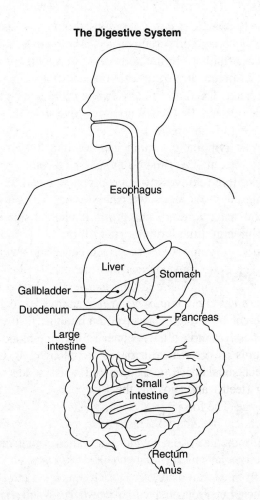

Circulatory System

The circulatory system is one of the transportation systems in your body. The main job of the circulatory system is to move oxygen, carbon dioxide, nutrients, waste products, immune components, and hormones through your body. The circulatory system is composed of vessels and muscles that control the flow of blood around the body. This process of blood flowing around the body is called *circulation*.

The main components of the circulatory system are the *heart*, *arteries*, *capillaries*, and *veins*.

There are three types of circulation, *coronary circulation*, *pulmonary circulation*, and *systemic circulation*. Coronary circulation is the circulation of blood within the heart itself by the coronary veins and arteries. If this circulation is blocked, it could result in a heart attack. Pulmonary circulation is the flow of blood from the heart to the lungs and back. Systemic circulation is the blood (with oxygen) moving through your body to your important organs.

The heart is a strong muscle that operates as the engine of the circulatory system. It has four compartments that are called *chambers*. The two upper chambers are called *atriums*, and the two lower chambers are called *ventricles*. When your heart beats, the two ventricles contract at the same time, followed by the two atria. Blood flows from an atrium to a ventricle and then from the ventricle to a blood vessel. The *pulmonary valves* keep the blood from flowing backward. There is a wall between the two atria and the two ventricles, keeping blood that has a lot of oxygen apart from blood that does not have as much oxygen.

Blood returns from the body to the right atrium of the heart. At this point, the blood is low on oxygen. When the right atrium contracts, it moves the blood to the right ventricle. The blood then moves via the *pulmonary artery* to the lungs, where it picks up oxygen and eliminates waste (carbon dioxide). The oxygenated blood leaves the lungs and comes into the heart through the left atrium. Blood leaves the heart from the left ventricle and goes into the biggest artery, called the *aorta*. Fresh blood from the aorta goes to various parts of your body,

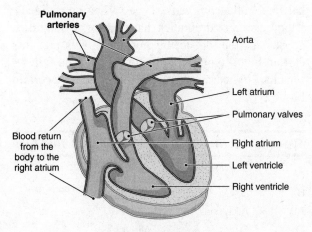

The Human Heart

including the brain, which needs a constant supply of oxygen. Blood returns to the heart through the veins, starting the cycle over.

Arteries are blood vessels that carry blood away from the heart. Veins carry blood to the heart. Arteries and veins are connected by thousands of miles of tiny vessels called capillaries.

Blood About five liters of blood flows through your body, delivering essential elements and removing harmful wastes. Blood transports oxygen from the lungs to body tissues and carbon dioxide from body tissues to the lungs. It also transports disease-fighting substances to the tissue and waste to the *kidneys*.

Blood contains *red blood cells* and *white blood cells*. These cells are responsible for nourishing and cleansing the body. Red blood cells are shaped like disks and contain *hemoglobin*, which carries oxygen and carbon dioxide. Unlike other cells, they do not have a nucleus. White blood cells fight bacteria, viruses, and other intruders in your body. The white blood cells are carried to the place where an intruder has invaded and go into that tissue. Their job is to destroy the bacteria or viruses.

Cell fragments called *platelets* are carried along with the red and white blood cells. Platelets plug holes in small blood vessels to stop bleeding. They help to clot blood.

Red and white blood cells and platelets are carried by a fluid called *plasma*. About 55 percent of the blood's volume comes from plasma. Nutrients, minerals, and oxygen are carried by the plasma to various parts of the body. Waste products are also carried by the plasma.

There are four different blood types: *A, B, AB,* and *O*. Types A, B, and AB have certain chemical tags called *antigens*. Type O has no antigens. Blood also has antibodies that destroy or neutralize substances that do not belong there. This prevents certain blood types from being mixed. The following chart indicates who can receive and give certain blood types.

Type	Can Receive	Can Donate to This Type
A	A, O	A, AB
B	B, O	B, AB
AB	All types	AB
O	O	All types

People with type O blood are called universal donors; those with type AB are called universal receivers.

Your blood also has Rh factors, making it even more unique. The Rh factor is an additional chemical tag. If the blood has the Rh factor, it is labeled Rh-positive. If the factor is not present, the blood is called Rh-negative. If the wrong blood is given to a person, the blood will try to destroy the other person's blood. That's why it is important to know your blood type.

Lymphatic System

The lymphatic system is composed of *lymph vessels*, *lymph nodes*, and certain organs. The system absorbs excess fluids from the body and returns them to the bloodstream. It also absorbs fat and transports it to the heart. The fluid contains *lymphocytes*, which are a type of white blood cell that tries to destroy disease-causing organisms.

The lymphatic system is a lot like the circulatory system. The fluid *lymph* passes through lymph nodes that remove any microorganisms and foreign materials. Lymph nodes generally occur in clusters in the neck, armpits, and groin. If you get sick with an infection, the lymphocytes fill the lymph nodes, and your lymph nodes may feel tender and swollen.

There are three organs that are part of the lymphatic system. These are the *tonsils*, the *thymus*, and the *spleen*. Your tonsils help keep out invaders that try to come in through your nose and mouth. The thymus makes lymphocytes. The spleen filters the blood and removes worn-out or damaged red blood cells. Cells in the spleen destroy bacteria and other invaders.

Immune System

The immune system defends our bodies from invading microorganisms and viruses called *pathogens*, as well as from cancerous cell growth. Immune-system components are grouped into *first-line defenses* and *second-line defenses*. First-line defenses include your skin and your respiratory, digestive, and circulatory systems.

Pathogens can't get through your skin unless it is cut or broken, but they can get though your mouth, nose, and eyes. The respiratory system uses *cilia*, little hairlike structures, and *mucus* to trap pathogens. When you cough or sneeze, you are expelling some mucus that contains pathogens. The digestive system uses saliva, enzymes, hydrochloric acid, and other substances to get rid of bacteria that can be harmful to you. The circulatory system uses white blood cells to surround and destroy foreign organisms and chemicals. Temperature destroys some organisms, so if your white blood cells cannot do the job fast enough, you might get a *fever.*

Second-line defenses are specific to the disease. Molecules that that are foreign to your body are called *antigens.* When your body determines that a foreign molecule has invaded, special lymphocytes, called *T cells,* attack. Special T cells stimulate other lymphocytes called *B cells* to form *antibodies.* Antibodies are made in response to a specific antigen.

With certain diseases, a lot of extra antibodies are formed, so that when your disease is cured, a few antibodies hang around and stay on watch. If the pathogen enters your body again, these antibodies can reproduce very rapidly and eliminate the disease. That's why some diseases, like chicken pox, you get only once. This is an example of *active immunity.*

Passive immunity occurs when antibodies are acquired from another person such as a newborn receiving antibodies from the mother or antibodies being injected. A *vaccination* injects a type of antigen that gives you active immunity against the disease. It does this by stimulating the production of antibodies. Vaccinations are specific to one kind of virus or bacteria. For example, there is a new flu vaccine every year because the virus is different each year. Common vaccines include those for measles, diphtheria, tetanus, mumps, rubella, and whooping cough.

Diseases caused by bacteria include tetanus, tuberculosis, strep throat, and bacterial pneumonia. Viruses cause colds, influenza (flu), measles, polio, mumps, and smallpox. *Antibiotics* can cure some bacterial diseases, but not viral diseases.

Excretory System

The excretory system removes waste. It removes undigested material through the digestive system by way of the large intestine. It removes waste gases through the circulatory and respiratory systems. It removes salts through the skin when we sweat. It removes excess water and waste through the urinary system. The *urinary system* is responsible for maintaining the fluid levels in our bodies.

The *kidneys* play a major role in the excretory system. They are two bean-shaped organs that are responsible for filtering blood that contains waste from the cells. Once the blood has been purified by tiny filtering units called *nephrons,* it is returned to

the circulatory system. The leftover water from this process is called *urine.* It is collected in the *bladder* and then eliminated through the *urethra* during urination. Persons who have kidney disease need to have dialysis to remove the waste from their blood. Without waste removal, a person will die.

Nervous System

The nervous system coordinates and controls such actions as memory, learning, and conscious thought. The nervous system also maintains such functions as heartbeat, breathing, and control of involuntary muscle actions. It is the most complex and delicate of all our body systems.

The largest organ in the nervous system is the *brain.* The brain is a sort of control center, as it sends and receives messages through a network of nerves. It is made up of a hundred billion *neurons,* or brain cells. The brain has three major parts: the *cerebrum,* the *cerebellum,* and the *brain stem.*

The cerebrum is the largest part of the brain; it takes care of our thinking processes. The outer layer of the cerebrum is called the *cortex* and has a lot of ridges and grooves. More ridges and grooves allow more complex thinking to occur.

The cerebellum is the second-largest part of the brain. Its job is to coordinate our muscle movements and maintain normal muscle tone and posture. The cerebellum coordinates our balance while walking, riding a bike, and so on.

The brain stem is closest to the *spinal cord.* It has three parts: the *midbrain,* the *pons,* and the *medulla.* The midbrain and pons coordinate various parts of the brain so that it acts together. The medulla is involved in coordinating our heartbeat, breathing, blood pressure, and the reflex centers for vomiting, coughing, sneezing, swallowing, and hiccupping.

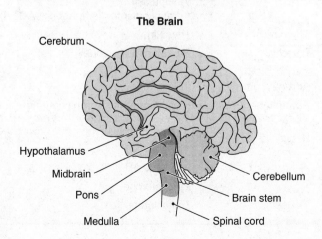

The Brain

Nerve Cells

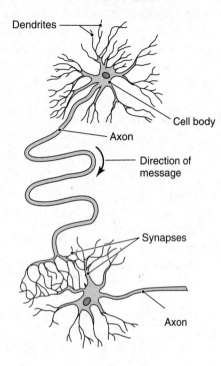

The *hypothalamus* regulates thirst, hunger, body temperature, water balance, and blood pressure, and links the nervous system to the endocrine system.

The spinal cord is a thick bundle of *nerves* running down the center of the spine. Along the spinal cord, smaller bunches of nerves branch out. From these bunches, still smaller bundles of nerves branch out again. Eventually they reach every part of the body. The spinal cord is protected by a column of vertebrae—part of the skeletal system.

The brain and the spinal cord make up the *central nervous system*. These are the nerves in your head and the nerves that come out from the spinal cord. The nerves outside the central nervous system are called the *peripheral nervous system*. The peripheral nervous system connects the central nervous system to the rest of the body. The peripheral nervous system has two parts: the *somatic system* and the *autonomic system*. The somatic system controls voluntary movements, like walking, running, and swiveling your hip. The autonomic system controls involuntary movements, such as heartbeat, breathing, digestion, and so on.

Messages that are transported through the nervous system are conducted by the *nerve cells*. Each microscopic nerve cell, or *neuron*, has a blob-shaped main part, the *cell body*, and thin, spiderlike *dendrites*. It has one lone fiber called the *axon*. The axon's branched ends have little bulbs that *almost* touch adjacent nerve cells. The spaces between the nerve cells are called *synapses*. Nerve signals travel in one direction only along the axon and jump across synapses to other nerve cells.

Gland	Hormone	What It Does
Pituitary gland	Growth hormone	Stimulates the growth of muscles and bones
	Follicle-stimulating hormone (FSH)	Stimulates the growth of reproductive organs, such as the ovaries and testes
	Thyroid-stimulating hormone (TSH)	Stimulates the thyroid gland, which controls metabolism
	Prolactin	Stimulates the secretion of milk
	Vasopressin	Helps the kidneys to absorb water
	Adrenocorticotropic hormone (ACTH)	Stimulates the adrenal cortex
Thyroid	Thyroxin	Regulates metabolism
Parathyroid	Parathyroid hormone	Increases the concentration of calcium in the blood
Adrenal cortex	Aldosterone	Helps the kidneys absorb water and sodium
Adrenal medulla	Epinephrine and norepinephrine	Get the body ready for strenuous activity by increasing the concentration of blood sugar
Pancreas	Insulin	Regulates the amount of sugar in the blood
	Glucagon	Increases the amount of sugar in the blood
Ovaries	Estrogen	Promotes female secondary sex characteristics
	Progesterone	Thickens endometrial lining
Testes	Testosterone	Promotes male secondary sex characteristics

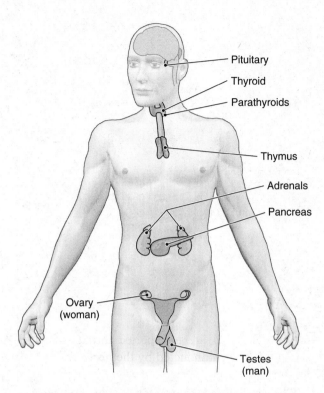

The Endocrine System

Endocrine System

Endocrine glands secrete hormones that regulate body metabolism, growth, and reproduction. These organs are not in contact with each other, but they communicate through chemical messages transported by the circulatory system. The preceding table lists the major glands in the endocrine system, the hormone(s) each one produces, and what the hormones do. On the ASVAB test, you probably will not need to know the specific hormones that are produced, but just in general what each gland does.

Reproductive System

The purpose of the reproductive system is to continue the species for another generation. The organs of this system, called *gonads*, produce *gametes* that combine in the female system to produce the next generation. The male gonads are the *testes*, which produce *sperm* and male sex hormones. The female gonads are the *ovaries*, which produce *eggs* (ova) and female sex hormones. The sperm fertilizes the egg, and reproduction begins. Fertilization takes place when the sperm, using its *flagellum* (a sort of whiplike tail), moves through fluid to reach the egg. Each egg or sperm contains 23 *chromosomes*. These chromosomes carry

DNA, which contributes to forming a new individual and determines the person's traits or characteristics.

Sex cells divide by a process called *meiosis*. Before this process begins, the nucleus divides twice, creating four cells, each with half the number of chromosomes of the original cell. So these cells have 23 chromosomes, half of what is needed. When a sperm and an egg combine, the fertilized egg contains the full complement of 46 chromosomes. These new cells keep dividing, growing, and developing over time, eventually creating a baby.

The Senses

The senses are sight, hearing, touch, taste, and smell. There are specialized organs for each sense.

Sight Let's suppose that you are looking at an object. Light waves from that object enter the eye first through the *cornea* (a transparent section of the eye) and then through the *pupil*, the opening in the *iris*. Light waves are brought to convergence first by the cornea, and then by the *lens*. The lens directs the light through the *vitreous humor* (a gelatinous substance) onto the *retina*. The retina has two types of cells, *rods* and *cones*. Rods detect light intensity, and cones respond to color. At this point, the light waves are changed to electrical signals and then sent along the optic nerve to the brain. The brain then interprets the signals as the picture of the object.

Some people have vision problems. Two typical problems are *nearsightedness* and *farsightedness*. Nearsighted people have trouble seeing distant objects. Farsighted people have trouble seeing things that are close up. Nearsighted people can have their vision corrected with a *concave* lens, and farsighted people can have their vision corrected with a *convex* lens.

Hearing Sound is vibrating air. Vibrating air creates sound waves. These waves can pass through solids, liquids, and gases to eventually reach your ear. When the sound waves reach your ear, they stimulate nerve cells that send signals to the brain. The brain interprets these signals as sound.

The ear is made up of several different parts, each contributing to the process of transforming sound waves into signals. The ear has three basic sections: the *outer ear*, the *middle ear*, and the *inner ear*.

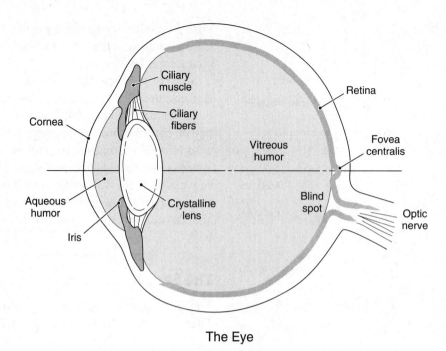

The Eye

The outer ear traps the sound waves and sends them down the ear canal to the middle ear, where the eardrum creates a vibration. This vibration then moves to some tiny specialized bones called the *hammer*, *anvil*, and *stirrup*. The stirrup bone rests against a membrane in the inner ear. The inner ear contains the *cochlea*, which is filled with fluid and is shaped like a snail. The cochlea vibrates when the stirrup vibrates, bending little hairs in the cochlea. The vibrating hairs send electrical signals to the brain, which in turn translates the signals into various sounds.

The semicircular canals in your inner ear are also responsible for maintaining your balance.

Smell Substances such as food, perfume, and gases give off molecules into the air. These molecules stimulate some nerve cells in your nose. These nerve cells are called *olfactory cells*. The olfactory cells are moist from mucus. Molecules are dissolved in the mucus, and, if there are a sufficient number of these molecules, a signal is sent to the brain. The brain then interprets these signals. If you have smelled this before, you may recognize the smell

The Ear

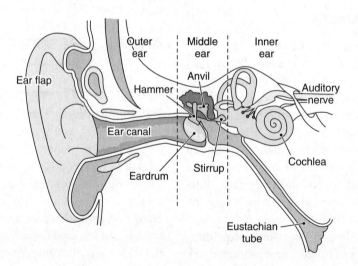

as a hamburger with onions, pumpkin pie, or your mother's favorite perfume.

Taste There are about 10,000 *taste buds* on your tongue. When you take food into your mouth, it begins to dissolve in liquid, your saliva. The mixture of saliva and food washes over your taste buds and stimulates the nerve fibers in the taste bud. The nerve fibers send a signal to your brain, and your brain translates the taste as sweet, sour, salty, bitter, or the taste of MSG (monosodium glutamate). The sense of smell and the sense of taste are related to each other.

Touch Your skin also has receptors allowing you to determine if something is hot, cold, rough, smooth, painful, hard, soft, and so on. The receptors send a signal to the brain, which in turn interprets the signals.

Genetics

All characteristics are inherited from genes of the mother and the father. Chromosomes come in pairs. The genes on a chromosome have information about the trait, but the information from the father and the mother is not necessarily exactly the same. Different forms of a gene are called *alleles*. For example, for the genes that determine hair color, the allele from your mother might be for blond hair and the allele from your father might be for black hair. Some alleles are *dominant* and some are *recessive*. The dominant allele will determine what traits actually become part of you.

Sometimes errors in mitosis or meiosis take place, altering a gene or chromosome. Some mutations are harmless, such as a four-leaf clover or a white tiger. Others can be harmful, setting the stage for certain diseases, conditions, or even death.

Determining the Probability of Certain Traits When describing genetic traits or alleles, a dominant allele is indicated with a capital letter (such as B). A recessive allele is indicated with a lowercase letter (such as b). In the genes, these alleles appear in pairs, such as BB, bb, or Bb. The sum of these genetic codes is the *genotype*, or genetic makeup of the organism. How the organism looks is called the *phenotype*. So if you have blond hair, that is your phenotype.

An organism that has two alleles that are the same, such as BB or bb, is called *homozygous*. An organism

that has one allele that is dominant and one that is recessive, such as Bb, is called *heterozygous*.

To determine the probability that an offspring will have a certain characteristic, you can use a device called a *Punnett square*.

Suppose a father has black hair with one dominant allele for black hair (B) and one recessive allele for blond hair (b). Then suppose a mother has blond hair with two recessive alleles (bb). The following Punnett square shows the probability that these parents will have a child with black or blond hair.

		Father	
		B	**b**
Mother	**b**	Bb	bb
	b	Bb	bb

There is a 2 in 4 (or 50 percent) probability that a child will have black hair (Bb) and a 2 in 4 (or 50 percent) probability that a child will have blond hair (bb).

Now suppose the father has two dominant alleles for black hair (BB).

		Father	
		B	**B**
Mother	**b**	Bb	Bb
	b	Bb	Bb

All offspring would have black hair (Bb).

Now suppose that the father and mother each have black hair with one dominant allele for black hair (B) and one recessive allele for blond hair (b).

		Father	
		B	**b**
Mother	**B**	BB	Bb
	b	Bb	bb

The probability of having a blond child (bb) would be 1 in 4, or 25 percent.

Determining the Sex of an Offspring The female carries two X chromosomes, and the male carries an X and a Y chromosome. The female egg contains an

Role of Some Important Vitamins

Vitamin	What It Does	Where to Get It
B	Helps in growth, use of carbohydrates, red blood cell production, and development of a healthy nervous system	Wheat germ, whole-grain cereals, poultry, eggs, fish, dairy products, green vegetables, pasta
A	Helps in growth, eyesight, and healthy skin	Fish and liver, green and yellow fruits and vegetables
E	Helps in the formation of cell membranes	Vegetable oils, whole grains, nuts and seeds, green vegetables
C	Helps in growth, good bones and teeth, and wound healing	Citrus fruits, tomatoes, vegetables, strawberries
D	Helps in absorption of calcium and phosphorus in bones and teeth	Milk, eggs, cheese
K	Helps with the clotting of blood and wound healing	Green vegetables, vegetable oils, pork, liver, egg yolks

X chromosome. A male sperm can contain either an X or a Y chromosome. Depending on which sperm fertilizes the egg, the result can be a female (XX) or a male (XY). The male parent determines the sex of the offspring.

Nutrition

You need to eat for energy and to maintain your biologic functions. Food provides you with the necessary nutrients to survive. There are six types of nutrients: *proteins, carbohydrates, fats, vitamins, minerals,* and *water.* Proteins, carbohydrates, fats, and vitamins are all *organic* nutrients. Minerals and water are *inorganic.* Organic means the substance contains carbon.

Proteins are used by the body for replacement and repair of body cells and for growth. They are made up of amino acids. Eggs, meat, and cheese are considered protein foods.

Carbohydrates are a good source of energy for your body. Three types of carbohydrates are sugar, fiber, and starch. Sugars are simple carbohydrates. Starches and fiber are complex carbohydrates. Foods like potatoes, pasta, beans, and breads are complex carbohydrates.

Fats provide energy and help to absorb vitamins. Fats contain twice as much energy as carbohydrates. Excess energy from the foods you eat is stored as fat.

Vitamins are nutrients that are needed for certain bodily functions and for preventing some diseases. Water-soluble vitamins, such as B and C, need to be taken in every day. Fat-soluble vitamins are also stored in fat cells. Examples are vitamins A, D, E, and K.

Minerals can regulate the chemical reactions in your body. You need some level of about 14 different minerals. Most minerals are needed only in small (trace) amounts. Others, like calcium and phosphorous, are needed in larger amounts. Perhaps the most

Mineral	What It Does	Where You Get It
Calcium	Creates strong bones and teeth, good muscle and nerve activity	Dairy products such as milk and yogurt, green vegetables, soy
Phosphorus	Creates strong bones and teeth, regulates contraction of muscles	Cheese, meat, cereal
Potassium	Regulates water balance in cells, muscle contraction, nerve impulse conduction	Bananas, potatoes, oranges, nuts, meat
Sodium	Regulates fluid balance in tissues, nerve impulse conduction	Meat, milk, cheese, beets, carrots, salt, most prepared foods
Iron	Transports oxygen in red blood cells	Red meat, raisins, beans, spinach, eggs
Iodine	Controls thyroid activity, metabolic stimulation	Seafood, iodized salt

important contribution of minerals is the production and maintenance of our bones.

The preceding table lists the most important minerals, their benefits, and the foods that provide each one.

About two-thirds of your body is *water*. Your cells need water to carry out their work. You would die if you didn't have water for a few days. Some of your water comes from foods, but you must also drink water. Your body loses about four pints of water every day. That needs to be replenished. People who exercise need even more water.

CHEMISTRY

Everything is made up of *matter*. Matter is anything that takes up space and has energy. *Energy* causes change. Matter can exist as a *solid*, *liquid*, or *gas*—the three states of matter. An *atom* is the smallest building block of matter. Atoms are made of *neutrons* (with no electric charge), *protons* (with a positive electric charge), and *electrons* (with a negative electric charge). The center of an atom is the *nucleus*. The nucleus contains protons and neutrons. The nucleus of an atom is tiny in comparison to the atom itself. Electrons fly around the nucleus in orbits. Most of an atom is empty space. Energy holds the atom together. Atoms have the same number of electrons and protons, making them stable.

Elements

If a substance is made up entirely of the same kind of atom, it is called an *element*. An element cannot be broken down into a simpler form. The element carbon is made up of only carbon atoms, and the element sulfur is made up of only sulfur atoms.

Scientists have given all elements a one- or two-letter symbol. For example, oxygen is O, sulfur is S, calcium is Ca, and magnesium is Mg. All elements are arranged in a periodic table according to their similarities, providing important information about each element. You will not need to know the periodic table for the ASVAB test, but you may need to know that each block of the table has certain information.

All elements in the periodic table are ordered by their *atomic number*. The atomic number is the number of protons in the atom. In an atom with a neutral charge, the number of electrons equals the number of protons. The *atomic mass* number is equal to the number of protons plus the number of neutrons.

Atomic number → 6
Chemical symbol → C
Element name → Carbon
Atomic mass → 12.0107

Presence of Elements Most of the human body is made up of water, H_2O. Your cells contain about 65 to 90 percent water by weight. As much as 99 percent of the mass of the human body is made up of just six elements: oxygen, carbon, hydrogen, nitrogen, calcium, and phosphorus.

Elements in the Human Body	Percent
Oxygen	65
Carbon	18
Hydrogen	9.5
Nitrogen	3.2
Calcium	1.5
Phosphorus	1
Potassium	0.35
Sulfur	0.25
Sodium	0.15
Magnesium	0.05
Copper, zinc, selenium, molybdenum, fluorine, chlorine, iodine, manganese, cobalt, iron	0.70
Lithium, strontium, aluminum, silicon, lead, vanadium, arsenic, bromine	Trace amounts

By contrast, Earth's crust is made up of lesser amounts of oxygen, but a lot of silicon and aluminum.

Elements in Earth's Crust	Percent
Oxygen	47.2
Silicon	28.2
Aluminum	8.2
Iron	5.1
Calcium	3.7
Sodium	2.9
Potassium	2.6
Magnesium	2.1

Periodic Table of the Elements

New / Original

Solid — C
Liquid — Br
Gas — H
Synthetic — Tc

Alkali Metals
Alkaline Earth Metals
Transition metals
Lanthanide series
Actinide series
Other Metals
Nonmetals
Noble gases

Atomic masses in parentheses are those of the most stable or common isotope.

Web Page Design Copyright © 1997 Michael Dayah. Last Modified: Fri May 06 2005 13:48:56

Note: The subgroup numbers 1-18 were adopted in 1984 by the International Union of Pure and Applied Chemistry. The names of elements 112-118 are the Latin equivalents of those numbers.

162

Compounds

In a *compound*, two or more elements combine chemically in a fixed proportion to create a new substance that has characteristics different from those of the combining elements. For example, water is a compound made up of two hydrogen atoms and one oxygen atom. It is commonly written as H_2O. This ratio holds whether you have a gram of water or an ocean full of water.

Common Compounds in the Human Body	Importance and Use
Water	Makes up of most of our body, including blood. Nearly all chemical reactions take place in water
Calcium phosphate	Strengthens bones
Hydrochloric acid	Breaks down food in the digestive system
Sodium bicarbonate	Helps with digestion
Various salts	Helps to send messages along the nerves

There are two types of compounds, *covalent compounds* and *ionic compounds*. A covalent compound is made up of *molecules* (in most cases). A molecule is a group of atoms that are held together by chemical bonds (mainly covalent bonds). *Chemical reactions* occur when the bonds are broken and new bonds form, making different molecules. *Ions* are atoms that are positively or negatively charged. If an ion has more electrons than protons, it is negatively charged. If it has more protons than electrons, it is positively charged. Ions that are positively charged are attracted to ions that are negatively charged. Often ions will come together to form neutral ionic compounds. Table salt is a good example of this, as it has a positive ion of sodium (Na^+) that is attracted to a negatively charged chlorine (Cl^-), forming NaCl.

Mixtures

A *mixture* is composed of two or more substances that do not combine with each other, but instead retain their original characteristics. Also, the substances in a mixture do not have to be in any fixed proportion. For example, if you poured flour and salt together into a bowl, you would create a mixture. Mixing a cup of sugar into a gallon of water would create a mixture called a *solution*, where the sugar dissolves into the water. Mixtures can be solids, liquids, or gases or any combination of those.

Another type of mixture is a *suspension*. A suspension is a mixture of a liquid or gas with another substance spread evenly through it. Common suspensions include salt in water, fine soot or dust in air, droplets of oil in air, and whole blood. Particles in a suspension precipitate to the bottom if the suspension is left standing.

PHYSICAL SCIENCE

The Laws of Motion

The English scientist Sir Isaac Newton (1642–1727) formulated three laws of motion.

Newton's First Law The first law reads as follows: *An object at rest tends to stay at rest and an object in motion tends to stay in motion with the same speed and in the same direction unless acted upon by an unbalanced force.* Basically, this means that an object will keep doing what it is doing unless something makes it change. The something that makes an object change its state is called a *force*. A force is a push or pull upon an object resulting from one object's interaction with another object. An example of this is a person pushing a swing or a person pulling a suitcase.

An object has *inertia* when it is moving. Inertia is merely the resistance to change. An example is the tendency of your body to keep moving forward when your car comes to a sudden stop. In a collision, a seatbelt can keep you in place when otherwise you might hurtle through the windshield because of inertia.

Friction is a force that results when the surface of one object touches the surface of another. Friction causes moving objects to slow down or stop. For example, if you shove a book across a table, it will soon slow to a stop because it is rubbing on the surface of the table. Friction between two objects causes *heat*.

Newton's Second Law According to Newton, *an object will accelerate only if there is an unbalanced force acting upon it.* The presence of an unbalanced force will accelerate an object, changing its speed, its direction, or both its speed and its direction. The second law states that the acceleration of an object is dependent upon two variables—the force acting upon the object and the mass of the object. The formula for acceleration is $a = \dfrac{F}{m}$.

Newton's Third Law Newton's third law reads: *For every action, there is an equal and opposite reaction.* When you sit in your chair, your body exerts a downward force on the chair and the chair exerts an upward force on your body. There are two forces resulting from this interaction—a force on the chair and a force on your body. When a bird flaps its wings downward, the air pushes it upward, allowing it to fly. A gun recoils when it is fired.

Describing Motion In physics, there are various ways to describe motion. *Speed* is how fast an object is moving. A fast-moving object has a high speed, while a slow-moving object has a low speed. An object with no movement at all has a zero speed. The average speed during the course of a motion can be calculated using the following equation:

$$\text{Speed} = \frac{\text{distance traveled}}{\text{time of travel}}$$

Velocity is defined as the rate and direction at which an object's position changes. Velocity includes both speed and direction, such as moving 55 miles/hour in a westerly direction or 6 meters/second upward.

Average velocity can be calculated using the equation:

$$\text{Velocity} = \frac{\text{change of position}}{\text{time}}$$

Acceleration is defined as "the rate at which an object changes its velocity." An object is accelerating if it is changing its velocity. If an object is not changing its velocity, then the object is not accelerating. A falling object accelerates as it falls. If you could measure the motion of a falling object, you would notice that the object has an average velocity of 5 m/s in the first second, 15 m/s in the second second, 25 m/s in the third second, 35 m/s in the fourth second, and so on. By pushing down the gas pedal, you can accelerate your car.

Work, Energy, and Power

Some of the most important concepts in physics are work, energy, and power.

Work Work results from a force acting upon an object, causing it to change position or move from one place to another. There are three key aspects to work: force, movement, and cause. In order for a force to qualify as having done work on an object,

there must be a change of position caused by the force. Here are some common examples of work: a person carrying a box of books upstairs, a horse pulling a plow through the fields, a weightlifter lifting barbells, a person pushing a grocery cart down the aisle of a grocery store, a shot putter launching the shot, and an ice skater lifting his partner overhead. In each case, there is a force exerted upon an object that causes the object to be displaced. Work is measured in *joules*.

Energy In physics, *energy* is defined as the ability to do work. Energy can be either potential or kinetic.

Potential Energy An object can store energy as the result of its position. A can of soup on a shelf has potential energy. When it falls from the shelf onto the floor, it releases its energy. A roller-coaster car has potential energy when it is at the top of the track. It releases the energy when it plunges downward. An arrow in a drawn bow has potential energy resulting from its position. If the bow is not drawn, or pulled back, the arrow has no potential energy. The can of soup and the roller-coaster car have potential energy that is caused by *gravitation*—being pulled toward Earth. The second form of potential energy is *elastic* potential energy. Elastic potential energy is the energy stored when an object is stretched or compressed. For example the arrow in a drawn bow has elastic potential energy. Other examples include stretched rubber bands, bungee cords, trampolines, and springs. The more stretch or compression that is exerted on the object, the more potential energy it holds.

Kinetic Energy Kinetic energy is the energy of motion. Any object that has motion has kinetic energy. The direction does not matter. A moving car has kinetic energy, as does a moving ice skater or a soup can falling off the shelf. When the soup can falls off the shelf, its potential energy is changed to kinetic energy.

Forms of Energy Energy cannot be created or destroyed; it merely changes from one form of energy to another. Forms of energy include:

Chemical	Electrical
Gravitational	Heat
Light	Mechanical
Nuclear	Solar
Sound	Wind

Power Power is how much work is done over a given period of time. Work can be done very quickly or very slowly. For example, a rock climber scaling a sheer cliff may take a long time to raise his or her body just a few meters. But a hiker who selects an easier, less vertical path might raise his or her body the same few meters in a much shorter period of time. Even though the amount of work is the same, the hiker does the work in considerably less time than the rock climber. The hiker has a greater power than the rock climber.

The formula for power is

$$Power = \frac{work}{time}$$

The standard metric unit of power is the *watt*. Watts are used to measure the amount of energy consumed by an electric device.

Waves

Sound waves, light waves, radio waves, microwaves, water waves, earthquake waves, and waves on a piece of string are just a few of the kinds of waves we are likely to encounter every day. Waves transport energy. Waves have different parts. This section will focus on sound and light waves.

The *crest* of a wave is the point where there is the maximum amount of upward displacement from the rest or equilibrium position. The *trough* of a wave is the point where there is the maximum amount of downward displacement from the rest or equilibrium position. The *amplitude* of a wave refers to the height of the wave from its equilibrium point.

The *wavelength* of a wave is simply the length of one complete wave cycle. The wavelength can be measured as the distance from crest to crest or from trough to trough or at any two similar points

on the wave. The *period* of a wave is the amount of time it takes to get from one point on the wave to the same point on the next wave.

The amount of energy carried by a wave is related to its amplitude (the distance from the wave's equilibrium position to the maximum height or depth). A high-energy wave is characterized by a high amplitude; a low-energy wave is characterized by a low amplitude.

Low-energy and amplitude wave

High-energy and amplitude wave

The *frequency* of a wave is the number of complete cycles per second that the wave makes, from equilibrium to its crest, then back through equilibrium to its trough, and back again to equilibrium.

The diagram of the *electromagnetic spectrum* shows that waves have a large range of frequencies. The diagram on page 166 depicts the electromagnetic spectrum and its various regions. The longer-wavelength, lower-frequency regions are located on the far left of the spectrum; shorter-wavelength, higher-frequency regions are on the far right. The different wavelengths of waves determine what we see and how we communicate.

Sound Waves Sound is a wave that is created by vibrating objects and that moves through a medium from one location to another. Sound cannot travel through a *vacuum*. The medium is usually air, but it could be any material, like a liquid or solid. The

The Electromagnetic Spectrum

| Radio | Microwave | Infrared | Visible | Ultraviolet | X-ray | Gamma Ray |

10^4 10^2 1 10^{-2} 10^{-5} 10^{-6} 10^{-8} 10^{-10} 10^{-12}

Wavelength in centimeters

About the size of ...

Buildings   Humans   Honey Bee   Pinhead   Protozoans   Molecules   Atoms   Atomic Nuclei

vibrating object could be the vocal chords of a person, the string of a guitar, or a tuning fork, or the vibrating diaphragm (see respiratory system earlier in this overview) of a television announcer.

The *loudness* of sound depends on the amplitude of the wave. The higher the amplitude, the louder the sound. Loudness is measured in *decibels*. The *pitch* of the sound depends on the frequency of the sound waves. A high-pitched sound is created by a high-frequency wave, and a low-pitched sound is created by a low-frequency wave.

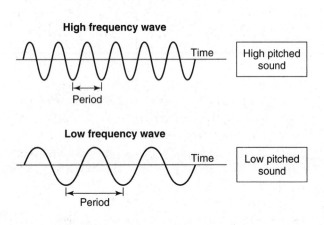

Sound travels faster in solids than in gases. Sound also travels faster in substances that have a higher temperature.

Sound waves are subject to a phenomenon called the *Doppler effect*. You may have heard the results of the Doppler effect without knowing it. Have you ever listened to an ambulance siren moving toward you and then detected a change in pitch when the siren started to move away from you? This is an example of the Doppler effect—a shift in the frequency of the waves coming from a moving object. As the object moves toward you, the pitch is higher; when it is moving away, the pitch is lower.

Light Waves *Visible light* occurs within a very tiny range of the electromagnetic spectrum. Each color in visible light has a distinct wavelength. This can be seen most clearly when you pass white light through a *prism* that separates the light into its "rainbow" of colors. Dispersion of visible light produces the colors red (R), orange (O), yellow (Y), green (G), blue (B), indigo (I), and violet (V). The red wavelengths of light are the longer wavelengths, and the violet wavelengths of light are the shorter wavelengths. The visible light spectrum is shown in the diagram below. To remember the order from long wavelengths to the shorter wavelengths, think of the letters *ROY G BIV*.

White is really not a color; rather, it is the combination of all the colors of the visible light spectrum. *Black* is not really a color, either. Black is

The Visible Spectrum

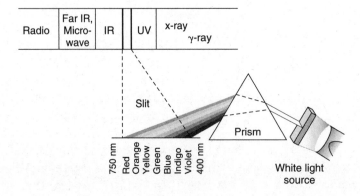

the absence of the wavelengths of the visible light spectrum or the absence of light or color. If you are in a room that is totally black/dark, it means that there are no wavelengths of visible light striking your eye.

Refraction Light *refracts*, or bends, when it passes through different media. Different substances bend light in different amounts. Every substance that can pass light has what is called a *refractive index*, the amount that the substance will bend light.

Refraction

Light is bent when it goes through *lenses*. Lenses can be *convex* or *concave*, and light behaves differently when it passes through each type of lens. Convex lenses are thicker in the middle than at the edges. Concave lenses are thicker at the edges than in the middle.

When light rays travel through a convex lens, the lens *converges* the light to a focal point. The more curved the lens, the closer the focal point is to the lens.

Refraction by a converging lens

Focal point

A concave lens, by contrast, *diverges* the light so that the light rays will never meet.

Refraction by a diverging lens

Reflection Light also has the property of reflection. A ray of light, perhaps coming from a flashlight or other light source, approaching a mirror is known as an *incident ray* (*I*). The ray of light that leaves the mirror is known as the *reflected ray* (*R*). At the point where the ray strikes the mirror, a perpendicular line can be drawn; this line is known as a *normal line* (*N*). The normal line divides the angle into two equal angles. The angle between the incident ray and the normal is known as the *angle of incidence*. The angle between the reflected ray and the normal is known as the *angle of reflection*.

Like lenses, mirrors can be *concave* (converging) and *convex* (diverging).

A converging mirror takes light rays and converges them to a focal point. The focal point is the point in space at which light will meet after reflection. Flashlights and headlights on a car use concave mirrors to produce direct light beams in a narrow area.

A diverging mirror spreads the light after it is reflected, so that the light beams will never intersect. For this reason, convex mirrors produce virtual images that appear to be located somewhere behind the mirror. Examples of these are the security mirrors you seen in stores so that clerks can see people in a large part of the store. They can also be found in the outside rearview mirrors in cars, which help you see a larger viewing area than a flat mirror. Convex mirrors make objects look farther away and smaller. That's why you have the warning in your outside rearview mirror that states that objects appear more distant than they really are.

Telescopes use both types of lenses to refract light and mirrors to reflect light.

Lasers Light from a *laser* is all of one wavelength, and all the waves are in *phase* (all crests and troughs are in tandem) and are traveling in the same direction. As a result, a laser beam of light does not spread out very much and directs its energy in a very small area. This characteristic allows lasers to be used as cutting tools in situations like eye surgery, for transferring digital music to CDs, and for reading bar codes in such places as grocery and department stores. Because laser light doesn't spread, lasers are used to carry information across long distances in space or through fiber-optic cable on land.

Blueshift and Redshift The *Doppler effect* is also a phenomenon of light. Scientists use this phenomenon to determine whether objects like stars and galaxies are moving toward Earth or away from it. If an object is moving toward Earth, the light from the object appears bluer (a blueshift). If an object is moving away from Earth, the light from the object appears redder (a redshift). Scientists have used this information to determine that the universe is expanding, creating a shift in wavelengths toward the red end of the spectrum

Heat

Heat is created by moving molecules. The faster the molecules move, the more heat is generated. Heat is basically *kinetic energy* (review the section on energy earlier in this chapter). Heat is measured by a *thermometer*.

Heat transfers or flows from warmer objects to colder objects when they are in contact. Transfer takes place in three ways: *radiation*, *conduction*, and *convection*.

Radiation The first method of heat transfer is *radiation*, which takes place via invisible waves through the air or even through a vacuum. The energy from the sun warms us through radiation, just as a fire in a fireplace warms our hands. A microwave oven heats food via radiation.

Conduction The second method of heat transfer is *conduction*, which refers to heat transferred between atoms bumping into each other in a substance. What happens if you put a spoon in boiling water? Eventually the handle of the spoon gets too hot to hold. The heat from the water causes the molecules in the spoon to move and collide, creating heat that eventually is conducted up the spoon handle to your hand.

Some materials are good conductors of heat, and some are not. Metals are good conductors of heat, with gold, silver, and copper being the best conductors. Copper is used more because it is cheaper and more plentiful. Some materials are called *insulators* because they are not very good at conducting heat. Materials made of cotton or wool, for example, are not good conductors of heat. If you wrap yourself in a wool blanket, rather than conducting the heat away from your body, it traps the heat and you get warmer. Air is a good insulator, as are plastic, wood, rubber, and tile (think of the tiles on the space shuttle that protect the shuttle from the heat of friction created when the shuttle strikes the atmosphere during its return to Earth).

Think about heat conduction when you get into a car on a hot sunny day when the windows are closed. Vinyl or leather seats will feel very hot, as they are better conductors of heat then fabric seats.

Convection Heat also transfers via a process called *convection*. Convection generally occurs in gases or liquids. For example, as the temperature of a pan of water on the stove increases, the molecules start to move around more quickly. As they do this, the distance between the molecules increases and the liquid expands. The denser, cooler water then sinks to the bottom of the pan and forces the warmer liquid upward. A circulation of the colder and warmer liquid begins. On a much larger scale, this is the process that helps to create currents in the oceans.

The same process creates currents in the atmosphere. When land is heated by the sun, it heats the air that is in contact with it. The warmer air expands and rises, and the cooler, heavier air sinks down. The rising air creates upward motion, which is used by birds and hang gliders to stay aloft. Sometimes these upward currents are called *thermals*. Thermals can reach many thousands of feet up and will give people in airplanes a bumpy ride.

Convection also creates land and sea breezes at a shoreline. Land heats faster than water. As the land heats up, it warms the air above it. The air expands and rises. It is then replaced by cooler air flowing in from over the water. This process creates a wind current that goes from the water to the land. We call this current a sea breeze. In the evening, the reverse happens. The land cools faster than the water, so the air current flows in the opposite direction. This creates what is called a land breeze—a breeze from the land to the sea.

Heated air expands and rises

925 mb

950 mb

975 mb

Cooler air replaces the heated air forming a sea breeze at the surface of the land.

Land (80°F)   Water (65°F)

Magnetism

Magnets can be made by placing a certain material, such as iron or steel, in a strong magnetic field. Pieces of the steel or iron are generally arranged in a random order. When these pieces, or *domains*, are placed in a strong magnetic field, they line up in the direction of the field. When most of the domains are aligned, the material becomes a magnet.

Before magnetization

After magnetization

N   S

A bar magnet has three-dimensional lines of force around it on all sides. If the lines were visible, they would look like the following diagram.

When opposite poles of two magnets are brought together, the lines of force join up and the magnets pull together.

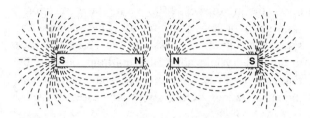

When like poles of two magnets are brought together, the magnets repel each other and the lines of force push away.

Earth as a Magnet Because of its iron-nickel core, Earth behaves like a giant magnet. It happens that Earth's magnetic poles are fairly close to the geographic poles. A compass has a needle that is attracted to the magnetic north pole and is repelled by the magnetic south pole.

Earth's magnetic field, called a *magnetosphere*, is produced by electric currents. Deep in Earth's core, there is convection as hot molten magma rises, cools, and sinks. The process repeats itself time and time again. Within these rising and falling masses of magma, the rotation of Earth creates organized patterns of circular electric currents, called eddies. The interior of Earth seems to act like a giant dynamo. Earth's magnetic field deflects most of the charged particles streaming from the sun.

Magnets are used to make electric motors and generators. Generators produce electricity, which supports our lifestyle in many ways.

Electricity and Magnetism The movement of electrons around the nucleus of an atom produces a *magnetic field*. The wire that contains an electric current is surrounded by a magnetic field. A wire with a current running through it that is wrapped around an iron core is called an *electromagnet*. Electromagnets are used in a variety of ways in our lives in everything from doorbells to magnetic high-speed trains.

GEOLOGY

Geology is the study of the solid Earth. It includes processes that have shaped Earth's surface, the ocean floors, and Earth's interior. It also involves the study of Earth's history from the past to the present.

Our planet has evolved since its creation about 4.6 billion years ago. Many processes have shaped Earth, some slow and others fast-acting. Slow processes include the formation of rocks, the chemical breakdown or weathering of rocks to form soil, the cementing of sand grains together to form rock, the metamorphosis of some kinds of rocks into other kinds of rocks through recrystallization, the uplifting of mountain ranges through tectonic activity, and the erosion of mountain ranges. Relatively faster processes include beach erosion during a storm, volcanic eruptions, landslides, dust storms, river flooding, and mudflows.

Earth's History

The chart below shows Earth's evolution over the past 4.6 billion years. On the ASVAB, you probably will not be asked about specific details on this chart, but you need to have a general idea of the history of Earth.

| **Phanerozoic Eon**
(543 mya* to present) | **Cenozoic Era**
(65 mya to today)

This era covers the last 10 percent of Earth's whole geologic history. After the disappearance of the dinosaurs, there were suddenly many empty places on Earth where other animals could live. Mammals diversified, and the Cenozoic Era became the "Age of Mammals." Whales took over the oceans; saber-tooth cats shared the land with elephants.

The global climate grew colder, and the last few million years saw the return of giant glaciers and ice caps to North America, Eurasia, and Antarctica. Ice ages occurred several times during this time period. There were mass extinctions during the Cenozoic Era, as there were during the Mesozoic and Paleozoic Eras.

Finally, humans appeared during the last 2 million years. In the last 10,000 years, humans spread across the planet. Humans changed the face of Earth with cities and farms, destroying some plants and animals and domesticating others. | **Quaternary**
(1.8 mya to today)
    Holocene (10,000 years to today)
    Pleistocene (1.8 mya to 10,000 yrs)

Tertiary
(65 to 1.8 mya)
    Pliocene (5.3 to 1.8 mya)
    Miocene (23.8 to 5.3 mya)
    Oligocene (33.7 to 23.8 mya)
    Eocene (54.8 to 33.7 mya)
    Paleocene (65 to 54.8 mya) |
| | **Mesozoic Era**
(248 to 65 mya)

The Mesozoic Era is divided into just three time periods: the Triassic, the Jurassic, and the Cretaceous. The supercontinents Gondwanaland and Laurasia collided to form a single super-super continent called Panagea. Plate tectonics continued, eventually causing Pangea to break up into the continents we know today.

Life was diversifying rapidly. The dominant animals on both land and sea were reptiles, the most famous of which are the dinosaurs. They are so prevalent in the Jurassic period that this is called "the Age of Reptiles." Birds and mammals also appeared during the Mesozoic | **Cretaceous**
(144 to 65 mya)

Jurassic (206 to 144 mya)

Triassic (248 to 206 mya) |

Phanerozoic Eon (*Continued*) (543 mya* to present)	**Mesozoic Era** (*Continued*) (248 to 65 mya)	
	Era, as well as deciduous trees and flowering plants.	
	The climate during the Mesozoic Era was so warm that there were no ice caps. Plants grew profusely with all the warmth and moisture.	
	At the end of the Mesozoic Era, more than half of all the existing life forms disappeared, including virtually all of the dinosaurs.	
	Paleozoic Era (543 to 248 mya)	**Permian** (290 to 248 mya)
		Carboniferous (354 to 290 mya) Pennsylvanian (323 to 290 mya) Mississippian (354 to 323 mya)
	Many different things happened during the Paleozoic Era. Earth's interior cooled down. Giant "hot-spot" type eruptions still occurred every hundred million years or so. Plate tectonics continued to push land masses across Earth's surface. At one particular time—the middle of the Silurian Period—most of the land was locked in two supercontinents called Gondwanaland (wandering over the southern hemisphere) and Laurasia (on the north side of the globe). Huge glaciers covered the interior of Gondwanaland, and Earth was experiencing one of its ice ages. Over the next hundred million years, Gondwanaland moved north over the equator and began to break up, and the climate warmed.	**Devonian** (417 to 354 mya)
		Silurian (443 to 417 mya)
		Ordovician (490 to 443 mya)
		Cambrian (543 to 490 mya) Tommotian (530 to 527 mya)
	The composition of the atmosphere continued to slowly change, mostly due to the increase in oxygen produced by photosynthetic algae floating on the ocean. By the Paleozoic Era, the composition of the air had reached something like what we breathe now: about 4/5 nitrogen, 1/5 oxygen, and small amounts of carbon dioxide, water vapor, and other gases. The air was capable of supporting large animals.	
	At the beginning of the Paleozoic Era, life existed only in or near the ocean. Trilobites, shellfish, corals, and sponges appeared, followed by the first fish. Land plants appeared near the end of the Ordovician Period.	
	The Paleozoic Era had several mass extinctions in which many life forms died out. Mass extinctions occurred at the end of the Ordovician and the Devonian Periods. During the Permian Period, about 95 percent of all life on Earth died! These mass changes were probably caused by volcanic eruptions and changes in the climate.	

(Continued)

Precambrian Time (4,500 to 543 mya)	Proterozoic Era (2,500 to 543 mya)	Neoproterozoic (900 to 543 mya) Vendian (650 to 543 mya)
This time period represents the very earliest rocks and fossils, and almost 90 percent of the entire history of Earth. It has been divided into three eras: the Hadean, the Archean, and the Proterozoic.		**Mesoproterozoic** (1,600 to 900 mya) **Paleoproterozoic** (2,500 to 1,600 mya)
This era began about 4.6 billion years ago with the formation of Earth from dust and gas orbiting the sun. Volcanoes were active, and asteroids kept pummeling the planet. The air was hot, thick, and steamy. It was not breathable by animals yet.	**Archaean Era** (3,800 to 2,500 mya)	
Later, cooling of Earth began and water in the atmosphere condensed to form the oceans. The air was now mostly nitrogen, like our air today. The lava had mostly cooled to form the ocean floor.		
Still later, blue-green algae came into existence. The surface of Earth was still very active. Continental collisions happened often. Life was still found only in the ocean. Eventually, multicelled creatures with no hard parts came into existence. Oxygen released by the algae floating in the oceans began to collect in the air. Earth at this time was also very cold, with huge, bluish glacial ice sheets visible across the planet.	**Hadean Era** (4,500 to 3,800 mya)	

*mya 5 million years ago

Earth's Structure

Earth is made up of three basic layers of rock: the crust, the mantle, and the core. The table on page 173 gives some characteristics of each of these layers.

Categories of Rocks

There are three categories of rock: *igneous*, *sedimentary*, and *metamorphic*. Igneous rocks are made of molten material that has solidified. Igneous rocks can be formed beneath Earth's surface (*intrusive*) or above Earth's surface (*extrusive*), as in the case of lava flows. When rock is subjected to weathering from chemical reactions, atmospheric conditions, or the results of gravity, the rock breaks into

Layers of the Earth

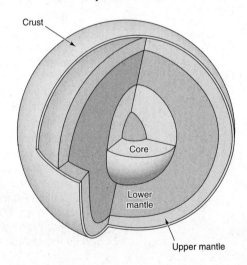

Characteristics of Earth's Layers

Layer	Characteristics	Composition
Crust	Crust is different on the continents and in the ocean; layers are very thin, only about 30 km; represents only 1 percent of Earth's volume; crust is lighter and floats on the mantle	Oceanic crust is dense rock called basalt; continental crust is made up of less dense andesite and granite Rich in the elements oxygen and silicon, with lesser amounts of aluminum, iron, magnesium, calcium, potassium, and sodium
Mantle	Represents about 85 percent of Earth by volume	Made of minerals rich in the elements iron, magnesium, silicon, and oxygen
Core	Two layers: a solid inner core and a liquid outer core; remains very hot after 4.5 billion years of cooling; represents about 15 percent of Earth's volume	Mostly iron and nickel

Common Elements Found in Earth's Rocks

Element	Chemical Symbol	Percent Weight in Earth's Crust
Oxygen	O	46.60
Silicon	Si	27.72
Aluminum	Al	8.13
Iron	Fe	5.00
Calcium	Ca	3.63
Sodium	Na	2.83
Potassium	K	2.59
Magnesium	Mg	2.09

smaller pieces, or sediments. These sediments can be compacted and cemented together to form solid rock called sedimentary rock. Both igneous and sedimentary rock can be placed under a great deal of heat and pressure. Under those conditions, the rock transforms into metamorphic rock. If the pressure and temperature are high enough, metamorphic rocks can melt and then solidify into igneous rock.

Igneous Rocks Igneous rocks are rocks that at one time were melted. They can form either underground or above ground. Melted rock underground is called *magma*, and it is sometimes trapped in pockets. As the melted magma cools, it forms masses of igneous rock. Igneous rocks form above ground when volcanoes erupt and magma reaches Earth's surface. When magma appears above Earth's surface, it is called *lava*. Typical igneous rocks are *pumice*, *obsidian*, and *granite*.

Pumice rocks are created when a volcano spews out lava that is filled with trapped gases. When the gases escape and the remaining materials harden, pumice is left. This rock is filled with air pockets

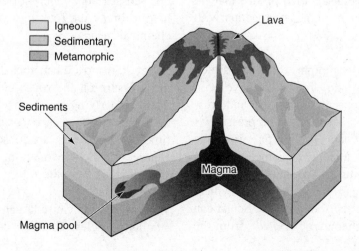

Igneous
Sedimentary
Metamorphic

Lava

Sediments

Magma

Magma pool

where the gases were once trapped. It is so light in weight that many pumice rocks will float in water. Obsidian rocks are created when lava is shot into the atmosphere and then cools so quickly that it forms a kind of glass. Slow cooling would give the lava time to form crystals like the ones in granite. Granite is an igneous rock formed by the slow cooling of magma beneath the earth's surface. The slower the magma cools, the larger the crystals.

Sedimentary Rocks Rock that is subjected to weathering from wind, water, gravity, and chemical reactions breaks down from larger pieces to smaller pieces. Gravity helps the pieces collect in low areas, such as valleys, ocean bottoms, lakes, and streams. Over thousands and even millions of years, these sediments form layer after layer of material, one on top of the other. As the layers get compressed under the weight of new layers of sediment, they eventually become rock. Typical sedimentary rocks include *sandstone*, *limestone*, *shale*, and *conglomerate*.

Sandstone rocks are made from small grains of the minerals quartz and feldspar. Sandstone typically forms in areas near ancient beaches and sand dunes. Limestone rocks are created over a long period of time in deep-water locations, such as the bottoms of oceans or deep lakes. The main mineral in limestone is calcite, which comes from the shells of sea animals and from minerals dissolved in the water. After the water evaporates, the calcite becomes sedimentary rock. Shale rock is formed from clays that are squeezed and compacted together by pressure. Conglomerates are made up of large sediments like sand and pebbles and are typically found in river beds, along a shoreline, or in valleys where pieces of rock of various sizes have gathered. The rock pieces are so large and varied in size that, in order to form rock, they are cemented together with dissolved minerals.

Metamorphic Rocks Metamorphic rocks are formed from igneous or sedimentary rocks that have been subjected to a tremendous amount of heat and pressure deep beneath Earth's surface. The pressure is so great that the rocks actually "morph" from one kind into another. By looking at some metamorphic rocks, you can actually see that the grains or crystals have been squeezed and flattened. Typical metamorphic rocks are *schist* and *gneiss*. Schist can be created from the igneous rock *basalt*, from the

sedimentary rock *shale*, or from the metamorphic rock *slate*. Slate itself is a metamorphic rock that was originally shale. Gneiss started out as the igneous rock called granite, but heat and pressure changed it. In some gneiss, you can see the flattened granite crystals.

Weathering and Erosion

Weathering and erosion are two processes by which nature works to flatten Earth's surface. *Erosion* involves the removal and transport of Earth's materials by natural agents, such as glaciers, wind, water, earthquakes, volcanoes, tornadoes, hurricanes, mud flows, and avalanches. *Weathering* is the breakup of rocks that are exposed to the atmosphere. Weathering includes both mechanical and chemical processes.

Causes Weathering and erosion take place as a result of various causes. The major ones are given here.

Freeze/Thaw Cycle Water collects in cracks in rocks. When the water freezes and expands, the crack grows larger, and eventually the rock breaks up into smaller pieces.

Wet/Dry Cycle This process occurs mostly in rocks that contain clay (i.e., shale and mudstone) when they are repeatedly wetted and dried. Clay expands when it is wet and contracts when it is dry. Eventually this process breaks up the rock into smaller parts.

Plants Plants can grow in the cracks in rocks. As their roots expand, the rocks can eventually break up. Mosses and lichens often grow on rocks and help to break the rock into smaller pieces through chemical means.

Sheet Jointing When rock layers are worn away, the pressure on the rocks below them is relieved. Those underlying rocks move up and expand. Joints or breaks in the rock occur. After some period of time, sheets of rock are loosened and fall away in a process called exfoliation. This typically occurs with domes of granite.

Wind Wind can cause larger rocks to break up into smaller particles. This happens in places where the winds are particularly strong and persistent. If winds are strong enough to carry particles like sand, larger rocks can be scoured.

Water Erosion takes place in water, such as streams where rocks are carried downstream, bumping into each other and making smaller particles. Strong rivers can carry very large boulders, which crash and smash, creating smaller pieces. Waves crashing on beaches cause erosion of the shoreline.

Chemical Processes When water is mixed with substances that form an acid, it can erode rock. Limestone is particularly vulnerable to this process, as seen in the formation of *caves* and *caverns*.

Glaciers Glaciers occur when the temperatures are so cold for so long that snow does not have a chance to completely melt. The snow accumulates and forms sheets of compressed snow or ice called glaciers. There are two categories of glaciers: *continental glaciers* and *mountain* or *alpine glaciers*.

Continental glaciers were prevalent during the Ice Ages, when massive sheets of ice covered much of the land. They spread from the poles down across the continents. At one time a large part of what is now the United States was covered by ice.

Mountain glaciers form high in the mountains and spread downward as a result of gravity.

Each type of glacier causes massive erosion through the scraping, plucking, scouring, and pushing of land material. Each produces distinctive land forms.

Continental glaciers act as sort of a conveyer belt, carrying rock and debris forward. When the glacier stops for a while and melts at its front, debris is dropped, forming a *moraine*. Continental glaciers have dammed up rivers to form lakes and have actually changed the direction of a river's flow. Alpine glaciers have distinct features as well. They scour mountains to form *cirques* (bowl-shaped depressions), block alpine rivers to form *hanging valleys*, and create the sharp peaks and characteristics shapes of *arêtes* and *horns*. Horns, like the Matterhorn in Switzerland, are pyramidal peaks that form when several cirques carve a mountain on three or more sides.

Plate Tectonics and Continental Drift

For many years, scientists discussed the theory of continental drift—the idea that the continents, as we know them now, were situated in different locations in the past and even were once combined into one large continent called Pangaea. This theory was based on fossil evidence, climatic evidence, the shapes of the continents and the way they seem to "fit together" like pieces of a gigantic jigsaw puzzle, and the similarity of geologic deposits found on different continents. But it was unclear how continental drift could take place.

Later, scientists developed the theory of *plate tectonics*, which provides the "how" for this worldwide geologic process. The theory is based on the assumption that Earth's crust is divided into several plates that move around and change over time. The places

Glaciers

where these plates bump into each other or meet are locations of very intense volcanic and earthquake activity and mountain building. The force behind this movement is *sea-floor spreading*, a process in which molten rock beneath the seabed moves upward and forms underwater ridges, then spreads laterally away from the ridges and along the ocean floor. Sea-floor spreading creates new oceanic crust that slowly moves away from the mid-ocean ridges.

Sea Floor Spreading

Further research indicated that sea-floor spreading is caused by very large convection currents within Earth's mantle. These currents cause the magma to rise up in the ocean floor, to spread outward, and to become *subducted* (sink back down), creating deep oceanic trenches. This process causes the plates on Earth's crust to move about Earth's surface. Where an oceanic plate *converges* with (bumps against) a continental plate, volcanic activity is prevalent and may create mountain ranges or volcanic islands like those in the Caribbean Sea. When two continental plates converge, mountains

Plate Tectonics

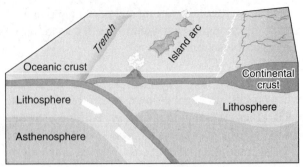

Oceanic-oceanic convergence

are formed on the land. (The Himalayas in Asia are one example.) The areas of convergence undergo tremendous stress, which is often relieved by earthquakes along fault lines.

THE ATMOSPHERE

Composition and Structure

Most of Earth's atmosphere is made up of nitrogen and oxygen.

Composition of Earth's Atmosphere

Gas	Formula	Abundance (percent by volume)
Nitrogen	N_2	78.084%
Oxygen	O_2	20.9476%
Argon	Ar	0.934%
Carbon dioxide	CO_2	0.0314%

The atmosphere is divided into various layers, determined by temperature. In the *troposphere*, the layer in which we live and in which our weather occurs, the temperature decreases dramatically as the altitude increases. The troposphere contains most of the atmosphere's mass and thus air pressure.

Above the troposphere is the *stratosphere*. Very little weather occurs in the stratosphere. Occasionally, the top portions of very large thunderstorms poke into this layer. The lower portion of the stratosphere is also influenced by the *polar jet stream* and the *subtropical jet stream*. Ozone gas molecules, which absorb ultraviolet sunlight, concentrate in this layer, causing this layer to experience a sharp rise in temperature.

The *mesosphere* contains the coldest temperatures, and the *thermosphere* has the highest temperatures. The highest temperatures come from the absorption of solar radiation by the oxygen molecules.

Layers of Earth's Atmosphere

The line along which two air masses meet is called a front. Much of our severe weather takes place at or near a front. A *cold front* is the interface in the atmosphere where a cold, dry, stable air mass displaces a warm, moist, unstable subtropical air mass. *Cirrus* clouds are found before the front reaches an area and are followed by precipitation from cumulus and cumulonimbus clouds. A *warm front* is located at the place where an advancing warm, subtropical, moist air mass replaces a retreating cold, dry, polar air mass. An *occluded* front is produced when a fast-moving cold front catches and overtakes a slower-moving warm front.

Types of Cloud Clouds are classified according to their appearance and height. Clouds form when water vapor condenses onto dust particles floating in the air. Cloud formation also occurs when warm and cold air (or land) meet.

Winds and Storms

Wind is the movement of air in our atmosphere. Wind occurs because of pressure differences between one part of the atmosphere and another. The greater the pressure difference (called the *gradient*), the stronger the wind. Atmospheric pressure is measured by *barometers* and is shown on maps as *isobars*, or areas of equal pressure.

Air Masses Air masses are large bodies of air that have similar temperature and humidity. They can be cold air masses (*polar*) or warm air masses (*tropical*). If they are formed over water, they are called *maritime* (with much moisture), and if they are formed over land, they are called *continental* (dryer).

Types of Clouds

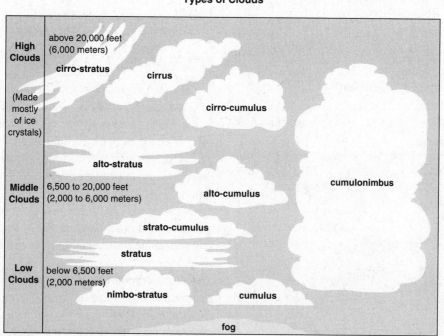

Wind Movements Wind does not necessarily travel in a straight line. In a high-pressure area (*anticyclone*), the wind flows out and around like water poured over an inverted bowl. In a low-pressure area (*cyclone*), the wind flows inward. Adding to the complexity, Earth's rotation creates another force called the *Coriolis force*. The Coriolis force deflects the air so that it moves to the right in the Northern Hemisphere and to the left in the Southern Hemisphere.

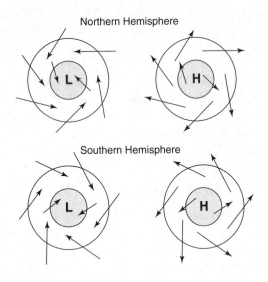

Effects of Mountains and Prevailing Winds When a prevailing wind meets up with an obstacle like a mountain range, the air rises and cools, forming clouds, and loses some moisture in the form of precipitation. This occurs on the windward side of the mountains. After the air passes over the mountain range, it descends and heats up. Thus the leeward side of a mountain range is often dry and sometimes will become a desert.

Storms Two important kinds of storms are thunderstorms and hurricanes.

Thunderstorms These occur when moist, unstable air is lifted vertically. When lifting begins, the air starts to cool until the dew point is reached and condensation takes place, forming a cumulus cloud. For a thunderstorm to form, the uplifting needs to continue until a cumulonimbus cloud forms. Within these clouds are found strong winds, downdrafts, hail, thunder, lightning, and even tornadoes.

Hurricanes These are large cyclonic storms (areas of very low pressure) that develop over the oceans in the tropics. Other names for hurricanes are cyclones, tropical cyclones, and typhoons. The center of the hurricane has the lowest air pressure. The magnitude of the pressure gradient at Earth's surface from the outside to the inside of the hurricane determines the strength of the winds. Around the clear and calm eye are bands of thunderstorms, severe rain, and winds. Damage from hurricanes comes from strong winds, flooding, and storm surge. Storm surge is created when strong winds push ocean water upward and inland, much like a huge water wall. The water crushes and often washes away many of the obstacles in its way.

Climate

Climate is the general temperature and humidity of a region over time. For example, a climate can be tropical, desert, or polar. Climate is dependent upon several factors, including

- The latitude of the area
- What air masses generally influence the area
- Proximity of oceans and ocean currents
- Location of mountain barriers
- Direction of the prevailing winds
- Altitude

Over Earth's history, the climate has changed. Sometimes the planet was warmer and more tropical; other times it was colder and covered with ice. Today scientists suspect that Earth is warming, primarily because of atmospheric pollution caused by human activities.

Climate changes have been tracked through the chemical composition of rocks, the types of animals that lived in the past, and indicators such as tree rings.

The Greenhouse Effect The greenhouse effect is a phenomenon of Earth's atmosphere. It is similar to the heat buildup in your car on a sunny day. A huge percentage of the rays of visible light from the sun pass through Earth's atmosphere, warming the planet's surface. Part of the energy is re-radiated or bounced back toward space by long-wave infrared radiation and is absorbed by carbon dioxide molecules and water vapor in the atmosphere. This energy is reflected back to Earth's surface in the form of heat. Basically, all this is a good thing; without it, Earth's surface would be too cold to allow us to survive. Even the oceans would freeze if it were not for the greenhouse effect.

However, scientists worry that as we increase the amount of carbon dioxide in the atmosphere through industrial pollutants and other particles, the greenhouse effect can intensify. A significant and persistent warming of the planet can cause long-term climate changes. An increase in chlorofluorocarbons, nitrous oxide, and methane from human activity can aggravate this situation.

The Greenhouse Effect

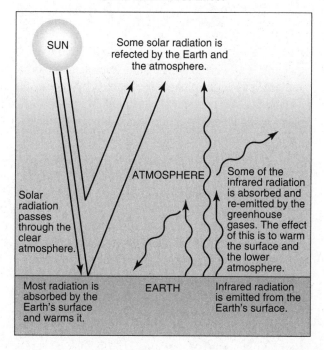

OCEANOGRAPHY AND WATER

The oceans cover 71 percent of the planet. Around the edges of the continents is the *continental shelf*. Further out is the *continental slope*, then the *rise*, and then the *ocean floor*. The shape of the continental shelf often determines the magnitude of the tides along the coast.

Tides

An ocean tide refers to the cycle of rising and falling seawater caused by the gravitational pull of the moon and the sun. The moon, being closer to Earth, has the strongest effect on tides. Tides during full and new moons, when Earth, the moon, and the sun are in a nearly straight line (*spring tides*), are the highest. When the sun is more or less perpendicular to Earth and the moon, less dramatic tides are created, called *neap tides*. Neap tides take place during the first and last quarter of the moon.

The continental slope has the steepest angle. The ocean floor contains a thin layer of basaltic rock. The ocean floor also has many interesting features, such as volcanoes, fissures, trenches, and ridges.

Surface water moves around the oceans with currents that are generated by winds. The friction between the ocean and the wind causes the water to move in the direction of the wind. Some currents are temporary and others are permanent, such as the Gulf Stream on the east coast of the United States (bringing warm water northward) and the California Current along the west coast of the United States (bringing colder water southward).

Water also moves around and up and down through the oceans as a result of temperature, density, salinity, and chemical differences between masses of water. Water that is denser (colder and/or saltier) sinks to the bottom, to be replaced by lighter

Undersea Features

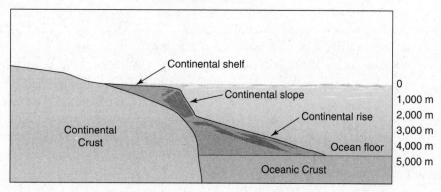

The Water Cycle
(The Hydrologic Cycle)

water. This creates internal circulation or convection and mixing of the oceans.

The Hydrologic Cycle

The diagram above shows the cycle of water as it moves between Earth's surface and the atmosphere and back. Water is stored in reservoirs, such as the ocean, lakes or rivers, glaciers, and groundwater. From these reservoirs, the water *evaporates* into the atmosphere. When conditions permit, the water in the atmosphere *condenses* and returns to Earth's surface in the form of *precipitation* like rain or snow. Water can also flow downward over the land in the form of runoff from rivers or groundwater, eventually ending up back in the ocean, where it too evaporates, condenses, and precipitates back to Earth. The process of *sublimation* can occur when water molecules from snow or ice pass directly into the atmosphere without becoming a liquid. Some 97 percent of Earth's water is held in the oceans.

Water also reaches the atmosphere through a process called *transpiration*—water loss from the stomata of plants (see the relevant section in biology). It is difficult to tell the difference between evaporation and transpiration. As a result, the word *evapotranspiration* is used to describe the entire process.

ASTRONOMY

The Solar System

Earth is the third planet from the sun and, so far as we know, the only planet that currently supports life as we know it. Earth is part of the *solar system*, a group of planets that revolve around the sun. The planets in order from the nearest to the sun to the furthest, are *Mercury*, *Venus*, *Earth*, *Mars*, *Jupiter*, *Saturn*, *Uranus*, *Neptune*, and *Pluto*. For the ASVAB, it is good to memorize this order. Pluto was recently determined not to be a planet but rather a member of a category of dwarf planets called "plutoids." So now there are only eight planets recognized by scientists.

There is a gap between the orbits of Mars and Jupiter that is filled by tens of thousands of minor planets, known as *asteroids*. A few asteroids are several hundred kilometers in diameter, but most are just a few meters across. Scientists speculate that these asteroids are part of a planet that failed to form because of Jupiter's strong gravitational pull. Some asteroids have a very elliptical orbit, taking them outside the solar system for part of their orbit. Some asteroids have entered Earth's atmosphere. Generally they burn up before hitting the planet's surface, but a few have collided with the Earth. These are called *meteorites*. You may have seen some fly through the atmosphere as bright *meteors*.

Some planets have *satellites*. Earth has one satellite, called the *moon*. Jupiter has the most satellites or moons; 39 are currently known. Saturn also has several moons and rings made up of millions of tiny particles. Mars has conditions that are most similar to Earth's, but Mars is not habitable because of its cold temperature and lack of an atmosphere that would support humans. Periodic visitors to the inner solar system are *comets*, which are believed to be made up of ice and dust particles. Comets have their own orbits. Comets can be recognized by their bright core and tail and can usually be observed for several days.

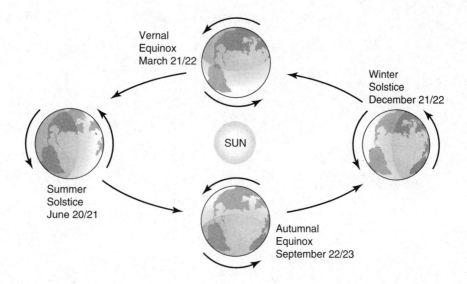

Motion of the Earth

Seasons The combination of Earth's revolution around the sun plus the tilt of Earth on its axis causes us to have *seasons*. Earth revolves around the sun in an elliptical fashion, as shown above. In January, Earth is closest to the sun, at a point called the *perihelion*. In July, it is farthest from the sun, at a point called the *aphelion*. On average, Earth is 93 million miles from the sun. The distance from sun to Earth is called an *astronomical unit*. The distance light travels in one year is called a *light-year*.

When it is summer in the Northern Hemisphere, Earth's axis points toward the sun at an angle of 23.5°, allowing the sun's rays to hit the northern part of the planet in a more direct fashion and thus raise temperatures in that part of the globe. When it is winter in the Northern Hemisphere, the axis points away from the sun, causing the rays to come in at more of an angle and thus lower temperatures in that part of the globe. The opposite happens in the Southern Hemisphere.

Day and Night Day and night are caused by Earth's rotation on its axis. One rotation occurs every 24 hours. Days are also longer in the summer and shorter in the winter because of the tilt of Earth's axis. At the *vernal* and *autumnal* equinoxes, days and nights are of equal length.

Eclipses The diagram opposite shows the lineup of the sun, Earth, and moon that results in a *lunar eclipse*. A *solar eclipse* occurs when the moon is in between the sun and Earth.

Eclipse of the Moon

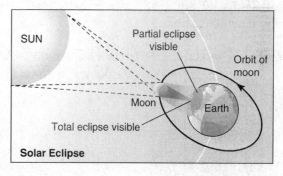

Solar Eclipse

Sun and Stars

Our Sun The *corona* is the outer layer of the sun's atmosphere. The corona extends for millions of miles, and its temperatures reach 1 million °C. The *chromosphere*, a reddish layer, is an area of rising temperatures. It appears red because hydrogen atoms are in an excited state and emit radiation near the red part of the visible spectrum. The chromosphere can be seen during solar eclipses. The next layer in is the *photo-sphere*, the part we can see, as it emits light in the visible range of wavelength. Next is the *radiative zone*, which emits radiation, and after that is the

The Structure of the Sun

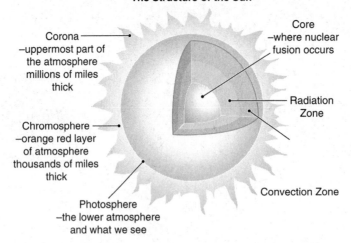

Corona —uppermost part of the atmosphere millions of miles thick

Core —where nuclear fusion occurs

Radiation Zone

Chromosphere —orange red layer of atmosphere thousands of miles thick

Convection Zone

Photosphere —the lower atmosphere and what we see

convective zone. The *core* is where nuclear fusion takes place. The temperature is about 15 million °C.

Our sun has *sunspots*, which are cool, dark patches on the surface. Individual sunspots last for one or two weeks, but they generally come in 11-year cycles. *Solar flares* are magnetic storms that appear to be an eruption of high-energy particles and gases. Solar flares are ejected thousands of miles from the surface of the sun.

Sometimes the sun's corona will emit a stream of ions called a *solar wind*. These ions can disrupt the working of artificial satellites, spacecraft, and radio communications.

Stars Stars are categorized by their composition, size, and temperature. Most stars, like our sun, are fueled by *nuclear fusion*, which converts hydrogen into helium. These stars are stable for most of their lives. When stars begin to die, they change into "red giants" or supergiants. Their hydrogen supply runs out, their core contracts, and eventually they explode into a *supernova*, later becoming a "white dwarf," a neutron star, or a black hole. Small stars like our sun will grow dim and will eventually become cold and dark "black dwarfs."

Galaxies Our solar system is part of a galaxy, a conglomeration of many stars. Our galaxy is called the Milky Way. The closest galaxy to ours is the Andromeda Galaxy. A galaxy is basically a huge group of stars and other celestial objects. Galaxies have between 100,000 and 3,000,000,000,000 (3 trillion) stars.

Chapter 8

Arithmetic Reasoning 1: The Basics

YOUR GOALS FOR THIS CHAPTER:

- Find out what arithmetic topics you need to know for the ASVAB.

- Review techniques and strategies for solving arithmetic problems.

- Study sample arithmetic problems and their step-by-step solutions.

- Measure your test readiness by taking an arithmetic quiz.

INTRODUCTION: ASVAB ARITHMETIC REASONING QUESTIONS

The ASVAB Arithmetic Reasoning test measures your ability to solve the kinds of arithmetic problems that you encounter every day at home or on the job. All of the questions on the test are word problems. That is, each one presents a real-life situation with a problem that must be solved using an arithmetic operation, such as addition, subtraction, multiplication, or addition. Arithmetic Reasoning problems also involve other arithmetic concepts, such as fractions, decimals, percents, exponents, and square roots.

It is important to do well on the Arithmetic Reasoning test because it is one of the four ASVAB tests that are used to calculate the AFQT—your military entrance score. That's why it pays to spend time reviewing topics in basic arithmetic and tackling plenty of sample ASVAB Arithmetic Reasoning questions.

The following pages offer a quick but important overview of the basic arithmetic you need to know to score well on the ASVAB. Make sure that you carefully review and test yourself on every topic covered in this section. Also make sure that you

---

ASVAB Arithmetic Reasoning Test

Number of Questions:

- Paper-and-pencil ASVAB: 30
- CAT-ASVAB: 16

Time Limit:

- Paper-and-pencil ASVAB: 36 minutes
- CAT-ASVAB: 39 minutes

Suggested Review Plan for Arithmetic

- Work through the arithmetic review at your own pace.
- Pay careful attention to the examples provided.
- After you complete the arithmetic review, take the arithmetic quiz.
- Score your quiz.
- Study any problems you answered incorrectly. Reread the corresponding review section, then try the problem again. Work until you understand how to solve the problem.

Remember that you probably won't get these exact problems on the ASVAB, but knowing how to solve them will help you do your best on the actual test.

---

learn how to use all of the problem-solving methods presented in the examples. There is much more to basic math, but if you master the core information presented here, you will be able to answer ASVAB Arithmetic Reasoning questions with relative ease. Note that your ASVAB arithmetic review should also include the next chapter of this book, which covers word problems.

ARITHMETIC REVIEW

Topics	
Place value	Decimals
Arithmetic operations	Percent
Positive and negative numbers	Finding a percent of a number
Multiplying and dividing by zero	Finding the percent increase or decrease
Factors	Exponents and square roots
Multiples	Scientific notation
Fractions	Mean, median, and mode
Mixed numbers	Graphs
Working with fractions and mixed numbers	Units of measure

Place Value

Each digit in a number occupies a particular place. In the number below, the digit 4 is in the hundreds and tens place.

32,768,445.123

The *value* of a digit in a number is that number multiplied by its place. In the number above, 4 is in the tens place. That indicates a value of $4 \times 10 = 40$, or 4 tens.

Example

23,456,789.247

2 (the first 2) is in the ten millions place

3 is in the millions place

4 (the first 4) is in the hundred thousands place

5 is in the ten thousands place

6 is in the thousands place

7 (the first 7) is in the hundreds place

8 is in the tens place

9 is in the ones place

2 is in the tenths place

4 is in the hundredths place

7 is in the thousandths place

ARITHMETIC OPERATIONS

The basic operations of arithmetic are addition, subtraction, multiplication, and division.

Addition There are two ways to show addition:

$$234 \quad \text{or} \quad 234 + 123 =$$
$$+\ 123$$

In either case, you need to add the two numbers to get the sum.

Subtraction There are also two ways to show subtraction:

$$234 \quad \text{or} \quad 234 - 123 =$$
$$-\ 123$$

Subtraction of Whole Numbers with Renaming Sometimes you have to "rename" numbers in order to complete subtraction.

$$731$$
$$-465$$

To subtract the 5 from the 1 in the ones place, "rename" the "31" in the top number as "2 tens and 11 ones." Write "2" above the 3 in the tens place and "11" above the 1 in the ones place. Subtract 5 from 11 to get 6.

$$\begin{array}{r} ^{2\ 11} \\ 7\cancel{3}\cancel{1} \\ -\ 465 \\ \hline 6 \end{array}$$

Next, you need to subtract the 6 from the (new) 2 in the tens place, so rename "72" as "6 hundreds and 12 tens." Write "6" above the 7 in the hundreds place and "12" above the 3 in the tens place. Subtract 6 from 12 to get 6. Then subtract 4 from 6 in the hundreds place to get 2, completing the subtraction.

$$\begin{array}{r} ^{6\ 12\ 11} \\ 7\cancel{3}\cancel{1} \\ -\ 465 \\ \hline 266 \end{array}$$

Multiplication Multiplication is a bit more complicated in that it can be shown in various ways.

$$10 \times 3 = 30$$
$$10(3) = 30$$
$$(10)3 = 30$$
$$10 \cdot 3 = 30$$
$$(10)(3) = 30$$

Division Division can also be shown in more than one way.

$$12 \div 3 = 4$$
$$12/3 = 4$$
$$\frac{12}{3} = 4$$

Symbols

= is equal to
≠ is not equal to
< is less than
≤ is less than or equal to
> is greater than
≥ is greater than or equal to
∥ is parallel to
≅ is approximately equal to
≈ is approximately
⊥ is perpendicular to
|−x| = x absolute value
± plus or minus
% percent
$a{:}b$ ratio of a to b or $\frac{a}{b}$

Order of Operations If addition, subtraction, multiplication, and division are all in the same mathematical statement, the order of operations (what you do first, second, third, and so on) is

1. Perform operations shown within Parentheses
2. Attend to Exponents and Square Roots
3. Perform Multiplication or Division from left to right
4. Perform Addition or Subtraction from left to right

You can use the sentence "Please Excuse My Dear Aunt Sally" to help you remember the order of operations.

HINT *Order is important!* You almost certainly will get an ASVAB math item that will require you to know order of operations rules.

Examples

$$2 + 3 \times 4 = 2 + 12$$
$$= 14$$

$$3^2 + 4(5 - 2) = 9 + 4(5 - 2)$$
$$= 9 + 4(3)$$
$$= 9 + 12$$
$$= 21$$

$$5(10 + 2) + 2 + 3 = 5(12) + 2 + 3$$
$$= 60 + 5$$
$$= 65$$

$$3^3(8 + 3) \times (15 \div 5) + (9 \times 2) - (298 + 300)$$
$$= 3^3(11) \times (3) + (18) - (598)$$
$$= 27(11) \times (3) + (18) - (598)$$
$$= 297 \times 3 + 18 - 598$$
$$= 891 + 18 - 598$$
$$= 909 - 598$$
$$= 311$$

REMINDER:
Order of Operations
1. Simplify groupings inside parentheses, brackets and braces first. Work with the innermost pair, moving outward.
2. Simplify the exponents.
3. Do the multiplication and division in order from left to right.
4. Do the addition and subtraction in order from left to right.

Rounding Often you will be asked to round to the nearest 10, 100, or 1,000 or to the nearest tenth, hundredth, or thousandth. A good way to do this is to underline the number in the place to which you are rounding. Identify the number immediately to the right. If it is 5 or greater, round up by 1. If it is 4 or less, leave it as is. Change everything to the right of that to zeros.

Examples

Round 123,756 to the nearest thousand.
Underline the number in the thousands place.

123,756

Look at the number in the place immediately to the right.
7 is greater than 5, so round the underlined number to 4 and change the rest to zeros.

Result = 124,000

Round 123,456 to the nearest thousand.
Underline the number in the thousands place.

123,456

Look at the number in the place immediately to the right.
4 is less than 5, so keep the number in the thousands place as it is and change all numbers to the right to zeros.

Result = 123,000

Round 123.456 to the nearest hundredth.
Underline the number in the hundredths place.

123.456

6 is greater than 5, so change the 5 to 6 and make all numbers to the right zeros.

Result = 123.46

Positive and Negative Numbers

Positive numbers are numbers that are greater than 0, such as +6. Negative numbers are numbers that are less than 0, such as −4. (See number line at bottom of page.)

The *absolute value* of a number is the distance of the number from 0 on a number line. For example, the absolute value of +6 is 6. The absolute value of −4 is 4.

Operations with Positive and Negative Numbers

For the ASVAB, you'll need to know how to add, subtract, multiply, and divide with positive and negative numbers.

Adding Positive and Negative Numbers To *add numbers with the same sign*, add their absolute values. The sum will have the same sign as the numbers you added.

Example

$$
\begin{array}{r}
\text{Add:} \ -4 \\
-3 \\
\hline
-7
\end{array}
$$

To add numbers with different signs, first find their absolute values. Subtract the lesser absolute value from the greater absolute value. Give the sum the same sign as the number with the greater absolute value.

Examples

$$
\begin{array}{r}
\text{Add:} \ +4 \\
-3 \\
\hline
+1
\end{array}
$$

$$
\begin{array}{r}
\text{Add:} \ +4 \\
-6 \\
\hline
-2
\end{array}
$$

> **HINT** *Know negative numbers!* Be sure to practice adding, subtracting, multiplying, and dividing using negative numbers.

Subtracting Positive and Negative Numbers Look again at the number line. (See number line at bottom of page.)

- When you subtract a positive number, you move *left* on the number line a distance equal to the absolute value of the number being subtracted.
- When you subtract a negative number, you move *right* on the number line a distance equal to the absolute value of the number being subtracted.

Examples

Subtract positive numbers (move *left* on the number line):

$$
\begin{array}{r}
+7 \\
-(+12) \\
\hline
-5
\end{array}
$$

$$
\begin{array}{r}
-7 \\
-(+12) \\
\hline
-19
\end{array}
$$

−12 −11 −10 −9 −8 −7 −6 −5 −4 −3 −2 −1 0 1 2 3 4 5 6 7 8 9 10 11 12

Subtract negative numbers (move *right* on the number line):

$$\begin{array}{r} +7 \\ -(-12) \\ \hline +19 \end{array}$$

$$\begin{array}{r} -7 \\ -(-12) \\ \hline +5 \end{array}$$

Note that when you subtract negative numbers, all you really need to do is change the sign of the number being subtracted from negative to positive, and then add.

Absolute Value A number regardless of its sign (+ or −) is called the *absolute value*. The absolute value of a number is shown as the number placed between two vertical parallel lines; for example, $|-4|$ or $|4|$. In each of these cases, the absolute value of the number is 4. When using absolute values, just ignore the sign.

Examples

$|-x| = x$
$|-5 - 6| = |-11| = 11$
$8 + |-9| = 17$

Multiplying and Dividing Negative Numbers These operations are easy if you use just one trick. To multiply or divide negative numbers, first treat all the numbers as positive and perform the operation is normally.

- If there is an *odd number of negative signs*, the answer will be negative.
- If there is an *even number of negative signs*, the number will be positive.

Examples

$(-5)(+6)(+2) = -60$

This expression has 1 negative sign. Since 1 is an odd number, the result is negative.

$(-5)(-6)(+2) = +60$

This expression has 2 negative signs. Since 2 is an even number, the result is positive.

$$\frac{-88}{-11} = +8$$

This expression has 2 negative signs. Since 2 is an even number, the result is positive.

$$\frac{-88}{+11} = -8$$

This expression has 1 negative sign. Since 1 is an odd number, the result is negative.

Subtracting Numbers within Parentheses If there is a minus sign in front of parentheses, change the sign of all the numbers within the parentheses and then add.

Examples

$11 - (+3 - 5 + 2 - 8)$

changes to

$$\begin{aligned} 11 + (-3 + 5 - 2 + 8) &= 11 + (-5 + 13) \\ &= 11 + (+8) \\ &= 19 \end{aligned}$$
$$\begin{aligned} 20 - (-3 + 5 - 2 + 8) &= 20 + (+3 - 5 + 2 - 8) \\ &= 20 + (+5 - 13) \\ &= 20 + -8 \\ &= 12 \end{aligned}$$

Multiplying and Dividing by Zero Remember the following rules:

- Any number multiplied by zero = zero.
- Zero divided by any number = zero.
- Dividing by zero is considered to be "undefined."

Examples

$45 \times 0 = 0$
$1{,}232{,}456 \times 0 = 0$
$10.45399 \times 0 = 0$
$0 \div 5 = 0$
$0 \div 500 = 0$
$7 \div 0$ is undefined
$\dfrac{32}{0}$ is undefined
$\dfrac{89}{0}$ is undefined

Factors

Factors are whole numbers that are multiplied together to create another number.

Examples

2 × 4 = 8 (2 and 4 are factors of 8.)
1 × 8 = 8 (1 and 8 are factors of 8.)
So 1, 2, 4, and 8 are all factors of 8.
1 × 32 = 32 (1 and 32 are factors of 32.)
2 × 16 = 32 (2 and 16 are factors of 32.)
8 × 4 = 32 (8 and 4 are factors of 32.)
So 1, 2, 4, 8, 16, and 32 are all factors of 32.

Types of Factors Knowing about factors will be very useful when solving equations.

Common Factors Common factors are factors that are shared by two or more numbers. As shown above, 8 and 32 share the common factors 1, 2, 4, and 8.

Multiples

Multiples of a number are found by multiplying the number by 1, 2, 3, 4, 5, 6, 7, 8, and so on. So multiples of 5 are 10, 15, 20, 25, 30, 35, 40, and so on.

Common Multiples Common multiples are multiples that are shared by two or more numbers.

Least Common Multiple The least common multiple is the smallest multiple that two numbers share. For example, 6, 12 and 18 are all common multiples of 2 and 3 because they are all evenly divisible by both 2 and 3. 6 is the least common multiple because it is the smallest number that 2 and 3 both divide evenly.

Fractions

Fractions have two numbers, a numerator and a denominator.

$$\frac{3}{6} = \frac{\text{numerator}}{\text{denominator}}$$

The denominator tells how many parts something is divided into. The numerator tells how many of those parts you have. The fraction as a whole tells the *proportion* of the parts you have to the parts there are in all.

So if a pie is divided into 8 pieces and you take 2 of them, the fraction telling the proportion of the

pie you have is $\frac{2}{8}$. The denominator (8) tells how many pieces of pie there are in all. The numerator (2) tells how many of those pieces you have.

$$\frac{2}{8} \text{ or a proportion of 2 to 8.}$$

Fractions can be positive or negative. A negative fraction is written like this:

$$-\frac{2}{8}$$

Types of Fractions For the ASVAB, you'll need to know about proper fractions, improper fractions, and mixed numbers.

Proper Fractions Fractions representing amounts smaller than 1 are called *proper fractions*. Fractions smaller than 1 have numerators that are smaller than the denominators.

Examples

$$\frac{1}{3} \qquad \frac{3}{7} \qquad \frac{5}{8} \qquad \frac{9}{11} \qquad \frac{6}{32} \qquad \frac{99}{100}$$

Improper Fractions *Improper fractions* are greater than 1. The numerator is larger than the denominator.

Examples

$$\frac{22}{3} \qquad \frac{3}{2} \qquad \frac{12}{5} \qquad \frac{17}{8} \qquad \frac{66}{3} \qquad \frac{11}{9}$$

Mixed Numbers

Expressions that include both whole numbers and fractions are called *mixed numbers*.

Examples

$$2\frac{7}{8} \qquad 3\frac{1}{2} \qquad 9\frac{2}{3} \qquad 27\frac{3}{4}$$

Renaming an Improper Fraction as a Mixed Number To rename an improper fraction as a mixed number, simply divide the numerator by the denominator.

Examples

$$\frac{22}{3} = 22 \div 3 = 7\frac{1}{3}$$

$$\frac{3}{2} = 3 \div 2 = 1\frac{1}{2}$$

$$\frac{12}{5} = 12 \div 5 = 2\frac{2}{5}$$

$$\frac{17}{8} = 17 \div 8 = 2\frac{1}{8}$$

HINT *You'll see these for sure!* On the ASVAB, you're sure to see items that require you to manipulate fractions and mixed numbers. Don't despair! Be sure to understand the procedures thoroughly and you should have no problem.

Renaming a Mixed Number as a Fraction To rename a mixed number as an improper fraction, simply multiply the whole number by the denominator and add the numerator. Put that number over the denominator.

Examples

$7\frac{1}{3}$

$3 \times 7 + 1 = 22$

Put 22 over the denominator $= \frac{22}{3}$

$2\frac{2}{5}$

$2 \times 5 + 2 = 12$

Put 12 over the denominator $= \frac{12}{5}$

Working with Fractions and Mixed Numbers

ASVAB problems are likely to require you to find equivalent fractions, reduce fractions to lowest terms, and add, subtract, multiply, and divide fractions and mixed numbers.

Finding Equivalent Fractions Two fractions are said to be *equivalent* (the same in value) if they use different numbers but represent the same proportion. For example, the following fractions are equivalent:

$$\frac{1}{2} \quad \frac{4}{8} \quad \frac{3}{6} \quad \frac{5}{10}$$

To change a fraction into an equivalent fraction, multiply or divide the numerator and denominator by the same number.

Examples

$$\frac{2 \times 3 = 6}{4 \times 3 = 12} \quad \text{so } \frac{2}{4} \text{ is equivalent to } \frac{6}{12}.$$

$$\frac{9 \div 3 = 3}{12 \div 3 = 4} \quad \text{so } \frac{9}{12} \text{ is equivalent to } \frac{1}{2}.$$

Reducing Fractions to Lowest Terms Fractions are commonly shown in their lowest terms, that is, the smallest numbers that still represent the original proportion. When a fraction is not in its lowest terms, you can reduce it to its lowest terms by dividing the numerator and denominator by the largest number that will divide into both evenly.

Examples

$\frac{40}{80}$ can be divided evenly by 40, giving a fraction of $\frac{1}{2}$

$\frac{9}{15}$ can be divided evenly by 3, giving a fraction of $\frac{3}{5}$

$\frac{21}{28}$ can be divided evenly by 7, giving a fraction of $\frac{3}{4}$

Adding and Subtracting Fractions To add and subtract fractions with *like denominators*, simply add or subtract the numerators. The result is often shown in lowest terms.

Examples

$$\frac{3}{10} + \frac{1}{10} = \frac{4}{10} = \frac{2}{5} \qquad \frac{9}{10} - \frac{1}{10} = \frac{8}{10} = \frac{4}{5}$$

To add and subtract fractions with *unlike denominators*, you first need to find equivalent fractions that all have the same denominator. To do this, you need to find the *least common denominator (LCD)*, the least common multiple of the denominators of all the fractions. Use the LCD to create new fractions equivalent to the original ones. Then add the new numerators.

Examples

$$\frac{6}{8} + \frac{1}{2} =$$

The least common denominator is 8, so $\frac{6}{8}$ does not need to be changed. However, $\frac{1}{2}$ is changed to the equivalent fraction $\frac{4}{8}$.

$$\frac{6}{8} + \frac{4}{8} = \frac{10}{8} = 1\frac{2}{8} = 1\frac{1}{4} \text{ (reduced to lowest terms)}$$

$$\frac{1}{3} + \frac{1}{2} + \frac{7}{8} =$$

Find the least common denominator. The least common multiple of 8, 3, and 2 is 24, so 24 is the least common denominator. Use the LCD to create new fractions equivalent to the original ones:

$$\frac{1}{3}+\frac{1}{2}+\frac{7}{8}=\frac{8}{24}+\frac{12}{24}+\frac{21}{24}$$
$$=\frac{41}{24}$$
$$=1\frac{17}{24}$$

Use the same approach to add and subtract positive and negative fractions. Refer to the section earlier in this math review on adding and subtracting positive and negative numbers.

Adding and Subtracting Mixed Numbers Add and subtract mixed numbers by following the same rules previously outlined. Change the fractions to equivalent fractions using the least common denominator. Add or subtract the fractions. Add or subtract the whole numbers. If the fractions add up to more than a whole number, add that to the whole numbers.

Example (Addition)

$$3\frac{3}{4}$$
$$+2\frac{1}{2}$$

changes to

$$3\frac{3}{4}$$
$$+2\frac{2}{2}$$

$$\frac{3}{4}+\frac{2}{4}=\frac{5}{4}=1\frac{1}{4}$$
3 and 2 = 5
$$5+1\frac{1}{4}=6\frac{1}{4}$$

Examples (Subtraction)

$$3\frac{3}{4}$$
$$-2\frac{1}{2}$$

changes to

$$3\frac{3}{4}$$
$$-2\frac{2}{4}$$

$$\frac{3}{4}-\frac{2}{4}=\frac{1}{4}$$
3 − 2 = 1
$$1+\frac{1}{4}=1\frac{1}{4}$$

$$3\frac{3}{4}$$
$$-5\frac{1}{2}$$

changes to

$$3\frac{3}{4}$$
$$-5\frac{2}{4}$$

Caution: Remember that subtraction means moving *left* on the number line. Start at $3\frac{3}{4}$ and move left $5\frac{2}{4}$ on the number line. The correct answer is $-1\frac{3}{4}$.

HINT *Subtracting mixed numbers: a special case.* Sometimes when you have mixed numbers, the fraction of the first mixed number is smaller than the fraction of the second mixed number. You need to rename before subtracting.

Example:

$$6\frac{1}{6}$$
$$-4\frac{3}{6}$$

Since you can't subtract $\frac{3}{6}$ from $\frac{1}{6}$ because $\frac{3}{6}$ is larger, you need to rename the whole number 6 as a 5 and rename the fraction as $\frac{7}{6}$. Now you can subtract:

$$5\frac{7}{6}$$
$$-4\frac{3}{6}$$

Subtract $\frac{3}{6}$ from $\frac{7}{6}$ to get $\frac{4}{6}$ and 4 from 5 to get 1. So the answer is $1\frac{4}{6}$. Since the fraction is not in lowest terms, change it to $\frac{2}{3}$, so the final answer is $1\frac{2}{3}$.

Multiplying Fractions To multiply fractions, just multiply the numerators and multiply the denominators. Reduce the resulting fraction to lowest terms.

Examples

$$\frac{5}{12}\times\frac{2}{3}=$$

Multiply the numerators: 5 × 2 = 10
Multiply the denominators: 12 × 3 = 36

Result: $\frac{10}{36}=\frac{5}{18}$

$$\frac{4}{5} \times \frac{7}{8} =$$

Multiply the numerators: $4 \times 7 = 28$

Multiply the denominators: $5 \times 8 = 40$

Result: $\frac{28}{40} = \frac{7}{10}$

HINT *Simplify, simplify.* Sometimes it is possible to simplify terms before performing any math operation. Take the same example that we have already completed:

$$\frac{4}{5} \times \frac{7}{8}$$

Find a number (or greatest common factor) that divides into one of the numerators and one of the denominators. In this example, the number 4 divides into 4 and into 8.

$$\frac{4}{5} \times \frac{7}{8} = \frac{{}^{1}\cancel{4}}{5} \times \frac{7}{\cancel{8}^{2}}$$

To finish the problem, multiply 1×7 and 5×2, making the final answer $\frac{7}{10}$.

Dividing Fractions To divide fractions, invert the second fraction and multiply. Reduce the result to lowest terms.

Examples

$$\frac{1}{2} \div \frac{1}{3} = \frac{1}{2} \times \frac{3}{1}$$

$$\frac{3}{2} = 1\frac{1}{2}$$

$$\frac{3}{4} \div -\left(\frac{1}{2}\right) = \frac{3}{4} \times -\left(\frac{2}{1}\right)$$

$$= -\left(\frac{6}{4}\right) = -1\frac{2}{4} = -1\frac{1}{2}$$

HINT *Dividing fractions.* Sometimes you might see division of fractions in this format:

$$\frac{\frac{1}{2}}{\frac{1}{3}}$$

Treat it the same as

$$\frac{1}{2} \div \frac{1}{3}$$

Multiplying Mixed Numbers To multiply mixed numbers, change each mixed number to a fraction and then multiply as usual. Reduce to lowest terms.

Examples

$$1\frac{1}{4} \times 2\frac{1}{2} = \frac{5}{4} \times \frac{5}{2}$$

$$= \frac{25}{8} = 3\frac{1}{8}$$

$$3\frac{2}{3} \times 9\frac{1}{2} = \frac{11}{3} \times \frac{19}{2}$$

$$= \frac{209}{6} = 34\frac{5}{6}$$

Dividing Mixed Numbers To divide mixed numbers, rename the mixed numbers as fractions and then follow the rule for dividing fractions: invert the second fraction and multiply.

Example

$$3\frac{1}{2} \div 1\frac{1}{4} = \frac{7}{2} \div \frac{5}{4}$$

$$= \frac{7}{2} \times \frac{4}{5}$$

$$= \frac{28}{10}$$

$$= 2\frac{8}{10}$$

Simplify the fraction.

$$2\frac{4}{5}$$

Decimals

A decimal is a number with one or more digits to the right of the decimal point. 0.862 and 3.12 are decimals. (Note that a zero is shown to the left of the decimal point when the decimal is between 0 and 1.)

Working with Decimals

On the ASVAB, you'll probably need to know how to add, subtract, multiply, and divide decimals. You'll also need to know how to change decimals to fractions.

Adding and Subtracting Decimals To add or subtract decimals, line up the decimal points one above the other. Then add or subtract as you would normally. Place a decimal point in the answer beneath the other decimal points.

Examples (Addition)

$$
\begin{array}{r}
14.50 \\
200.32 \\
+1{,}245.89 \\
\hline
1{,}460.71
\end{array}
$$

$$
\begin{array}{r}
14.50 \\
200.047 \\
48.0075 \\
+10.6 \\
\hline
\end{array}
$$

Add zeros in the blank decimal places to make this problem easier to tackle.

$$
\begin{array}{r}
14.5000 \\
200.0470 \\
48.0075 \\
+10.6000 \\
\hline
273.1545
\end{array}
$$

Examples (Subtraction)

$$
\begin{array}{r}
475.89 \\
-62.45 \\
\hline
413.44
\end{array}
$$

$$
\begin{array}{r}
\overset{7\;\;14}{475.\cancel{8}4} \\
-62.69 \\
\hline
413.15
\end{array}
$$
Since 9 is larger than 4, rename 84 as 7 tens and 14 ones.

Multiplying Decimals To multiply decimals, follow the usual multiplication rules. Count the number of places to the right of the decimal point in each factor. Add the numbers of places. Put that many decimal places in the answer.

Examples

12.43	(two decimal places)
× 2.4	(one decimal place)
29.832	(total of three decimal places in the answer)
6.624	(three decimal places)
× 1.22	(two decimal places)
8.08128	(total of 5 decimal places)

Dividing Decimals To divide decimals, follow the usual division rules. If the divisor (the number you are dividing by) has decimals, move the decimal point to the right as many places as necessary to make the divisor a whole number. Then move the decimal point of the dividend (the number you are dividing) that same number of places to the right. (You may

have to add some zeros to the dividend to make this work.) Put the decimal point in the answer directly above the decimal point in the dividend.

Examples

$$
12.76)\overline{58.696} = 1276)\overline{5{,}869.6}^{\;\;4.6}
$$

Note that the decimal point is moved two places to the right in each term. The decimal point in the answer is directly above the decimal point in the dividend.

$$
1.25)\overline{50} = 125)\overline{5{,}000}^{\;\;40}
$$

In this example, the decimal point is moved two places to the right in 1.25 to make 125. The dividend 50 can also be expressed as 50.00 (adding zeros), and moving the decimal point the same number of places to the right makes 5,000. No decimal point needs to be shown in the answer because the answer is a whole number.

Changing Decimals to Fractions Read the decimal and then write the fraction. Reduce the fraction to its lowest terms.

Examples

0.5 = five tenths or five over ten; $\dfrac{5}{10} = \dfrac{1}{2}$

0.66 = 66 hundredths or 66 over 100; $\dfrac{66}{100} = \dfrac{33}{50}$

0.75 = 75 hundredths or 75 over 100; $\dfrac{75}{100} = \dfrac{3}{4}$

0.006 = 6 thousandths or 6 over 1000; $\dfrac{6}{1000}$ $= \dfrac{3}{500}$

0.0006 = 6 ten thousandths or 6 over 10,000; $\dfrac{6}{10{,}000} = \dfrac{3}{5{,}000}$

Changing Fractions to Decimals To change a fraction to a decimal, divide the numerator by the denominator.

Examples

$\dfrac{1}{2} = 1 \div 2 = 0.5$

$\dfrac{3}{4} = 3 \div 4 = 0.75$

$\dfrac{6}{1{,}000} = 6 \div 1{,}000 = 0.006$

$\frac{2}{3} = 2 \div 3 = 0.6\bar{6}$ (The bar over the final 6 indicates that this is a *repeating decimal*. That means that you could keep on dividing forever and always have the same remainder.)

Percent

Percent means "out of 100" or "per hundred." For example, "70%" is read as "70 percent," meaning 70 out of 100 equal parts. Percents are useful ways to show parts of a whole. They can also be easily changed into decimals or fractions.

Working with Percent

On the ASVAB, you'll probably need to know how to change percents to decimals and fractions, and how to solve problems involving percent.

Changing Percents to Decimals Percent means "per 100." So 70% means "70 per 100," which is 70/100 or 70 ÷ 100, which is 0.70. So to change percents to decimals, delete the percent sign and place the decimal point two places to the left. You may need to add zeros.

Examples

        67% = 0.67
         6% = 0.06 (A zero was added to the left of
              the 6.)
       187% = 1.87
      0.14% = 0.0014 (Two zeros were added to the
              left of the 14.)

Changing Decimals to Percents To change decimals to percents, merely move the decimal point two places to the right and add a percent sign. (You may need to add a zero on the right.)

Examples

       0.67 = 67%
        0.4 = 40% (A zero was added to the right of
              the 4.)
       1.87 = 187%
     28.886 = 2888.6%
     0.0014 = 0.14%

Changing Percents to Fractions A percent is some number over (divided by) 100. So every percent is also a fraction with a denominator of 100. For example, $45\% = \frac{45}{100}$.

To change percents to fractions, remove the percent sign and write the number over 100. Reduce the fraction to lowest terms.

Examples

$50\% = \frac{50}{100} = \frac{5}{10} = \frac{1}{2}$

$25\% = \frac{25}{100} = \frac{1}{4}$

$30\% = \frac{30}{100} = \frac{3}{10}$

Changing Fractions to Percents To change fractions to percents, change the fraction to a decimal and then change the decimal to a percent.

Examples

$\frac{1}{2} = 0.5 = 50\%$

$\frac{1}{4} = 0.25 = 25\%$

$\frac{1}{10} = 0.10 = 10\%$

$\frac{6}{20} = \frac{3}{10} = 0.3 = 30\%$

$\frac{1}{3} = 0.33 = 33\%$

Time Savers: Fractions, Decimals, and Percents Memorizing some of these relationships might save you some calculation time.

Fraction(s)	= Decimal	= Percent (%)
$\frac{1}{100}$	0.01	1%
$\frac{1}{10}$	0.1	10%
$\frac{1}{5} = \frac{2}{10}$	0.2	20%
$\frac{3}{10}$	0.3	30%
$\frac{2}{5} = \frac{4}{10}$	0.4	40%
$\frac{1}{2} = \frac{5}{10}$	0.5	50%
$\frac{3}{5} = \frac{6}{10}$	0.6	60%
$\frac{4}{5} = \frac{8}{10}$	0.8	80%
$\frac{1}{4} = \frac{2}{8} = \frac{25}{100}$	0.25	25%
$\frac{3}{4} = \frac{75}{100}$	0.75	75%
$\frac{1}{3} = \frac{2}{6}$	$0.33\frac{1}{3}$	$33\frac{1}{3}\%$

Fraction(s)	= Decimal	= Percent (%)
$\frac{2}{3}$	$0.66\frac{2}{3}$	$66\frac{2}{3}\%$
$\frac{1}{8}$	0.125	12.5%
$\frac{3}{8}$	0.375	37.5%
$\frac{5}{8}$	0.625	62.5%
$\frac{1}{6}$	$0.16\frac{2}{3}$	$16\frac{2}{3}\%$
1	1.00	100%
1.5	1.50	150%

Finding a Percent of a Number The ASVAB Math Knowledge test and Arithmetic Reasoning test frequently include problems that ask you to find a percent of a number. Problems are often worded like this: "What is 25% of 1,000?" There are two ways you can solve this kind of problem. You can start by changing the percent into a fraction, or you can change it into a decimal.

If you change 25% into a fraction, solve the problem like this:

$$\frac{25}{100} \times 1,000 = \frac{25,000}{100} = 250$$

If you change 25% into a decimal, solve the problem like this:

$$0.25 \times 1,000 = 250$$

You should use the approach that is easiest and best for you.

Percent problems are sometimes stated in another way. For example, a problem may ask, "25 is what percent of 200?" When you see a problem like this, make it into an equation:

$$25 = x(200) \text{ where } x \text{ is the percent}$$
$$x = \frac{25}{100} = \frac{1}{8} = 0.125 = 12.5\%$$

Examples

30 is what percent of 90?

$$30 = x(90)$$
$$\frac{30}{90} = \frac{1}{3} = 0.33 = 33\%$$

You can also solve the problem by setting up a proportion:

$$\text{Some unknown percent } (x\%) = \frac{20}{25}.$$

$x\%$ is really $\frac{x}{100}$. So the equation becomes

$$\frac{x}{100} = \frac{20}{25}$$

Reduce the fraction and solve:

$$\frac{x}{100} = \frac{4}{5}$$
$$5x = 400$$
$$x = 80$$

So 20 is 80 percent of 25.

Example

30 is what percent of 120?

$$\frac{x}{100} = \frac{30}{120}$$
$$\frac{x}{100} = \frac{3}{12}$$
$$12x = 300$$
$$x = \frac{300}{12} = 25$$
$$x = 25\%$$

Finding the Percent Increase or Decrease You will likely also encounter these types of percent problems on the ASVAB. Here is an example: "What is the percent increase in Kim's salary if she gets a raise from $12,000 to $15,000 per year?" Set this up as an equation with the following structure

$$\frac{\text{Amount of change}}{\text{Original number}} = \text{percent of change}$$

Example (Increase)

For the problem above about Kim's salary, the amount of change is 3,000 because Kim's salary increased by that amount. The original number is 12,000. Plug those numbers into the formula:

$$\frac{3,000}{12,000} = \frac{3}{12} = 0.25 = 25\%$$

Kim's salary increased by 25%.

Example (Decrease)

A CD player has its price reduced from $250 to $200. What is the percent decrease? Use the same process as with the previous problem.

$$\frac{\text{Amount of change}}{\text{Original number}} = \text{percent of change}$$

The amount of change (decrease) is 50 (250 minus 200). The original number (original price) is \$250. Plug these numbers into the formula:

$$\frac{50}{250} = \frac{5}{25} = \frac{1}{5} = 0.20$$

The CD price decreased by 20%.

Exponents and Square Roots

Arithmetic problems on the ASVAB may deal with exponents and square roots. One or two may even involve scientific notation, which is a way of writing large numbers using exponents.

Exponents An *exponent* is a number that tells how many times another number is multiplied by itself. In the expression 4^3, the 3 is an exponent. It means that 4 is multiplied by itself three times or $4 \times 4 \times 4$. So $4^3 = 64$. The expression 4^2 is read "4 to the second power" or "4 squared." The expression 4^3 is read "4 to the third power" or "4 cubed." The expression 4^4 is read "4 to the fourth power." In each of these cases, the exponent is called a "power" of 4. In the expression 5^2 ("5 to the second power" or "5 squared"), the exponent is a "power" of 5.

Examples

$3^5 = 3 \times 3 \times 3 \times 3 \times 3 = 243$
$6^2 = 6 \times 6 = 36$

Negative Exponents Exponents can also be negative. To interpret negative exponents, follow this pattern:

$$2^{-3} = \frac{1}{2^3} \quad \text{or} \quad \frac{1}{8}$$

Examples

$$3^{-2} = \frac{1}{3^2} = \frac{1}{9}$$

$$4^{-3} = \frac{1}{4^3} = \frac{1}{64}$$

Multiplying Numbers with Exponents To multiply numbers with exponents, multiply out each number and then perform the operation.

Examples

$3^4 \times 2^3 = (3 \times 3 \times 3 \times 3) \times (2 \times 2 \times 2)$
$= 81 \times 8$
$= 648$

$2^9 \times 12^2 =$
$(2 \times 2 \times 2 \times 2 \times 2 \times 2 \times 2 \times 2 \times 2) \times (12 \times 12)$
$= 512 \times 144$
$= 73,728$

Square Roots The *square* of a number is the number times the number. The square of 2 is $2 \times 2 = 4$. The *square root* of a number is the number whose square equals the original number. One square root of 4 (written $\sqrt{4}$) is 2, since $2 \times 2 = 4$. −2 is also a square root of 4, since $-2 \times -2 = 4$.

Examples

$\sqrt{1} = 1$ or −1
$\sqrt{4} = 2$ or −2
$\sqrt{9} = 3$ or −3
$\sqrt{16} = 4$ or −4
$\sqrt{25} = 5$ or −5
$\sqrt{36} = 6$ or −6
$\sqrt{49} = 7$ or −7
$\sqrt{64} = 8$ or −8
$\sqrt{81} = 9$ or −9
$\sqrt{100} = 10$ or −10
$\sqrt{121} = 11$ or −11
$\sqrt{144} = 12$ or −12
$\sqrt{169} = 13$ or −13
$\sqrt{196} = 14$ or −14
$\sqrt{225} = 15$ or −15

REMINDER
Watch the signs! Remember that a negative number multiplied by itself results in a positive number.

Scientific Notation

For convenience, very large or very small numbers are sometimes written in what is called *scientific notation*. In scientific notation, a number is written as the product of two factors. The first factor is a number greater than or equal to 1 but less than 10. The second factor is a power of 10. (Recall that in an expression such as 10^3, which is read "10 cubed" or "10 to the third power," the exponent 3 is a power of 10.)

For example, here is how to write the very large number 51,000,000 in scientific notation. This number can also be written 51,000,000.00. Move the decimal point to the left until you have a number between 1 and 10. If you move the decimal point 7 places to the left, you have the number 5.1000000 or 5.1. Since you moved the decimal point 7 places, you would have to multiply 5.1 by 10^7 (a power of 10) to recreate the original number. So in scientific notation, the original number can be written as 5.1×10^7.

For very small numbers, move the decimal point to the right until you have a number between 1 and 10. Then count the decimal places between the new position and the old position. This time, since you moved the decimal point to the right, the power of 10 is a negative. That is, the exponent is a negative number.

Examples (Large Numbers)

698,000,000,000 can be written 6.98×10^{11}
45,000,000 can be written 4.5×10^7

Examples (Small Numbers)

0.00000006 can be written 6×10^{-8}
0.0000016 can be written 1.6×10^{-6}
To change back to the original number from scientific notation, merely move the decimal point the number of places indicated by the "power of 10" number.

Example (Large Numbers)

2.35×10^5 becomes 235,000. The decimal point moved 5 places to the right.

6×10^8 becomes 600,000,000. The decimal point moved 8 places to the right.

Example (Small Numbers)

2.3×10^{-4} becomes 0.00023. The decimal point moved 4 places to the left.

7×10^{-12} becomes 0.000000000007. The decimal point moved 12 places to the left.

Multiplying in Scientific Notation To multiply numbers written in scientific notation, multiply the numbers and add the powers of 10.

Examples

$(2 \times 10^8) \times (3.1 \times 10^2) = 6.2 \times 10^{10}$

$(3.3 \times 10^{12}) \times (4 \times 10^{-3}) = 13.2 \times 10^9$

Here you are adding a 12 and a −3, giving you 9 for the power of 10. But remember the rule that the decimal point must be after a number that is between 1 and 9,

so you have to move the decimal place one more place to the left to put it after the 1, and you have to increase the power of 10 accordingly. So the final result of the multiplication is 1.32×10^{10}.

Dividing in Scientific Notation To divide in scientific notation, divide the numbers and subtract the powers of 10.

Examples

$$(9 \times 10^7) \div (3 \times 10^3) = 3 \times 10^4$$

Here you divide 9 by 3 (= 3), and you subtract the exponent 3 from the exponent 7 to get the new exponent 4.

$$(1.0 \times 10^4) \div (4 \times 10^{-3}) = 0.25 \times 10^7$$

Since the number in the first position must be between 1 and 9, move the decimal to the right one place and decrease the exponent accordingly, so the final result is 2.5×10^6.

Mean, Median, and Mode

The mean, median, and mode are mathematical measures that are used to understand and describe a given set of numbers.

Mean or Average The *mean* of a set of numbers is the average. Add the numbers and divide by the number of numbers.

Examples

What is the mean of the numbers 2, 4, 7, 4, and 5? The sum is 22. Since there are 5 numbers, divide 22 by 5 to get a mean or average of 4.4.

What is the mean of the numbers 3, 4, 2, 6, 7, 12, 56, and 104?
The sum is 194. There are 8 numbers, so divide 194 by 8 to get 24.25.

Median Order a set of numbers from least to greatest. If there is an odd number of numbers, the *median* is the number in the middle of that sequence of numbers. If there is an even number of numbers, the median is the mean or average of the two middle numbers.

Examples

What is the median of the following numbers?

14, 999, 75, 102, 456, 19, 10

Reorder the numbers from least to greatest: 10, 14, 19, 75, 102, 456, 999

The middle number is 75, so that is the median.
What is the median of the following numbers?

15, 765, 65, 890, 12, 1, 10

Reorder the numbers from least to greatest: 1, 12, 15, 65, 765, 890

Since there is an even number of numbers, find the average of the middle two numbers.

15 + 65 = 80
80 ÷ 2 = 40
40 is the median

HINT *When the median helps.* If there are extremes (a few very high or very low numbers) in a set of numbers, the median is a good way to describe the "central tendency" of the number set.

Mode The *mode* of a set of numbers is the number that appears most frequently in that set.

Example

What is the mode of the following set of numbers?

12, 14, 15, 15, 15, 17, 18

The number 15 appears most often in this set, so it is the mode of the set.

Graphs

Often it is helpful to represent numbers in a visual form called a *graph*. The most common types of graphs are circle graphs, bar graphs, and line graphs. You probably won't be asked to construct such graphs on the ASVAB, but you are likely to have to interpret one or more of them on the math and/or science sections of the test.

Types of Graphs Some of the most common types of graphs are circle graphs, bar graphs, and line graphs.

Circle Graph This kind of graph uses a circle divided into parts to show fractional or percentage relationships.

Example

In a survey at a local high school, students were asked to name their favorite lunch food. The results of that survey are shown in the circle graph below.

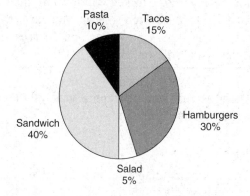

Favorite Lunch Food of High School Students

Questions such as the following are typical.

- Which food was most (or least) popular with the students? (Most: sandwich; least: salad)
- Which two food selections of the students make up 50% of the total? (Sandwich and pasta: 40% and 10% = 50%)
- What is the ratio of the students who selected sandwiches to the students who selected hamburgers? (4:3)
- If the total number of students surveyed was 2,500, how many chose salad as their favorite lunch? (125; 2,500 × 0.05 = 125)

Bar Graph This kind of graph uses bars to provide a visual comparison of different quantities.

Example

The following bar graph compares the number of different types of sandwiches sold on Monday at a certain sandwich shop.

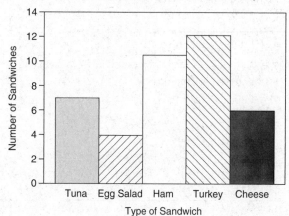

Number of Sandwiches Sold on Monday

Questions such as the following are typical.

- Which kind of sandwich did the store sell the most of on Monday? (Turkey)
- How many more turkey sandwiches than egg salad sandwiches were sold on Monday? (8)
- How many tuna sandwiches and cheeses sandwiches were sold on Monday? (13)

Line Graph This kind of graph is generally used to show change over time.

Example

The following line graph shows the change in attendance at this year's football games.
Questions such as the following are typical.

- How many more people attended game 2 than game 1? (2,000)

Attendance at This Year's Football Games

- Which game had the highest attendance? (Game 7)
- How many people attended the last game of the year? (6,000)

Units of Measure

If you don't know the following units of measure, you just need to memorize them.

Customary System

Length
12 inches (in.) = 1 foot (ft)
3 feet = 1 yard (yd)
36 inches = 1 yard
5,280 feet = 1 mile (mi)

Area
1 square foot (ft^2) = 144 square inches ($in.^2$)
9 square feet = 1 square yard (yd^2)

Weight
16 ounces (oz) = 1 pound (lb)
2,000 pounds = 1 ton (t)

Liquid Volume
2 cups (c) = 1 pint (pt)
2 pints = 1 quart (qt)
4 quarts = 1 gallon (gal)

Time
60 seconds = 1 minute
60 minutes = 1 hour
24 hours = 1 day
7 days = 1 week
4 weeks = 1 month
12 months = 1 year
52 weeks = 1 year
10 years = 1 decade

Metric System

Length
100 centimeters (cm) = 1 meter (m)
1,000 meters = 1 kilometer (km)

Volume
1,000 milliliters (mL) = 1 liter (L)

Mass
1,000 grams (g) = 1 kilogram (kg)
1,000 kilograms = 1 metric ton

Converting Between Systems
1 meter ≈ 39.37 inches
1 kilometer ≈ 0.62 mile
1 centimeter ≈ 0.39 inch
1 kilogram ≈ 2.2 pounds
1 liter ≈ 1.057 quarts
1 gram ≈ 0.035 ounce

ARITHMETIC QUIZ

Circle the letter that represents the correct answer. Check your answers with those on page 204. If any of your answers were wrong, go back and study the relevant section of the math review.

1. Add:

   $336 + 789$

   A. 1,025
   B. 1,110
   C. 1,125
   D. 1,126

2. Subtract:

   $\begin{array}{r} 475 \\ -397 \\ \hline \end{array}$

   A. 83
   B. 82
   C. 78
   D. 68

3. Which of the following symbols means "is less than"?
   A. $\approx$
   B. $\neq$
   C. $<$
   D. $\perp$

4. Which of the following means to multiply 3 times 6?
   A. $(3)(6)$
   B. $3 \div 6$
   C. $\dfrac{3}{6}$
   D. 3 ± 6

5. $3 + 5(6 - 3) =$
   A. 18
   B. 24
   C. 30
   D. 32

6. $4 + (19 - 4^2)^2 =$
   A. −240
   B. 13
   C. 85
   D. 240

7. $2^3 - (2 \times 3) + (-4) =$
   A. −2
   B. 7
   C. 17
   D. 19

8. $3(10 - 6)(3 - 7) =$
   A. −48
   B. −43
   C. 18
   D. 48

9. Round to the nearest thousand:

   34,578

   A. 34,000
   B. 34,080
   C. 34,600
   D. 35,000

10. Round to the nearest tenth:

    12.8892

    A. 12.0
    B. 12.890
    C. 12.9
    D. 13.0

11. $4 + (-8) + 2 + (-6) =$
    A. 10
    B. 4
    C. −8
    D. −20

12. Subtract:

    $\begin{array}{r} 18 \\ --2 \\ \hline \end{array}$

    A. 20
    B. 16
    C. 12
    D. −16

13. Subtract:

$$\begin{array}{r} -15 \\ - \underline{-12} \end{array}$$

   A. −27
   B. −3
   C. 3
   D. 27

14. $(-5)(-3)(-2) =$
   A. 30
   B. 13
   C. −10
   D. −30

15. $(14)(2)(0) =$
   A. 28
   B. 16
   C. 0
   D. −28

16. Reduce to lowest terms:

$$\frac{18}{36} =$$

   A. $\frac{1}{4}$

   B. $\frac{1}{2}$

   C. $\frac{2}{4}$

   D. $\frac{3}{6}$

17. Rename this fraction as a mixed number:

$$\frac{22}{7} =$$

   A. $2\frac{4}{7}$

   B. $2\frac{6}{7}$

   C. $3\frac{1}{7}$

   D. 4

18. Rename this mixed number as a fraction:

$$5\frac{3}{4} =$$

   A. $\frac{4}{15}$

   B. $\frac{15}{4}$

   C. $\frac{19}{4}$

   D. $\frac{23}{4}$

19. Add the following fractions:

$$\frac{1}{2} + \frac{3}{4} + \frac{3}{12} =$$

   A. $\frac{7}{24}$

   B. $\frac{7}{12}$

   C. $1\frac{1}{2}$

   D. $1\frac{3}{4}$

20. Subtract the following fractions:

$$\frac{3}{4} - \frac{1}{2} =$$

   A. $\frac{1}{4}$

   B. $\frac{1}{2}$

   C. $\frac{4}{4}$

   D. 1

21. Subtract the following fractions:

$$3\frac{1}{2}$$
$$-2\frac{7}{8}$$

 A. $-1\frac{7}{8}$

 B. $\frac{5}{8}$

 C. $\frac{7}{8}$

 D. $1\frac{7}{8}$

22. Multiply the following fractions:

$$\frac{3}{8}\times\frac{9}{18} =$$

 A. $\frac{27}{144}$

 B. $\frac{3}{16}$

 C. $\frac{1}{5}$

 D. $\frac{78}{54}$

23. Divide the following fractions:

$$\frac{1}{9}\div\frac{2}{3} =$$

 A. $\frac{2}{27}$

 B. $\frac{1}{6}$

 C. $\frac{3}{11}$

 D. $\frac{2}{6}$

24. Multiply the following mixed numbers:

$$2\frac{3}{4}\times4\frac{1}{3} =$$

 A. $8\frac{1}{3}$

 B. $8\frac{2}{3}$

 C. $11\frac{11}{12}$

 D. $12\frac{1}{6}$

25. Divide the following mixed numbers:

$$3\frac{1}{3}\div4\frac{2}{9} =$$

 A. $3\frac{1}{7}$

 B. $\frac{45}{57}$

 C. $\frac{16}{21}$

 D. $\frac{15}{19}$

26. Change the following fraction to a decimal:

$$\frac{3}{4} =$$

 A. 0.34
 B. 0.50
 C. 0.75
 D. 0.80

27. Change the following decimal to a fraction:

0.008 =

 A. $\frac{8}{50}$

 B. $\frac{8}{100}$

 C. $\frac{4}{100}$

 D. $\frac{1}{125}$

28. Add the following decimals:

    $12.51 + 3.4 + 6.628 =$

    A. 21.52
    B. 22.528
    C. 22.538
    D. 223.258

29. Subtract the following decimals:

    $23.51 - 20.99 =$

    A. 3.62
    B. 3.49
    C. 2.52
    D. 2.42

30. Divide the following decimals.

    $40.896 \div 12.78 =$

    A. 5.6
    B. 4.4
    C. 3.6
    D. 3.2

31. Change the following percent to a decimal:

    9%

    A. 0.009
    B. 0.09
    C. 0.9
    D. 9.0

32. Change the following decimal to a percent:

    0.32

    A. 32%
    B. 3.2%
    C. 0.32%
    D. 0.032%

33. What is 75% of 1,250?
    A. 937.5
    B. 950
    C. 975
    D. 1000

34. 25 is what percent of 200?
    A. 10%
    B. 12%
    C. 12.5%
    D. 15%

35. Write the following number in scientific notation:

    $0.0002392 =$

    A. $2,392 \times 10^{-7}$
    B. 23.92×10^{-5}
    C. 23×10^{5}
    D. 2.392×10^{-4}

36. Multiply:

    $(2.3 \times 10^{5}) \times (7.1 \times 10^{-3}) =$

    A. 9.4×10^{-8}
    B. 9.4×10^{8}
    C. 16.33×10^{2}
    D. 16.33×10^{8}

37. What is the square root of 100?
    A. 0.05
    B. 5
    C. 10
    D. 75

38. What is the mean (average) of the following set of numbers?

    12 14 18 22 45 78

    A. 27.5
    B. 31.5
    C. 32.0
    D. 45.5

39. Last month, the librarian at a certain library kept track of all books checked out. The graph below shows the results by type of book. What percentage of all the books checked out last month were travel books?

A. 15.3%
B. 15%
C. 8%
D. 7.5%

40. How many feet are in 2 miles?
A. 10,000
B. 10,560
C. 11,954
D. 16,439

41. How many square inches are in 3 square feet?
A. 144
B. 278
C. 432
D. 578

42. How many quarts are in 3 gallons?
A. 3
B. 9
C. 12
D. 16

43. How many meters are in 4 kilometers?
A. 40
B. 400
C. 4,000
D. 40,000

44. How many grams are in 2.5 kilograms?
A. 250
B. 2,500
C. 25,000
D. 250,000

45. 4 kilograms is about how many pounds?
A. 8.8
B. 9
C. 9.6
D. 10.6

ARITHMETIC QUIZ—ANSWERS

Number	Answer	Number	Answer
1.	C	24.	C
2.	C	25.	D
3.	C	26.	C
4.	A	27.	D
5.	A	28.	C
6.	B	29.	C
7.	A	30.	D
8.	A	31.	B
9.	D	32.	A
10.	C	33.	A
11.	C	34.	C
12.	A	35.	D
13.	B	36.	C
14.	D	37.	C
15.	C	38.	B
16.	B	39.	D
17.	C	40.	B
18.	D	41.	C
19.	C	42.	C
20.	A	43.	C
21.	B	44.	B
22.	B	45.	A
23.	B		

Chapter 9

Arithmetic Reasoning 2: Word Problems

YOUR GOALS FOR THIS CHAPTER:

- **Find out what kinds of arithmetic word problems are on the ASVAB.**

- **Learn effective procedures for solving arithmetic word problems.**

- **Study sample word problems and their step-by-step solutions.**

- **Measure your test readiness by taking a word problem quiz.**

INTRODUCTION: ASVAB ARITHMETIC WORD PROBLEMS

What is a word problem? Basically it is a description of a real-life situation that requires a mathematical solution. To solve a word problem, you need to translate the situation into mathematical terms and then calculate the answer.

All of the questions on the ASVAB Arithmetic Reasoning test are word problems. To do well, you need to learn good word problem–solving skills. The following pages will show you many different kinds of arithmetic word problems. For each kind, you'll learn how to translate the facts of the problem into mathematical terms. Then you'll see how to use those terms to set up an equation. Finally, you'll see how to solve that equation for the missing piece of information that you're looking for. To start your study program, look at the following word problem-solving tips.

How to Tackle Word Problems

Here are some helpful suggestions for dealing with word problems.

- Read the problem all the way through before you start making any calculations. That way, you will better understand what the problem is about and what you are supposed to find out.

- Be sure you understand what the problem is asking. Are you supposed to find a distance? How fast something is moving? When someone will arrive at point A? How much something costs? How many items you can buy if you have a certain amount of money? How much older Kim is than Kay? Draw a picture if that helps.
- List the information that the problem gives you. Note any units of measure (meters, pounds, feet per second, and the like).
- Look for key words in the problem that define relationships or indicate what mathematical operation you need to use. (See the list of key words that follows.)
- Figure out what unit of measure you must use to express your answer. Cubic meters? Centimeters per second? Dollars? Minutes? Number of items?
- Weed out unnecessary information that will not help you solve the problem.
- Use the information you have gathered to create an equation to help you solve the problem.
- Solve the equation.

Key Words

Many word problems contain key words that tell you what mathematical operation you need to use to solve the problem. It pays to know these key words, so be sure you study the following list.

These key words tell you to *add*.

Key Words	Example Phrases
Increased by	If the temperature is increased by
More than	If the bicycle costs $75 more than
Sum	If the sum of the paychecks is
Total	The total number of payments equals
Added	If *a* is added to *b*
Plus	If the interest plus the principal is
Combined	If the volume of the cube is combined with
In all	How many pounds in all
Successive	The cost of eight successive phone bills

These key words tell you to *subtract*.

Key Words	Example Phrases
Less than	The interest payment was less than
Difference	The difference between the time it takes to
Are left	How many pieces of pie are left if
Fewer than	If there are 15 fewer scholarships this year than
Minus	Some number minus 36
Reduced by	If the federal budget is reduced by

These key words tell you to *multiply*.

Key Words	Example Phrases
Times	There are 3 times as many red tiles as blue tiles
Product	The product of *a* and *b* is
Increased by a factor of	If the speed is increased by a factor of
Decreased by a factor of	If the temperature is decreased by a factor of
At	If you buy 12 cameras at $249 each
Per	If a ferry can carry 20 cars per trip, how many cars can it carry in six trips?
Total	If you spend $10 a week on movies for a total of 5 weeks
Twice	The house covers twice as many square feet as

These key words tell you to *divide*.

Key Words	Example Phrases
Quotient	What is the quotient if the numerator is 500?
Divided equally among	If 115 tickets are divided equally among 5 groups
Divided into equal groups	If the students were divided into 6 equal groups
Ratio of	If the ratio of oxygen to hydrogen is
Per	If a ferry can carry 24 cars per trip, how many trips will it take to carry 144 cars?
Percent	What percent of 100 is 30?
Half	If half the profits go to charity, then how much

These key words tell you to use an *equal sign*.

Key Words	Example Phrases
Is	If the total bill is $19.35
Sells for	If the car sells for $26,000
Gives	If multiplying a^2 and b^2 gives c^2

SETTING UP AN EQUATION AND SOLVING FOR AN UNKNOWN

Before you start tackling word problems, you need to know how to set up an equation and solve for an unknown. For each problem, you will be given certain pieces of information ("*what you know*"). You first need to translate this information into mathematical terms. Then you can use those terms to set up an equation. An *equation* is nothing more than a mathematical expression that indicates that one mathematical term is equal to another. The terms in an equation are shown on opposite sides of an equal sign. The missing piece of information that you are looking for ("*what you need to find*") is called the *unknown*. In your equation, you can represent an unknown by a letter such as x or *a*.

In the pages that follow, you will see how to set up equations for many different kinds of word problems. The process of solving an equation for an unknown is pretty simple. Work through these examples until you get perfectly comfortable with the process.

Examples

Solve for x.

$$25x = 200$$

This equation is read, "25 times some unknown number x equals 200." Your task is to determine what number x is. Here is how to solve this equation.

Divide both sides of the equation by 25:

$$\frac{25x}{25} = \frac{200}{25}$$
$$x = \frac{200}{25}$$
$$x = 8$$

Solve for x:

$$\frac{x}{5} = \frac{3}{45}$$

To solve this type of problem, cross-multiply (45 times x and 3 times 5).

$$45x = 15$$
$$x = \frac{15}{45} = \frac{1}{3} = 0.33$$

Solve for x:

$$\frac{10}{x} = \frac{50}{350}$$

To solve this problem, cross-multiply (10 times 350 and 50 times x).

$$50x = 3,500$$
$$x = 70$$

To check your answer, merely substitute 70 back into the equation and see if it works. $\frac{10}{70} = \frac{50}{350}$ Reduce the fractions to $\frac{1}{7} = \frac{1}{7}$ or cross-multiply (10 times 350 and 70 times 50), making $3,500 = 3,500$. Either way, you are correct.

TYPES OF ASVAB ARITHMETIC WORD PROBLEMS

In the pages that follow, you will learn about many different kinds of word problems that you are likely to see on the ASVAB Arithmetic Reasoning test. For each kind, you will see how to use the information you are given to set up an equation. Then you will see how to solve the equation for the unknown that is the answer to the problem. The following chart shows the different kinds of word problems discussed in this chapter.

Arithmetic Word Problem Types
Simple interest
Compound interest
Ratio and proportion
Motion
Percent
Percent change
Numbers and number relationships
Age
Measurement

Simple Interest

Interest is an amount paid for the use of money. *Interest rate* is the percent paid per year. *Principal* is the amount of money on which interest is paid. *Simple interest* is interest that is computed based only on the principal, the interest rate, and the time. To calculate simple interest, use this formula:

$$\text{Interest} = \text{principal} \times \text{rate} \times \text{time}$$
$$I = prt$$

Examples

Martina has $300 in a savings account that pays simple interest at a rate of 3% per year. How much interest will she earn on that $300 if she keeps it in the account for 5 years?

Procedure

What must you find? Amount of simple interest
What are the units? Dollars
What do you know? Rate = 3% per year, time = 5 years, principal = $300
Create an equation and solve.

$$I = (\$300)(0.03)(5)$$
$$I = \$45$$

Five years ago, Robin deposited $500 in a savings account that pays simple interest. She made no further deposits, and today the account is worth $750. What is the rate of interest?

Procedure

What must you find? Rate of simple interest
What are the units? Percent per year
What do you know? Interest = $250 ($750 − $500); principal = $500; time = 5 years

Create an equation and solve.

$$250 = (500)(x)(5)$$
$$250 = 2,500x$$
$$\frac{250}{2500} = x$$
$$x = \frac{250}{2,500} = 0.10 \text{ or } 10\%$$

Compound Interest

Compound interest is the interest paid on the principal and also on any interest that has already been paid. To calculate compound interest, you can use the formula $I = prt$, but you must calculate the interest for each time period and then combine them for a total.

Example

Ricardo bought a $1,000 savings bond that earns 5% interest compounded annually. How much interest will he earn in two years?

Procedure

What must you find? Amount of compound interest
What are the units? Dollars
What do you know? Principal = $1,000; rate = 5%; time = 2 years
Create an equation and solve.

To find the compound interest, calculate the amount earned in the first year. Add that amount to the principal, then calculate the interest earned in the second year. Total the amount of interest earned in the two years.

Year 1:

$$I = prt$$
$$I = (\$1,000)(0.05)(1)$$
$$I = \$50$$

New principal = $1,050

Year 2:

$$I = prt$$
$$I = (\$1,050)(0.05)(1)$$
$$I = \$52.50$$

So the total compound interest paid in two years is $50 + $52.50 = $102.50.

Ratio and Proportion

On the ASVAB, you will almost certainly encounter word problems that will require you to work with ratios and proportions.

Examples

Kim reads an average of 150 pages per week. At that rate, how many weeks will it take him to read 1,800 pages?

Procedure

What must you find? How long it will take to read 1,800 pages.
What are the units? Weeks
What do you know? 150 pages read each week; 1,800 pages to be read
Set up a proportion and solve.

$$\frac{\text{Number of pages}}{1 \text{ week}} = \frac{\text{number of pages}}{x \text{ weeks}}$$

Substitute values into the equation.

$$\frac{150 \text{ pages}}{1 \text{ week}} = \frac{1,800 \text{ pages}}{x \text{ weeks}}$$

Cross-multiply:

$$150x = 1,800$$
$$x = 12 \text{ weeks}$$

It takes 8 hours to fill a swimming pool that holds 3,500 gallons of water. At that rate, how many hours will it take to fill a pool that holds 8,750 gallons?

Procedure

What must you find? How long it will take to fill the 8,750-gallon pool
What are the units? Hours
What do you know? Number of hours for 3,500 gallons
Set up a proportion and solve.

$$\frac{\text{Number of gallons}}{\text{Number of hours}} = \frac{\text{number of gallons}}{\text{number of hours}}$$

$$\frac{3,500 \text{ gallons}}{8 \text{ hours}} = \frac{8,750 \text{ gallons}}{x}$$

Cross-multiply:

$$3,500x = (8)(8,750)$$
$$x = 20 \text{ hours}$$

An airplane travels the 1,700 miles from Phoenix to Nashville in 2.5 hours. Flying at the same speed, the plane could travel the 2,550 miles from Phoenix to Boston in how many hours?

Procedure

What must you find? Time it would take to fly 2,550 miles
What are the units? Hours
What do you know? The plane traveled 1,700 miles in 2.5 hours
Set up a proportion and solve.

$$\frac{\text{Number of miles}}{\text{Number of hours}} = \frac{\text{number of miles}}{\text{number of hours}}$$

Substitute values.

$$\frac{1,700 \text{ miles}}{2.5 \text{ hours}} = \frac{2,550 \text{ miles}}{x}$$

Cross-multiply:

$1,700x = (2.5)(2,550)$
$1,700x = 6,375$
$x = 3.75$ hours

Motion

Motion problems deal with how long it will take to get from point a to point b if you are traveling at a certain steady rate. To solve them, use this formula:

$$\text{Distance} = \text{rate} \times \text{time}$$
$$d = rt$$

Example

If a racing boat travels at a steady rate of 80 miles per hour, how many miles could it travel in 3.5 hours?

Procedure

What must you find? Distance traveled in 3.5 hours
What are the units? Miles
What do you know? Rate = 80 miles per hour; time = 3.5 hours

Create an equation and solve.

$d = rt$

Substitute values into the formula:

$d = (80)(3.5)$

$d = 280$ miles

Percent

There are likely to be word problems involving percent on both the Arithmetic Reasoning and Math Knowledge tests of the ASVAB.

Examples

Lilly's bill at a restaurant is $22.00, and she wants to leave a 15% tip. How much money should her tip be?

Procedure

What must you find? Amount of tip
What are the units? Dollars and cents
What do you know? Total bill = $22.00; Percent of tip = 15

Create an equation and solve.

Tip = 15% × 22.00

Substitute and solve.

$t = (0.15)(22.00)$
$t = \$3.30$

Frederick earns $1,500 per month at his job, but 28% of that amount is deducted for taxes. What is his monthly take-home pay?

Procedure

What must you find? Monthly take-home pay
What are the units? Dollars and cents
What do you know? Monthly pay before taxes = $1,500; percent deducted = 28%

Create an equation and solve.

Take-home pay is 1,500 minus 28% × 1,500.

$T = 1,500 - (1,500 \times 0.28)$
$T = 1,500 - (420)$
$T = \$1,080$

40 is 80% of what number?

Procedure

What must you find? Number of which 40 is 80%
What are the units? Numbers

What do you know? 40 is 80% of some larger number

Create an equation and solve.

$$40 = 0.8x$$
$$0.8x = 40$$
$$x = \frac{40}{0.8}$$
$$x = 50$$

Percent Change

Some ASVAB word problems ask you to calculate the percent change from one number or amount to another.

Examples

Samantha now earns $300 per month working at a cosmetics store, but starting next month her monthly salary will be $375. Her new salary will be what percent increase over her current salary?

Procedure

What must you find? Percent change from current salary
What are the units? Percent
What do you know? Current pay = $300/month; pay after the raise = $375/month
Create an equation and solve.

$$\text{Percent change} = \frac{\text{amount of change}}{\text{starting point}}$$

Substitute values and solve:

$$\text{Percent change} = \frac{(375 - 300)}{300}$$

$$\text{Percent change} = \frac{75}{300}$$

$$\text{Percent change} = 0.25 \text{ or } 25\%$$

On his sixteenth birthday, Brad was 60 inches tall. On his seventeenth birthday, he was 65 inches tall. What was the percent increase in Brad's height during the year?

Procedure

What must you find? Percent change in height
What are the units? Percent
What do you know? Starting height = 60 inches; height after a year = 65 inches

Create an equation and solve.

$$\text{Percent change} = \frac{\text{amount of change}}{\text{starting point}}$$

Substitute values and solve.

$$\text{Percent change} = \frac{5 \text{ inch}}{60 \text{ inch}}$$

$$\text{Percent change} = 0.08 \text{ or } 8\%$$

At a certain store, every item is discounted by 15% off the original price. If Kevin buys a CD originally priced at $15.00 and a baseball cap originally priced at $11.50, how much money will he save?

Procedure

What must you find? Total amount saved
What are the units? Dollars and cents
What do you know? Percent change = 15%; original price for two items = $15.00 + $11.50 = $26.50
Create an equation and solve.

$$\text{Percent change} = \frac{\text{amount of change}}{\text{starting point}}$$

Substitute values and solve.

$$0.15 = \frac{x}{26.50}$$
$$x = 0.15(26.50)$$
$$x = \$3.98 \text{ (Note, this answer is rounded to}$$
$$\text{the nearest tenth.)}$$

Numbers and Number Relationships

Pay attention to the key words in this type of word problem.

Examples

If the sum of two numbers is 45 and one number is 5 more than the other, what are the two numbers?

Procedure

What must you find? Value of each number
What are the units? Numbers
What do you know? Sum of two numbers is 45; one number is 5 more than the other
Create an equation and solve.
Let x be the smaller number.

$$x + (x + 5) = 45$$

Solve for x:

$$x + x + 5 = 45$$
$$2x = 40$$
$$x = 20$$

So the two numbers are 20 and 20 + 5 = 25.

One number is twice the size of another, and the two numbers together total 150. What are the two numbers?

Procedure

What must you find? Value of each number
What are the units? Numbers
What do you know? One number is twice the size of the other, and the sum of the numbers is 150.
Create an equation and solve.
Let x be the smaller number.

$$x + 2x = 150$$
$$3x = 150$$
$$x = 50$$

So the smaller number is 50 and the larger number is 100.

Age

Some word problems ask you to calculate a person's age given certain facts.

Examples

Jessica is 26 years old. Two years ago she was twice as old as her brother Ned. How old is Ned now?

Procedure

What must you find? Ned's age now
What are the units? Years
What do you know? When Jessica was 24, she was 2 times as old as Ned

Create an equation and solve.

Prepare an equation that shows the relationship.
Let x = Ned's age two years ago.

$$2x = 24$$
$$x = 12$$

Ned's age two years later = 12 + 2 = 14 years

Measurement

Some word problems will ask you to use what you know about units of measure to solve problems. If necessary, review the table of units of measure in Chapter 8, "Arithmetic Reasoning 1: The Basics."

Example

How many cups of milk are in 5 pints of milk?

Procedure

What must you find? The number of cups of milk in 5 pints
What are the units? Cups
What do you know? According to the chart in Chapter 8, there are 2 cups in 1 pint.
Create an equation and solve.
Let x = the number of cups in 5 pints.

$$5 \text{ pints} = x \text{ cups}$$
$$1 \text{ pint} = 2 \text{ cups}$$
$$5 \times 1 \text{ pint} = 5 \times 2 \text{ cups (Multiply both sides of the equation by 5)}$$
$$5 \text{ pints} = 10 \text{ cups} = x \text{ cups}$$
$$x = 10$$

So there are 10 cups in 5 pints.

WORD PROBLEMS QUIZ

1. The U.S. Treasury Department spends 3.5 cents to manufacture every quarter. 3.5 cents is what percent of the value of the coin?
    A. 3%
    B. 7%
    C. 12%
    D. 14%

2. A person's recommended weight can be calculated using the following formula:

    $$w = \frac{11(h-40)}{2} \text{ where } w = \text{weight and}$$

    $$h = \text{height in inches.}$$

    If Stuart is 5 feet 10 inches tall, what is his recommended weight?
    A. 135 lb
    B. 155 lb
    C. 165 lb
    D. 167 lb

3. It takes 200 lb of sugar cane to produce 5 lb of refined sugar. How many pounds of sugar cane does it take to produce 200 lb of refined sugar?
    A. 2,500 lb
    B. 7,500 lb
    C. 7,700 lb
    D. 8,000 lb

4. Rudy is training for a race. On Monday he ran 2 km. On Tuesday he ran 15% farther than on Monday. If he increases his running distance by the same percentage each day, on which day will he first run more than 4 km?
    A. Wednesday
    B. Thursday
    C. Friday
    D. Saturday

5. Julie's salary is $600 per month, but after taxes and insurance are deducted, her monthly paycheck is $444. What percent of her monthly salary goes for taxes and insurance?
    A. 15%
    B. 26%
    C. 33%
    D. 34%

6. Keisha worked 75 hours during July at a pay rate of $12.50/hour. What were her total earnings for the month before taxes and insurance were deducted?
    A. $447.50
    B. $937.50
    C. $1,447.50
    D. $1,667.50

7. Debbie is walking to raise money for her favorite charity. She is being sponsored by Sally at 10 cents per mile, by Lucie at 12 cents per mile, and by Kelsey at 14 cents per mile. If she walks 8 miles, how much money will she raise?
    A. $2.88
    B. $3.12
    C. $5.25
    D. $10.75

8. Mark has saved 150 quarters in a jar. Of that total, 25 were minted before 1970, 35 were minted between 1970 and 1980, and the remaining quarters were minted after 1980. If Mark picks a quarter out of the jar without looking, what is the probability that he will pick a quarter minted after 1980?
    A. 3:5
    B. 1:2
    C. 7:8
    D. 9:5

9. The bar graph shows the results of a survey asking workers in a company to tell what means of transportation they use to get to work. Based on the graph, what percent of all the workers surveyed said that they take the bus to work?
    A. 16%
    B. 20%
    C. 31%
    D. 35%

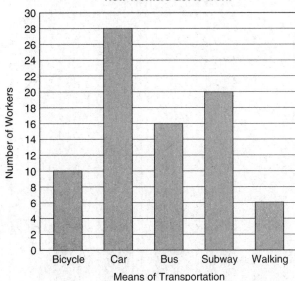

10. Jennifer was elected state senator with 60% of the vote. Which of the following represents that percent as a fraction in simplest form?
    A. $\dfrac{60}{100}$
    B. $\dfrac{6}{10}$
    C. $\dfrac{3}{5}$
    D. $\dfrac{3}{2}$

11. Samuel's current salary is $30,000. He has been promised a raise to $31,500 next year. His raise will be what percent increase over his current salary?
    A. 3%
    B. 3.5%
    C. 4%
    D. 5%

12. Phillip deposited $450 in an account that earns 5% interest, compounded yearly. If he makes no further deposits, how much will be in the account after 2 years?
    A. $472.50
    B. $491.14
    C. $496.13
    D. $512.24

13. If Kevin saves $4.75 per week, how many weeks will it take him to save $266?
    A. 27
    B. 34
    C. 51
    D. 56

14. If an airplane flies at an average speed of 320 miles per hour, how long will it take to fly 1,200 miles?
    A. 2.50 hours
    B. 3.25 hours
    C. 3.75 hours
    D. 4.5 hours

15. What is the difference between 2 meters and 180 centimeters?
    A. 2 cm
    B. 12 cm
    C. 18 cm
    D. 20 cm

ANSWERS TO WORD PROBLEMS QUIZ

Number	Answer
1.	D
2.	C
3.	D
4.	D
5.	B
6.	B
7.	A
8.	A
9.	B
10.	C
11.	D
12.	C
13.	D
14.	C
15.	D

Chapter 10

Word Knowledge

YOUR GOALS FOR THIS CHAPTER:

- **Find out what you can do to build a better vocabulary.**

- **Study common prefixes, suffixes, and word roots.**

- **Learn how to use context to figure out the meaning of an unfamiliar word.**

- **Make your own list of vocabulary words and their meanings.**

INTRODUCTION: ASVAB WORD KNOWLEDGE QUESTIONS

The ASVAB Word Knowledge test measures your ability to understand the meaning of words through synonyms. *Synonyms* are words that have the same or nearly the same meaning as other words. Your ability to recognize synonyms is an indicator of how well you comprehend what you read. Word Knowledge, along with Paragraph Comprehension, is part of the verbal ability portion of the AFQT.

Some Word Knowledge questions present a vocabulary word and ask you which of four answer choices the word "most nearly means." Other Word Knowledge questions present a vocabulary word in a sentence. You can use the meaning of the sentence to help you decide which of the four answer choices has the same meaning as the vocabulary word. The tested vocabulary words are not difficult scientific or technical terms. They are words that

you are likely to encounter in your ordinary reading or conversation but which may be unfamiliar to you. This chapter will teach you ways to figure out the meaning of unfamiliar words and improve your score on the Word Knowledge test.

If you take the CAT-ASVAB, you have only about half a minute to answer each Word Knowledge question. If you take the paper-and-pencil ASVAB, you'll have even less time, so you'll have to work fast if you want to get a good score. That's why it pays to spend time studying ways to build your vocabulary and tackling plenty of sample ASVAB Word Knowledge questions.

How Good Is Your Vocabulary Now?

Start your preparation for the Word Knowledge test by taking this short quiz. It will determine your level of strength in the area of vocabulary. Beside each word, write a word or phrase that helps to define the word. Correct definitions are given at the end of this chapter. Compare your definitions to the correct definitions. If your definition is the same or nearly the same as the correct definition, give yourself 1 point. If your definition is very different from the correct definition, give yourself 0 points.

18–20 points: pretty good work

15–17 points: not too bad

Below 15 points: you need some work

ASVAB Word Knowledge Test

Number of Questions:

- Paper-and-pencil ASVAB: 35
- CAT-ASVAB: 16

Time Limit:

- Paper-and–pencil ASVAB: 11 minutes
- CAT-ASVAB: 8 minutes

Vocabulary Quiz

Word	Definition	Score
abscond		
antagonist		
complacent		
consensus		
defensive		
didactic		
docile		
dormant		
exorbitant		
fidelity		
hyperbole		
intermittent		
neophyte		
parity		
pivotal		
reticent		
succinct		
tenacious		
unilateral		
venerate		
Total Points		

START BUILDING A BETTER VOCABULARY

If it's clear that you need to brush up on your vocabulary for the ASVAB, here's what you can do to start studying for this test.

Memorize (Not!)

It may help you to memorize some common prefixes, suffixes, and word roots. However, memorizing word lists will not be particularly helpful, especially if your study time is limited. You need to use study methods that are far more useful than memorizing words and definitions.

Read, Read, Read, and Read Some More

Read everything you can get your hands on, including school books, newspapers, magazines, and fiction and nonfiction books. The more you read, the more new words you'll come across that you can add to your vocabulary.

Develop a Word List

As you read and find words you don't know, start developing a word list. Use the Word List Chart provided at the end of this section. Write down each word you don't know. Take a guess at the meaning. Write down your guess. Then go to a dictionary, your thesaurus, or your word processing program to find synonyms (words that mean the same thing). Write the synonyms in the last column of the chart. You don't need to write down the formal dictionary definition because the synonyms are what the ASVAB asks for. Also use the Word List Chart for words that you hear people say, but that you do not know.

Often just writing down a word and some synonyms will help you retain the meaning. You may also want to use the Word List Chart to create flash cards that you can take with you anywhere to study when you have some free time. Using something like 3" × 5" cards, write the word on one side and some synonyms on the other. Later in this section, you will have a set of words that can be used for these flash cards or whatever other study system you decide to use.

Review, Review, Review

Once you have developed your word list, listed synonyms, and worked through the sample tests, you still need to keep reviewing. Review on the bus to work or school. Review during TV commercials. Review during your spare time. Review during study sessions. Review before you go to sleep at night. Review with your parents. Review with your friends. Review with a study group. Review in whatever way is most convenient and efficient for you. Be realistic. If reviewing with your friends ends up as a chat session or a party, then that's not helping you reach your goal of scoring high on the ASVAB. Stay disciplined. Stay focused. Stay on track.

USE WORD PARTS TO FIGURE OUT MEANING

Many words are made up of several parts: a *root* (the basic idea) and a *prefix* and/or a *suffix* (short letter combinations that change the meaning in some way). A prefix is attached to the root at the beginning of the word. A suffix is attached to the root at the end of the word. Not all words have prefixes and suffixes, but many do. On the ASVAB test, you will find many words that have roots with prefixes and/or suffixes. If you learn the most common word roots, prefixes, and suffixes, you can use what you know to pick apart unfamiliar words and figure out what they mean.

On the following pages you will find tables of common prefixes, common word roots, and common suffixes. Study these tables carefully. The more you know about these word parts, the better able you will be to figure out the meaning of unfamiliar words.

Study Some Examples

Now that you have studied these common word parts, you can start using what you know to figure out the meaning of unfamiliar words. Here are a few examples of picking words apart to find their meaning.

- *Antibiotic. Anti-* is a prefix that means "against," and *bio* is a root that means "life," so the word has something to do with "against life." An *antibiotic* is a substance that is designed to kill germs.
- *Inaudible. In-* is a prefix that means "not," *aud* has something to do with sound, and the suffix *-ible* mans "capable of," so the word means something like "not capable of being heard."
- *Audiovisual. Audio-* is a prefix that has something to do with hearing, and *visual* relates to seeing, so *audiovisual* involves both hearing and seeing.
- *Precede. Pre-* is a prefix that means "before," and *cede* is a root that means "to go," so the word means something like "going before."
- *Captain. Capit* is a root that means "head," so the word relates to the head of something (in this case, a ship's crew).
- *Capital. Capit* is a root that means "head," so the word has something to do with the head of something (in this case, the symbolic "head" of a country, the location of the government).
- *Chronometer. Chron-* is a prefix that has to do with time, and *meter* relates to measuring, so the word has to do with measuring time.
- *Pedicure. Pedi-* is a prefix that has to do with "foot," so this word has to do with something related to feet.
- *Visage. Vis* has something to do with seeing or looking, so the meaning of this word is "how a person looks."
- *Transform. Trans-* is a prefix that means "go across," so this word means "going across" or "changing form."
- *Microbiology. Micro-* is a prefix that means "small," *bio* is a root that has to do with life, and *-ology* is a suffix that means "the study of," so the word has to do with studying small living things.
- *Multitalented. Multi-* is a prefix that means "many," so this word has to do with many talents.
- *Thermometer. Therm-* has to do with heat, and *meter* means measuring, so this word has to do with measuring heat.
- *Geology. Geo* is a root that means "earth," and *-ology* is a suffix that means "the study of," so this word has to do with studying the earth.
- *Revolve. Re-* is a prefix that means "again," and *volve* means "to turn," so this word has something to do with turning again or turning repeatedly.
- *Mispronounce. Mis-* is a prefix that means "wrong" or "to do wrongly," so this word has to do with pronouncing something in a wrong way.
- *Vacate. Vac* means "empty," so this word has to do with making something empty or leaving an empty space.
- *Aerate. Aero* is a root that has to do with air, so this word has to do with putting or placing air in a particular place.

Look up each of these words in a dictionary to see the precise definition.

Common Prefixes

Prefix	Meaning	Examples
a-, an-	without	amoral, anaerobic
ante-	before	antedate, antechamber
anti-	against, opposing	antipollution, antipathy
auto-	self	autobiography, autopilot
bene-	good or well	beneficial, benediction
bi-	two	bicycle, bipolar
cen-	hundred, hundredth	century, centimeter
circum-	around	circumnavigate, circumvent
co-	together, with	coauthor, copilot
com-	bring together	complete, compile
contra-	against	contradict, contraband
counter-	opposite, against	counterclockwise, counterterrorism
de-	away from, down, undoing	deactivate, detract
dis-	the opposite, undoing	disagree, disarm
ex-	out of, away from	exhale, expropriate
hetero-	different	heterogeneous, heterodox
homo-	same	homogenized, homonym
hyper-	above, excessive	hyperactive, hypertension
il-/in-/ir-	not	illiquid, inaudible, irregular
inter-	between	intercontinental, interject
intra-	within	intramural, intranet
mal-	bad or ill	maladjusted, malevolent
micro-	small	microbiology, microscope
milli-	thousand, thousandth	millennium, millisecond
mis-	bad, wrong	misbehave, misunderstand
mono-	one	monosyllable, monorail
neo-	new	neoclassical, neophyte
non-	not	nonessential, nonconformist
paleo-	old, ancient	paleontology, paleobiology
pan-	all, all over	pandemic, panorama
poly-	many	polygon, polynomial
post-	after, behind	postpone, postnasal
pre-	before	preview, premeditate
pro-	forward, before, in favor of	promote, projection
re-	back, again	rewrite, retract
retro-	backward	retrofit, retroactive
semi-	half	semiannual, semifinal
sub-	under, below	submarine, subway
super-	above, over	supersede, supervise
sym-/syn-	together, at the same time	symbiosis, synchronize
tele-	from a distance	telecommute, telemetry
therm-	heat	thermal, thermometer
tor	twist	torsion, contort
trans-	across	transcontinental, transatlantic
un-	not	unannounced, unnoticed
uni-	one	unicycle, unify
vert, verse	change	revert, reverse

Common Word Roots

Root	Meaning	Examples
act	do	transact, activate
aero	air	aerobics, aerospace
ambu	walk	ambulate, ambulatory
anthrop	human	anthropology, philanthropy
annu, anni	year	annual, anniversary
aster, astr	star	astronomy, asterisk
audi	hear	audible, auditory
biblio	book	bibliography, bibliographic
bio	life	biosphere, biography
brev	short	brevity, abbreviate
capit	head	decapitate, capital
card, cord, cour	heart	cardiology, discord
carn	flesh	carnivorous, carnage
cede	go	recede, precede
chron	time	chronology, synchronize
cide	killing	suicide, homicide
cis	cut	precise, scissors
claim	shout, cry out	exclaim, proclaim
cogn	know	cognition, recognize
crat	rule	autocratic, democrat
culp	blame	culpable, exculpate
dem	people	democracy, demographics
dic, dict	speak	dictation, predict
dorm	sleep	dormant, dormitory
fer	carry	transfer, refer
fuge	flee	refuge, centrifugal
geo	earth	geography, geologic
gram	something written or recorded	telegram, cardiogram
graph	to write	graphic, calligraphy
jac, ject	throw	eject, trajectory
jur	law	jury, jurisprudence
labor	work	laboratory, collaborate
loc	place	location, collocate
luc	light	translucent, illuminate
manu	hand	manuscript, manufacture
meter, metr	measure	barometer, metric
morph	form	morphology, amorphous
mort	die	mortuary, mortal
omni	all	omnipresent, omnipotent
op, oper	work	cooperate, operator
path	feeling, suffering	empathy, pathetic
ped, pod	foot	pedal, podiatry
philo, phil	like, love	philanthropy, philosophy
phobe	fear	phobic, claustrophobia
phon	sound	phonograph, stereophonic
photo	light	photographic, telephoto
phys	nature, body	physique, physical
scrib	write	scribble, scribe
stro, stru	build	destroy, construction
ter	earth	extraterrestrial, territory
vac	empty	vacuous, evacuate
verb	word	verbose, proverb
vid, vis	see	video, television
vol, volv	turn, roll	revolve, evolution

Common Suffixes

Suffix	Meaning	Examples
-able, -ible	capable or worthy of	likable, possible
-ful	full of	healthful, joyful
-fy, -ify	to make or cause	purify, glorify
-ish	like, inclined to, somewhat	impish, devilish
-ism	act of, state of	capitalism, socialism
-ist	one who does	conformist, cyclist
-ize	make into	formalize, legalize
-logue, -log	discourse	dialogue, travelogue
-logy	discourse	paleontology, dermatology
-ment	state of being	entertainment, amazement
-oid	like, resembling	humanoid, trapezoid
-ty, -ity	state of being	purity, acidity

Start Using What You Know

Use the following activity to further expand and strengthen your vocabulary.

USE CONTEXT CLUES TO FIGURE OUT MEANING

One good way to figure out the meaning of an unfamiliar word is to use what are called *context clues*. The *context* of a word is the phrases and sentence or sentences that surround it. Often, even if you have never heard a word before, you can guess its meaning by looking at the context in which it appears. The context may give you clues to help you figure out the meaning.

Study Some Examples

Here are some examples of how to use context clues to figure out the meaning of an unfamiliar word.

- During the snowstorm, the government sent home all *nonessential* personnel. (*Nonessential* must mean "not important" or "not needed.")
- When giving a person driving directions, you must be very *explicit*, or else the person may make a wrong turn. (*Explicit* must mean "precise" or "exact.")
- Even though the club members disagreed about the project, their conversation was *amicable*. (*Amicable* must mean something that is the opposite of disagreeing.)
- The chairperson *convened* a panel of experts to discuss global warming. (*Convened* must mean something related to bringing together a group of people.)

- They *commemorated* the end of the war by holding a big parade. (*Commemorate* must mean something like "get together to remember.")
- Even though there was no sign of a problem, Kisha had a *premonition* that something would go wrong. (A *premonition* must be a suspicion or feeling about something that is going to happen.)
- Gene was only in fourth grade, but he was *precocious* in his school subjects because he studied with his older brothers. (*Precocious* must mean something related to being advanced or ahead of what is expected.)
- Scientists are worried that this new disease, which spreads rapidly and for which there is no vaccine, may cause a *pandemic*. (A *pandemic* must be a disease outbreak that is widespread and out of control.)
- Brad was usually stable and predictable, but to our surprise, his behavior in this instance was *unorthodox*. (*Unorthodox* must mean something like "different from stable and predictable.")
- Though most people in the audience were calm and quiet, Sally was bubbly and *loquacious*. (*Loquacious* must mean the opposite of calm and quiet.)
- Brian took *vicarious* pleasure in Joan's debut on stage, even though he was not able to attend the performance. (*Vicarious* must have something to do with experiencing pleasure without being there.)
- Even though the hurricane is expected to arrive on shore at any moment, the sea is still *placid*. (*Placid* must have something to do with not being stirred up with high surf and waves. It may mean "calm.")
- The weapons and stolen cash were *tangible* evidence that the defendant was guilty. (*Tangible* must mean "real" or "concrete.")

Start Using What You Know

Use the following activity to further expand and strengthen your vocabulary.

Word Meaning Activity: Prefixes, Roots, and Suffixes

The words below use common prefixes, roots, and suffixes. Read the word and try to guess its meaning. Write down your guess. Then look up the dictionary meaning and write it down. From the dictionary or a thesaurus, list at least one synonym.

Word	My Guess	Dictionary Meaning	Synonym(s)
achromatic			
ambidextrous			
antipathy			
apathetic			
atypical			
benefit			
biography			
cacophony			
chronicle			
chronological			
cognizant			
contiguous			
contradict			
contrarian			
decompress			
defile			
democracy			
demography			
deregulate			
devalue			
geography			
geopolitics			
hemisphere			
interject			
judicial			
metrics			
microwave			
patricide			
polychrome			
preamble			
prologue			
retrofire			
retrograde			
subterranean			
subversive			
sympathy			
terrestrial			
translate			
ungainly			

Word Meaning Activity: Guess the Meaning of Words in Context

In this activity, a sentence is given and a word is italicized. By reading the sentence, guess the meaning of the word. Then look up the dictionary meaning and list at least one synonym.

Sentence	My Guess	Dictionary Meaning	Synonym(s)
Even though Bill did not believe he was at fault, he made the *magnanimous* gesture of apologizing.			
Valerie and Samuel were usually friendly and polite, but on the subject of politics, their discussions were *acrimonious*.			
After at first insisting on watching television, Edie finally *acquiesced* to her sister's wish to play a board game.			
During the storm, it was difficult to hold the umbrella because the wind was so *erratic*.			
Leon was mildly enthusiastic about football and baseball, but he cheered the hockey team with great *fervor*.			
Margaret usually spoke up in class discussions, but that day she was *reticent* about expressing her opinion.			
Generally, Mr. Smith considered the input of others before making a decision, but on the subject of overtime, he made a *unilateral* determination.			
The threat from the invading army *galvanized* the soldiers into preparing for battle.			

USE IT OR LOSE IT

Many experts say that the best way to learn a new word is to use the word in your speech and writing. When you learn a new word, use it in different sentences. Say the word out loud. Do this several times. If you don't use it, you are likely to forget it. Make up new sentences with the word. Find ways to use the word in your daily life. The following activities will help you practice these skills.

Answering ASVAB Word Knowledge Items

When you take the ASVAB Word Knowledge test, use the knowledge and skills you have learned in this chapter to figure out the meanings of unfamiliar words. Here are seven steps you can follow to attack Word Knowledge items:

1. When you read the item, see if there are any context clues.
2. Mentally guess at the meaning of the word.
3. Scan the possible answers.
4. Eliminate those that are clearly wrong.
5. Pick the word that is the closest match—the *best* answer.
6. If you can't make an initial determination, try picking the word apart. Look for the prefixes, roots, and suffixes.
7. Give it your best shot and don't be afraid of guessing, as there is no penalty for a wrong answer on the paper-and-pencil version.

WORD LIST CHART

Use the following chart to record unfamiliar words that you read or hear. Write down your guess at the meaning of the word. Then look up the word in a dictionary or thesaurus to identify synonyms.

Word Meaning Activity: Using New Words in a Sentence

In the activity below, you are given several words. If you don't know the meaning of the word, look it up in the dictionary. Then create a sentence using the word.

Word	Dictionary Definition	My Sentence
adapt		
attire		
automation		
calamitous		
cursory		
defile		
digress		
evade		
futile		
garner		
mundane		
overbearing		
pensive		
peripheral		
solvent		
thwart		
undermine		
wary		

Word Meaning Activity: Create Synonyms

For each word, list at least one synonym for it. A *synonym* is a word that has the same or nearly the same meaning. Use a dictionary or thesaurus if necessary.

Word	Synonyms
abate	
abhor	
acquit	
cajole	
disdain	
erroneous	
facade	
feasible	
ghastly	
haughty	
incognito	
incriminate	
legitimate	
leverage	
liaison	
meander	
opulent	
purge	
rebuke	
rescind	
sanction	
simulate	
stooped	
tangible	
truncate	
ultimate	
undermine	
vacillate	
vie	
viscous	

Word List Chart

Word	My Guess	Synonyms

Vocabulary Quiz: Correct Definitions

Word	Definition
abscond	escape quickly and secretly
antagonist	adversary; someone who opposes
complacent	contented or satisfied
consensus	general agreement; an opinion agreed upon by most or all
defensive	protecting; defending
didactic	instructive; moralizing
docile	willing to obey
dormant	quiet; sleeping
exorbitant	well beyond reasonable or normal
fidelity	faith; loyalty
hyperbole	a large exaggeration
intermittent	periodic; irregular
neophyte	a beginner or novice
parity	equal in status or value
pivotal	referring to a turning point; of critical importance
reticent	reserved; inclined to keep feelings to oneself
succinct	clear and brief
tenacious	holding on firmly; stubborn
unilateral	by one person or group only; one-sided
venerate	to honor or hold in deep reverence

Paragraph Comprehension

INTRODUCTION: ASVAB PARAGRAPH COMPREHENSION QUESTIONS

The ASVAB subtest called Paragraph Comprehension is designed to find out how well you obtain information from written material. Basically, it measures your reading comprehension skills. Paragraph Comprehension is especially important because it is part of the AFQT, the primary score for entering the military. To get in and get good job and training opportunities, you need to score well on this test. Just think about it: During your basic and specialized training, you will need to understand written material provided to you by your instructors. You will need to read and understand manuals that relate to your job. The military, regardless of branch, needs you to have a good understanding of everything you read.

ASVAB Paragraph Comprehension Test

Number of questions:

- Paper-and-pencil ASVAB: 15
- CAT-ASVAB: 11

Time limit:

- Paper-and-pencil ASVAB: 13 minutes
- CAT-ASVAB: 22 minutes

Item format: paragraphs with multiple-choice questions

Subjects covered: history, health, science, social studies, sports, current events, culture

Each item on the Paragraph Comprehension test consists of a paragraph or paragraphs followed by multiple-choice questions. You will need to read the paragraphs in order to answer the questions. The paragraphs will cover a wide variety of topics. Note, however, that you won't need to know anything about each topic other than what is in the paragraph. The paragraph will contain everything you need to know to answer the questions.

If you do the math, you will see that on the paper-and-pencil ASVAB, you have only 52 seconds to answer each item, including reading the passage. That means that you will need a test-taking strategy that allows you to approach the test both quickly and accurately. This chapter gives you some practical advice on how to approach the test, what kinds of questions to expect, and how to prepare yourself to get your best score on the ASVAB Paragraph Comprehension test.

BUILD YOUR READING COMPREHENSION SKILLS

Start your preparation for the ASVAB Paragraph Comprehension test by learning what you can do to build your reading comprehension skills. Here are some suggestions.

Read

The best way to improve your reading comprehension skills is to *read, read, read*. The more you read and practice your reading comprehension skills, the better off you will be on the test. The following list suggests a variety of materials that you should be reading.

What to Read

- *Books on subjects you like.* Whatever topic interests you, there are books about it—and reading those books will help you. If you are a sports fan, read books about great teams and famous games. If you love science fiction, read this year's most popular science fiction stories. If you are a history buff, read about the famous people and events of the past that made our world what it is today. Read autobiographies, books on politics, health books, science books, books on bicycling, nutrition, ice skating, organizing your life, and more. The list is endless. You don't need to buy these books; use your local library. The library is also a great place to read because it is quiet and you won't get distracted.

- *School books.* If you are in school, devour those textbooks. Focus on paragraph headings, see how the information is organized, and highlight critical statements and facts. Reading the textbook will not only expand your knowledge base for the other ASVAB tests, but also improve your vocabulary and your ability to understand what you are reading.

- *Newspapers.* Daily newspapers, especially those from a large town or city, offer plenty of reading opportunity on a variety of subjects.

- *The Internet.* Be selective about what you read on the Internet. Look for more lengthy passages, such as articles from a newspaper or extracts from a book. Avoid Internet sites where information is short, choppy, and abbreviated. That kind of reading will probably not help your reading comprehension skills. Reading Internet material can be helpful if you select the right stuff.

Learn New Words

The better your vocabulary, the easier it will be to understand what you are reading. The previous chapter of this book explained how to improve your vocabulary for the ASVAB Word Knowledge test. Following those suggestions will help you on the Paragraph Comprehension test as well. (You may wish to go back to the earlier chapter and review.)

How to Learn Words

- *Develop a word list.* As you are reading, identify words that you don't know or don't know very well. Based on the sentence or paragraph that contains the word, try to guess its meaning. Look up the meaning in a dictionary to be sure that you are correct. The previous chapter of this book gave you a word list chart for recording these words and their definitions. Use it to help your vocabulary grow.

- *Use context clues.* The *context* of a word is the other words and sentences that surround it. Often you can determine the meaning of a word from its context. One way to determine the meaning is to see how the word is used in the sentence.

- *Use prefixes, suffixes, and roots.* These word parts can help you decode a word's meaning. The Word Knowledge chapter gives you a whole laundry list of common prefixes, suffixes, and roots.

LEARN HOW TO ANSWER EACH QUESTION TYPE

There are four different types of Paragraph Comprehension questions. Each type asks you something different about the paragraph you read. Here is a list of the question types, along with tips for answering each type.

Type 1: Words in Context Questions

Some Paragraph Comprehension questions will ask you to determine the meaning of an unfamiliar word in the paragraph by looking at the context in which that word appears.

Example

Space flight is a somewhat common experience these days. Nowadays the International Space Station generally is the home of several astronauts from the United States and Russia. Astronauts generally spend several months in a weightless condition. They sleep, eat, and work without the effects of gravity. One of the effects of lengthy space travel is the atrophy of major muscle groups and the stress of travel on the heart and lungs. When these space travelers return to Earth, it takes several days for them to adjust back to gravity and to walk normally.

In this instance the word <u>atrophy</u> means

A. strengthening.
B. defining.
C. weakening.
D. breaking.

If the correct meaning was "strengthening" (choice A), then it probably wouldn't take several days for the space travelers to adjust back to gravity. If choice D, "breaking," was the correct answer, then the space travelers would probably not adjust at all, as their muscles would be in very poor shape. Muscles that are "defining," choice B, would result from exercise performed against gravity, not in a weightless environment. Choice C, "weakening," is the correct answer, because when muscles do not have a chance to work out, they get weaker.

Type 2: Main Idea Questions

Another kind of Paragraph Comprehension question asks about the main idea of the paragraph. In this kind of question, you may be asked to identify the main idea, to choose the best title for the paragraph (which is simply another way of stating the main idea), to identify the theme of the paragraph, or to identify the author's purpose in writing the paragraph.

Example

Bologna, Italy, is a city with 26 miles of covered walkways dating from the 1200s. The atmosphere of this beautiful city and its residents envelop you like a warm hug. In the center piazza of the city are two leaning towers, forming the most notable landmarks. Around the corner is the famous Roxy coffee bar, a hangout for many of the young university students who are studying medicine and political science. The nearby open marketplace bustles with color and excitement. Listening closely, you can hear many languages spoken by the tourists who visit each year.

In the paragraph above, which of the following best states the main idea of the passage?

A. Bologna is an old city.
B. University students love Bologna.
C. Bologna is an interesting place to visit.
D. Bologna has two leaning towers.

Clearly, choice C is the best and correct answer. The main idea is that Bologna is an interesting and vibrant city that attracts visitors from many places.

The other answers may be true, but they do not sum up the gist of the entire passage.

Often in a paragraph there will be one sentence that sums up the main idea of the paragraph as a whole. The question may ask you to choose which sentence that is. A sentence that sums up the main idea of a paragraph is called the *topic sentence*. In the following example, the sentences are numbered. As you read, try to pick out the topic sentence.

Example

(1) It was 6 p.m. on a cloudy, frigid day in the forest. (2) It had been sleeting the entire afternoon. (3) Simone was worried because her son hadn't returned home, as he usually did by this time. (4) Todd was always punctual, but tonight was different. (5) Todd had a basketball game after school, and a friend was supposed to drive him home. (6) Simone waited by the window in hopes of seeing Todd's smiling face as he came up the stairs.

Which of the following sentences best reflects the main idea of the paragraph?

A. 1
B. 3
C. 4
D. 5

The best and correct answer is choice B. In most paragraphs, the topic sentence is the first sentence. But in this case, as you might have noticed, it is not. Of the six sentences, sentence 3 best conveys the meaning of the entire paragraph. It tells you that for some reason, Todd was supposed to be home and wasn't, and that Simone was worried. Sentence 3 is the topic sentence. Sentences 1 and 2 just give an indication of the setting. Sentences 4 and 5 tell us that Todd was usually on time and that this day he had a basketball game. These sentences don't reflect the basic idea of the paragraph: that Simone was worried and why she was worried. Sentence 6 conveys no sense that there was any kind of problem or reason for worry, only that Simone was looking out the window hoping to see Todd.

"Best Title" Questions Another kind of main idea question will ask you to choose the best title for the paragraph. The best title is the one that best expresses the main idea of the paragraph as a whole. Here is an example.

Example

Visiting New York City and taking in a Broadway musical has always been a dream of Kevin's, but he knew a visit to the big city would be very expensive. He wanted to plan a short vacation to the city over a holiday weekend. Could he visit the city on a limited budget? Searching the Internet, he found opportunities for reduced-price hotels, half-price Broadway play tickets, and a special on train transportation. He was ecstatic as he started to pack his bags.

> For the paragraph above, which of the following is the best title?
> A. New York—An Expensive City
> B. Kevin's Budget
> C. Finding Cheap Tickets
> D. Kevin Goes to the Big City

Of the options, choice D is the best and correct answer. You don't know about Kevin's actual budget, so choice B is not correct. You do know that New York City is expensive to visit, but that is not the major point of the paragraph. Finding cheap tickets is part of the process, but it is not by any means the major thrust of the paragraph. Kevin's dream and all its parts is the most important theme of the paragraph.

Note that there are a number of other possible good titles for this paragraph. A few include *Kevin Goes to the Big City*, *New York City on a Budget*, and *Kevin's Dream Comes True*. Each of these titles conveys the main idea of the paragraph and would make a possible correct answer choice.

Author's Purpose Questions   Another kind of main idea question will ask you to identify the author's purpose in writing the paragraph. Authors write for a variety of purposes: to describe, to raise issues or concerns, to move readers to action, to persuade readers to think in a particular way, to frighten, to give directions, to describe steps or procedures, to compare and contrast, or to entertain. Here is an example of this kind of question.

Example

Global warming is an increasingly serious environmental problem. It is caused by "greenhouse gases," which are created by things we do to the environment every day. But there are many little things people can do to reduce greenhouse gas emissions. You can do your part by carpooling to save gasoline. Four people can ride to school or work in a carpool instead of each person taking a car and driving alone. Save electricity by turning off the lights, the television, and the computer when you are through with them. Save energy by taking the bus or by riding your bicycle to school or to run errands. Walk to where you want to go. Recycle your cans, bottles, plastic bags, and newspapers. If you care about the future of this planet, help protect the environment! Get with the program!

> In the paragraph above, what is the author's purpose?
> A. To entertain readers
> B. To describe global warming
> C. To offer directions
> D. To move readers to action

The best answer is choice D. The purpose of the paragraph is to move you to act to protect the environment. The paragraph makes no attempt to entertain readers (choice A), nor does it really describe what global warming is (choice B). It does give suggestions for fixing global warming, but these are not really directions, so choice C is also incorrect.

Author's Attitude or Tone Questions   Another kind of main idea question will ask you to identify the author's attitude or tone. In other words, you will need to determine how the author feels toward the subject of the paragraph. Is the author angry? Discouraged? Excited? Happy? For clues to how the author feels, look at the words he or she has chosen to use. Here is an example.

Example

Shooting a cat with a BB gun or anything else is animal cruelty and is illegal. The recent incident in our neighborhood should be reported to the Society for the Prevention of Cruelty to Animals, the local humane society, or the police. We must as a community band together to find the perpetrators, prosecute them, and get the person or persons into some serious counseling program. It's important for all of us to be watchful and to speak up about this horrific behavior. These incidents *must* be stopped before these individuals cause even more serious harm.

> In the above paragraph, which of the following best describes the author's tone?

A. Happy about the situation
B. Biased in favor of cats
C. Angry about the situation
D. Depressed about the situation

The correct answer is choice C, "angry about the situation." The author's anger is apparent in words and phrases like "horrific," "we must as a community band together," "prosecute them," and "these incidents *must* be stopped," There is nothing in the paragraph to support any of the other choices.

Type 3: Specific Details Questions

The third kind of ASVAB Paragraph Comprehension question will ask you to pick out specific details in the paragraph that you have read. In these paragraphs, a lot of information is often provided. You have to find the specific item or detail that the question asks about. For this kind of question, it is very helpful to read the question before you read the paragraph. Here is an example.

Example

Dental assistants perform a variety of patient care, office, and laboratory duties. They work chairside as dentists examine and treat patients. They make patients as comfortable as possible in the dental chair, prepare them for treatment, and obtain their dental records. Assistants hand instruments and materials to dentists and keep patients' mouths dry and clear by using suction or other devices. Assistants also sterilize and disinfect instruments and equipment, prepare trays of instruments for dental procedures, and instruct patients on postoperative and general oral health care.

In the above paragraph, where is the dental assistant when the doctor is examining the patient?
A. Right next to the dentist and the patient
B. In the laboratory
C. Finding dental records
D. Sterilizing instruments

The correct answer is choice A. The detail you are looking for is found in the sentence, "They work chairside as dentists examine and treat patients." So the correct answer is "right next to the dentist and the patient." At other times, a dental assistant may be in the laboratory (choice B), finding dental records (choice C), or sterilizing instruments (choice D),

but when the dentist is working with the patient, the assistant is right by the dentist's side.

Sequence of Steps Questions One type of specific details question will ask you about the sequence (order) of steps in a process. The process may be something in nature, or it may be preparing a food item, operating a machine, making a repair, or something similar. To answer this kind of question correctly, you need to pay close attention to the order in which things happen or in which things are done. Reading the question before reading the passage is a very good strategy with this type of item. Here is an example.

Example

Making a Brownie

Preheat the oven to 350° and lightly spray the pan with cooking oil. In a saucepan, combine the butter and chopped chocolate. Set this over a low heat until melted. Stir the mixture and set aside to cool. In a mixing bowl, mix together the flour, cocoa, baking powder, salt, and cinnamon. Measure the sugar into a large bowl and mix in the cooled butter-chocolate mixture. Add the eggs, vanilla, and water. Mix very well. Add the dry ingredients and mix until blended. Spoon the batter into the pan and bake for 23 to 25 minutes. Cool in the pan and cut into squares.

When should you add the eggs, vanilla, and water?
A. After melting the chocolate
B. Before cooling the melted butter and chocolate
C. After spooning the batter into the pan
D. Before adding the dry ingredients

The correct answer is choice D. There is a lot of detail in this paragraph, but the time for adding the eggs, vanilla, and water is before combining the melted butter and chocolate with the dry ingredients.

Type 4: Interpretation Questions

The fourth type of ASVAB Paragraph Comprehension question will ask you to interpret something that you read. Often an author will suggest or hint at a certain idea, but will not state it directly. It is up to you to figure out the author's meaning by "reading between the lines" and drawing your own conclusion. When you do this, you analyze the author's words, you think about what they mean, and you put your ideas together to create something new and original. This process is called *making an inference*. Here is an example of a question that asks you to make an inference.

Example

The dinosaurs became extinct at the end of the Cretaceous Period. Reasons for this event are still undetermined. Some scientists attribute it to a cataclysmic occurrence, such as a meteor that struck the Earth, kicking up vast quantities of dust. Another possibility is the great increase in volcanic activity that is known to have taken place at the end of the Cretaceous period. Either cause could have filled the atmosphere with enough dust and soot to block out the sunlight, producing a dramatic climate change. Recent discoveries indicate that in many places on several continents, there is a layer of iridium in geologic strata associated with the Cretaceous Period. Iridium is an element associated with lava flows.

An inference test item might look like this:

According to this passage, the dinosaurs became extinct because of which of the following conditions?
A. Disappearance of vegetation
B. Radiation from the sun
C. Climate changes
D. Volcanic activity

The best answer is choice C, climate changes. The paragraph does not come to a conclusion about which of the two events caused the extinction of the dinosaurs, but both seem to point to the fact that climate changes were the eventual cause of their disappearance. This conclusion is not stated in the passage. You needed to infer this from reading the passage.

Answering ASVAB Paragraph Comprehension Questions

Here are a few basic tips for answering ASVAB Paragraph Comprehension questions.

1. *Read the questions before reading the paragraph.* This is an absolute must—no exceptions. You need to do this so that you can focus on the pertinent parts of the paragraph and ignore the remainder. Remember that you have a very limited amount of time and you need to get to the right answer as quickly as possible.

2. *Read the paragraph next.* When you read the paragraph, focus on the answers to the questions and ignore all the extraneous information that might be in the paragraph. There will be a lot of fluff in the passage that has nothing to do with the questions you are being asked. Don't try to fully understand all the information that is given. Your job is to answer the question, not to be an expert on the subject at hand.

3. In your mind, *try to answer the question* as you read each paragraph. Try to guess the answers in your own mind. Your answer will probably be similar to one of the answer choices.

4. *Now look at the answer choices* to see which one matches the answer you reached in your mind. Pick the choice that is closest.

5. *Guess if you must.* If you cannot decide which answer choice is correct, try to eliminate choices that are clearly wrong. Then guess, even if you cannot eliminate more than one or two choices. The more choices you eliminate, the better your chance of guessing correctly. There is no penalty for wrong answers on the paper-and-pencil version, so be sure to mark an answer for every question, even if you have to guess.

Chapter 12

Mathematics Knowledge 1: Algebra and Probability

YOUR GOALS FOR THIS CHAPTER:

- **Find out what algebra and probability topics you need to know for the ASVAB.**

- **Review techniques and strategies for solving algebra and probability problems.**

- **Study sample algebra and probability problems and their step-by-step solutions.**

- **Measure your test readiness by taking an algebra and probability quiz.**

INTRODUCTION: ASVAB MATHEMATICS KNOWLEDGE QUESTIONS

The ASVAB Mathematics Knowledge test measures your ability to solve problems using concepts taught in high school math courses. These concepts include various topics in algebra, probability, and geometry. You'll need to know about solving equations, setting up ratios and proportions, graphing on a coordinate plane, determining the probability of a given event, identifying plane and solid geometric figures, and calculating perimeter, area, and volume.

It is important that you do well on the Mathematics Knowledge test because it is one of the four ASVAB tests that are used to calculate the AFQT—your military entrance score. That's why it pays to spend time reviewing topics in algebra, probability, and geometry and tackling plenty of sample ASVAB Mathematics Knowledge questions.

The following pages offer a quick but important overview of the basic algebra and probability that you need to know if you are to score well on the ASVAB. Make sure that you carefully review and test yourself on every topic covered in this section. Also make sure that you learn how to use all

---

ASVAB Mathematics Knowledge Test

Number of Questions:

- Paper-and-pencil ASVAB: 25
- CAT-ASVAB: 16

Time Limit:

- Paper-and-pencil ASVAB: 24 minutes
- CAT-ASVAB: 20 minutes

Suggested Review Plan for Algebra and Probability

- Work through the algebra and probability review at your own pace.
- Pay careful attention to the examples provided.
- After you complete the review, take the algebra and probability quiz.
- Score your quiz.
- Study any problems you answered incorrectly. Reread the corresponding review section, then try the problem again. Work until you understand how to solve the problem.

Remember that you probably won't get these exact problems on the ASVAB, but knowing how to solve them will help you do your best on the actual test.

---

of the problem-solving methods presented in the examples. Chapter 13 will provide a similar review of basic concepts and problem-solving methods in geometry. If you master the core information presented in these two chapters, you will be able to answer ASVAB Mathematics Knowledge questions with relative ease.

ALGEBRA AND PROBABILITY REVIEW

Topics	
The language of algebra	Monomials, binomials, and polynomials
Evaluating expressions	Solving quadratic equations
Solving equations for one unknown	Algebraic fractions
Inequalities	Graphing on a number line
Ratios and proportions	Graphing on a coordinate plane
Solving equations for two unknowns	Probability

The Language of Algebra

Algebra uses arithmetic functions and processes, but some of the numbers are replaced by letters. The letters merely represent numbers that are currently unknown or that can change in value according to circumstances. In algebra, a letter representing a number that can change in value is called a *variable*.

- An expression such as $6x$ means "6 times some number, currently unknown" or "some number, currently unknown, times 6."
- An expression such as $x + 7$ means "some number, currently unknown, plus 7."
- An expression such as $x - 12$ means "some number, currently unknown, less 12."
- An expression such as $\frac{x}{5}$ means "some number, currently unknown, divided by 5," or "the ratio of some number and 5."

Very often verbal expressions in word problems need to be translated into algebraic expressions before they can be solved. Here are some examples of verbal expressions and their algebraic counterparts.

Verbal Expression	Algebraic Expression
Some number plus 7	$x + 7$
Some number subtracted from 8	$8 - x$
8 subtracted from some number	$x - 8$
The product of some number and 12	$12x$
The product of 5 and the sum of x and y	$5(x + y)$
Some number divided by 4	$\frac{x}{4}$
The ratio of 6 and some number	$\frac{6}{x}$
9 times some number plus the sum of 5 and y	$9x + (5 + y)$
12 less the sum of 3 and some number	$12 - (3 + x)$

Evaluating Expressions

To evaluate an algebraic expression, substitute the given value for the unknown and then perform the arithmetic as indicated.

Examples

Evaluate $a + b + c$ if $a = 2$, $b = 4$, and $c = 3$.

Substitute each value for the corresponding letter and then do the addition as indicated.

$$2 + 4 + 3 = 9$$

Evaluate $2x^2 + 4y + 5$ if $x = 2$ and $y = 3$.

$$2(2)^2 + 4(3) + 5 = 2(4) + 12 + 5$$
$$= 8 + 12 + 5$$
$$= 25$$

Evaluate $\dfrac{a+b}{4} + \dfrac{a}{b+c}$ if $a = 2$, $b = 6$, and $c = 10$.

$$\frac{2+6}{4} + \frac{2}{6+10} = \frac{8}{4} + \frac{2}{16}$$
$$= 2 + \frac{2}{16}$$
$$= 2\frac{1}{8}$$

HINT *Don't forget:* Order of operations is critical!
- Simplify anything within the parentheses.
- Apply the powers or exponents.
- Multiply and divide in order from left to right.
- Add and subtract in order from left to right.

Solving Equations for One Unknown

An *equation* is a mathematical statement that contains an equal (=) sign. When an equation contains a letter standing for an unknown number, you can use the equation to find the value of that unknown. This is called *solving the equation for the unknown*.

Think of an equation as a balanced scale. Everything to the right of the = sign has to balance with everything on the left side of the = sign.

Because an equation is balanced, it will stay in balance if you do the same thing to the numbers on both sides of the = sign. For example, the equation $10 = 10$ will stay balanced if you add 3 to both sides. The new equation will be $13 = 13$. Similarly, the equation $x + y = x + y$ will stay balanced if you subtract 10 from both sides. The new equation will be $x + y - 10 = x + y - 10$.

Similarly, the equation $x + y = a + b$ will stay balanced if you subtract 8 from both sides. The new equation will be $x + y - 8 = a + b - 8$.

To solve an equation and find the value of an unknown, you need to get the *unknown* on one side of the equation and *all the other terms* on the other side of the equation. Consider this example.

Solve: $y - 4 = 20$

Add 4 to both sides:

$$y - 4 + 4 = 20 + 4$$
$$y = 20 + 4$$
$$y = 24$$

> **HINT** *Another way to think about it.* Here is a simple way to think about using addition or subtraction to solve an equation: Just move the number you are adding or subtracting from one side of the = sign to the other and change its sign (either − to + or + to −). So in the equation shown, move the − 4 to the other side of the = sign and make it + 4. This makes the equation $y = 20 + 4$ or 24.

An equation will also stay balanced if you multiply or divide both sides by the same number. So you can also use these operations to solve equations.

Example (Division)

Solve: $3x = 18$

You want to get x all alone on the left side of the equation, so divide $3x$ by 3. Since $3/3 = 1$, $3x/3 = x$. To maintain the balance, divide the right side of the equation by 3 as well: $\frac{18}{3} = 6$. So $x = 6$.

> **HINT** *Another way to think about it.* Here is another way to think about using division to solve an equation: In a problem such as $3x = 18$, instead of trying to divide both sides by 3, simply move the 3 across the = sign and make it the denominator of the other side of the equation:
>
> $$3x = 18$$
> $$x = \frac{18}{3}$$
> $$x = 6$$

Example (Multiplication)

$$\frac{x}{3} = 12$$

Multiply both sides by 3.

$$3\frac{x}{3} = 3(12)$$
$$x = 3(12)$$
$$x = 36$$

> **HINT** *Another way to think about it.* Here is another way to think about using multiplication to solve an equation: In a problem such as $\frac{x}{2} = 20$, move the denominator 2 across the = sign and make it the multiplier on the other side.
>
> $$\frac{x}{2} = 20$$
> $$x = 2(20)$$
> $$x = 40$$

Examples

Solve for z:

$$16 + z = 24$$

Subtract 16 from both sides.

$$z = 24 - 16 = 8$$

Solve for x:

$$\frac{x}{5} - 4 = 2$$

Add 4 to both sides.

$$\frac{x}{5} = 2 + 4$$
$$\frac{x}{5} = 6$$

Multiply each side by 5 to isolate x on the left side.

$$x = 5(6) = 30$$

Solve for a:

$$\frac{2}{3}a - 5 = 9$$

Add 5 to both sides.

$$\frac{2}{3}a = 9 + 5$$

$$\frac{2}{3}a = 14$$

Multiply each side by $\frac{3}{2}$.

$$a = 14\left(\frac{3}{2}\right)$$

$$a = \frac{42}{2} = 21$$

HINT *Divide out common factors.* Another way to do this final step is to divide out common factors.

$$\frac{\overset{7}{\cancel{14}}}{1} \times \frac{3}{\underset{1}{\cancel{2}}} = 21$$

Solve for y:

$$7y = 3y - 12$$
$$7y - 3y = -12$$
$$4y = -12$$
$$y = -\frac{12}{4}$$
$$y = -3$$

Inequalities

Unlike equations, inequalities are statements that show that certain relationships between selected variables and numbers are *not* equal. Instead of using the equal sign, you use the "greater than" sign (>) or the "less than" sign (<). At times you may see signs for "greater than or equal to" (≥) or "less than or equal to" (≤).

Examples

$x > 13$ means that the value of x is greater than 13.

$y < 45$ means that the value of y is less than 45.

$x - y < 33$ means that when y is subtracted from x, the result is less than 33.

$\frac{x}{5} \geq z$ means that when x is divided by 5, the result is greater than or equal to the value of z.

Solving Inequalities If you work problems with inequalities, you can treat them much like equations. If you multiply or divide both sides by a negative number, you must reverse the sign.

Examples

Solve for x:

$$3x + 5 > 8$$
$$3x + 5 - 5 > 8 - 5 \text{ Subtract 5 from both sides.}$$
$$3x > 3 \text{ Divide each side by 3.}$$
$$x > 1$$

Solve for x:

$$5 - 2x > 9$$
$$5 - 5 - 2x > 9 - 5 \text{ Subtract 5 from both sides.}$$
$$-2x > 4 \text{ Divide by } -2 \text{ (Be sure to reverse the sign, since you are dividing by a negative number.)}$$
$$x < -2$$

Ratios and Proportions

A *ratio* is a comparison of one number to another. A ratio can be represented by a fraction.

Example

On a certain road, there are 6 cars for every 4 trucks. The ratio is $\frac{6}{4}$ or $\frac{3}{2}$.

A *proportion* is an equation stating that two ratios are equivalent. Ratios are equivalent if they can be represented by equivalent fractions. A proportion may be written

$$\frac{a}{b} = \frac{c}{d}$$

where a/b and c/d are equivalent fractions. This proportion can be read "a is to b as c is to d."

Like any other equation, a proportion can be solved for an unknown by isolating that unknown on one side of the equation. In this case, to solve for a, multiply both sides by b:

$$\frac{(b)a}{b} = \frac{(b)c}{d}$$

$$a = \frac{bc}{d}$$

Examples

Solve for p:

$$\frac{c}{p} = \frac{h}{j}$$

Multiply both sides by p.

$$(p)\frac{c}{p} = (p)\frac{h}{j}$$

$$c = \frac{ph}{j}$$

Solve for a:

$$\frac{a}{4} = \frac{3}{6}$$

$$(4)\frac{a}{4} = (4)\frac{3}{6}$$

$$a = \frac{12}{6}$$

$$a = 2$$

HINT *Another way to solve it.* Another way to solve proportion problems is to find the cross products.

Solve for a:

$$\frac{a}{4} = \frac{3}{6}$$

Cross-multiply:

$$a \times 6 = 4 \times 3$$

$$6a = 12$$

$$a = 2$$

Solve for k:

$$\frac{2}{5} = \frac{8}{k}$$

$$2k = 40$$

$$k = 20$$

Solving Equations for Two Unknowns

An equation may have two unknowns. An example is $3a + 3b = 9$. If you are given two equations with the same unknowns, you can solve for each unknown. Here is how this process works:

Solve for a and b:

$$3a + 4b = 9$$
$$2a + 2b = 6$$

Follow these steps:

Step 1. Multiply one or both equations by a number that makes the number in front of one of the unknowns the same in both equations.

Multiply the second equation by 2 to make $4b$ in each equation.

$$2(2a + 2b = 6)$$
$$4a + 4b = 12$$

Step 2. Add or subtract the two equations to eliminate one unknown. Then solve for the remaining unknown.

$$3a + 4b = 9$$
$$\underline{-(4a + 4b = 12)}$$
$$-a = -3$$
$$a = 3$$

Step 3. Insert the value for the unknown that you have found into one of the two equations. Then solve for the other unknown.

$$3a + 4b = 9$$
$$3(3) + 4b = 9$$
$$9 + 4b = 9$$
$$4b = 0$$
$$b = 0$$

Answer: $a = 3$, $b = 0$

Examples

Solve for j and k: $j + k = 7$

$$j - k = 3$$

You can skip Step 1 of the solution process because the number in front of each of the unknowns is understood to be 1.

Step 2. Add the equations.

$$j + k = 7$$
$$\underline{j - k = 3}$$
$$2j = 10$$
$$j = 5$$

Step 3. Substitute the solution for j into one of the equations and solve for k.

$$5 + k = 7$$
$$k = 7 - 5$$
$$k = 2$$

Solve for c and d: $3c + 4d = 2$
$$6c + 6d = 0$$

Step 1. Multiply the first equation by 2.

$$2(3c + 4d = 2)$$
$$6c + 8d = 4$$

Step 2. Subtract the two equations and solve for one unknown.

$$6c + 8d = 4$$
$$\underline{-(6c + 6d = 0)}$$
$$2d = 4$$
$$d = 2$$

Step 3. Substitute the solution for d into one of the equations and solve for c.

$$3c + 4(2) = 2$$
$$3c + 8 = 2$$
$$3c = -6$$
$$c = -2$$

Answer: $d = 2$, $c = -2$

Monomials, Binomials, and Polynomials

You can guess by the prefix *mono-* that a monomial has something to do with "one." A *monomial* is a mathematical expression consisting of only one term. Examples include $12x$, $3a^2$, and $9abc$.

A *binomial* (the prefix *bi-* means "two") has exactly two terms: $12z + j$.

A *polynomial*, as indicated by the prefix *poly-*, meaning "many," has two or more terms. Examples include $x + y$, $x + y + z$, and $y^2 - 2z + 12$.

Adding and Subtracting Monomials   If the variables are the same, just add or subtract the numbers.

Examples

Add:

$$\begin{array}{r} 9y \\ 11y \\ \hline 20y \end{array}$$

Subtract:

$$\begin{array}{r} 30b \\ -15b \\ \hline 15b \end{array}$$

Add:

$$\begin{array}{r} 12a^2bc \\ 4a^2bc \\ \hline 16a^2bc \end{array}$$

Subtract:

$$\begin{array}{r} 12a^2bc \\ -4a^2bc \\ \hline 8a^2bc \end{array}$$

Multiplying Monomials   When multiplying monomials, multiply any numbers, then multiply unknowns.

Add any exponents. Keep in mind that in a term like x or $2x$, the x is understood to have the exponent 1 even though the 1 is not shown.

Examples

$$(2k)(k) = 2k^2$$
$$(3x)(2y) = 6xy$$
$$(k^2)(k^3) = k^5$$
$$(j^3k)(j^2k^3) = j^5k^4$$
$$-5(b^4c)(-3b^3c^5) = 15b^7c^6$$

Dividing Monomials   To divide monomials, divide the numbers and subtract any exponents (the exponent of the divisor from the exponent of the number being divided).

Examples

$$\frac{2g^5}{6g^3} = \frac{1}{3}g^2$$

$$3\frac{g^5}{g^3} = 3g^2$$

$$\frac{12a^6b^2}{3a^3b} = 4a^3b$$

$$\frac{m^5}{m^8} = m^{-3} = \frac{1}{m^3}$$

$$\frac{-5(ab)(ab^2)}{ab} =$$

This example can be handled in two ways. One way is to simplify the numerator:

$$\frac{-5a^2b^3}{ab} = -5ab^2$$

Another way is to divide out similar terms:

$$\frac{-5(\cancel{ab})(ab^2)}{\cancel{ab}} = -5ab^2$$

Either way will give you the correct answer.

Adding and Subtracting Polynomials   Arrange the expressions in columns with like terms in the same column. Add or subtract like terms.

Examples (Addition)

Add:

$$\begin{array}{r} j^2 + jk + k^2 \\ 3j^2 + 4jk - 2k^2 \\ \hline 4j^2 + 5jk - k^2 \end{array}$$

Add:

$$3p^3 + 2pq + p^2 + r^3$$
$$2p^3 - 6pq + 2p^2 + 3r^3$$
$$-p^3 + pq + 3p^2 - 6r^3$$
$$\overline{4p^3 - 3pq + 6p^2 - 2r^3}$$

Examples (Subtraction)

Remember that when you subtract negative terms, you change the sign and add.

Subtract:

$$j^2 + jk + k^2$$
$$-(3j^2 + 4jk - 2k^2)$$
$$\overline{-2j^2 - 3jk + 3k^2}$$

Subtract:

$$9pq^3 + 3ab - 12m^2$$
$$-(3pq^3 + 2ab - 15m^2)$$
$$\overline{6pq^3 + ab + 3m^2}$$

Multiplying Polynomials To multiply polynomials, multiply each term in the first polynomial by each term in the second polynomial. The process is just like regular multiplication. For example, if you multiply 43 times 12, the problem looks like this:

```
   43
  ×12
 ────
   86   Multiply 2×3 and 2×4 to make 86
   43   Then multiply 1×3 and 1×4 to make 43.
 ────
  516   Add the results.
```

Using polynomials, the process is just the same.

Examples

Multiply:

$$2g - 2h$$
$$\times 3g + h$$
$$\overline{2gh - 2h^2}$$ Multiply $h \times 2g$ and $h \times -2h$ to make $2gh - 2h^2$.
Multiply $3g \times 2g$ and $3g \times -2h$ to make $+6g^2 - 6gh$.
$$\underline{6g^2 - 6gh}$$
$$6g^2 - 4gh - 2h^2$$ Add.

Multiply:

$$3b + a$$
$$2b - 2a$$
$$\overline{-6ab - 2a^2}$$ Multiply $-2a \times 3b$ and $-2a \times a$ to make $-6ab - 2a^2$.
Multiply $2b \times 3b$ and $2b \times a$ to make $6b^2 + 2ab$.
$$\underline{6b^2 + 2ab}$$
$$6b^2 - 4ab - 2a^2$$ Add.

Dividing a Polynomial by a Monomial Just divide the monomial into each term of the polynomial.

Examples

Divide:

$$\frac{8b^2 + 2b}{2b} = \frac{8b^2}{2b} + \frac{2b}{2b}$$
$$= 4b + 1$$

Divide:

$$\frac{9c^3 + 6c^2 + 3c}{3c} = \frac{9c^2}{3c} + \frac{6c^2}{3c} + \frac{3c}{3c}$$
$$= 3c^2 + 2c + 1$$

Dividing a Polynomial by a Polynomial To divide a polynomial by another polynomial, first make sure the terms in each polynomial are in descending order (i.e., cube → square → first power).

For example, $6c + 3c^2 + 9$ should be written $3c^2 + 6c + 9$.

$10 + 2c + 5c^2$ should be written $5c^2 + 2c + 10$.

Then use long division to solve the problem.

Example

Divide $(a^2 + 18a + 45)$ by $(a + 3)$

$$a + 3 \overline{)a^2 + 18a + 45}$$

$$\begin{array}{r} a + 15 \\ a + 3 \overline{)a^2 + 18a + 45} \\ \underline{a^2 + 3a} \\ + 15a + 45 \\ \underline{+ 15a + 45} \\ 0 \end{array}$$

Multiply a times $a + 3$ and subtract the result, leaving $15a$. Bring down the 45 and continue by dividing a into $15a$. Subtracting $15a + 45$ from $15a + 45$ gives zero.

Check your work by multiplying $(a + 3)(a + 15)$ to get $a^2 + 18a + 45$.

Factoring a Polynomial A *factor* is a number that is multiplied to get a product. *Factoring* a mathematical expression is the process of finding out which numbers, when multiplied together, produce the expression.

To factor a polynomial, follow these two steps:

- Find the largest common monomial in the polynomial. This is the first factor.
- Divide the polynomial by that monomial. The result will be the second factor.

Examples

Factor the following expression:

$$5y^2 + 3y$$

y is the largest common monomial.

$$\frac{(5y^2 + 3y)}{y} = 5y + 3$$

y and $5y + 3$ are the two factors.

Factor the following expression:

$$8x^3 + 2x^2$$

$2x^2$ is the largest common monomial.

$$\frac{(8x^2 + 2x^2)}{2x^2} = 4x + 1$$

$2x^2$ and $4x + 1$ are the two factors.

To check your work, multiply the two factors. The result should be the original expression.

$$2x^2 \times (4x + 1) = 8x^3 + 2x^2$$

Special Case: Factoring the Difference between Two Squares

Examples

Factor the following expression:

$$y^2 - 100$$

In this expression, each term is a perfect square; that is, each one has a real-number square root. The square root of y^2 is y, and the square root of 100 is 10.

When an expression is the difference between two squares, its factors are the sum of the squares ($y + 10$)

and the difference of the squares ($y - 10$). Multiplying the plus sign and the minus sign in the factors gives the minus sign in the original expression.

Factoring Polynomials in the Form $ax^2 + bx + c$, Where a, b, and c Are Numbers Remember that you want to find two factors that when multiplied together produce the original expression.

Examples

Factor the expression:

$$x^2 + 5x + 6$$

First, you know that x times x will give x^2, so it is likely that each factor is going to start with x.

$$(x \quad)(x \quad)$$

Now you need to find two factors of 6 that when added together give the middle term of 5. Some options are 1 and 6 and 2 and 3. 2 and 3 add to 5, so add those numbers to your factors. Now you have

$$(x \quad 2)(x \quad 3)$$

Finally, deal with the sign. Since the original expression is all positive, both signs in the factors must be positive. So the two factors must be

$$(x + 2)(x + 3)$$

Check your work by multiplying the two factors to see if you come up with the original expression.

$$(x + 2)(x + 3) = x^2 + 5x + 6$$

Factor the expression:

$$6x^2 + 8x - 8$$

$6x^2$ can be factored into either $(6x)(x)$ or $(2x)(3x)$. Using the latter, the first terms in our factors are as follows:

$$(2x \quad)(3x \quad)$$

Now let's consider the -8. Factors of 8 can be $(8)(1)$ or $(2)(4)$. Let's try 2 and 4, so our factors are now:

$$(2x \quad 2)(3x \quad 4)$$

Now for the signs. In order to get a minus 8 in the original expression, one of the numbers must be a negative and the other a positive. Let's try making the 4 negative, making the factors:

$$(2x + 2)(3x - 4) = 6x^2 - 2x - 8$$

That's close, but the original expression was $6x^2 + 8x - 8$, not $6x^2 - 2x - 8$. What if we switched the numbers 2 and 4?

$$(2x + 4)(3x - 2) = 6x^2 + 8x - 8$$

Now the factors give the original expression when multiplied together, so this is the correct answer.

> **HINT** *It helps to practice.* Don't worry about factoring. Factoring is a little bit of intuition and a lot of practice. Once you do a lot of these kinds of problems, factoring will become almost second nature.

Solving Quadratic Equations

A quadratic equation is one that is written in the form $ax^2 + bx + c$, where a, b, and c are numbers.

To solve an equation in this form for x, set the expression equal to zero. Note that x will have more than one value.

Follow these steps:

- Put all the terms of the expression on one side of the = sign and set it equal to zero.
- Factor the equation.
- Set each factor equal to zero.
- Solve the equations.

Examples

Solve:

$$x^2 + 7x = -10$$
$$x^2 + 7x + 10 = 0 \qquad \text{Add 10 to both sides}$$

in order to get all the terms on one side of the = sign. Now the expression is equal to 0.

$$(x + 5)(x + 2) = 0 \qquad \text{Factor the equation.}$$
$$x + 5 = 0 \quad x + 2 = 0 \qquad \text{Set each factor equal to zero.}$$
$$x = -5 \qquad x = -2 \qquad \text{Solve the equations.}$$

Check your answer by substituting each value back into the original equation.

$$x^2 + 7x = -10$$
$$(-5)^2 + 7(-5) = -10$$
$$25 - 35 = -10$$
$$(-2)^2 + 7(-2) = -10$$
$$4 - 14 = -10$$

Solve for y:

$$y^2 - 4y = 12$$
$$y^2 - 4y - 12 = 0 \qquad \text{Move all terms to one}$$

side and set the equation equal to zero.

$$(y - 6)(y + 2) = 0 \qquad \text{Factor.}$$
$$y - 6 = 0 \quad y + 2 = 0 \qquad \text{Set each factor equal to zero.}$$
$$y = 6 \qquad y = -2 \qquad \text{Solve the equations.}$$

Algebraic Fractions

An algebraic fraction is a fraction containing one or more unknowns.

Reducing Algebraic Fractions to Lowest Terms   To reduce an algebraic fraction to lowest terms, factor the numerator and the denominator. Cancel out or divide common factors.

Example

Reduce to lowest terms:

$$\frac{3y - 3}{4y - 4} = \frac{3(y - 1)}{4(y - 1)} \qquad \text{Factor each expression.}$$

$$= \frac{3\cancel{(y-1)}}{4\cancel{(y-1)}} \qquad \text{Divide out common terms.}$$

$$= \frac{3}{4} \qquad \text{Reduce the fraction to lowest term}$$

> **HINT** *Division reminder:* Don't divide out common terms from a term that includes an addition or subtraction sign.
>
> For example, in a term such as $\frac{x + 2}{2}$, you cannot divide out the 2s.
>
> **Wrong:** $\frac{x + \cancel{2}}{\cancel{2}}$

Example

Reduce to lowest terms:

$$\frac{k^2 + 2k + 1}{3k + 3} = \frac{(k + 1)(k + 1)}{3(k + 1)} \qquad \text{Factor each expression.}$$

$$= \frac{(k + 1)\cancel{(k+1)}}{3\cancel{(k+1)}} \qquad \text{Divide out common terms.}$$

$$= \frac{k + 1}{3}$$

Adding or Subtracting Algebraic Fractions with a Common Denominator To add or subtract algebraic functions that have a common denominator, combine the numerators and keep the result over the denominator. Reduce to lowest terms.

Examples

$$\frac{3y+9y}{m} = \frac{12y}{m}$$

$$\frac{9y-8}{z} - \frac{6y-6}{z} = \frac{9y-8-6y-(-6)}{z}$$

$$= \frac{9y-6y-8+6}{z}$$

$$= \frac{3y-2}{z}$$

Adding or Subtracting Algebraic Fractions with Different Denominators To add or subtract algebraic fractions that have different denominators, examine the denominators and find the least common denominator. Then change each fraction to the equivalent fraction with that least common denominator. Combine the numerators as shown in the previous section. Reduce the result to lowest terms.

Examples

$$\frac{7}{a} + \frac{12}{b} = \frac{7b}{ab} + \frac{12a}{ab}$$

$$= \frac{(12a+7b)}{ab}$$

Note that ab is the least common denominator.

In this example, $12x$ is the least common denominator, as $4x$ and $6x$ both divide into it.

$$\frac{g+2}{4x} + \frac{g-5}{6x} = \frac{3}{3} \times \frac{g+2}{4x} + \frac{2}{2} \times \frac{g-5}{6x}$$

$$= \frac{3g+6}{12x} + \frac{2g-10}{12x}$$

$$= \frac{3g+6+2g-10}{12x}$$

$$= \frac{5g-4}{12x}$$

Note that you have to multiply in order to make each term contain the least common denominator.

Multiplying Algebraic Fractions When multiplying algebraic fractions, factor any numerator and denominator polynomials. Divide out common terms where possible. Multiply the remaining terms in the numerator and denominator together. Be sure that the result is in lowest terms.

Examples

Multiply the following fractions:

$$\frac{y^2}{2j} \times \frac{2j}{3y} = \frac{2y^2 j}{6yj}$$

$$= \frac{2y^2 j}{6yj} = \frac{1y}{3} = \frac{y}{3}$$

Divide out common terms, then multiply. Reduce to lowest terms.

Multiply the following fractions:

$$\frac{6}{x+1} \times \frac{3x+3}{6} = \frac{6}{x+1} \times \frac{3(x+1)}{6}$$ Factor where possible.

$$= \frac{6}{x+1} \frac{3(x+1)}{6}$$ Divide out common terms and multiply.

$$= 3$$

Dividing Algebraic Fractions To divide algebraic fractions, follow the same process used to divide regular fractions: invert one fraction and multiply.

Examples

Divide the following fractions:

$$\frac{3k^2}{5} \div \frac{2k}{z} = \frac{3k^2}{5} \times \frac{z}{2k}$$ Invert the second fraction and multiply.

$$= \frac{3k^2}{5} \times \frac{z}{2k}$$ Simply where possible.

$$= \frac{3kz}{10}$$

Divide the following fractions:

$$\frac{8m^3}{15} \div \frac{6m^2}{3} = \frac{8m^3}{15} \times \frac{3}{6m^2}$$ Invert and multiply.

$$= \frac{8m^3}{15} \times \frac{3}{6m^2}$$ Simply where possible.

$$= \frac{4m}{5} \times \frac{1}{3} = \frac{4m}{15}$$

Graphing on a Number Line

You can represent a number as a point on a number line, as shown in the following examples. Representing a number on a number line is called *graphing*.

Note that whole numbers on the line are equally spaced. Note too that in these examples, both positive and negative numbers are represented.

On the number line, positive numbers are shown to the right of zero. Negative numbers are shown to the left of zero. The positive number +3 is three

units to the right of zero. The negative number −2 is two units to the left of zero.

Graphing on a Coordinate Plane

A coordinate plane is based on an *x* axis (horizontal number line) and a *y* axis (vertical number line). The axes intersect at their zero points. This point of intersection is called the *origin*. Every point on the plane has both an *x* coordinate and a *y* coordinate. The *x* coordinate tells the number of units to

the right of the origin (for positive numbers) or to the left of the origin (for negative numbers). The *y* coordinate tells the number of units above the origin (for positive numbers) or below the origin (for negative numbers).

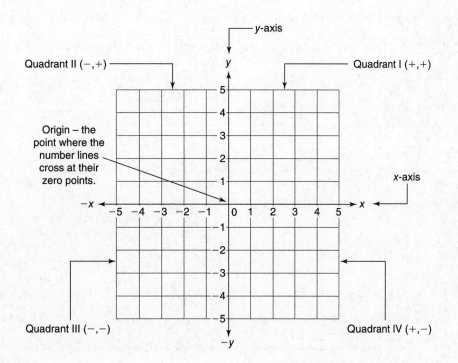

The coordinates of each point are often shown in what is called an *ordered pair* of numbers. An ordered pair looks like this: (2, 3). In every ordered pair, the first number is the *x* coordinate, and the second number is the *y* coordinate. So the ordered pair (2, 3) identifies a point with an *x* coordinate of 2 and a *y* coordinate of 3. The point is located at the intersection of the vertical line that is 2 units to the right of the origin (*x* = +2) and the horizontal line that is 3 units above the origin (*y* = +3). The point (2, −3) is located at the intersection of the vertical line that is 2 units to the right of the origin (*x* = +2) and the horizontal line that is 3 units below the origin (y = −3). The origin is identified by the ordered pair (0, 0).

The *x* and *y* axes separate the graph into four parts called quadrants.

- Points in Quadrant I have positive numbers for both the *x* and the *y* coordinates.
- Points in Quadrant II have a negative number for the *x* coordinate but a positive number for the *y* coordinate.
- Points in Quadrant III have negative numbers for both the *x* and the *y* coordinates.
- Points in Quadrant IV have a positive number for the *x* coordinate but a negative number for the *y* coordinate.

Examples

The graph below shows the following points:

(2,3), (−3,2), (−4,−4), and (0,−2)

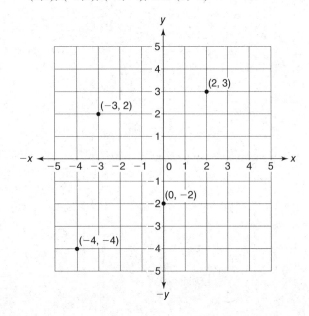

The graph below shows the following points:

A (4,−2), B (−1,1), C (3,3), and D (−4,−3).

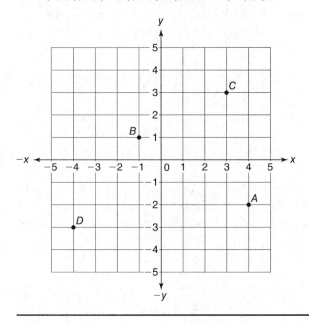

Graphing Equations on the Coordinate Plane An equation with two variables *x* and *y* can be graphed on a coordinate plane. Start by plugging in values for either *x* or *y*. Then solve the equation to find the value of the other variable. The *x* and *y* values make ordered pairs that you can plot on the graph.

Examples

Graph the equation $x + y = 4$

Solving for *x*, the equation becomes $x = 4 - y$

If $y = 1$, then $x = 3$.
If $y = 2$, then $x = 2$.
If $y = 3$, then $x = 1$.
If $y = 4$, then $x = 0$.

HINT *Use a function machine to generate ordered pairs!* Plug in numbers for *x* to get *y*.
If $x =$ _____, then $y =$ _____.

Function Machine

x	y
3	1
2	2
1	3
0	4

Plot the ordered pairs (3,1), (2,2), (1,3), and (0,4) on a graph. If you connect the points, you will see that the result is a straight line.

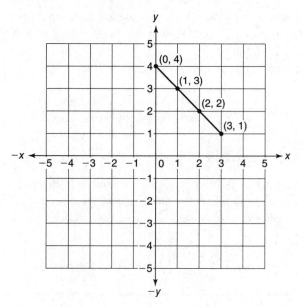

Graph the equation $y - x^2 = 2$

$$y = 2 + x^2$$

If $x = 0$, then $y = 2$.
If $x = 1$, then $y = 3$.
If $x = 2$, then $y = 6$.
If $x = 3$, then $y = 11$.
If $x = 4$, then $y = 18$.

Graph these points and connect the points with a line. Note that when you connect the points, you get a curved line.

Probability

When every event in a set of possible events has an equal chance of occurring, probability is the chance that a particular event (or "outcome") will occur. Probability is represented by the formula

$$\text{Probability} = \frac{\text{number of positive outcomes}}{\text{number of possible outcomes}}$$

Let's say you have a spinner with an arrow that spins around a circle that is divided into six equal parts. The parts are labeled from 1 to 6. When you spin the arrow, what is the probability that it will land on the part labeled 4? Following the formula:

$$\text{Probability} = \frac{\text{number of positive outcomes}}{\text{number of possible outcomes}}$$

$$\text{Probability} = \frac{1}{6} \text{ or 1 in 6}$$

Let's take that same spinner. What is the probability that the arrow will land on the number 2 or the number 3 when it is spun? Using the formula:

$$\text{Probability} = \frac{\text{number of positive outcomes}}{\text{number of possible outcomes}}$$

$$\text{Probability} = \frac{2}{6} = \frac{1}{3} \text{ or 1 in 3}$$

Examples

Solve: The National Fruit Growers' Association is conducting a random survey asking people to tell their favorite fruit. The chart shows the results so far.

Favorite Fruit	Number of People
Apples	236
Peaches	389
Oranges	250
Pears	125

What is the probability that the next randomly selected person will say that pears are his or her favorite fruit?

To solve probability problems, follow the word problem solution procedure outlined in Chapter 9.

Procedure

What must you find? The probability that a certain event will occur

What are the units? Fractions, decimals, or percents

What do you know? The number of people selecting each fruit as their favorite.

Create an equation and solve.

$$\text{Probability} = \frac{\text{number of positive outcomes}}{\text{number of possible outcomes}}$$

Substitute values and solve.

Number of positive outcomes = 125 people who named pears as their favorite fruit
Number of possible outcomes = all people surveyed = 236 + 389 + 250 + 125 = 1,000

$$\text{Probability} = \frac{125}{1,000} = \frac{1}{8}$$
$$= 1:8 = 0.125 = 12.5\%$$

Solve: A box is filled with 25 black balls, 50 white balls, and 75 red balls. If Wendell reaches into the box and picks a ball without looking, what is the probability that he will pick a black or a white ball?

Procedure

What must you find? The probability that either of two events will occur
What are the units? Fractions, decimals, or percents
What do you know? How many of each kind of ball are in the box
Create an equation and solve.

$$\text{Probability} = \frac{\text{number of positive outcomes}}{\text{number of possible outcomes}}$$

Substitute values and solve.

Number of positive outcomes = number of black balls + number of white balls = 25 + 50 = 75
Number of possible outcomes = 25 + 50 + 75 = 150

$$\text{Probability} = \frac{75}{150} = \frac{1}{2} = 1:2 = 0.5 = 50\%.$$

ALGEBRA AND PROBABILITY QUIZ

Circle the letter that represents the best or correct answer. Check your answers with those on page 249. If any of your answers were wrong, go back and study the relevant section of the algebra review.

1. The phrase "some number plus 20" is the same as
   A. $j + 20$
   B. $j - 20$
   C. $\dfrac{j}{20}$
   D. $j \times 20$

2. Evaluate: $a + 2(b) - c$ if $a = 5$, $b = 3$, and $c = 2$
   A. 7
   B. 9
   C. 10
   D. 11

3. Solve for z: $32 + z = 12$
   A. -20
   B. -12
   C. 12
   D. 20

4. The proportion "a is to b is as 3 is to 6" can be represented as
   A. $a + b = 3 + 6$
   B. $a \times b = 3 \times 6 + 45$
   C. $a(3) + b(6)$
   D. $\dfrac{a}{b} = \dfrac{3}{6}$

5. Solve for each variable.

   $y + g = 12$ and $2y + 3g = 16$

   A. $g = 15$, $y = -3$
   B. $g = 5$, $y = 7$
   C. $g = 1$, $y = 11$
   D. $g = -8$, $y = 20$

6. Add:

   $45g$
   $\underline{-90g}$

   A. $-45g$
   B. $45g$
   C. $45g^2$
   D. $135g$

7. Subtract:

   100
   $\underline{130}$

   A. -230
   B. -30
   C. 30
   D. 230

8. Multiply:

   $(g^3)(g^{12})$

   A. g^{-3}
   B. g^{15}
   C. g^{-15}
   D. g^{36}

9. Add:

   $g^2 + gh + h^2 + 3g^2 + 4gh + 3h^2 =$

   A. $2g^2 + 3gh + 2h^2$
   B. $2g^2 + 5gh + 4h^2$
   C. $4g^2 + 5gh + 4h^2$
   D. $4g^2 + 3gh + 2h^2$

10. Multiply:

    $3h - 2m$
    $\underline{\times\ 2h + m}$

    A. $5h^2 + 3m^2$
    B. $6h^2 - hm - 2m^2$
    C. $6h^2 + 5hm + 2m^2$
    D. $6h^2 + 4hm + 2m^2$

11. Factor: $x^2 + 4x - 12$
    A. $(2x^2 + 1 + 6)(-x^2 + 3x - 2)$
    B. $(x + 6)(x - 2)$
    C. $(x + 4)(x + 3)$
    D. $(x^2 + 2)(x^{-2} + 4)$

12. Reduce to lowest terms:

    $$\frac{6x - 6}{8x - 8}$$

    A. $x - 2$

    B. $\dfrac{3x}{4x}$

    C. $\dfrac{6x}{8x}$

    D. $\dfrac{3}{4}$

13. Multiply:

    $$\frac{j^2}{2j} \times \frac{2j}{3g}$$

    A. $\dfrac{3j^2}{6j}$

    B. $\dfrac{2j^3}{6jg}$

    C. $\dfrac{2j^2}{6jg}$

    D. $\dfrac{j^2}{3g}$

14. Divide:

    $$\frac{8g^3}{15} \div \frac{6g^2}{3}$$

    A. $\dfrac{48g^5}{45}$

    B. $\dfrac{2g^5}{12}$

    C. $\dfrac{4g}{15}$

    D. $\dfrac{4g^3}{15g^2}$

15. Which equation is represented by the following graph?

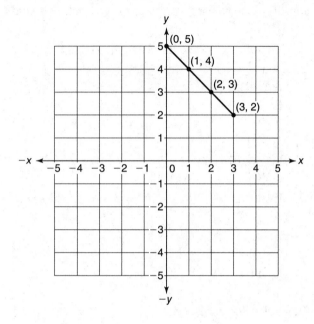

    A. $2x + y = 0$
    B. $x^2 + 1 = 0$
    C. $x + y = 5$
    D. $2x + y = 7$

16. Using a number cube with sides labeled 1 through 6, what is the probability of throwing a 3 or a 4?
    A. 2 in 4
    B. 1 in 3
    C. 2 in 8
    D. 1 in 9

ALGEBRA QUIZ ANSWERS

Number	Answer
1.	A
2.	B
3.	A
4.	D
5.	D
6.	A
7.	B
8.	B
9.	C
10.	B
11.	B
12.	D
13.	D
14.	C
15.	C
16.	B

Chapter 13

Mathematics Knowledge 2: Geometry

YOUR GOALS FOR THIS CHAPTER:

- **Find out what geometry topics you need to know for the ASVAB.**

- **Review techniques and strategies for solving geometry problems.**

- **Study sample geometry problems and their step-by-step solutions.**

- **Measure your test readiness by taking a Geometry Quiz.**

INTRODUCTION: GEOMETRY ON THE ASVAB MATHEMATICS KNOWLEDGE TEST

Along with problems in algebra and probability, the ASVAB Mathematics Knowledge test also includes problems in geometry. To do well on this portion of the test, you'll need to know the basic geometry concepts taught in high school math courses. Topics tested include classifying angles, identifying different kinds of triangles and parallelograms, calculating perimeter and area, finding the circumference and area of circles, identifying different kinds of solid figures, and solving geometry word problems.

It is important that you do well on the Mathematics Knowledge test because it is one of the four ASVAB tests that are used to calculate the AFQT—your military entrance score. That's why it pays to spend time reviewing topics in algebra, probability, and geometry and tackling plenty of sample ASVAB Mathematics Knowledge questions.

The following pages offer a quick but important overview of the basic geometry you need to know to score well on the ASVAB. Make sure that you carefully review and test yourself on every topic covered in this section. Also make sure that you learn how to

use all of the problem-solving methods presented in the examples. Chapter 12 provides a similar review of basic concepts and problem-solving methods in algebra and probability. If you master the core information presented in these two chapters, you will be able to answer ASVAB Mathematics Knowledge questions with relative ease.

Suggested Review Plan for Geometry

- Work through the geometry review at your own pace.
- Pay careful attention to the examples provided.
- After you complete the review, take the geometry quiz.
- Score your quiz.
- Study any problems you answered incorrectly. Reread the corresponding review section, then try the problem again. Work until you understand how to solve the problem.

Remember that you probably won't get these exact problems on the ASVAB, but knowing how to solve them will help you do your best on the actual test.

GEOMETRY REVIEW

Topics
Points, lines, and angles
Triangles
Quadrilaterals
Circles
Perimeter and area
Three-dimensional (solid) figures
Geometry word problems

Points, Lines, and Angles

To work with geometry, you need to understand points, lines, and angles.

- A *point* is an exact location in space. It is represented by a dot and a capital letter.

- A *line* is a set of points that form a straight path extending in either direction without end. A line that includes points *B* and *D* is represented as follows: *BD*.

- A *ray* is a part of a line that has one endpoint and continues without end in the opposite direction. A ray that ends at point *A* and includes point *B* is represented as follows: $\overrightarrow{AB}$.

- A *line segment* is a part of a ray or a line that connects two points. A line connecting points *A* and *B* is represented as follows: $\overline{AB}$.

An *angle* is a figure formed by two rays that have the same endpoint. That endpoint is called the *vertex* (plural: *vertices*) of the angle. An example is shown below.

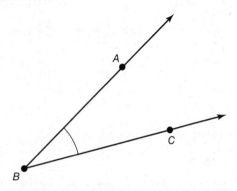

In this example, rays $\overline{BA}$ and $\overline{BC}$ have the same endpoint, which is point *B*. So point *B* is the vertex of the angle. The two line segments $\overline{BA}$ and $\overline{BC}$ are called the *sides* of the angle. The symbol ∠ is used to indicate an angle.

An angle is labeled or identified in several different ways:

- By the vertex: ∠*B*
- By the letters of the three points that form it: ∠*ABC* or ∠*CBA*. (The vertex is always the middle of the three letters.)

The measure of the size of an angle is expressed in *degrees* (°).

Classifying Angles There are three types of angles that you should know for the ASVAB test. They are right angles, acute angles, and obtuse angles.

Right Angles A right angle measures exactly 90°. Right angles are found in squares, rectangles, and certain triangles. ∠*ABC* is a right angle.

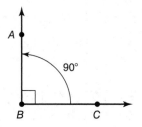

Examples

The angles below are both right angles.

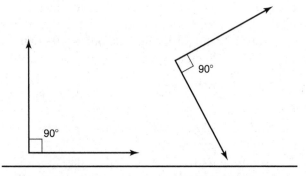

> **HINT** *Look for the "box."* A little "box" tucked into the corner of an angle always means that the angle is a right angle.

Acute Angles An angle that measures less than 90° is called an acute angle. ∠*STU* is an acute angle.

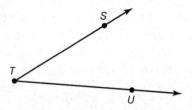

Examples

The angles below are all acute angles.

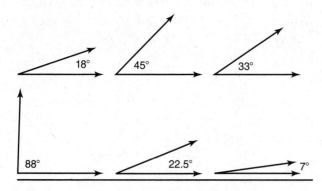

Obtuse Angles An angle with a measure that is greater than 90° but less than 180° is called an obtuse angle. ∠*MNO* is an obtuse angle.

Examples

The angles below are all obtuse angles.

Straight Angles A straight angle is one that measures exactly 180°. This kind of angle forms a straight line. ∠*EFG* is a straight angle.

Classifying Pairs of Lines

Intersecting Lines Intersecting lines are lines that meet or cross each other.

Line *DF* intersects line *GH* at point *E*.

Parallel Lines Parallel lines are lines in a plane that never intersect.

Line *MN* is parallel to line *OP*. In symbols, *MN* ∥ *OP*.

Perpendicular Lines Perpendicular lines intersect to form right angles.

Line *ST* is perpendicular to line *UV*. In symbols, *ST* ⊥ *UV*.

Classifying Pairs of Angles

Adjacent Angles Adjacent angles have the same vertex and share one side. ∠*ABC* and ∠*CBD* are adjacent angles.

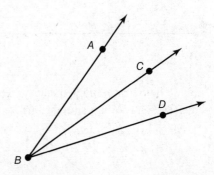

Complementary Angles Two adjacent angles whose measures total 90° are called complementary angles.

∠*MNO* and ∠*ONP* are complementary. Their measures total exactly 90°.

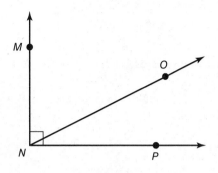

> **HINT**   Figures on the ASVAB are not necessarily drawn exactly to scale.

Example

These two angles are complementary. Together they measure 90°.

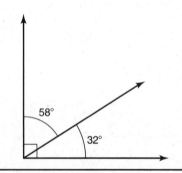

Supplementary Angles   Two adjacent angles whose measures total 180° are called supplementary angles. Together they make a straight line. ∠*KHG* and ∠*GHJ* are supplementary because together they add to 180° or a straight line.

Example

The two angles below are supplementary. Together they measure 180° and form a straight line.

Vertical Angles   Two angles formed by intersecting lines are called vertical angles if they are not adjacent. In the figure below, ∠*AED* and ∠*BEC* are vertical angles. ∠*AEB* and ∠*DEC* are also vertical angles. Vertical angles are often said to be "opposite" to each other, as shown in the figure.

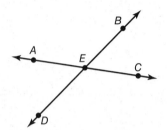

Vertical angles are *congruent*. That is, their measures are the same. ∠*AED* = ∠*BEC* and ∠*AEB* = ∠*DEC*.

Example

Identifying Congruent (Equal) Angles   In the figure below, lines *AC* and *DF* are parallel. They are intersected by a third line *GH*. This third line is called a *transversal*.

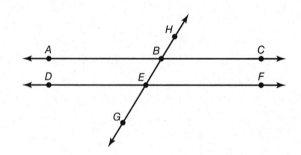

This intersection creates eight angles. There are four pairs of vertical congruent angles:

$$∠ABH = ∠EBC$$
$$∠ABE = ∠HBC$$
$$∠DEB = ∠GEF$$
$$∠DEG = ∠BEF$$

Alternate Interior Angles In addition, four of these angles make two pairs of alternate interior angles. These are angles that are on opposite sides of the transversal, are between the two parallel lines, and are not adjacent. When parallel lines are intersected by a transversal, alternate interior angles are congruent. The two pairs are:

$$\angle ABE = \angle BEF$$
$$\angle DEB = \angle EBC$$

Alternate Exterior Angles Four of the angles also make two pairs of alternate exterior angles. These are angles that are on opposite sides of the transversal, are outside the two parallel lines, and are not adjacent. When parallel lines are intersected by a transversal, alternate exterior angles are congruent. The two pairs are:

$$\angle ABH = \angle GEF$$
$$\angle HBC = \angle DEG$$

Corresponding Angles Eight of the angles also make four pairs of corresponding angles. These are angles that are in corresponding positions. When parallel lines are intersected by a transversal, corresponding angles are congruent. The four pairs are:

$$\angle ABH = \angle DEB$$
$$\angle HBC = \angle BEF$$
$$\angle ABE = \angle DEG$$
$$\angle EBC = \angle GEF$$

> **HINT** *Angles count!* Pay attention to these angle relationships! They are almost certain to appear in some form on the ASVAB.

Solving Angle Problems On the ASVAB, you will most likely be asked to use what you know about angles and angle relationships to solve problems. You may be asked to tell which angles in a figure are congruent. Or you may be given the measure of one angle and asked for the measure of an adjacent angle or some related angle in a figure.

Examples

In the following diagram, parallel lines *MO* and *RT* are intersected by transversal *WV*.

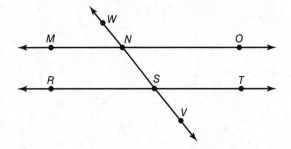

Which angle is congruent to ∠*MNW*?

A. ∠*MNS*
B. ∠*WNO*
C. ∠*RSV*
D. ∠*VST*

Of the choices, the only one that is congruent to ∠*MNW* is ∠*VST* because they are alternate exterior angles.

Which angle is congruent to ∠*MNS*?

A. ∠*RSV*
B. ∠*SNO*
C. ∠*VST*
D. ∠*MNW*

Of the choices, the only one that is congruent to ∠*MNS* is ∠*RSV* because they are corresponding angles.

If ∠*RSN* measures 50°, what is the measure of ∠*RSV*?

A. 90°
B. 110°
C. 130°
D. 150°

∠*RSN* and ∠*RSV* are supplementary angles. That is, together they form a straight line and their measures add up to 180°. So if ∠*RSN* measures 50°, then ∠*RSV* measures 180 − 50 = 130°.

Triangles

A *polygon* is a closed figure that can be drawn without lifting the pencil. It is made up of line segments (sides) that do not cross. A *triangle* is a polygon with three sides. Every triangle has three angles that total 180°.

HINT *Look for tick marks and arcs.* When sides of a polygon are congruent (equal), they may be marked with an equal number of tick marks. When angles are congruent, they may be marked with an equal number of arcs.

Example

The tick marks indicate that sides *AB* and *AC* have the same length. The arcs indicate that ∠*ABC* and ∠*ACB* are congruent.

If sides have different numbers of tick marks, they are not congruent. If angles have different numbers of arcs, they are not congruent.

Identifying the Longest Side of a Triangle   The longest side of a triangle is always opposite the largest angle. So, if a triangle has angles of 45°, 55°, and 80°, the side opposite the 80° angle would be the longest.

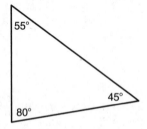

Types of Triangles   There are four main types of triangles. They are equilateral, isosceles, scalene, and right. Each has special characteristics that you should know.

Equilateral Triangle   This kind of triangle has three congruent (equal) sides and three congruent (equal) angles. In an equilateral triangle, each angle measures 60°.

Isosceles Triangle   This type of triangle has at least two congruent sides, and the angles opposite the congruent sides are also congruent. In the isosceles triangle shown below, sides *AB* and *BC* are congruent. ∠*BAC* and ∠*BCA* are also congruent. In an isosceles triangle, if you know the measure of any one angle, you can calculate the measures of the other two.

Examples

In this isosceles triangle, if ∠1 measures 30°, what is the measure of ∠3?

Since ∠1 and ∠2 are congruent, ∠2 must also measure 30°. Together, ∠1 and ∠2 add up to 60°. Since the sum of all three angles in any triangle is 180°, ∠3 must be 180 − 60 = 120°.

If ∠3 measures 100°, what are the measures of ∠1 and ∠2?

Since the sum of all three angles in any triangle is 180°, the sum of the measures of ∠1 and ∠2 must be 180 − 100 = 80°. Since angles 1 and 2 are congruent, each one must measure 80° ÷ 2 = 40°.

Scalene Triangle   This kind of triangle has no equal sides or angles.

Right Triangle   This kind of triangle has one angle that measures 90°. This angle is the *right angle*. It is identified in the figure by the little "box." Since the sum of all three angles in any triangle is 180°, the sum of the two remaining angles in a right triangle is 180 − 90 = 90°.

In a right triangle, there is a special relationship among the lengths of the three sides. This relationship is described by the *Pythagorean Theorem*.

In the right triangle below, ∠*C* is the right angle. The side opposite the right angle is called the *hypotenuse* (*c*). It is always the longest side. The other two sides (*a* and *b*) are called *legs*.

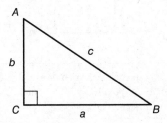

According to the Pythagorean Theorem, in any right triangle, the sum of the squares of the legs equals the square of the hypotenuse. In symbols:

$$a^2 + b^2 = c^2$$

So if you know the lengths of any two sides of a right triangle, you can calculate the length of the third side.

Examples

If *a* = 2 and *b* = 3, what is *c*?
Following the Pythagorean Theorem,

$$2^2 + 3^2 = c^2$$
$$4 + 9 = c^2$$
$$13 = c^2$$
$$\sqrt{13} = c$$

If *a* = 3 and *b* = 4, what is *c*?

$$3^2 + 4^2 = c^2$$
$$9 + 16 = c^2$$
$$25 = c^2$$
$$5 = c$$

If *a* = 6 and *c* = 10, what is *b*?

$$6^2 + b^2 = 10^2$$
$$36 + b^2 = 100$$
$$b^2 = 100 - 36$$
$$b^2 = 64$$
$$b = \sqrt{64}$$
$$b = 8$$

Base and Height of a Triangle   Any side of a triangle can be called the *base*. The *height* is the length of a line segment that connects a base to the vertex opposite that base and is perpendicular to it.

Look at the triangle below. Dashed line *CD* is the height. Line *CD* is perpendicular to the base *AB*.

Where line *CD* meets base *AB*, it creates two right angles, ∠*CDA* and ∠*CDB*.

> **HINT** Sometimes you will see the word *perpendicular* represented by the symbol ⊥. So in the picture above, $\overline{CD} \perp \overline{AB}$.

Median of a Triangle   A *median* of a triangle is a line drawn from any vertex to the middle of the opposite side. This line splits the opposite side into two equal lengths.

Example

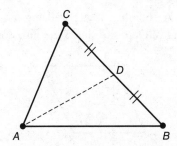

Dashed line *AD* is a median of triangle *ABC*. It splits side *BC* into two equal lengths, $\overline{CD}$ and $\overline{BC}$.

Quadrilaterals

A quadrilateral is a polygon with four sides and four angles. The sum of the four angles is always 360°.

Types of Quadrilaterals   There are several different kinds of quadrilaterals. Each type is classified according to the relationships among its sides and angles. The square, rectangle, parallelogram, and rhombus are all types of quadrilaterals.

Parallelogram   A parallelogram is a quadrilateral with both pairs of opposite sides parallel and congruent. The opposite angles are also congruent. Around the edge of the parallelogram, each pair of consecutive angles is supplementary; that is, their sum is 180°. Diagonal lines drawn from opposite vertices *bisect* each other (divide each other exactly in half), but the diagonals themselves are not equal in length.

$$\angle A = \angle D$$
$$\angle C = \angle B$$

$$\angle A + \angle B = 180°$$
$$\angle B + \angle D = 180°$$
$$\angle D + \angle C = 180°$$
$$\angle C + \angle A = 180°$$

Like triangles, quadrilaterals have bases and height. Any side of this parallelogram can be a base. Dashed line $\overline{AE}$ is a height of this parallelogram. The *height* is a line originating at a vertex and drawn perpendicular to the opposite base. The height forms two right angles where it meets the base.

Rhombus A rhombus is a parallelogram with four congruent sides. Opposite angles are also congruent.

HINT Watch out for ASVAB questions that use parallelograms, rhomboids, or trapezoids, but involve the Pythagorean Theorem. In the trapezoid, for example, you might be asked to calculate the hypotenuse by knowing the length of $\overline{CE}$ and $\overline{AE}$.

Rectangle A rectangle is a parallelogram with four right angles. Diagonal lines drawn from opposite vertices of a rectangle bisect each other (divide each other exactly in half) and are equal in length.

Square A square is a rectangle with four congruent sides. Diagonal lines drawn from opposite vertices of a rectangle bisect each other (divide each other exactly in half) and are equal in length.

HINT In any square like the one shown, if you draw diagonals from point A to point D and from point C to point B, the lines are equal in length and bisect each other.

Trapezoid A trapezoid is a quadrilateral with only one pair of parallel sides. Like other quadrilaterals, it has bases and height. In the example below, dashed line CE is the height. Sides AB and CD are parallel, but sides AC and BD are not parallel.

Circles

A circle is a closed figure with all points the same distance from a *center*. A circle with its center at point A is called circle A.

Parts of a Circle A *chord* is a line segment that has endpoints on a circle. A *diameter* is a chord that passes through the center of a circle. A *radius* is a line segment that connects the center of a circle and a point on the circle. Its length equals half the length of the diameter. In the figure below, A is the center of the circle. EF is a chord. BC is a diameter of the circle. AC and AB are each a radius of the circle.

An *arc* is two points on a circle and the part of the circle between the two points. In the figure below, CD is an arc of the circle. A *central angle* is an angle whose vertex is the center of a circle. In the figure below, $\angle CAD$ is a central angle. Its measure is 50°. The sum of the measures of the central angles in a circle is 360°.

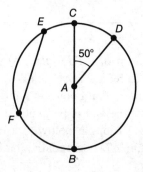

Perimeter and Area

The *perimeter* is the distance around a closed two-dimensional figure. The *area* is the amount of surface a two-dimensional figure covers. Area is measured in square units such as square inches (in^2) or square centimeters (cm^2). A square inch is the area of a square with sides 1 inch long.

Finding the Perimeter of a Polygon   To find the perimeter of a polygon, just add the length of each side to find the total.

Example

$\triangle ABC$ is an isosceles triangle. If side AB has a length of 25 cm and side BC has a length of 15 cm, what is the perimeter?

Since $\triangle ABC$ is an isosceles triangle, side AB = side AC. So if side AB has a length of 25 cm, side AC also has a length of 25 cm. Thus, the perimeter is 25 + 25 + 15 = 65 cm.

Finding the Area of a Polygon   There are special formulas you can use to calculate the areas of various types of polygons. You will want to memorize these, as you will almost certainly be asked a question about area on the ASVAB.

Area of a Triangle   The area (A) of a triangle is one-half the base (b) multiplied by the height (h), or

$$A = \frac{1}{2}bh$$

> **HINT**   *Watch the squares!* Anytime you see units squared, you are dealing with area. Examples: square inches (in^2), square centimeters (cm^2), square yards (yd^2), and so on.

Example

If a triangle has a height that measures 30 cm and a base that measures 50 cm, what is its area?

$$b = 50 \text{ cm}$$
$$h = 30 \text{ cm}$$
$$A = \frac{1}{2}bh$$
$$A = \frac{1}{2}(50)(30)$$
$$A = \frac{1}{2}(1{,}500)$$
$$A = 750 \text{ cm}^2$$

Area of a Square or Rectangle   The area (A) of a square or rectangle is its length (l) multiplied by its width (w), or $A = lw$

Example

If this rectangle is 10 miles long and 6 miles wide, what is its area?

$$A = lw$$
$$A = (10)(6)$$
$$A = 60 \text{ square miles } (60 \text{ mi}^2)$$

Area of a Parallelogram (Including a Rhombus)   The area (A) of a parallelogram is its base (b) multiplied by its height (h), or $A = bh$.

Example

If a parallelogram has a base of 6 meters and a height of 4 meters, what is the area?

$$A = bh$$
$$A = (6)(4)$$
$$A = 24 \text{ square meters } (24 \text{ m}^2)$$

Area of a Trapezoid   The area (A) of a trapezoid is one-half the sum of the two bases (b_1 and b_2) multiplied by the height (h), or $A = \frac{1}{2}(b_1 + b_2)h$.

Example

If a trapezoid has one base of 30 meters and another base of 60 meters, and its height is 20 meters, what is the area?

$$A = \frac{1}{2}(b_1 + b_2)h$$

$$A = \frac{1}{2}(30 + 60)20$$

$$A = \frac{1}{2}(90)20$$

$$A = \frac{1}{2}(1,800)$$

$$A = 900 \text{ square meters } (900 \text{ m}^2)$$

Finding the Circumference and Area of a Circle   The *circumference* of a circle is the distance around the circle. The circumference (C) divided by the diameter (d) always equals the number π (pi). Pi is an infinite decimal, meaning that its decimal digits go on forever. When you use it to solve problems, you can approximate as π 3.14 or 22/7.

To find the circumference of a circle, use the formula $C = \pi d$.

Example

If a circle has a radius of 3 inches, what is the circumference?

Since the diameter is twice the radius $(2r)$, the diameter is 6 inches.

$$C = \pi d$$
$$C = 3.14(d)$$
$$C = 3.14(6)$$
$$C = 18.84 \text{ in.}$$

To find the area of a circle, multiply π times the square of the radius: $A = \pi r^2$

Example

If a circle has a radius of 4 centimeters, what is its area?

$$A = \pi r^2$$
$$A = 3.14(4)^2$$
$$A = 3.14(16)$$
$$A = 50.24 \text{ cm}^2$$

Three-Dimensional (Solid) Figures

A figure is *two-dimensional* if all the points on the figure are in the same plane. A square and a triangle are two-dimensional figures. A figure is *three-dimensional* (solid) if some points of the figure are in a different plane from other points in the figure.

On solid figures, the flat surfaces are called *faces*. *Edges* are line segments where two faces meet. A point where three or more edges intersect is called a *vertex*.

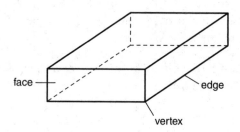

Types of Solid Figures   On the ASVAB, you may see problems related to these solid figures: rectangular solid (prism), cube, cylinder, and sphere.

Rectangular Solid (Prism)   On a rectangular solid (also called a prism), all of the faces are rectangular. The top and bottom faces are called *bases*. All opposite faces on a rectangular solid are parallel and congruent.

Cube A cube is a rectangular solid on which every face is a square.

Cylinder A cylinder is a solid figure with two parallel congruent circular bases and a curved surface connecting the boundaries of the two faces.

Sphere A sphere is a solid figure that is the set of all points that are the same distance from a given point, called the center. The distance from the center is the radius (r) of the sphere.

center

Finding the Volume of Solid Figures Volume is the amount of space within a three-dimensional figure. Volume is measured in cubic units, such as cubic inches (in^3) or cubic centimeters (cm^3). A cubic inch is the volume of a cube with edges 1 inch long.

Volume of a Rectangular Solid To find the volume (V) of a rectangular solid, multiply the length (l) times the width (w) times the height (h). The formula is $V = lwh$.

Example

If a rectangular solid has a length of 3 yards, a height of 1.5 yards, and a width of 1.5 yards, what is its volume?

$V = lwh$
$V = (3)(1.5)(1.5)$
$V = 6.75$ cubic yards (6.75 yd^3)

Volume of a Cube On a cube, the length, width, and height are all the same: Each one equals 1 side (s). To find the volume (V) of a cube, multiply the length $\times$ width $\times$ height. This is the same as multiplying side $\times$ side $\times$ side. The formula is $V = s \times s \times s = s^3$.

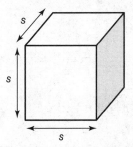

Example

If each side of a cube measures 9 feet, what is its volume?

$V = s^3$
$V = (9)^3$
$V = 729$ cubic feet (729 ft^3)

Volume of a Cylinder To find the volume (V) of a cylinder, first find the area of the circular base by using the formula $A = \pi r^2$. Then multiply the result times the height (h) of the cylinder. The formula is $V = (\pi r^2)h$.

Example

If a cylinder has a height of 7 meters and a radius of 2 meters, what is its volume?

$V = (\pi r^2)h$
$V = 3.14(2)^2(7)$
$V = 3.14(4)(7)$
$V = 87.92$ cubic meters (87.92 m^3)

Volume of a Sphere To find the volume of a sphere, multiply 4/3 times π times the radius cubed. The formula is $V = \frac{4}{3}\pi r^3$.

Example

If the radius of a sphere measures 12 inches, what is the volume?

$V = \frac{4}{3}\pi r^3$

$V = \frac{4}{3}\pi(12)^3$

$V = \frac{4}{3}(3.14)(1728)$

$V = \frac{4}{3}(5{,}425.92)$

$V = 7{,}234.56$ cubic inches (7,234.56 in.^{3})

Geometry Word Problems

Word problems on the ASVAB may deal with geometry concepts such as perimeter, area, and volume. To solve these problems, you may also need to use information about different units of measure. To review units of measure, see Chapter 8.

Just as with other kinds of word problems, you can solve geometry problems by following a specific procedure. In the examples that follow, pay special attention to the procedure outlined in each solution. Follow this same procedure whenever you need to solve this kind of word problem.

Examples

Sally is buying wood to make a rectangular picture frame measuring 11 in. × 14 in. The wood costs 25 cents per inch. How much will Sally have to pay for the wood?

Procedure

What must you find? Cost of the wood for the frame
What are the units? Dollars and cents
What do you know? Cost of the wood per inch; shape of the frame, measure of the frame
Create an equation and solve.

Length of wood needed for rectangular frame $= 2l + 2w$

Substitute values and solve:

Length of wood = 2(14) + 2(11)
Length of wood = 28 + 22 = 50 in.

If each inch costs 0.25, then

0.25 × 50 = $12.50

Sergei is planting rosebushes in a rectangular garden measuring 12 ft × 20 ft. Each rosebush needs 8 ft^2 of space. How many rosebushes can Sergei plant in the garden?

Procedure

What must you find? Number of rosebushes that can be planted in the garden
What are the units? Numbers
What do you know? Shape of the garden, garden length and width, amount of area needed for each rosebush
Create an equation and solve.

$A = lw$

Substitute values and solve.

$A = 12 \times 20 = 240$ ft^2

Each rosebush needs 8 ft^2

240 ÷ 8 = 30

Sergei can plant 30 rosebushes in the garden.

Shapes and Formulas: Summary

Shapes	Formulas

Triangle
Area = 1/2 of the base × the height
$A = 1/2\ bh$
Perimeter = $a + b + c$

Square
Area = length × width
$A = lw$
Perimeter = side + side + side + side
$P = 4s$

Rectangle
Area = length × width
$A = lw$
Perimeter = 2 × length + 2 × width
$P = 2l + 2w$

Parallelogram and Rhombus
Area = base × height
$A = bh$
Perimeter = 2 × length + 2 × width
$P = 2l + 2w$

Trapezoid
Area = the sum of the two bases divided by 2 × height

$$A = \left(\frac{b_1 + b_2}{2}\right)h$$

Perimeter = $a + b_1 + b_2 + c$

$P = a + b_1 + b_2 + c$

Circle
The distance around the circle is its circumference (C). The length of a line segment passing through the center with endpoints on the circle is the diameter (d). The length of a line segment connecting the center to a point on the circle is the radius (r). The diameter is twice the length of the radius ($d = 2r$).
$C = \pi d = 2\pi r$
$A = \pi r^2$
$\pi = 3.14$ or $22/7$

Cube
Volume = side × side × side
$V = s^3$

(Continued)

Shapes and Formulas: Summary (*Continued*)

Shapes	Formulas
	Rectangular Solid Volume = length × width × height $V = lwh$
	Cylinder Volume = πr^2 × height $V = \pi r^2 h$
	Sphere Volume = $4/3\pi r^3$ $V = 4/3\pi r^3$

GEOMETRY QUIZ

1. The endpoint shared by two rays that form an angle is called a
   A. line segment.
   B. degree.
   C. vertex.
   D. straight line.

2. A right angle is an angle that measures
   A. exactly 90°.
   B. greater than 90°.
   C. less than 90°.
   D. 45°.

3. An acute angle is an angle that measures
   A. exactly 90°.
   B. greater than 90°.
   C. less than 90°.
   D. exactly 180°.

4. An obtuse angle is an angle that measures
   A. exactly 90°.
   B. between 90° and 180°.
   C. exactly 180°.
   D. greater than 180°.

5. In the figure shown, if angle 1 measures 65°, what is the measure of angle 2?

   A. 120°
   B. 90°
   C. 25°
   D. 10°

6. In the figure shown, if angle 1 measures 35°, what is the measure of angle 2?

   A. 145°
   B. 95°
   C. 65°
   D. 45°

7. In the figure shown, if angle 2 measures 45°, what is the measure of angle 4?

   A. 135°
   B. 75°
   C. 45°
   D. 35°

8. In the figure shown, lines *AB* and *CD* are parallel and angle 1 measures 120°. What is the measure of angle 2?

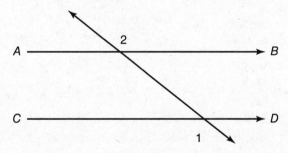

   A. 60°
   B. 90°
   C. 120°
   D. 180°

9. A certain triangle has exactly two equal sides, and the angles opposite those sides are also equal. This triangle is a(n)
   A. isosceles triangle.
   B. scalene triangle.
   C. equilateral triangle.
   D. right triangle.

10. In the equilateral triangle shown, what is the measure of each angle?

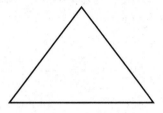

 A. 60°
 B. 90°
 C. 120°
 D. 180°

11. In the triangle shown, ∠*ACB* measures 55° and ∠*CAB* measures 65°. What is the measure of ∠*CBA*?

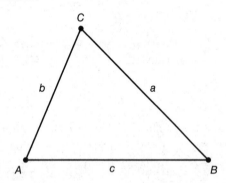

 A. 50°
 B. 60°
 C. 80°
 D. 90°

12. In the triangle shown, side *a* is 5 in. long and side *b* is 6 in. long. How long is side *c*?

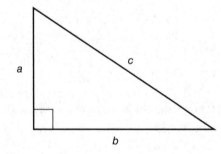

 A. 7.81 in.
 B. 8.51 in.
 C. 9.11 in.
 D. 10.71 in.

13. In the rectangle shown, side *a* measures 13 cm and side *b* measures 36 cm. What is the perimeter of the rectangle?

 A. 49 cm
 B. 98 cm
 C. 469 cm
 D. 512 cm

14. In the triangle shown, side *a* is 4 ft long, side *b* is 6 ft long, and side *c* is 8 ft long. What is the area of the triangle?

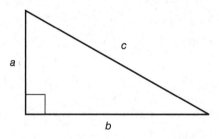

 A. 12 ft²
 B. 18 ft²
 C. 24 ft²
 D. 36 ft²

15. In which of the following circles is the line segment a diameter?

A.

B.

C.

D.

16. The circle shown has a diameter of 12 m. What is the area of the circle?

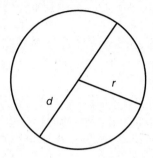

A. 452.16 m²
B. 360 m²
C. 144 m²
D. 113.04 m²

17. In the trapezoid shown, $b_1 = 4$ ft, $b_2 = 8$ ft, and $h = 5$ ft. What is the area of the trapezoid?

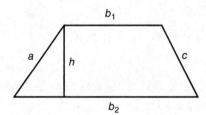

A. 16 ft²
B. 30 ft²
C. 90 ft²
D. 160 ft²

18. Figure *WXYZ* is a parallelogram. Which of the following is NOT necessarily true?

A. Side *WX* is parallel to side *ZY*.
B. Side *XY* is parallel to side *WZ*.
C. ∠*W* has the same measure as ∠*Y*.
D. Side *WX* is the same length as side *XY*.

19. Which of the following figures contains line segments that are perpendicular?

A.

B.

C.

D.

20. What is the ratio of the length of a side of an equilateral triangle to the triangle's perimeter?
A. 1:1
B. 1:2
C. 1:3
D. 3:1

21. Jules needs to purchase a ladder that just reaches the top of a 16-foot building. If the bottom of the ladder will be placed 12 feet from the base of the building, how long should Jules's ladder be?
A. 18 ft
B. 20 ft
C. 25 ft
D. 30 ft

22. Kai must buy canvas to make a sail for his sailboat. The sail will have the shape of a right triangle. It will be as tall as the mast (the vertical pole) and as wide at the bottom as the boom (the horizontal pole). If the mast measures 18 meters and the boom measures 9 meters, about how much canvas does Kai need to buy?
A. 27 m²
B. 61 m²
C. 81 m²
D. 103 m²

23. Renee wants to carpet her living room. If the room measures 15 feet × 18 feet, how many square yards of carpet must she purchase?
    A. 20 yd^2
    B. 30 yd^2
    C. 32 yd^2
    D. 35 yd^2

24. Saul wants to wallpaper one wall in his dining room. The wall is 11 ft high and 14 ft long. It has a window that measures 3 ft by 4 ft. About how many square feet of wallpaper must Saul buy?
    A. 25 ft^2
    B. 32 ft^2
    C. 112 ft^2
    D. 142 ft^2

25. In the following figure, line *AB* intersects two parallel lines. If angle 1 measures 35°, what is the measure of angle 4?

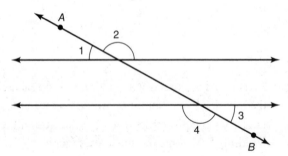

    A. 35°
    B. 55°
    C. 90°
    D. 145°

26. The Lakeville skating rink is a perfect circle. If the diameter of the rink is 50 ft, which of the following best represents its area? (Use π = 3.14)
    A. 78.5 ft^2
    B. 157 ft^2
    C. 1,962 ft^2
    D. 7,850 ft^2

27. A tomato paste can has a diameter of 8 cm and a height of 20 cm. Which of the following tells about how much tomato paste it will hold?
    A. 4,019 cm^3
    B. 1,005 cm^3
    C. 201 cm^3
    D. 50 cm^3

28. In the figure shown, what is the area of the rectangle if the radius of each circle is 6 cm?

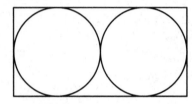

    A. 72 cm^2
    B. 112 cm^2
    C. 288 cm^2
    D. 310 cm^2

29. A square garden is doubled in length and 4 feet is added to its width. Which of the following expressions represents the new area of the garden?
    A. $2x(x + 4)$
    B. $4x^2$
    C. $4x + 4$
    D. $(2x)(4x)$

30. A rectangular garden is 40 yards long and 15 yards wide. Darryl runs once around the edge of the garden. How far does Darryl run?
    A. 55 yards
    B. 80 yards
    C. 100 yards
    D. 110 yards

GEOMETRY QUIZ ANSWERS

Number	Answer
1.	C
2.	A
3.	C
4.	B
5.	C
6.	A
7.	C
8.	C
9.	A
10.	A
11.	B
12.	A
13.	B
14.	A
15.	A
16.	D
17.	B
18.	D
19.	A
20.	C
21.	B
22.	C
23.	B
24.	D
25.	D
26.	C
27.	B
28.	C
29.	A
30.	D

Chapter 14

Electronics Information

YOUR GOALS FOR THIS CHAPTER
• Find out what Electronics Information topics are covered on the ASVAB.
• Learn basic facts about electricity, electric circuits, and electrical devices and systems.
• Study examples of ASVAB Electronics Information questions and learn ways to solve them.
• Take an Electronics Information quiz.

INTRODUCTION: ASVAB ELECTRONICS INFORMATION QUESTIONS

The electronics information questions that appear on the ASVAB measure how much you understand about electricity, electric circuits, and electrical and electronic devices and systems.

The questions may ask you to identify a particular device on a circuit diagram, explain how to measure voltage or current, or identify particular types of circuits. If you have tinkered with electricity or electronics at home or in school, you may be familiar with some of the topics covered here.

Whichever ASVAB version you take, you'll have only about half a minute to answer each electronics information question, so you'll have to work fast if you want to get a good score. That's why it pays to spend time studying the test topics and tackling plenty of sample ASVAB Electronics Information questions.

The topic review that follows will help prepare you to answer ASVAB Electronics Information questions. At the end of the chapter there is a short quiz with questions modeled on those on the actual test. Read carefully through the review materials in this chapter, then use the quiz to find out how well you have mastered this subject area. Go back and reread the review materials for any quiz items you miss.

ELECTRICITY

Basics

Let's start by getting acquainted with some basic concepts in electricity. To understand electricity, you need to know the following:

ASVAB Electronics Information Test
Number of Questions:
• Paper-and-pencil ASVAB: 20
• CAT-ASVAB: 16
Time Limit:
• Paper-and-pencil ASVAB: 9 minutes
• CAT-ASVAB: 8 minutes
Topics covered:
• Electric current
• Electric circuits
• Electrical devices and systems

- *Electricity* is a form of energy that can travel invisibly through conductors. It can be used in so many ways that we could call it the most versatile form of energy. Electricity is carried by moving charged particles, especially by electrons. Electrons are tiny negative charges that orbit the nucleus of an atom.
- A *conductor* is a material that allows an easy flow of electrons. Silver, copper, and aluminum are all good conductors.
- An *insulator* is a material that resists the flow of electrons. Rubber, plastic, and ceramic are good insulators.

- A *circuit* is a loop of conductor that takes electricity from its source to the load (the place where it does some work) and back to the source.
- A *load* is anything in the circuit, such as a heater, a light, or a motor, that uses power.
- *Direct current* (DC) is a steady-flowing type of electricity, produced by batteries and used in flashlights, boom boxes, and computers.
- *Alternating current* (AC) is a type of current that changes direction many times per second. AC is used in home wiring, mainly because it can be transported long distances over transmission wires.
- *Electronics* is a branch of science that deals with complicated uses of electricity, such as in radios, televisions, and computers.

Technical Terms

To understand electricity, you also need to know a few technical terms. Study the following list.

- *Electric current* is the amount of electrons flowing through a conducting material.
- *Electric power* is the amount of power consumed by an electrical device.
- *Voltage* is a force that affects the rate at which electricity flows through a conductor. It is sometimes called electrical pressure. The higher the voltage, the more likely electricity is to "leak" across an insulator or an air gap. That's one reason higher voltages are more dangerous. *Voltage drop* tells how much electrical pressure is used in a part of the circuit.

- *Frequency* is the number of complete alternations—from one direction to the other and then back again—that alternating current makes per second. Each complete alternation is called a cycle.
- *Resistance* is the opposition of a material to the flow of electricity through it. All circuits must have a resistance. If they don't, they are called *short circuits*, and wires can overheat.

Units of Measure and Measuring Devices

Different aspects of electricity are measured using different units of measure. Special measuring devices are used. The following table shows the different units and devices.

Ohm's Law

Ohm's law describes the relationship among electrical pressure (voltage), current strength (amperage), and resistance (ohms) in any circuit:

$$\text{Amperes} = \text{volts/ohms}$$
$$A = V/\Omega$$

If you know two of these three quantities, you can always calculate the third.

$$\text{Amperes} = \text{volts/ohms}$$
$$\text{Volts} = \text{amperes} \times \text{ohms}$$
$$\text{Ohms} = \text{volts/amperes}$$

What Is Measured	Unit of Measure	Unit Definition	Symbol	Measuring Device
Electric power (*amount of energy consumed*)	Watt	Watts = volts × amperes 1 *kilowatt* = 1,000 watts 1 *kilowatt hour* = 1,000 watts flowing for 1 hour.	W	Electric meter
Electric current (*strength*)	Ampere	1 ampere = the flow of 1 coulomb of electricity past a given point per second (1 coulomb = 6.25×10^{18} electrons)	A	Ammeter
Voltage (*electrical pressure*)	Volt	Volts = watts/amperes	V	Voltmeter
Resistance	Ohm	1 ohm = 1 volt per ampere	Ω	Ohmmeter
Frequency	Hertz	Number of cycles per second (in North America, AC is delivered at 60 Hz)	Hz	

Here's an easy way to remember how to use Ohm's law to find the third quantity if you know two already. On the circle (below), place your finger over the quantity you want to find. Look at the remaining two quantities to see how to calculate the third quantity.

$$\frac{\text{Volts}}{\text{Amps} \times \text{Ohms}} = \frac{V}{A \times \Omega}$$

Ohm's Law Circle.

Memorize the equations on the circle; you'll need them on the ASVAB. Let's look at a couple of examples of how to use the Ohm's law circle.

Examples

Find the amperes if a 120-volt current runs through 6 ohms.

Amperes = volts/ohms
Amperes = 120/6 = 20 amperes

Or cover amperes in the circle. Notice that what remains is volts divided by ohms (the same result you would get by remembering the three formulas above).

Amperes = 120/6 = 20 amperes

In a 6-volt circuit with 24 amperes flowing, what is the resistance?

Ohms = volts/amperes
Ohms = 6/24 = 1/4 ohms

The Law of Electric Power

The amount of power consumed by an electrical or electronic device can be calculated using the following formula:

Watts = volts × amperes

You can use this equation to find any one of the three factors as long as you know the other two. Here are two examples.

Examples

How much power is consumed by a lamp that draws 10 amperes of current at 120 volts?

Watts = volts × amperes
Watts = 120 × 10 = 1,200 watts

A clothes dryer is rated at 2,400 watts. At 120 volts, how much current does it draw?

Amperes = watts/volts
Amperes = 2400/120 = 20 amperes

ELECTRICITY AND MAGNETISM

Electricity and magnetism are tightly connected: It's easy to change from an electric current to a magnetic field and back again. This close relationship explains electromagnets, transformers, motors, and generators. Let's start with electromagnets.

A current passing through a conductor creates a magnetic field around it. In most electromagnets, the conductor (wire) is wrapped around an iron core.

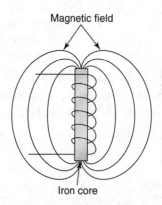

Magnetic field

Iron core

An Electromagnet with Magnetic Field Shown.

A transformer is like two electromagnets placed next to each other. If the transformer has more turns of wire on the output side, it is a *step-up* transformer, and the output voltage will be greater than the input voltage. If there are more turns on the input side, it's a *step-down* transformer, and the output voltage is smaller than the input voltage.

Bolt

Wire coil

Wire coil

Steel "Flatbar"

Transformer.

Motors and Generators

Electromagnetism also explains motors and generators. In fact, motors and generators are really the same machines, operating backwards.

- A *generator* changes rotating (kinetic) energy into electric energy.

- A *motor* changes electric energy into kinetic energy.

Here's how a motor works. Each magnet has two poles: north and south. Opposite poles attract, and like poles repel: North attracts south, but repels north. A motor has two magnets: a *rotor* that spins inside a *stator*, a fancy name for a stationary magnet. One of these magnets, usually the rotor, is an electromagnet. It is wired so that the magnetic field changes twice per rotation. When the rotor starts rotating, the rotor and the stator repel each other, forcing the rotor to start turning. At just about the point where the magnets would stop repelling, the rotor changes polarity, and it again repels the stator. This change in polarity is what drives the motor. We call them electric motors, but motors are all about magnetism.

Electric Motor.

ELECTRICAL DEVICES AND SYMBOLS

Electrical devices are the guts of many electrical and electronic systems. You'll need a basic acquaintance with these devices. You should also know the symbols used for them in electrical diagrams.

A *capacitor* is a device that can briefly store electricity.

This Is the Symbol for a Capacitor.

A *resistor* creates resistance to the flow of electrons. If a circuit does not have any resistance, it's called a short circuit. Excess current will cause such a circuit to heat up, which may cause a fire.

This Is the Symbol for a Resistor.

A *transformer* changes the voltage and amperage of a current. Transformers work by changing electricity into magnetism, then back into electricity. As you can see from the diagram, transformers have two coils. One gets current (usually AC) from a source; the other supplies the output. The first coil creates a magnetic field, which rises and falls as the current alternates. The second coil is inside a changing electric field, and any wire in a changing magnetic field will pick up current from that magnetism.

This Is the Symbol for a Transformer.

A *battery* stores electricity as chemical energy that can be readily converted into electric current. Batteries may be wet (like the lead-acid storage batteries used in cars) or dry (like the nickel-cadmium or metal hydride batteries used in flashlights, computers, and the like). Batteries always make direct current. Depending on their chemistry, some batteries can be recharged.

The electrochemical reactions between the cathode and the electrode result in free electrons, which can travel through a circuit to make an electric current.

This Is the Symbol for a Battery.

This Is the Symbol for Alternating Current.

SERIES, PARALLEL, AND SERIES-PARALLEL CIRCUITS

Electric current exists only when electrons can flow through a circuit. There are two basic types of circuits, and a third type that blends the two.

Let's start with the basics: the series and parallel circuits.

In a *series circuit*, all moving electrons pass through every part of the circuit, including all the loads and switches. Current (the quantity of electrons) is the same at all points of the circuit, but voltage drops as the current goes through each device. The total voltage of the loads must equal the voltage of the circuit: In a series circuit supplied by a 12-volt car battery, a single light bulb must have a 12-volt drop. If the circuit has two lights, their combined voltage drop is 12 volts.

When a series circuit is used in a string of Christmas tree bulbs, the whole string goes dark if any bulb burns out. Thus, although they are simple, series circuits are less common than the next basic type, the parallel circuit.

Series Circuit.

In a *parallel circuit*, the loads are placed between the two supply wires, so that they all get the same voltage. A second advantage of the parallel circuit is this: Current can flow through any of the loads, even if one is switched off. (In a series circuit, a switch controls the current in the entire circuit.)

Parallel Circuit.

Remember this rule: Current is the same at all points in a series circuit. Voltage is the same at all points in a parallel circuit.

To find the *total resistance* in a series circuit, add the resistance of each load. For example, in a series circuit with one 12-Ω and one 8-Ω resistor, total resistance = 12 + 8 = 20 Ω.

It's more complicated to calculate total resistance in a parallel circuit since you must add the inverse of the resistances. What is the total resistance in a parallel circuit with one 12-Ω and one 8-Ω resistor?

$$1/R_{total} = 1/12 + 1/8 = 2/24 + 3/24 = 5/24 = 1/R_{total}$$

Solve for R_{total}:

Multiply both sides by R_{total}: $5 \times R_{total}/24 = 1$

Multiply both sides by 24: $5 \times R_{total} = 24$

Divide both sides by 5: $R_{total} = 24/5$ ohms

Note that R_{total}, 24/5, is simply the inverse of 5/24, the fraction equaling $1/R_{total}$.

The third type of circuit is the *series-parallel circuit*, which combines features of series and parallel circuits. The series-parallel circuit is a hybrid with many advantages of each. You'll find series-parallel circuits throughout your house. The branch circuits that bring electric power to the lights and outlets are series-parallel: All the current goes through a fuse or circuit breaker, but then it is distributed in parallel. Why is this circuit needed? Because voltage must be the same for all outlets and lights, and because the circuit must work whether any particular light is switched on or not.

Series-Parallel Circuit.

SEMICONDUCTORS

So far, we've talked about insulators and conductors. But there is an important category of materials between these two categories.

A semiconductor can act as a conductor or as an insulator. Silicon, the main semiconductor, is the basis for computer memory and logic boards. Chemicals called *dopants* are applied to the silicon to determine whether it will act as an insulator or as a conductor. They do this by making electrons available or not available to flow. (When electrons can flow, a material becomes a conductor.)

The basis for computer applications is a group of components, particularly transistors and diodes.

Transistors are devices that can switch a current, regulate its flow, or amplify a current, all based on the presence of a smaller current. Millions of tiny transistors are built on small pieces of semiconductor, which are the basis of computer logic and memory.

This Is the Symbol for a Transistor.

Diodes are devices that allow a current to flow in one direction only. In addition to electronics, diodes are also used in devices called *rectifiers*, which convert AC into DC.

Diode

This Is the Symbol for a Diode.

PRACTICAL ELECTRICITY

The ASVAB will also ask you about more practical matters, including simple electric circuits. You'll have an advantage here if you've ever worked on your home wiring (which is usually much easier than most people think).

In a simple electric circuit like the one in your home, electricity is distributed at a fuse box or circuit breaker box. The box has two functions:

- Breaking up the load in the building into a number of circuits
- Preventing excess current from flowing into the circuits

Many simple circuits have two separate conductors: hot and grounded. The hot conductor is usually black, but it can be red or another color. The grounded (sometimes called neutral) conductor is white. Together, the black and white wires are called the *supply* wires, because they form the circuit that electric current needs to travel.

To work safely on any electric circuit, you need to shut off the electricity, and check that it is off. The fuses and circuit breakers can shut off the circuit. Before starting work, use an electrical tester to test whether the hot wires are energized.

Bigger (heavier) wires can carry more current. Home wiring systems are usually rated for 15 or 20 amperes. 15-ampere circuits require 14-gauge wires. Larger, 12-gauge wires are needed for 20-ampere circuits.

Grounding Systems

Electricity always "wants" to complete a circuit, to get back to where it came from. The wiring in a building always includes two options for returning current to the circuit breaker or fuse box. The white (grounded) wire is the normal return path for electricity. The bare (equipment grounding) wire is the alternative path, available if something goes wrong with the grounded wire. In many systems, the alternative return path is provided by a steel sheath on the wires, called a *conduit*.

Black (hot)

Bare (equipment grounding)

White (ground)

House Wiring.

Because the two supply wires are different (black brings the current, and white drains it away), modern electric plugs are *polarized*. This means that they can fit into the socket in only one way, because one lug on the plug is bigger than the other.

Polarized Plug.

Switches and Rheostats

Switches turn electric circuits on and off. One single-pole switch controls a circuit. Two *three-way* switches can work together to control a circuit from either of two locations, such as at the top and bottom of a stairway. A rheostat continuously controls the voltage, and is used to dim lights. In home wiring, switches always control the hot side of the circuit—the one that supplies the current.

Electrical Connections

Electrical connections must be secure and tight. Otherwise, electric arcs will develop, causing heat and ruining the connection. One of the best connections comes from solder, a metal that is melted over a connection. Solder joints must have flux, a chemical that prevents oxidation from happening when the wires get heated. Solder can be used to join wires to other wires or wires to terminals.

Circuit Breakers and Fuses

Because electric circuits get hot when something goes wrong, circuit breakers and fuses are used in most circuits. Both have the same job: breaking the circuit (cutting off the power) when something goes wrong. A circuit breaker usually has an electromagnet that opens a circuit when the current gets too high. A fuse has an element that melts when the current is too high. Fuses are easier to make, but circuit breakers can just be reset after they trip, whereas a fuse must be replaced. If a fuse continually blows, do not replace it with a larger-capacity fuse; this invites fire. Find the problem and fix it.

Coaxial Cables

Coaxial means "having the same axis." Coaxial cables, usually used in cable TV systems, have an inner and an outer conductor.

ELECTRONICS INFORMATION QUIZ

Take the following quiz to check your understanding of ASVAB Electronics Information topics. There is no time limit. Answers and explanations are given immediately after the quiz.

1. Alternating current is so called because
   A. it is an alternative to direct current.
   B. it alters the magnetic field.
   C. resistance alternates many times per second.
   D. the current changes direction many times per second.

2. An electric current is
   A. a form of energy.
   B. a flow of electrons.
   C. the ability to do work.
   D. both A and B.

3. A battery
   A. always produces direct current.
   B. may produce alternating current.
   C. converts electric energy into chemical energy.
   D. must have a liquid electrolyte.

4. In a series circuit, total voltage drop equals
   A. the drop produced by the biggest resistance in the circuit.
   B. the sum of the individual voltage drops.
   C. one-half the total individual voltage drops.
   D. the inverse of the largest individual voltage drop.

5. A volt is a unit of electric(al)
   A. current.
   B. resistance.
   C. pressure.
   D. capacitance.

6. If a 120-volt current is running through a circuit with a resistance of 6 Ω, what is the current strength in amperes?
   A. 15 A
   B. 20 A
   C. 30 A
   D. 60 A

7. The transformer depends on the relationship between electricity and
   A. voltage.
   B. amperage.
   C. chemical energy.
   D. magnetism.

8. In an electric motor, magnets
   A. repel each other.
   B. attract each other.
   C. cancel each other.
   D. amplify each other.

9. A circuit without resistance is called
   A. an open circuit.
   B. a short circuit.
   C. a closed circuit.
   D. a hot circuit.

10. A transformer changes the _____ in a circuit.
    A. resistance
    B. current
    C. voltage
    D. both B and C

11. In a series circuit, a switch controls
    A. all devices on the circuit.
    B. only devices with a positive charge.
    C. only devices with a negative charge.
    D. voltage, but not current.

12. Which is the same at all points in a parallel circuit?
    A. Voltage
    B. Resistance
    C. Current
    D. Ohms

13. A switch in a series-parallel circuit controls
    A. all devices.
    B. some or all devices.
    C. only electronic devices.
    D. only nonelectronic devices.

14. The purpose of dopant in a semiconductor is to make it act as a(n)
    A. insulator.
    B. resistor.
    C. conductor.
    D. A or C.

15. In a parallel circuit, what is the total resistance if the individual resistances are 3 Ω and 12 Ω?
    A. 5/12 Ω
    B. 12/5 Ω
    C. 12 Ω
    D. 5 Ω

ANSWERS AND EXPLANATIONS

1. **D.** The polarity, or direction of electron flow, alternates in AC. Choice B is something that happens with alternating current, but this is not the reason for the name.

2. **D.** Electricity is a form of energy, and a current is defined as a flow of electrons.

3. **A.** Batteries always produce direct current (DC).

4. **B.** Total voltage drop is the sum of the individual voltage drops.

5. **C.** Electrical pressure is what "pushes" current through a circuit.

6. **B.** Amperes = volts/ohms = 120/6 = 20.

7. **D.** When electricity goes through a coil of wire in a transformer, it creates a magnetic field. When this field interacts with another coil of wire, it induces an electric current.

8. **A.** Electric motors are based on magnetic repulsion.

9. **B.** A short circuit has no resistance.

10. **D.** A transformer changes both current and voltage.

11. **A.** A series circuit has only one pathway, so when a switch is open, the whole circuit shuts down.

12. **A.** Voltage is the same at all points of a parallel circuit.

13. **B.** A switch in a series-parallel circuit can control some or all devices, depending on the way it's wired.

14. **D.** Dopants control the electrical properties of a semiconductor.

15. **B.** $1/R_{total} = 1/R_1 + 1/R_2 + 1/R_3 = 1/3 + 1/12 = 5/12$. Solve for R_{total} to get 12/5 ohms.

Chapter 15

Auto Information

YOUR GOALS FOR THIS CHAPTER

- **Find out what automobile topics are covered on the ASVAB.**

- **Learn basic facts about automobile components and systems.**

- **Study examples of ASVAB auto information questions and learn ways to solve them.**

- **Take an auto information quiz.**

INTRODUCTION: ASVAB AUTO INFORMATION QUESTIONS

The automobile questions that appear on the ASVAB measure how much you understand about automobile components and systems, and how much you know about maintaining and repairing them. The questions may ask you to describe the function of a particular part, to tell what might be causing a given problem, or to explain how to repair a given malfunction. You won't necessarily be asked to explain *why* auto parts function as they do, but you will be asked *what to do* and *how to do it* when a part needs maintenance or repair. If you own a car and maintain it yourself, you may already be familiar with many of the topics covered on the test. You may also have learned about cars by watching

or helping family members or friends maintain an automobile, or by working in a garage yourself.

On the paper-and-pencil version of the ASVAB, automobile questions are one part of the Auto and Shop Information test. On the CAT-ASVAB, they form a separate test of their own.

Whichever ASVAB version you take, you'll have only about a minute to answer each automobile question, so you'll have to work fast if you want to get a good score. That's why it pays to spend time studying the test topics and tackling plenty of sample ASVAB automobile questions.

The topic review that follows will help prepare you to answer ASVAB automobile questions. It describes each of the major systems of today's automobiles and reviews the functions of all the most important automobile parts. At the end of the chapter, there is a short quiz with questions modeled on those on the actual test. Read carefully through the review materials in this chapter, then use the quiz to find out how well you have mastered this subject area. Go back and reread the review materials for any quiz items you miss.

ASVAB Auto Information Questions

Number of Questions:
- Paper-and-pencil ASVAB: 10–12 (as part of the Auto and Shop Information test)
- CAT-ASVAB: 11 (as a separate test)

Time Limit:
- Paper-and-pencil ASVAB: 5–6 minutes (as part of the 11-minute Auto and Shop Information test)
- CAT-ASVAB: 7 minutes

AUTOMOBILE ENGINES

The engine is the heart of an automobile. Cars use an internal-combustion engine, meaning that the fuel is burned inside the engine. (Steam engines are "external-combustion engines" that burn fuel outside the engine; steam is piped to a turbine that creates the rotary motion.) All car engines, including diesel engines, use the Otto cycle, named for Nicholas Otto, the German who invented the four-stroke gasoline engine in the 1870s.

Here is an overview of what happens inside an Otto-cycle engine: A mix of fuel and air is brought inside a closed space, called a cylinder. The mix is compressed and then explodes. The explosion moves a piston, which rotates the crankshaft. The crankshaft is connected through the drive train to the driving wheels, which move the car. Waste heat from the explosions is removed by the cooling system.

Cylinders are located in the large, cast-iron engine block. Cylinders are laid out in a straight line or a V shape. Straight-line engines usually have four cylinders. For a six- or eight-cylinder engine, the V design (called a V-6 or V-8) saves space.

Piston, Connecting Rod, and Crankshaft.

Cylinder and Piston

The *cylinder* is the heart of the internal combustion engine, since it's where combustion takes place. The cylinder is a finely machined chamber that holds a *piston* as it slides up and down. Thin rings called *piston rings* seal the gap between the cylinder and the piston, containing the explosions and increasing efficiency.

- If the piston rings wear, oil can enter the cylinder. Burning oil makes blue smoke and cuts power output. When an engine starts to burn oil, a major repair called an engine overhaul is needed.
- Changing the oil regularly is the best way to prevent excess wear to piston rings.

Cylinder Head

The *cylinder head* is a complex metal casting that closes the top of the cylinders. The head is bolted to the engine block. A *head gasket* separates the

head and the block. Like all gaskets, the head gasket creates a seal between two rigid objects that would leak if there were not something compressible between them.

Each cylinder needs at least one intake valve and one exhaust valve. These valves close off a port that allows intake gases to enter or exhaust gases to leave. Many engines increase their power output by using two intake valves and/or two exhaust valves. The cylinder head also has passages for coolant and holes for the bolts that hold it to the engine block.

When you bolt a cylinder head to the engine block, both the order of tightening and the torque (tightening force) are important. Tightening bolts in the correct order prevents the head from warping. Tightening to the right torque ensures that the head is tight enough to seal the gasket evenly. For American cars, torque is measured in foot-pounds. For other cars, it is measured in newton-meters.

The cylinder head also has threaded holes for the *spark plug*. These electrical devices create a spark when they get a high-voltage jolt of electricity from the ignition system. Spark plugs are screwed into the cylinder head and should be replaced periodically.

Crankshaft

Pistons move in a straight line, but the engine produces rotating motion. The *connecting rods* and *crankshaft* change linear motion into rotary motion. Think of the knee of a bicyclist. It moves up and down in a straight line, just like a piston. The knee is connected to the pedal by the lower leg, which acts like a connecting rod. The pedals and cranks act like a crankshaft to convert linear motion to rotary motion.

Connecting rods are attached to the crankshaft by the *main bearings*. The crankshaft itself rotates on *journal bearings* attached to the engine block. The crankshaft is housed inside an *oil pan*, and the bearings also get lubrication from oil tubes or channels in the block.

How the Four-Cycle Engine Works

Understanding an Otto-cycle engine starts with firing order. Memorize this order: intake, compression, power, exhaust.

- *Intake.* The piston moves down, creating a partial vacuum in the cylinder. The fuel-air mixture enters the cylinder through the open intake valve. The exhaust valve is closed.

- *Compression.* Both valves are closed. The piston moves up, compressing the fuel-air mixture to about 10 times atmospheric pressure.
- *Power.* The spark plug fires, starting an explosion inside the cylinder. The resulting high pressure pushes the piston down.
- *Exhaust.* The piston moves up again, with the exhaust valve open and the intake valve closed. The piston pushes burned exhaust gases into the exhaust manifold and out of the engine.

fuel and air. Valves must open and close precisely and quickly, several thousand times a minute when an engine is running at full throttle. Valves, particularly the exhaust valve, are in the hottest part of the engine. They cannot be cooled by water, but must conduct away their heat by contact with the valve seat in the cylinder head.

Helix-shaped *valve springs* hold valves against the *valve seat*, a polished, sloping surface that closely fits the outside edge of the valve.

Intake Stroke.   **Compression Stroke.**

Power Stroke.   **Exhaust Stroke.**

Overhead Camshaft and Valve.

In overhead-camshaft engines, the top of the valve rides against the *camshaft*. Once every two revolutions of the crankshaft, the *camshaft lobe* pushes against the valve stem, opening the valve.

Valves and Valve Train

Valves play a critical part in the Otto engine because they admit fresh fuel and air and discharge burned

Conventional Camshaft and Valve.

In conventional-camshaft engines, the camshaft pushes against a *push rod*, which pushes the *rocker arm*. The rocker arm pivots on the *rocker-arm shaft*, so the ends move in opposite directions. When the push rod raises one end of the rocker arm, the other end pushes down on the valve, so it opens.

The camshaft is driven by a *timing chain* from a sprocket on the crankshaft. The chain keeps the camshaft perfectly in sync with the crankshaft. A broken timing chain is one of the most serious of all problems that can affect an Otto-cycle engine.

Firing Order

To make the engine run more smoothly, nearby cylinders do not ignite in sequence. Instead, the firing is spread around the engine. A typical four-cylinder engine might fire in the order 1-3-2-4. Firing order gets a bit more complicated in V-type engines, but the general rule is the same.

Lubrication System

Engines contain hundreds of metal parts that rotate or slide against metal. Pistons and piston rings slide against the cylinder. The crankshaft rotates inside journal bearings. Camshafts, push rods, rocker arms, and valves must also be protected against friction with a thin film of lubricant—engine oil.

Engines have a complicated set of tubes and internal passages that bring oil to the contact points. A gear-driven *oil pump* pushes oil through these passages. Oil also splashes onto the cylinder walls, lubricating the piston rings and making compression more effective.

- Oil gets dirty and wears out, so it must be replaced periodically. Oil filters clean the oil, but they must also be replaced.
- Oil and filter manufacturers estimate their product lifetime in miles and/or months. Replace the oil or filter when you reach the first of these milestones.
- To change oil, warm up the engine, place a pan under the oil plug in the crankcase, remove the plug, and drain the oil. Replace the plug and refill the oil through the filler cap on top.
- Recycle used oil; do not dump it down the drain or in a field.
- New cars should not need a top-up of oil between oil changes. But as cars age, engines wear and oil consumption increases, so it makes sense to check the oil periodically. Much of this wear occurs at the piston rings and cylinders.
- When a car starts "burning oil," blue smoke indicates wear of the rings and/or cylinders.
- If the oil pressure light comes on while you are driving, pull over as soon as possible and check for trouble. If you are lucky, the oil level may simply be low, and adding oil should take care of the problem. Otherwise, to prevent severe engine damage, get the car towed to a shop. Sudden loss of oil pressure can also result from oil-pump failure, or other serious engine problems.

Viscosity Oil, like most fluids, gets thicker as the temperature drops. You can see this with molasses. In the refrigerator, it is almost solid. But if you heat molasses on the stove, it starts to flow like water. The viscosity, or thickness, of oil is measured by S.A.E. numbers, which range from a very light S.A.E. 5 to a molasses-like S.A.E. 90. Typically, for summer driving, oil is rated at S.A.E. 30 to 40.

Auto engines start out cold and warm up as they operate. Thick, cold oil creates a lot of resistance when you try to start a cold engine. But if the oil is too thin at operating temperature, it won't separate the metal parts. To resolve this dilemma, lubrication engineers created "multiweight" oil, which is rated with two S.A.E. numbers, for low/high-temperature viscosity. Thus S.A.E. 10W-40 flows more easily at low temperatures (where it's S.A.E. 10) and is thicker when it warms up (where it's S.A.E. 40).

Transmissions and differentials also need lubrication, usually from heavier oil, such as S.A.E. 80 or 90. (These transmission oils or transmission greases are different from automatic transmission fluid, which is used only in automatic transmissions.)

Cooling System

Internal-combustion engines develop a great deal of heat from all those explosions. Only about 30 percent of the energy in gasoline is converted into energy to drive the car. The rest becomes waste heat. Unless the engine can get rid of this heat quickly, it will overheat. Waste heat is removed and delivered to the atmosphere by coolant. At first, water was used as the coolant. But water freezes in winter, and the expansion when it does so can crack the engine block. Chemicals called *antifreeze* are added to prevent freezing. Dissolving most chemicals in water usually lowers the freezing point. Water can also rust—corrode—the iron in an engine. Coolants also contain a chemical that halts rust, called, logically, *rust inhibitor.* Because rust inhibitor eventually breaks down, coolant must be replaced every few years.

Coolant flows through hollow passages in the engine block and cylinder head. These *water jackets* must bring enough coolant to every part of the engine block and cylinder head. From the engine block, coolant flows to the radiator, which has many small tubes covered by fins. The radiator is located on the front of the engine, where it can get plenty of fresh air.

A *radiator fan* pulls air through the radiator, removing heat from the tubes. The radiator is connected to the engine block through a series of hoses, which can wear out or leak.

- Checking hose and fan belt condition is good preventive maintenance, although modern engines are packed so tightly that the hoses and belts may be hard to see.
- Don't fill the radiator through the cap. Instead, add coolant to the translucent reservoir that's attached by hoses to the radiator. The reservoir has "low" and "full" markings; just keep coolant between these marks.
- Repair shops have testers to determine the freezing point of coolant. If you always add coolant (50-50 antifreeze and water), your coolant should stay liquid down to about −30°F. But if you top up the radiator with water, get the freezing point checked in the fall; you may have to replace the coolant to protect the engine.

A *water pump*, often located on the front of the crankshaft, circulates coolant through the engine. If the water pump fails for even a few minutes, overheating and severe engine damage can result. To increase heat removal, the coolant is pressurized. Pressurized liquids stay liquid at higher temperatures, and hotter liquids can move more heat.

Although we've talked about the need to cool an engine, engines operate best after they have warmed up. To help an engine reach operating temperature, a *thermostat* prevents the circulation of cold coolant. Thermostats are usually located on the top of the engine, inside a housing that connects the engine block to the top radiator hose. Inside the thermostat, a metal valve opens when the coolant reaches operating temperature.

In newer cars, the fan may also help with engine warm-up. In older cars, the fan was driven from a pulley on the crankshaft by a *fan belt.* These fans rotated when the engine ran. Now, electrically driven fans start running only when the engine is warm.

- Cars have either a warning light to indicate engine overheating or a gauge that measures engine temperature. Another sign of overheating is the smell of antifreeze; overheating raises engine pressure, and eventually coolant blows out through the radiator cap, releasing a cloud of sweet-smelling, greasy steam.
- A stuck thermostat is probably the largest cause of engine overheating. If you don't drive until you correct the problem, it's usually an inexpensive one as well. Problems with fan belts, radiators, coolant level, and sensors can also cause overheating.

Engine Troubleshooting

Engines are getting more complex all the time, but it helps to know a few troubleshooting hints to score big on the ASVAB:

- A "ping" or "knocking" sound on acceleration usually means that you need a higher-octane gasoline. The noise indicates that the fuel-air mixture is igniting too soon inside the cylinder.
- A squealing noise that increases with engine speed indicates a loose or worn fan belt.
- An engine that runs extremely rough may have a failed spark plug or some other problem in the ignition system.

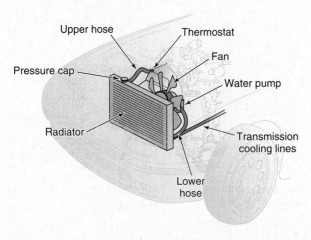

Cooling System.

- General sluggishness, roughness, or poor fuel mileage all indicate the need for a tune-up.
- Loud clanking sounds may indicate major engine problems that will only get worse if you ignore them.

DRIVE TRAIN

The *drive train* gets power from the engine to the wheels. The drive train includes the transmission, driveshaft, differential, and axles on the driving wheels, which may be in front, in back, or both. In cars with front-wheel drive, the transmission and differential are combined in a "transaxle."

The drive train must

- Provide different gears so that the engine can always work at an efficient rpm (revolutions per minute), no matter what the driving speed.
- Allow the car to move backward (in reverse gear).
- Allow the engine to run when the car is not moving.
- Drive two or four wheels.
- Allow the car to turn without tire slippage.

Manual Transmission

In a manual transmission, you change gears with a *clutch* and *gearshift*. Manuals, which once had only two or three speeds, today generally have five forward speeds plus reverse. In general, transmissions have an input shaft, a layshaft, and an output shaft. The input shaft is connected to the clutch, and the output shaft is connected to the driveshaft and eventually the driving wheels.

When a transmission "changes gears," it changes the ratio of input speed to output speed. In first gear, roughly four revolutions of the input shaft turn the output shaft once. First gear is used to accelerate from a stop, and the engine must turn fast while the wheels turn slowly. First gear allows fast acceleration because it multiplies torque at slow driving speed.

When you shift gears in a manual transmission, the gears do not engage or disengage; all the gears are always engaged. Instead, the gears are shifted by a small collar attached to the output shaft. *Dog teeth* on the side of this collar catch holes in the side of the gear, connecting the gear to the output shaft. When the collar is disengaged, the gears spin freely on the output shaft.

The gearshift moves the collar, and synchronizers between the collar and the gear allow the dog teeth to engage the gears. If you shift too fast, these synchronizers don't have time to engage, and the gears clash.

To change direction for reverse gear, there is an *idler gear* between the layshaft and the output shaft. In forward gears, the input and output shafts rotate in opposite directions. But the idler gear causes the output shaft to turn in the same direction as the input shaft.

Five-Speed Manual Transmission.

Clutch The clutch disconnects the engine from the transmission, so that you can shift gears. The clutch also allows you to idle at a traffic light without shifting into neutral. A clutch usually has three plates, which are controlled by the clutch pedal.

Clutch, Engaged.

The clutch is *engaged* when the clutch pedal is up and *disengaged* when the pedal is down.

When the clutch is engaged, springs push the pressure plate against the clutch disk, pressing the clutch disk against the flywheel. Because of friction between the pressure plate and the flywheel, the input shaft and flywheel rotate together. In this position, neither the throwout bearing nor the clutch plates wear.

When the clutch is disengaged, a cable or hydraulic piston moves the release fork, pressing the throwout bearing against the diaphragm spring, moving the pressure plate away from the clutch disk, and disconnecting the flywheel from the input shaft. The throwout bearing does get wear in this position. The pressure plate wears when the clutch is partly engaged, mainly when starting from a standstill in first gear.

Automatic Transmission

Automatic transmissions change gears automatically to suit driving conditions. Modern automatics often have four forward gears, plus reverse, park, and neutral. The transmission itself uses a complex set of gears to do the shifting.

Instead of the manual clutch just described, automatics link the engine to the transmission with a hydraulic mechanism called a *torque converter*. The torque converter has two blades that look much like propellers. The drive blade, attached to the engine output shaft, churns up hydraulic fluid the way a propeller moves water. The driven blade is caught by the stream of hydraulic fluid and turns like a pinwheel in a breeze.

When the engine is idling at a stoplight, little hydraulic fluid is pumped, little energy is transmitted to the driven blade, and just a bit of pressure on the brake holds the car still. When the engine speeds up, the drive blade pumps more fluid, and more energy is transferred to the driven blade. At highway speeds, almost all of the energy is transmitted to the driven blade. Because of inefficiencies, automatics waste more gasoline than manual transmissions, but they are "hands-free" and much more popular.

Differential

When a car turns a corner, the outside wheels must drive further than the inside wheels. If both driving wheels were locked to the axle, the tires would be

Torque Converter.

forced to slip against the pavement. The differential solves this problem.

The differential has three jobs:

- *Allow different (differential) movement of the two axles*, so that the car can turn a corner.
- *Change drive directions.* In rear-wheel-drive cars, the differential connects to a driveshaft that runs from front to back and powers the axles, which run from side to side.
- *Increase power.* The differential usually reduces the drive speed, so that three to four input revolutions create one turn of the axles.

Normally, if one wheel is slipping, the differential will direct all power to it, allowing the other wheel to sit still without doing any work. This causes problems when traction is poor. "Limited-slip" or "positraction" differentials limit this slip.

Front-Wheel or Rear-Wheel Drive

Traditionally, cars steered with the front wheels and drove with the rear wheels. Driving with the front wheels is more complicated, but it offers many advantages:

- The engine weight is on the driving wheels, increasing traction.
- The steering wheels also drive, pulling the car to follow the steering wheels on ice, snow, or sand.
- There is no driveshaft, saving interior room.

The disadvantage is complexity. Stacking the transmission and differential together in a "transaxle" makes front-wheel-drive systems harder to design and repair.

Cars with four-wheel drive, of course, have both a conventional driveshaft and a transaxle, and a front-back differential. They have the most complicated drive trains.

ELECTRICAL SYSTEM

The first cars had barely any electrical system. A hand crank started them, and gas or oil lamps lit the road for those foolhardy enough to drive after dark. The only electrical mechanism was the magneto that fed electric current to the spark plugs. Let's start our examination of the electrical system by looking at the ignition system.

Ignition System

The key parts of the ignition system are the breaker points, the coil, the distributor cap, and the distributor rotor. The breaker points ride against a lobed shaft inside the distributor. The shaft completes one revolution for every two strokes of the crankshaft (intake, compression, power, exhaust).

A Connection to coil-1/2 volt
B Breaker points
C Adjusting screw
D Cam follower
E Distributor Camp
F Condenser

Breaker Points.

When the breaker points close, they complete a circuit, and a pulse of 12-volt current goes through the primary winding of the ignition coil, creating a

brief magnetic field. This changing magnetic field induces a current in any nearby wire. The voltage of this induced (output) current depends on the ratio of the primary and secondary windings. In an ignition coil, the primary winding has few loops, and the secondary winding has many.

The ignition coil is a direct-current transformer. The induced current, which creates the spark at the spark plugs, is at 10,000 volts or higher. This high-voltage output goes via heavy, high-voltage cable to the center of the distributor cap.

High-voltage coil cable
To breaker points
To ground
Primary winding
Secondary winding

Ignition Coil.

The distributor cap and rotor direct the high-voltage current to the spark plugs. The rotor is on top of the distributor shaft. The rotor receives the high-voltage current from the coil wire and directs it to the spark plug wires connected to the distributor cap. Because the shaft rotation is synchronized with the crankshaft rotation, the spark occurs at the right time.

All the important parts of the electrical system—the breaker points, rotor, distributor cap, and high-voltage wires—can wear out. That's why tune-ups are needed every few thousand miles. Distributor ignition has largely been replaced by electronic ignition, which we'll get to shortly.

Spark Plug The spark plug receives the high-voltage spark current from the distributor and creates an electric spark that sets off the explosion in the cylinder. Spark plugs operate in hot conditions, and they must be replaced occasionally.

- If a spark plug is coated with a greasy black substance, the cylinder is leaking oil, probably because of worn piston rings. Oil burns incompletely in the cylinders, leaving this black deposit.
- Spark plugs must have the correct gap, measured in thousandths of an inch. Feeler gauges are used to set the correct gap.
- When spark plug electrodes get thin, the plug should be replaced.

Terminal nut

Ceramic insulator

Gasket

Thread

Plug gap

Spark Plug.

Diesel engines need no spark plug because the fuel-air mixture ignites when it is compressed. Diesels don't need a coil or distributor. They are somewhat more fuel-efficient, but also more polluting, than gasoline engines. Diesels require fuel injectors and special fuel, but otherwise are quite similar to gasoline engines.

Electronic Ignition

Electronic ("solid-state") *ignitions* have been introduced over the last 20 years to eliminate the many weak points of distributor ignition. Instead of one centrally located coil, there is a coil at each spark plug, and instead of a mechanical distributor, an electronic unit directs a low-voltage current to those coils. The system allows precise spark timing, which increases power and gasoline mileage, while reducing pollution.

Battery

Cars use a 12-volt battery to store electric energy for starting. These lead-acid batteries are compact and affordable electricity storage devices that last for several years. Lead-acid batteries can quickly deliver the large current needed by the starter motor. They are easily recharged, because the electrochemical reaction that makes electricity is reversible, allowing electricity to be stored as chemical energy.

Inside a lead-acid battery, a chemical reaction between sulfuric acid (the *electrolyte*) and lead plates (the *electrodes*) creates extra electrons at the negative pole. When you connect the starter motor to the negative and positive electrodes, a current flows, discharging the battery and turning the starter motor. Each battery cell makes about 2 volts, so a 12-volt battery has six cells. During charging, a 12-volt battery requires about a current of about 14 volts.

- Lead-acid batteries eventually wear out. However, the biggest problem with a lead-acid battery is often the simplest. Corrosion on the battery terminals or battery cables can break the circuit, causing a fully charged battery to appear "dead."
- Corrosion-preventing chemicals can avoid problems blamed on "dead batteries." These chemicals often appear as a red spray on the terminal.
- Older lead-acid batteries had a tendency to run dry, but modern batteries really need no checking. They do wear out after a few years, however. Repair shops have battery testers that can measure how much life is left in a battery.

Starter Motor

The battery is connected to a large direct-current motor called the *starter motor*. When the starter spins, its gear is inserted against teeth on the flywheel, cranking the engine until (we hope) it starts. When you release the ignition key, the starter motor disengages from the flywheel and the motor stops.

If you've ever tried to start a car that was already running, you've heard a loud grinding noise. This racket comes from the starter-motor gear clashing against the spinning flywheel.

Starter motors require a very large current, which requires a large cable. Instead of running a large cable from the battery to the ignition switch and then to the starter, cars use a *relay*. This electromagnetic switch closes a circuit between the battery and the starter motor. Because they save weight and money, these *solenoid relays* are also used in other circuits.

Alternator

Batteries don't create electricity, they only store it, and they must be recharged while the engine runs. On early cars, a generator made electricity to run the lights and recharge the battery. These generators made direct-current (DC) electricity, the kind used in a car, and were most effective at higher engine rpms. Nowadays, the *alternator* handles this essential task. Alternators make alternating-current (AC) electricity, which must be "rectified" to DC for use in a car. Alternators, however, make more power at lower rpms.

An alternator is basically an electric motor working in reverse. Instead of converting electricity *into* rotary motion, it makes electricity *from* rotary motion. The rotation comes from the engine, via a fan belt.

The principle of an alternator is similar to the principle of an ignition coil: Electricity is induced in a wire that moves in a magnetic field. In a coil, although the wires don't move, the magnetic field does.

To make an electric current, you can rotate a magnet inside a coil or rotate a coil inside a magnet. In an alternator, a magnet rotates inside a stationary coil, called a *stator*. The magnet is called the *rotor* because it rotates.

As the name implies, alternators create AC. To make the DC that the car needs, the AC goes through a device called a *diode*. Diodes, housed inside the alternator, are a common source of trouble. The rest of the alternator is more reliable, because it has three separate circuits for creating AC.

- If an alternator circuit fails, you may not notice it until you place a heavy demand on the electrical system.
- Alternators can fail suddenly if a belt breaks.
- If the alternator goes out, the battery must supply all electricity. By cutting off all unnecessary electrical devices, you may be able to get home or to a repair shop before the engine dies.

Engine Control Unit

Auto engines are now run by a small computer called the *engine control unit,* or ECU. The ECU

is the car's brain, and while it is not serviceable, technicians can diagnose trouble by connecting the ECU to a computer.

ECUs get information from sensors that detect

- The mass of air going into the engine
- Engine speed
- The position of the throttle (showing how much power the driver wants)
- The amount of oxygen in the exhaust (showing whether the fuel mix is right)
- Coolant temperature (cold engines need a different mix from warm ones)
- Pressure in the intake manifold (showing how hard the engine is working)
- Alternator voltage (whether the engine needs to speed up to make more current)

Electrical System Troubleshooting

Electrical problems were once about the most common source of driving complaints. Fortunately, all of the big problems have been improved over the years through better materials, better design, and the elimination of problematic parts, especially the distributor and coil. Here are a few troubleshooting points for electrical systems:

- Loose and corroded connections are a major source of intermittent problems. Corrosion is an insulator, remove it with fine sandpaper to ensure a good contact.
- Many times, the best diagnosis for electrical problems comes from hooking a car up to a diagnostic computer.

FUEL SYSTEM

The fuel system contains the fuel tank, the fuel filter, and the carburetor or fuel injector. To increase reliability and reduce pollution, fuel systems have changed radically over the years.

The fuel tank, usually located at the rear of the car, stores gasoline. A charcoal filter in the tank absorbs gasoline fumes, reducing pollution. A fuel pump delivers gas through a different fuel filter to the fuel injectors.

A throttle plate controls how much air enters the engine. In older cars, the plate was connected directly to the gas pedal. The plate controls how fast the engine is running and how much power it puts out.

Carburetor

Carburetors are another "old-style" component that has largely been replaced. Carburetors combine gasoline with air in a *venturi*, where a rapid stream of air flows past a small fuel port. The partial vacuum in the fast-moving air draws fuel into the airstream, where it vaporizes and mixes with air.

The exact ratio of fuel to air is critical to performance. A mixture with too much fuel (a "rich" mixture) will waste gas and increase pollution. A mixture with too little fuel (a "lean" mixture) will burn too hot and be short on power. Carburetors always struggled to create the perfect mix for constantly varying driving conditions. Now, fuel injectors have solved that problem through a combination of electronic control and quick response.

Fuel Injector

Fuel injectors are electronically controlled valves that squirt fuel into the cylinder. The valve is closed until the injector receives an electric current and an electromagnet opens the valve. Fuel sprays into the cylinder until the valve closes.

The first fuel injectors were called *throttle-body* injectors. One injector sprayed fuel into the intake manifold. Newer, *multiport* injectors spray fuel directly upstream of the intake valve. The injectors, one per cylinder, get fuel from the *fuel rail*, a supply pipe filled with high-pressure liquid fuel.

The key advantages of injectors over carburetors are accuracy and reliability. By precisely timing the moment and quantity of spray, injectors allow engine designers to improve fuel mileage and performance while cutting pollution. And since injectors have few moving parts, they are more reliable than carburetors.

Fuel systems have improved greatly over the decades. Most problems stem from dirty or stale gasoline. While problems are rare, they still arise:

- Water or dirt in the fuel can clog lines or filters.
- Water can freeze in the fuel line.
- Vapor lock, a condition caused by overheated fuel lines, is no longer a problem with modern vehicles.

EXHAUST SYSTEM

After combustion, burned gases enter the *exhaust system*. The *exhaust manifold* connects the cylinders to the muffler, tailpipe, and parts of the pollution control equipment. Exhaust systems operate at high temperatures, and must protect the car and its occupants from heat.

The *muffler* is a chamber with baffles that deaden the noise of the explosions inside the engine. It's something that you take for granted until you hear a car with a hole in the muffler—and then you realize how loud an internal-combustion engine can be!

POLLUTION CONTROL

When gasoline burns cleanly, it produces mainly carbon dioxide and water vapor. While carbon dioxide is a cause of global warming, it is not usually considered a pollutant. However, gasoline engines make several types of pollutants, especially when combustion is incomplete. One goal of the ECU is to cut pollution by allowing complete combustion.

Engines can produce these kinds of pollution:

- *Carbon monoxide*, a product of partial combustion, is a colorless, odorless, but poisonous gas.
- *Partially burned hydrocarbons*, also known as particulate matter, include various pollutants. In large quantities, small pieces of hydrocarbon make black soot that you can see.
- *Volatile organic compounds* are another group of pollutants made by partial combustion. Some cause cancer, others irritate lung tissue, and many are a source of smog.
- Air is 79 percent nitrogen, and several *nitrogen oxides* are created in the high temperatures and pressures inside an engine. Sunlight can convert nitrogen oxides into *ozone*, a molecule with three oxygen atoms that is a key part of smog. Ozone damages the lungs. Nitrogen oxides also cause acid rain, which damages forests and surface waters.

Positive Crankcase Ventilation

The bottom of an internal-combustion engine is full of a smoky, polluted gas made from the burning of oil and gasoline. To prevent crankcase gases from polluting the atmosphere, the *positive crankcase ventilation* system pipes this gas to the intake manifold, where the gas is burned in the cylinders. These simple, effective controls were the first pollution controls on gasoline engines.

Catalytic Converter

Catalysts—rare metals like platinum, rhodium, and palladium—cause other chemicals to react without being consumed themselves. Catalysts are embedded in heat-resistant ceramic elements. Pollutants in the exhaust gases are converted to simpler, less toxic compounds in the catalytic converter. From the outside, catalytic converters look like mufflers.

A *three-way* catalytic converter deals with carbon monoxide, volatile organic compounds, and nitrogen oxides. Often, two separate catalysts are needed to perform these chemical reactions:

A *reduction catalyst* reduces nitrogen oxides to oxygen and nitrogen.

An *oxidation catalyst* oxidizes carbon monoxide into carbon dioxide, and volatile organic compounds into carbon dioxide and water.

SUSPENSION

The job of the suspension is to hold the wheels to the road and make the ride safe and comfortable. *Axles* connect the car to the wheels. Driving axles move the wheels and must rotate themselves. In rear-wheel-drive cars, the driving axles connect the differential to the wheel. In front-wheel-drive cars, the axles are part of the transaxle. These are quite complicated.

Steering Gear

Steering gear connects the steering wheel to the front wheels. In *rack-and-pinion* steering, a small *pinion* gear at the end of the steering shaft turns against a flattened gear called a *rack*. In other systems, a steering gearbox converts rotary motion of the steering wheel to a linear motion that steers the wheels.

Rack-and-Pinion Steering Gear.

Modern steering equipment can be quite complex, especially with front-wheel or all-wheel drive.

Steering may be power-assisted, where the steering wheel does only part of the work, or manual, in which case the driver provides all the effort. Generally, larger cars have power steering, while in smaller cars, the driver's force is sufficient. Power steering can supply a varying level of assistance. A type of hydraulic fluid called *power steering fluid* is used in the hydraulic system in power steering.

Suspension

Autos use many types of suspension, but the two key categories are *leaf spring* or *coil spring*. Springs are made of a kind of steel that is tough and resilient.

Shock absorbers ("shocks") prevent axles from bouncing back, which makes for an uncomfortable ride. Springs resist movement when the car is moving downward, and shocks resist the rising motion. Ideally, after hitting a bump, the axle will move up toward the frame, then return to its original position.

When shocks wear out, a car tends to wander on the road because the springs aren't limited by the shocks.

Bearings

Bearings are mechanical gadgets that allow a part to rotate with almost no friction. Cars have bearings wherever rotating parts are found: in the steering wheel, engine, transmission, drive shaft, differential, and axles. Wheel bearings hold a wheel to a stationary (not driving) axle. Axle bearings hold driving axles. The individual bearings may be shaped like balls (*ball bearings*) or like tiny cylinders (*roller bearings*). Many individual bearings are housed together in an assembly that is also called a bearing.

Wheels and Tires

As we reach the end of the suspension, we meet two familiar objects: the *wheel* and the *tire*. Wheels are usually made of steel, and are bolted to the axle (for a driving wheel) or the brake apparatus (for a nondriving wheel). Most tires are called *radial-ply*, meaning that their plies (the invisible reinforcing belts that hold the tire together) run radially—in a line starting at the center of the wheel. Radials offer better life and performance than older *bias-ply* tires.

Tires are made of artificial rubber, inflated to a pressure of 30 or 40 pounds per square inch. Air pressure holds the tire's shape, and also permits it to absorb road shock.

- Proper inflation is important for critical gas mileage, long tire life, and safe handling. The suggested pressures are listed on a tire sidewall or inside the glove compartment. Normally, hot air expands. But air trapped inside a tire cannot expand, so its pressure rises instead. Suggested tire pressures apply only to a cold tire. Do not release air from a hot tire if it seems overpressurized. Instead, wait until the tire is cold to check the pressure.
- Tires may gradually lose pressure without having a major problem. But if you have to pump up a tire frequently, it's got a problem that needs attention.

BRAKE SYSTEM

Mechanically, brakes are the opposite of engines. Engines convert heat that originates in fuel into motion; brakes use friction to convert motion into heat. Brake systems have two key parts: the hydraulics and the braking mechanism at the wheel that does the actual stopping. The hydraulics transfer motion from the driver's foot to the brake mechanism.

A Dual Braking System Has Two Master Cylinders and Two Sets of Tubes to the Individual Brakes.

Hydraulic systems are based on the fact that hydraulic fluid cannot be compressed. In the simplest hydraulic mechanism, two cylinders are connected by a tube. When a piston moves in the first cylinder, the piston in the second cylinder must also move. Why? Because the fluid is not compressible and must always occupy the same volume.

Air is easily compressed. If air enters the hydraulic system, the brake pedal will get "spongy." The cure is to "bleed" out the air through bleeder valves located at each brake.

In a car, the brake pedal is connected to the *master cylinder*, and four tubes run to the *slave* or *wheel cylinders*. These are located in the brake mechanism at the wheels. Cars now have dual master cylinders and dual hydraulic lines. If one part of the system fails, the other half should still work.

In This Simple Hydraulic System, Moving the Piston in the Master Cylinder Causes the Piston to Move in the Slave (Wheel) Cylinder.

Drum Brakes

Drum brakes operate by expanding two *brake shoes* inside a large cylinder called a *drum*. The drum rotates with the wheel, but the shoes do not rotate. A *wheel cylinder* operates the brake by moving the shoes toward the drum. Friction between the shoes and the drum creates the stopping power.

- When the shoes wear, a self-adjusting mechanism moves them closer to the drum. Wheel cylinders have rubber pistons that must be replaced when they wear out.
- Brake shoes and drums must also be replaced occasionally. If you let the shoes wear too far, they will damage the drums, forcing a more expensive repair.

Disk Brakes

A disk brake has a rotor, or disk, that revolves with the wheel and a pair of stationary pads that create

Typical Drum Brake.

friction when they press against the rotor. Disk brakes are a big improvement over drum brakes because they offer shorter stopping distances and better control.

Typical Disk Brake.

The horseshoe-shaped *caliper* holds the pads. Hydraulic force squeezes the pads against the disk.

- Over time, pads wear out. Many disk brakes make a warning noise when the pads are wearing out. You usually will hear the noise when your foot is not on the brake pedal.
- Eventually, the pads wear concentric grooves in the disk. Before putting on new pads, the disks must be machined flat so that the new pads press against a flat surface. After being machined several times, the disks become too thin, risking a heat buildup and reduced stopping power ("fading"). For safety's sake, these disks must be replaced.

Parking Brakes

Parking brakes need a separate mechanical system to operate the brakes; they cannot use hydraulics. Usually, cables from the parking-brake lever to a drum brake operate the parking brake. Disk brakes require a more complicated parking brake. They may have a miniature drum brake built inside them. In other cases, a corkscrew mechanism pushes the brake pads against the rotor.

Antilock Brakes

When tires skid, they lose braking power, and steering becomes difficult or impossible. To improve safety during sudden stops, many cars have an antilock braking system (ABS). An ABS uses sensors to detect wheel rotation. If a wheel starts to skid during braking, the ABS reduces pressure to that brake, then starts pumping the brake. Pumping may produce a vibration in the brake pedal. Other wheels get full braking pressure until they too start to skid. ABS is a good feature on ice or snow.

AUTO INFORMATION QUIZ

Take the following quiz to check your understanding of ASVAB Auto Information topics. Circle each answer that you choose. There is no time limit. Answers and explanations are given immediately after the quiz.

1. If the shock absorbers are defective,
   A. the springs will wear out too soon.
   B. the front wheels will go out of alignment.
   C. the brakes will lock up too soon.
   D. the wheels will rebound excessively after the car hits a bump.

2. Some cylinder heads are made of aluminum because
   A. it is light and inexpensive.
   B. it is heavy and inexpensive.
   C. cast iron warps too easily.
   D. it is light and conducts heat well.

3. Disk brakes are sometimes used only on the front wheels because
   A. disk brakes are easier to steer.
   B. the front wheels provide most of the stopping force.
   C. disk brakes are cheaper to make than drum brakes.
   D. disk brakes are less likely to seize up than drum brakes.

4. In a 12-volt system, when the electric current is 12 volts, the battery is
   A. charging.
   B. discharging.
   C. neither charging nor discharging.
   D. I cannot tell. There is not enough information to answer the question.

5. In a hydraulic system, a 2-inch-diameter master cylinder drives a 1-inch-diameter wheel cylinder. If we move the piston 3 inches into the master cylinder,
   A. the force will be multiplied at the wheel cylinder.
   B. the force will be reduced at the wheel cylinder.
   C. the force will be the same at the wheel cylinder.
   D. nothing will happen. This hookup will not work because the slave cylinder needs to have a larger diameter than the master cylinder.

6. A higher viscosity rating is applied to oil that is
   A. thicker.
   B. thinner.
   C. less likely to freeze in winter.
   D. more likely to overheat.

7. If a car has a fuel injector, it will not have
   A. a regulator.
   B. a carburetor.
   C. an Otto-cycle engine.
   D. a fuel filter.

8. When the brake shoes wear down too much, you are likely to see _____ in the drums.
   A. glazing
   B. scoring (gouges)
   C. shot spots
   D. rust

9. When you see blue smoke coming from the tail-pipe, you should check the
   A. piston rings.
   B. intake valves.
   C. positive crankcase ventilation system.
   D. fuel system.

10. If a car suddenly stops responding to the starter and the headlights do not light, what would be the most likely problem?
    A. The battery terminals or cables are corroded.
    B. The battery has gone dead.
    C. The starter switch is bad.
    D. The starter motor has died.

11. If a manual transmission is in neutral,
    A. the wheels cannot turn.
    B. the engine can run without moving the car.
    C. the differential is locked up.
    D. the transmission cannot be shifted.

12. When you bolt a cylinder head into place, you should
    A. align the cylinders with the pistons.
    B. align the carburetor.
    C. check the main bearings.
    D. observe proper tightening torque.

13. If the oil light comes on while you are driving,
    A. drive home and check for problems.
    B. replace the oil within 1,000 miles.
    C. do not worry unless you see other evidence of trouble; the light is probably defective.
    D. as soon as it's safe, pull over to find the problem.

14. Which components are not found in a car with electronic ignition?
    A. Coil wire and distributor
    B. Coil and alternator
    C. Distributor and ECU
    D. ABS and ECU

15. If it's hard to shift gears in a car with manual transmission,
    A. add transmission oil.
    B. check the free play on the clutch.
    C. don't worry, the oil is probably cold.
    D. try starting in gear.

ANSWERS AND EXPLANATIONS

1. **D.** Without shock absorbers, the axle and wheel would continue to bounce (think of a weight bouncing up and down on a long spring). That would cause an unstable, unpleasant ride. The other answers are partly correct, but D is the most accurate answer.

2. **D.** Why are the other answers incorrect? A, aluminum is relatively expensive; B, aluminum is light; C, cast iron does not warp easily (it is commonly used in engine blocks).

3. **B.** Vehicles lurch forward while braking, and the engines are in front, so up to two-thirds of the stopping force occurs on the front wheels. Because disk brakes are more effective than drum brakes, a cost-saving compromise is to put disks in front and drums in the rear.

4. **B.** Despite the name, a 12-volt battery is actually discharging at 14 volts. To charge the battery, the alternator must supply a higher voltage.

5. **B.** When a larger cylinder drives a smaller one, the smaller one moves further, but with less force.

6. **A.** Viscosity measures resistance to flow. Oils with higher viscosity are thicker, and flow more slowly.

7. **B.** Fuel injectors replace carburetors. (Internal-combustion engines do use the Otto cycle, named for the German who invented the gasoline engine.)

8. **B.** Worn brake shoes can score, or gouge, the brake drums, which then must be machined to produce good stopping power.

9. **A.** Worn piston rings allow oil to enter the cylinder, causing blue smoke.

10. **A.** Oxidized metal (corrosion) is often an insulator. So corroded battery terminals or cables can cause a sudden loss of current to the starter and lights. Why are the other answers incorrect? B is possible, but batteries seldom go completely dead this quickly. C, a bad starter switch, and D, a dead starter motor, would not affect the headlights.

11. **B.** The purpose of neutral gear in any transmission is to allow the engine to run while the car stands still.

12. **D.** Proper tightening torque prevents warping of the cylinder head.

13. **D.** Low oil pressure can quickly destroy an engine; pull over and determine the cause of the problem as soon as it's safe to do so.

14. **A.** Electronic ignition replaces the coil wire, which feeds high-voltage current from the coil to the distributor. It also replaces the distributor, which routes high-voltage current to the spark plugs. Why are the other answers incorrect? The car would still have an alternator, ECU (engine control unit), and ABS (antilock braking system).

15. **B.** If the clutch does not have the right amount of free travel at the top of the stroke, it may not be disengaging completely, and shifting may become more difficult.

Chapter 16

Shop Information

YOUR GOALS FOR THIS CHAPTER
• Find out what shop topics are covered on the ASVAB.
• Learn basic facts about shop tools, practices, materials, and procedures.
• Study examples of ASVAB shop questions and learn ways to solve them.
• Take a shop information quiz.

INTRODUCTION: ASVAB SHOP INFORMATION QUESTIONS

The shop information questions that appear on the ASVAB measure how much you understand about shop tools, practices, materials, and procedures. The questions may ask you to identify a particular shop tool, to tell how it is used, or to choose the correct procedure when working with wood, metal, or construction materials. If you took shop courses in high school, or if you have done any woodworking or metalworking on your own, you may already be familiar with many of the topics covered on the test. You

may also have learned shop and construction tools and procedures on the job.

On the paper-and-pencil version of the ASVAB, shop questions are one part of the Auto and Shop Information test. On the CAT-ASVAB, they form a separate test of their own.

Whichever ASVAB version you take, you'll have only about half a minute to answer each shop information question, so you'll have to work fast if you want to get a good score. That's why it pays to spend time studying the test topics and tackling plenty of sample ASVAB shop information questions.

The topic review that follows will help prepare you to answer ASVAB shop information questions. It lists and describes the different tools you should know, with an emphasis on traditional hand tools. It also covers common fasteners and materials. There is also important information about tool safety. At the end of the chapter, there is a short quiz with questions modeled on those on the actual test. Read carefully through the review materials in this chapter, then use the quiz to find out how well you have mastered this subject area. Go back and reread the review materials for any quiz items you miss.

MEASUREMENT AND LAYOUT

New projects and many repairs start with measurement and layout. This is where you amass the proper tools and materials, and mark out the cutting and drilling.

ASVAB Shop Information Questions

Number of Questions:

• Paper-and-pencil ASVAB: 13–15 (as part of the Auto and Shop Information test)
• CAT-ASVAB: 11 (as a separate test)

Time Limit:

• Paper-and-pencil ASVAB: 5–6 minutes (as part of the 11-minute Auto and Shop Information test)
• CAT-ASVAB: 6 minutes

Topics Covered:

• Tools
• Wood and metal shop practices
• Construction materials and procedures

Measuring Tools

Carpenters usually use a *tape measure*, marked in 1/16-inch increments. The tape retracts automatically into the case, but locks in place when it must be extended for a while. The tape has a hook on the end that moves slightly for accurate inside and outside measurements. Retractable tape measures range from 6 feet to 25 feet long.

When greater accuracy is needed, machinists use a rigid *steel rule*. These rules are often marked in 1/32- or 1/64-inch increments and are often 1 foot long. A metric steel rule would usually be marked in 1-millimeter increments.

Inside Caliper.

Outside Caliper.

Vernier Caliper.

When even greater accuracy is needed, machinists use *calipers* or *micrometers*. Some calipers are simply two legs that can transfer a measurement to a steel rule. These calipers can take inside or outside measurements, depending on the shape of the legs. Calipers can also have straight legs.

The Vernier caliper is even more accurate, thanks to the clever Vernier system. First identify the Vernier scale and the main scale. Now look at the "0" on the Vernier scale (see Figure below). This is just past the third mark on the main scale, indicating 3 millimeters (mm) on this metric caliper. So the measurement is a bit more than 3 mm, but how much more? Notice that line 3 on the Vernier scale lines up with a line on the main scale. That means that you should add 0.3 mm to the measurement, making a total of 3.3 mm. (Only one mark on the Vernier scale will line up with the main scale, and it doesn't matter which line it lines up with. Remember, read the number *on the Vernier scale* to get the right-hand digit in the measurement.)

Close-up of Vernier Scale.

Micrometer.

Micrometers are even more accurate than Vernier calipers, but they are usually designed to read only in a certain range, say up to 1 inch, or 1 inch to 2 inches. Unlike a Vernier caliper, where you slide the adjuster, you turn a screw on a micrometer.

Layout often calls for square (90°) lines. A *carpenter's square* is used to draw these lines: When you hold one leg against the edge of a board, the second makes a square line across the board. A smaller version is called the *try square*.

Carpenter's Square.

You may also see a *sliding bevel*, which has a metal leg fastened to a wooden block. By loosening the adjustment screw, you can set the tool to mark almost any angle. Sliding bevels can be used to transfer angles from place to place.

Sliding Bevel.

The easiest way to tell if something is level (horizontal) or vertical (plumb) is with a *level*, sometimes called a spirit level. Levels use glass or plastic tubes that are curved or slightly swollen in the middle. When the bubble in the liquid (spirit) is centered, the level is horizontal or vertical.

Level.

CUTTING AND SHAPING

After the layout step is done, it's time to cut and shape the materials. We'll take up woodworking tools first, then metalworking tools.

Woodworking Tools

Sharp hand saws are the most basic way to cut wood. Saws cut a *kerf* that is wider than the blade itself;

the kerf allows the saw to move freely through the cut. *Crosscut saws* are designed to cut at 90° to the grain, while *ripsaws* cut parallel to the grain. Ripsaws have larger teeth. *Backsaws* have a rigid steel backing that improves accuracy; they are used in miter boxes that guide them for 45° or 90° cuts.

Hand Saw.

Keyhole saws are made to cut complicated profiles. An electric version is called the *jigsaw*. A *coping saw* has a thin blade held in a P-shaped handle. The saw is used to cut molding.

Keyhole Saw.

An electric *circular saw*, usually with a 7-1/4-inch-diameter blade, is much faster for cutting wood, especially for ripsawing, and for sawing plywood or other panels. These saws are dangerous; read the instruction manual carefully.

Circular Saw.

Wood chisels, sold in widths from 1/4 inch to 1-1/2 inches, cut wood when they are struck with a hammer or mallet.

Wood Chisel.

A *hand plane* removes thin strips of wood and is used to shape, smooth, or reduce the size of boards. It's especially useful for removing saw marks from the edge of a board. The "jack" plane is a general-purpose type of hand plane.

Jack Plane.

Metalworking Tools

A *hacksaw* has a replaceable metal blade with small teeth and is used for cutting iron, steel, and other, softer metals. Choose a blade with finer teeth for thinner metal, and one with larger teeth for thicker metal. The hacksaw should cut on the forward stroke.

Hacksaw.

Tin snips cut steel, copper, or aluminum sheet metal, using a shearing action. Some snips have replaceable blades; others can be sharpened. Special snips are designed to cut curves.

Tin Snips.

A *right-angle grinder* can polish metal before painting, or otherwise smooth or shape metal. Grind toward the edge of the wheel; do not hold it flat to the surface of the metal. The same tool will also drive a wire brush for removing rust.

A *pipe cutter*—used for copper, not steel, pipe—has a sharp cutting wheel. Gradually tighten the handle as you rotate the tool around the pipe.

Pipe Cutter.

Taps and *dies* cut or restore threads in metal. A die cuts threads on a rod; a tap cuts threads in a hole drilled in a plate. Either tool can be used to restore mangled threads. Both taps and dies cut only one diameter and pitch (number of threads per inch). To select a die, you must know the outside diameter (O.D.) of the pipe.

Thread-Cutting Die.

Thread-Cutting Tap.

DRILLS AND DRILLING TOOLS

Electric *drills* have become a centerpiece of all workshops, for making holes, driving screws, and other purposes. Drills are sized by the largest diameter of bit that will fit in the chuck (the rotating clamp that holds the bit). You sometimes see 1/4-inch drills, but 3/8-inch drills are an all-around tool for the home workshop. Larger drills handle bits of 1/2- or 3/4-inch diameter. However, the shank (the part that gets grabbed in the chuck) can be smaller than the tip of the drill bit, so it's possible to drill 1-inch holes in wood with a 3/8-inch drill.

Iron and steel are much harder to drill than wood, and thus call for a larger, more powerful drill. Often, it's best to drill a small "pilot" hole in metal. This is because metal-cutting drill bits have a blind spot near the center where they don't drill very well. The pilot hole makes a clear space for the blind spot on the larger drill. While drilling metal, it often helps to oil the bit for cooling; excess heat can destroy the heat treatment that makes a bit hard enough to cut metal.

The chuck may be tightened with a chuck key, as shown. Newer, self-tightening chucks do not use a key. Instead, the parts tighten when they are turned against each other.

Drill Chuck with Chuck Key.

3/8-Inch Drill.

Drill Bit.

The helix on a twist drill brings chips up out of the hole. Twist drills will start accurately in wood, but they wander across the surface in metal. A *center punch* makes a dimple in metal to locate the bit as it starts to drill. Use a hammer to hit the center punch.

Center Punch.

Auger bits are made only for wood, which they cut much faster than twist drills. Auger bits were originally driven by a brace and bit, but they can also be used in electric drills.

Auger Bit.

Brace and Bit.

A *countersink* is a conical depression in a surface that allows a flat-head screw to sit flush (flat) to the surface. A special drill bit, also called a countersink, makes the countersink.

Countersink.

A *hole saw* makes large-diameter holes in wood and some metals. The type of hole saw shown screws onto a mandrel, allowing one mandrel to handle several size saws. Hole saws are more economical than big drills for drilling wood, but they do not work in hard metal.

Hole Saw.

POUNDING TOOLS

Many of the oldest tools are designed to hit something. A *claw* (carpenter's) *hammer* pounds nails with the face and pulls them with the claw. A straight claw is better for longer nails, and is also handier for doing demolition. Some hammer faces have a checkered pattern, called a *waffle head*, to increase the grip on the nails. The standard size of claw hammer is 16 oz. Hammers 24 oz. in size are used for large nails.

Claw Hammer.

Metal workers use a *ball-peen hammer*. One face is flat, like a claw hammer, the other face has a ball peen, used for shaping metal and riveting. Ball-peen hammers may weigh up to 3 lb.

Ball-Peen Hammer.

Sledgehammers are used for heavy purposes. Some people can swing the hand sledge shown here with one hand. True sledgehammers have a 32-inch handle and require two hands.

Hand Sledge.

A *rubber mallet* may be used to adjust parts without damage, or to drive wooden-handled chisels. Wooden mallets are also used for striking chisels. Many modern chisels, however, have steel shanks and can safely be struck with a hammer.

Rubber Mallet.

TOOLS FOR TURNING OR GRABBING

Shop work, including maintenance and repair, requires a good assortment of tools that turn or grab. An *adjustable* (Crescent) *wrench* can be adjusted to hold various sizes of hexagonal or square bolts. Typical overall lengths range from 6 to 12 inches.

Adjustable Wrench.

A *combination wrench* combines two basic types of wrench: the box-end and the open-end wrench. Each end of a combination wrench fits the same size bolt. Because most bolt heads have six faces (called *hexagonal bolts* or hex bolts) the box end has 6 or 12 facets. With 12 facets, you can turn the wrench 1/12 of a turn, which is handy in tight quarters. That's why they are offset 15° at the end.

Open end

Box end

Combination Wrench.

A *socket wrench* holds a bolt or nut from above. The deep socket, shown, allows you to grab a nut even if some threads are sticking out above it. Socket wrenches connect to the sockets with a square drive; possible drive dimensions include 1/4, 3/8, 1/2, or 3/4 inch. Larger drives are available for heavier-duty use.

Deep Socket.

A *ratchet wrench* is one way to drive a socket. It will grab when it swings in one direction and slip in the other, for convenient tightening or loosening.

Square drive

Ratchet Wrench.

A *torque wrench* fits a socket and drives bolts to a specified tightness. You can buy them marked in American or metric units.

Torque Wrench.

An *Allen wrench* fits screws with a hexagonal recess in the head. Allen wrenches are sold in inches and millimeters.

Allen Wrench.

Arc-joint pliers (often called Channel Locks) are used to grab various sizes of material. To adjust the jaws, open them wide and engage a different set of arcs. Arc-joint pliers are not good for grabbing bolts or nuts, as they will scar the metal.

Arc-Joint Pliers.

Locking pliers (often called Vise Grips) have a lever system that gives a very strong, locking grab. They are one of the handiest tools in the box, but they can damage bolts and nuts.

Locking Pliers.

A *needle-nose* (longnose) *pliers* gets at small parts and is especially handy for electric wiring.

Needle-Nose Pliers.

A *bar clamp,* among other types of clamp, can hold parts in position while you work or hold joints while the glue sets.

Bar Clamp.

A *pipe wrench* has steel teeth that hold steel pipe. They are sold in lengths ranging from 12 to 48 inches. Flip the wrench over to turn the pipe in the other direction.

Pipe Wrench.

Flat-bladed (standard) *screwdrivers* are a major part of any toolbox. They come in many sizes. A long shank will protect your hands when you are pressing hard.

Standard Screwdriver.

A *Phillips screwdriver* drives Phillips screws—the ones with a cross-shaped head. They also are sold in various sizes.

Phillips Screwdriver.

FASTENERS AND FASTENING TECHNIQUES

Keeping things together requires a variety of different types of fasteners. We'll start with threaded fasteners and nails, then move to fasteners that use molten metal.

Threaded Fasteners

Some threaded fasteners—*screws* and *bolts*—are designed to cut threads in the material. These wood and sheet-metal screws come in many sizes and materials, with any number of head styles. Sheet-metal screws cut threads in sheet-metal.

Round-Head Wood Screw.

Wood screws are sized by length and diameter. Length is measured in inches; diameter by a numbering system (#6, #8, #10, and so on). Larger numbers indicate a larger diameter.

Sheet-Metal Screw.

A separate category of threaded fasteners uses what are called *machine threads*. These screws and bolts must be screwed into a nut with the same diameter and number of threads per inch (also called pitch). Most machine threads are right-hand, meaning that they tighten when you turn the top to the right—clockwise. Left-hand bolts tighten in the opposite direction. Machine screws often use lock washers to prevent the nut from loosening. The lock washer is compressed under the nut and holds the nut tight.

Machine Screw.

A *hex bolt* is a machine screw. It can range in diameter from 1/4 inch on up, and in length from 1/2 inch on up.

Hex Bolt.

A *carriage bolt* is a machine screw with a round head and a square shank. The shank fits a square slot, so the bolt does not turn while being tightened. The large head substitutes for a flat washer, distributing the bolt's force across a wider area.

Carriage Bolt.

Nails

Nails are an ancient form of fastener, but they have gotten a lot more complicated over the past 20 years. Let's start with some terminology:

- *Brad*: A small, thin nail with a small head, used for picture frames and other light fastening.
- *Tack*: A small nail with a big head, used to attach carpet and upholstery.
- *Finishing nail*: A sturdy, small-diameter nail with a small head, used to attach trim and molding.
- *Common nail*: A big, large-headed nail used for rough construction.
- *Sinker*: A smaller-diameter version of the common nail that causes less splitting.
- *Spike*: A heavy, large nail for fastening timbers.
- *Ring-shank*: A nail with rings that improve grip.
- *Spiral*: A nail with a spiral on the shank, used to increase grip, for example, on flooring nails.

Nails are sized by length and by pennies ("d"). A 4d nail is 1-1/2 inches long, while a 16d nail is 3-1/2 inches long. Nails are sometimes coated with zinc (*galvanized*) to resist rust. These days, nails are often driven with pneumatic devices called *nail guns*.

When selecting a nail, choose a large head to hold soft materials and a small head for an exposed location. In construction, structural nails must grab about

1-1/2 inches. A larger diameter gets a stronger grip, but is also more likely to split the wood. Finally, for strength, a ring- or spiral-shank nail is a good choice.

Welding, Soldering, and Brazing

Welding, soldering, and brazing are fastening methods that use molten metal. *Welding* melts the metal that is being fastened. *Soldering* and *brazing* melt a separate metal, called *solder* or *brazing rod*, to make the attachment. Soldering is used for plumbing and for electrical or electronic equipment. Solder was traditionally a mixture of tin and lead, but lead is toxic, so in modern solder, tin is now mixed with other metals, such as antimony.

To solder, clean the parts, apply flux, heat, and then touch the solder to the heated parts (do not just melt it with the iron and drip it over the joint). *Flux* is needed to prevent oxidation during heating and to allow the solder to flow into the joint. A good solder joint makes a tight seal in copper pipe and a durable connection in electronics.

Soldering Iron.

Brazing is similar to soldering except that the joining material is bronze, and the metal must be heated hotter. This is usually done with an oxyacetylene torch, which burns acetylene gas and oxygen. The same torch can be used to weld steel. An oxyacetylene cutting torch heats the steel, then floods it with oxygen, causing the steel to rapidly oxidize, or burn.

An arc welder heats metal with an electric current and is widely used for welding. The current, the composition of the welding rod, and the gas surrounding the weld can all be controlled to get the desired results. Arc welders such as TIG (tungsten inert gas) are highly versatile machines that can weld a wide variety of metals, including steel, tungsten, and aluminum.

SHOP INFORMATION QUIZ

Take the following quiz to check your understanding of ASVAB Shop Information topics. Circle each answer that you choose. There is no time limit. Answers and explanations are given immediately after the quiz.

1. The reason for a long shaft on a screwdriver is to
   A. give leverage for opening paint cans.
   B. protect your fingers when you're pushing hard on a screw.
   C. allow plenty of room to grab the shaft with a locking pliers.
   D. hang easily on the tool board.

2. What is the purpose of a saw kerf?
   A. To make room for the saw blade in the cut
   B. To increase tension on the saw blade, to make a straight cut
   C. To reduce space between the teeth, so that the saw cuts faster
   D. To hold the blade straight so that the saw will cut straight

3. What is the purpose of a 15° offset on an open-end wrench?
   A. To protect your knuckles
   B. To "torque down" the bolt to the correct tightness
   C. To allow the wrench to grab the nut when working in tight quarters
   D. To allow a hex wrench to fit a square bolt head

4. An electric drill used to drive wood screws should be
   A. reversible.
   B. variable speed.
   C. a plug-in type.
   D. variable speed and reversible.

5. Tin snips are a type of
   A. nipper.
   B. wrench.
   C. shear.
   D. torque wrench.

6. A common nail has a _____ than a finishing nail.
   A. smaller head and smaller diameter
   B. smaller head and larger diameter
   C. larger head and smaller diameter
   D. larger head and a larger diameter

7. In a wood screw labeled #8 × 1-1/4", "#8" indicates that the
   A. screw is #8 galvanized steel.
   B. screw has threads per inch.
   C. screw threads are at an 8° angle.
   D. the screw is #8 diameter.

8. If a steel pipe has an inside diameter (I.D.) of 3/4 inch,
   A. you have enough information to select a thread-cutting die.
   B. the outside diameter must be larger than 3/4 inch.
   C. the pipe is legal for carrying natural gas, but not potable water.
   D. the inside diameter must be smaller than 3/4 inch.

9. If a bolt has a left-hand thread,
   A. it requires a right-hand-thread nut.
   B. a clockwise turn will tighten the nut.
   C. the switch on a ratchet wrench should be pushed to the left side.
   D. a counterclockwise turn will tighten the nut.

10. The purpose of a lock washer is to
    A. prevent vibration from loosening the joint.
    B. hold the flat washer in position.
    C. prevent anyone from taking the nut off.
    D. keep the screw threads clean.

11. An arc welder
    A. creates heat with an electric arc.
    B. is used to make curved welds.
    C. can be used only on stainless steel.
    D. can also be used to solder.

12. The best tool for making accurate layout measurements is
    A. a try square.
    B. a steel rule.
    C. a tape measure.
    D. a spirit level.

13. A machine screw
    A. will fit any nut with the right diameter.
    B. can also be used to cut threads in sheet metal.
    C. cannot cut threads in wood.
    D. is used only in autos and related machinery.

14. In a Vernier caliper, the Vernier scale is used to
    A. find the rough measurement.
    B. find the most accurate digit in the measurement.
    C. find the fractional measurement.
    D. convert fractions to decimals.

15. What is the purpose of a center punch?
    A. To find the center of a dowel
    B. To locate the starting point for a circular chisel (gouge)
    C. To start a drill hole in wood
    D. To start a drill hole in metal

ANSWERS AND EXPLANATIONS

1. **B.** With a long shaft, your hands are a long way from the screw, protecting you from injury if something slips.

2. **A.** The kerf, or overall width of a cut, must be wider than the blade, or else the blade will jam in the cut.

3. **C.** In tight quarters, the 15° allows you to turn the wrench over after moving the bolt slightly to get another grab on the bolt.

4. **D.** A variable-speed, reversible electric drill is best for driving and removing wood screws.

5. **C.** Tin snips cut with a shearing action. A is incorrect; the cutting blades of nippers meet instead of sliding past each other. B and D are incorrect; tin snips are not made to turn nuts or bolts.

6. **D.** A common nail has a larger head and a larger diameter than a finishing nail.

7. **D.** The diameter of wood screws is sized by these numbers; larger numbers indicate larger diameter.

8. **B.** If the inside diameter is 3/4 inch, the outside diameter (O.D.) must be larger than 3/4 inch. Why are the other answers incorrect? A, to choose a thread-cutting die, you also must know the number of threads per inch (the pitch). C, in most places, steel pipe is acceptable for carrying potable (drinking) water. D, 3/4 inch is the inside diameter.

9. **D.** A left-hand thread works opposite to the usual thread, so a counterclockwise turn will tighten, not loosen, the nut. Why are the other answers incorrect? A, bolts with left-hand threads require left-hand nuts. B, a clockwise turn will loosen the nut. C, it depends on the ratchet wrench.

10. **A.** Lock washers spring out against the nut, to prevent unwanted loosening.

11. **A.** An arc welder creates heat with an electric arc.

12. **B.** A steel rule makes the most accurate measurements.

13. **C.** Machine screws do not cut threads in wood. Why are the other answers incorrect? A, the pitch and diameter must be the same. B, a machine screw cannot cut threads in sheet metal. D, machine screws can be used in building and other applications.

14. **B.** The Vernier scale provides the most accurate digit in the measurement.

15. **D.** Center punches make a dimple that locates the drill bit as you start to drill.

Chapter 17

Mechanical Comprehension

YOUR GOALS FOR THIS CHAPTER

- **Find out what topics are covered on the ASVAB Mechanical Comprehension test.**

- **Learn basic facts about mechanical devices and mechanical motion.**

- **Study examples of Mechanical Comprehension questions and learn ways to solve them.**

- **Take a Mechanical Comprehension quiz.**

INTRODUCTION: ASVAB MECHANICAL COMPREHENSION QUESTIONS

The ASVAB Mechanical Comprehension test is all about the basic materials and mechanical devices that you see around you every day. The questions deal with things like levers, pipes, water wheels, gears, pulleys, and the like. This is not a test of high school physics, so don't worry if you can't explain things in terms of Newton's laws or use words like *inertia* and *elastic rebound*. You won't have to know *why* machines function as they do. You won't have to know a lot of complicated scientific terms. But you will have to know *what* simple machines and materials are and *how* they operate. Most questions on the Mechanical Comprehension test can be answered using simple common sense, but you may need to do a few calculations. Many questions include a picture of some kind of simple machine, and you can use the picture to help you answer the question. Spinning gears, heat transfer from one material to another, and barrels rolling up inclined planes are all standard situations that you'll find on the Mechanical Comprehension test.

Whichever ASVAB version you take, you'll have only about a minute to answer each Mechanical Comprehension question, so you'll have to work fast if you want to get a good score. That's why it pays to spend time studying the test topics and tackling plenty of sample Mechanical Comprehension questions.

ASVAB Mechanical Comprehension Test

Number of Questions:

- Paper-and-pencil ASVAB: 25
- CAT-ASVAB: 16

Time Limit:

- Paper-and-pencil ASVAB: 19 minutes
- CAT-ASVAB: 20 minutes

MECHANICAL COMPREHENSION QUESTION TOPICS

The topics covered on the Mechanical Comprehension test will probably be familiar to you if you have ever operated machines or taken them apart to repair them. (See the box on the next page.)

This chapter will help you prepare for the Mechanical Comprehension test. It starts by listing the important simple machines and explaining how they operate. Then it covers other important topics, such as properties of materials, mechanical motion, and fluid dynamics. At the end of the chapter, there is a short quiz with questions modeled on those on the actual test. Read carefully through the review materials in this chapter, then use the quiz to find out how well you have mastered this subject area. Go back and reread the review materials for any quiz question you miss.

Mechanical Comprehension Question Topics

Principles of Mechanical Devices

- Mechanical advantage
- Simple machines
- Compound machines
- Structural support
- Properties of materials

Mechanical Motion

- Systems of pulleys
- Systems of gears
- Rotating wheels and disks
- Cams and cam followers
- Cranks and pistons

Fluid Dynamics

- Air pressure
- Water pressure
- Filling and emptying tanks

SOME BASIC CONCEPTS: WORK, ENERGY, AND FORCE

To do well on Mechanical Comprehension questions, you'll need to understand just a few basic concepts. For starters, you should know that in mechanics, *work* refers to a specific force applied over a specific distance. For example, your arm does work when it uses force to pick up a book. A lever does work when it uses force to lift a heavy object.

The ability to do work is called *energy*. Energy comes in several forms:

- *Kinetic energy*: Energy in a moving object.
- *Potential energy*: Energy that can be released under certain conditions. For example, potential energy is stored in objects when they are lifted off the ground. It is released when the objects fall.
- *Chemical energy*: Energy stored in chemicals, such as in a flashlight battery. Chemical energy is potential until it is released in a chemical reaction.
- *Electric energy*: Energy in moving electrons in an electric current.
- *Nuclear energy*: Energy released by reactions in the nucleus of an atom.
- *Solar energy*: Energy in the heat and light from the sun.

On the ASVAB, you may be asked to tell which kind of energy is present in a given situation. For example, when a child's swing reaches its highest

point and pauses momentarily before swinging back down, the swing has only potential energy and no kinetic energy. When it swings through its lowest point, the opposite is true: The swing has no potential energy (because it cannot fall any further) and all kinetic energy. As it swings back up the other side, the kinetic energy is converted back into potential energy.

Potential energy → Kinetic energy → Potential energy

Similarly, a battery stores electric energy as chemical energy. When the flashlight is turned on, electric energy passes through the filament in the flashlight bulb, where it is converted into heat and light.

Forces are powers that push or pull objects. A force has a *magnitude* (strength) that you can measure, and it has a *direction*. Some forces are obvious—when a bat hits a baseball, you can even hear the force being applied. Other forces, like gravity and air pressure, are much less obvious, but they are still real.

One kind of force is *gravity*. Gravity is an attractive force between objects. All objects create a gravitational attraction for each other. On Earth, gravity causes objects to fall toward the center of the Earth. Falling objects accelerate (fall faster) as they fall. (*Acceleration* is defined as the change in velocity, or speed in a particular direction.) If you discount air resistance, all objects fall at the same rate—a fact proved centuries ago by the Italian scientist Galileo. In real life, however, air resistance often disguises the fact that objects fall at the same rate.

Air resistance is a kind of friction. *Friction* is a force that results from the interaction between two surfaces that are touching each other. Friction acts as a resistance to the movement of an object. For example, friction makes it harder to push a heavy crate up a ramp. Friction also helps to keep the crate from sliding back down the ramp. Without friction, a car would slide all over the place because the tires could not get a grip on the pavement. Tables would slide all over the room, and billiard balls would never stop rolling! In machinery, friction can often be a problem. It can prevent machines from running smoothly and efficiently. That's why lubricants are used to reduce friction.

Two other forces are *compression* and *tension*. Compression is a force that pushes materials together. Tension is a force that pulls materials apart. Air pressure and water pressure are forms of compression. The force exerted by the cable in a pulley is a kind of tension. In a bridge, some parts are in compression and others in tension. The weight of the structure squeezes (compresses) the top and puts tension on the bottom. Steel reinforcing is strong in tension, so it is placed at the bottom of a bridge, where its tensile strength can support the load.

PRINCIPLES OF MECHANICAL DEVICES

Machines are devices that multiply force or motion. Some machines are simple devices that involve only a single force. A lever is an example. Other machines involve combinations of devices working together. A bicycle is an example. The essential thing about all machines is that in order to make them multiply your force, you must exert that force over a longer distance. You'll see how this works in the following section, which describes the main simple machines one by one. First, however, you need to learn how to calculate how much a machine multiplies your force.

Mechanical Advantage

The amount your force is multiplied by a machine is called the *mechanical advantage*, or MA. There are two ways to calculate MA.

1. Divide the output force (called the *load* or sometimes the *resistance*) by the input force (called the effort): Load/effort = MA.

Example

With a lever, you use a 50-lb force (the effort) to lift a 200-lb weight (the load). What is the mechanical advantage of the lever? 200/50 = 4. MA = 4.

2. Divide the length of the effort (called the *effort distance*) by how far the load moves (called the *load distance*): Effort distance/load distance = MA.

Example

With a pulley, you use 5 feet of rope (the effort distance) to lift a load 1 foot (the load distance). What is the mechanical advantage of the pulley? 5/1 = 5. MA = 5

Simple Machines

The simple machines are a group of very common, basic devices that have all been in use for a very long time. They are called *simple* because each one is used to multiply just one single force. The simple machines include the lever, the pulley, the inclined plane, the gear, the wedge, the wheel and axle, and the screw. You can count on the ASVAB to test your knowledge of simple machines.

Levers The first kind of simple machine is the lever, a device that helps you apply force to lift a heavy object. To understand levers, you'll need to know the following terms:

* *Fulcrum*: The stationary element that holds the lever but still allows it to rotate.
* *Load*: The object to be lifted or squeezed.
* *Load arm (load distance)*: The part of the lever from load to fulcrum.
* *Effort*: The force applied to lift or squeeze.
* *Effort arm (effort distance)*: The part of the lever from force to fulcrum.

There are three classes of levers. Let's examine them one at a time and see how to calculate MA for each.

Class 1 Lever In a class 1 lever, the fulcrum is between the load and the effort. If the fulcrum is closer to the load than to the effort (as it usually is), the lever has a mechanical advantage.

Mechanical advantage
= effort distance/load distance = load/effort

Class 1 lever

Effort

150 lb

Load

MA = 3

Example

The figure shows a class 1 lever. What force (effort) is needed to lift the load? Since you know that MA = 3, use this formula to find the effort.

$$MA = \text{load/effort}$$
$$3 = 150 \text{ lb/effort}$$
$$3 \times \text{effort} = 150 \text{ lb}$$
$$\text{effort} = 50 \text{ lb}$$

Class 2 Lever In a class 2 lever, the load is between the effort and the fulcrum. The effort arm is as long as the whole lever, but the load arm is shorter. So a class 2 lever always has a mechanical advantage.

Example

The wheelbarrow shown is a class 2 lever. What is its mechanical advantage?

$$MA = \text{effort distance/load distance} = 3/1.5 = 2$$

Class 2 lever

Effort distance: 3 ft

Load distance (to center of load): 1.5 ft

Load →

Fulcrum →

Effort

Class 3 Lever In a class 3 lever, the effort is between the load and the fulcrum. Tweezers and tongs are good examples of class 3 levers. The length of the effort arm and the load arm are calculated from the fulcrum, as with the class 2 lever.

Example

The figure shows a class 3 lever. What is the mechanical advantage?

$$MA = \text{load/effort} = 1/2 = 0.5$$

In other words, 2 pounds of effort would produce 1 pound of "squeeze" on the orange. We could call this a fractional mechanical advantage, or a mechanical disadvantage. But in return for reducing the squeezing force, each inch of effort movement produces 2 inches of load movement.

Class 3 lever

Effort = 2 lb

Fulcrum

Load: 1 lb

Balancing a Lever Some ASVAB problems may show you a diagram of a lever with various parts marked and ask you what force or weight is needed to balance the lever. To answer this kind of question, keep in mind that the moments of force (effort or load × distance) on either side of the fulcrum must be equal. Here is an example.

8 ft

6 ft

2 ft

F

2 kg 4 kg

Example

What is the force *F*, in kilograms, needed to balance the lever? Add up the moments of force on either side of the fulcrum:

$$(2 \text{ kg} \times 8 \text{ ft}) + (4 \text{ kg} \times 6 \text{ ft}) = (8 \text{ ft} \times F)$$
$$16 + 24 = 8F$$
$$40 = 8F$$
$$F = 5 \text{ kg}$$

Pulleys Another kind of simple machine that helps you lift a heavy object is the pulley, also called a block and tackle. In pulleys, the mechanical advantage is found in either of the following two ways:

- MA = effort distance/load distance.
- MA = number of supporting strands. Supporting strands of rope or cable get shorter when you hoist the load. We'll return to this, but don't just count strands—some do not shorten as you hoist.

Example

The figure shows a pulley attached to a beam that is used to hoist a heavy crate. Each foot of pull on the rope lifts the crate 1 foot. Effort distance = load distance, so MA = 1. Although this pulley allows you to pull down instead of up, it gives no mechanical advantage.

Example

The figure shows two pulleys. When you hoist, two strands of the rope must be shortened. So for every 2 feet of pull (effort distance), you get 1 foot of lift (load distance).

MA = effort distance/load distance = 2/1
MA = 2

The simplest way to find the pulley MA is to count the strands of rope on the movable pulley (in

this case, the one attached to the load). MA = number of supporting strands.

Until now, we have ignored friction and the weight of the movable pulley and extra rope. As MA increases, these factors also increase, so there is a practical limit to the mechanical advantage of pulleys.

Gears Gears are a simple machine used to multiply rotating forces. Finding the MA of a gear is simplicity itself. Identify the driving gear (the one that supplies the force) and count the teeth. Count the teeth on the driven gear. Then use this formula:

Number of teeth on driven gear/number of teeth on driving gear = MA

Example

The figure shows a driving gear with 9 teeth and a driven gear with 36 teeth.

36/9 = 4
MA = 4

You will learn more about systems of driving and driven gears later in this chapter.

Sheaves Sheaves (often also called pulleys) and belts are a simple machine closely related to gears. To calculate the MA of a sheave system, divide the diameter of the driven sheave by the diameter of the drive sheave:

MA = driven diameter/drive diameter

Whenever the driven sheave is larger than the drive sheave, you get a mechanical advantage.

Example

The figure shows a sheave system. What is the MA?

9/3 = 3

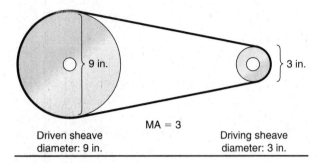

MA = 3

Driven sheave
diameter: 9 in.

Driving sheave
diameter: 3 in.

You will learn more about systems of sheaves (pulleys) later in this chapter.

Inclined Plane *Inclined plane* is a fancy term for "ramp." An inclined plane is another simple machine that is used to lift heavy objects. The formula for finding the mechanical advantage of an inclined plane is as follows:

MA = length of the slope/vertical rise

To find the mechanical advantage, measure vertically and diagonally along the ramp.

Example

The figure shows an inclined plane. What is the mechanical advantage?

MA = 12/3 = 4

If the load weighs 400 lb, how much force is needed to push it up the ramp?

MA = load/effort
4 = 400/effort
4 × effort = 400
Effort = 100 lb

In real life, friction can play a huge role in ramps if the load is not on wheels. Most ASVAB problems will allow you to ignore friction in dealing with all simple machines.

Wedge The wedge is a type of inclined plane. It is one of the rarer simple machines. As always, MA = effort distance/load distance. The wedge is essentially two inclined planes, and the MA calculation also requires you to measure perpendicular to the long axis of the wedge.

Example

The figure shows a wedge. What is the MA?

Every time the wedge moves 5 inches, the load will move 2 inches. MA = 5/2 = 2.5. In reality, friction plays a major role in wedges.

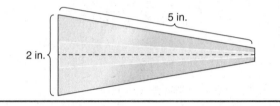

Screw Screws are some of the handiest simple machines, although we usually think of a screw as a fastener rather than as a way to multiply force. Finding mechanical advantage can be complicated because it comes from two sources: the threads and the wrench you use to tighten the screw. But if you consider effort distance and load distance, the calculation is simple.

MA = effort distance/load distance

Example

The figure shows an 8-inch wrench turning a screw with 8 threads per inch. This screw has a *pitch* (movement per turn of the screw) of 1/8 inch. The effort distance is π × diameter = 3.14 × 16 inches = about 50 inches. The load distance per turn of the wrench is 1/8 inch, so MA = 50/1/8 = 400. In reality, the MA is much less, because of friction and because you don't push on the

Screw with
8 threads
per inch

8 inch wrench turns in a circle
with a 16 inch diameter

absolute end of the wrench. But this still demonstrates the power of screws as simple machines!

Most ASVAB questions will not require this much calculation, but it never hurts to be prepared!

Wheel and Axle Wheels are a common and essential part of daily life, but most of these wheels are not simple machines. Instead, they are a way to reduce friction by the use of bearings. A wheel and axle is a simple machine only when the wheel and axle are fixed and rotate together.

A typical wheel-and-axle simple machine is the screwdriver. The screwdriver's handle is the wheel, and the screwdriver's blade is the axle. For wheel-and-axle machines, mechanical advantage is calculated as follows:

MA = effort distance (radius of the wheel)/load distance (radius of the axle)

So for a screwdriver, MA = radius of the handle/ radius of the blade.

Example

The figure shows a brace and bit, a kind of heavy-duty screwdriver that is an example of a wheel and axle as a simple machine. What is the MA?

Effort distance/load distance = MA
6 in./0.25 in. = 24
MA = 24

A wheel and axle can also give a mechanical disadvantage. In a car or a bicycle, where the axle drives the wheel instead of the wheel driving the axle, a small motion at the axle creates a large motion at the circumference of the rim. In these cases, you need a larger force, but you get more motion in return.

Compound Machines

A *compound machine* is one in which two or more simple machines work together. For example, a screwdriver (wheel and axle) driving a screw is a compound machine. To find the mechanical advantage of a compound machine, multiply the MA of the simple machines together.

Example

The axe shown is a compound machine. The handle is a lever, and the head is two inclined planes. Find the combined MA by multiplying the individual MA of each simple machine.

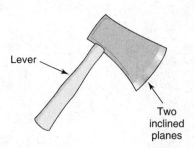

Structural Support

Some Mechanical Comprehension questions ask about the load carried by support structures such as beams or bridges—or sometimes by people. You will be given a diagram showing support structures and asked which one is strongest or weakest, or which support in the diagram is bearing the lesser or greater part of the load. To answer this kind of question, keep this in mind: When a load of any kind is supported by two support beams, posts, or people, the load is perfectly balanced if it is exactly centered. In that case, each beam, post, or person is bearing exactly half the load. However, if the load is not centered, then the beam, post, or person nearer to the load is bearing the greater part of the weight.

Example

The figure shows two people carrying a load. The load is centered. Each person is bearing half the load, or 75 lb.

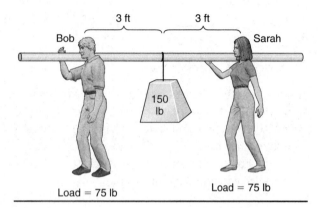

Example

The figure shows two people carrying a load. Which person is bearing the greater part of the load? Common sense tells you that it's the woman, because she is closer to the load.

Questions about structural support may also ask you to decide which of several support structures is the strongest (or weakest). For this kind of question, you can often use your common sense. If a diagram shows several different structures, look for the one with the most brackets or other support elements. Also look for the one that leaves the least horizontal area (for example, the front part of a flat bookshelf) unsupported. A bracket that runs the whole width of the shelf provides better support than one that does not.

Example

Which of these four shelves can bear the most weight?

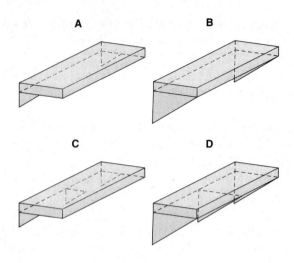

Choice D can bear the most weight. Of the four shelves, it is the strongest because it has the largest brackets, and because it has the most brackets.

Shape can also make a difference in the strength of a support structure. For example, a structure in which the support beams form rectangular shapes is not as strong as one in which the beams form triangular shapes. The reason is that while rectangular supports can easily bend out of shape, a triangle keeps its shape unless it falls apart entirely. That's why triangular shapes are used in support structures such as shelf brackets. That is also why you often see triangular shapes in the support structures of bridges, towers, and other buildings.

Example

Which bridge is the strongest?

In the diagram, bridge C is the strongest because its framework is made of many triangles.

Properties of Materials

Tools, machines, and structures can be made of many different materials, such as wood, metal, plastic, and the like. Each material has its own *properties*, or characteristics. Some Mechanical Comprehension questions will ask you about those properties, or ask you to compare the properties of different materials. Most questions of this type can be answered with simple common sense, based on your everyday experience. For some, you may need to recall some of the basic ideas you learned in high school science.

One of the most important properties of materials is the ability to conduct heat. Here is an example of a question about this property.

Example

Three pots are cooking on a stove. Pot A has a wooden handle, pot B has a metal handle, and pot C has a plastic handle. Which handle will feel hottest to the touch?

A. A
B. B
C. C
D. All three will feel equally hot

To answer this question, think about your everyday experience. For which pot would you need a potholder? You might also remember from a high school science class that metal is a better conductor of heat than either wood or plastic. The correct answer is choice B.

Another important property of some materials is the ability to bend without breaking. This is called *flexibility*. The springs on a car can bend millions of times without breaking because they are made of spring steel. A ceramic cup, on other hand, cannot flex even once without breaking. Materials that are somewhat flexible include regular steel, copper, and wood. Some flexible materials will spring back to their original shape after bending. Others will stay in the new shape.

Example

Which object shown will resume its original shape after bending?

The spring (choice C) will resume its original shape. Nails, screws, and bolts are not made of spring steel, and while you can bend them, they will not spring back into their original shape.

Another important property of some materials is the ability to be formed into a new shape through repeated blows from a hammer. This property is called *malleability*. You will probably not need to be able to recall this term, but you should be able to identify substances that have this property. Metals like steel and copper are malleable and can thus be formed into the shapes of tools, containers, and other objects. Glass and ceramics, on the other hand, are not malleable.

Still another important property of some materials is the ability to stretch without breaking. Rubber can stretch in this way. Metal, glass, and plastic can stretch when heated. Wood and paper, on the other hand, will not stretch.

MECHANICAL MOTION

Many Mechanical Comprehension questions have to do with things that move or rotate: gears, pulleys, and other mechanisms.

Systems of Pulleys

You have already learned about pulleys as simple machines used to hoist heavy objects. Pulleys are also used as drive mechanisms. That is, systems of interconnected pulleys are used to transfer power, and often rotational speed, from one shaft to another. Two pulleys (sheaves) that are connected by a belt will run at the same speed if they are the same size. When the sheaves are of different sizes, the smaller one will run faster than the larger one because the smaller one must make more turns to move the belt the same distance.

In most cases on the ASVAB, you will simply be asked which of two or more interconnected pulleys runs fastest or slowest, and you can easily solve these problems by identifying the smallest or largest pulley. However, if you are asked to calculate the speed of a particular pulley in a system of pulleys, you can easily do so by using the following formula:

$$\text{Speed}_1 \times \text{diameter}_1 = \text{speed}_2 \times \text{diameter}_2$$

(Note that pulley speed is measured in revolutions per minute, or rpm.)

Example

Pulley 1 measures 9 inches in diameter. Pulley 2 measures 3 inches in diameter. If pulley 1 rotates at 1,200 rpm, how fast will pulley 2 rotate?

$$\text{Speed}_1 \times \text{diameter}_1 = \text{speed}_2 \times \text{diameter}_2$$
$$1,200 \times 9 = 10,800 = \text{speed}_2 \times 3$$
$$\text{Speed}_2 = 10,800/3 = 3,600$$

Another way to calculate the speed of pulley 2 is to look at the ratio between the two diameters. A ratio of 9:3, or 3:1, will multiply speed × 3. So 1,200 rpm × 3 = 3,600 rpm. Remember that the pulley with the smaller diameter is always the one that rotates faster!

Using these methods, you can calculate the speed of any pulley system as long as you know the diameters of both pulleys and the speed of either pulley.

Example

When pulley A runs at 400 rpm, what will be the speeds of pulleys B, C, and D?

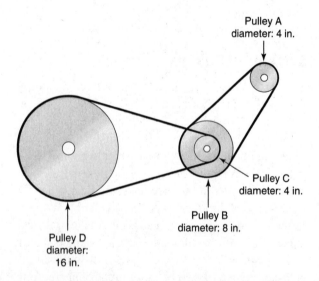

Pulley A diameter: 4 in.

Pulley C diameter: 4 in.

Pulley B diameter: 8 in.

Pulley D diameter: 16 in.

In this system, assume that the linked pulleys (B and C in the example) run at the same rpm, since they are

attached to the same shaft. Break the problem down into parts, and calculate them in order:

- Diameter of pulley A/diameter of pulley B = 4/8, so pulley B will run 1/2 as fast as pulley A.

  400/2 = 200 rpm

- You already know that pulley C runs at the same speed as pulley B.
- Diameter of pulley C/diameter of pulley D = 4/16 = 1/4, so pulley D will run 1/4 as fast as pulley C.

  200/4 = 50 rpm

Systems of Gears

Another way to transfer power between shafts is through systems of gears. The gears in a system typically have different diameters and different numbers of teeth per gear. The teeth of one gear mesh with the teeth of another, and as one gear (the *driving* gear) turns, it turns the other gear (the *driven* gear). When interlocking gears have different numbers of teeth, the gear with fewer teeth will rotate more times in a given period than the gear with more teeth. To see how this works, look at the following example.

Example

Gear A and gear B make up a system of gears. If gear A makes 6 revolutions, how many revolutions will gear B make?

9 teeth   27 teeth

A

B

To solve this problem, use the picture and your common sense. Count the teeth on each gear. Gear A has 9 teeth. Gear B has 27 teeth. The ratio of the teeth on the two gears is 9:27 or 1:3. Common sense should tell you that gear A must rotate 3 times to make gear B rotate once. So if gear A rotates 6 times, gear B will rotate twice. Always keep in mind that in this kind of system, the gear with more teeth makes fewer rotations in the same period than the gear with fewer teeth.

Notice, too, that gears change the rotation direction, while pulleys usually do not. To rotate a gear in the same direction as the driving gear, you need a third gear, called an *idler* gear.

Example

In this system, gear A (the driving gear) is rotating clockwise. Gear B is the idler gear. Gear A makes gear B rotate counterclockwise. Gear B then makes gear C rotate clockwise, the same direction as gear A.

Rotating Wheels and Disks

Another way to drive shafts is to use what is called a *pin and slot arrangement*. In this arrangement, a pin is attached to a driving shaft, and a slotted disk is attached to a driven shaft. When the driving shaft rotates, the pin enters a slot on the disk and turns the driven shaft.

Example

In this pin and slot arrangement, each time the driving shaft turns one full revolution, the disk on the driven shaft will make 1/4 revolution. How far will the disk rotate when the pin turns three complete revolutions?

3 × 1/4 = 3/4 turn.

You may also be asked simple questions about what happens to points on a wheel when the wheel turns.

Example

How many rotations will point A make when point C makes 5 rotations? Point A will make 5 rotations

because point A and point C are both fixed on the same wheel.

Example

Which point will travel farthest as the wheel makes 10 rotations? Point B will travel farthest because it is farthest from the center. The distance it travels in each rotation is greater than the distance traveled by the other points.

Cams and Cam Followers

Cams are lobes attached to rotating shafts to push separate pieces, called *cam followers*. Cams are often found in engines, where they push intake and exhaust valves open when the engine turns. For every complete rotation of the camshaft, the cam follower will move away from and then back to its original position. A spring pushes the follower tight to the cam.

Cranks and Pistons

Cranks are used to change motion in a straight line to motion in a circle. You'll find cranks connected to pedals on a bike, and to pistons in a car engine. When a crank makes one complete revolution, the piston must go up and down and return to its original position.

FLUID DYNAMICS

Fluids are substances that take the shape of their container. Gases and liquids are both fluids. The behavior of fluids is called *fluid dynamics*, and it can get rather complicated, but not on the ASVAB. Let's start with air, and move on to hydraulics—the engineering of liquids.

Air Pressure

Air pressure is measured in pounds per square inch. Atmospheric pressure at sea level is 14.7 lb/in^2, which is actually quite a bit of pressure. Since it's present all around us, we don't notice it. However, if you create a vacuum inside a weak container, the container will be crushed by all that pressure.

Pneumatics and the Gas Laws Systems that use compressed air to do work are called *pneumatic systems*. Air is easily compressed, and the calculations are more complicated than they are with liquids, which usually can't be compressed. The larger the driven cylinder, the more air pressure it is exposed to, and the greater the force it can exert.

The "gas laws" apply to air as it is compressed and expanded.

- When a gas is compressed, it gains thermal energy—it warms up. The gas also gains potential energy, which is why compressed air can be used to drive nail guns and pneumatic hammers.
- When a given amount of gas expands, its pressure drops and the gas cools.
- When a gas cools without a change in outside pressure, it loses volume.

What happens when you increase the air pressure outside a balloon? The balloon shrinks until the pressure inside becomes great enough to balance the pressure outside.

Air pressure is also what keeps airplanes aloft. The bulge on the top of an airplane wing increases the speed of air passing over the wing, and that

causes a reduction in pressure. Because air pressure does not change below the wing, the result is an unbalanced upward force. This force lifts the airplane.

Refrigerators Refrigerators and air conditioners provide interesting applications of the gas laws. A compressor compresses a fluid, called a *refrigerant*. The refrigerant warms up, as predicted by the gas laws. Then the refrigerant loses heat (but not pressure) in the condenser. The refrigerant is piped into an evaporator, where it goes through a small hole and evaporates under reduced pressure. Expansion causes the temperature to drop, and the cold refrigerant can pick up heat from the surroundings. This is why the evaporator is placed in the area to be cooled. The condenser is placed where it's easy to get rid of excess heat—in the backyard for an air conditioner, or in back for a refrigerator.

Water Pressure

On the ASVAB, water pressure questions often involve flow through pipes. Keep these principles in mind:

1. Total flow through a pipe system must be the same everywhere because water cannot be compressed.
2. When liquid speeds up, pressure falls.
3. When liquid slows down, pressure rises.

In the diagram, the same amount of water is flowing everywhere in the pipe system. For this to be true, water must be flowing faster at point B than at point A. That means that pressure is lower at point B.

Water in a container also exerts pressure on the bottom of the container. The deeper the water, the greater the pressure. To find the amount of water pressure in a tank, calculate the total weight of the water and divide by the area of the base of the tank.

Example

A tank with a base that measures 2 feet × 4 feet holds 1,600 pounds of water. What is the water pressure at the base of the tank?

$$2 \text{ ft} \times 4 \text{ ft} = 8 \text{ ft}^2$$
$$1,600/8 = 200 \text{ lb/ft}^2$$

Remember too that $1 \text{ ft}^2 = 144 \text{ in}^2$. To convert pressure between pounds per square inch and pounds per square foot, divide or multiply by 144.

Filling and Emptying Tanks

The Mechanical Comprehension test often includes problems about filling and emptying tanks. Usually the filling and emptying take place at different rates, as in the following examples.

Example

Water is being piped into a tank at the rate of 2 gallons per second. At the same time, it is being piped out of the tank at the rate of 60 gallons per minute. How many gallons will be added in 5 minutes?

Convert the inflow rate so that you are working only with gallons per minute.

$$\text{gal/sec} \times 60 = \text{gal/min}$$
$$2 \text{ gal/sec} \times 60 = 120 \text{ gal/min}$$

Subtract:

$$120 \text{ gal/min inflow} - 60 \text{ gal/min outflow}$$
$$= 60 \text{ gal/min net gain}$$

The net gain in 5 minutes is $5 \times 60 = 300$ gallons.

2 gal/sec

60 gal/min

Example

A 100-gallon tank contains 10 gallons of water. Water is added through one pipe at the rate of 3 gallons per minute. It is drained away through another pipe at the rate of 2 gallons per minute. How long will it take to fill the tank?

Find the net gain of water per minute:

$$3 \text{ gal/min} - 2 \text{ gal/min} = 1 \text{ gal/min}$$

It will take $100 - 10 = 90$ gallons to fill the tank. At the rate of 1 gal/min, it will take 90 minutes to fill the tank.

CHAPTER GLOSSARY

chemical energy. Energy stored in chemicals or released in a chemical reaction

compound machine. A machine made up of two or more simple machines working together

compression. A force that pushes materials together

effort. In a lever, the point where you apply force

effort arm. In a lever, the distance from the force to the fulcrum

electrical energy. Energy in moving electrons

flexibility. The ability of a material to bend without breaking

friction. The force that resists the relative motion of two surfaces in contact

fulcrum. The stationary element that holds a lever but also allows it to rotate

gravity. An attractive force between objects

kinetic energy. Energy in a moving object

load. In a lever, the part where output force lifts or squeezes

load arm. In a lever, the distance from the load to the fulcrum

mechanical advantage. The amount by which a machine multiplies the force applied to it

potential energy. Energy that can be released under certain conditions

tension. A force that pulls materials apart

LAWS AND FORMULAS TO KNOW

How to calculate mechanical advantage (MA):

- *Lever*: MA = load/effort = effort distance/load distance
- *Pulley*: MA = load/effort = number of supporting strands
- *Gears*: MA = number of teeth on driven gear/number of teeth on driving gear

324 MCGRAW-HILL EDUCATION: ASVAB

- *Sheaves*: MA = driven diameter/drive diameter
- *Inclined plane*: MA = horizontal length/vertical rise
- *Wheel and axle*: MA = radius of wheel/radius of axle

Speed of pulleys in a system:

$$\text{Speed}_1 \times \text{diameter}_1 = \text{speed}_2 \times \text{diameter}_2$$

The gas laws:

- When a gas is compressed, it heats up.
- When a given amount of gas expands, its pressure drops and the gas cools.
- When a gas cools without a change in outside pressure, it loses volume.

Water pressure:

- Total flow through a pipe system is the same everywhere.
- When liquid speeds up, pressure falls.
- When liquid slows down, pressure rises.

MECHANICAL COMPREHENSION QUIZ

Take the following quiz to check your understanding of ASVAB Mechanical Comprehension topics. Circle each answer that you choose. There is no time limit. Answers and explanations are given immediately after the quiz.

1. The diagram shows a class 1 lever. Which of the following is the same kind of lever?
   A. A pair of tweezers
   B. A pair of scissors
   C. A wheelbarrow
   D. A pair of tongs

2. The diagram shows a class 2 lever. Which of the following is the same kind of lever?
   A. A seesaw
   B. A pair of scissors
   C. The human forearm
   D. A wheelbarrow

3. When a mass of air expands, which of the following is most likely to happen?
   A. The air warms up.
   B. The air cools down.
   C. The air stays at the same temperature.
   D. The air contracts.

4. The diagram shows a class 3 lever. Which of the following is the same kind of lever?
   A. A pair of tweezers
   B. A wheelbarrow
   C. A seesaw
   D. A wedge

5. Which of the following would feel hottest to the touch if one end were placed in a pot of boiling water?
   A. A wooden spoon
   B. A metal fork
   C. A plastic knife
   D. A plastic cup

6. A lever lifts 300 lb with an effort of 60 lb. What is the mechanical advantage?
   A. 3
   B. 4
   C. 5
   D. 8

7. In a class 1 lever with an MA of 4, if the effort distance measures 8 ft, how long is the load distance?
   A. 2 ft
   B. 4 ft
   C. 8 ft
   D. 16 ft

8. Water is flowing into a tank at the rate of 180 gallons per minute. However, the tank has a leak, and water is leaking out at the rate of 2 gallons per second. How long will it take to add 120 gallons?
   A. 1 min
   B. 2 min
   C. 3 min
   D. 4 min

9. Water is flowing from a 3-inch pipe into a 1-inch pipe. Which statement is true?
   A. Pressure is lower in the 3-inch pipe.
   B. Pressure is higher in the 1-inch pipe.
   C. More water is passing through the 3-inch pipe than through the 1-inch pipe.
   D. The same amount of water is passing through every part of the piping system.

10. Gear A, with 18 teeth, meshes with gear B, which has 12 teeth. When gear A rotates 3 times, gear B will rotate
    A. 3 times.
    B. 4.5 times.
    C. 6 times.
    D. 9 times.

11. What is the mechanical advantage in this pulley system?

    A. 2
    B. 3
    C. 4
    D. 6

12. In the diagram, what can you tell about the load on posts A and B?

    A. Post B carries more weight.
    B. Post A carries more weight.
    C. Post A carries no weight.
    D. The load is equal on posts A and B.

13. Water is flowing through this pipe. Which statement is true?

    A. Water is moving faster at point A than at point B.
    B. Water pressure is equal at points A and B.
    C. Water pressure is greater at point A than at point B.
    D. Water pressure is greater at point B than at point A.

14. What is the advantage of using triangle shapes in constructing a bridge?
    A. Triangles are sturdier than other shapes.
    B. Triangles are very flexible.
    C. Triangles are inexpensive to manufacture.
    D. Triangles are attractive to look at.

15. Which formula will calculate the mechanical advantage of a lever?
    A. Load/effort
    B. Effort distance/load distance
    C. Both A and B
    D. Load × effort

ANSWERS AND EXPLANATIONS

1. **B.** In a class 1 lever, the fulcrum is between the effort and the load. Of the choices, only the pair of scissors has the same arrangement of elements. The tweezers (choice A) and tongs (choice B) are examples of class 3 levers. The wheelbarrow (choice C) is a class 2 lever.

2. **D.** In a class 2 lever, the fulcrum is at one end, the effort is at the other end, and the load is between the fulcrum and the effort. Of the choices, only the wheelbarrow has this arrangement of elements. The seesaw (choice A) and the scissors (choice B) are class 1 levers. The human forearm (choice C) is a class 3 lever.

3. **B.** Air is a gas, so according to the gas laws, when a mass of warm air expands, it will most likely cool down.

4. **A.** In a class 3 lever, the fulcrum is at one end, the load is at the other, and the effort is between the fulcrum and the load. Of the choices, only the tweezers have this arrangement of elements. The wheelbarrow (choice B) is a class 2 lever. The seesaw (choice C) is a class 1 lever. The wedge (choice D) is not a lever at all but an inclined plane.

5. **B.** Metal is a better conductor of heat than wood or plastic, so the metal fork would feel hottest to the touch.

6. **C.** MA = load/effort. 300/60 = 5

7. **A.** MA = effort distance/load distance. 4 = 8/load distance. 4 = 8/2. The load distance is 2 ft.

8. **B.** The leak of 2 gal/sec = 120 gal/min. Net gain is 60 gal/min, so it will take 2 minutes to add 120 gallons to the tank.

9. **D.** Because water cannot be compressed, the same amount of water must be flowing through both parts of the pipe system. This makes choice C incorrect. If the same amount of water is flowing through all parts of the system, then the water must be flowing faster in the 1-inch section, reducing pressure in that section. That makes choices A and B both incorrect.

10. **B.** The ratio of teeth is 18 to 12. Each turn of gear A will turn gear B 1.5 times. $1.5 \times 3 = 4.5$.

11. **A.** Count the supporting strands (the strands of rope that will be shortened as the load is lifted). There are two supporting strands, so MA = 2.

12. **D.** Since the load is centered between the posts, each post carries equal weight.

13. **C.** When fluid speed increases, pressure decreases. Because the same amount of water must be in these pipes, water must be moving faster at point B. Therefore pressure is lower at point B.

14. **A.** The only way to distort the form of a triangular-shaped structure is to break the legs or angles. That makes triangles sturdier than other structural shapes, which is a good reason to use triangle shapes when constructing a bridge.

15. **C.** Either load/effort or effort distance/load distance will calculate the mechanical advantage.

Assembling Objects

INTRODUCTION: ASVAB ASSEMBLING OBJECTS QUESTIONS

The Assembling Objects (AO) subtest of the ASVAB was added to the battery of tests in 2002. This subtest is designed to test your skills in spatial orientation. It is not part of the Armed Forces Qualification Test (AFQT) and does not determine your eligibility for enlistment.

> The Assembling Objects test is found on all versions of the ASVAB, but at this time AO scores are used only by the Navy, for determining eligibility for certain kinds of jobs.

The types of questions you will see on the Assembling Objects (AO) subtest will likely not be familiar to you from tests you took in high school. They require the ability to comprehend the sizes and orientations of various shapes and to picture how those objects can be maneuvered to be joined together. In order to do well on this subtest, you will need a method to follow, common sense, and practice, in addition to your spatial ability.

There are two types of AO questions:

- **Puzzle:** In this question type, you are given several individual objects in a box. Then you will have four choices of what those objects could look like when they are assembled together into one figure. This is a bit like fitting together pieces in a jigsaw puzzle.

- **Connection:** In this question type, you are given objects that each have a point that is marked. You will again have four choices and you must choose which one shows the objects joined by a line between the correct points. This is a bit like connect-the-dots.

Let's look at strategies for each type of question.

PUZZLE QUESTIONS

In this question type, you are given several individual objects and you choose the answer that shows what they could look like when assembled together into one figure.

For example, if you are given these objects:

The correct choice might look like this:

Rules

1. **The correct answer must have the exact same objects as the original (and no additional ones).** For example, this would be incorrect because it has an additional triangle that the original did not.

2. **The objects must remain the same size.** For example, this would be incorrect because the rectangle at the bottom is smaller than the original one.

3. **The objects can be rotated.** For example, this shape in the original:

might look like this in the answer:

4. **The objects must remain in their original orientation: they can rotate but not be flipped over.** In other words, do not choose an answer that shows a mirror image of the original object.

For example, this shape in a question:

CANNOT look like this in the answer:

Strategies

1. First, count the number of objects and eliminate any answer choice that does not match. If the original figure has six objects, then the correct answer must also have six objects.
2. Look for one object at a time and eliminate any answer choice that does not include it.
3. Choose the most distinctive (unique) object to look for. For example, it is easier to look for a weird-looking object such as this:

than a more common one like this:

4. Keep choosing new objects until you have eliminated all but one answer choice. Once you are down to only one choice, you know you have found the correct answer.

Examples

1. *Which figure best shows how the objects in the box will appear if they are fit together?*

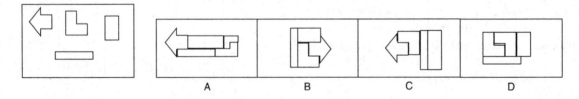

2. *Which figure best shows how the objects in the box will appear if they are fit together?*

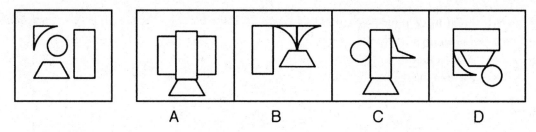

A   B   C   D

Explanations

1. **B.** First, count the number of objects. There are four in the original. Choice A has five, so eliminate A. The others each have four, so move on to the next strategy. Choose the most distinctive object to look for first—perhaps the arrow. Choice D does not have an arrow, so eliminate D. Now look for the L-shaped object. Choices B and C both have it, so choose another object. The long thin rectangle is in both choices as well. The rectangle at the top right of the original figure is the last object left. Choice C has another rectangle, but it is not the same size as the original, so eliminate C. That leaves only choice B. **The correct answer is B.**

2. **D.** First, count the number of objects. There are four in the original and in all the answer choices. Move on to the next strategy. Choose the most distinctive object to look for first: the object that looks like a triangle with one concave side. Choice A does not have it, so eliminate A. Choice B has two of them, so eliminate B as well. Choice C has a similar shape, but it is not the same as the original. Eliminate C. That leaves only choice D. **The correct answer is D.**

CONNECTION QUESTIONS

In this question type, you are given individual objects that each have a point labeled with a letter. You choose the answer that shows what the objects would look like when the labeled points are connected by a line.

For example, if you are given these objects:

The correct choice might look like this:

Rules

1. **Follow the same rules as Puzzle questions.**
   Plus
2. **Each object must connect at the exact same point that was labeled in the original.**
3. **Points may be located anywhere on the object— on the perimeter or within the area.**

Strategies

1. Look for one labeled point at a time.

2. Start with whichever shape has the easier point to find. For example, it is easier to look for a point in a distinctive location like a corner, such as this:

than one in a less distinct location such as this:

3. Once you have eliminated choices that do not connect at the first point correctly, repeat the process for the other point. Both points must be connected at the place they were labeled in the original.

Examples

1. *Which figure best shows how the objects in the box will touch if the letters for each object are matched?*

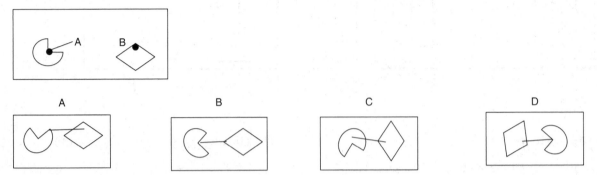

2. *Which figure best shows how the objects in the box will touch if the letters for each object are matched?*

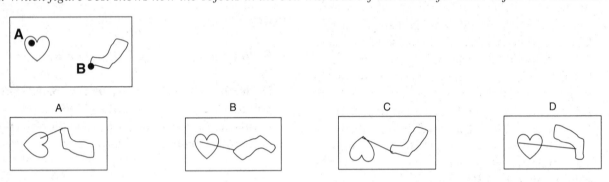

Explanations

1. **D.** The first object has point A located at the center of the ¾ circle. Choices A and C do not connect there, so eliminate them. The second object has point B located within the figure, in the wider angle of the rhombus. Choice B does not connect at that point. **The correct answer is D.**

2. **A.** The heart has point A located within the upper left rounded part. Choices C and D do not connect there, so eliminate them. Point B is located at the "toe" of the boot shape. Choice B does not connect at that point. That leaves only choice A. **The correct answer is A.**

ASVAB PAPER VERSION

Paper-and-pencil versions of the ASVAB are given at Military Entrance Test (MET) sites around the country or on high school and some college campuses.

On the paper-and-pencil version of the ASVAB, there are 25 questions and you will have 15 minutes to complete them.

Every candidate receives the same test questions, and questions range from very easy to very difficult.

Strategies for the Paper Version

- **Skip around:** You do not necessarily have to do the questions in order, as long as you fill in your answer sheet correctly. This will enable you to focus on your personal strengths. If, for example, you find that you perform better on the connection questions, you can seek those out and answer them first. That way you will not run out of time without doing all the questions you are best at. Save harder questions for last to maximize the number of correct answers you get.

- **Don't leave any blanks:** Since there is no penalty for guessing on the paper-and-pencil version of the test, be sure to keep an eye on the clock so that you can fill in an answer on any question you didn't get a chance to work. Do not leave anything blank. Wrong answers do not hurt you, but a blank question is a missed chance for points.

- **Use the process of elimination:** The easiest way to approach Assembling Objects questions is by using the process of elimination. Cross out choices that you know cannot be correct and you will get to the correct answer more quickly. If you are taking a paper version of the test, this is easy to do.

- **Practice:** Working 25 questions in only 15 minutes is tough. The more you practice, the faster you will get. The Assembling Objects practice tests in this book are paper-and-pencil format, so you will have plenty of opportunity to work on your speed and accuracy. Answers and explanations are provided so that you can review your work and learn from your mistakes.

ASVAB COMPUTER VERSION (CAT)

Computer Adaptive Test (CAT) versions of the ASVAB are given at Military Entrance Processing Stations (MEPS) around the country.

On the CAT-ASVAB, there are 16 questions and you will have 16 minutes to complete them.

The CAT-ASVAB provides questions that adapt to each tester's ability. Questions are selected from a large pool of items that range in difficulty from very easy to very difficult. The first question presented will be of medium difficulty. If you answer correctly, you will get a slightly more difficult question next. If you answer incorrectly, you will be given a slightly easier question next. This process continues after each question, allowing the computer to quickly home in on your highest level of ability. For that reason, CATs generally have fewer questions than paper exams and provide more score-level precision.

Strategies for the CAT-ASVAB

- **Take your time:** You can't skip around on the CAT and earlier questions are very important since they determine the level of difficulty (and score level) of later questions. Do not rush. You have more time per question on the CAT than you would on the paper version, so use it wisely. Work carefully.

- **Use the process of elimination:** The easiest way to approach Assembling Objects questions is by using the process of elimination. Cross out choices that you know cannot be correct and you will get to the correct answer more quickly. This is easier to do on the paper version of the test, but it can be done on the CAT as well. You will need to use your scratch paper to write "ABCD," and then you can cross out choices as you eliminate them. Do this for each question.

- **Double-check:** Once you submit an answer, you cannot return to that question to change it. Be sure you get each question correct before you submit and confirm your answer.

- **Finish the test:** There are only 16 items and most testers are able to finish them in the time allowed. However, if you should happen to run out of time, there is a penalty. Any questions that were not completed are scored as though they were answered at random. This will have an effect on your score, but not as much of an effect as would rushing through the test in order to finish and missing early questions. Work on your pacing while you practice so that this will not be an issue for you on test day.

- **Practice:** The more you practice, the faster you will get. The Assembling Objects practice tests in this book are paper-and-pencil format, but that will give you even more opportunity to work on your speed and accuracy. Answers and explanations are provided so that you can review your work and learn from your mistakes.

Part 4

THREE
ASVAB
PRACTICE
TEST
FORMS

ASVAB PRACTICE TEST FORM 1

Try to take this practice test under actual test conditions. Find a quiet place to work, and set aside a period of approximately 2½ hours when you will not be disturbed. Work on only one section at a time, and use your watch or a timer to keep track of the time limits for each section. Mark your answers on the answer sheet, just as you will when you take the real exam.

At the end of the test you'll find an answer key and explanations for every question. After you check your answers against the key, you can complete a chart that will show you how you did on the test and what test topics you might need to study more. Then review the explanations, paying particular attention to the ones for the questions that you answered incorrectly.

GENERAL DIRECTIONS

IF YOU ARE TAKING THE PAPER-AND-PENCIL VERSION OF THE ASVAB, THE TEST ADMINISTRATOR WILL READ THE FOLLOWING ALOUD TO YOU:

DO NOT WRITE YOUR NAME OR MAKE ANY MARKS in this booklet. Mark your answers on the separate answer sheet. Use the scratch paper which was given to you for any figuring you need to do. Return this scratch paper with your other papers when you finish the test.

If you need another pencil while taking this test, hold your pencil above your head. A proctor will bring you another one.

This booklet contains 9 tests. Each test has its own instructions and time limit. When you finish a test, you may check your work in that test ONLY. Do not go on to the next test until the examiner tells you to do so. Do not turn back to a previous test at any time.

For each question, be sure to pick the BEST ONE of the possible answers listed. Each test has its own instructions and time limit. When you have decided which one of the choices given is the best answer to the question, blacken the space on your answer sheet that has the same number and letter as your choice. Mark only in the answer space. BE CAREFUL NOT TO MAKE ANY STRAY MARKS ON YOUR ANSWER SHEET. Each test has a separate section on the answer sheet. Be sure you mark your answers for each test in the section that belongs to that test.

Here is an example of correct marking on an answer sheet.

S1. A triangle has

A. 2 sides
B. 3 sides
C. 4 sides
D. 5 sides

PRACTICE

S1 Ⓐ ● Ⓒ Ⓓ
S2 Ⓐ Ⓑ Ⓒ Ⓓ
S3 Ⓐ Ⓑ Ⓒ Ⓓ

The correct answer to sample question S1 is B.

Next to the item, note how space B opposite number S1 has been blackened. Your marks should look just like this and be placed in the space with the same number and letter as the correct answer to the question. Remember, there is only ONE BEST ANSWER for each question. If you are not sure of the answer, make the BEST GUESS you can. If you want to change your answer, COMPLETELY ERASE your first answer mark.

Answer as many questions as possible. Do not spend too much time on any one question. Work QUICKLY, but work ACCURATELY. DO NOT TURN THE PAGE UNTIL TOLD TO DO SO. Are there any questions?

ASVAB PRACTICE TEST FORM 1

ANSWER SHEET

ANSWER SHEET   PAGE 3
ARMED SERVICES VOCATIONAL
APTITUDE BATTERY

DD FORM 1304-5AS   FOR OFFICIAL USE ONLY (WHEN COMPLETED)

PART 1. GENERAL SCIENCE

THE TEST ADMINISTRATOR WILL READ THE FOLLOWING ALOUD TO YOU:

Turn to Part 1 and read the directions for General Science silently while I read them aloud. This test has questions about science. Pick the BEST answer for each question and then blacken the space on your separate answer sheet that has the same number and letter as your choice. Here are three practice questions.

S1. A rose is a kind of
   A. animal.
   B. bird.
   C. flower.
   D. fish.

S2. A cat is a
   A. plant.
   B. mammal.
   C. reptile.
   D. mineral.

S3. The earth revolves around the
   A. sun.
   B. moon.
   C. meteorite.
   D. Mars.

Now look at the section of your answer sheet labeled "PRACTICE." Notice that answer space C has been marked for question S1. Now do practice questions S2 and S3 by yourself. Find the correct answer to the question, then mark the space on your answer sheet that has the same letter as the answer you picked. Do this now.

   You should have marked B for question S2 and A for question S3. If you make any mistakes, erase your mark carefully and blacken the correct answer space. Do this now.

   Your score on this test will be based on the number of questions you answer correctly. You should try to answer every question. If you finish before time is called, go back and check your work in this part ONLY. Now find the section of your answer sheet that is marked PART 1. When you are told to begin, start with question number 1 in Part 1 of your test booklet and answer space number 1 in Part 1 on your separate answer sheet. DO NOT TURN THE PAGE UNTIL TOLD TO DO SO. This part has 25 questions in it. You will have 11 minutes to complete it. Most of you should finish in this amount of time. Are there any questions?

   Turn the page and begin.

1. A major difference between a plant cell and an animal cell is
   A. plant cells do not reproduce.
   B. plant cells do not have cell walls.
   C. plant cells have chloroplasts.
   D. plant cells die after a year.

2. Sponges, worms, insects, and amphibians belong to which of the following kingdoms?
   A. Monera
   B. Protista
   C. Plantae
   D. Animalia

3. What name is given to the global ecosystem?
   A. Atmosphere
   B. Hydrosphere
   C. Lithosphere
   D. Biosphere

4. Which of the following parts of a plant is (are) not digestible by humans?
   A. Cell wall
   B. Stomata
   C. Root hairs
   D. Tap root

5. In fish, respiration takes place in which of the following body parts?
   A. Gills
   B. Spinal cord
   C. Tail
   D. Circulatory system

6. If a seed is planted upside down, the roots will still grow downward because of which of the following plant responses?
   A. Respiration
   B. Gravitropism
   C. Osmosis
   D. Turgidity

7. When a plant like mistletoe lives by stealing the nutrients from the tissue of living trees, the condition is called which of the following?
   A. Mutualism
   B. Commensalism
   C. Predation
   D. Parasitism

8. Which of the following organs contains smooth muscle cells?
   A. Biceps
   B. Heart
   C. Stomach
   D. Thyroid

9. Bacteria and viruses can invade your body from all except which of the following?
   A. Mouth
   B. Nose
   C. Eyes
   D. Skin

10. Most of the absorption of nutrients takes place in which part of the digestive system?
    A. Small intestine
    B. Mouth
    C. Large intestine
    D. Stomach

11. The autonomic system is not involved in controlling which of the following?
    A. Walking
    B. Digestion
    C. Heart rate
    D. Breathing

12. If one parent has two dominant genes for tallness (TT) and the other parent has two recessive genes for shortness (tt), what is the probability that the offspring will be tall?
    A. 25%
    B. 50%
    C. 75%
    D. 100%

13. If an object is more than two focal lengths away from a convex lens, which of the following best represents what the image would look like?
    A. The image is larger and inverted.
    B. The image is smaller and inverted.
    C. The image is larger and upright.
    D. The image is smaller and upright.

14. An element's atomic mass is determined by which of the following?
    A. The number of protons and the number of electrons
    B. The number of protons, electrons, and neutrons
    C. The number of protons only
    D. The number of protons and the number of neutrons

15. A rainbow is the outcome of which of the following behaviors of light?
    A. Diffusion
    B. Refraction
    C. Reflection
    D. Interference

16. Which of the following features indicate that continents such as Africa were once situated near the South Pole?
    A. Fault lines
    B. Glacial deposits
    C. Snow-capped mountains
    D. River deposits

17. Pumice formed from a volcano is considered to be which of the following types of rock?
    A. Intrusive igneous rock
    B. Extrusive igneous rock
    C. Intrusive metamorphic rock
    D. Extrusive metamorphic rock

18. Which of the following causes ocean waves?
    A. Persistent surface winds
    B. Excessive rainfall in one part of the ocean
    C. Steep slopes near the shoreline
    D. The relative alignment of the moon and the sun with Earth

19. Earth is closest to the sun during which of the following months?
    A. July
    B. June
    C. January
    D. September

20. Which planet is eighth in order from the sun?
    A. Venus
    B. Saturn
    C. Jupiter
    D. Neptune

21. Which of the following is NOT a possible effect of the global warming of Earth's atmosphere?
    A. Warmer weather might support an increase in tropical diseases such as malaria.
    B. Sea level might rise due to the melting of the polar ice caps.
    C. Earth's mesosphere might become more ionized, hindering space travel.
    D. The number of storms and hurricanes might increase.

22. Severe storms are most likely to be created under which of the following conditions?
    A. A cold front when the warm air it replaces rises quickly
    B. A warm front that is replacing cold air
    C. An occluded front where a fast-moving cold air mass replaces a slower warm air mass
    D. A stationary front that remains in place for several days

23. Which of the following are features associated with glaciers?
    A. Cirques, aràtes, moraines
    B. Sinkholes, groundwater flow, stalactites
    C. Sedimentary rocks, conglomerates, shale
    D. Vents, calderas, hot spots

24. A sea breeze is caused by which of the following conditions?
   A. The sea is warmer than the air.
   B. The sea is warmer than the land.
   C. The land is warmer than the sea.
   D. The sea is colder than the air.

25. An atom of the same element that has different numbers of neutrons is called a(n)
   A. ion.
   B. isotope.
   C. compound.
   D. mixture.

STOP! DO NOT TURN THIS PAGE UNTIL TIME IS UP FOR THIS TEST. IF YOU FINISH BEFORE TIME IS UP, CHECK OVER YOUR WORK ON THIS TEST ONLY.

PART 2. ARITHMETIC REASONING

Turn to Part 2 and read the directions for Arithmetic Reasoning silently while I read them aloud. This is a test of arithmetic word problems. Each question is followed by four possible answers. Decide which answer is CORRECT, and then blacken the space on your answer sheet that has the same number and letter as your choice. Use your scratch paper for any figuring you wish to do.

Here is a sample question. DO NOT MARK your answer sheet for this or any further sample questions.

S1. A student buys a sandwich for 80 cents, milk for 20 cents, and pie for 30 cents. How much did the meal cost?
   A. $1.00
   B. $1.20
   C. $1.30
   D. $1.40

The total cost is $1.30; therefore, C is the right answer. Your score on this test will be based on the number of question you answer correctly. You should try to answer every question. DO NOT SPEND TOO MUCH TIME on any one question. If you finish before time is called, go back and check your work in this part <u>ONLY</u>.

Now find the section of your answer sheet that is marked PART 2. When you are told to begin, start with question number 1 in Part 2 of your test booklet and answer space number 1 in Part 2 on your separate answer sheet.

DO NOT TURN THIS PAGE UNTIL TOLD TO DO SO. You will have 36 minutes for the 30 questions. Are there any questions?

Begin.

1. At an electronics store, Sal bought a CD for $14.99, another CD for $19.99, a CD player for $49.75, and a software program for his computer for $56.59. What was his total bill?
   A. $121.45
   B. $125.42
   C. $139.72
   D. $141.32

2. Brad placed several calls on his cell phone during the first half of the month. The calls were 15 minutes, 46 minutes, 59 minutes, 83 minutes, and 114 minutes. If his plan authorizes 400 minutes, how many minutes does he have left?
   A. 47
   B. 83
   C. 113
   D. 147

3. A math class has 32 students. Fourteen are females. What percent of the class is female?
   A. 24.22%
   B. 37.25%
   C. 43.75%
   D. 52.75%

4. Tim has run a 500-meter race four times. His times are 169 seconds, 212 seconds, 198 seconds, and 201 seconds. What is his average speed?
   A. 182 seconds
   B. 195 seconds
   C. 198 seconds
   D. 201 seconds

5. Trinidad earns $2,700 per month. If she spends $1,100 on the rent for her apartment, to the nearest percent what percent is spent on rent?
   A. 20%
   B. 41%
   C. 51%
   D. 65%

6. A restaurant had a delivery of 12 cartons of vegetables and 36 cartons of fruit. What is the ratio of vegetable cartons to fruit cartons?
   A. $\dfrac{1}{4}$
   B. $\dfrac{1}{8}$
   C. $\dfrac{1}{3}$
   D. $\dfrac{6}{12}$

7. A manufacturer can produce 112 shirts per hour. If a work day is 8 hours, how many shirts can be produced in 3.5 days?
   A. 392
   B. 1,125
   C. 1,236
   D. 3,136

8. Vanessa has a drawer full of headbands. Twenty are pink, 32 are blue, and 16 are black. If she reaches into the drawer and picks out a headband at random, what is the probability that the headband will not be black?
   A. $\dfrac{17}{32}$
   B. $\dfrac{13}{17}$
   C. $\dfrac{16}{32}$
   D. $\dfrac{1}{2}$

9. Five years ago, Ruth made a deposit of $500 into a savings account that pays simple interest. She made no further deposits, and now her account is worth $750. What was the rate of interest per year?
   A. 2%
   B. 4%
   C. 9%
   D. 10%

10. If Gary earns $53/hour during a regular workday of 8 hours and $57/hour for any work he does after 5 P.M., how much does he earn if he worked 5 regular work days and 6.5 overtime hours?
    A. $1,870.50
    B. $2,292.25
    C. $2,490.50
    D. $2,597.50

11. Ellen baked 112 cookies and shared them equally with her 23 classmates. How many whole cookies each can Ellen and her classmates have?
    A. 4
    B. 5
    C. 6
    D. 7

12. Leon wants to paint the four walls in his dining room. Each wall is 8 feet high by 30 feet wide. A quart of paint covers 40 ft^2. How many gallons of paint must he purchase?
    A. 6
    B. 8
    C. 12
    D. 15

13. A family goes to a restaurant, and the bill is $112.00. If the parents want to leave the waitperson a 15 percent tip, how much should they leave?
    A. $15.40
    B. $16.80
    C. $17.25
    D. $17.85

14. At the local department store, a flat screen television retails for $4,250. Manuel finds the same television for sale on the Internet for $450 less. What percent will Manuel save if he purchases the television via the Internet site?
    A. 5.2%
    B. 10.6%
    C. 12.8%
    D. 15%

15. Jenny is 34 years old. Two years ago she was twice as old as her cousin. How old is her cousin now?
    A. 15
    B. 17
    C. 18
    D. 21

16. Simon's garden is 12 by 24 feet. He will plant bushes that require 8 sq ft of space. How many bushes can he plant?
    A. 16
    B. 24
    C. 27
    D. 36

17. Jake is riding a bicycle on a circular track. The distance from the center of the track to the outside of the circle is 10 meters. How far will Jake ride if he goes around the track one time?
    A. 62.8 m
    B. 145.5 m
    C. 157.8 m
    D. 162.8 m

18. Robby is twice as old as Greg. If Robby is 46 years old, how old is Greg?
    A. 15
    B. 23
    C. 25
    D. 27

19. Karin is as old as her two cousins combined. If Karin is 54 and one cousin is 21, how old is the second cousin?
    A. 13
    B. 22
    C. 33
    D. 37

20. Ned works after school. When he cuts grass, he earns $6.25 per hour. When he delivers papers, he earns $5.95 per hour and when he runs errands for people, he earns $5.50 per errand. If in one week he cut grass for 6 hours, delivered papers for 11 hours, and ran 6 errands, how much money did he earn?
    A. $114.95
    B. $135.95
    C. $144.15
    D. $156.05

21. Gerard throws a discus distances of 10 meters, 14.5 meters, 14.8 meters, 16.7 meters, and 15.4 meters. On his last attempt he faults, which counts as 0 meters. What is his average throwing distance?
    A. 11.9 meters
    B. 12.8 meters
    C. 13.78 meters
    D. 14.28 meters

22. An aquarium is 12 inches high, 24 inches long, and 10 inches wide. A goldfish needs 144 cubic inches of space to live. How many goldfish can this aquarium support?
    A. 15
    B. 20
    C. 22
    D. 24

23. The movie *Gladiator* earned $6 million in the first week of its showing. All movies shown that week earned $114 million. Which of the following shows the ratio of the earnings of *Gladiator* to the earnings of all movies that week?
    A. 1:4
    B. 2:13
    C. 1:19
    D. 3:8

24. A soup can is 6 inches high with a diameter of 4 inches. How much soup can it hold?
    A. 44.6 in^3
    B. 57.2 in^3
    C. 75.4 in^3
    D. 81.3 in^3

25. Sylvia wants to plant flowers in a window box that measures 48 inches long, 10 inches high, and 18 inches wide. If a bag of potting soil holds 1,440 cubic inches of soil, how many bags should she purchase?
    A. 2
    B. 4
    C. 6
    D. 8

26. During the first year of life, a whale gains about 30 tons of weight. What is the average weight gain per month?
    A. 1.2 tons
    B. 2.5 tons
    C. 2.9 tons
    D. 3.1 tons

27. Sally's rent is $750.00 each month. After two years of paying rent, how much has she spent?
    A. $12,000
    B. $18,000
    C. $21,000
    D. $24,000

28. Jonathan's monthly take-home pay is $2,556.36. If 28 percent is routinely taken out of his pay for taxes and insurance, what is his original pay before the deductions?
    A. $3,550.50
    B. $3,665.72
    C. $4,175.50
    D. $4,278.50

29. Rita earns an annual salary of $30,000. Her boss promised her that next year she will earn $32,500. What percent increase is the new salary?
    A. 5.2%
    B. 6.3%
    C. 8.3%
    D. 9.1%

30. Elaine was born on December 15 and has lived in Minneapolis, MN, all her life. Weather records show that over the last 100 years, it has snowed on December 15 60 percent of the time. If this trend continues and Elaine lives to be 85, on how many birthdays will she probably have snow?
    A. 47
    B. 51
    C. 54
    D. 62

STOP! DO NOT TURN THIS PAGE UNTIL TIME IS UP FOR THIS TEST. IF YOU FINISH BEFORE TIME IS UP, CHECK OVER YOUR WORK ON THIS TEST ONLY.

PART 3. WORD KNOWLEDGE

THE TEST ADMINISTRATOR WILL READ THE FOLLOWING ALOUD TO YOU:

Now turn to Part 3 and read the directions for Word Knowledge silently while I read them aloud.

This is a test of your knowledge of word meanings. These questions consist of a sentence or phrase with a word or phrase underlined. From the four choices given, you are to decide which one MEANS THE SAME OR MOST NEARLY THE SAME as the underlined word or phrase. Once you have made your choice, mark the space on your answer sheet that has the same number and letter as your choice.

Look at the sample question.

S1. The weather in this geographic area tends to be <u>moderate</u>.
   A. Severe
   B. Warm
   C. Mild
   D. Windy

The correct answer is "mild," which is choice C. Therefore, you would have blackened in space C on your answer sheet.

Your score on this test will be based on the number of questions you answer correctly. You should try to answer every question. DO NOT SPEND TOO MUCH TIME on any one question. If you finish before time is called, go back and check your work in this part <u>ONLY</u>.

Now find the section of your answer sheet that is marked PART 3. When you are told to begin, start with question number 1 in Part 3 of your test booklet and answer space number 1 in Part 3 on your separate answer sheet.

DO NOT TURN THE PAGE UNTIL TOLD TO DO SO. You will have 11 minutes to complete the 35 questions in this part. Are there any questions?

Begin.

1. At the time, the situation seemed <u>calamitous</u>.
   A. Ruthless
   B. Joyous
   C. Controlled
   D. Disastrous

2. <u>Lure</u> most nearly means
   A. prepare.
   B. drift.
   C. attract.
   D. repel.

3. Based on the facts, his solution was <u>judicious</u>.
   A. Mistaken
   B. Fantastic
   C. Misguided
   D. Sensible

4. He did not understand the <u>enormity</u> of his decision.
   A. Perfection
   B. Size
   C. Fluidity
   D. Logic

5. Before the storm, there was a definite feeling of <u>foreboding.</u>
   A. Serenity
   B. Calm
   C. Fear
   D. Distance

6. After his dog was lost for a week, Kevin was <u>forlorn</u>.
   A. Nervous
   B. Hopeless
   C. Happy
   D. Anxious

7. <u>Haughty</u> most nearly means
   A. proud.
   B. angry.
   C. naive.
   D. important.

8. Filling out those forms seemed to be an unnecessary bureaucratic <u>impediment</u>.
   A. Requirement
   B. Step
   C. Obstacle
   D. Challenge

9. She was <u>steadfast</u> in her belief about the causes of crime.
   A. Wrong
   B. Correct
   C. Wavering
   D. Firm

10. <u>Vilify</u> most nearly means
    A. respect.
    B. abuse.
    C. enhance.
    D. believe.

11. He was appreciated for his <u>wry</u> sense of humor.
    A. Clever
    B. Nasty
    C. Funny
    D. Tedious

12. Even though they had never won any championships, the team members were still <u>arrogant</u> about their skills.
    A. Forlorn
    B. Disappointed
    C. Conceited
    D. Ignorant

13. <u>Estranged</u> most nearly means
    A. together.
    B. strange.
    C. punished.
    D. separated.

14. Krista was <u>gratified</u> that the problem had been worked out.
    A. Hopeful
    B. Satisfied
    C. Thankful
    D. Disappointed

15. <u>Irascible</u> most nearly means
    A. smooth.
    B. heavy.
    C. testy.
    D. agreeable.

16. After the tornado, the town was <u>obliterated</u>.
    A. Destroyed
    B. Rebuilt
    C. Saved
    D. Warned

17. The apartment was <u>ransacked</u>.
    A. Decorated
    B. Furnished
    C. Plundered
    D. Rented

18. <u>Vendor</u> most nearly means
    A. outlaw.
    B. buyer.
    C. machine.
    D. salesperson.

19. <u>Scavenger</u> most nearly means
    A. employer.
    B. authority.
    C. gatherer.
    D. relative.

20. The speech given by the politician created <u>repercussions</u> around the world.
    A. Votes
    B. Consequences
    C. Applause
    D. Discontent

21. It took a while to <u>extricate</u> the victim from the burning house.
    A. Hear
    B. Find
    C. Elevate
    D. Remove

22. She <u>floundered</u> through the first reading of the play.
    A. Stumbled
    B. Rushed
    C. Mumbled
    D. Slept

23. <u>Mortify</u> most nearly means
    A. support.
    B. question.
    C. kill.
    D. humiliate.

24. Bob was simply <u>inept</u> with mechanical things.
    A. Superb
    B. Sloppy
    C. Incompetent
    D. Funny

25. Due to a busy schedule, Brad had to <u>forgo</u> his exercise.
    A. Increase
    B. Skip
    C. Reduce
    D. Change

26. <u>Foster</u> most nearly means
    A. encourage.
    B. abandon.
    C. scold.
    D. waver.

27. The day was <u>fraught</u> with excitement.
    A. Electrified
    B. Started
    C. Targeted
    D. Filled

28. The costume was <u>frivolous</u>.
    A. Skimpy
    B. Colorful
    C. Serious
    D. Playful

29. The boat tipped over in a <u>gale</u>.
    A. Lake
    B. Ocean
    C. Windstorm
    D. Panic

30. The new designer fabrics seemed <u>gaudy</u>.
    A. Skimpy
    B. Expensive
    C. Flashy
    D. Basic

31. The e-mail message contained <u>gibberish</u>.
    A. Photos
    B. Nonsense
    C. Warnings
    D. Errors

32. <u>Glower</u> most nearly means
    A. gleam.
    B. shirk.
    C. enrage.
    D. scowl.

33. <u>Grapple</u> most nearly means
    A. struggle.
    B. explain.
    C. interpret.
    D. define.

34. She filed a <u>grievance</u> over the way the issue was handled.
    A. Understanding
    B. Annoyance
    C. Complaint
    D. Question

35. To prevent them from communicating with each other, the brothers were <u>sequestered</u>.
    A. Praised
    B. Separated
    C. Questioned
    D. Encouraged

STOP! DO NOT TURN THIS PAGE UNTIL TIME IS UP FOR THIS TEST. IF YOU FINISH BEFORE TIME IS UP, CHECK OVER YOUR WORK ON THIS TEST ONLY.

PART 4. PARAGRAPH COMPREHENSION

THE TEST ADMINISTRATOR WILL READ THE FOLLOWING ALOUD TO YOU:

Turn to Part 4 and read the directions for Paragraph Comprehension silently while I read them aloud.

This is a test of your ability to understand what you read. In this section you will find one or more paragraphs of reading material followed by incomplete statements or questions. You are to read the paragraph and select one of four lettered choices which BEST completes the statement or answers the question. When you have selected your answer, blacken the space on your answer sheet that has the same number and letter as your answer.

Your score on this test will be based on the number of questions you answer correctly. You should try to answer every question. DO NOT SPEND TOO MUCH TIME on any one question. If you finish before time is called, go back and check your work in the part ONLY.

Now find the section of your answer sheet that is marked PART 4. When you are told to begin, start with question number 1 in Part 4 of your test booklet and answer space number 1 in Part 4 on your separate answer sheet.

DO NOT TURN THE PAGE UNTIL TOLD TO DO SO. You will have 13 minutes to complete the 15 questions in this part. Are there any questions?

Begin.

Anyone who pans for gold hopes to be rewarded by the glitter of colors in the fine material collected in the bottom of the pan. Although the exercise and outdoor activity experienced in prospecting are rewarding, there are few thrills comparable to finding gold. Even an assay report showing an appreciable content of gold in a sample obtained from a lode deposit is exciting. The would-be prospector hoping for financial gain, however, should carefully consider all the pertinent facts before deciding on a prospecting venture.

Only a few prospectors among the many thousands who searched the western part of the United States ever found a valuable deposit. Most of the gold mining districts in the West were located by pioneers, many of whom were experienced gold miners from the southern Appalachian region, but even in colonial times only a small proportion of gold seekers were successful. Over the past several centuries the country has been thoroughly searched by prospectors. During the depression of the 1930s, prospectors searched the better-known gold-producing areas throughout the nation, especially in the West, and the little-known areas as well. The results of their activities have never been fully documented, but incomplete records indicate that an extremely small percentage of the total number of active prospectors supported themselves by gold mining. Of the few significant discoveries reported, nearly all were made by prospectors of long experience who were familiar with the regions in which they were working.

The lack of outstanding success in spite of the great increase in prospecting during the depression of the 1930s confirms the opinion of those most familiar with the occurrence of gold and the development of gold mining districts that the best chances of success lie in systematic studies of known productive areas rather than in efforts to discover gold in hitherto unproductive areas. The development of new, highly sensitive, and relatively inexpensive methods of detecting gold, however, has greatly increased the possibility of discovering gold deposits which are too low grade to have been recognized earlier by the prospector using only a gold pan.

1. According to the passage, which of the following is true?
   A. Panning for gold in the western United States is a useful and profitable activity.
   B. Many prospectors got rich by panning for gold.
   C. There are many places in the United States where gold can be found.
   D. Prospectors who were successful knew the areas where they worked.

2. In this passage the word <u>pertinent</u> means
   A. confusing.
   B. contradictory.
   C. relevant.
   D. identifiable.

3. According to the passage, which of the following is true?
   A. Prospectors were hopeless people looking to strike it rich.
   B. Prospectors could not earn enough to support a family.
   C. Only a few prospectors found gold.
   D. The only successful prospectors were from the southern Appalachian region.

4. Which of the following would be the best title for the passage?
   A. Prospectors Strike It Rich
   B. Technology Finds Gold in the United States
   C. The Gold Rush—A Big Hoax
   D. Few Find It—Many Have Tried

5. With regard to the future of gold mining, the passage suggests which of the following?
   A. Gold mining will never be profitable.
   B. Only the prospectors from the southern Appalachian region seem to be able to find gold.
   C. There is no more gold to be found in the United States.
   D. New technologies will help to find more gold.

Organic food is produced by farmers who emphasize the use of renewable resources and the conservation of soil and water to enhance environmental quality for future generations. Organic meat, poultry, eggs, and dairy products come from animals that are given no antibiotics or growth hormones. Organic food is produced without using most conventional pesticides, petroleum-based fertilizers or sewage sludge-based fertilizers, bioengineering, or ionizing radiation. Before a product can be labeled "organic," a Government-approved certifier inspects the farm where the food is grown to make sure the farmer is following all the rules necessary to meet federal organic standards. Companies that handle or process organic food before it gets to your local supermarket or restaurant must be certified, too.

No organization claims that organically produced food is safer or more nutritious than conventionally produced food. Organic food differs from conventionally produced food in the way it is grown, handled, and processed. At the supermarket, in order to distinguish organically produced food from conventionally produced food, consumers must look at package labels and watch for display signs. Along with the national organic standards, there are strict labeling rules to help consumers know the exact organic content of the food they buy. An official seal also tells you that a product is at least 95 percent organic.

The word "organic" and a small sticker version of the Official Organic seal will be on organic vegetables or pieces of fruit, or they may appear on the sign above the organic produce display. The word "organic" and the seal may also appear on packages of meat, cartons of milk or eggs, cheese, and other single-ingredient foods.

"Natural" foods are not necessarily organic foods. Truthful claims, such as "free-range," "hormone-free," and "natural," can still appear on food labels. However, this does not mean that they are "organic." Only food labeled "organic" has been certified as meeting government organic standards.

6. According to this passage, organic farming is helpful because
   A. food grown organically is generally healthier than conventional food.
   B. organic food uses no fertilizers or harmful rays.
   C. growing organic food is cheaper and easier for the farmer.
   D. organic farming tends to improve environmental quality for the future.

7. According to the passage, to be considered organic, a farmer must do which of the following?
   A. Use special fertilizers.
   B. Use special bioengineering techniques.
   C. Show that the foods produced on the farm are healthier than those produced using conventional methods.
   D. Follow certain rules and standards set by the federal government.

8. According to the passage, how can a person identify an organically produced food?
   A. There will be a label or a sign with the word "organic."
   B. There is no way to tell.
   C. Organic labels are prohibited.
   D. A label will indicate "Safe to Eat."

9. In this passage the word <u>renewable</u> most nearly means which of the following?
   A. Fresh
   B. New
   C. Replaceable
   D. Ignored

10. According to the passage, which of the following ensures that foods are organic?
    A. The foods are naturally grown and produced.
    B. The foods are hormone-free.
    C. The foods are grown without chemicals.
    D. The foods are grown according to government standards.

To understand what the Everglades is today, you need to know what it once was. The pristine Everglades was a wetland that spanned the state of Florida south of Lake Okeechobee, about 2.9 million acres of mostly peatland covered by tall saw grass growing in shallow water. When the lake was full, water overflowed into the northern Everglades and moved slowly to the south in a 50-mile-wide sheet, a foot deep. In the 1880s people began to drain the Kissimmee River–Lake Okeechobee–Everglades watershed. Drainage exposed the organic muck soil, which produced extraordinary crop yields.

Today more than 50 percent of the historic Everglades has been eliminated. More than 1,400 miles of drainage canals and levees have been constructed in and around the Everglades for flood control. Widespread population growth and land-use modification for agriculture and industry have altered the natural wetlands, affecting the quantity and quality of drinking water and increasing human exposure to hydrologic hazards such as floods. Chemicals used in farming, including fertilizers, insecticides, herbicides, and fungicides, now often leak into the groundwater or nearby surface waters. Storm-water runoff from urban areas commonly transports heavy metals and nutrients into canals and the Biscayne aquifer.

The last 100 years have seen tremendous change in the Everglades. Today the flow of water is controlled by a complex management system that includes canals, levees, and pumps. The Everglades has been called "the biggest artificial plumbing system in the world."

11. From this passage it can be inferred that
A. people have harmed their own environment by changing it.
B. the peatlands have been eliminated.
C. people living near the Everglades need to use bottled water.
D. the Everglades is overpopulated.

12. According to the passage, which of the following has been the cause of the shrinking of the Everglades?
A. Loss of peatlands
B. Draining of the watershed
C. Home building in Florida
D. Overgrowth of saw grass

13. Why is the Everglades called "the biggest artificial plumbing system in the world"?
    A. It is managed by a system of canals, levees, and pumps.
    B. Industrial fluids and chemicals flow into the aquifer.
    C. Insecticides and pesticides leak into the water.
    D. The extensive saw grass tends to block drainage.

14. According to the passage, what was the first event resulting in the elimination of much of the Everglades?
    A. Farming of the peatlands
    B. Flooding of Lake Okeechobee
    C. Draining of the Everglades
    D. Installation of pumps and levees

15. In this passage, what is the meaning of hydrologic?
    A. Catastrophic
    B. Chemical
    C. Water-based
    D. Electronic

STOP! DO NOT TURN THIS PAGE UNTIL TIME IS UP FOR THIS TEST. IF YOU FINISH BEFORE TIME IS UP, CHECK OVER YOUR WORK ON THIS TEST ONLY.

PART 5. MATHEMATICS KNOWLEDGE

THE TEST ADMINISTRATOR WILL READ THE FOLLOWING ALOUD TO YOU:

Now turn to Part 5 and read the directions for Mathematics Knowledge silently while I read them aloud.

This is a test of your ability to solve general mathematics problems. You are to select the correct response from the choices given. Then mark the space on your answer sheet that has the same number and letter as your choice. Use your scratch paper to do any figuring you wish to do.

Your score on this test will be based on the number of questions you answer correctly. You should try to answer every question. DO NOT SPEND TOO MUCH TIME on any one question. If you finish before time is called, go back and check your work in this part ONLY.

Now find the section of your answer sheet that is marked PART 5. When you are told to begin, start with question number 1 in Part 5 of your test booklet and answer space number 1 in Part 5 on your separate answer sheet.

DO NOT TURN THE PAGE UNTIL TOLD TO DO SO. You will have 24 minutes to complete the 25 questions in this part. Are there any questions?

Begin.

1. If $y - 12 = 24$, $y = ?$
   A. 12
   B. 15
   C. 17
   D. 36

2. $2^3 + 2\,(2 + 5) =$
   A. 12
   B. 17
   C. 19
   D. 22

3. $\dfrac{9}{12} \times 1\dfrac{1}{4} =$
   A. $\dfrac{12}{48}$
   B. $\dfrac{1}{8}$
   C. $\dfrac{15}{16}$
   D. $\dfrac{24}{5}$

4. $(2 \times 10^3)(4.3 \times 10^5) =$
   A. 6.3×10^8
   B. 6.3×10^{-2}
   C. 8.6×10^{-2}
   D. 8.6×10^8

5. Change the fraction $\frac{5}{2}$ to a percent.
   A. 2.5%
   B. 52%
   C. 250%
   D. 252%

6. Subtract:
   $$24\dfrac{1}{8}$$
   $$-15\dfrac{3}{4}$$
   A. $7\dfrac{1}{4}$
   B. $8\dfrac{3}{8}$
   C. $9\dfrac{2}{8}$
   D. $10\dfrac{7}{8}$

7. Subtract:
   $$(4x^2 + 5y + 6)$$
   $$-(6x^2 + 3y + 8)$$
   A. $10x^2 + 8y + 14$
   B. $2x^2 + 2y + 2$
   C. $10x^2 - 2y - 2$
   D. $-2x^2 + 2y + 2$

8. Solve for x.
   $7x = 4x - 12$
   A. 2
   B. −2
   C. −4
   D. 4

9. Solve for the two unknowns.
   $6c - 2d = 32$
   $3c + 2d = 22$
   A. $c = 2$; $d = 4$
   B. $c = 6$; $d = 3$
   C. $c = 6$; $d = 2$
   D. $c = 2$; $d = 6$

10. Divide h^6 by h^8.
    A. h^{-2}
    B. h^{14}
    C. h^2
    D. h^{48}

11. Solve for y.

    $y^2 - 25 = 0$

    A. $y = -2$
    B. $y = 5$
    C. $y = 6$
    D. $y = \dfrac{6}{5}$

12. Multiply:

    $\dfrac{8a}{5} \times \dfrac{3}{4y} =$

    A. $24a + 12$
    B. $\dfrac{6a}{5y}$
    C. $\dfrac{32ay}{15}$
    D. $\dfrac{27a}{20y}$

13. Divide:

    $\dfrac{6a^2}{5b} \div \dfrac{2b}{9a}$

    A. $\dfrac{12a^2b}{45ab}$
    B. $\dfrac{27a^3}{5b^2}$
    C. $\dfrac{27a^3}{10b^2}$
    D. $\dfrac{12a}{45b}$

14. $\sqrt[3]{512} =$
    A. 2
    B. 4
    C. 6
    D. 8

15. Solve for y.

    $gy - n = x$

    A. $y = g\,(nx)$
    B. $y = \dfrac{x - n}{g}$
    C. $y = \dfrac{g}{xn}$
    D. $y = \dfrac{x + n}{g}$

16. Which of the following is an isosceles triangle?

    A.
    B.
    C.
    D.

17. What is the perimeter of the following square?

    4 in

    A. 8 in
    B. 10 in
    C. 14 in
    D. 16 in

18. What is the circumference of a circle with a radius of 8 in.?
    A. 12.25 in
    B. 25.12 in
    C. 30.24 in
    D. 50.24 in

19. In the following isosceles triangle, what is the measure of $\angle 1$?

    35°

    A. 30°
    B. 85°
    C. 90°
    D. 110°

20. If ∠1 is 142°, what is the measure of ∠2?

A. 24°
B. 38°
C. 142°
D. 218°

21. In the following right triangle, what is the length of side *AB*?

A. 5 m
B. 9 m
C. 10 m
D. 14 m

22. What is the area of the following triangle?

25 in   25 in
20 in
30 in

A. 80 in.²
B. 300 in.²
C. 420 in.²
D. 530 in.²

23. What is the area of the following circle?

10 mi

A. 78.5 mi²
B. 145.5 mi²
C. 240.5 mi²
D. 314 mi²

24. If lines *A* and *B* are parallel and are intersected by line *C* and ∠1 is 145°, what is the sum of the measures of angles 1, 2, 5, and 6?

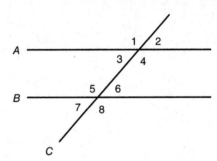

A. 160°
B. 180°
C. 240°
D. 360°

25. What is the volume of a cylinder with a radius of 4 cm and a height of 6 cm?
A. 75.36 cm³
B. 150.72 cm³
C. 301.44 cm³
D. 602.88 cm³

STOP! DO NOT TURN THIS PAGE UNTIL TIME IS UP FOR THIS TEST. IF YOU FINISH BEFORE TIME IS UP, CHECK OVER YOUR WORK ON THIS TEST ONLY.

PART 6. ELECTRONICS INFORMATION

THE TEST ADMINISTRATOR WILL READ THE FOLLOWING ALOUD TO YOU:

Now turn to Part 6 of your test booklet and read the directions for Electronics Information silently while I read them aloud.

This is a test of your knowledge of electrical, radio, and electronics information. You are to select the correct response from the choices given and then mark the space on your answer sheet that has the same number and letter as your choice.

Your score on this test will be based on the number of questions you answer correctly. You should try to answer every question. DO NOT SPEND TOO MUCH TIME on any one question. If you finish before time is called, go back and check your work in this part ONLY.

Now find the section of your answer sheet that is marked PART 6. When you are told to begin, start with question number 1 in Part 6 of your test booklet and answer space number 1 in Part 6 on your separate answer sheet.

DO NOT TURN THE PAGE UNTIL TOLD TO DO SO. You will have 9 minutes to complete the 20 questions in this part. Are there any questions?

Begin.

1. If you were installing lighting in a backyard, you might choose 12-volt equipment because it
   A. carries more energy than 120-volt equipment.
   B. does not need to be supplied through a transformer.
   C. would be less likely to "leak" through a wet insulator.
   D. would be more likely to "leak" through a wet insulator.

2. Of the following, the best conductor is
   A. copper.
   B. rubber.
   C. ceramic.
   D. glass.

3. On an electrical circuit diagram, the symbol shown below usually represents a

   A. resistor.
   B. capacitor.
   C. transformer.
   D. battery.

4. In residential wiring, you would use steel conduit to
   A. protect the wires.
   B. ground the system.
   C. protect the wires and ground the system.
   D. serve as a backup hot wire.

5. When you are hooking up an electric light, the switch should
   A. control the hot side of the circuit.
   B. control the ground side of the circuit.
   C. control the equipment grounding side of the circuit.
   D. be wired in parallel with the light.

6. In which kind of circuit is current always the same at all points?
   A. Series
   B. Parallel
   C. Series-parallel
   D. Series-series circuit

7. A battery makes which kind of current?
   A. Direct or alternating
   B. Alternating
   C. Direct
   D. No current

8. An electric current is made of moving
   A. ohms.
   B. neutrons.
   C. protons.
   D. electrons.

9. Which of the following materials would make the best insulator?
   A. Silver
   B. Gold
   C. Rubber
   D. Salt water

10. If you wanted to convert AC to DC, you might use
    A. an electromagnet.
    B. a transformer.
    C. a rectifier.
    D. a resistor.

11. On an electrical circuit diagram, the symbol shown below usually represents a

    A. resistor.
    B. capacitor.
    C. transformer.
    D. battery.

12. Which of these is a correct statement of Ohm's law?
    A. ohms = volts × amps
    B. volts = amps × ohms
    C. amps = volts × ohms
    D. volts × amps = ohms

13. If resistors R_1 and R_2 are both of equal size, what is the voltage at the arrow in the diagram below?

A. 6V
B. 9V
C. 18V
D. 24V

14. To find out if a circuit is live or shut off, you would connect
A. an ohmmeter between hot and ground.
B. a test light to the hot side.
C. a test light to the ground side.
D. a voltmeter between hot and ground.

15. How many amperes would flow in a 120-volt circuit with 12 ohms of resistance?
A. 0.5
B. 1.0
C. 5
D. 10

16. The purpose of a switch in a series circuit is to
A. shut off all current.
B. reduce the voltage.
C. increase the amperage.
D. reduce the amperage.

17. If you were choosing a fuse for a circuit supplying a large air compressor, you would most likely look for a fuse that would allow
A. high resistance.
B. low resistance.
C. a heavy surge of voltage.
D. heavy surge of current.

18. What is the reading on the voltmeter in this series circuit?

voltmeter

A. 0
B. 120
C. 240
D. 480

19. Which tells how much power an electric device requires?
A. Amperes/ohms
B. Volts/amperes
C. Volts × amperes
D. Amperes × ohms

20. In an electrical circuit diagram, the symbol shown below represents a

A. transistor.
B. diode.
C. rectifier.
D. transformer.

STOP! DO NOT TURN THIS PAGE UNTIL TIME IS UP FOR THIS TEST. IF YOU FINISH BEFORE TIME IS UP, CHECK OVER YOUR WORK ON THIS TEST ONLY.

PART 7. AUTO AND SHOP INFORMATION

THE TEST ADMINISTRATOR WILL READ THE FOLLOWING ALOUD TO YOU:

Now turn to Part 7 and read the directions for Auto and Shop Information silently while I read them aloud.

This test has questions about automobiles, shop practices, and the use of tools. Pick the BEST answer for each question and then mark the space on your answer sheet that has the same number and letter as your choice.

Your score on this test will be based on the number of questions you answer correctly. You should try to answer every question. DO NOT SPEND TOO MUCH TIME on any one question. If you finish before time is called, go back and check your work in this part <u>ONLY</u>.

Now find the section of your answer sheet that is marked PART 7. When you are told to begin, start with question number 1 in Part 7 of your test booklet and answer space number 1 in Part 7 on your separate answer sheet.

DO NOT TURN THE PAGE UNTIL TOLD TO DO SO. You will have 11 minutes to complete the 25 questions in this part. Are there any questions?

Begin.

1. If a diesel engine runs roughly, which device might be causing the problem?
   A. Carburetor
   B. Fuel injector
   C. Cooling system
   D. Spark plugs

2. If a tire label says it should be inflated to 32 lb/square inch,
   A. the pressure should be 32 lb/square inch when the tire is hot.
   B. the pressure should be 32 lb/square inch when the tire is cold.
   C. tire temperature does not matter; you can measure the pressure at any time.
   D. pressure should be within 10 lb/square inch.

3. When you step on the clutch pedal,
   A. the clutch engages.
   B. the clutch disengages.
   C. the throwout bearing engages.
   D. the throwout bearing disengages.

4. If an engine is overheating, the engine thermostat
   A. is allowing too much water to flow through the cooling system.
   B. is helping the heater work.
   C. may be preventing hot coolant from flowing through the cooling system.
   D. should not be inspected.

5. An engine control unit is basically a(n)
   A. linkage between the throttle and the camshaft.
   B. older method of controlling power output.
   C. substitute for the ignition switch.
   D. computer.

6. If black soot is gathering in the tailpipe,
   A. the fuel-air mix is not burning completely.
   B. the positive crankcase ventilator should be replaced.
   C. the fuel injectors must be replaced.
   D. the catalytic converter is working correctly.

7. If oil is puddling on the ground underneath a vehicle,
   A. check the piston rings immediately.
   B. it is time to change the oil.
   C. a gasket may be loose or defective.
   D. the oil filter is plugged.

8. If antilock brakes fail, the wheel sensor may not be
   A. sensing brake-pad position.
   B. detecting wheel rotation.
   C. opening the brake line.
   D. closing the brake line.

9. The torque converter shown below contains two parts that act as

   A. fans.
   B. propellers.
   C. sieves.
   D. flywheels.

10. If a fan belt breaks, which of the following may stop functioning?
    A. Air-conditioning compressor, alternator, or power-steering pump
    B. Camshaft, generator, and distributor
    C. Generator and alternator
    D. Brakes

11. During periodic maintenance, which system(s) may need replacement oil?
    A. Air conditioner and carburetor
    B. Differential
    C. Fuel injection and brakes
    D. Brakes and power steering

12. If a valve stops opening, which of these parts should be inspected?
    A. Drive shaft
    B. Main bearing
    C. Cylinder head
    D. Camshaft, timing belt, and rocker arm

13. Which tool would you be most likely to use after sawing wood?
    A. Wood file
    B. Plane
    C. Belt sander
    D. Wood chisel

14. A countersink is
    A. a gauge used to check drill sharpness.
    B. a conical hole that allows a screw head to sit flat with a surface.
    C. a plumbing tool used to check flow through a sink drain.
    D. a specialized masonry drill bit.

15. The tool shown below is used for

    A. opening paint cans.
    B. chiseling metal.
    C. drilling metal.
    D. locating a drill hole in metal.

16. What is one advantage of a Phillips screwdriver?
    A. It is less likely to slip off the screw.
    B. It gets a stronger grip.
    C. It has a longer shaft.
    D. It is more symmetrical.

17. Which measuring device is generally not used for carpentry?
    A. Dividers
    B. Marking gauge
    C. Tape measure
    D. Dial gauge

18. Why is the end of a box wrench angled slightly to the body?
    A. To allow better access in tight quarters
    B. To grab square and hexagonal bolt heads
    C. To get a better grip on the bolt
    D. To allow the wrench to clear nearby obstructions

19. The tool shown below is a(n)

    A. arc-joint pliers.
    B. can-do clamp.
    C. Crescent® (adjustable) wrench.
    D. come-along.

20. Which of these tools are likely to be used together?
    A. Center punch and drill bit
    B. Phillips screwdriver and slot screwdriver
    C. Wood plane and coping saw
    D. Nail set and center punch

21. Which two tools are best for cutting plywood?
    A. Hand saw and coping saw
    B. Jigsaw and circular saw
    C. Hand saw and hacksaw
    D. Jigsaw and hacksaw

22. Rivets are used to
    A. make permanent connections.
    B. join wood to metal.
    C. replace glue.
    D. make joints that can be taken apart.

23. The tool shown below is used for

   A. cutting curves.
   B. aligning hinges.
   C. sawing molding.
   D. sawing metal.

24. Tightening the screw on the handle of a locking pliers will
   A. make the pliers stronger.
   B. open the jaws.
   C. adjust the pliers for smaller objects.
   D. allow the jaws to open wider.

25. The teeth on a hacksaw
   A. point away from the handle.
   B. must be sharpened frequently.
   C. are usually made of tungsten carbide.
   D. cut when you pull the saw toward you.

STOP! DO NOT TURN THIS PAGE UNTIL TIME IS UP FOR THIS TEST. IF YOU FINISH BEFORE TIME IS UP, CHECK OVER YOUR WORK ON THIS TEST ONLY.

PART 8. MECHANICAL COMPREHENSION

THE TEST ADMINISTRATOR WILL READ THE FOLLOWING ALOUD TO YOU:

Now turn to Part 8 and read the directions for Mechanical Comprehension silently while I read them aloud.

This test has questions about mechanical and physical principles. Study the picture and decide which answer is CORRECT and then mark the space on your separate answer sheet that has the same number and letter as your choice.

Your score on this test will be based on the number of questions you answer correctly. You should try to answer every question. DO NOT SPEND TOO MUCH TIME on any one question. If you finish before time is called, go back and check your work in this part ONLY.

Now find the section of your answer sheet that is marked PART 8. When you are told to begin, start with question number 1 in Part 8 of your test booklet and answer space number 1 in Part 8 on your separate answer sheet.

DO NOT TURN THE PAGE UNTIL TOLD TO DO SO. You will have 19 minutes to complete the 25 questions in this part. Are there any questions?

Begin.

1. Pipes A and B are carrying water with the same amount of water pressure. Pipe A is carrying how much more water than pipe B?
   A. Ten times as much
   B. Nine times as much
   C. Three times as much
   D. Two times as much

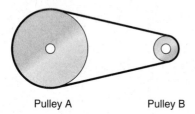

Pulley A   Pulley B

2. Pulleys A and B run on the same belt. Which pulley is rotating faster?
   A. Pulley A and pulley B rotate at the same rate.
   B. Pulley A rotates faster.
   C. Pulley B rotates faster.
   D. First pulley A rotates faster, then pulley B rotates faster.

3. The lever shown is used to lift a 300-lb weight. What force is needed to lift the weight?
   A. 60 lb
   B. 50 lb
   C. 45 lb
   D. 30 lb

600 lb

4. The rope shown must be able to lift at least
   A. 150 lb
   B. 200 lb
   C. 300 lb
   D. 1,200 lb

5. Which of the following is a type of lever?

A.

B.

C.

D.

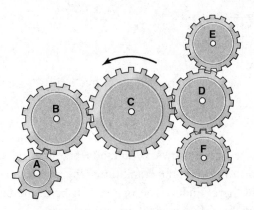

6. In the gear system shown, gear C is rotating in the direction shown. Which other gears are rotating in the same direction?
   A. A and D
   B. B, D, and F
   C. B and E
   D. A, E, and F

7. In a pulley system, the easiest way to find the theoretical mechanical advantage is to
   A. count the supporting strands.
   B. count the pulleys.
   C. count the number of rope strands you see.
   D. measure effort and load.

8. Gear A, with 24 teeth, is meshed with gear B, with 12 teeth. For every complete rotation of gear B, how many complete rotations will gear A make?
   A. ½
   B. 1
   C. 2
   D. 4

9. If all these items are the same temperature, which one will feel coldest to the touch?

A.

B.

C.

D.

10. To lift one side of the piano, how much force must be applied to the lever?
    A. 150 lb
    B. 200 lb
    C. 250 lb
    D. 300 lb

Crank

11. Water is flowing into the tank through pipe A at 6 gallons per minute and through pipe B at 7 gallons per minute. It is flowing out of the tank through pipe C at 8 gallons per minute. How much more water will be in the tank at the end of 5 minutes?
A. 13 gallons
B. 15 gallons
C. 21 gallons
D. 25 gallons

12. The diagram shows a cross section of an airplane wing in flight, with air passing above and beneath it. Lift is created because
A. air pressure above the wing is less than air pressure below the wing.
B. air pressure above the wing is equal to air pressure below the wing.
C. the wing pushes air down, and the opposing force lifts the plane.
D. air pressure above the wing is greater than air pressure below the wing.

13. The figure shows a crank attached to a rod and piston. When the crank turns, the piston moves in the cylinder. The piston will be at the base of the cylinder if the crank makes a
A. ¼ turn
B. ½ turn
C. ¾ turn
D. complete turn

14. A tank 4 feet wide by 4 feet long holds 800 lb of water. What is the water pressure at the bottom in lb/ft^2?
A. 10
B. 12.5
C. 25
D. 50

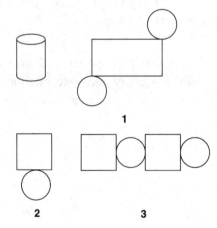

15. The flat sheet metal pattern that can be bent to form the completely closed cylinder shown is
A. 1
B. 2
C. 3
D. None of the Above

1   2

3   4

Bob   Sarah

16. Which of the gear types shown is used to transmit motion between shafts that form a 90° angle?
    A. 1
    B. 2
    C. 3
    D. 4

17. If gear A and gear B are meshed, and gear B rotates twice as fast as gear A, the gear ratio of A:B is
    A. 2:1
    B. 1:1
    C. 0.5:1
    D. 1:2

18. Oxygen gas stored in a metal cylinder exerts a pressure of 6 pounds per square inch on the inside of the cylinder. If you pump additional oxygen into the cylinder, which of the following could be the new pressure inside the cylinder?
    A. 4 pounds per square inch
    B. 5 pounds per square inch
    C. 6 pounds per square inch
    D. 8 pounds per square inch

19. In the diagram, who is carrying more of the load?
    A. Sarah
    B. Bob
    C. They are carrying equal loads.
    D. Sarah, then later Bob

20. What happens when this screw is turned 8 complete turns tight?
    A. The screw moves in by 2/3 in.
    B. The screw moves out by 3/4 in.
    C. The screw moves in by 1/2 in.
    D. The screw moves in by 3/4 in.

21. The mechanical advantage in the pulley system shown is
A. 2
B. 3
C. 4
D. 6

22. In the diagram, pressure in the main tank is 50 lb/in^2. What is the pressure in tank B in lb/in^2?

A. 25
B. 50
C. 100
D. 200

23. A nut and a bolt exert compression on this board. You run the parts through a degreaser and tighten the nut to 100 ft/lbs. What happens if you take the assembly apart, grease the threads, and retighten to 100 ft/lbs?

A. Compression increases.
B. Compression decreases.
C. Compression does not change.
D. Compression decreases while tightening, then increases.

24. How much effort will be needed to roll a 350-lb drum up a ramp 25 feet long and 5 feet high? (Ignore the effect of friction.)
A. 35 lb
B. 60 lb
C. 70 lb
D. 100 lb

25. In the hydraulic system shown, how much will the piston in cylinder B move when you move the piston in cylinder A by 6 inches?

    A. 1.5 inches
    B. 2 inches
    C. 3 inches
    D. 6 inches

STOP! DO NOT TURN THIS PAGE UNTIL TIME IS UP FOR THIS TEST. IF YOU FINISH BEFORE TIME IS UP, CHECK OVER YOUR WORK ON THIS TEST ONLY.

PART 9. ASSEMBLING OBJECTS

Now turn to Part 9 and read the directions for Assembling Objects silently while I read them aloud.

This test has questions that will measure your spatial ability. Study the diagram, decide which answer is CORRECT, and then mark the space on your separate answer sheet that has the same number and letter as your choice.

Your score on this test will be based on the number of questions you answer correctly. You should try to answer every question. DO NOT SPEND TOO MUCH TIME on any one question. If you finish before time is called, go back and check your work in this part ONLY.

Now find the section of your answer sheet that is marked PART 9. When you are told to begin, start with question 1 in Part 9 of your test booklet and answer space number 1 in Part 9 on your separate answer sheet.

DO NOT TURN THE PAGE UNTIL TOLD TO DO SO. You will have 15 minutes to complete the 25 questions in this part. Are there any questions?

Begin.

For Questions 1–18, which figure best shows how the objects in the left box will appear if they are fit together?

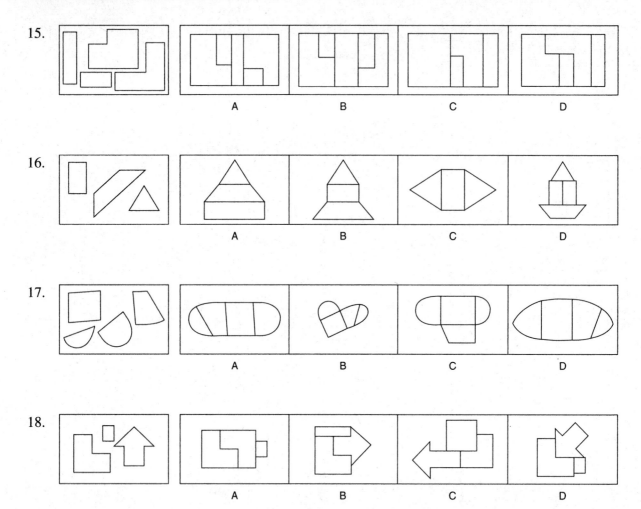

For Questions 19-25, which figure best shows how the objects in the left box will touch if the letters for each object are matched?

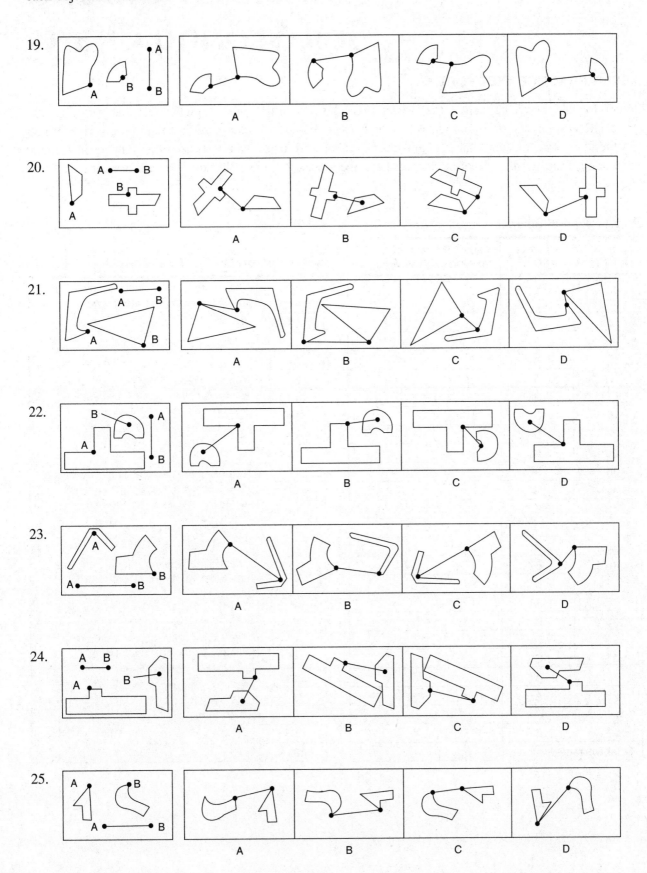

Answer Keys and Self-Scoring Charts

ASVAB PRACTICE TEST FORM 1

The following answer keys show the correct answers for each part of the practice test that you just took. For each question, compare your answer to the correct answer. Mark an × in the column to the right if you got the item correct. Then total the number correct for each part of the test. Find that number in the corresponding chart to the right of the answer key. See the suggestions listed for your performance.

Part 1. General Science

Item Number	Correct Answer	Mark X If You Picked the Correct Answer
1	C	
2	D	
3	D	
4	A	
5	A	
6	B	
7	D	
8	C	
9	D	
10	A	
11	A	
12	D	
13	B	
14	D	
15	B	
16	B	
17	B	
18	A	
19	C	
20	D	
21	C	
22	A	
23	A	
24	C	
25	B	
Total Correct		

Score Interpretation—Total Correct

25	This is pretty good work. Review the explanations for the answers you got incorrect.
24	
23	
22	
21	
20	You are doing pretty well. Review the explanations for the items you answered incorrectly. If you have time, review the other explanations and you will learn even more.
19	
18	
17	
16	
15	You need to keep studying. Pay close attention to the explanations for each item, even for the ones you got correct.
14	
13	
12	
11	
10	Spend time working on the General Science review in Part 3 of this book.
9	
8	
7	
6	If you have copies of your school science textbooks, it would be a good idea to study those.
5	
4	
3	
2	
1	
0	

Part 2. Arithmetic Reasoning

Item Number	Correct Answer	Mark X If You Picked the Correct Answer
1	D	
2	B	
3	C	
4	B	
5	B	
6	C	
7	D	
8	B	
9	D	
10	C	
11	A	
12	A	
13	B	
14	B	
15	C	
16	D	
17	A	
18	B	
19	C	
20	B	
21	A	
22	B	
23	C	
24	C	
25	C	
26	B	
27	B	
28	A	
29	C	
30	B	
Total Correct		

Score Interpretation—Total Correct

30, 29, 28, 27, 26	This is pretty good work. Review the explanations for the answers you got incorrect. This test is a part of the AFQT, and you must do well.
25, 24, 23, 22, 21	You are doing pretty well. Review the explanations for the items you answered incorrectly. If you have time, review the other explanations and you will learn even more.
20, 19, 18, 17, 16	You need to keep studying. Pay close attention to the explanations for each item, even for the ones you got correct.
15, 14, 13, 12	Spend time working on the Arithmetic Reasoning reviews in Part 3 of this book.
11, 10, 9, 8, 7, 6, 5, 4, 3, 2, 1, 0	Keep working and reworking problems until you are comfortable with the processes.

Part 3. Word Knowledge

Item Number	Correct Answer	Mark X If You Picked the Correct Answer
1	D	
2	C	
3	D	
4	B	
5	C	
6	B	
7	A	
8	C	
9	D	
10	B	
11	A	
12	C	
13	D	
14	C	
15	C	
16	A	
17	C	
18	D	
19	C	
20	B	
21	D	
22	A	
23	D	
24	C	
25	B	
26	A	
27	D	
28	D	
29	C	
30	C	
31	B	
32	D	
33	A	
34	C	
35	B	
Total Correct		

Score Interpretation—Total Correct

Score	Interpretation
35	This is pretty good work. Review the explanations for the answers you got incorrect. This is an important test that contributes to your AFQT.
34	
33	
32	
31	
30	You are doing pretty well. Review the explanations for the items you answered incorrectly. If you have time, review the other explanations and you will learn even more.
29	
28	
27	
26	
25	You need to keep studying. Pay close attention to the explanations for each item, even for the ones you got correct.
24	
23	
22	
21	
20	Spend time working on the Word Knowledge review in Part 3 of this book.
19	
18	
17	
16	Keep reading and identifying words you don't know.
15	
14	
13	
12	
11	
10	
9	
8	
7	
6	
5	
4	
3	
2	
1	
0	

Part 4. Paragraph Comprehension

Item Number	Correct Answer	Mark X If You Picked the Correct Answer
1	D	
2	C	
3	C	
4	D	
5	D	
6	D	
7	D	
8	A	
9	C	
10	D	
11	A	
12	B	
13	A	
14	C	
15	C	
Total Correct		

Score Interpretation—Total Correct

Score	
15	This is pretty good work. Review the explanations for the answers you got incorrect. This test is a part of the AFQT, and you must do well.
14	You are doing pretty well. Review the explanations for the items you got incorrect. This test is a part of the AFQT, and you must do well.
13	You need to keep studying. Pay close attention to the explanations for each item, even for the ones you got correct. This will help you understand why the answer is correct.

Spend time reviewing the Paragraph Comprehension and Word Knowledge reviews in Part 3 of this book. Keep reading books and newspapers. |
12	
11	
10	
9	
8	
7	
6	
5	
4	
3	
2	
1	
0	

Part 5. Mathematics Knowledge

Item Number	Correct Answer	Mark X If You Picked the Correct Answer
1	D	
2	D	
3	C	
4	D	
5	C	
6	B	
7	D	
8	C	
9	C	
10	A	
11	B	
12	B	
13	B	
14	D	
15	D	
16	C	
17	D	
18	D	
19	D	
20	B	
21	C	
22	B	
23	A	
24	D	
25	C	
Total Correct		

Score Interpretation—Total Correct

Score	Interpretation
25	This is pretty good work. Review the explanations for the answers you got incorrect.
24	
23	
22	You are doing pretty well. Review the explanations for the items you answered incorrectly. If you have time, review the other explanations and you will learn even more.
21	
20	
19	This test is part of the AFQT. You must perform well on this test.
18	
17	
16	You need to keep studying. Pay close attention to the explanations for each item, even for the ones you got correct.
15	
14	
13	
12	Spend time working on the Mathematics Knowledge reviews in Part 3 of this book, and work and rework the problems until you fully understand the processes.
11	
10	
9	
8	
7	
6	
5	
4	
3	
2	
1	
0	

Part 6. Electronics Information

Item Number	Correct Answer	Mark X If You Picked the Correct Answer
1	C	
2	A	
3	D	
4	C	
5	A	
6	A	
7	C	
8	D	
9	C	
10	C	
11	A	
12	B	
13	B	
14	D	
15	D	
16	A	
17	D	
18	A	
19	C	
20	A	
Total Correct		

Score Interpretation—Total Correct

20	This is pretty good work. Review the explanations for the answers you got incorrect.
19	
18	
17	You are doing pretty well. Review the explanations for the items you answered incorrectly. If you have time, review the other explanations and you will learn even more.
16	
15	
14	
13	
12	You need to keep studying. Pay close attention to the explanations for each item, even for the ones you got correct.
11	
10	
9	
8	Spend time working on the Electronics Information review in Part 3 of this book.
7	
6	
5	Your school electronics or physics books may have some helpful information as well.
4	
3	
2	
1	
0	

Part 7. Auto and Shop Information

Item Number	Correct Answer	Mark X If You Picked the Correct Answer
1	B	
2	B	
3	B	
4	C	
5	D	
6	A	
7	C	
8	B	
9	B	
10	A	
11	B	
12	D	
13	B	
14	B	
15	D	
16	A	
17	D	
18	D	
19	C	
20	A	
21	B	
22	A	
23	D	
24	C	
25	A	
Total Correct		

Score Interpretation—Total Correct

Score	Interpretation
25, 24, 23, 22, 21	This is pretty good work. Review the explanations for the answers you got incorrect.
20, 19, 18, 17, 16, 15	You are doing pretty well. Review the explanations for the items you answered incorrectly. If you have time, review the other explanations and you will learn even more.
14, 13, 12, 11, 10, 9, 8, 7, 6, 5, 4, 3, 2, 1, 0	You need to keep studying. Pay close attention to the explanations for each item, even for the ones you got correct.\n\nSpend time working on the Auto and Shop Information reviews in Part 3 of this book.

Part 8. Mechanical Comprehension

Item Number	Correct Answer	Mark X If You Picked the Correct Answer
1	B	
2	C	
3	A	
4	B	
5	D	
6	D	
7	A	
8	A	
9	B	
10	A	
11	D	
12	A	
13	C	
14	D	
15	A	
16	C	
17	A	
18	D	
19	A	
20	A	
21	A	
22	B	
23	A	
24	C	
25	A	
Total Correct		

Score Interpretation—Total Correct

Score	Interpretation
25	This is pretty good work. Review the explanations for the answers you got incorrect.
24	
23	
22	
21	
20	You are doing pretty well. Review the explanations for the items you answered incorrectly. If you have time, review the other explanations and you will learn even more.
19	
18	
17	
16	
15	You need to keep studying. Pay close attention to the explanations for each item, even for the ones you got correct.
14	
13	
12	
11	Spend time working on the Mechanical Comprehension review in Part 3 of this book
10	
9	
8	
7	
6	
5	
4	
3	
2	
1	
0	

Part 9. Assembling Objects

Item Number	Correct Answer	Mark X if You Picked the Correct Answer
1	C	
2	B	
3	A	
4	B	
5	C	
6	B	
7	A	
8	D	
9	C	
10	C	
11	A	
12	B	
13	B	
14	C	
15	D	
16	B	
17	A	
18	D	
19	D	
20	D	
21	A	
22	D	
23	C	
24	A	
25	C	
Total Correct		

Score Interpretation–Total Correct

Score	Interpretation
25	This is pretty good work. Review the explanations of the answers you got incorrect.
24	
23	
22	
21	
20	You are doing pretty well. Review the explanations for the items you answered incorrectly. If you have time, review the other explanations and you will learn even more.
19	
18	
17	
16	
15	Keep studying. Pay close attention to the explanations for each item, even for the ones you got correct.
14	
13	
12	
11	Spend time working on the Assembling Objects review in Part 3 of this book.
10	
9	
8	
7	
6	
5	
4	
3	
2	
1	
0	

Answers and Explanations

PART 1. GENERAL SCIENCE

1. **C.** Plant cells do reproduce and they do have cell walls. Plant cells do not necessarily die after one year. Plant cells do contain chloroplasts, and animal cells do not. The correct answer is therefore choice C.

2. **D.** All these creatures are animals and are part of the kingdom Animalia.

3. **D.** An ecosystem is the collection of organisms, living and nonliving, along with the factors that affect them such as heat, light, landforms, gases, and the like. The atmosphere (choice A) is the air that surrounds Earth, the hydrosphere (choice B) is the water found in and on Earth, and the lithosphere (choice C) is the land on Earth. Biosphere is the name given to the global ecosystem. Choice D is the correct answer.

4. **A.** Stomata (choice B) are parts of a leaf and should be digestible in most plants. Root hairs (choice C) and roots (choice D) should be digestible as well. The cell wall (choice A) is made of cellulose, which is not digestible by humans. Choice A is the correct answer.

5. **A.** The process of respiration takes place in the gills of a fish. Choice A is the correct answer.

6. **B.** Respiration (choice A) is the series of chemical reactions that release energy that is stored in food molecules. Osmosis (choice C) is the process by which water diffuses through a cell membrane. Turgidity (choice D) is the swelling of a plant stem as it fills with water and stands up. A plant that is not turgid is limp. Choice B, gravitropism, is a plant's response to gravity. Roots have a positive reaction to gravity and grow downward regardless of how the plant is situated.

7. **D.** A predator is an animal that seeks out another animal for food. Choice C is not correct. Mutualism is a condition in which both organisms benefit from their cooperation. Choice A is not the correct answer. Commensalism is a situation in which one organism benefits by living off another, but without harming the other organism. Choice B is not the correct answer. Mistletoe is a parasite, an organism that steals nutrients from another organism. Choice D is the correct answer.

8. **C.** The biceps and the heart contain certain muscle cells, but the stomach has specialized, smooth muscle cells. Choice C is the correct answer.

9. **D.** Pathogens can enter your body from areas that are open and related to mucus like the mouth (choice A), nose (choice B), and eyes (choice C). The skin (choice D) is the first line of defense against viruses and bacteria, unless it is cut in some way. Choice D is the correct answer.

10. **A.** The mouth (choice B) is the starting place of the digestive system where food begins to break down, but it is not the place where nutrients are absorbed. The large intestine (choice C) absorbs a lot of the liquid, but not much in the way of nutrients. The stomach (choice D) is important for the chemical breakdown of food into absorbable particles that can be absorbed by the small intestine (choice A). Choice A is the correct answer.

11. **A.** The autonomic system controls functions that are involuntary, such as breathing (choice D), heart rate (choice C), and digestion (choice B). Voluntary movements, such as walking (choice A) and other purposeful actions, are not controlled by the autonomic system. Choice A is the correct answer.

12. **D.** You can use Punnett Squares to determine the probability of offspring having certain characteristics. The dominant trait or allele is shown in capital letters, and the recessive allele is in lower case letters.

		Father	
		T	T
Mother	t	Tt	Tt
	t	Tt	Tt

From this it can be seen that every offspring will be tall. Choice D, 100%, is the correct answer.

13. **B.** If an object is more than two focal lengths away from a convex lens, the image would be smaller and inverted. The correct answer is choice B.

14. **D.** An element's atomic mass is determined by the number of protons and neutrons it contains. Choice D is the correct answer.

15. **B.** Light has many characteristics; one is that it bends when it changes speed as it passes through various materials. The degree of bending depends on the original frequency and the medium through which the light is passing. When a light wave moves through water (for example, through a raindrop), it forms a spectrum of colors we know as a rainbow. Although light diffuses (choice A) or spreads and can be reflected (choice C), these do not cause a rainbow. Bending of light is refraction, so choice B is the correct answer.

16. **B.** In the past, when the continents were connected in a megacontinent called Pangaea, areas that are currently tropical or temperate, like Africa, South America, and India were closer to the South Pole. Parts of these continents were covered by glaciers where there are no glaciers now. Evidence of glacial deposits, along with the scouring of rocks typical of glaciers, is present. Choice B, glacial deposits, is the correct answer.

17. **B.** Pumice is formed when molten rock is shot out of a volcano by high concentrations of gases. It is extrusive because it is above the surface of the earth and igneous because it is formed from volcanic activity. The correct answer is choice B, extrusive igneous rock.

18. **A.** The alignment of Earth, the moon, and the sun (choice D) causes oceanic tides, not waves. Excessive rainfall (choice B) does not cause waves. Steep slopes near the shoreline (choice C) can cause waves to crash forming breakers, but the slopes are not the cause of wave formation. Persistent surface winds over the ocean are the chief cause of wave formation. Choice A is the correct answer.

19. **C.** Earth's orbit around the sun is elliptical, not circular. As a result there are times of the year when Earth is closer to the sun than at other times. It is January when Earth is closest to the sun. For people in the northern hemisphere, this may seem odd because it is winter in the northern hemisphere in January. In the southern hemisphere, however, January is in the middle of the summer. Choice C is the correct answer.

20. **D.** Know your planetary order: Mercury, Venus, Earth, Mars, Jupiter, Saturn, Uranus, and Neptune. The eighth from the sun is Neptune (choice D).

21. **C.** If the atmosphere heats up over time to the point where the climate is changed (called global warming), that could have severe environmental effects. The warmer weather could indeed help increase the amount of area considered tropical, thus spreading tropical diseases such as malaria (choice A). If the temperature rises high enough, polar ice caps and glaciers would melt, thus raising the level of the oceans and seas (choice B). Since hurricanes are initiated by low pressure systems over warm waters, the number and severity of hurricanes could increase (choice D). All these are possibilities. We are seeing some evidence of global warming already. Scientists are debating whether the increase in global temperature is

part of a natural cycle or whether some human actions are causing this to happen. There is no known relationship between Earth's mesosphere being ionized and global warming. Choice C is the correct answer.

22. **A.** A stationary front (choice D) means a front is not moving or not moving very fast. When a warm air mass is replacing cold air (choice B) or when an occluded front overtakes a warm air mass (choice C), the weather tends to be rainy across large areas around the front. The weather is not necessarily severe. A cold front that replaces warm air causing the warm air to uplift rapidly generally causes severe weather. Choice A is the correct answer.

23. **A.** Sinkholes, groundwater flow, and stalactites (choice B) are features related to groundwater. Sedimentary rocks, conglomerates, and shale (choice C) are related to a category of rocks called *sedimentary rocks*. Vents, calderas, and hot spots (choice D) are all associated with volcanism. Choice A, cirques, arètes, and moraines, are features of glaciers. Choice A is the correct answer.

24. **C.** Land heats faster than water. As the land heats up, it warms the air above it. The air expands and rises, creating an upward current. The rising warm air is replaced by cooler air flowing in from over the water. This process creates a wind current that goes from the water to the land, called a *sea breeze*. In the evening the reverse takes place because the land cools faster than the water. The air current moves in the opposite direction, from the land to the sea, and is called a *land breeze*. Choice C is the correct answer.

25. **B.** An atom of the same element that has a different number of neutrons is called an *isotope*. Choice B is the correct answer.

PART 2. ARITHMETIC REASONING

1. **D.** This is a simple addition problem. Add the amounts to get the total of $141.32.

2. **B.** This problem has two steps. First you need to add the number of minutes Brad used. Then you need to subtract that amount from his allocation of 400 minutes. The total number of minutes used was 317, so subtracting that from 400 leaves 83 minutes.

3. **C.** In order to calculate the percent, you need to divide the number of female students by the total number of students. In this case you would divide 14 by 32 to get 0.4375. To change that to a percent, move the decimal point two places to the right and add the percent sign to get the correct answer of 43.75%.

4. **B.** To find the average, add the numbers and divide by the number of numbers. In this problem Tim's times add up to 780 seconds. Dividing that number by 4 gives an average of 195 seconds.

5. **B.** To determine the percent, you need to divide the amount Trinidad spends on rent by the amount that she earns. In this problem, $1,100 is divided by $2,700 with the result coming to 40.7%. Rounding to the nearest percent gives the correct answer of 41%.

6. **C.** To find the ratio of one number to another, create a fraction to show the relationship. In this problem 12 cartons of vegetables are compared to 36 cartons of fruit. The resulting fraction is $\frac{12}{36}$. Simplifying this fraction results in a ratio of $\frac{1}{3}$. You might see this as 1:3 on the ASVAB test. $\frac{1}{3}$ and 1:3 mean the same thing.

7. **D.** Set this up as a proportion. If 112 shirts can be produced in 1 hour, then [x] shirts can be produced in 8 hours. The proportion would look like this: $\frac{112}{1} = \frac{x}{8}$. Cross-multiply and solve for x. 1x = 896. So 896 shirts can be produced in one 8-hour day. The question asks how many can be produced in 3.5 days, so multiply 896 by 3.5 to get the final answer of 3,136.

8. **B.** Probability = number of favorable outcomes/ number of possible outcomes. In this problem the number of possible outcomes equals

$20 + 32 + 16 = 68$. The number of favorable outcomes is the sum of pink and blue or $20 + 32 = 52$. $\frac{52}{68} = \frac{13}{17}$, the correct answer when simplified.

9. **D.** Simple interest problems use the formula $I = prt$, where I is the amount of interest, p is the principal or the amount saved or invested, r is the rate of interest, and t is the amount of time in which the interest is accruing. In this problem you are asked to find the rate of interest given that Ruth has earned $250 in interest over 5 years. Substitute the information into the formula to get $\$250 = \$500(r)5$ and solve for r. $\$250 = \$2,500r$; $r = 0.10$ or 10%.

10. **C.** Multiply the number of hours worked by the regular rate of $53 per hour and add that to the overtime hours multiplied by the overtime rate. The number of regular hours worked is 5×8 or 40.

$$40(\$53) + 6.5(\$57) = \$2,490.50$$

11. **A.** If Ellen baked 112 cookies for herself and her 23 classmates, divide 24 into 112 to get 4.67. The question asks for the number of whole cookies, so there are 4 per person plus some fraction of a cookie left over. The correct answer is 4.

12. **A.** Leon has four walls that are 8 ft by 30 ft. That's an area of 240 ft^2 for each of four walls. For all four walls, multiply 240 by 4, giving a total square footage of 960 ft^2. If a quart of paint covers 40 ft^2, then you need to divide 960 by 40, which results in 24 quarts of paint. The question asks for the number of gallons. Since there are 4 quarts in a gallon, divide 24 by 4 to get 6 gallons.

13. **B.** If the bill is $112.00, a tip of 15% is calculated by multiplying $112.00 by 0.15.

$$\$112.00 \times 0.15 = \$16.80$$

14. **B.** Use the following formula:

$$\text{percent of change} = \frac{\text{amount of change}}{\text{original amount}}.$$

In this problem we know that the amount of change is $450 if Manuel purchases the TV online. The starting point is the cost of the TV at the local department store, $4,250. Substitute that information into the formula:

$$\text{percent of change} = \frac{\$450.00}{\$4,250.00} = 0.106.$$

Change the result to a percent by moving the decimal place two places to the right and adding the percent sign.

$$0.106 = 10.6\%$$

15. **C.** Two years ago Jenny was 32 years old. She was twice the age of her cousin. Set this up as an equation.

$$2c = 32.$$

Solve for c.

$$c = 16$$

Since we want the cousin's age now, which is two years later, it would be 18 $(16 + 2)$.

16. **D.** To calculate the area of Simon's garden, use the formula $A = lw$.

$$A = 12 \text{ ft} \times 24 \text{ ft}$$
$$A = 288 \text{ ft}^2$$

If each bush needs 8 ft^2 of space, divide 288 by 8.

$$\frac{288 \text{ ft}^2}{8} = 36 \text{ bushes}$$

17. **A.** To find the circumference of a circle, use the formula $C = 2\pi r$. The radius is given as 10 meters. Substitute that information into the formula $C = 2(3.14)10$.
Solve for C. $C = 62.8$ meters.

18. **B.** Create an equation to solve this problem: Robby $= 2$(Greg).
You are told that Robby is 46. Substitute that information into the formula: $46 = 2$(Greg).
Solve for Greg by dividing both sides by 2.

$23 = $ Greg, so Greg is 23 years old.

19. **C.** Create an equation to solve this problem.

$$\text{Karin} = \text{cousin } 1 + \text{cousin } 2.$$

You are told that Karin is 54 and one cousin is 21. Substitute that information into the formula.

$$54 = 21 + \text{cousin } 2$$

Solve for cousin 2 by subtracting 21 from both sides.

$$33 = \text{cousin } 2$$

20. **B.** Create an equation to solve this problem. This problem requires both multiplication and addition.

$$6(\$6.25) + 11(\$5.95) + 6(\$5.50)$$
$$= \$37.50 + \$65.45 + \$33.00 = \$135.95$$

21. **A.** To find the average, add the numbers and divide by the number of numbers. In this problem add 10, 14.5, 14.8, 16.7, 15.4, and 0 to get 71.4. Divide this by 6.

$$\frac{71.4}{6} = 11.9$$

Caution: Don't forget that the zero counts as a number, so be sure to divide by 6, not 5.

22. **B.** To solve this problem, use the formula $V = lwh$. You have been given the dimensions of $l = 24$ inches, $w = 10$ inches, and $h = 12$ inches. Substitute that information into the formula.

$$V = (24)(10)(12) = 2{,}880 \text{ in}^3$$

If a goldfish needs 144 in^3 to exist in the aquarium, divide that number into the total amount of volume.

$$2880 \text{ in}^3 \div 144 \text{ in}^3 = 20 \text{ goldfish.}$$

23. **C.** The ratio would be stated as 6:114 or $\frac{6}{114}$. Simplify this fraction to get $\frac{1}{19}$.

24. **C.** To calculate the volume of a cylinder, use the formula $V = \pi r^2 h$. In this problem the diameter is 4 in, so the radius is 2 in. The height is given as 6 in. Substitute that information into the formula.

$$V = (3.14)(2^2)(6)$$
$$V = (3.14)(4)(6)$$
$$V = 75.36 \text{ or } 75.4 \text{ in}^3$$

Be sure to pay attention to the information you are given. You could have made an error by using the diameter rather than the radius because the diameter was given in the problem.

25. **C.** To calculate the volume of a rectangular solid, use the formula $V = lwh$. In this problem you are given a length of 48 inches, a width of 18 inches, and a height of 10 in.

$$V = (48)(18)(10)$$
$$V = 8{,}640 \text{ in}^3$$

Next you need to determine how many bags of soil measuring 1,440 in^3 are needed to fill the container. Calculate the answer by dividing 8,640 in^3 by 1,440 in^3.

$$\frac{8{,}640}{1{,}440} = 6 \text{ Bags of Soil}$$

26. **B.** To calculate the average, take the number of tons and divide by the number of months.

$$\frac{30}{12} = 2.5 \text{ tons per month}$$

27. **B.** Multiply the monthly rent by the number of months. There are 24 months in two years.

$$24 \times \$750 = \$18{,}000$$

28. **A.** Create an equation.

$$\$2{,}556.36 = x - 0.28x$$

Solve for x.

$$\$2{,}556.36 = 0.72x$$
$$\frac{\$2{,}556.36}{0.72} = \$3{,}550.50$$

29. **C.** Use the formula percent of change = $\frac{\text{amount of change}}{\text{starting point}}$. The amount. of change is the difference between \$30,000 and \$32,500 or \$2,500. The starting point is the original salary of \$30,000. Substitute the information into the formula.

$$\text{percent of change} = \frac{\$2,500}{\$30,000} = 0.083$$

or an 8.3% raise

30. **B.** Multiply 85 years by 0.60 to get 51 years with snow.

PART 3. WORD KNOWLEDGE

1. **D.** *Calamitous* means "relating to misfortune or disaster." The words *ruthless*, *joyous*, and *controlled* do not match the definition. *Disastrous*, choice D, is the correct answer.

2. **C.** To *lure* means "to tempt or entice." The word *repel* is the opposite of this concept. *Drift* also means moving away, not attracting or enticing. *Prepare* is not related to the definition. *Attract*, choice C, is the correct answer.

3. **D.** *Judicious* means "having sound judgment." The words *mistaken* and *misguided* are opposite to that meaning. *Fantastic* is unrelated. *Sensible*, choice D, is the correct answer.

4. **B.** *Enormity* means "great size, scale, or impact." *Perfection*, *fluidity*, and *logic* are unrelated. *Size*, choice B, is the correct answer.

5. **C.** A *foreboding* is a feeling that something bad will happen. The words *serenity* and *calm* are somewhat opposite to this definition. *Distance* is unrelated. *Fear* is closest in meaning to *foreboding*. Choice C is the correct answer.

6. **B.** Kevin probably would not be *happy* if his dog was lost for a week, so clearly that is not correct. He might be *anxious* or *nervous* about the situation, but since *forlorn* means

"miserable and wretched and without hope," choice B, *hopeless*, is the best answer.

7. **A.** *Haughty* means "being full of oneself, feeling self-important, or being arrogant." The words *correct*, *wavering*, and *fixed* do not seem related to that idea. *Proud*, choice A, is the closest word to the correct meaning.

8. **C.** To *impede* means "to block or obstruct." An *impediment* is something that blocks or discourages movement or progress. The words *requirement* and *step* do not match the definition. An impediment could be a *challenge*, but the word that most closely reflects the idea of blocking or obstructing is *obstacle*. The correct answer is choice C.

9. **D.** To be *steadfast* means "to be unwavering and sure of one's beliefs or actions." *Wavering* is the opposite of this idea, so it is clearly the wrong answer. The words *correct* and *wrong* seem unrelated, so *firm*, choice D, is the correct answer.

10. **B.** *Vilify* relates to the word *vile,* which means "morally evil, wicked, and degrading." To *vilify* is to say wicked or degrading things about a person or situation. *Respect* and *enhance* are somewhat the opposite in meaning. *Believe* does not relate to the definition, but *abuse* does. Choice B is the correct answer.

11. **A.** *Wry* means "ironic, dry, or sarcastic." *Tedious, funny,* and *nasty* do not relate to the definition, so *clever*, choice A, is the best answer.

12. **C.** *Arrogant* means "proud and full of oneself." *Forlorn, disappointed,* and *ignorant* have no relation to the definition. *Conceited*, choice C, is the correct answer.

13. **D.** *Estranged* means "changed in one's view from affectionate to indifferent" or "at odds with another person." The word *together* conveys the opposite meaning. The words *strange* and *punished* do not match the definition.

Separated is the word that is closest to the meaning. Choice D is the correct answer.

14. **C.** *Gratified* means "pleased or be grateful." The words *hopeful*, *satisfied*, and *disappointed* are not descriptions of being pleased or grateful. *Thankful* is the most appropriate answer. Choice C is correct.

15. **C.** *Irascible* means "easily angered or hot-tempered." *Smooth*, *heavy*, and *agreeable* are clearly not correct. Choice C, *testy*, is correct.

16. **A.** *Obliterated* means "blotted out or destroyed." The words *rebuilt* and *saved* are somewhat opposite to this definition. *Warned* has no relationship to the correct definition. Choice A, *destroyed*, is the correct answer.

17. **C.** *Ransacked* means "searched thoroughly" or "plundered." The words *decorated, furnished,* and *rented* do not fit that meaning. *Plundered*, choice C, is the correct answer.

18. **D.** *Vend* means "to sell." A *vendor* is a person or organization that sells. The word *buyer* is opposite to the word *vendor*. *Outlaw* and *machine* are not related. *Salesperson* is the most correct answer from among the options presented. Choice D is the best answer.

19. **C.** A *scavenger* collects or gathers things that are discarded by others. The words *employer*, *authority*, and *relative* are not related to this definition. The word most closely related to this concept is *gatherer*. Choice C is the correct answer.

20. **B.** *Repercussions* are far-reaching effects or reactions to some event. *Applause* and *discontent* are certainly reactions, but they are not necessarily far-reaching. The word *votes* doesn't seem to fit the definition of *repercussions*. The correct answer, *consequences*, matches the meaning of a far-reaching effect. Choice B is the correct answer.

21. **D.** *Ex-* is a prefix that means "out of." *Extricate* means "to remove or set free." The words *hear, find,* and *elevate* do not relate to the stated definition. *Remove*, choice D, is clearly the correct answer.

22. **A.** *Floundered* means "struggled" or "acted in an awkward way." The words *rushed* and *slept* do not relate to the definition. The word *mumbled* could be a result of floundering, but choice A, *stumbled*, is the correct answer.

23. **D.** To *mortify* means "to humiliate." The words *support*, *question*, and *kill* do not relate to the definition, so choice D, *humiliate*, is the correct answer.

24. **C.** *Inept* means "clumsy or foolish." *Superb* seems to be the opposite of that meaning, and *sloppy* and *funny* do not relate to the definition. *Incompetent*, choice C, is the correct answer.

25. **B.** To *forgo* means "to relinquish, miss, or give up on something." The words *increase, reduce,* and *change* do not carry that meaning. Choice B, *skip*, is the best answer.

26. **A.** To *foster* means "to nourish, help develop, or promote." The word *abandon* means somewhat the opposite of *foster*. The words *scold* and *waver* do not match the definition. Choice A, *encourage*, has a similar meaning and is the correct answer.

27. **D.** *Fraught* means "full of or loaded with something." The words *electrified, started,* and *targeted* do not relate to the definition. *Filled*, choice D, is the correct answer.

28. **D.** *Frivolous* means "silly, giddy, or of little value." The words *skimpy* and *colorful* do not match the definition. The word *serious* conveys an idea opposite the meaning of *frivolous*. *Playful*, choice D, is the correct answer.

29. **C.** A *gale* is a strong wind. The words *lake, ocean,* and *panic* do not match the definition, so *windstorm*, choice C, is the correct answer

30. **C.** *Gaudy* means "bright and showy but lacking in good taste." The words *skimpy*, *expensive*, and *basic* do not share that meaning, so choice C, *flashy*, is the correct answer.

31. **B.** *Gibberish* is spoken or written communication that is unintelligible. The words *photos*, *warnings*, and *errors* do not share that idea, so *nonsense*, choice B, is the correct answer.

32. **D.** To *glower* means "to look angrily or glare at someone." Don't be fooled by the word *enrage*. *Glower* does not mean "to make someone angry," but to look angrily at someone. *Gleam* and *shirk* are clearly incorrect, so *scowl*, choice D, is the correct answer.

33. **A.** To *grapple* means "to wrestle with or to try to cope with a situation or condition." *Struggle*, choice A, has the same meaning and is the correct answer.

34. **C.** A *grievance* is an accusation that something is thought to be unjust or unfair. *Understanding*, *annoyance*, and *question* do not relate to this idea, so choice C, *complaint*, is the correct answer.

35. **B.** *Sequestered* means "set apart or isolated." The only word that shares that meaning is choice B, *separated*.

PART 4. PARAGRAPH COMPREHENSION

1. **D.** The passage indicates that panning for gold was profitable for only a few people, so choices A and B cannot be correct. Only the western United States is mentioned, and the passage does not indicate that gold could be found in many places, so choice C is not correct. The last sentence of the passage states that discoveries of gold were made by people who were familiar with the regions in which they were working. That makes choice D the correct answer.

2. **C.** The word *pertinent* means "having some connection with the subject mentioned." The correct answer is choice C, *relevant*.

3. **C.** There is no indication that prospectors were hopeless people (choice A) or that they could not afford to support a family (choice B). Though some successful prospectors were from the southern Appalachian region (choice D), there is nothing in the passage to suggest that they were the only successful prospectors. Choice C, that only a few prospectors were successful, is the correct answer.

4. **D.** The major idea of the passage is that a lot of people have tried to find gold in the United States, but few people have been successful. The only title that reflects that idea is choice D, "Few Find It—Many Have Tried."

5. **D.** The passage suggests that new, highly sensitive, and relatively inexpensive methods of detecting gold have greatly increased the possibility of discovering gold deposits. Choice D is the correct answer.

6. **D.** The first sentence indicates that farmers who emphasize the use of renewable resources and the conservation of soil and water do so to enhance environmental quality for future generations. So choice D is the correct answer. There is no mention that the food is healthier (choice A) or cheaper (choice C), so those cannot be correct. Choice B is true, but it does not refer to an aspect of organic farming that is helpful. So choice B cannot be correct.

7. **D.** The passage clearly indicates that to be considered organic, food must be grown according to all the rules that meet government standards. Choice D is the correct answer. Choice A is partly true, but it is only one aspect of organic farming. Choice B, using bioengineering, is clearly forbidden by the standards, and there is no claim that the food is healthier (choice C).

8. **A.** The passage indicates that any organic product is required to have a label stating that it is an organic product. The label appears on the product or on a sign above the product display. Choice A is the correct answer.

9. **C.** *Renewable* means "replaceable." Choice C is the correct answer.

10. **D.** Foods that are naturally grown and produced (choice A), that are hormone-free (choice B), and that are grown without chemicals (choice C) might be organic, but the passage indicates that much more is involved. Only foods that are grown according to specific government standards can be labeled organic. Choice D is the correct answer.

11. **A.** The passage does not suggest that the peatlands have been eliminated (choice B) or that people near the Everglades need to use bottled water (choice C). Overpopulation in Florida may have contributed to the problem (choice D), but the passage mostly suggests that activities such as draining and land-use changes have caused the problem. These are human activities, so choice A is the best and correct answer.

12. **B.** The passage indicates that the Everglades is shrinking because of the draining of the water. Choice B is the correct answer.

13. **A.** The passage clearly indicates that the Everglades is controlled by a complex management system that includes canals, levees, and pumps, making it the world's largest artificial plumbing system. Choice A is the correct answer.

14. **C.** Although all the answer options have taken place, the first one mentioned in the passage is the draining of the Everglades. Choice C is the correct answer.

15. **C.** The passage gives you a direct hint at the meaning of *hydrologic*. The passage mentions "hydrologic hazards such as floods." This suggests that *hydrologic* has to do with water. Choice C is the correct answer.

PART 5. MATHEMATICS KNOWLEDGE

1. **D.** Isolate the unknown on one side.
Add 12 to each side.

$$y = 24 + 12$$
$$y = 36$$

2. **D.** Perform operations in the parentheses first, then the exponents, and then the remaining operations.

$$8 + 2(7)$$
$$8 + 14 = 22$$

3. **C.** Change the mixed numbers to improper fractions. Carry out the operation by multiplying the two numerators and the two denominators. In this case you can reduce the $\frac{9}{12}$ to $\frac{3}{4}$.

$$\frac{9}{12} \times \frac{5}{4}$$
$$= \frac{3}{4} \times \frac{5}{4}$$
$$= \frac{15}{16}$$

4. **D.** When multiplying numbers in scientific notation, multiply the numbers and add the exponents.

$$2 \times 4.3 = 8.6$$

Add the two exponents.

$$3 + 5 = 8$$

The answer is 8.6×10^8

5. **C.** Change the fraction to a decimal, which is 2.50. Move the decimal point two places to the right and add the percent sign. The result is 250%.

6. **B.** In order to subtract the fractions, they need to be changed to the least common denominator. In this instance the least common denominator is 8, so the fraction $\frac{3}{4}$ becomes $\frac{6}{8}$. But $\frac{6}{8}$ is larger than $\frac{1}{8}$, so, using the notion of regrouping, we can change the 24 to a 23 and add the $\frac{8}{8}$ to the $\frac{1}{8}$, making the fraction $\frac{9}{8}$. Now the $\frac{6}{8}$ can be subtracted from $\frac{9}{8}$ leaving $\frac{3}{8}$. Now subtract the whole numbers, 15 from 23, leaving $8\frac{3}{8}$ as the correct answer.

7. **D.** When subtracting, change the minus sign to a plus sign and change the sign of ALL of the terms/numbers that follow. In this

problem the signs for $-(6x^2 + 3y + 8)$ becomes: $+ (-6x^2 - 3y - 8)$.

$$4x^2 + 5y + 6$$
$$+ (-6x^2 - 3y - 8)$$

Now add like terms and get: $-2x^2 + 2y - 2$.

8. **C.** To solve such problems, move all the terms with an unknown to one side of the equals sign and the numbers to the other. In this problem, subtract $4x$ from both sides. This results in $7x - 4x = -12$. Combine the terms to give $3x = -12$, so $x = -4$.

9. **C.** Set each equation to equal zero. Next, arrange the equations so that when one is subtracted from or added to the other, one of the terms results in a zero and drops out of the result. Next, solve for the remaining unknown.
   In this problem,

$$6c - 2d - 32$$
$$3c + 2d - 22$$

Set each equation to zero.

$$6c - 2d - 32 = 0$$
$$3c + 2d - 22 = 0$$

Note that if you add the two equations, the d term drops out, leaving $9c - 54 = 0$. Solve for c: $9c = 54$; $c = 6$

Substitute for c in one of the equations to solve for d.

$$6(6) - 2d - 32 = 0$$
$$36 - 2d - 32 = 0$$
$$-2d = 32 - 36$$
$$-2d = -4$$
$$d = 2$$

The correct answer is $c = 6$; $d = 2$.

10. **A.** To divide numbers with exponents, subtract the exponents. In this instance, subtracting 8 from 6 leaves -2. So the correct answer is h^{-2}. This also can be written as $\frac{1}{h^2}$.

11. **B.** In this problem you should see two squares. Solve for y:

$$y^2 = 25$$
$$y = 5.$$

12. **B.** To multiply fractions, multiply the numerators and denominators. Simplify where possible.

$$\frac{8a}{5} \times \frac{3}{4y} = \frac{24a}{20y}$$

Simplify to $\frac{6a}{5y}$.

13. **B.** To divide fractions, invert the second term and multiply. Simplify where possible.

$$\frac{6a^2}{5b} \div \frac{2b}{9a} \text{ becomes } \frac{6a^2}{5b} \times \frac{9a}{2b}.$$

Multiply the numerators and denominators.

$$\frac{54a^3}{10b^2}$$

Simplify.

$$\frac{27a^3}{5b^2}$$

14. **D.** The cube root is the number that, when multiplied by itself three times, results in the answer. In this instance, $8 \times 8 \times 8 = 512$, so the cube root of $512 = 8$.

15. **D.** Isolate the variable of interest on one side of the equation. In this problem the variable of interest is y. First add n to both sides, resulting in $gy = x + n$. Next, divide each side by g to isolate y. The correct answer is $y = \frac{x+n}{g}$.

16. **C.** An isosceles triangle has at least two equal sides and two equal angles, so C is the correct answer.

17. **D.** To find the perimeter of a quadrilateral, add the lengths of the four sides. In this problem, each side measures 4 inches, so the correct answer is 16 in. For a square, just multiply the length of one side by 4 to obtain the correct answer.

18. **D.** The formula for the circumference of a circle is πd. The problem gives the radius, which is $\frac{1}{2}$ the length of the diameter. The diameter is 16, so the correct answer is 16π, or approximately 50.24 inches.

19. **D.** The two known angles total 70°. Subtracting that from 180° gives the correct answer of 110°.

20. **B.** A straight line or straight angle is 180°. If $\angle 1$ is 142°, then $\angle 2$ must be the difference between 180° and 142° or 38°.

21. **C.** $\angle C$ is a right angle, so you can employ the Pythagorean Theorem $a^2 + b^2 = c^2$ to get your answer. $6^2 + 8^2 = c^2$. So $36 + 64 = 100$. $c = 10$, the square root of 100.

22. **B.** In an isosceles triangle, the base is the unequal side and the height is the length of a line from the base to the opposite angle. In this problem the base is 30 inches and the height is 20 inches. The indication that the other two sides are 25 inches each, is irrelevant to this problem.

    The formula for the area of a triangle is $\frac{1}{2}bh$. Substituting the information into the formula gives $\frac{1}{2}(30)(20)$, making the correct answer 300 in^2.

23. **A.** The formula for the area of a circle is πr^2. In this problem you are given the diameter, 10 miles. The radius is half the diameter, 5 miles. Substituting the information into the formula gives $3.14\,(5)^2$, or 78.5 mi^2.

24. **D.** $\angle 1$ and $\angle 2$ make up a straight line of 180°. $\angle 5$ and $\angle 6$ also make up a straight line of 180°. That adds up to 360°.

25. **C.** The formula for finding the volume of a cylinder is $V = \pi r^2 h$. In this problem you are given a radius of 4 cm and a height of 6 cm. Substituting that information into the formula gives $\pi(4)^2\,(6)$, or 301.44 cm^3.

PART 6. ELECTRONICS INFORMATION

1. **C.** Higher voltage is more likely to "push" electricity across air gaps and faulty insulation.

2. **A.** Copper is an excellent conductor; the other materials are all insulators.

3. **D.** This is the symbol for a battery.

4. **C.** Steel conduit both protects wires and supplies the backup ground.

5. **A.** Switches should turn the hot side on and off. They should never control the ground or equipment grounding side.

6. **A.** Current must flow through the entire series circuit, so it must be the same at all points.

7. **C.** Batteries make direct current.

8. **D.** When electrons move in a circuit, an electric current exists.

9. **C.** Rubber is a good insulator; the other materials listed are conductors.

10. **C.** A rectifier converts alternating current to direct current.

11. **A.** This is the symbol for a resistor.

12. **B.** Ohm's law is important, and you should memorize it before taking the ASVAB.

13. **B.** The total voltage drop in the circuit must equal the voltage across the battery, 18V. Because the resistors are the same size, each creates half that voltage drop, or 9V apiece. Thus the voltage at the arrow is 9V.

14. **D.** If the meter detects voltage when connected between hot and ground, the circuit is live.

15. **D.** According to Ohm's law, amperes = volts/ohms = 120/12 = 10

16. **A.** A switch shuts off all current in a series circuit.

17. **D.** Motors often require a brief surge of current when they start; special motor fuses can handle this surge without blowing.

18. **A.** The switch is open, so the potential across the voltmeter is 0V.

19. **C.** Volts × amps = watts. The watt is the unit that measures electrical power.

20. **A.** This is the symbol for a transistor.

PART 7. AUTO AND SHOP INFORMATION

1. **B.** Diesel engines contain fuel injectors and neither carburetor nor spark plugs. In a diesel engine, the piston compresses the fuel-air mixture hot enough to cause ignition. A cooling system problem is unlikely to cause roughness.

2. **B.** Tire pressure should always be measured when the tire is cold.

3. **B.** Stepping on the clutch disengages the clutch, so you can shift gears.

4. **C.** The thermostat must open after the coolant warms up. If the thermostat is stuck closed, coolant cannot circulate through the engine and radiator to cool the engine, and overheating will result.

5. **D.** The control unit gets input from sensors about gas pedal position and engine conditions. Then it controls the ignition and fuel systems for optimum performance and minimum pollution.

6. **A.** Soot is a sign of incomplete combustion. Why are the other answers incorrect? Choice C: the problem may be with the fuel injectors or ECM, but incomplete combustion is the immediate cause of soot. Choice D: The converter may not be working correctly, but it would not be the first thing to check.

7. **C.** Leaking gaskets are the primary cause of leaks in a stationary vehicle.

8. **B.** The wheel sensor detects wheel rotation and "tells" the antilock brake control that one wheel has stopped turning. The control immediately eases off on that brake, to prevent skidding.

9. **B.** The wheels in a torque converter act like propellers. One wheel moves the transmission fluid, and the other catches the moving fluid and is forced to spin. Choice A is the second-best answer; choice B is better because fans move air, while propellers move water.

10. **A.** Why are the other answers incorrect? Choice B: the camshaft and distributor are not driven by belts. Choice C: a car would not have both a generator and an alternator. Choice D: a belt does not drive the brakes.

11. **B.** The differential is lubricated with a high-viscosity oil.

12. **D.** The camshaft, timing belt, and rocker arm all work together to lift the valve off its seat. Why are the other answers incorrect? Choices A and B: The drive shaft and main bearing have nothing to do with the valves. Choice D: The cylinder head is not a moving part.

13. **B.** Planes remove minor roughness from board edges. Why are the other answers incorrect? Choice A: A wood file leaves a rougher surface. Choice C: A belt sander is hard to use on an edge. Choice D: A wood chisel is not used to smooth wood.

14. **B.** A countersink bit makes a conical hole (a countersink) so a screw head can sit flush.

15. **D.** A center punch prevents the drill bit from wandering before you drill.

16. **A.** Phillips screwdrivers are no stronger than slotted screwdrivers, but they do stay in place on the screw head.

17. **D.** Machinists use a dial gauge to measure surface irregularities; the gauge is too accurate for carpentry.

18. **D.** The wrench is angled so that it does not lie flat against a surface. This improves access in tight quarters and protects your fingers.

19. **C.** This wrench can be adjusted to fit a bolt or nut.

20. **A.** A center punch is used to mark metal before drilling.

21. **B.** A hand saw is awkward for cutting plywood. A coping saw will cut only near the edge. A hacksaw is for cutting metal, not wood.

22. **A.** Rivets can be taken apart only by destroying them.

23. **D.** Hacksaws have fine teeth, and they are only good for cutting metal.

24. **C.** Tightening the screw makes the jaws close tighter.

25. **A.** Hacksaws cut on the down (away) stroke. Why are the other answers incorrect? Choice B: Hacksaw blades are discarded, not sharpened. Choice C: They are made of steel, not tungsten carbide. Choice D: They cut on the away stroke.

PART 8. MECHANICAL COMPREHENSION

1. **B.** The volume of water depends on the cross-sectional area of the pipe. For the 1-inch pipe, the cross-sectional area is $\pi r^2 = \pi(1^2) = \pi$. For the 3-inch pipe, the cross sectional area is $\pi r^2 = \pi(3^2) = 9\pi$. So the 3-inch pipe can carry nine times as much water as the 1-inch pipe.

2. **C.** Pulley B is smaller, so it must rotate faster than Pulley A.

3. **A.** MA = effort arm/load arm = 5/1 = 5. So the force needed to move the 300-lb weight is 300/5 = 60 lb.

4. **B.** The pulley has three working strands and a mechanical advantage of 3. Each strand must support 200 lb.

5. **D.** The tongs shown in choice D are a type of class 3 lever. The screwdriver (choice A) is a type of wheel and axle. The bolt (choice B) is a type of inclined plane. The eggbeater (choice C) is a system of meshed gears.

6. **D.** In this gear system, gear C is rotating counterclockwise. That means that gears B and D are rotating clockwise, and gears A, E, and F are rotating counterclockwise.

7. **A.** Count the supporting strands—the ones that are shortened as you hoist.

8. **A.** If gear A has 24 teeth and gear B has 12 teeth, every time gear B makes one complete revolution, gear A will make 12/24 = ½ of a complete revolution.

9. **B.** Of the items shown, only the pliers are made of metal. Since metal conducts heat better than other substances, when you touch the pliers, heat will be conducted away from your fingers. As a result, the metal pliers will feel colder to the touch than the other items pictured, even though all are actually at the same temperature.

10. **A.** The piano weighs 600 lb so one side carries 300 lb The mechanical advantage is 2, so a 150-lb effort will lift 300 lb.

11. **D.** The amount of water flowing into the tank each minute is 6 + 7 = 13 gallons. At the same time, 8 gallons are flowing out each minute, so the net gain per minute is 13 − 8 = 5 gallons. So in 5 minutes the tank will gain 5 × 5 = 25 gallons of water.

12. **A.** The curved upper surface of the wing forces the air going over it to travel a longer distance.

The air speeds up, moving faster than the air that is going under the wing. This makes the air pressure pressing down on the wing from above less than the air pressure pressing up on the wing from below. The result is the lift force that keeps the airplane airborne.

13. **C.** If the crank makes a ¼ turn, the piston will be at the top of the cylinder. If the crank makes a ½ turn, it will return to the position shown. If the crank makes a ¾ turn, the piston will be at the base of the cylinder. If the crank makes one complete turn, the cylinder will return to the position shown.

14. **D.** Pressure = force/area. Area = $4 \times 4 = 16$ ft^2. Pressure = $800/16 = 50$ lb/ft^2.

15. **A.** Of the patterns shown, the only one that could form a completely closed cylinder is pattern number 1. The rectangle can be rolled to form the one continuous side of the cylinder, and the two circles form its top and bottom.

16. **C.** The gear labeled 3 is called a *miter gear*. This kind of gear is used to transmit motion between shafts that form a 90° angle.

17. **A.** If gear B rotates twice as fast as gear A, then gear B must have fewer teeth than gear A. The gear ratio of A:B is 2:1.

18. **D.** Pressure = force/area. When more gas is added, it creates more force. Therefore, choice D is the only possible answer.

19. **A.** The load is closer to Sarah, so she is carrying more of it.

20. **A.** This screw has 12 threads per inch, so each turn tight moves it 1/12 in. in the "in" direction.

$$1/12 \times 8 = 8/12 = 2/3 \text{ in}$$

21. **A.** There are two supporting strands, so the MA is 2. To find the number of supporting strands, look at how many parts of the rope will get shorter as you tighten the rope.

22. **B.** Pressure is the same at all points in a closed system, so the pressure is 50 lb/in^2 in tank B.

23. **A.** Friction causes the simple machine to be less efficient, so less of the rotating force is transferred into compressive force on the board.

24. **C.** The ramp is an inclined plane. The mechanical advantage is $25/5 = 5$. So the effort required is $350/5 = 70$ lb.

25. **A.** Volume of a cylinder equals height $\times \pi \times$ radius^2. The same volume of fluid that leaves cylinder A must enter cylinder B. So $h \times \pi \times r^2$ for A $= h \times \pi \times r^2$ for B. Dividing both sides by π gives $h \times r^2 = h \times r^2$ (radius = diameter/2).

Now substitute:

$$6 \times 1 \times 1 = h \times 2 \times 2$$
$$6 = 4h$$
$$1.5 = h$$

Notice that you can just look at the ratio of the diameters to quickly get this answer: $2^2/4^2 = 1/4$. The large piston moves 1/4 as far as the small piston.

PART 9. ASSEMBLING OBJECTS

1. **C.** The original figure has four objects and choice B has five, so eliminate B. Focus on the most distinctive object, perhaps the long triangle with one jagged side at the bottom right of the original. Choice A does not have the squared-off jagged object. Look for the right triangle. Choice D does not have it. Choice C is the correct answer.

2. **B.** The original figure has three objects and choice C has only 2, so eliminate C. Look for the two identical teardrop shapes. Choices A and D have circles instead. Choice B is the correct answer.

3. **A.** The original has four objects and choice B has five, so eliminate it. Look for the small triangle. Choice D does not have a triangle. Look for the two curved objects. Choice C only has one and it is bigger than either of the original objects. Choice A is the correct answer.

4. **B.** The original has five objects and choice A has four, so eliminate it. Look for the large object with a curved side and a right angle. Choice C does not have that object. Choices B and D have that object, but in choice D the curved object is a mirror image of the original. Choice B is the correct answer.

5. **C.** The original has four objects and choice D has five, so eliminate D. Now find a distinct shape. The large curved object should stand out. In choice A, this object does not have two straight-edged ends. Look for the two equal circles. Choice B does not have circles of equal size. Choice C is the correct answer.

6. **B.** There are five objects in the original and seven in choice D, so eliminate it. Look at the large dome-shaped object on the right. It is not present in choice A. In choice C, the dome is too thin. Choice B is the correct answer.

7. **A.** There are five objects in the original and six in choice B, so eliminate it. Look for the small right triangle. Choice C has an equilateral triangle and choice D does not have a triangle at all. Choice A is the correct answer.

8. **D.** There are three objects in the original and four in choice C, so eliminate C. Look for the long rectangle. It is not present in choice A. Look for the large circle. Choice B has two circles of equal size. Choice D is the correct answer.

9. **C.** The original has four objects, while choice B has only three. Look for the small hexagon. It is not present in choice D. Look for the parallelogram. Choice A has a rectangle. Choice C is the correct answer.

10. **C.** The original figure contains four objects, so eliminate choice A, which has only three. Now focus on one shape at a time. Look for the largest object: the quadrilateral at the lower right. It is not present in choice B. Look for the isosceles triangle. The one in choice D is a right triangle. Choice C is the correct answer.

11. **A.** There are three objects in the original and two in choice C, so eliminate C. Look at the large arch. There are two of them in choice B and it is not present in choice D. Choice A is the correct answer.

12. **B.** The original figure has three objects and choice C has four, so eliminate C. Focus on the most distinctive object: the five-sided object on the right. In choice D there is a square instead. Look for the two identical thin rectangles. Choice A has one that is too wide. Choice B is the correct answer.

13. **B.** Since each figure has four objects, look for each shape. There is one long thin rectangle, but each figure has it. There are two identical rhombuses. Choice C does not have them, so eliminate it. Choice A has three identical rhombuses, so eliminate it as well. Choices B and D have the correct objects, but in choice D the irregular quadrilateral is a mirror image of the original. Choice B is the correct answer.

14. **C.** Since each figure has four objects, look for the most distinctive shape. The object at the bottom of the figure looks like a rectangle with a bump in the middle. Choice A has a similar shape, but the bump is much taller. Look for the small equilateral triangle. Choice D has a tall isosceles triangle instead. Finally, look for the two trapezoids. Choice B has quadrilaterals that are shaped differently. Choice C is the correct answer.

15. **D.** The original has four objects, but choices A and B have five. Look for the large L-shaped object at the lower right. Choice C does not have the same shape. Choice D is the correct answer.

16. **B.** There are three objects in the original and four in choice D, so eliminate D. Look for the most distinctive shape: the isosceles trapezoid. It is not present in choice C. Look for the rectangle. Choice A has a rectangle, but it is much too long. Choice B is the correct answer.

17. **A.** Since each choice has the same number of objects as the original, focus on one object at a time. There is a rounded dome shape in the original that is not the same in choice D. Choice B has a dome, but it is much too small. Look for the quadrilateral with the slanted side at the top right. Choice C has a quadrilateral, but it is not the same shape. Choice A is the correct answer.

18. **D.** Since all the choices have three objects, look for the most distinctive object: the arrow. Choice A does not have it. Look for the small rectangle. Choices B and C do not have one of the proper size. Choice D is the correct answer.

19. **D.** Start with the smaller second object because it is easier to orient. The small object has point B on the center of the smaller curved line. Choices A and B do not join at that point. Choice C is joined at the correct spots, but the larger object is a mirror image of the original. Choice D is the correct answer.

20. **D.** If you picture the first object lying on its larger base, then point A is at the lower right corner. Choice A connects on the lower left corner of that object, and Choice B connects in the middle of that object. On the second object point B is at an internal angle. Choice C has point B at the end of the t-shaped object. Choice D is the correct answer.

21. **A.** With the first object in its original orientation, point A is at the bottom right. This is not true in choices B and C. Point B is at the right angle of the triangle. Choice D does not connect the triangle at that point. Choice A is the correct answer.

22. **D.** Point A is on the inside left corner of the T-shaped object. This point is in the wrong location in choice A (here it is in the inside right corner) and choice B. Point B is in the center of the arch object. Choice C places point B on the perimeter of that object. Choice D is the correct answer.

23. **C.** Point A is at the center of the inside edge on the first object. Point A is not at the correct spot in choices B or D, so eliminate them. Point B is at the lower right point of the second object (in its current orientation). Point B does not connect at this spot in choice A. Choice C is the correct answer.

24. **A.** Since point B is quite distinctive, look for it first. It should be in the center of the large end of the second object. Choice C does not connect at this spot. Now look for point A. In choice B, it is on the wrong corner of the bump on the rectangle. Choice D may appear to connect the objects in the correct spots, but the object with point A is a mirror image of the original. Choice A is the correct answer.

25. **C.** Each object has its designated point at the top tip. Choice A does not connect the second object at that point. Choice B does not connect the first object at the correct point. Choice D may appear to connect the objects in the correct spots, but the second object is a mirror image of the original. Choice C is the correct answer.

ASVAB PRACTICE TEST FORM 2

Try to take this practice test under actual test conditions. Find a quiet place to work, and set aside a period of approximately $2\frac{1}{2}$ hours when you will not be disturbed. Work on only one section at a time, and use your watch or a timer to keep track of the time limits for each section. Mark your answers on the answer sheet, just as you will when you take the real exam.

At the end of the test you'll find an answer key and explanations for every question. After you check your answers against the key, you can complete a chart that will show you how you did on the test and what test topics you might need to study more. Then review the explanations, paying particular attention to the ones for the questions that you answered incorrectly.

GENERAL DIRECTIONS

IF YOU ARE TAKING THE PAPER-AND-PENCIL VERSION OF THE ASVAB, THE TEST ADMINISTRATOR WILL READ THE FOLLOWING ALOUD TO YOU:

DO NOT WRITE YOUR NAME OR MAKE ANY MARKS in this booklet. Mark your answers on the separate answer sheet. Use the scratch paper which was given to you for any figuring you need to do. Return this scratch paper with your other papers when you finish the test.

If you need another pencil while taking this test, hold your pencil above your head. A proctor will bring you another one.

This booklet contains 9 tests. Each test has its own instructions and time limit. When you finish a test, you may check your work in that test ONLY. Do not go on to the next test until the examiner tells you to do so. Do not turn back to a previous test at any time.

For each question, be sure to pick the BEST ONE of the possible answers listed. Each test has its own instructions and time limit. When you have decided which one of the choices given is the best answer to the question, blacken the space on your answer sheet that has the same number and letter as your choice. Mark only in the answer space. BE CAREFUL NOT TO MAKE ANY STRAY MARKS ON YOUR ANSWER SHEET. Each test has a separate section on the answer sheet. Be sure you mark your answers for each test in the section that belongs to that test.

Here is an example of correct marking on an answer sheet.

S1. A triangle has

A. 2 sides
B. 3 sides
C. 4 sides
D. 5 sides

PRACTICE

S1 Ⓐ ● Ⓒ Ⓓ
S2 Ⓐ Ⓑ Ⓒ Ⓓ
S3 Ⓐ Ⓑ Ⓒ Ⓓ

The correct answer to sample question S1 is B.

Next to the item, note how space B opposite number S1 has been blackened. Your marks should look just like this and be placed in the space with the same number and letter as the correct answer to the question. Remember, there is only ONE BEST ANSWER for each question. If you are not sure of the answer, make the BEST GUESS you can. If you want to change your answer, COMPLETELY ERASE your first answer mark.

Answer as many questions as possible. Do not spend too much time on any one question. Work QUICKLY, but work ACCURATELY. DO NOT TURN THE PAGE UNTIL TOLD TO DO SO. Are there any questions?

ASVAB PRACTICE TEST FORM 2

ANSWER SHEET

ANSWER SHEET   PAGE 3
ARMED SERVICES VOCATIONAL
APTITUDE BATTERY

LAST   FIRST   MI   SSN

PART 1-GS
PART 2-AR
PART 3-WK
PART 4-PC
PART 5-MK
PART 6-EI
PART 7-AS
PART 8-MC
PART 9-AO

PRACTICE
S1 (A) (B) (C) (D)
S2 (A) (B) (C) (D)
S3 (A) (B) (C) (D)

DD FORM 1304-5AS   FOR OFFICIAL USE ONLY (WHEN COMPLETED)

PART 1. GENERAL SCIENCE

THE TEST ADMINISTRATOR WILL READ THE FOLLOWING ALOUD TO YOU:

Turn to Part 1 and read the directions for General Science silently while I read them aloud. This test has questions about science. Pick the BEST answer for each question and then blacken the space on your separate answer sheet that has the same number and letter as your choice. Here are three practice questions.

S1. A rose is a kind of
    A. animal.
    B. bird.
    C. flower.
    D. fish.

S2. A cat is a
    A. plant.
    B. mammal.
    C. reptile.
    D. mineral.

S3. The earth revolves around the
    A. sun.
    B. moon.
    C. meteorite.
    D. Mars.

Now look at the section of your answer sheet labeled "PRACTICE." Notice that answer space C has been marked for question S1. Now do practice questions S2 and S3 by yourself. Find the correct answer to the question, then mark the space on your answer sheet that has the same letter as the answer you picked. Do this now.

You should have marked B for question S2 and A for question S3. If you make any mistakes, erase your mark carefully and blacken the correct answer space. Do this now.

Your score on this test will be based on the number of questions you answer correctly. You should try to answer every question. If you finish before time is called, go back and check your work in this part ONLY. Now find the section of your answer sheet that is marked PART 1. When you are told to begin, start with question number 1 in Part 1 of your test booklet and answer space number 1 in Part 1 on your separate answer sheet. DO NOT TURN THE PAGE UNTIL TOLD TO DO SO. This part has 25 questions in it. You will have 11 minutes to complete it. Most of you should finish in this amount of time. Are there any questions?

Turn the page and begin.

1. Parts of a cell that store food, waste, and/or water are called
   A. vacuoles.
   B. alleles.
   C. DNA.
   D. bacteria.

2. The organelle responsible for holding hereditary information is the
   A. cell wall.
   B. chloroplasts.
   C. nucleus.
   D. vacuole.

3. Which of the following is not a function of the plant root?
   A. Conduct photosynthesis
   B. Absorb nutrients
   C. Anchor the plant to the soil
   D. Store food

4. Which of the following parts of a plant controls the amount of water within the plant?
   A. Stem
   B. Xylem
   C. Stomata
   D. Flower

5. The eating habits of humans would classify them as
   A. herbivores.
   B. carnivores.
   C. omnivores.
   D. arachnids.

6. Kangaroos and other animals with pouches are considered to be
   A. placentals.
   B. amphibians.
   C. marsupials.
   D. endotherms.

7. Which of the following is not a function of the human skeletal system?
   A. Produce red blood cells
   B. Protect body organs
   C. Create nutrients
   D. Store minerals for later use

8. When you lift a weight with your biceps, which of the following occurs?
   A. Your bicep sends electrical charges to your bone marrow.
   B. Your biceps contract, and your triceps relax.
   C. Your muscle increases in weight.
   D. Your abdominals tighten and relax alternatively.

9. Sunlight promotes the development of which of the following vitamins important for bone development?
   A. Vitamin A
   B. Vitamin C
   C. Vitamin D
   D. Vitamin E

10. Which of the following are the vessels through which blood moves from your heart to other parts of your body?
    A. Veins
    B. Capillaries
    C. Atriums
    D. Arteries

11. The part of the eye that responds to light intensity and color is called the
    A. retina.
    B. iris.
    C. vitreous humor.
    D. lens.

12. What a person actually looks like as a result of his or her genetic makeup is called which of the following?
    A. Genotype
    B. Phenotype
    C. Mutation
    D. Variation

13. Which of the following reasons makes the laser such a good surgical cutting tool?
    A. It makes incisions less prone to bacterial infection.
    B. It makes an incision quickly.
    C. A lot of energy can be directed to a small area.
    D. The light is made of different wavelengths.

14. Which of the following is required in order to change a solid to a liquid?
    A. Chemical compounds
    B. Neutrons
    C. Thermal energy
    D. Extra molecules

15. The tendency of Earth's winds and surface water currents to flow in a clockwise direction in the northern hemisphere is a result of which of the following?
    A. Doppler effect
    B. Convection effect
    C. Coriolis effect
    D. Compression effect

16. Which type of volcano is the steepest, forming from alternating layers of lava and volcanic ash, cinders, and other materials from volcanic explosions?
    A. Composite volcano
    B. Fissure eruptions
    C. Cinder cone
    D. Shield volcano

17. Which of the following represents the way the oceans were formed?
    A. Water flowed from the land to the lower areas of Earth's surface.
    B. Volcanoes released water vapor that eventually condensed to form rain that filled the ocean basins.
    C. Organisms during photosynthesis released oxygen, which then combined with hydrogen creating water that filled the ocean basins.
    D. Water trapped underground was released to the ocean basins after Earth's crust cooled.

18. The strongest and highest tides occur under which of the following conditions?
    A. Hurricane force winds and heavy rains
    B. The perpendicular alignment of the sun, Earth, and moon
    C. The vertical alignment of the sun, Earth, and moon
    D. An earthquake caused by faulting in the ocean floor

19. The term that describes the time when the sun's rays are directly over the equator is
    A. season.
    B. solstice.
    C. equatorial tilt.
    D. equinox.

20. The space between Mars and Jupiter is occupied by which of the following?
    A. Uranus
    B. Asteroids
    C. Comets
    D. Gas nebulas

21. If there were no greenhouse effect, which would likely happen to Earth?
    A. Pollution would decrease.
    B. Earth would get colder.
    C. The ozone layer would increase.
    D. Plant and animal diversity would increase.

22. Which of the following conditions is necessary to create a hurricane?
    A. A cold front in the tropics
    B. A low-pressure area over the tropical ocean
    C. A downdraft caused by air circulation
    D. Surface winds that form over the ocean and move toward land

23. The process by which moisture from a lake enters the atmosphere is called
    A. transpiration.
    B. condensation.
    C. evaporation.
    D. precipitation.

24. The south pole of a magnet is attracted to which of the following?
    A. The geographic south pole
    B. The magnetic north pole
    C. The magnetic south pole
    D. The geographic north pole

25. Which of the following is a substance that speeds up chemical reactions?
    A. Catalyst
    B. Ionic converter
    C. Inhibitor
    D. Rising temperature

STOP! DO NOT TURN THIS PAGE UNTIL TIME IS UP FOR THIS TEST. IF YOU FINISH BEFORE TIME IS UP, CHECK OVER YOUR WORK ON THIS TEST ONLY.

PART 2. ARITHMETIC REASONING

THE TEST ADMINISTRATOR WILL READ THE FOLLOWING ALOUD TO YOU:

Turn to Part 2 and read the directions for Arithmetic Reasoning silently while I read them aloud. This is a test of arithmetic word problems. Each question is followed by four possible answers. Decide which answer is CORRECT, and then blacken the space on your answer sheet that has the same number and letter as your choice. Use your scratch paper for any figuring you wish to do.

Here is a sample question. DO NOT MARK your answer sheet for this or any further sample questions.

S1. A student buys a sandwich for 80 cents, milk for 20 cents, and pie for 30 cents. How much did the meal cost?

   A. $1.00
   B. $1.20
   C. $1.30
   D. $1.40

The total cost is $1.30; therefore, C is the right answer. Your score on this test will be based on the number of questions you answer correctly. You should try to answer every question. DO NOT SPEND TOO MUCH TIME on any one question. If you finish before time is called, go back and check your work in this part ONLY.

Now find the section of your answer sheet that is marked PART 2. When you are told to begin, start with question number 1 in Part 2 of your test booklet and answer space number 1 in Part 2 on your separate answer sheet.

DO NOT TURN THIS PAGE UNTIL TOLD TO DO SO. You will have 36 minutes for the 30 questions. Are there any questions?

Begin.

1. Lyn had a birthday party and spent $9.98 on balloons, $47.23 on party favors, $16.97 on a cake, $21.77 on ice cream, and $15.15 on invitations. How much did Lyn spend on the party?
   A. $97.20
   B. $111.10
   C. $125.20
   D. $127.30

2. Ned's physical fitness program includes a goal of 175 minutes of jogging per week. He ran 35 minutes on Monday, 44 minutes on Wednesday, 17 minutes on Thursday, and 62 minutes on Friday, how many more minutes does he need to run to reach his goal?
   A. 17
   B. 29
   C. 37
   D. 42

3. Bob's CD collection totals 200. If 30 CDs contain jazz music, what percent of his collection is jazz?
   A. 2%
   B. 15%
   C. 27%
   D. 35%

4. Dave is on a kayaking trip. On the first day he travels 15 miles. On the second day he travels 35 miles, and the third day he rests. On the fourth day he travels 57 miles, and on the fifth day he travels 43 miles. What is the average number of miles that he travels per day?
   A. 25
   B. 27
   C. 30
   D. 32

5. Blair plays football. In the last game he threw completed passes of 3 yards, 22 yards, 45 yards, 19 yards, and 16 yards. What is his average?
   A. 17 yards
   B. 19 yards
   C. 21 yards
   D. 22 yards

6. A volleyball team won 25 games during a season of 55 games. What is the ratio of wins to losses?
   A. $\dfrac{5}{11}$
   B. $\dfrac{5}{6}$
   C. $\dfrac{1}{3}$
   D. $\dfrac{1}{2}$

7. A certain relay team is made up of eight members. If each team member runs 1.2 kilometers, how many meters is the race?
   A. 9.6
   B. 116.6
   C. 5,280
   D. 9,600

8. The Ice Cream Manufacturers Association is conducting a survey of favorite ice cream flavors. The results so far are as follow:

Flavor	Number of Persons
Chocolate	602
Rocky Road	411
Vanilla	589
Strawberry	214
Peach	78
Pistachio	514

   If these numbers are representative, what is the probability that the next randomly selected person will say that his or her favorite flavor is chocolate?
   A. $\dfrac{1}{4}$
   B. $\dfrac{1}{3}$
   C. $\dfrac{4}{5}$
   D. $\dfrac{6}{7}$

9. Sally and Peter are saving to buy a car. They deposit $10,000 into a savings account that pays simple interest at a rate of 15% per year. If a car costs $17,500, in how many years will they have enough money to buy the car?
    A. 3
    B. 5
    C. 6
    D. 7

10. A manufacturing plant in Detroit makes 80 cars on Monday, 78 on Tuesday, 84 on Wednesday, 77 on Thursday, and 86 on Friday. What is the average number of cars made each day?
    A. 81
    B. 82
    C. 83
    D. 84

11. Wayne has 256 pieces of candy that he needs to pack into boxes that hold 30 pieces each. How many pieces of candy are left over after he fills as many boxes as he can?
    A. 4
    B. 16
    C. 18
    D. 22

12. Leroy wants to tile the floor in his kitchen. The floor is 10 feet by 12 feet. Each tile is 6 by 8 inches. How many tiles will he need to finish the job?
    A. 124 tiles
    B. 360 tiles
    C. 412 tiles
    D. 514 tiles

13. The Metro Fitness Center has a joining fee of $125.00 per person. The Center runs a special promotion every December with a discount of 25% off the usual fee. What is the special joining fee in December?
    A. $80.00
    B. $93.75
    C. $100.00
    D. $112.25

14. Blythe sees a computer that she wants to buy. It costs $1,600. The store manager says that next week the computer will be on sale for $350 less. What percent will Blythe save if she waits a week before purchasing the computer?
    A. 12.8%
    B. 15.3%
    C. 21.9%
    D. 31.3%

15. Two numbers add to 1,500. One number is 4 times the size of the other. What are the two numbers?
    A. 300; 1,200
    B. 200; 1,300
    C. 500; 1,000
    D. 750; 750

16. Miles is starting a tree farm. His plot of land is triangular with one side 36 feet and the other two sides 30 feet each. The height of this triangle-shaped plot is 24 feet. If each tree needs 8 square feet of space to grow, how many trees can Miles plant?
    A. 35
    B. 42
    C. 54
    D. 76

17. A meteor made a circular crater with a circumference of 56.52 meters. What is the diameter of the crater?
    A. 9 m
    B. 12 m
    C. 15 m
    D. 18 m

18. Jamie is three times as old as Francis. If Francis is 14, how old is Jamie?
    A. 39
    B. 42
    C. 44
    D. 47

19. In 1968 the population of the Chicago metropolitan area was 8,435,978. In 1998, the population was 10,544,972. By about what percent did the population increase in 30 years?
    A. 13%
    B. 18%
    C. 21%
    D. 25%

20. Sandra has a piece of ribbon that is 5 yards long. She needs to cut the ribbon into pieces of 18 inches each in order to wrap presents. How many presents can she wrap with the ribbon that she has?
    A. 8
    B. 10
    C. 12
    D. 18

21. Randy is training to run a 12-kilometer race. His training program starts at him running 3 kilometers per day for the first week and increasing that amount by 15% each week. How many kilometers will he be running per day in the fourth week?
    A. 3.45 km
    B. 3.97 km
    C. 4.12 km
    D. 4.57 km

22. A swimming pool is 3 meters deep, 50 meters long, and 25 meters wide. If it takes 0.25 pounds of chlorine for every 15 cubic meters of water to keep the pool clean and healthy, how many pounds of chlorine are needed?
    A. 27.2 pounds
    B. 35.7 pounds
    C. 45.4 pounds
    D. 62.5 pounds

23. A person needs 1,500 milligrams of calcium each day. For breakfast, Joel eats a bowl of cereal with milk that has 250 milligrams of calcium, a bagel with cream cheese that has 100 milligrams of calcium, and a small container of yogurt that has 225 milligrams of calcium. What percent of the daily calcium requirement does he get at breakfast?
    A. 24%
    B. 38%
    C. 44%
    D. 49%

24. A circular baking pan is 4 inches high with a diameter of 16 inches. How much cake batter can it hold?
    A. 404.2 in^3
    B. 512.7 in^3
    C. 788.8 in^3
    D. 803.8 in^3

25. A basketball has a diameter of 12 inches. What is the volume?
    A. 76.2 in^3
    B. 89.52 in^3
    C. 904.32 in^3
    D. 1068.12 in^3

26. A box of cereal contains 45.6 oz of cereal. If the cost for one ounce is 12 cents, how much does the box of cereal cost?
    A. $4.12
    B. $4.56
    C. $5.47
    D. $5.97

27. Melanie's credit card bill was $4,000 in February. If her monthly interest is 18%, what will her bill be in March if she makes no payments and no new purchases?
    A. $4,440
    B. $4,570
    C. $4,720
    D. $4,890

28. In a jar, there are 45 green marbles, 32 red marbles, 13 purple marbles, 16 orange marbles, and 29 yellow marbles. If Duke selects one marble at random, what is the probability that the marble will be red or purple?
    A. 1:3
    B. 2:5
    C. 3:5
    D. 3:7

29. A corner table is the shape of a right triangle. One side is 3 feet, another side is 4 feet, and the third side is 5 feet. What is the area of the table top?
    A. 6 ft^2
    B. 7.2 ft^2
    C. 8 ft^2
    D. 8.5 ft^2

30. Arnold signs an agreement with the A-1 car rental company for a car at $25 per day plus 15 cents per mile driven. If Arnold rents the car for 2 days and drives 200 miles, how much does he owe the company?
    A. $55
    B. $75
    C. $80
    D. $95

STOP! DO NOT TURN THIS PAGE UNTIL TIME IS UP FOR THIS TEST. IF YOU FINISH BEFORE TIME IS UP, CHECK OVER YOUR WORK ON THIS TEST ONLY.

PART 3. WORD KNOWLEDGE

THE TEST ADMINISTRATOR WILL READ THE FOLLOWING ALOUD TO YOU:

Now turn to Part 3 and read the directions for Word Knowledge silently while I read them aloud.

This is a test of your knowledge of word meanings. These questions consist of a sentence or phrase with a word or phrase underlined. From the four choices given, you are to decide which one MEANS THE SAME OR MOST NEARLY THE SAME as the underlined word or phrase. Once you have made your choice, mark the space on your answer sheet that has the same number and letter as your choice.

Look at the sample question.

S1. The weather in this geographic area tends to be <u>moderate</u>.

    A. Severe
    B. Warm
    C. Mild
    D. Windy

The correct answer is "mild," which is choice C. Therefore, you would have blackened in space C on your answer sheet.

Your score on this test will be based on the number of questions you answer correctly. You should try to answer every question. DO NOT SPEND TOO MUCH TIME on any one question. If you finish before time is called, go back and check your work in this part <u>ONLY</u>.

Now find the section of your answer sheet that is marked PART 3. When you are told to begin, start with question number 1 in Part 3 of your test booklet and answer space number 1 in Part 3 on your separate answer sheet.

DO NOT TURN THE PAGE UNTIL TOLD TO DO SO. You will have 11 minutes to complete the 35 questions in this part. Are there any questions?

Begin.

1. The comedy was <u>hilarious</u>.
   A. Confusing
   B. Repellent
   C. Serious
   D. Funny

2. Richard was <u>wary</u> about what he was being told.
   A. Enthusiastic
   B. Cautious
   C. Nervous
   D. Happy

3. He felt a <u>tremor</u> in his hand.
   A. Trembling
   B. Pain
   C. Warmth
   D. Object

4. <u>Ingenious</u> most nearly means
   A. destructive.
   B. threatening.
   C. clever.
   D. sorrowful.

5. <u>Illusory</u> most nearly means
   A. real.
   B. first.
   C. deceptive.
   D. bright.

6. <u>Thrive</u> most nearly means
   A. move.
   B. separate.
   C. think.
   D. flourish.

7. He was able to <u>articulate</u> the meaning of the paragraph.
   A. Explain
   B. Change
   C. Contradict
   D. Support

8. Tom felt <u>reticent</u> about expressing his opinion.
   A. Hopeful
   B. Encouraged
   C. Restrained
   D. Hopeless

9. Carrying those packages was <u>cumbersome</u> for Julie.
   A. Clumsy
   B. Easy
   C. Difficult
   D. Annoying

10. The argument was <u>coherent</u>.
    A. Misguided
    B. Logical
    C. Mixed
    D. Unfavorable

11. The discussion between the two was <u>contentious</u>.
    A. Quarrelsome
    B. Agreeable
    C. Laughable
    D. Interesting

12. The data started to <u>converge</u> into a possible theory.
    A. Dissolve
    B. Join
    C. Form
    D. Slide

13. <u>Invert</u> most nearly means
    A. rebuke.
    B. lecture.
    C. overturn.
    D. break.

14. Judy <u>feigned</u> interest in the subject.
    A. Lost
    B. Showed
    C. Pretended
    D. Disregarded

15. The new measurements <u>refute</u> the original hypothesis.
    A. Disprove
    B. Support
    C. Question
    D. Direct

16. <u>Impetuous</u> most nearly means
    A. natural.
    B. impulsive.
    C. slow.
    D. severe.

17. He had a <u>propensity</u> for taking criticism to heart.
    A. Fault
    B. Awareness
    C. Aversion
    D. Tendency

18. He <u>spurned</u> the accusation.
    A. Moved
    B. Rejected
    C. Scattered
    D. Accepted

19. During the fall, squirrels tend to <u>hoard</u> acorns.
    A. Eat
    B. Stockpile
    C. Share
    D. Hide

20. Their relationship was <u>tempestuous</u>.
    A. Friendly
    B. Adversarial
    C. Stormy
    D. Calm

21. <u>Charade</u> most nearly means
    A. pretense.
    B. nervousness.
    C. subtlety.
    D. contamination.

22. The speech he made was <u>incoherent.</u>
    A. Jumbled
    B. Nasty
    C. Simple
    D. Incorrect

23. His attitude <u>inhibited</u> him from moving forward.
    A. Pushed
    B. Prevented
    C. Scared
    D. Questioned

24. The atmosphere in the boardroom was one of <u>levity</u>.
    A. Seriousness
    B. Lightheartedness
    C. Anger
    D. Distrust

25. <u>Malady</u> most nearly means
    A. illness.
    B. heart.
    C. comedy.
    D. strength.

26. In the rainstorm, the umbrella was <u>unwieldy</u>.
    A. Heavy
    B. Useless
    C. Cumbersome
    D. Colorful

27. His action was a serious <u>transgression</u> of their agreement.
    A. Mistake
    B. Misspelling
    C. Diversion
    D. Violation

28. The paragraph was a <u>preamble</u> to the story.
    A. Summary
    B. Preface
    C. Ending
    D. Interruption

29. <u>Artificial</u> most nearly means
    A. false.
    B. creative.
    C. faithful.
    D. late.

30. The new rules caused a <u>rebellion</u> in the office.
    A. Meeting
    B. Parade
    C. Revolt
    D. Celebration

31. <u>Benefactor</u> most nearly means
    A. supporter.
    B. partner.
    C. employer.
    D. counselor.

32. The beach was <u>secluded</u>.
    A. Windy
    B. Rocky
    C. Narrow
    D. Hidden

33. Good health is a <u>prerequisite</u> for a physically active life.
    A. Requirement
    B. Outcome
    C. Cause
    D. Desire

34. The grade was a <u>blemish</u> on her perfect record.
    A. Notation
    B. Inspiration
    C. Defect
    D. Entry

35. His argument was based on <u>hearsay</u>.
    A. Facts
    B. Statements
    C. Rumor
    D. Measurements

STOP! DO NOT TURN THIS PAGE UNTIL TIME IS UP FOR THIS TEST. IF YOU FINISH BEFORE TIME IS UP, CHECK OVER YOUR WORK ON THIS TEST ONLY.

PART 4. PARAGRAPH COMPREHENSION

THE TEST ADMINISTRATOR WILL READ THE FOLLOWING ALOUD TO YOU:

Turn to Part 4 and read the directions for Paragraph Comprehension silently while I read them aloud.

This is a test of your ability to understand what you read. In this section you will find one or more paragraphs of reading material followed by incomplete statements or questions. You are to read the paragraph and select one of four lettered choices which BEST completes the statement or answers the question. When you have selected your answer, blacken the space on your answer sheet that has the same number and letter as your answer.

Your score on this test will be based on the number of questions you answer correctly. You should try to answer every question. DO NOT SPEND TOO MUCH TIME on any one question. If you finish before time is called, go back and check your work in this part ONLY.

Now find the section of your answer sheet that is marked PART 4. When you are told to begin, start with question number 1 in Part 4 of your test booklet and answer space number 1 in Part 4 on your separate answer sheet.

DO NOT TURN THE PAGE UNTIL TOLD TO DO SO. You will have 13 minutes to complete the 15 questions in this part. Are there any questions?

Begin.

Everyone wants to protect children. Yet when it comes to the sensitive issue of childhood obesity, too often we fall silent. We need to break the silence and lay open for the country the hard facts and necessary choices we need to make to deal with what has become a quiet epidemic in America. The simple fact is that more people die in the United States of too much food than of too little, and the habits that lead to this epidemic become ingrained at an early age.

Everyone knows the statistics: obesity and excessive weight affect 10 million U.S. children. That's a record, and there's no real sign that it won't be broken again soon. In the past 20 years, the number of obese children has doubled, placing more Americans at risk of high cholesterol, high blood pressure, heart disease, diabetes, arthritis, and cancer—all at an earlier age. Obesity contributes to 300,000 deaths each year. That's close to 1,000 lives lost each day at a cost to our healthcare system of $70 billion a year, or 8 percent of all medical bills.

We need to take this issue seriously. For at least one in five kids, excessive weight is not a cute phase that will be outgrown. It's the start of a lifetime of serious health problems. It is time we elevate this issue to its rightful place near the top of the public health agenda alongside cancer, heart disease, and other leading killers of Americans today.

Solving the problem is a complex issue because it involves some very sensitive areas: personal choice, culture, and economic status. Children soak up the wrong lessons not just from TV, but also from the one in three adults who is overweight. The apple isn't falling far from the tree, here. So we can't blame only fast food restaurants or the media for the problem. We need to have a strong educational program so that children and their parents know the facts.

The only way kids will succeed is if they have easier access to healthy foods, fewer temptations, and role models that set the right example both with eating habits and exercise. Success almost always hinges on changing the whole family's eating habits, and that is good for everyone.

1. In this passage, the author is attempting to point out which of the following?
   A. Reasons to combat childhood obesity
   B. Statistics about obesity
   C. The causes of obesity
   D. The definition of the word *obesity*

2. Which of the following does the passage suggest as a solution to the obesity problem?
   A. Education of parents and children
   B. Mass media campaigns
   C. Elimination of school vending machines
   D. Personal choice

3. According to the passage, childhood obesity
   A. is influenced mostly by parents and schools.
   B. will probably continue to set records.
   C. will not be a problem in the future.
   D. can be eliminated with exercise.

4. The passage indicates that obesity results in
   A. 300,000 deaths per day.
   B. a society that does not exercise.
   C. public admiration for cute children.
   D. $70 billion in healthcare costs.

5. The passage indicates that the number of adults who are overweight is
   A. one in three.
   B. one in four.
   C. one in five.
   D. one in ten.

Pocahontas was the daughter of Powhatan, an important chief of the Algonquian Native Americans (the Powhatans) who lived in the Virginia region. Her real name was Matoaka. Pocahontas was a nickname meaning "playful" or "mischievous one."

Pocahontas was only about 10 years old when her world changed forever. English settlers arrived from far across the ocean and created a settlement at Jamestown, Virginia. These new English settlers looked and acted very differently from Powhatan's tribe. Some of Pocahontas's people were afraid or even hateful of the newcomers. But the chief's daughter had a curious mind and a friendly manner. She wanted to know more about these newcomers.

Pocahontas got to know and make friends with the new colonists. Her warm nature and natural curiosity led the English to like and trust her as well. One of the colonists, Captain John Smith, said that her appearance, intelligence, and friendly personality "much exceedeth any of the rest of Powhatan's people." But not all of Powhatan's people were so curious and friendly. In December 1607, Captain Smith was captured and held at Chief Powhatan's capital, Werowocomoco.

Pocahontas is most famous for reportedly saving the life of English Captain John Smith. Throughout her short life (she died at the age of 22), however, she was important in other ways as well. Pocahontas tried to promote peace between the Powhatans and the English colonists. She even converted to Christianity and married John Rolfe, a Jamestown colonist, a union which helped bring the two groups together. Her untimely death in England hurt the chance for continued peace in Virginia between the Algonquians and the colonists.

6. According to the passage, Pocahontas might best be remembered as a
   A. warrior.
   B. mediator.
   C. daughter.
   D. child.

7. According to the passage, the nickname "Pocahontas" means
   A. beautiful child.
   B. white rose.
   C. playful cloud.
   D. mischievous one.

8. Pocahontas can be described by which of the following words?
   A. Baby
   B. Friendly
   C. Superior
   D. Hateful

9. According to the passage, what was one of the major reasons Pocahontas married John Rolfe?
   A. To promote peace
   B. To bear children
   C. To increase her influence
   D. To ensure her status in her tribe

10. According to the passage, John Rolfe was which of the following?
    A. A messenger
    B. A warrior
    C. A trader
    D. A colonist

Conflict over issues of how much control the federal government should have over the states, industrialization, trade, and especially slavery had increased tension between Northern and Southern states. After Abraham Lincoln was elected president in 1860, turmoil arose. One after another, Southern states were seceding from the United States of America.

On January 10, 1861, Florida delegates who were meeting in the state capital, Tallahassee, voted to secede from the United States. Florida then became one of six Southern states that formed a new independent government, the Confederate States of America. Five more Southern states would soon join the original six, making a total of 11 Confederate states. These events led to the outbreak of the Civil War—a brutal, bloody, four-year conflict that left the South defeated and ended slavery at the cost of more than half a million lives.

Though Florida had the smallest population of the Southern states, some 16,000 Floridians fought in the Civil War. While this was a small number when compared to the forces provided by other Southern states, it was the highest percentage of available men of military age from any Confederate state. The state also provided resources valuable to the Confederate cause. Florida's coastline had important harbors, and its products, such as sugar, pork, and salt, helped to feed the Southern soldiers.

Very little military action took place in Florida, except in a couple of coastal cities. When Confederate General Robert E. Lee surrendered in 1865, Tallahassee was the only Southern capital held by rebel forces. What do you and your family think of when you think of Florida? The Sunshine State? Oranges? Beaches? Walt Disney World? You might not think of Florida's Civil War history.

11. Which of the following would be the best title for this passage?
   A. Sunny State—Confederate History
   B. Florida Secedes
   C. Florida Leaves the Union
   D. Florida Feeds the Soldiers

12. According to the passage, what was the major reason Florida seceded from the Union?
   A. Territorial issues related to its borders
   B. Issues related to feeding Confederate soldiers
   C. Florida's weather
   D. Disagreements over slavery

13. According to the passage, how many Floridians fought in the Civil War?
    A. 5,000
    B. 7,500
    C. 11,000
    D. 16,000

14. How many states eventually left the Union?
    A. 6
    B. 9
    C. 10
    D. 11

15. According to the passage, which of the following is true?
    A. Florida was the first state to leave the Union.
    B. Florida provided the highest percentage of soldiers of any Confederate state.
    C. Most of the battles in the South took place in Florida's coastal cities.
    D. Florida's position on slavery and government control contributed to the end of the Civil War.

STOP! DO NOT TURN THIS PAGE UNTIL TIME IS UP FOR THIS TEST. IF YOU FINISH BEFORE TIME IS UP, CHECK OVER YOUR WORK ON THIS TEST ONLY.

PART 5. MATHEMATICS KNOWLEDGE

THE TEST ADMINISTRATOR WILL READ THE FOLLOWING ALOUD TO YOU:

Now turn to Part 5 and read the directions for Mathematics Knowledge silently while I read them aloud.

This is a test of your ability to solve general mathematics problems. You are to select the correct response from the choices given. Then mark the space on your answer sheet that has the same number and letter as your choice. Use your scratch paper to do any figuring you wish to do.

Your score on this test will be based on the number of questions you answer correctly. You should try to answer every question. DO NOT SPEND TOO MUCH TIME on any one question. If you finish before time is called, go back and check your work in this part <u>ONLY</u>.

Now find the section of your answer sheet that is marked PART 5. When you are told to begin, start with question number 1 in Part 5 of your test booklet and answer space number 1 in Part 5 on your separate answer sheet.

DO NOT TURN THE PAGE UNTIL TOLD TO DO SO. You will have 24 minutes to complete the 25 questions in this part. Are there any questions?

Begin.

1. If $z + 12 = 24$, $z = ?$
   A. 6
   B. 12
   C. 24
   D. 36

2. $4^2 + 3(2 - 5) =$
   A. 7
   B. 12
   C. −4
   D. −12

3. 30 is what percent of 90?
   A. 30
   B. 33
   C. 45
   D. 50

4. What is the mean of the following numbers?

   14, 24, 12, 16, 34, 104

   A. 14
   B. 24
   C. 34
   D. 44

5. Divide $\frac{1}{3}$ by $\frac{5}{6}$.

   A. $\frac{2}{5}$

   B. $\frac{5}{18}$

   C. $\frac{15}{6}$

   D. $2\frac{1}{2}$

6. Factor the following expression:

   $x^2 - 100$

   A. $(x + 10)(x + 10)$
   B. $2x(100)$
   C. $(x - 10)(x - 10)$
   D. $(x - 10)(x + 10)$

7. Subtract:

   $$12x^2 + 6y - 3$$
   $$-(3x^2 - 2y + 12)$$

   A. $9x^2 + 8y - 15$
   B. $15x^4 + 4y + 9$
   C. $15x^2 + 4y + 9$
   D. $9x^2 + 4y + 9$

8. Solve for x.

   $$\frac{r}{j} = \frac{x}{y}$$

   A. $\frac{yr}{j} = x$

   B. $x = \frac{rx}{jy}$

   C. $x = \frac{rx}{jy}$

   D. $jy = x$

9. Solve for the two unknowns.

   $3a + 4b = 12$
   $2a + 2b = 15$

   A. $a = 12$; $b = 10$
   B. $a = -10$; $b = 12$
   C. $a = -4$; $b = 9.5$
   D. $a = 18$; $b = -10.5$

10. $\dfrac{x^4 y^6}{x^7 y^2} =$

    A. $x^{-3}y^8$

    B. x^3y^8

    C. $\dfrac{y^4}{x^3}$

    D. $\dfrac{y^4}{x^4}$

11. Solve for g.

    $3g^2 + 4g + 1 = 0$

    A. $g = 4$; $g = -1$
    B. $g = 4$; $g = 1$
    C. $g = 1/3$; $g = -1$
    D. $g = -1/3$; $g = -1$

12. Multiply:

$$\frac{6}{x+1} \times \frac{3x+3}{5}$$

A. $\dfrac{18x+18}{5x+1}$

B. $3\dfrac{3}{5}$

C. $30(3x^2 + 1)$

D. $18x^2 + 30$

13. Divide:

$$\frac{5}{x+1} \div \frac{6}{3x+3}$$

A. $\dfrac{30}{3x^2+6x+3}$

B. $\dfrac{30}{(x+1)(3x+3)}$

C. $\dfrac{15x}{6x^2}$

D. $2\dfrac{1}{2}$

14. $\sqrt[2]{121} =$
   A. 3
   B. 5
   C. 6
   D. 11

15. Solve for y.

$$\frac{v}{y} = \frac{s}{t}$$

A. $y = \dfrac{vs}{yt}$

B. $y = \dfrac{s}{vt}$

C. $y = \dfrac{vt}{s}$

D. $y = vst$

16. Which of the following is a hexagon?

A.

B.

C.

D.

17. What is the perimeter of the following parallelogram?

6 mi

2 mi

A. 9 mi
B. 12 mi
C. 16 mi
D. 20 mi

18. Round the following number to the nearest hundredth.

1,478.964

A. 1,478.99
B. 1,500.00
C. 1,478.96
D. 1,478.970

19. If the following is a right triangle and $\angle 2$ is 35°, what is the measure of $\angle 1$?

1

2

A. 25°
B. 55°
C. 65°
D. 75°

20. In the following figure, if ∠2 is 29°, what is the measure of ∠4?

   A. 61°
   B. 85°
   C. 90°
   D. 119°

21. In the following right triangle, what is the length of side *AC*?

   A. 6 in
   B. 12 in
   C. $\sqrt{24}$ in
   D. $\sqrt{35}$ in

22. What is the area of the following rectangle?

   A. 36 cm²
   B. 99 cm²
   C. 121.5 cm²
   D. 243 cm²

23. What is the area of the following circle?

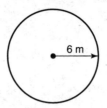

   A. 18.84 m²
   B. 97.02 m²
   C. 113.04 m²
   D. 452.16 m²

24. What is 1% of 5,000?
   A. 5
   B. 10
   C. 50
   D. 105

25. What is the volume of a sphere that has a radius of 3 meters?
   A. 12.56 m³
   B. 37.68 m³
   C. 75.36 m³
   D. 113.04 m³

STOP! DO NOT TURN THIS PAGE UNTIL TIME IS UP FOR THIS TEST. IF YOU FINISH BEFORE TIME IS UP, CHECK OVER YOUR WORK ON THIS TEST ONLY.

PART 6. ELECTRONICS INFORMATION

THE TEST ADMINISTRATOR WILL READ THE FOLLOWING ALOUD TO YOU:

Now turn to Part 6 of your test booklet and read the directions for Electronics Information silently while I read them aloud.

This is a test of your knowledge of electrical, radio, and electronics information. You are to select the correct response from the choices given and then mark the space on your answer sheet that has the same number and letter as your choice.

Your score on this test will be based on the number of questions you answer correctly. You should try to answer every question. DO NOT SPEND TOO MUCH TIME on any one question. If you finish before time is called, go back and check your work in this part ONLY.

Now find the section of your answer sheet that is marked PART 6. When you are told to begin, start with question number 1 in Part 6 of your test booklet and answer space number 1 in Part 6 on your separate answer sheet.

DO NOT TURN THE PAGE UNTIL TOLD TO DO SO. You will have 9 minutes to complete the 20 questions in this part. Are there any questions?

Begin.

1. When an air compressor starts up, other lights on the circuit often dim because
   A. motors need large amperage to start.
   B. motors need large voltage when starting.
   C. motors need large resistance when starting.
   D. most circuits are not designed for motors.

2. A capacitor is used to store
   A. voltage.
   B. current.
   C. capacitance.
   D. resistance.

3. A 480-volt circuit has a resistance of 24 ohms. How much current is flowing?
   A. 0.05 amperes
   B. 20 amperes
   C. 48 amperes
   D. Can't tell from this information

4. The electrical property that is usually referred to as pressure is
   A. current.
   B. resistance.
   C. amperage.
   D. voltage.

5. A meter at point A will read

   A. voltage.
   B. resistance.
   C. current.
   D. capacitance.

6. In an electrical diagram, the following symbol represents a(n)

   A. transformer.
   B. electromagnet.
   C. battery.
   D. capacitor.

7. How much power is being carried in a 120-volt circuit when the current is 12 amps?
   A. 10 watts
   B. 240 watts
   C. 1,200 watts
   D. 1,440 watts

8. A dishwasher on a 120-volt circuit is consuming 1,800 watts of power. What is the amperage?
   A. 1.5
   B. 15
   C. 120
   D. 1,680

9. An electrical wire is usually made by
   A. stretching a conductor until it's thin enough to make wire.
   B. wrapping a conductor around an insulator.
   C. wrapping an insulator around a conductor.
   D. transforming a conductor into an insulator.

10. Many computer parts use gold-plated contacts because gold
    A. resists corrosion, ensuring a good contact.
    B. has a high impedance.
    C. adds prestige to the computer.
    D. is heat-resistant.

11. Which of these devices would you use to control the flow of current?
    A. Generator
    B. Transistor
    C. Alternator
    D. Capacitor

12. A material that allows free flow of electrons is called a(n)
    A. insulator.
    B. resistor.
    C. semiconductor.
    D. conductor.

13. A lead-acid storage battery presents an explosion hazard if you
    A. undercharge it.
    B. add too much water.
    C. add too little water.
    D. get a spark near it.

14. One kilowatt hour is the same as
    A. 1,000 watts for 1 hour
    B. 10 watts for 10 hours
    C. 1,000 watts for 1,000 hours
    D. 1 watt for 1 hour

15. 12-gauge wire is _____ than 16-gauge wire.
    A. more flexible
    B. longer
    C. thicker
    D. thinner

16. What is the total resistance in this circuit?

$R_1 = 400\Omega$

$R_2\ 300\Omega$

$R_3\ 400\Omega$

    A. 0.11 ohm
    B. 11 ohms
    C. 425 ohms
    D. 1,100 ohms

17. What is the approximate total resistance in this circuit?

$R_1\ 400\Omega$ $R_2\ 400\Omega$ $R_3\ 400\Omega$

    A. 0.133 ohm
    B. 33 ohms
    C. 133.3 ohms
    D. 3,300 ohms

18. When the primary side of a transformer has more turns than the secondary side, the output voltage will be _____ the input voltage.
    A. lower than
    B. higher than
    C. the same as
    D. a multiple of

19. Which of these devices contains an electromagnet?
    A. Incandescent light bulb
    B. Fluorescent light bulb
    C. Light switch
    D. Doorbell

20. Current that changes polarity many times per second is called
    A. direct current.
    B. alternating current.
    C. AC/DC current.
    D. reverse-polarity current.

STOP! DO NOT TURN THIS PAGE UNTIL TIME IS UP FOR THIS TEST. IF YOU FINISH BEFORE TIME IS UP, CHECK OVER YOUR WORK ON THIS TEST ONLY.

PART 7. AUTO AND SHOP INFORMATION

THE TEST ADMINISTRATOR WILL READ THE FOLLOWING ALOUD TO YOU:

Now turn to Part 7 and read the directions for Auto and Shop Information silently while I read them aloud.

This test has questions about automobiles, shop practices, and the use of tools. Pick the BEST answer for each question and then mark the space on your answer sheet that has the same number and letter as your choice.

Your score on this test will be based on the number of questions you answer correctly. You should try to answer every question. DO NOT SPEND TOO MUCH TIME on any one question. If you finish before time is called, go back and check your work in this part ONLY.

Now find the section of your answer sheet that is marked PART 7. When you are told to begin, start with question number 1 in Part 7 of your test booklet and answer space number 1 in Part 7 on your separate answer sheet.

DO NOT TURN THE PAGE UNTIL TOLD TO DO SO. You will have 11 minutes to complete the 25 questions in this part. Are there any questions?

Begin.

1. If you hear a "ping" or knocking sound on acceleration, what is the most likely cause?
   A. The fuel-air mixture is too rich.
   B. The fuel-air mixture is too lean.
   C. The gasoline octane is too low.
   D. The gasoline octane is too high.

2. If the antifreeze is defective,
   A. the engine may overheat.
   B. the engine block or cylinder head may crack.
   C. the engine may not warm up enough.
   D. the defroster will stop working.

3. Problems with this system
   A. can prevent a vehicle from stopping fast enough.
   B. should be checked out when convenient.
   C. may cause engine overheating.
   D. will always cause steering problems.

4. What is not an advantage of front-wheel drive?
   A. Improved traction in mud, rain, and snow
   B. Greater traction on the driving wheels
   C. More interior room
   D. Better tire life on the front wheels

5. If engine oil gets too low, you can expect more
   A. corrosion.
   B. friction.
   C. noise.
   D. exhaust.

6. If there are problems with the valve train, you can expect
   A. overheating.
   B. loss of power.
   C. engine roughness.
   D. B and C.

7. If a vehicle loses acceleration,
   A. check the fuel.
   B. horsepower is falling off for some reason.
   C. torque is falling off for some reason.
   D. press harder on the gas pedal.

8. All other things being equal, a heavier car will
   A. have more headroom.
   B. be harder to start in winter.
   C. use more gasoline per mile.
   D. have more gears.

9. If an engine turns over too slowly in the winter,
   A. the starter motor may need replacement.
   B. the battery may be losing its charge.
   C. the oil may be too heavy.
   D. B and C.

10. When jump starting a car, be sure to
    A. connect the ground cable to the front axle.
    B. remove all the battery caps.
    C. connect the terminals positive to positive, and negative to negative.
    D. keep the transmission in drive.

11. If a manual transmission "grinds" during a normal gearshift, check the
    A. synchronizers.
    B. clutch adjustment.
    C. fluid in the torque converter.
    D. A and B.

12. If an engine seizes up (cannot turn), you might suspect problems with the
    A. lubrication system.
    B. cooling system.
    C. main bearings.
    D. all the above.

13. What type of screw head would best hold a flat plate to a joist?
    A. Round head or pan head
    B. Phillips head
    C. Flat head
    D. Any head

14. The tool shown below is a

    A. hacksaw.
    B. prybar saw.
    C. dowel saw.
    D. keyhole saw.

15. When applying a glossy paint to wood, what is the correct order of operations?
    A. Prime, paint, repaint
    B. Prime, sand, paint
    C. Sand, prime, sand, paint
    D. Sand, prime, paint

16. When fastening drywall,
    A. all joints should occur on top of a stud.
    B. vertical joints should occur on top of a stud.
    C. joints should overlap slightly.
    D. joints should be avoided.

17. When sanding drywall, always
    A. use a belt sander.
    B. start with medium sandpaper.
    C. sand with the grain.
    D. wear a dust mask.

18. The tool shown below is a(n)

    A. box wrench.
    B. open-end wrench.
    C. arc-joint wrench.
    D. combination wrench.

19. When an electric grinder spins at 4,500 rpm,
    A. it should not use fine-grained wheels.
    B. it would be smart to use a 3,000 rpm wheel, which would cut even faster at 4,500 rpm.
    C. you must use water to cool the metal you are grinding.
    D. the metal you are grinding will heat up quickly.

20. For which group of operations would you use a wire brush?
    A. Removing paint from metal, removing rust, cleaning bolt threads
    B. Stripping paint, dulling paint before repainting, cleaning a wood deck
    C. Preparing drywall for painting, removing rust
    D. Cleaning threads inside a nut, removing paint from metal, dulling paint before repainting

21. The tool shown below is best used for

    A. turning bolts.
    B. clamping.
    C. cutting sheet metal.
    D. pounding a chisel.

22. The standard size of a sheet of plywood, drywall, or oriented-strand board
    A. varies
    B. is 4×8 ft
    C. is 1/2 in thick
    D. is 5/8 in $\times$ 4 ft $\times$ 8 ft

23. What is the purpose of galvanizing?
    A. To prevent oxidation on steel
    B. To smooth a steel surface to reduce friction
    C. To harden steel
    D. To sharpen steel

24. Which items have a similar mechanical role?
    A. Sheet-metal screw, screen door operator
    B. Deadbolt in lock, toggle in wall switch
    C. Door hinge pin, auto axle
    D. Door weather-strip, door lock

25. Which group of tools has the same function?
    A. Rasp, plane, sandpaper
    B. Screwdriver, awl, prybar
    C. Drill, auger, jigsaw
    D. Band saw, hole saw, jigsaw

STOP! DO NOT TURN THIS PAGE UNTIL TIME IS UP FOR THIS TEST. IF YOU FINISH BEFORE TIME IS UP, CHECK OVER YOUR WORK ON THIS TEST ONLY.

PART 8. MECHANICAL COMPREHENSION

THE TEST ADMINISTRATOR WILL READ THE FOLLOWING ALOUD TO YOU:

Now turn to Part 8 and read the directions for Mechanical Comprehension silently while I read them aloud.

This test has questions about mechanical and physical principles. Study the picture and decide which answer is CORRECT and then mark the space on your separate answer sheet that has the same number and letter as your choice.

Your score on this test will be based on the number of questions you answer correctly. You should try to answer every question. DO NOT SPEND TOO MUCH TIME on any one question. If you finish before time is called, go back and check your work in this part ONLY.

Now find the section of your answer sheet that is marked PART 8. When you are told to begin, start with question number 1 in Part 8 of your test booklet and answer space number 1 in Part 8 on your separate answer sheet.

DO NOT TURN THE PAGE UNTIL TOLD TO DO SO. You will have 19 minutes to complete the 25 questions in this part. Are there any questions?

Begin.

1. A tank holds 480 gallons of fuel. If it is drained at a rate of 120 gallons per minute, it will be empty in _____ seconds.
   A. 60
   B. 120
   C. 240
   D. 480

2. If the lever balances as shown, what is the mechanical advantage?

   A. 2
   B. 3
   C. 4
   D. 8

3. When a pump compresses air, the air
   A. gets hotter.
   B. gets colder.
   C. becomes a liquid.
   D. becomes a solid.

4. In a hydraulic system, the driving cylinder has a radius of 4 inches and the driven cylinder has a radius of 8 inches. The mechanical advantage is
   A. 2
   B. 4
   C. 6
   D. 8

5. For two gears to mesh properly, they must
   A. have the same number of teeth.
   B. rotate at the same speed.
   C. have teeth that are the same size.
   D. be made of the same material.

6. A screwdriver is used to turn a screw with a pitch of ¼ inch. After 10 complete turns of the screwdriver, the screw will have moved
   A. 1 inch
   B. 1 1/2 inches
   C. 2 inches
   D. 2 1/2 inches

7. Five gears are shown below. If gear A turns as shown, the other gears that turn in the same direction are

   A. Gears A and B
   B. Gears B and C
   C. Gears C and D
   D. Gears A and D

8. Which bookshelf is supported most securely?
   A. 1

   B. 2
   C. 3
   D. 2 and 3 are equally secure.

9. Which flat cardboard pattern can be folded along the dotted lines to form the complete, totally enclosed, three-sided pyramid shown?

1

2

3

4

A. 1
B. 2
C. 3
D. 4

10. Which of these is not a simple machine?
A. Lever
B. Inclined plane
C. Pulley
D. Electric motor

11. A tank 2 feet wide by 6 feet long holds 600 pounds of water. What is the water pressure at the bottom in lb/ft²?
A. 25
B. 35
C. 40
D. 50

12. The figure shows a crank attached to a rod and piston. When the crank turns, the piston moves in the cylinder. The piston will be at the top of the cylinder if the crank makes

A. a ¼ turn
B. a ½ turn
C. a ¾ turn
D. one complete turn

13. How much effort is needed to roll a 120-lb drum up a ramp 30 ft long and 3 ft high at its high end? (Ignore the effect of friction.)
A. 6 lb
B. 9 lb
C. 10 lb
D. 12 lb

14. If you pulled the following objects from a pot of hot water, which would seem hottest to your hand?
A. wooden spoon
B. metal spoon
C. plastic spoon
D. paper straw

15. A gear and pinion have a ratio of 6 to 1. If the gear is rotating at a speed of 150 revolutions per minute (rpm), the speed of the pinion is most nearly
A. 900 rpm
B. 750 rpm
C. 150 rpm
D. 25 rpm

16. A spring, a device that can resume its original shape after bending, is best made from which of the following materials?
    A. ceramic
    B. paper
    C. steel
    D. wood

17. What is the mechanical advantage in this pulley system?

    A. 2
    B. 3
    C. 4
    D. 6

18. If pulley A rotates as shown, pulley C will rotate

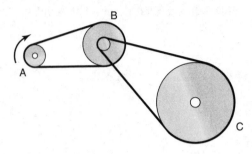

    A. faster, in the same direction.
    B. slower, in the same direction.
    C. faster, in the opposite direction.
    D. slower, in the opposite direction.

19. If you wanted to hit a heavy nail, you might choose a hammer with a
    A. lighter head.
    B. longer handle.
    C. lead head.
    D. shiny striking surface.

20. A sheet metal screw is likely to be _____ than a wood screw.
    A. longer
    B. shorter
    C. harder
    D. softer

21. The tank shown below holds 100 gallons of water. The pipe is delivering 5 gallons/second at the top, and the pipe at the bottom is removing 100 gallons/minute. How many gallons will remain in the tank after 2 minutes?

    A. 200
    B. 300
    C. 500
    D. 700

22. On the bicycle wheel shown, A and B are fixed points. When the wheel turns, which of the following is true?

A. Point A travels farther than point B in each turn of the wheel.
B. Point A makes fewer complete turns per minute than does point B.
C. Point B travels farther than point A in each turn of the wheel.
D. Point A turns in complete circles, but point B does not turn.

23. If gear A is rotating at 200 rpm, how fast will gear C be rotating?

Gear A 18 teeth   Gear B 12 teeth   Gear C 24 teeth

A. 100 rpm
B. 150 rpm
C. 300 rpm
D. 400 rpm

24. When water flows in the direction shown, pressure at point B will be

A   B

A. higher, and water velocity will be higher.
B. higher, and water velocity will be lower.
C. lower, and the water velocity will be higher.
D. lower, but velocity will not change.

25. Gear X, which has 60 teeth, meshes with gear Y, which has 12 teeth. Each time gear X makes one complete rotation, how many rotations does gear Y make?
A. 6
B. 5
C. 4
D. 3

STOP! DO NOT TURN THIS PAGE UNTIL TIME IS UP FOR THIS TEST. IF YOU FINISH BEFORE TIME IS UP, CHECK OVER YOUR WORK ON THIS TEST ONLY.

PART 9. ASSEMBLING OBJECTS

THE TEST ADMINISTRATOR WILL READ THE FOLLOWING ALOUD TO YOU:

Now turn to Part 9 and read the directions for Assembling Objects silently while I read them aloud.

This test has questions that will measure your spatial ability. Study the diagram, decide which answer is CORRECT, and then mark the space on your separate answer sheet that has the same number and letter as your choice.

Your score on this test will be based on the number of questions you answer correctly. You should try to answer every question. DO NOT SPEND TOO MUCH TIME on any one question. If you finish before time is called, go back and check your work in this part ONLY.

Now find the section of your answer sheet that is marked PART 9. When you are told to begin, start with question 1 in Part 9 of your test booklet and answer space number 1 in Part 9 on your separate answer sheet.

DO NOT TURN THE PAGE UNTIL TOLD TO DO SO. You will have 15 minutes to complete the 25 questions in this part. Are there any questions?

Begin.

For Questions 1–17, which figure best shows how the objects in the left box will appear if they are fit together?

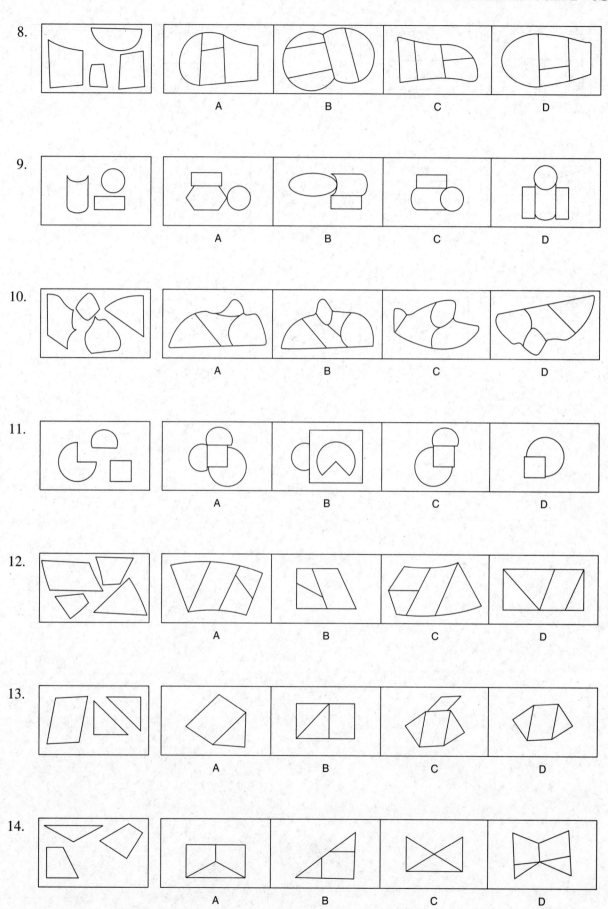

8.   A   B   C   D

9.   A   B   C   D

10.   A   B   C   D

11.   A   B   C   D

12.   A   B   C   D

13.   A   B   C   D

14.   A   B   C   D

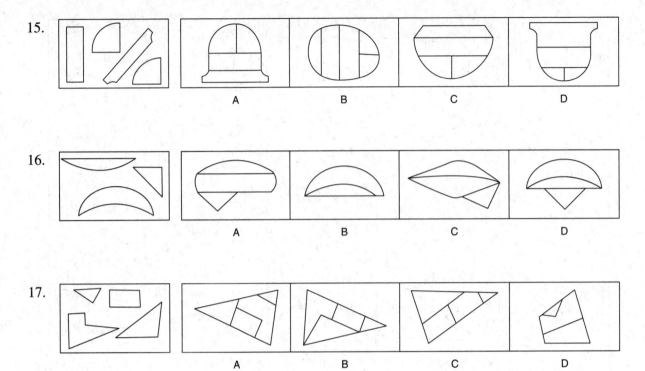

15. A   B   C   D

16. A   B   C   D

17. A   B   C   D

For Questions 18-25, which figure best shows how the objects in the left box will touch if the letters for each object are matched?

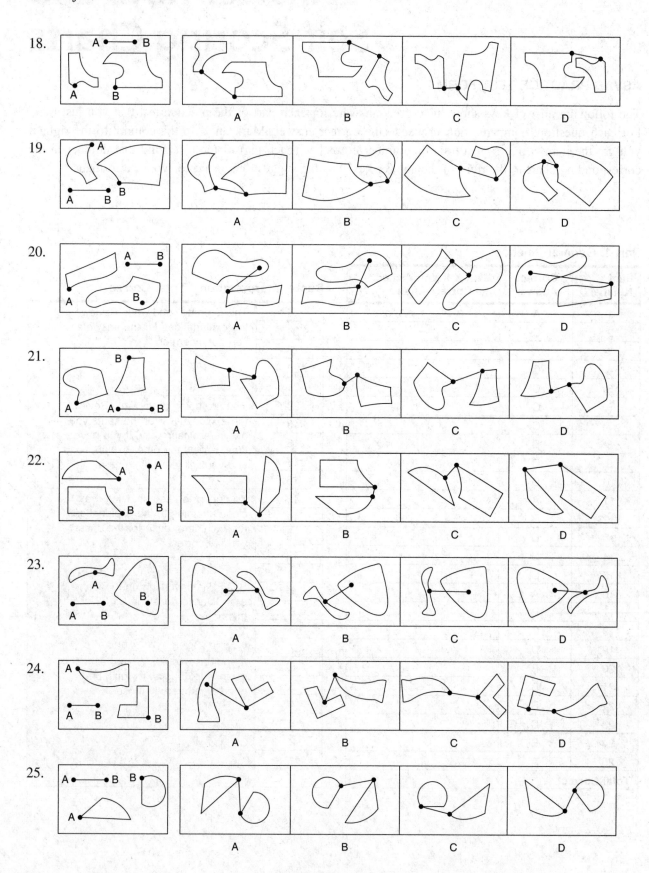

Answer Keys and Self-Scoring Charts

ASVAB PRACTICE TEST FORM 2

The following answer keys show the correct answers for each part of the practice test that you just took. For each question, compare your answer to the correct answer. Mark an X in the column to the right if you got the item correct. Then total the number correct for each part of the test. Find that number in the corresponding chart to the right of the answer key. See the suggestions listed for your performance.

Part 1. General Science

Item Number	Correct Answer	Mark X If You Picked the Correct Answer
1	A	
2	C	
3	A	
4	C	
5	C	
6	C	
7	C	
8	B	
9	C	
10	D	
11	A	
12	B	
13	C	
14	C	
15	C	
16	A	
17	B	
18	C	
19	D	
20	B	
21	B	
22	B	
23	C	
24	B	
25	A	
Total Correct		

Score Interpretation—Total Correct

25	This is pretty good work. Review the explanations for the answers you got incorrect.
24	
23	
22	
21	
20	You are doing pretty well. Review the explanations for the items you answered incorrectly. If you have time, review the other explanations and you will learn even more
19	
18	
17	
16	
15	You need to keep studying. Pay close attention to the explanations for each item, even for the ones you got correct.
14	
13	
12	
11	
10	Spend time working on the General Science review in Part 3 of this book.
9	
8	
7	
6	If you have copies of your school science textbooks, it would be a good idea to study those.
5	
4	
3	
2	
1	
0	

Part 2. Arithmetic Reasoning

Item Number	Correct Answer	Mark X If You Picked the Correct Answer
1	B	
2	A	
3	B	
4	C	
5	C	
6	B	
7	D	
8	A	
9	B	
10	A	
11	B	
12	B	
13	B	
14	C	
15	A	
16	C	
17	D	
18	B	
19	D	
20	B	
21	D	
22	D	
23	B	
24	D	
25	C	
26	C	
27	C	
28	A	
29	A	
30	C	
Total Correct		

Score Interpretation—Total Correct

Score	Interpretation
30	This is pretty good work. Review the explanations for the answers you got incorrect. This test is a part of the AFQT, and you must do well
29	
28	
27	
26	
25	You are doing pretty well. Review the explanations for the items you answered incorrectly. If you have time, review the other explanations and you will learn even more.
24	
23	
22	
21	
20	You need to keep studying. Pay close attention to the explanations for each item, even for the ones you got correct.

Spend time working on the Arithmetic Reasoning reviews in Part 3 of this book.

Keep working and reworking problems until you are comfortable with the processes. |
19	
18	
17	
16	
15	
14	
13	
12	
11	
10	
9	
8	
7	
6	
5	
4	
3	
2	
1	
0	

Part 3. Word Knowledge

Item Number	Correct Answer	Mark X If You Picked the Correct Answer
1	D	
2	B	
3	A	
4	C	
5	C	
6	D	
7	A	
8	C	
9	A	
10	B	
11	A	
12	B	
13	C	
14	C	
15	A	
16	B	
17	D	
18	B	
19	B	
20	C	
21	A	
22	A	
23	B	
24	B	
25	A	
26	C	
27	D	
28	B	
29	A	
30	C	
31	A	
32	D	
33	A	
34	C	
35	C	
Total Correct		

Score Interpretation—Total Correct

35	This is pretty good work. Review the explanations for the answers you got incorrect. This is an important test that contributes to your AFQT.
34	
33	
32	
31	
30	You are doing pretty well. Review the explanations for the items you answered incorrectly. If you have time, review the other explanations and you will learn even more.
29	
28	
27	
26	
25	You need to keep studying. Pay close attention to the explanations for each item, even for the ones you got correct.
24	
23	
22	
21	
20	
19	Spend time working on the Word Knowledge review in Part 3 of this book.
18	
17	
16	
15	Keep reading and identifying words you don't know.
14	
13	
12	
11	
10	
9	
8	
7	
6	
5	
4	
3	
2	
1	
0	

Part 4. Paragraph Comprehension

Item Number	Correct Answer	Mark X If You Picked the Correct Answer
1	A	
2	A	
3	B	
4	D	
5	A	
6	B	
7	D	
8	B	
9	A	
10	D	
11	A	
12	D	
13	D	
14	D	
15	B	
Total Correct		

Score Interpretation—Total Correct

15	This is pretty good work. Review the explanations for the answers you got incorrect. This test is a part of the AFQT, and you must do well.
14	You are doing pretty well. Review the explanations for the items you got incorrect. This test is a part of the AFQT, and you must do well.
13 12 11 10 9 8 7 6 5 4 3 2 1 0	You need to keep studying. Pay close attention to the explanations for each item, even for the ones you got correct. This will help you understand why the answer is correct. Spend time reviewing the Paragraph Comprehension and Word Knowledge reviews in Part 3 of this book. Keep reading books and newspapers.

Part 5. Mathematics Knowledge

Item Number	Correct Answer	Mark X If You Picked the Correct Answer
1	B	
2	A	
3	B	
4	C	
5	A	
6	D	
7	A	
8	A	
9	D	
10	C	
11	D	
12	B	
13	D	
14	D	
15	C	
16	A	
17	C	
18	C	
19	B	
20	C	
21	C	
22	D	
23	C	
24	C	
25	D	
Total Correct		

Score Interpretation—Total Correct

25	This is pretty good work. Review the explanations for the answers you got incorrect.
24	
23	
22	You are doing pretty well. Review the explanations for the items you answered incorrectly. If you have time, review the other explanations and you will learn even more.
21	
20	
19	This test is part of the AFQT. You must perform well on this test.
18	
17	
16	You need to keep studying. Pay close attention to the explanations for each item, even for the ones you got correct.
15	
14	
13	
12	Spend time working on the Mathematics Knowledge reviews in Part 3 of this book, and work and rework the problems until you fully understand the processes.
11	
10	
9	
8	
7	
6	
5	
4	
3	
2	
1	
0	

Part 6. Electronics Information

Item Number	Correct Answer	Mark X If You Picked the Correct Answer
1	A	
2	B	
3	B	
4	D	
5	C	
6	A	
7	D	
8	B	
9	C	
10	A	
11	B	
12	D	
13	D	
14	A	
15	C	
16	D	
17	C	
18	A	
19	D	
20	B	
Total Correct		

Score Interpretation—Total Correct

20	This is pretty good work. Review the explanations for the answers you got incorrect.
19	
18	
17	You are doing pretty well. Review the explanations for the items you answered incorrectly. If you have time, review the other explanations and you will learn even more.
16	
15	
14	
13	
12	You need to keep studying. Pay close attention to the explanations for each item, even for the ones you got correct.
11	
10	
9	
8	Spend time working on the Electronics Information review in Part 3 of this book.
7	
6	
5	Your school electronics or physics books may have some helpful information as well.
4	
3	
2	
1	
0	

Part 7. Auto and Shop Information

Item Number	Correct Answer	Mark X If You Picked the Correct Answer
1	C	
2	B	
3	A	
4	D	
5	B	
6	D	
7	C	
8	C	
9	D	
10	C	
11	D	
12	D	
13	A	
14	D	
15	C	
16	B	
17	D	
18	D	
19	D	
20	A	
21	B	
22	B	
23	A	
24	C	
25	A	
Total Correct		

Score Interpretation—Total Correct

Score	Interpretation
25	This is pretty good work. Review the explanations for the answers you got incorrect.
24	
23	
22	
21	
20	You are doing pretty well. Review the explanations for the items you answered incorrectly. If you have time, review the other explanations and you will learn even more.
19	
18	
17	
16	
15	
14	You need to keep studying. Pay close attention to the explanations for each item, even for the ones you got correct.
13	
12	
11	
10	Spend time working on the Auto and Shop Information reviews in Part 3 of this book.
9	
8	
7	
6	
5	
4	
3	
2	
1	
0	

Part 8. Mechanical Comprehension

Item Number	Correct Answer	Mark X If You Picked the Correct Answer
1	C	
2	C	
3	A	
4	B	
5	C	
6	D	
7	C	
8	C	
9	A	
10	D	
11	D	
12	B	
13	D	
14	B	
15	A	
16	C	
17	A	
18	B	
19	B	
20	C	
21	C	
22	A	
23	B	
24	C	
25	B	
Total Correct		

Score Interpretation—Total Correct

Score	Interpretation
25	This is pretty good work. Review the explanations for the answers you got incorrect.
24	
23	
22	
21	
20	You are doing pretty well. Review the explanations for the items you answered incorrectly. If you have time, review the other explanations and you will learn even more.
19	
18	
17	
16	
15	You need to keep studying. Pay close attention to the explanations for each item, even for the ones you got correct.
14	
13	
12	
11	Spend time working on the Mechanical Comprehension review in Part 3 of this book
10	
9	
8	
7	
6	
5	
4	
3	
2	
1	
0	

Part 9. Assembling Objects

Item Number	Correct Answer	Mark X if You Picked the Correct Answer
1	B	
2	A	
3	A	
4	C	
5	C	
6	B	
7	B	
8	A	
9	C	
10	D	
11	C	
12	A	
13	D	
14	A	
15	A	
16	D	
17	B	
18	D	
19	C	
20	D	
21	C	
22	D	
23	B	
24	C	
25	D	
Total Correct		

Score Interpretation–Total Correct

Score	Interpretation
25	This is pretty good work. Review the explanations of the answers you got incorrect.
24	
23	
22	
21	
20	You are doing pretty well. Review the explanations for the items you answered incorrectly. If you have time, review the other explanations and you will learn even more.
19	
18	
17	
16	
15	Keep studying. Pay close attention to the explanations for each item, even for the ones you got correct.
14	
13	
12	Spend time working on the Assembling Objects review in Part 3 of this book.
11	
10	
9	
8	
7	
6	
5	
4	
3	
2	
1	
0	

Answers and Explanations

PART 1. GENERAL SCIENCE

1. **A.** Vacuoles are the parts of a cell that are the storage containers, holding water, waste, and food. The correct answer is choice A.

2. **C.** The nucleus contains the hereditary information for a cell. Choice C is the correct answer.

3. **A.** Root hairs have several functions including absorbing nutrients from the soil (choice B), helping the root system to anchor the plant (choice C), and storing food (choice D). The root hairs do not conduct photosynthesis because they do not contain chloroplasts. Choice A is the correct answer.

4. **C.** The flower (choice D) is not associated with controlling water. The stem (choice A) helps to transport water, but does not really control it. Xylem (choice B) is a tissue that makes up vessels in plants that help to support the plant and transport water; however, those vessels do not control the amount of water. The stomata are holes in the leaf that are surrounded by guard cells. The guard cells open and close the stomata, depending on how much water is contained in the plant and how much humidity there is in the atmosphere, thus controlling the amount of water that is released to the atmosphere. Choice C is the correct answer.

5. **C.** Arachnids, choice D, are spiders and this does not relate to the question. Herbivores (choice A) are plant eaters, carnivores (choice B) are meat eaters, and omnivores (choice C) eat both plants and animals as do humans. Choice C is the correct answer.

6. **C.** Kangaroos are marsupials. Choice C is the correct answer.

7. **C.** Your bones do indeed produce red blood cells (choice A), protect your body organs (choice B), and store minerals like calcium (choice D). Bones do not create nutrients. Choice C is the correct answer.

8. **B.** Any time you lift a weight or move a muscle, one muscle contracts, and the opposing muscle relaxes. So when you contract your biceps, your triceps relax. Choice B is the correct answer.

9. **C.** Sunlight promotes the development of vitamin D, which is important for the development of bones. Choice C is the correct answer.

10. **D.** Arteries (choice D) are structures that move the blood from the heart to other parts of the body. Veins (choice A) bring blood into the heart. Atriums (choice C) are not part of the circulatory system. Capillaries (choice B) are the tiny blood vessels found throughout the body. Choice D is the correct answer.

11. **A.** The retina (choice A) contains rods and cones that respond to light intensity and color. Choice A is the correct answer.

12. **B.** What a person actually ends up looking like based on his or her genetic makeup is called the *phenotype*. Choice B is the correct answer.

13. **C.** A laser emits light rays that are all the same wavelength; the waves are in phase. As a result, the light can travel great distances with very high energy without spreading. A laser can direct a lot of energy to a very small area and do it accurately, making it a great cutting tool. Choice C is the correct answer.

14. **C.** In order to change a solid to a liquid, thermal energy is necessary. Choice C is the correct answer.

15. **C.** The Doppler effect (choice A) relates to the change in the frequency of wavelengths. It is not the correct answer. Winds and surface water currents are affected by the Earth's rotation, which bends them in the clockwise direction in the northern hemisphere and counterclockwise in the southern hemisphere. This condition is called the Coriolis effect. Choice C is the correct answer.

16. **A.** A fissure eruption (choice B) is merely magma that flows out from a crack in the Earth's surface and can flood a large part of the land with basalt. Cinder cones (choice C) are volcanoes formed by explosive events, throwing cinders, lava, and ash into the air. When these materials drop back to the ground, they form a small cone. A shield volcano (choice D) is formed by lava flows of layers of basalt. A shield volcano is not very steep. The volcano type that forms from alternating layers of explosive materials and lava flows and is the steepest of all the volcanoes is a composite volcano. Choice A is the correct answer.

17. **B.** Earlier in the history of the Earth there was much more volcanic activity than there is now. The volcanoes spewed molten material and also gases. The gases included water vapor. When the atmosphere cooled to a certain point, it began to rain. It rained heavily and for a very long time. The water collected in the low areas which are now the oceans. The best answer is choice B.

18. **C.** Tides are caused by the relative positions of the Earth, the moon, and the sun. When the moon and the sun are in a straight line with Earth, the gravitational pull is the strongest. Choice C is the correct answer.

19. **D.** When the sun's rays are directly over latitude $23\frac{1}{2}°$ N (the Tropic of Cancer), it is the summer solstice for the northern hemisphere and the winter solstice for the southern hemisphere. When the sun's rays are directly over latitude $23\frac{1}{2}°$ S (the Tropic of Capricorn), it is the winter solstice for the northern hemisphere and the summer solstice for the southern hemisphere. When the sun's rays are directly over the equator, it is the equinox, when days and nights are nearly equal all over the Earth. Choice D, equinox, is the correct answer.

20. **B.** Asteroids are small rocky bodies that revolve around the sun between the orbits of Mars and Jupiter. Scientists speculate that Jupiter's strong gravitational pull prevented a larger planet from forming in that plane. Choice B is the correct answer.

21. **B.** Without the greenhouse effect, Earth would get colder. Choice B is the correct answer.

22. **B.** A low-pressure area in the tropics is the cause of hurricanes. Choice B is the correct answer.

23. **C.** Water enters the atmosphere through transpiration from plants and evaporation from bodies of water like rivers, lakes, and oceans. Choice C is the correct answer.

24. **B.** The geographic pole is the axis point around which Earth rotates. The magnetic and geographic poles differ by about $11\frac{1}{2}$ degrees at the current time. The magnetic poles have reversed many times during Earth's long history. Opposite magnetic poles attract. The magnetic south pole of a magnet is attracted to the magnetic north pole. Choice B is the correct answer.

25. **A.** A substance that speeds up chemical reactions is called a catalyst. Choice A is the correct answer.

PART 2. ARITHMETIC REASONING

1. **B.** This is a simple addition problem. Add the amounts to get the total of $111.10.

2. **A.** This problem has two steps. First you need to add the number of minutes that Ned ran and then subtract that amount from the goal of 175 minutes. He ran 158 minutes, so he needs to run 17 minutes more to reach 175.

3. **B.** In order to calculate the percent, you need to divide the total number of CDs into the number of jazz CDs. In this case you would divide 200

into 30 to get 0.15. To change that to a percent, move the decimal point two places to the right and add the percent sign to get the correct answer of 15%.

4. **C.** To find the average, add the numbers and divide by the number of numbers. In this instance the number of miles Dave has traveled add up to 150. The number of numbers is 5, so the average number of miles per day he has traveled is 30. Don't make the mistake of dividing by 4 because on one day his number of miles was 0. That number needs to be used in calculating the average.

5. **C.** To find the average, add up the numbers and divide by the number of numbers. In this problem the number of yards in Blair's completed passes adds to 105 yards. Since he has thrown 5 times, his average pass is 21 yards.

6. **B.** To find the ratio of one number to another, create a fraction to show the relationship. In this problem, there are 25 wins in a total of 55 games. The question asks for the ratio of wins to losses, so you need to calculate the number of losses. Subtracting 25 from 55 gives the result of 30 losses. Representing this as a fraction would be $\frac{25}{30}$. Simplifying this results in the fraction $\frac{5}{6}$.

7. **D.** Set this up as a proportion. If one member runs 1.2 km, how many km would eight members run? The proportion would look like this: $\frac{1}{1.2} = \frac{8}{x}$. Cross-multiply and solve.

$$x = 8(1.2) \text{ or } x = 9.6 \text{ km}$$

However, the problem asks for the number of meters. Realizing that 1 km = 1,000 meters, change 9.6 km to 9,600 meters.

8. **A.**

$$\text{Probability} = \frac{\text{number of favorable outcomes}}{\text{number of possible outcomes}}$$

In this problem the number of favorable outcomes is the number of people selecting chocolate as a favorite flavor. The number of possible outcomes is the number of all those surveyed or $602 + 411 + 589 + 214 + 78 + 514 = 2,408$.

So substitute into the formula: $\frac{602}{2,408}$. This simplifies to $\frac{1}{4}$, the correct ratio.

9. **B.** Simple interest problems use the formula $I = prt$, where I is the amount of interest, p is the principal or the amount saved or invested, r is the rate of interest, and t is the amount of time that the interest is accruing. In this problem, the interest needed is the difference between what was invested and the amount needed to buy the car: $\$17,500 - \$10,000 = \$7,500$. The principal is $10,000 and the rate is 15%. Substitute that information into the formula to get $\$7,500 = \$10,000(0.15)t$ and solve for t. $\$7,500 = \$1500t$; $t = 5$ years.

10. **A.** To find the average, add the numbers and divide by the number of numbers. In this case you would add $80 + 78 + 84 + 77 + 86$, and then divide by 5 to get an average of 81 cars per day.

11. **B.** If Wayne has 256 pieces of candy that he packs into boxes of 30 each, he can fill $256 \div 30 = 8$ boxes with 16 pieces left over—not enough to fill another box.

12. **B.** The formula for calculating area is $A = lw$. Since we are working with the result in tiles that are measured in inches, calculate the area of the floor in square inches. 10 feet × 12 inches = 120 inches. 12 feet × 12 inches = 144 inches. So the area of the floor is 17,280 in². Each tile has an area of 6×8 inches or 48 in². Dividing 17,280 in² by 48 in² = 360 tiles.

13. **B.** The cost of the joining fee is $125.00. Reduce that amount by 25% by multiplying the total cost by 0.25.

$$\$125.00 \times 0.25 = \$31.25$$

Subtract $31.25 from the original cost.

$$\$125.00 - \$31.25 = \$93.75$$

A faster way to do this (and speed is important on the ASVAB) is to multiply the original cost by 75% or 0.75 because that is the cost of the items after the discount.

$$\$125.00 \times 0.75 = \$93.75$$

14. **C.** Use the following formula

$$\text{Percent of Change} = \frac{\text{Amount of Change}}{\text{Starting Point}}$$

In this problem we know that the amount of change is $350 and that the starting price of the computer is $1,600. Substitute that information into the formula:

$$\text{Percent of Change} = \frac{\$350.00}{\$1,600.00} = 0.219.$$

Change that number to a percent by moving the decimal place two places to the right and add the percent sign: $0.219 = 21.9\%$

15. **A.** You are told that two numbers add up to 1,500, with one number being 4 times the size of other. Create an equation.

$$x + 4x = 1,500$$

Solve for x.

$$5x = 1,500$$
$$x = 300$$
$$4x = 1,200$$

So the two numbers are 300 and 1,200.

16. **C.** To calculate the area of a triangle, use the formula $A = \frac{1}{2}bh$. In this instance the base is 36 feet and the height is 24 feet.

$$A = \frac{1}{2}(36)(24)$$
$$A = \frac{1}{2}864$$
$$A = 432 \text{ ft}^2$$

If each tree needs 8 ft², divide that into the area.

$$\frac{432 \text{ ft}^2}{8 \text{ ft}^2} = 54$$

17. **D.** Use the formula $C = 2\pi r$ or $C = \pi d$.

If the circumference is 56.52 meters, substitute that into the formula: $56.52 = \pi d$

Solve for d by dividing both sides by π.

$$\frac{56.52}{3.14} = d$$
$$d = 18 \text{ m}$$

18. **B.** Create an equation to solve this problem: Jamie = 3(Francis). You are told that Francis is 14. Substitute that information into the formula.

$$\text{Jamie} = 3(14)$$

Solve for Jamie.

$$\text{Jamie} = 42$$

19. **D.** Use the following formula

$$\text{Percent of Change} = \frac{\text{Amount of Change}}{\text{Starting Point}}.$$

The starting point is 8,435,978. The amount of change is the difference between 10,544,972 and 8,435,978. You find the difference by subtracting:

$$10,544,972 - 8,435,978 = 2,108,994$$

Substitute that information into the equation.

$$\text{Percent of Change} = \frac{2,108,994}{8,435,978} = 0.2499 \text{ or } 25\%$$

20. **B.** Watch the units in this problem. Change the yards to inches.

$$5 \text{ yards} = 15 \text{ feet} = 180 \text{ inches.}$$

The problem asks for the number of 18-in-long pieces. To find the answer, you need to divide 180 by 18.

$$\frac{180}{18} = 10 \text{ pieces}$$

21. **D.** Treat this like a compound interest problem where you calculate the increase in kilometers

each week, using the increased amount as the amount to use in the calculations the next week.

Week One

3 km

Week Two

3 km + 0.15(3) = 3.45 km

Week Three

3.45 km + 0.15(3.45) = 3.97 km

Week Four

3.97 km + 0.15(3.97) = 4.57 km

22. **D.** To solve this problem, use the formula $V = lwh$. You have been given the dimensions of $l = 50$, $w = 25$ m, and $h = 3$ m. Substitute that information into the formula.

$$V = (50)(25)(3)$$
$$V = 3,750 \text{ m}^3$$

If 0.25 lb of chlorine are required for every 15 m³, calculate how many units of 15 m³ there are in the total volume of 3,750 m³.

$$3,750 \text{ m}^3 \div 15 \text{ m}^3 = 250 \text{ quarter-pound units}$$

The question asks for pounds, so divide that number by 4.

$$250 \div 4 = 62.5 \text{ lb}$$

23. **B.** In this problem you need to add the amounts of calcium that Joel eats at breakfast. Add 250, 100, and 225 to get his calcium intake of 575 mg. To calculate the percentage, divide the required amount into 575.

$$\frac{575}{1,500} = 38\%$$

24. **D.** To calculate the volume of a cylinder, use the formula $V = \pi r^2 h$. In this problem the diameter is 16 in, so the radius is 8 in. The height is given as 4 in. Substitute that information into the formula.

$$V = (3.14)(8^2)(4)$$
$$V = (3.14)(64)(4)$$
$$V = 803.84 \text{ or } 803.8 \text{ in}^3$$

Be sure to pay attention to the information you are given. You could have made an error by using the diameter rather than the radius, because the diameter was given in the problem.

25. **C.** To calculate the volume of a sphere, use the formula $V = \frac{4}{3}\pi r^3$. You are given a diameter of 12 inches, so the radius is 6 in. Substitute that information into the formula.

$$V = \frac{4}{3}\pi(6)^3$$
$$V = \frac{4(3.14)(216)}{3}$$
$$V = \frac{2,712.96}{3} = 904.32 \text{ in}^3$$

26. **C.** To calculate the answer, multiply 45.6 by 0.12.

$$45.5 \times 0.12 = \$5.47$$

27. **C.** Melanie's charge will be \$4,000 plus interest of 18%. Multiply \$4,000 by 1.18 to get \$4,720. Her bill will be \$4,720 if she makes no payments and no new purchases.

28. **A.**

$$\text{Probability} = \frac{\text{number of favorable outcomes}}{\text{number of possible outcomes}}$$

Favorable outcomes would be red or purple.

$$\text{Probability} = \frac{32+13}{45+32+13+16+29}$$
$$= \frac{45}{135} = \frac{1}{3} = 1:3$$

29. **A.** Use the following formula for finding the area of a right triangle: $A = \frac{1}{2}bh$. The height of the triangle is 3 feet, and the base is 4 feet. Substitute that into the formula.

$$A = \frac{1}{2}(4)(3)$$
$$A = 6 \text{ ft}^2$$

30. **C.** The basic rental is $25 \times 2 = $50. For the mileage, multiply 200 miles times 15 cents. $200 \times 0.15 = $30. Combined the costs are $50 + $30 = $80.

PART 3. WORD KNOWLEDGE

1. **D.** *Hilarious* means "highly amusing." *Serious* has the opposite meaning and is clearly incorrect. The words *confusing* and *repellent* don't share the meaning, so choice D, *funny*, is the best answer.

2. **B.** To be *wary* means "to be guarded or mistrustful of something or someone." To mistrust something might make someone *nervous*, but that is not a synonym for *wary*. *Enthusiastic* and *happy* are not related to the meaning of *wary*, so choice B, *cautious*, is the correct answer.

3. **A.** A *tremor* is a shaking, quivering, or vibration. The words *pain*, *warmth*, and *object* are not related to the definition. The word that most closely relates to these is *trembling*. Choice A is the correct answer.

4. **C.** To be *ingenious* is to be smart and resourceful. The words *destructive*, *threatening*, and *sorrowful* do not seem like good matches. *Clever* is the word closest to the meaning of *ingenious*. Choice C is the correct answer.

5. **C.** *Illusory* means "misleading or false." *Real* is somewhat the opposite of this meaning, while the words *first* and *bright* are unrelated to the definition. *Deceptive*, choice C, is the correct answer.

6. **D.** To *thrive* means "to prosper or be successful." The words *move*, *separate*, and *think* do not seem to fit this meaning. *Flourish*, choice D, is the correct answer.

7. **A.** To *articulate* means "to speak clearly or to clarify." The words *change*, *contradict*, and *support* do not fit this meaning. *Explain*, choice A, is the word that most closely fits the meaning of *articulate*.

8. **C.** *Reticent* means "reserved, silent, or hesitant." The words *hopeful* and *hopeless* do not relate to the definition of *reticent*. *Encouraged* is somewhat the opposite in meaning. Choice C, *restrained*, is the word that most closely resembles the meaning of *reticent*.

9. **A.** *Cumbersome* means "unwieldy or awkward." That might make carrying packages *difficult*, but the best word to replace *cumbersome* is *clumsy*, choice A.

10. **B.** The prefix *co-* means "together." To be *coherent* means "to bring together ideas in a clear and logical way." The ideas "stick together" well. The words *misguided*, *mixed*, and *unfavorable* are not related to the definition of *coherent*. *Logical*, choice B, is the only answer that conveys this idea.

11. **A.** *Contentious* relates to strife or arguments—people in disagreement. The word *agreeable* suggests the opposite of that meaning and cannot be correct. Although contentious discussions might be *laughable* and even *interesting*, the best synonym for *contentious* is *quarrelsome*, choice A.

12. **B.** The prefix *con-* means "together or together with." To *converge* means "to come together at a point or place." The words *dissolve* and *slide* seem somewhat opposite of the concept of bringing together. The word *form* relates somewhat to the meaning of *converge*, but *join*, choice B, is the best answer.

13. **C.** To *invert* something means "to turn it over, turn it upside down, or reverse it." *Rebuke*, *lecture*, and *break* do not share the same meaning. *Overturn*, choice C, is the correct answer.

14. **C.** *Feigned* means "made up, faked, or invented." *Showed*, *disregarded*, and *lost* are not related to this idea. *Pretended*, choice C, is the best synonym for *feigned*.

15. **A.** To *refute* means "to prove something false or wrong." The word *support* conveys the opposite

meaning. *Direct* is also incorrect. To *question* the hypothesis seems to come close, but the best answer is choice A, *disprove*.

16. **B.** *Impetuous* means "hasty, spontaneous, or reckless." The words *natural*, *slow*, and *severe* are not related to the definition of *impetuous*. Only choice B, *impulsive*, conveys the correct meaning and is the best answer.

17. **D.** *Propensity* means "a leaning toward or a tendency to do something." *Aversion* conveys the opposite message as that word means "to move away from something." *Fault* and *awareness* are unrelated to the meaning of *propensity*. *Tendency*, choice D, is the best answer.

18. **B.** *Spurned* means "scorned, snubbed, or rebuffed." *Accepted* conveys the opposite meaning and cannot be correct. *Scattered* and *moved* do not relate to the definition of *spurned*. *Rejected*, choice B, is the correct answer.

19. **B.** To *hoard* means "to store or accumulate." The words *eat* and *share* do not relate to the meaning of *hoard*. In order to store or accumulate acorns, a squirrel probably does have to *hide* them, but the best answer is choice B, *stockpile*.

20. **C.** A *tempest* is a storm, so to be *tempestuous* certainly cannot mean *calm* or *friendly*. An *adversarial* relationship certainly can be tempestuous, but *stormy*, choice C, is the best synonym for *tempestuous*.

21. **A.** *Charade* means "a farce or fake." The words *nervousness*, *subtlety*, and *contamination* are not related to that idea. *Pretense*, choice A, is the best answer.

22. **A.** The prefix *in-* means "not." To be "not coherent" means to be illogical, disjointed, or not logically connected. The words *nasty*, *simple*, and *incorrect* are not related to the idea of being illogical. Choice A, *jumbled*, is the best answer.

23. **B.** To be *inhibited* means "to be repressed, held back, hindered, or restrained." The words *pushed*, *scared*, and *questioned* do not relate to this definition. *Prevented*, choice B, is the best answer.

24. **B.** *Levity* means "gaiety or frivolity." An atmosphere of levity would have laughter, jokes, and humorous comments. It would not be characterized by *seriousness*, *anger*, and *distrust*. *Lightheartedness*, choice B, is the best answer.

25. **A.** The prefix *mal-* means "bad, ill, or wrong." The words *comedy*, *heart*, and *strength* do not relate to this idea. A *malady* is an *illness*. Choice A is the correct answer.

26. **C.** *Unwieldy* means "hard to manage, awkward, or clumsy." *Colorful* does not relate to this idea. Though a *heavy* and *useless* umbrella may be unwieldy, the best answer is choice C, *cumbersome*.

27. **D.** *Transgression* means "a crime or offense." The words *misspelling* and *diversion* do not seem to relate to this definition. Although a transgression may be a *mistake*, choice D, *violation*, is the best synonym.

28. **B.** The prefix *pre-* means "before." *Preamble* means "a statement before or introduction to a longer narrative." It is certainly not an *ending* or an *interruption*. A preamble may well be a *summary*, but the word closest in meaning is choice B, *preface*.

29. **A.** *Artificial* means "not made by natural means; an imitation or a fake." *Creative*, *faithful*, and *late* do not relate to this idea. Choice A, *false*, is the best answer.

30. **C.** A *rebellion* is an uprising or upheaval. The words *celebration*, *parade*, and *meeting* do not share the same meaning of *uprising* or *upheaval*. Choice C, *revolt*, is the best answer.

31. **A.** The prefix *bene-* means "good or well." A *benefactor* is one who does something good or helpful for another. A *partner*, an *employer*, or a *counselor* might do good deeds for another person, but choice A, *supporter*, is the best answer.

32. **D.** *Secluded* means "shut off from others or isolated." The words *windy*, *rocky*, and *narrow* do not relate to this definition. *Hidden*, choice D, is the best answer.

33. **A.** The prefix *pre-* means "before." *Requisite* means "necessary or indispensable." Thus a *prerequisite* is a condition that needs to be fulfilled before another step or action can be taken. Choice A, *requirement*, is the best answer

34. **C.** A *blemish* is a spot, mark, or imperfection. The words *entry* and *inspiration* are clearly not correct answers. A blemish on the record could be in the form of a *notation*, but that word does not convey the meaning of being an imperfection. *Defect*, choice C, is the best answer.

35. **C.** *Hearsay* means "based on unsubstantiated statements or information, or on gossip." As a result, *facts*, *statements*, and *measurements* cannot be correct. In this case, the best answer is choice C, *rumor*.

PART 4. PARAGRAPH COMPREHENSION

1. **A.** In this passage the author's major intent is not to define obesity or point out obesity statistics or even the causes of obesity. The author spends most of the passage listing all the detrimental effects of obesity on health. Choice A is the correct answer.

2. **A.** The passage indicates that mass media might be a possible cause of obesity, but not part of the solution. Choice B is not the correct answer. The passage does not mention school vending machines, so choice C is not the correct answer. The passage suggests that personal choice is a factor in suggesting solutions, but it is not a solution by itself, so Choice D is not the correct answer. In several places, the passage indicates that knowledge of the facts by parents and children is the solution to the problem. Choice A is the correct answer.

3. **B.** The passage indicates that obesity is likely to be a problem in the future, so choice C cannot be correct. The passage does not suggest that exercise will eliminate obesity, so choice D cannot be correct. Although it is suggested that parents and schools have an influence on children's health (choice A), the best answer is stated directly in the passage—childhood obesity will likely continue to set records. Choice B is the correct answer.

4. **D.** The passage indicates that there are 300,000 deaths per year, not per day, from obesity-related causes, so choice A is not correct. Nothing in the passage suggests that obesity results in a society that does not exercise, although the passage does suggest that exercise is part of the solution. Choice B is not correct. Nothing indicates that obesity results in public admiration of cute children, so choice C is not correct. The passage specifically says that obesity is associated with $70 billion in healthcare costs, so choice D is the correct answer.

5. **A.** The passage says that "children soak up the wrong lessons not just from TV, but also from the one in three adults who is overweight." So choice A is the correct answer.

6. **B.** There is no indication that Pocahontas was a warrior (choice A). She certainly was a daughter (choice C), and she was only a child (choice D) when the English colonists first arrived. The passage, however, indicates that Pocahontas took various actions, such as promoting peace between the Powhatans and the English colonists and actually marrying one of the colonists, in hopes of bringing the colonists and Algonquians together. These actions made her a mediator, a person who tries to bring together people who disagree on some issue. Choice B is the correct answer.

7. **D.** The passage specifies that "Pocahontas" means "mischievous one." Choice D is the correct answer.

8. **B.** Pocahontas was young, but she is not described as a baby (choice A), as "superior" (choice C) or as "hateful" (choice D). The correct answer is "friendly," choice B.

9. **A.** There is no mention that Pocahontas married to have children (choice B), to increase her influence (choice C), or to ensure her status in her tribe (choice D). The correct answer is choice A, to promote peace.

10. **D.** Not much is said in the passage about John Rolfe. He is mentioned only as a colonist. Choice D is the correct answer.

11. **A.** Although Florida seceded from the United States (choice B), left the Union (choice C), and helped to feed the soldiers (choice D), these are not the major ideas in the passage. The passage indicates that we think of Florida as a sunny vacation state, but it has a history regarding the issues between the northern and southern states. This would lead to the best title: Sunny State—Confederate History. Choice A is the best answer.

12. **D.** There is no mention that issues about Florida's borders (choice A), the weather (choice C), or feeding soldiers (choice B) led to Florida's secession from the Union. These are all incorrect. The major sticking point between Florida and the Union was a disagreement about slavery. Choice D is the correct answer.

13. **D.** The passage indicates that 16,000 Floridians fought in the Civil War. The correct answer is choice D.

14. **D.** The passage states that 11 states left the Union. Choice D is the correct answer.

15. **B.** Although Florida did leave the Union, the passage does not state that it was the first to do so. Choice A is not correct. Although the passage states that there were some battles on the Florida coast, it does not state that most of the battles in the South took place there. Choice C is not correct. Clearly, Florida's position on government control and slavery were the cause of the beginning, not the end, of the Civil War. Choice D is not correct. The correct answer is B, that although Florida's contribution in total numbers was small, its percentage of soldiers among available men of military age was the highest of any Confederate state.

PART 5. MATHEMATICS KNOWLEDGE

1. **B.** Isolate the unknown on one side. Subtract 12 from both sides.

$$z = 24 - 12$$
$$z = 12$$

2. **A.** Perform operations in the parentheses first, then the exponents, and then the remaining operations.

$$16 + 3(-3)$$
$$16 + (-9) = 7$$

3. **B.** $30 = x\%$ of 90.

$$30 = x90$$

Solve for x.

$$x = \frac{30}{90}$$
$$x = \frac{1}{3} \text{ or } 33\%$$

4. **C.** When calculating the average or mean, add the numbers and then divide by the number of numbers. The sum of 14, 24, 12, 16, 34 and 104 is 204 divided by 6 which comes to 34.

5. **A.** When dividing fractions, invert and multiply. Then see if you can simplify the fractions.

$$\frac{1}{3} \div \frac{5}{6} = \frac{1}{3} \times \frac{6}{5} = \frac{6}{15} = \frac{2}{5}$$

6. **D.** In this problem you should note three things. First, x times x gives x^2. Second, 10×10 gives 100. Last, note that there are only two terms in the expression and that there is a minus sign. The minus sign tells you that the term in one factor needs to be a minus sign. This results in two factors: $(x - 10)(x + 10)$.

7. **A.** When subtracting, change the sign and add. In this problem, $3x^2 - 2y + 12$ is changed to $-3x^2 + 2y - 12$ and then added to the first term.

$$12x^2 + 6y - 3$$
$$-3x^2 + 2y - 12$$

Add the terms. This results in the correct answer of $9x^2 + 8y - 15$.

8. **A.** For this problem you want to isolate the x on one side of the equals sign. To do this, multiply each side by y, giving the correct answer: $\frac{yr}{j} = x$.

9. **D.** Set each equation to equal zero. Next, arrange the equations so that when one is subtracted from or added to the other, one of the terms results in a zero and drops out of the result. Next, solve for the remaining unknown. In this problem,

$$3a + 4b = 12$$
$$2a + 2b = 15$$

Set the equations to zero:

$$3a + 4b - 12 = 0$$
$$2a + 2b - 15 = 0$$

Note that neither adding nor subtracting will eliminate a term, but if you multiply one equation by an appropriate term to make two terms equal, you can add or subtract as necessary to eliminate a term. For this problem, if you multiply the second equation by -2 and then add the equations, the b term can be eliminated.

$$3a + 4b - 12 = 0$$
$$-2(2a + 2b - 15) = 0$$

$$3a + 4b - 12 = 0$$
$$-4a - 4b + 30 = 0$$

Add the two equations:

$$-a + 18 = 0$$
$$-a = -18$$
$$a = 18$$

Substitute the value of a into one of the original equations.

$$2(18) + 2b - 15 = 0$$
$$36 + 2b - 15 = 0$$
$$21 + 2b = 0$$
$$2b = -21$$
$$b = -10.5$$

The correct answer is choice D, $a = 18$, $b = -10.5$.

10. **C.** To divide numbers with exponents, subtract the exponents. In this problem, subtract 7 from 4 giving -3 as the exponent for x, and 2 from 6, giving 4 as the exponent for y. The term thus becomes $x^{-3} y^4$. This also can be written as $\frac{y^4}{x^3}$, which is choice C.

11. **D.** Factor this equation, resulting in $(3g + 1)$ $(g + 1)$. Set each factor to equal zero and solve for g.

$$3g = -1; \; g = -\frac{1}{3}$$
$$g = -1$$

The correct answer is $g = -\frac{1}{3}$; $g = -1$.

12. **B.** To multiply fractions, multiply the numerators and denominators. Simplify where possible.

$$\frac{6}{x+1} \times \frac{3x+3}{5}$$
$$= \frac{18x+18}{5x+5}$$

Factor this fraction to get:

$$\frac{18\,\cancel{(x+1)}}{5\,\cancel{(x+1)}}$$

To simplify, cancel the $x + 1$ terms, leaving $\frac{18}{5}$ or $3\frac{3}{5}$.

13. **D.** To divide fractions, invert the second term and multiply. Simplify where possible.

$$\frac{5}{x+1} \div \frac{6}{3x+3} \text{ becomes } \frac{5}{x+1} \times \frac{3x+3}{6}.$$

Multiply the numerators and denominators.

$$\frac{15x+15}{6x+6}$$

Simplify by factoring.

$$\frac{15\,\cancel{(x+1)}}{6\,\cancel{(x+1)}}$$

Simplify by canceling.

$$\frac{15}{6} = \frac{5}{2} = 2\frac{1}{2}$$

14. **D.** The square root is the number that, when multiplied by itself, results in the original number. In this case, $11 \times 11 = 121$, so 11 is the correct answer.

15. **C.** In this type of problem, where two fractions are separated by an equals sign, you can cross multiply and then solve for the variable of interest. Cross multiply to get $sy = vt$. Solving for y gives $\frac{vt}{s}$, the correct answer.

16. **A.** A hexagon has six sides, so A is the correct answer.

17. **C.** A parallelogram has two equal lengths and two equal widths. The perimeter is the sum of the widths and lengths, or $2(l) + 2(w)$. In this problem, the perimeter is 16 miles.

18. **C.** The hundredths place is two places to the right of the decimal point. Underline the hundredths place. If the number to the right of it is less than 5, keep the number in that place the same. If it is 5 or greater, increase the number in the hundredths place by one. In this problem, the number to the right of the hundredths place is 4 so the number is rounded to 1,478.96, which is the correct answer.

19. **B.** A right triangle has one angle that measures 90°. If a second angle measures 35°, that accounts for 125°. Subtracting that total from 180° (the total number of degrees in a triangle) gives the result of 55°.

20. **C.** In this problem, information on angles 1 and 2 is irrelevant. Since you know that $\angle 3$ is a right angle, $\angle 4$ must be $180° - 90°$ or 90°, another right angle.

21. **C.** $\angle C$ is a right angle, so you can employ the Pythagorean Theorem $a^2 + b^2 = c^2$ to get your answer. In this problem, you know that side c, the side opposite the right angle, has a length of 7. $c = 7$ and $c^2 = 49$. You also know that one other side has a length of 5.

$$a^2 + 5^2 = 7^2$$
$$a^2 + 25 = 49.$$

Solve for a:

$$a^2 = 49 - 25$$
$$a^2 = 24$$
$$a = \sqrt{24} \text{ in.}$$

22. **D.** The area of a rectangle is length × width. In the figure, the length is 27 cm, and the width is 9 cm. Multiplying 27×9 gives the correct answer of 243 cm².

23. **C.** The formula for the area of a circle is πr^2. You are given the radius of 6 meters. Substituting the information into the formula gives $3.14\,(6)^2$, or 113.04 m².

24. **C.** 1% is the equivalent of 0.01.

$$0.01 \times 5,000 = 50$$

25. **D.** The volume of a sphere is found by using the formula $\frac{4}{3}\pi r^3$. Substituting the information into the formula gives $\frac{4}{3}(3.14)(3)^3$ or $4 \times 3.14 \times 27 \div 3$, making the correct answer 113.04 m^3.

PART 6. ELECTRONICS INFORMATION

1. **A.** An electric motor makes a short but heavy current demand while starting. Current is measured in amperes.

2. **B.** Capacitors store current.

3. **B.** Current = volts/resistance = 480/24 = 20 amperes.

4. **D.** Voltage measures electrical "pressure."

5. **C.** To measure current, the meter must become part of the circuit, as it is at point A.

6. **A.** This is the standard symbol for a transformer.

7. **D.** Watts = amperes × volts = 120 × 12 = 1,440 watts.

8. **B.** Watts = volts × amperes. 1,800 = 120 × amperes. Amperes = 1,800/120 = 15 amperes.

9. **C.** An electrical wire is usually a copper conductor wrapped with a plastic insulator.

10. **A.** Corrosion (oxidation) is usually a good insulator. By resisting corrosion, gold ensures a low-resistance contact.

11. **B.** A transistor can slow or stop current.

12. **D.** Current is the flow of electrons, and current flows through a conductor.

13. **D.** Under certain conditions, lead-acid batteries generate hydrogen gas, which is explosive. Keep cigarettes and sparks away from these batteries!

14. **A.** In the metric system, "kilo" means 1,000, so 1 kilowatt hour translates into 1,000 watt hours, or 1,000 watts for 1 hour.

15. **C.** Wire gauge is sized backwards; the higher the gauge, the smaller the diameter.

16. **D.** In a series circuit like this, total resistance is the sum of the individual resistances. 400 + 400 + 300 = 1,100.

17. **C.** In a parallel circuit like this, $1/R_{total} = 1/R_1 + 1/R_2 + 1/R_3 = 1/400 + 1/400 + 1/400 = 3/400$. That equals $1/R_{total}$, so invert: 400/3 = 133.3 ohms.

18. **A.** The change in voltage is determined by the ratio of windings. If the output side has fewer windings, the transformer reduces the voltage.

19. **D.** An electromagnet moves the clapper that bangs against the bell in a doorbell (and in older telephones).

20. **B.** The polarity of alternating current goes through 60 complete cycles per second in 60-hertz current.

PART 7. AUTO AND SHOP INFORMATION

1. **C.** Knocking or "pinging" usually means that the octane of your gasoline is too low. The noise indicates that the fuel-air mixture is igniting too soon inside the cylinders.

2. **B.** Water expands as it freezes, and that could destroy the engine block and cylinder head.

3. **A.** Brake problems reduce stopping ability. Why are the other answers incorrect? Choice B: it's vital to check brake problems right away, not when it's convenient. Choices C and D: these can result from brake problems, but are less complete answers than choice A.

4. **D.** Front tire life is lower with front-wheel drive because the wheels are driving, steering,

and braking. However, front-wheel drive pulls the car in the direction you steer, and it is especially helpful in slippery conditions. Because the engine is above the driving wheels, the wheels get better traction. Because there is no driveshaft, there is more room in the interior.

5. **B.** The primary job of oil is to reduce friction. More friction also increases noise and temperature, but without oil, an engine would barely rotate at all.

6. **D.** Correct valve operation helps an engine run smoothly, with maximum power.

7. **C.** Torque, not horsepower, is what accelerates a vehicle, and so it's the most likely problem. Torque is defined as a twisting force, and it is measured in foot-pounds; one pound of force acting through one foot of rotary motion.

8. **C.** Because a heavier car needs more energy, it also needs more gasoline, which is its source of energy.

9. **D.** Batteries lose some of their power when they get cold, and high-viscosity oil gets thick in winter, requiring more force to turn the engine over. Choice A: starter motor, may be a problem, but either choice B or choice C is much more likely to be the cause.

10. **C.** When jump-starting a car, the battery cables must be connected positive to positive, and negative to negative. Why are the other answers incorrect? Choice A: the ground cable should be connected to the engine block or the ground terminal on the battery. Choice B: battery caps should remain in place. Choice D: the transmission should be in neutral or park.

11. **D.** Problems with the synchronizers or clutch adjustment can cause poor shifting. Choice C is incorrect: a torque converter is found in automatic, not manual, transmissions.

12. **D.** Problems with lubrication, cooling, or main bearings can all cause an engine to seize.

13. **A.** Both round and pan heads are flat on the bottom, so they will securely fasten a flat plate to a joist or other flat piece of wood. Why are the other answers incorrect? Choice B: a Phillips head is not necessarily flat on the bottom. Choice C: a flat head screw is cone-shaped on the bottom and would not hold the plate securely. Choice D: as explained above, the best screw head will be flat on the bottom.

14. **D.** The tool shown is a keyhole saw.

15. **C.** Sanding smoothes the wood, priming prevents it from absorbing too much paint, sanding again smoothes the primer, making it ready for painting.

16. **B.** Why are the other answers incorrect? Choice A: it's impossible to make vertical and horizontal joints occur on top of studs. Choice C: joints cannot overlap. D: joints are needed in any wall larger than one sheet of drywall.

17. **D.** Sanding drywall creates lots of dust. Why are the other answers incorrect? Choice A: a belt sander is much too aggressive for drywall. Choice B: medium sandpaper would gouge drywall; use fine paper. Choice C: drywall has no grain.

18. **D.** The tool shown is a combination wrench.

19. **D.** Metal always heats quickly on an electric grinder. Why are the other answers incorrect? Choice A: a fine-grained wheel would be acceptable if it's rated at 4,500 rpm. Choice B: it is *unsafe* to use a 3,000 rpm wheel on a 4,500 rpm grinder. Choice C: use water only on a grinder designed for water cooling.

20. **A.** A wire brush will remove paint from metal, remove rust, and clean bolt threads. It will not clean a wood deck, prepare drywall for painting, clean threads inside a nut, or dull paint before repainting.

21. **B.** The tool shown is best used for clamping.

22. **B.** Almost all sheets of plywood, drywall, and oriented-strand board are 4 feet by 8 feet. The thickness can vary.

23. **A.** Galvanizing is a zinc coating designed to prevent rusting (oxidation) on steel. Why are the other answers incorrect? Galvanizing does not smooth, harden, or sharpen steel.

24. **C.** A door hinge pin and auto axle both hold rotating objects in place.

25. **A.** A rasp, a plane, and sandpaper are all used to smooth wood surfaces.

PART 8. MECHANICAL COMPREHENSION

1. **C.** 480/120 = 4 minutes until drained. 4 × 60 = 240 seconds.

2. **C.** MA = load/effort = 8/2 = 4.

3. **A.** When a gas is compressed, it warms up because the energy that runs the pump is converted into heat.

4. **B.** Compare the areas of the bases of the cylinders to find mechanical advantage of a hydraulic system. Cylinder base area = $\pi \times$ radius^2. So the area of two cylinders is proportional to the square of their radii (plural of radius). $8^2 = 64$, $4^2 = 16$. 64/16 = 4.

5. **C.** For two gears to mesh properly, they must have teeth that are the same size. The gears can be of different sizes, they can rotate at different speeds, and they can be made of different materials.

6. **D.** If the screw has a pitch of ¼ inch, then with 4 complete turns of the screwdriver it will move 4 × ¼ = 1 inch. After 10 complete turns it will have moved 10 × ¼ = 10/4 = 2¼ = 2½ inches.

7. **C.** Gear A is turning clockwise. That means that gear B is turning counterclockwise. Gears C and D turn clockwise, the same direction as gear A. Gear E turns counterclockwise, the same as gear B.

8. **C.** Of the support brackets shown, choice C, which creates a triangle with the vertical wall, provides the most secure support.

9. **A.** Of the patterns shown, choice A is the only one that, when folded on the dotted lines, will make a three-sided pyramid.

10. **D.** Levers, inclined planes, and pulleys are all simple machines.

11. **D.** To find the water pressure in lb/ft^2, first find the area of the bottom of the tank: $2 \times 6 = 12$ ft^2. Then divide the total weight of the water by the area of the bottom: $600 \div 12 = 50$ lb/ft.^{2}

12. **B.** If the crank makes 1/2 turn, the piston will move up to the top of the cylinder.

13. **D.** The ramp (inclined plane) is a simple machine. To calculate its mechanical advantage, divide the length by the height: $30 \div 3 = 10$. To find how much effort is needed, divide the weight of the drum by the mechanical advantage: $120 \div 10 = 12$ lb of effort.

14. **B.** Metal conducts heat better than does wood or plastic, so it would feel hottest.

15. **A.** The gear is rotating at a speed of 150 rpm. At a ratio of 6:1, the pinion makes 6 revolutions for each revolution of the gear. So the speed of the pinion is $150 \times 6 = 900$ rpm.

16. **C.** A spring is a device that can be twisted or stretched by some force applied to it, and it will resume its original shape when the force is released. Of the choices, the only one that can be made to act in this manner is choice C, steel.

17. **A.** The system has 2 supporting strands, so MA = 2.

18. **B.** The larger pulley in a system will rotate slower than the smaller one, but both pulleys will rotate in the same direction.

19. **B.** A longer handle allows you to move the hammer head faster, producing more striking force.

20. **C.** Sheet metal screws must cut threads in metal, so they must be made of hard steel. They may be longer or shorter than wood screws.

21. **C.** If water is flowing into the tank at a rate of 5 gal/sec, then the amount flowing in per minute is $5 \times 60 = 300$ gallons. The amount flowing out per minute is 100 gallons, so the net gain per minute is $300 - 100 = 200$ gallons. In 2 minutes, the tank will gain 400 gallons more than the 100 gallons already present, so the total amount in the tank after 2 minutes will be $400 + 100 = 500$ gallons.

22. **A.** Point A, located on the outside of the wheel, travels farther than point B each time the wheel makes a complete turn.

23. **B.** In gear systems with an idler gear, you can discount the idler gear and just look at the number of teeth on the drive gear (A) and the driven gear (C). Here, the ratio is 18 to 24, or 3 to 4. So the driven gear will be rotating slower than the drive gear. $3/4 \times 200 = 150$.

24. **C.** The same quantity of water must be flowing past every point in the system, but the water must speed up through the smaller pipe. Fluid pressure falls when velocity increases.

25. **B.** Gear X has 60 teeth and gear Y has 12 teeth. $60 \div 12 = 5$, so for each complete rotation by gear X, gear Y makes 5 rotations.

PART 9. ASSEMBLING OBJECTS

1. **B.** The original figure has four objects, while choices A and C have five. Look for the object shaped like a large comma. Choice D does not have this object. Choice B is the correct answer.

2. **A.** The original figure has three objects, while choice C has four and choice D has only two. Look for the long thin rectangle. It is not present in choice B (there is a longer parallelogram there). Choice A is the correct answer.

3. **A.** The original figure has five objects, while choices B and D have six. Look for the small square. There is no square in choice C. Choice A is the correct answer.

4. **C.** The original figure has four objects, while choice A has five. Look for the largest piece. Choice B has a mirror image of this piece, so eliminate B. Look for the piece that looks like a right triangle with the right angle rounded off. Choice D has an actual right triangle instead. Choice C is the correct answer.

5. **C.** The original figure has three objects, while choice A has only two. Look for the pair of identical triangles. Choice B has only one triangle. Choice D has a rectangle rather than a parallelogram. Choice C is the correct answer.

6. **B.** The original figure has five objects, while choice A has six. Look for the wedge shape at the top middle of the original box. Choices C and D have wedges that are much too large. Choice B is the correct answer.

7 **B.** The original figure has three objects, while choice C has only two. Look for the moon shape. Choice A does not have it. Look for the triangle. Choice D does not have it. Choice B is the correct answer.

8. **A.** The original figure has four objects, while choice B has five. Look for the object shaped like a segment of a circle. Choice C does not have it. Look at the large shape on the left in the original. It is too small in choice D. Choice A is the correct answer.

9. **C.** The original figure has three objects and choice D has four, so eliminate D. Look for the distinctive object at the left. Choice A does not have it. Look for the circle. Choice B has an oval instead. Choice C is the correct answer.

10. **D.** The original figure contains four objects. Choice B has five, so eliminate it. Look for the distinctive shape on the left of the original figure. Choices A and C do not have that shape. Choice D is the correct answer.

11. **C.** The original figure has three objects, while choice A has four and choice D has two. Choice B has a square that is much larger than the original. Choice C is the correct answer.

12. **A.** The original figure has four objects, while choice B has only three. Look for the most distinctive object: the top left object looks like a parallelogram but with a curved right side. Choice D has a similar object, but it does not have this curved side. That leaves choices A and C. Look for the triangle. The one in choice C may be too large, but if you can't tell, look at the two quadrilaterals. In choice C, they are not the same shapes. Choice A is the correct answer.

13. **D.** The original figure contains three objects. Choice A has two and choice C has four, so eliminate them. Look for the parallelogram. Choice B does not have a parallelogram. Choice D is the correct answer.

14. **A.** The original figure has three objects, while choice D has four. None of the objects are really distinctive, but choose one to look for first. The isosceles triangle at the top left might be a good choice. Choice B does not have it. Look for the pair of quadrilaterals. Choice C has only triangles. Choice A is the correct answer.

15. **A.** The original figure has four objects, while choice B has five. Look for the most distinctive object: the one that looks like the base of a column. Choice C does not have it and in choice D it is much too tall. Choice A is the correct answer.

16. **D.** The original figure has three objects and choice B only has two, so eliminate B. Look for the most distinctive object—perhaps the one that looks like a banana. Choices A and C do not have that object. Choice D is the correct answer.

17. **B.** The original figure has four objects and choice D has three, so eliminate D. Look for the most distinctive object—perhaps the one at the lower left that looks like a pointed boot. Choice C does not have an object like that. There is a vaguely similar object in choice A, but it is not the same pointed-boot shape. Choice B is the correct answer.

18. **D.** Point A is in the center of the bottom left base of the first object in its original orientation. Choices A, B, and C do not connect the first object at that point. Choice D is the correct answer.

19. **C.** Point A is at the top right corner in the original orientation. In choice A this point is at the bottom right corner. Point B is at the bottom left corner in the original orientation. In choice B it is at the pointed corner. In choice D it is not at a corner at all. Choice C is the correct answer.

20. **D.** In this set of objects, the larger object with point B is more distinctive, so start with that one. The object looks like the head of a duck (upside down) with point B as the eye. Choices A and C do not have point B at this spot. Choice B has point B in the correct spot, but the object is a mirror image of the original, so eliminate it. Choice D is the correct answer.

21. **C.** The first object looks like a mitten with point A at the thumb. Choices A and B do not have point A at the correct spot. Point B is at the top left of the second object in its original orientation. In choice D, point B is at the bottom right of the object. Choice C is the correct answer.

22. **D.** In this set of objects, the object on bottom with point B is more distinctive, so start with that one. Point B is at the sharp tip of this object. Choice A does not connect at that point. The object on top has point A at the sharpest point as well. Choices B and C do not connect at that point. Choice D is the correct answer.

23. **B.** Point A is at the middle of the base of the first object (in its original orientation). Choice D places point A on the top side of the object. Picture the second object sitting on the flat base. In this orientation, point B is located in the center of the bottom right corner, not on the edge, but within the object. Choice A has point B located in the center of the bottom left corner. Choice C has point B located in the center of the object (plus the object with point A is shown in mirror image). Choice B is the correct answer.

24. **C.** Point A is at the pointed tip of the first object. Choice A does not connect at that point. Point B is at the pointed outside corner of the second object. Choice B has point B at the inside corner. Choice D has point B on one leg of the object. Choice C is the correct answer.

25. **D.** Point A is at the sharpest of the three corners. Choices A and C do not connect at that point. If you orient the second object with the flat base on the bottom, then point B is at the left bottom corner. Choice B has point B at the bottom right corner. Choice D is the correct answer.

ASVAB PRACTICE TEST FORM 3

Try to take this practice test under actual test conditions. Find a quiet place to work and set aside a period of approximately 2½ hours when you will not be disturbed. Work on only one section at a time, and use your watch or a timer to keep track of the time limits for each section. Mark your answers on the answer sheet, just as you will when you take the real exam.

At the end of the test, you'll find an answer key and explanations for every question. After you check your answers against the key, you can complete a chart that will show you how you did on the test and what test topics you might need to study more. Then review the explanations, paying particular attention to the ones for the questions that you answered incorrectly.

GENERAL DIRECTIONS

IF YOU ARE TAKING THE PAPER AND PENCIL VERSION OF THE ASVAB, THE TEST ADMINISTRATOR WILL READ THE FOLLOWING ALOUD TO YOU:

DO NOT WRITE YOUR NAME OR MAKE ANY MARKS in this booklet. Mark your answers on the separate answer sheet. Use the scratch paper which was given to you for any figuring you need to do. Return this scratch paper with your other papers when you finish the test.

If you need another pencil while taking this test, hold your pencil above your head. A proctor will bring you another one.

This booklet contains 9 tests. Each test has its own instructions and time limit. When you finish a test, you may check your work in that test ONLY. Do not go on to the next test until the examiner tells you to do so. Do not turn back to a previous test at any time.

For each question, be sure to pick the BEST ONE of the possible answers listed. Each test has its own instructions and time limit. When you have decided which one of the choices given is the best answer to the question, blacken the space on your answer sheet that has the same number and letter as your choice. Mark only in the answer space. BE CAREFUL NOT TO MAKE ANY STRAY MARKS ON YOUR ANSWER SHEET. Each test has a separate section on the answer sheet. Be sure you mark your answers for each test in the section that belongs to that test.

Here is an example of correct marking on an answer sheet.

S1. A triangle has

    A. 2 sides

    B. 3 sides

    C. 4 sides

    D. 5 sides

PRACTICE

S1 Ⓐ ● Ⓒ Ⓓ

S2 Ⓐ Ⓑ Ⓒ Ⓓ

S3 Ⓐ Ⓑ Ⓒ Ⓓ

The correct answer to Sample Question S1 is B.

Next to the item, note how space B opposite number S1 has been blackened. Your marks should look just like this and be placed in the space with the same number and letter as the correct answer to the question. Remember, there is only ONE BEST ANSWER for each question. If you are not sure of the answer, make the BEST GUESS you can. If you want to change your answer, COMPLETELY ERASE your first answer mark.

Answer as many questions as possible. Do not spend too much time on any one question. Work QUICKLY, but work ACCURATELY. DO NOT TURN THE PAGE UNTIL TOLD TO DO SO. Are there any questions?

ASVAB PRACTICE TEST FORM 3

ANSWER SHEET

ANSWER SHEET   PAGE 3
ARMED SERVICES VOCATIONAL
APTITUDE BATTERY

SSN

MI

FIRST

LAST

PART 9-AO

PART 8-MC

PART 7-AS

PART 6-EI

PART 5-MK

PART 4-PC

PART 3-WK

PART 2-AR

PART 1-GS

PRACTICE
S1
S2
S3

DD FORM 1304-5AS   FOR OFFICIAL USE ONLY (WHEN COMPLETED)

PART 1. GENERAL SCIENCE

THE TEST ADMINISTRATOR WILL READ THE FOLLOWING ALOUD TO YOU:

Turn to Part 1 and read the directions for General Science silently while I read them aloud.

This test has questions about science. Pick the BEST answer for each question and then blacken the space on your separate answer sheet that has the same number and letter as your choice. Here are three practice questions.

S1. A rose is a kind of
   A. animal.
   B. bird.
   C. flower.
   D. fish.

S2. A cat is a
   A. plant.
   B. mammal.
   C. reptile.
   D. mineral.

S3. The earth revolves around the
   A. sun.
   B. moon.
   C. meteorite.
   D. Mars.

Now look at the section of your answer sheet labeled "PRACTICE." Notice that answer space C has been marked for question S1. Now do practice questions S2 and S3 by yourself. Find the correct answer to the question, then mark the space on your answer sheet that has the same letter as the answer you picked. Do this now.

You should have marked B for question S2 and A for question S3. If you make any mistakes, erase your mark carefully and blacken the correct answer space. Do this now.

Your score on this test will be based on the number of questions you answer correctly. You should try to answer every question. If you finish before time is called, go back and check your work in this part ONLY. Now find the section of your answer sheet that is marked PART 1. When you are told to begin, start with question number 1 in Part 1 of your test booklet and answer space number 1 in Part 1 on you separate answer sheet. DO NOT TURN THE PAGE UNTIL TOLD TO DO SO. This part has 25 questions in it. You will have 11 minutes to complete it. Most of you should finish in this amount of time. Are there any questions?

Turn the page and begin.

1. The part of a cell that determines what enters and exits the cell is called the
   A. cell membrane.
   B. vacuoles.
   C. mitochondria.
   D. chlorophyll.

2. Roses, apple trees, and other plants that produce flowers are called
   A. angiosperms.
   B. annuals.
   C. deciduous.
   D. vascular.

3. A stalk of green celery has been placed in a glass with 2 inches of water with purple food coloring. Two hours later parts of the stalk and leaves of the celery are purple. Which of the following plant systems does this situation demonstrate?
   A. Vascular system
   B. Reproductive system
   C. Hereditary system
   D. Lymphatic system

4. Which of the following terms best represents a whale?
   A. Exoskeleton, cold-blooded
   B. Vertebrate, mammal
   C. Warm-blooded, invertebrate
   D. Carnivore, invertebrate

5. Which of the following is classified as a mammal?
   A. Fish
   B. Snake
   C. Crocodile
   D. Ape

6. Which of the following is considered to be a food producer?
   A. Frog
   B. Tree
   C. Parrot
   D. Manatee

7. The joints in bones are held together by which of the following?
   A. Cartilage
   B. Ligaments
   C. Hinges
   D. Marrow

8. Which of the following is the largest organ in your body?
   A. Skin
   B. Liver
   C. Kidney
   D. Lymph

9. Which of the following nutrients contain the most energy?
   A. Carbohydrates
   B. Proteins
   C. Minerals
   D. Fats

10. Most of your blood is made up of which of the following?
    A. Plasma
    B. White blood cells
    C. Red blood cells
    D. Platelets

11. Which part of your ear is responsible for your balance?
    A. Outer ear
    B. Middle ear
    C. Inner ear
    D. Olfactory membrane

12. Which of the following represents the basic difference between mitosis and meiosis?
    A. Cells divide twice as fast in mitosis as in meiosis.
    B. In mitosis each cell produced has 46 chromosomes, but in meiosis each cell produced has only 23 chromosomes.
    C. More nutrients are produced in mitosis than in meiosis.
    D. Mitosis occurs only with sexual reproduction, while meiosis can occur with sexual or asexual reproduction.

13. Which of the following characteristics describe ultraviolet radiation as compared to visible light?
    A. Less energy; lower frequency
    B. More energy; lower frequency
    C. Less energy; higher frequency
    D. More energy; higher frequency

14. A candle burns for 2 hours. What happens to the total mass as a result of the burning?
    A. It decreases.
    B. It increases.
    C. It stays the same.
    D. It first decreases and then increases.

15. Which of the following layers of Earth takes up the least amount of Earth's volume?
    A. Crust
    B. Mantle
    C. Lithosphere
    D. Core

16. Tectonic plates that are moving away from one another create which of the following features?
    A. Rifts
    B. Ridges
    C. Currents
    D. Land bridges

17. Sinking water that forms density currents is likely to have which of the following characteristics?
    A. Warm temperature and many animal inhabitants
    B. Swift-moving surface currents
    C. Cold temperatures and high salt content
    D. A high concentration of dissolved gases

18. The tilt of Earth's axis as the planet orbits around the sun causes which of the following?
    A. Tides
    B. Day and night
    C. Bulging of Earth at the equator
    D. Seasons

19. What causes the same side of the moon to always face Earth?
    A. Earth's gravitational pull on the moon
    B. The fast rotation of Earth in comparison to the moon
    C. The phases of the moon in comparison to the sun
    D. The friction of the moon in space

20. Which of the following elements is not naturally a gas at room temperature?
    A. Sulfur
    B. Oxygen
    C. Neon
    D. Fluorine

21. Most of Earth's weather takes place in which of the following atmospheric zones?
    A. Troposphere
    B. Stratosphere
    C. Thermosphere
    D. Exosphere

22. Which layer in the atmosphere reflects radio waves and allows long-distance communication on Earth?
    A. Troposphere
    B. Stratosphere
    C. Thermosphere
    D. Ionosphere

23. Which of the following is not an agent of erosion?
    A. Freezing and thawing
    B. Rivers
    C. Lava flows
    D. Lichen and mosses

24. The sun's energy comes from which of the following processes?
    A. Sunspot formation
    B. Magnetic fields
    C. Fusion of hydrogen to make helium
    D. Prominences that eject highly charged solar particles

25. When the nucleus of an atom gives up a particle and its energy in order to become more stable, the process is called which of the following?
    A. Ionization
    B. Refraction
    C. Radioactive decay
    D. Half-life

STOP! DO NOT TURN THIS PAGE UNTIL TIME IS UP FOR THIS TEST. IF YOU FINISH BEFORE TIME IS UP, CHECK OVER YOUR WORK ON THIS TEST ONLY.

PART 2. ARITHMETIC REASONING

THE TEST ADMINISTRATOR WILL READ THE FOLLOWING ALOUD TO YOU:

Turn to Part 2 and read the directions for Arithmetic Reasoning silently while I read them aloud.

This is a test of arithmetic word problems. Each question is followed by four possible answers. Decide which answer is CORRECT, and then blacken the space on your answer sheet that has the same number and letter as your choice. Use your scratch paper for any figuring you wish to do.

Here is a sample question. DO NOT MARK your answer sheet for this or any further sample questions.

S1. A student buys a sandwich for 80 cents, milk for 20 cents, and pie for 30 cents. How much did the meal cost?

A. $1.00
B. $1.20
C. $1.30
D. $1.40

The total cost is $1.30; therefore, C is the right answer. Your score on this test will be based on the number of question you answer correctly. You should try to answer every question. DO NOT SPEND TOO MUCH TIME on any one question. If you finish before time is called, go back and check your work in this part ONLY.

Now find the section of your answer sheet that is marked PART 2. When you are told to begin, start with question number 1 in Part 2 of your test booklet and answer space number 1 in Part 2 on your separate answer sheet.

DO NOT TURN THIS PAGE UNTIL TOLD TO DO SO. You will have 36 minutes for the 30 questions. Are there any questions?

Begin.

1. Len bought several books for school at $25.16, $28.99, $35.15, $42.27, and $62.12. How much did Len spend?
   A. $147.16
   B. $154.29
   C. $193.69
   D. $199.39

2. Marty is driving from Nashville, TN, to Mobile, AL. The distance is 527 miles. If Marty drives 111 miles on Monday, 67 miles on Tuesday, and 211 miles on Wednesday, how many miles must he drive if he wants to reach Nashville on Thursday?
   A. 28 miles
   B. 118 miles
   C. 138 miles
   D. 168 miles

3. Gene was up to bat 72 times during the baseball season. If he got 54 hits, what percent of the time was he successful?
   A. 56%
   B. 75%
   C. 79%
   D. 81%

4. Phil is monitoring his calorie consumption. On Monday he eats meals totaling 1,700 calories. On Tuesday he eats meals totaling 3,000 calories. On Wednesday he eats meals totaling 2,500 calories, and on Thursday his meals total 3,200 calories. What is his average calorie consumption per day?
   A. 1,600 calories
   B. 1,885 calories
   C. 2,100 calories
   D. 2,600 calories

5. If there are 450 members of a sports club and 60 percent are males, how many members are males?
   A. 210
   B. 225
   C. 255
   D. 270

6. On a map of the United States, 1 inch represents a distance of 50 miles. If the distance between New Town and Old Town is 450 miles, how far apart are they on the map?
   A. 2.5 inches
   B. 8.3 inches
   C. 9 inches
   D. 12 inches

7. Phil bought two hamburgers and a milk shake for $10.30. Janice bought three hamburgers and a milk shake for $14.80. What is the cost of the two milk shakes?
   A. $1.30
   B. $1.45
   C. $2.60
   D. $4.50

8. A box contains 35 white balls, 75 red balls, and 45 black balls. If Nikki picks out a ball at random, what is the probability that the ball will be white or black?
   A. $\frac{5}{12}$
   B. $\frac{6}{11}$
   C. $\frac{16}{31}$
   D. $\frac{18}{47}$

9. Jose bought a $3,000 savings bond that earns 5 percent compounded interest per year. How much will his bond be worth after 3 years?
   A. $3,150.00
   B. $3,307.50
   C. $3,348.88
   D. $3,472.88

10. After five science tests, Sonya's average score is 89. If she gets a 95 on the sixth test, what is her new average?
    A. 89.50
    B. 89.90
    C. 90.00
    D. 90.50

11. A pasta recipe calls for $\frac{2}{3}$ cup of tomato paste for each batch of lasagna. If Victor has 18 cups of tomato paste, how many batches of lasagna can he make?
    A. 12
    B. 21
    C. 26
    D. 27

12. Natalie wants to carpet her living room floor. The floor measures 12 feet by 24 feet. How many square yards of carpeting must she purchase?
    A. 12
    B. 22
    C. 24
    D. 32

13. Joanne earns $3,000 per month at her job at the department store. If her taxes are 28 percent of her pay, what is her monthly take-home pay?
    A. $2,160
    B. $2,280
    C. $2,370
    D. $2,780

14. On his 16th birthday Gene was 60 inches tall. On his 19th birthday he was 69 inches tall. What percent increase in height did Gene experience in the three years from his 16th to his 19th birthday?
    A. 10%
    B. 12%
    C. 13%
    D. 15%

15. Patrick took a trip on his motorcycle. He drove at a steady speed of 50 mph, and the trip took him 3 hours. How long would the trip have taken if his speed was 40 mph?
    A. 3.75 hr
    B. 4.00 hr
    C. 4.25 hr
    D. 4.45 hr

16. Troy is building a patio. He will make it 360 inches by 480 inches. If one bag of cement makes 16 sq feet of patio, how many bags will Troy need to complete the job?
    A. 32.5 bags
    B. 75 bags
    C. 95 bags
    D. 97.5 bags

17. A sprinkler sprays water in a circular region with a radius of 20 feet. What area can it cover?
    A. 1,256 ft²
    B. 1,596 ft²
    C. 1,996 ft²
    D. 2,056 ft²

18. Suzie is twice as old as Will, plus 4 years. If Will is 9, how old is Suzie?
    A. 19
    B. 21
    C. 22
    D. 29

19. Barry is saving quarters in a jar so that he can buy a computer. The computer costs $950. How many quarters must Barry save in order to purchase the computer?
    A. 1,200
    B. 3,800
    C. 4,200
    D. 4,276

20. Suzie has a piece of ribbon 6 yards long. She needs to cut the ribbon into lengths of 1½ feet. How many pieces will she be able to cut?
    A. 10
    B. 11
    C. 12
    D. 13

21. Randy is training to cycle in a 15-kilometer race. His training program starts at cycling 5 kilometers per day for the first week and increases that amount by 20 percent each week. How many kilometers will he be cycling per day in the fourth week?
    A. 7.20 km
    B. 8.64 km
    C. 9.33 km
    D. 9.98 km

22. A mother is sending a box of brownies to her daughter. The box is 6 inches high, 6 inches wide, and 15 inches long. If each brownie is 2 inches wide, ½ inch high, and 3 inches long, how many brownies will fit into the box?
    A. 25
    B. 55
    C. 90
    D. 180

23. If a pound of potatoes make 24 cups of hash browns, how many pounds of potatoes would it take to make 36 cups of hash browns?
    A. 1.5
    B. 2.0
    C. 3.4
    D. 4.4

24. A can of tomato paste is 10 cm high and has a diameter of 8 cm. How much tomato paste can the cans hold?
    A. 202.8 cm^3
    B. 347.0 cm^3
    C. 502.4 cm^3
    D. 538.4 cm^3

25. A circular balloon has a diameter of 18 inches. What is the volume?
    A. 114.24 in^3
    B. 3,052.08 in^3
    C. 5,624.10 in^3
    D. 8,416.34 in^3

26. Christy orders 1 pound of meat from the butcher. She wants it cut into slices each weighing 0.25 oz. About how many slices will Christy receive?
    A. 24
    B. 44
    C. 64
    D. 84

27. If Kent reads an average of 55 pages per day, how many days will it take him to read a book of 880 pages?
    A. 16
    B. 18
    C. 22
    D. 25

28. James took a trip of 448 miles in 8 hours. What was his average speed?
    A. 45 miles per hour
    B. 56 miles per hour
    C. 62 miles per hour
    D. 65 miles per hour

29. Kiki has been asked to decorate a square room with an area of 576 sq feet. What is the length of each side of the room?
    A. 17 feet
    B. 24 feet
    C. 26 feet
    D. 29 feet

30. A diver's score is determined by the degree of difficulty of each dive multiplied by the points awarded for that dive. The table below shows the points Wayne earned for five dives and the degree of difficulty for each dive. What was Wayne's total score?

Points	Difficulty
8.2	1.2
9.0	1.4
8.3	1.5
9.5	1.4
9.5	1.2

    A. 47.59
    B. 59.59
    C. 64.29
    D. 66.29

STOP! DO NOT TURN THIS PAGE UNTIL TIME IS UP FOR THIS TEST. IF YOU FINISH BEFORE TIME IS UP, CHECK OVER YOUR WORK ON THIS TEST ONLY.

PART 3. WORD KNOWLEDGE

THE TEST ADMINISTRATOR WILL READ THE FOLLOWING ALOUD TO YOU:

Now turn to Part 3 and read the directions for Word Knowledge silently while I read them aloud.

This is a test of your knowledge of word meanings. These questions consist of a sentence or phrase with a word or phrase underlined. From the four choices given, you are to decide which one MEANS THE SAME OR MOST NEARLY THE SAME as the underlined word or phrase. Once you have made your choice, mark the space on your answer sheet that has the same number and letter as your choice.

Look at the sample question.

S1. The weather in this geographic area tends to be <u>moderate</u>.

    A. severe
    B. warm
    C. mild
    D. windy

The correct answer is "mild" which is choice C. Therefore, you would have blackened in space C on your answer sheet.

Your score on this test will be based on the number of questions you answer correctly. You should try to answer every question. DO NOT SPEND TOO MUCH TIME on any one question. If you finish before time is called, go back and check your work in this part <u>ONLY</u>.

Now find the section of your answer sheet that is marked PART 3. When you are told to begin, start with question number 1 in Part 3 of your test booklet and answer space number 1 in Part 3 on your separate answer sheet.

DO NOT TURN THE PAGE UNTIL TOLD TO DO SO. You will have 11 minutes to complete the 35 questions in this part. Are there any questions?

Begin.

1. The hot afternoon sun made them <u>listless</u>.
   A. Active
   B. Energized
   C. Limp
   D. Thirsty

2. It was a <u>potent</u> combination of chemicals.
   A. Movable
   B. Powerful
   C. Colorful
   D. Explosive

3. They felt <u>compelled</u> to fulfill the request.
   A. Forced
   B. Happy
   C. Honored
   D. Free

4. He had a <u>vivid</u> imagination.
   A. Poor
   B. Stagnant
   C. Dull
   D. Colorful

5. His attempt to escape was <u>futile</u>.
   A. Successful
   B. Useless
   C. Easy
   D. Powerful

6. The patient <u>solicited</u> the advice of the doctor.
   A. Ignored
   B. Followed
   C. Requested
   D. Rejected

7. <u>Appease</u> most nearly means
   A. satisfy.
   B. hurt.
   C. scare.
   D. wonder.

8. <u>Abhor</u> most nearly means
   A. adore.
   B. worship.
   C. hate.
   D. reject.

9. Sally was <u>prudent</u> in the way she spent her allowance.
   A. Reckless
   B. Careful
   C. Stingy
   D. Wasteful

10. The family was a <u>staunch</u> supporter of the candidate.
    A. Steadfast
    B. Part-time
    C. Talkative
    D. Periodic

11. Her <u>zealous</u> beliefs contradicted the norm.
    A. Whimsical
    B. Incorrect
    C. Unusual
    D. Passionate

12. He had a <u>volatile</u> temper.
    A. Motivated
    B. Humorous
    C. Explosive
    D. Acceptable

13. The note she received was <u>terse</u> in its explanation.
    A. Expansive
    B. Concise
    C. Confusing
    D. Wordy

14. The living quarters were <u>austere</u>.
    A. Extravagant
    B. Fancy
    C. Simple
    D. Crowded

15. Brian was <u>meticulous</u> about his finances.
    A. Painstaking
    B. Careless
    C. Doubtful
    D. Persistent

16. Her contribution was <u>vital</u> to the success of the project.
    A. Unimportant
    B. Unrelated
    C. Harmful
    D. Essential

17. John was <u>timid</u> when asked to answer in class.
    A. Talkative
    B. Hesitant
    C. Upset
    D. Present

18. Her words were <u>inaudible.</u>
    A. Unheard
    B. Loud
    C. Funny
    D. Suspicious

19. The best time to plant bushes is when they are <u>dormant</u>.
    A. Growing
    B. Inactive
    C. Dry
    D. Seedless

20. I <u>relinquished</u> my place in line because I had to go back to work.
    A. Saved
    B. Transferred
    C. Surrendered
    D. Enjoyed

21. <u>Delegated</u> most nearly means
    A. absolved.
    B. assigned.
    C. withheld.
    D. promoted.

22. The new administrative assistant proved to be <u>indispensable</u> to the law firm.
    A. Hurtful
    B. Annoying
    C. Crucial
    D. Energizing

23. The employee gave a <u>plausible</u> explanation for the missing equipment.
    A. Ridiculous
    B. Lengthy
    C. Lofty
    D. Credible

24. The tax cut was <u>advantageous</u> to the middle class.
    A. Beneficial
    B. Harmful
    C. Useless
    D. Compromising

25. The court decision <u>aroused</u> the anger of many parents and teachers.
    A. Reduced
    B. Increased
    C. Appeased
    D. Awakened

26. The board gave <u>provisional</u> approval for the new airport.
    A. Initial
    B. Lasting
    C. Tentative
    D. Final

27. Marty's musical ability was <u>unparalleled</u>.
    A. Equaled
    B. Unmatched
    C. Appreciated
    D. Misunderstood

28. <u>Intermittent</u> most nearly means
    A. periodic.
    B. constant.
    C. disruptive.
    D. annoying.

29. Joan was <u>obstinate</u> about her decision to enroll in a creative writing class.
    A. Positive
    B. Unsure
    C. Hopeful
    D. Stubborn

30. Ramon was <u>tactful</u> when he told her the news.
    A. Unruly
    B. Thoughtless
    C. Diplomatic
    D. Forceful

31. Natalie was hired because she was <u>proficient</u> in computers.
    A. Superior
    B. Unschooled
    C. Trained
    D. Skilled

32. <u>Augment</u> most nearly means
    A. reduce.
    B. supplement.
    C. invent.
    D. forget.

33. The person's critique of the movie was <u>vindictive</u>.
    A. Gentle
    B. Accurate
    C. Mistaken
    D. Spiteful

34. The computer system was <u>obsolete</u>.
    A. Vibrant
    B. State-of-the-art
    C. Outdated
    D. Broken

35. Because of his victory, he was <u>inundated</u> with phone calls.
    A. Awakened
    B. Flooded
    C. Interrupted
    D. Greeted

STOP! DO NOT TURN THIS PAGE UNTIL TIME IS UP FOR THIS TEST. IF YOU FINISH BEFORE TIME IS UP, CHECK OVER YOUR WORK ON THIS TEST ONLY.

PART 4. PARAGRAPH COMPREHENSION

THE TEST ADMINISTRATOR WILL READ THE FOLLOWING ALOUD TO YOU:

Turn to Part 4 and read the directions for Paragraph Comprehension silently while I read them aloud.

This is a test of your ability to understand what you read. In this section you will find one or more paragraphs of reading material followed by incomplete statements or questions. You are to read the paragraph and select one of four lettered choices which BEST completes the statement or answers the question. When you have selected your answer, blacken the space on your answer sheet that has the same number and letter as your answer.

Your score on this test will be based on the number of questions you answer correctly. You should try to answer every question. DO NOT SPEND TOO MUCH TIME on any one question. If you finish before time is called, go back and check your work in this part ONLY.

Now find the section of your answer sheet that is marked PART 4. When you are told to begin, start with question number 1 in Part 4 of your test booklet and answer space number 1 in Part 4 on your separate answer sheet.

DO NOT TURN THE PAGE UNTIL TOLD TO DO SO. You will have 13 minutes to complete the 15 questions in this part. Are there any questions?

Begin.

More than 50 volcanoes in the United States have erupted one or more times in the past 200 years. The most volcanically active regions of the nation are in Alaska, Hawaii, California, Oregon, and Washington. Volcanoes produce a wide variety of hazards that can kill people and destroy property. Large explosive eruptions can endanger people and property hundreds of miles away and even affect global climate. Some volcanic hazards can occur even when a volcano is not erupting.

An explosive eruption blasts solid and molten rock fragments and volcanic gases into the air with tremendous force. The largest rock fragments, called *bombs*, usually fall back to the ground within 2 miles of the vent. Small fragments (less than about 0.1 inch across) of volcanic glass, minerals, and ash rise high into the air, forming a huge, billowing eruption column.

Eruption columns can grow rapidly and reach more than 12 miles above a volcano in less than 30 minutes, forming an eruption cloud. The volcanic ash in the cloud can pose a serious hazard to aviation. During the past 15 years, about 80 commercial jets have been damaged by inadvertently flying into ash clouds, and several have nearly crashed because of engine failure. Large eruption clouds can extend hundreds of miles downwind, resulting in ash fall over enormous areas; the wind carries the smallest ash particles the farthest. Ash from the May 18, 1980, eruption of Mount St. Helens, Washington, fell over an area of 22,000 square miles in the western United States. Heavy ash fall can collapse buildings, and even minor ash fall can damage crops, electronics, and machinery.

Volcanoes emit gases during eruptions. Even when a volcano is not erupting, cracks in the ground allow gases to reach the surface through small openings. Common volcanic gases are carbon dioxide, sulfur dioxide, hydrogen sulfide, hydrogen, and fluorine. Sulfur dioxide gas can react with water droplets in the atmosphere to create acid rain, which causes corrosion and harms vegetation. Carbon dioxide is heavier than air and can be trapped in low areas in concentrations that are deadly to people and animals.

1. According to this passage, fragments that fall close to the volcano itself during an eruption are referred to as
   A. bombs.
   B. vents.
   C. volcanic ash.
   D. rocks.

2. From the passage you can infer that
   A. areas a long distance from the volcano can be damaged by an eruption.
   B. volcanoes hurt the farming industry in many ways.
   C. it's best for airplanes to fly around volcanoes even when they are not erupting.
   D. volcanic ash has caused a few airlines to go bankrupt.

3. According to the passage, most volcanoes in the United States are located in which part of the country?
   A. The central states
   B. The western states
   C. Along the East Coast
   D. The southern states

4. According to the passage, which of the following creates acid rain?
   A. Volcanic glass
   B. Ash combined with water
   C. Fluorine
   D. Sulfur dioxide

5. In this passage, the word *billowing* most nearly means which of the following?
   A. Tall
   B. Dense
   C. Imploding
   D. Swelling

Langston Hughes was born in Joplin, Missouri, to two bookkeepers. His parents separated when he was very young. His father moved to Mexico, and his mother left him for long periods of time while she searched for steady employment. Hughes's grandmother raised him in Lawrence, Kansas, until he was 12, when he moved to Illinois to live with his mother and stepfather. The family later moved to Ohio. From these humble origins, Langston developed a deep admiration for those he called "low-down folks," poor people who had a strong sense of emotion and pride.

To express his feeling and emotions, Hughes began writing poetry in high school. He gained some early recognition and support among important black intellectuals such as James Weldon Johnson and W. E. B. DuBois. While working as a busboy at the Wardman Park Hotel in Washington, D.C., Hughes gave three of his poems to Vachel Lindsay, a famous critic. Lindsay's enthusiastic praise won Hughes an even wider audience.

Hughes spent the summers of 1919 and 1920 with his father in Mexico. While on a train on his second trip, he wrote his first great poem, "The Negro Speaks of Rivers." The poem was published in *The Crisis*, a magazine of the National Association for the Advancement of Colored People.

Langston Hughes became one of the most important writers and thinkers of the Harlem Renaissance, which was the African American artistic movement in the 1920s that celebrated black life and culture. Hughes's creative genius was influenced by his life in New York City's Harlem, a primarily African American neighborhood. His literary works helped shape American literature and politics. Hughes, like others active in the Harlem Renaissance, had a strong sense of racial pride. Through his poetry, novels, plays, essays, and children's books, he promoted equality, condemned racism and injustice, and celebrated African American culture, humor, and spirituality.

6. Of the following, which is the best title for the passage?
   A. A Kid from Missouri
   B. An Extraordinary Poet
   C. From Busboy to Poet
   D. A Poet Is Praised

7. Who was Vachel Lindsay?
   A. A restaurant worker
   B. A family friend
   C. One of the "low-down folks"
   D. A literary critic

8. According to the passage, what was the Harlem Renaissance?
   A. The neighborhood were Langston Hughes was born
   B. His grandmother's home in Illinois
   C. An African American artistic movement
   D. The topic of Hughes' first great poem

9. Why was Langston Hughes considered a great poet?
   A. His literary works helped shape American politics and literature.
   B. He came from a humble background to reach fame and fortune.
   C. His poems were published in many countries around the world.
   D. His poems were praised by Vachel Lindsay.

10. According to the passage, why did Langston Hughes live with his grandmother?
    A. He didn't want to stay in Missouri.
    B. He didn't want to move to Ohio.
    C. He wanted to continue to write his poems.
    D. His parents were not able to care for him.

Laura Ingalls Wilder was born on February 7, 1867, in the Big Woods of Wisconsin. Reflecting the pioneer spirit of the era, Laura's family moved several times throughout her childhood. She lived for periods in Kansas, Minnesota, Iowa, and South Dakota. Life on the frontier was difficult, and members of Laura's family experienced many hardships that threatened their survival. For example, grasshoppers destroyed their crops two seasons in a row, and a winter of continuous blizzards threatened their supplies. Laura's brother died nine months after his birth, and Laura's sister Mary lost her eyesight at the young age of 15 because of a stroke. The lessons of life on the prairie in America's heartland made a lasting impression on Laura.

Laura and her sisters attended nearby schools during their childhood, and Laura's love for learning sparked her interest in teaching. At age 15 while living in De Smet, South Dakota, Laura earned her teaching certificate. In a rural area just 12 miles from De Smet, she began her first teaching job. During this time, she met and married Almanzo Wilder.

Following in the pioneer footsteps of their families, Laura and Almanzo struggled to establish homes first in South Dakota and later in Minnesota. They along with their daughter, Rose, suffered through droughts, hail storms, fires, and diseases. Laura and Almanzo eventually settled on a farm in Missouri called "Rocky Ridge."

While living at Rocky Ridge, Laura developed her writing abilities, and for 12 years she edited the *Missouri Ruralist*. As she grew older, Laura became interested in sharing her pioneer experiences with the next generation. Unable to find a publisher for her autobiography called *Pioneer Girl*, Laura rewrote a section of the book and called it *Little House in the Big Woods*, which was published in 1932 when she was 65 years old. Soon after the book was released, *Little House* became a success. Children everywhere wanted to read more stories about the Ingalls family. Laura continued to write books about her family and finished her 18-volume series in 1943. Her desire to share her family's history painted a picture of life on the frontier for generations of children.

11. According to this passage what profession did Laura choose?
    A. Farmer
    B. Daughter
    C. Teacher
    D. Student

12. According to this passage, why did Laura choose to write about her childhood?
    A. She was otherwise unoccupied.
    B. She was too old to be considered a credible author.
    C. She wanted to share her experiences with others.
    D. She wanted to become a success.

13. According to the passage, where did Laura and Almanzo finally settle down?
    A. South Dakota
    B. Missouri
    C. Minnesota
    D. Iowa

14. Which of the following was *not* one of the hardships that Laura faced while growing up?
    A. Death of her brother
    B. Invasion of grasshoppers
    C. Blizzards
    D. Volcanic eruptions

15. Which of the following is the best title for this passage?
    A. Laura Ingalls Wilder—a Great Author
    B. Pioneer Woman and Writer
    C. Hardships of Farmers
    D. Little House in the Big Woods

STOP! DO NOT TURN THIS PAGE UNTIL TIME IS UP FOR THIS TEST. IF YOU FINISH BEFORE TIME IS UP, CHECK OVER YOUR WORK ON THIS TEST ONLY.

PART 5. MATHEMATICS KNOWLEDGE

THE TEST ADMINISTRATOR WILL READ THE FOLLOWING ALOUD TO YOU:

Now turn to Part 5 and read the directions for Mathematics Knowledge silently while I read them aloud.

This is a test of your ability to solve general mathematics problems. You are to select the correct response from the choices given. Then mark the space on your answer sheet that has the same number and letter as your choice. Use your scratch paper to do any figuring you wish to do.

Your score on this test will be based on the number of questions you answer correctly. You should try to answer every question. DO NOT SPEND TOO MUCH TIME on any one question. If you finish before time is called, go back and check your work in this part ONLY.

Now find the section of your answer sheet that is marked PART 5. When you are told to begin, start with question number 1 in Part 5 of your test booklet and answer space number 1 in Part 5 on your separate answer sheet.

DO NOT TURN THE PAGE UNTIL TOLD TO DO SO. You will have 24 minutes to complete the 25 questions in this part. Are there any questions?

Begin.

1. $k - 37 = -10$

   $k = ?$

   A. 27
   B. 29
   C. −29
   D. −12

2. $(4 - 7)(6 - 2)^2 =$
   A. −6
   B. −12
   C. −48
   D. −65

3. 45 is what percent of 180?
   A. 12
   B. 16
   C. 21
   D. 25

4. What percent is equivalent to $\frac{1}{8}$?
   A. 8%
   B. 12.5%
   C. 15%
   D. 17%

5. Divide $3\frac{1}{2}$ by $\frac{3}{4}$.

   A. $\frac{21}{8}$

   B. $2\frac{5}{8}$

   C. $4\frac{2}{3}$

   D. $5\frac{1}{8}$

6. Factor the following expression:

   $y^2 + 8y + 15$

   A. $(y + 1)(y + 15)$
   B. $2y^2 (y + 4)$
   C. $(y + 3)(y + 5)$
   D. $(y + 2)(y + 6)$

7. Subtract:

   $4x^3 - 2x^2 + 6$
   $-(4x^3 + 5x^2 - 12)$

   A. $8 + 3x^2 - 12$
   B. $3x^2 + 12$
   C. $8x^3 - 6$
   D. $-7x^2 + 18$

8. Solve for h.

   $$\frac{3}{h} = \frac{1}{11}$$

   A. $h = \frac{3}{11h}$

   B. $h = 33$
   C. $3h = 33$
   D. $h = 11$

9. Solve for the two unknowns.

   $3m + 3p = 24$
   $2m + p = 13$

   A. $m = 5; p = 3$
   B. $m = 2; p = 1\frac{1}{2}$
   C. $m = 5; p = 2$
   D. $m = 3; p = 5$

10. $\dfrac{3r^5 s^3}{12r^3 s^2} =$

    A. $4r^2 s$

    B. $\dfrac{1r^8 s^5}{4}$

    C. $\dfrac{r^2 s}{4}$

    D. $0.25r^2 s^5$

11. Solve for x.

    $x^2 - 18x = -45$

    A. $x = 9; x = 5$
    B. $x = 15; x = 3$
    C. $x = -3; x = -15$
    D. $x = 8; x = 2$

12. Multiply:

$$\frac{6g}{2} \times \frac{3}{4y}$$

A. $\dfrac{18g}{8g}$

B. $\dfrac{6g}{6y}$

C. $\dfrac{24gy}{6}$

D. $\dfrac{9g}{4y}$

13. Divide:

$$\frac{x^2}{3y} \div \frac{3x}{2y}$$

A. $\dfrac{2x}{9}$

B. $\dfrac{3x}{12y}$

C. $-\dfrac{3x^3}{12y^2}$

D. $\dfrac{x^3}{4}$

14. $\sqrt[3]{1,000} =$

A. 5
B. 10
C. 20
D. 25

15. Solve for g.

$$\frac{g}{8} = \frac{1}{4}$$

A. $g = 2$

B. $g = \dfrac{2}{4}$

C. $g = \dfrac{1}{2}$

D. $g = \dfrac{1}{32}$

16. Which of the following is a quadrilateral?

A.

B.

C.

D.

17. What is the perimeter of the following isosceles triangle?

A. 27 m
B. 30 m
C. 51 m
D. 72 m

18. Multiply −4.5 by −6.25.
A. −28.13
B. 24.23
C. 28.13
D. −24.23

19. In the following triangle, ∠1 is 30°, and ∠2 is 45°. What is the measure of ∠3?

A. 5°
B. 25°
C. 95°
D. 105°

20. Which of the following is true about the sides of the following triangle?

   A. $AB + BC > AC$
   B. $BC + AC < AB$
   C. $AB + AC = BC$
   D. $AC - BC = AB$

21. If the following figure is an isosceles right triangle, what is the measure of $\angle A$?

   A. 30°
   B. 45°
   C. 65°
   D. 90°

22. What is the area of the following parallelogram?

   A. 30 units²
   B. 40 units²
   C. 50 units²
   D. 200 units²

23. If lines A and B are parallel and are intersected by line C and $\angle 2$ is 25°, what is the measure of $\angle 4$?

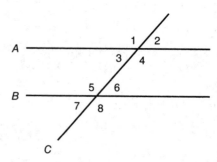

   A. 25°
   B. 45°
   C. 110°
   D. 155°

24. The edges of the following cube each measure 3 cm. What is its volume?

   A. 3 cm³
   B. 9 cm³
   C. 27 cm³
   D. 32 cm³

25. What is the volume of a sphere that has a diameter of 10 cm?
   A. 104.67 cm³
   B. 140 cm³
   C. 418.67 cm³
   D. 523.33 cm³

STOP! DO NOT TURN THIS PAGE UNTIL TIME IS UP FOR THIS TEST. IF YOU FINISH BEFORE TIME IS UP, CHECK OVER YOUR WORK ON THIS TEST ONLY.

PART 6. ELECTRONICS INFORMATION

THE TEST ADMINISTRATOR WILL READ THE FOLLOWING ALOUD TO YOU:

Now turn to Part 6 of your test booklet and read the directions for Electronics Information silently while I read them aloud.

This is a test of your knowledge of electrical, radio, and electronics information. You are to select the correct response from the choices given and then mark the space on your answer sheet that has the same number and letter as your choice.

Your score on this test will be based on the number of questions you answer correctly. You should try to answer every question. DO NOT SPEND TOO MUCH TIME on any one question. If you finish before time is called, go back and check your work in this part ONLY.

Now find the section of your answer sheet that is marked PART 6. When you are told to begin, start with question number 1 in Part 6 of your test booklet and answer space number 1 in Part 6 on your separate answer sheet.

DO NOT TURN THE PAGE UNTIL TOLD TO DO SO. You will have 9 minutes to complete the 20 questions in this part. Are there any questions?

Begin.

1. Which of these materials is a good insulator?
   A. Silver
   B. Copper
   C. Aluminum
   D. Neoprene

2. Voltage measures electrical
   A. current.
   B. pressure.
   C. resistance.
   D. frequency.

3. Which formula calculates the amount of power in an electrical circuit?
   A. Amps^2
   B. Watts/ohms
   C. Amps $\times$ volts
   D. Watts $\times$ amps

4. Four amps are flowing in a 12-volt circuit. How much power is being used?
   A. 1/3 watt
   B. 3 watts
   C. 8 watts
   D. 48 watts

5. A transformer changes the _____ in a circuit.
   A. voltage
   B. ohms
   C. capacitance
   D. polarity

6. A semiconductor gets its name because it can be used as a(n)
   A. generator or an alternator.
   B. switch or a transformer.
   C. insulator or a conductor.
   D. insulator or a capacitor.

7. Electric motors depend on
   A. capacitance.
   B. inductance.
   C. resistance.
   D. magnetic repulsion.

8. The purpose of a generator is to
   A. convert rotary motion into electric current.
   B. convert electric current into rotary motion.
   C. convert potential energy into kinetic energy.
   D. None of the above.

9. All circuits must have a
   A. load.
   B. current.
   C. voltage.
   D. switch.

10. If the electrochemical reaction in a battery is reversible, the battery is
    A. fully charged.
    B. dead.
    C. rechargeable.
    D. not rechargeable.

11. In the circuit shown, the total resistance is:

A. 9/24 ohm
B. 24/9 ohms
C. 32 ohms
D. 40 ohms

12. What is the total resistance in the circuit shown?

A. 0.066 ohm

B. 6 2/3 ohms

C. 30 ohms

D. 66 2/3 ohms

13. The type of circuit shown is

A. series.

B. parallel.

C. series-parallel.

D. parallel-parallel.

14. Silicon is commonly used in electronics because it is a

A. good conductor.

B. good insulator.

C. semiconductor.

D. resistor.

15. If you needed to ensure that current was flowing in one direction only, you would use a(n)

A. diode.

B. resistor.

C. capacitor.

D. alternator.

16. If the equipment grounding leg of a home circuit is not hooked up, what could happen?

A. Devices could get twice as much voltage as required because the ground is absent.

B. You could get a shock if something goes wrong with the wiring.

C. The circuit will be disconnected.

D. No significant change will be seen.

17. The major use of a simple circuit tester is to test

A. the voltage in a circuit.

B. the current in a circuit.

C. the resistance in a circuit.

D. whether a circuit is hot or cold.

18. How many three-way switches would you use to control a hallway light from both ends of the hallway?

A. 2

B. 3

C. 2 or 3

D. None of the above

19. In a circuit breaker, a(n) _____ shuts off the current when too much current flows.

A. rheostat

B. thermostat

C. electromagnet

D. resistor

20. In a circuit with 40 ohms of resistance, how much voltage would be present when the current is 10 amperes?

A. 0.25 v

B. 25 v

C. 200 v

D. 400 v

STOP! DO NOT TURN THIS PAGE UNTIL TIME IS UP FOR THIS TEST. IF YOU FINISH BEFORE TIME IS UP, CHECK OVER YOUR WORK ON THIS TEST ONLY.

PART 7. AUTO AND SHOP INFORMATION

THE TEST ADMINISTRATOR WILL READ THE FOLLOWING ALOUD TO YOU:

Now turn to Part 7 and read the directions for Auto and Shop Information silently while I read them aloud.

This test has questions about automobiles, shop practices, and the use of tools. Pick the BEST answer for each question and then mark the space on your answer sheet that has the same number and letter as your choice.

Your score on this test will be based on the number of questions you answer correctly. You should try to answer every question. DO NOT SPEND TOO MUCH TIME on any one question. If you finish before time is called, go back and check your work in this part ONLY.

Now find the section of your answer sheet that is marked PART 7. When you are told to begin, start with question number 1 in Part 7 of your test booklet and answer space number 1 in Part 7 on your separate answer sheet.

DO NOT TURN THE PAGE UNTIL TOLD TO DO SO. You will have 11 minutes to complete the 25 questions in this part. Are there any questions?

Begin.

1. If you hear a squealing noise that rises in pitch as the engine turns faster, what would you inspect?
   A. Distributor shaft
   B. Timing chain
   C. Fan belt
   D. Flywheel

2. The job of a spark plug is to
   A. make a spark every time the piston reaches top dead center.
   B. spark the catalytic converter.
   C. plug a hole in the cylinder head.
   D. ignite the fuel mixture.

3. If you smell a sickly sweet odor after the engine warms up, what would you suspect is the problem?
   A. Oil leak
   B. Transmission fluid leak
   C. Antifreeze leak
   D. Gasoline leak

4. The purpose of a flywheel is to
   A. smooth out crankshaft motion.
   B. help the brakes when the car is on a rough road.
   C. seal the wheel cylinder.
   D. increase friction between the tires and the road.

5. Gaskets are used to
   A. seal between two rigid surfaces.
   B. prevent overpressure in the crankcase.
   C. seal the two halves of the gas tank.
   D. seal between the piston and the cylinder wall.

6. When an ignition coil goes bad,
   A. the engine will overheat.
   B. the heater will not work.
   C. the timing chain is probably broken.
   D. cylinders may misfire because the spark plugs are not getting enough voltage.

7. The purpose of the connecting rod and crankshaft is to
   A. start the engine during cold weather.
   B. enable the power steering.
   C. change linear motion into rotary motion.
   D. transfer energy from the engine to the clutch.

8. When you step on the brake pedal,
   A. slave cylinders press on the master cylinder, causing the wheel cylinders to press against the brake pads.
   B. the brake lights come on, and an electrical signal is passed to the brakes, which stop the car.
   C. a servo-actuator in the hydraulic system creates pressure on the brake hoses, which press the brake pads against the brake drums.
   D. the master cylinder pushes brake fluid through the brake lines, causing the wheel cylinders to expand and push the brake pads against the disk or drum.

9. When replacing a cylinder head,
   A. tighten the bolts as much as possible.
   B. tighten the bolts in any order, as long as you tighten them with the correct torque.
   C. tighten the bolts to the correct torque, in the correct order.
   D. use the original bolts.

10. A fan belt should be tightened until
    A. the belt is slightly stretched.
    B. the bolts read 48 foot-pounds.
    C. it resists any deflection.
    D. it deflects slightly when you press midway between the pulleys.

11. If the tube feeding a fuel injector leaks,
    A. you may see a spray of gasoline.
    B. air will leak into the engine.
    C. air and gasoline will leak into the engine.
    D. methane will leak into the cylinder.

12. In a four-cylinder, four-stroke engine, how many explosions occur in one minute when the engine is running at 2,000 rpm?
    A. 1,000
    B. 2,000
    C. 4,000
    D. 8,000

13. Which list of fasteners is organized from weakest to strongest?
    A. Carriage bolt, lag bolt, screw
    B. Nail, screw, lag bolt, carriage bolt
    C. Screw, nail, lag bolt, carriage bolt
    D. Staple, carriage bolt, nail, lag bolt

14. The tool shown below is a(n)

    A. eight-point wrench.
    B. box wrench.
    C. open-end wrench.
    D. bar clamp.

15. When using carpenter's glue, it is necessary to
    A. wait 30 minutes for the glue to dry.
    B. clamp the parts for 30 minutes.
    C. clamp the parts overnight.
    D. put primer on the wood before gluing.

16. Flux is needed for soldering because it
    A. transfers heat to the metal.
    B. melts the solder.
    C. prevents oxidation during heating.
    D. holds the joint tight.

17. What kind of force does this tool create?

    A. Shearing
    B. Grinding
    C. Slicing
    D. Twisting

18. Unreinforced concrete
    A. has great compressive strength but little tensile strength.
    B. has great compressive strength and great tensile strength.
    C. has little compressive strength and little tensile strength.
    D. has little compressive strength but great tensile strength.

19. The tool shown below is a(n)

    A. punch.
    B. awl.
    C. Phillips screwdriver.
    D. slot screwdriver.

20. A center punch
    A. finds the center of a hole.
    B. replaces a drill when drilling wood.
    C. prevents a drill from wandering as it starts in metal.
    D. lines up hinge holes.

21. In which building material does actual size equal nominal size?
    A. 2 × 4
    B. 1 × 4
    C. 8-inch concrete block
    D. plywood

22. The tool shown below is a

    A. putty knife.
    B. paint scraper.
    C. wood chisel.
    D. tang chisel.

23. When using a lag-shield anchor in concrete, it is necessary to
    A. use a power-actuated tool.
    B. drill a hole first.
    C. set the anchor in wet cement.
    D. use construction adhesive.

24. A pipe wrench
    A. has two fixed jaws.
    B. has one fixed jaw and one movable jaw.
    C. can be used on pipe, but not on pipe fittings.
    D. is always 16 inches long.

25. The purpose of pipe-joint compound is to
    A. seal the joint only.
    B. hold Teflon tape in place while the tape dries.
    C. prevent rust in steel threads.
    D. seal the joint and prevent it from seizing up.

STOP! DO NOT TURN THIS PAGE UNTIL TIME IS UP FOR THIS TEST. IF YOU FINISH BEFORE TIME IS UP, CHECK OVER YOUR WORK ON THIS TEST ONLY.

PART 8. MECHANICAL COMPREHENSION

THE TEST ADMINISTRATOR WILL READ THE FOLLOWING ALOUD TO YOU:

Now turn to Part 8 and read the directions for Mechanical Comprehension silently while I read them aloud.

This test has questions about mechanical and physical principles. Study the picture and decide which answer is CORRECT and then mark the space on your separate answer sheet that has the same number and letter as your choice.

Your score on this test will be based on the number of questions you answer correctly. You should try to answer every question. DO NOT SPEND TOO MUCH TIME on any one question. If you finish before time is called, go back and check your work in this part ONLY.

Now find the section of your answer sheet that is marked PART 8. When you are told to begin, start with question number 1 in Part 8 of your test booklet and answer space number 1 in Part 8 on your separate answer sheet.

DO NOT TURN THE PAGE UNTIL TOLD TO DO SO. You will have 19 minutes to complete the 25 questions in this part. Are there any questions?

Begin.

1. The mechanical advantage in the pulley system shown is
   A. 1
   B. 2
   C. 3
   D. 4

2. This object is a mechanical governor for an engine. What would cause the balls to move outward?
   A. Spring tension
   B. Slower rotation
   C. Faster rotation
   D. Linear momentum

3. When you drag a concrete block across the pavement, one way to reduce the amount of pulling force needed would be to
   A. get a heavier block.
   B. use a better rope.
   C. pull harder.
   D. lubricate the pavement.

4. What type of simple machine is shown?
   A. Class 1 lever
   B. Class 2 lever
   C. Class 3 lever
   D. Two inclined planes

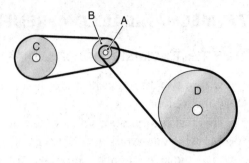

5. Which sheave would be rotating the slowest in this system?
   A. A
   B. B
   C. C
   D. D

6. A fuel tank is receiving fuel at the rate of 1 gallon per minute. It is supplying an engine that uses 3 gallons per hour. How many gallons of fuel will be in the tank after 1/2 hour, assuming the tank was empty at the start?
   A. 18.5
   B. 28.5
   C. 31.5
   D. 57

200 lb

7. What amount of effort would be required to pull on this rope?
   A. 25 lb
   B. 50 lb
   C. 100 lb
   D. 200 lb

100 lb

400 lb

8. Using the weights given, what mechanical advantage would allow a 100 lb effort to raise the 400 lb weight? (Note: fhe figure is not drawn to scale.)
   A. 2
   B. 4
   C. 8
   D. 16

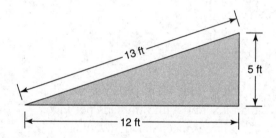

13 ft

5 ft

12 ft

9. What is the mechanical advantage of this inclined plane?
   A. 13/12
   B. 12/13
   C. 13/5
   D. 12/5

10. Gear A, with 24 teeth, is meshed with gear B, with 36 teeth. When gear A rotates 3 times, how many times will gear B rotate?
    A. 2
    B. 3
    C. 4
    D. 6

11. This tool combines which simple machines?
    A. Lever and wheel and axle
    B. Inclined plane and pulley
    C. Lever and wedge
    D. Pulley and wheel and axle

4 ft — 6 ft

12. What is the mechanical advantage of this lever?
    A. 0.5
    B. 1.5
    C. 2
    D. 3

13. In this figure, pulling 12 feet of rope will raise the weight
    A. 2 feet
    B. 3 feet
    C. 4 feet
    D. 8 feet

14. When two gears are engaged,
    A. the driving gear must be smaller than the driven gear.
    B. one must rotate faster than the other.
    C. they always rotate at the same speed.
    D. they always rotate in opposite directions.

15. How much force would be needed to balance this lever?
    A. 12 lb
    B. 25 lb
    C. 35 lb
    D. 45 lb

16. Which of these items would return to its original shape after being deformed?

A.

B.

C.

D.

17. What would help the beam carry a heavier load?
    A. Split the beam in two.
    B. Add a post under the load.
    C. Coat the beam with oil.
    D. Remove one post and turn the other into a fulcrum.

18. A bolt has 8 threads per inch. How far does it move if you tighten it five turns, and then loosen it three turns?
    A. 1/8 in
    B. 1/4 in
    C. 3/8 in
    D. 5/8 in

19. A screw with 12 threads per inch has _____ than a screw with 8 threads per inch.
    A. a larger mechanical advantage
    B. a smaller mechanical advantage
    C. more strength
    D. less strength

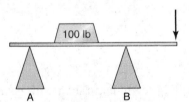

20. What would happen if you added a force at the arrow?
    A. Load would not change at A, and it would increase at B.
    B. Load would not change at A, but it would increase at B.
    C. Load would increase at A and decrease at B.
    D. Load would decrease at A and increase at B.

21. When you add water to a tank, water pressure on the bottom will
    A. stay the same.
    B. decrease.
    C. increase.
    D. depend on temperature.

22. If a bicycle rider changes to a smaller gear on the rear of the bike and wants to go the same speed,
    A. The rider must place more force on the pedals.
    B. The rider can put less force on the pedals.
    C. The rider need not change the force on the pedals.
    D. The rider should put more force on the left pedal and less force on the right pedal.

23. In the hydraulic system shown, where is the greatest pressure?
    A. A
    B. B
    C. C
    D. Pressure is the same at all points.

24. Moving the fulcrum closer to the load will
    A. increase the mechanical advantage.
    B. decrease the mechanical advantage.
    C. not change the mechanical advantage.
    D. allow you to lift farther with the lever.

25. What would you use to prevent a nut from moving on a bolt?
    A. Lock washer
    B. Lock nut
    C. Degreaser
    D. A and B

STOP! DO NOT TURN THIS PAGE UNTIL TIME IS UP FOR THIS TEST. IF YOU FINISH BEFORE TIME IS UP, CHECK OVER YOUR WORK ON THIS TEST ONLY.

PART 9. ASSEMBLING OBJECTS

THE TEST ADMINISTRATOR WILL READ THE FOLLOWING ALOUD TO YOU:

Now turn to Part 9 and read the directions for Assembling Objects silently while I read them aloud.

This test has questions that will measure your spatial ability. Study the diagram, decide which answer is CORRECT, and then mark the space on your separate answer sheet that has the same number and letter as your choice.

Your score on this test will be based on the number of questions you answer correctly. You should try to answer every question. DO NOT SPEND TOO MUCH TIME on any one question. If you finish before time is called, go back and check your work in this part ONLY.

Now find the section of your answer sheet that is marked PART 9. When you are told to begin, start with question 1 in Part 9 of your test booklet and answer space number 1 in Part 9 on your separate answer sheet.

DO NOT TURN THE PAGE UNTIL TOLD TO DO SO. You will have 15 minutes to complete the 25 questions in this part. Are there any questions?

Begin.

For Questions 1–17, which figure best shows how the objects in the left box will appear if they are fit together?

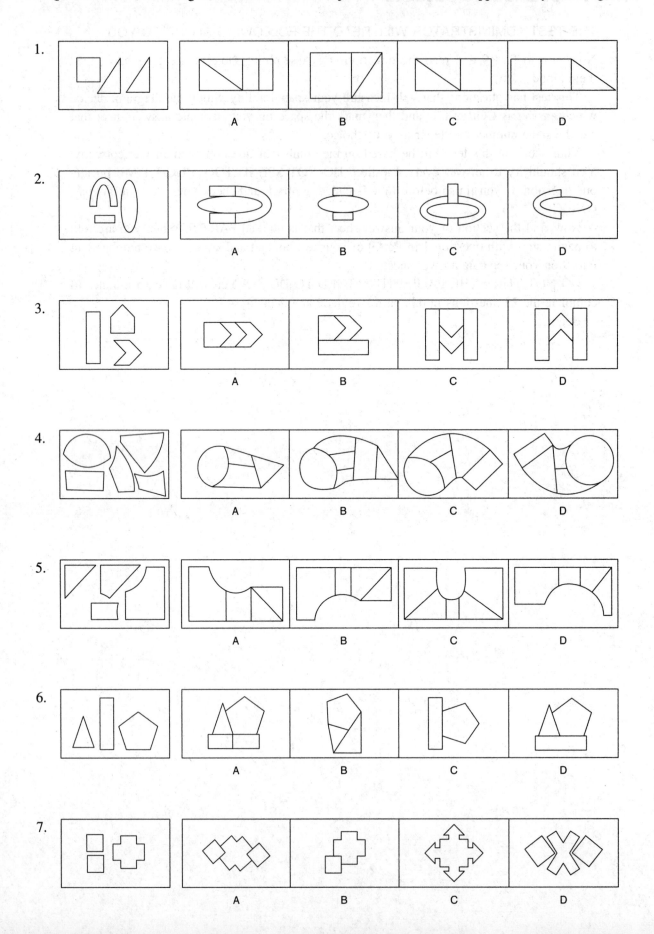

8.

9.

10.

11.

12.

13.

14.

15.

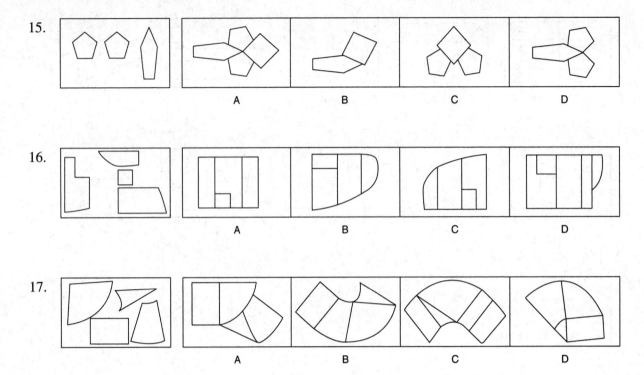

16.

17.

For Questions 18-25, which figure best shows how the objects in the left box will touch if the letters for each object are matched?

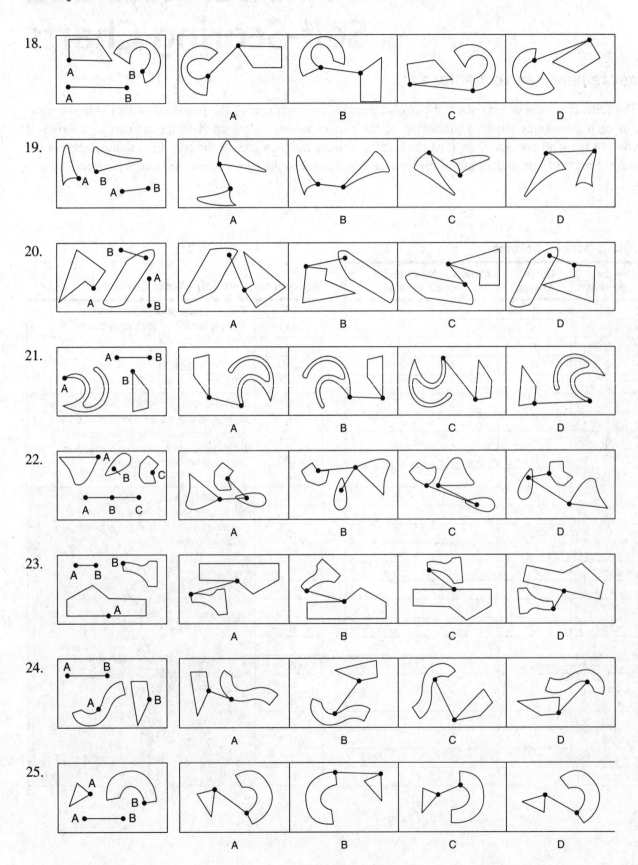

Answer Keys and Self-Scoring Charts

ASVAB PRACTICE TEST FORM 3

The following answer keys show the correct answers for each part of the practice test that you just took. For each question, compare your answer to the correct answer. Mark an X in the column to the right if you got the item correct. Then total the number correct for each part of the test. Find that number in the corresponding chart to the right of the answer key. See the suggestions listed for your performance.

Part 1. General Science

Item Number	Correct Answer	Mark X If You Picked the Correct Answer
1	A	
2	A	
3	A	
4	B	
5	D	
6	B	
7	B	
8	A	
9	D	
10	A	
11	C	
12	B	
13	D.	
14	C	
15	A	
16	A	
17	C	
18	D	
19	A	
20	A	
21	A	
22	D	
23	C	
24	C	
25	C	
Total Correct		

Score Interpretation—Total Correct

25	This is pretty good work. Review the explanations for the answers you got incorrect.
24	
23	
22	
21	
20	You are doing pretty well. Review the explanations for the items you answered incorrectly. If you have time, review the other explanations and you will learn even more.
19	
18	
17	
16	
15	You need to keep studying. Pay close attention to the explanations for each item, even for the ones you got correct.
14	
13	
12	
11	
10	Spend time working on the General Science review in Part 3 of this book.
9	
8	
7	
6	If you have copies of your school science textbooks, it would be a good idea to study those.
5	
4	
3	
2	
1	
0	

Part 2. Arithmetic Reasoning

Item Number	Correct Answer	Mark X If You Picked the Correct Answer
1	C	
2	C	
3	B	
4	D	
5	D	
6	C	
7	C	
8	C	
9	D	
10	C	
11	D	
12	D	
13	A	
14	D	
15	A	
16	B	
17	A	
18	C	
19	B	
20	C	
21	B	
22	D	
23	A	
24	C	
25	B	
26	C	
27	A	
28	B	
29	B	
30	B	
Total Correct		

Score Interpretation—Total Correct

Score	Interpretation
30	This is pretty good work. Review the explanations for the answers you got incorrect. This test is a part of the AFQT, and you must do well
29	
28	
27	
26	
25	You are doing pretty well. Review the explanations for the items you answered incorrectly. If you have time, review the other explanations and you will learn even more.
24	
23	
22	
21	
20	You need to keep studying. Pay close attention to the explanations for each item, even for the ones you got correct.
19	
18	
17	
16	
15	Spend time working on the Arithmetic Reasoning reviews in Part 3 of this book.
14	
13	
12	
11	Keep working and reworking problems until you are comfortable with the processes.
10	
9	
8	
7	
6	
5	
4	
3	
2	
1	
0	

Part 3. Word Knowledge

Item Number	Correct Answer	Mark X If You Picked the Correct Answer
1	C	
2	B	
3	A	
4	D	
5	B	
6	C	
7	A	
8	C	
9	B	
10	A	
11	D	
12	C	
13	B	
14	C	
15	A	
16	D	
17	B	
18	A	
19	B	
20	C	
21	B	
22	C	
23	D	
24	A	
25	D	
26	C	
27	B	
28	A	
29	D	
30	C	
31	D	
32	B	
33	D	
34	C	
35	B	
Total Correct		

Score Interpretation—Total Correct

35	
34	This is pretty good work. Review the explanations for the answers you got incorrect. This is an important test that contributes to your AFQT.
33	
32	
31	
30	You are doing pretty well. Review the explanations for the items you answered incorrectly. If you have time, review the other explanations and you will learn even more.
29	
28	
27	
26	
25	You need to keep studying. Pay close attention to the explanations for each item, even for the ones you got correct.
24	
23	
22	
21	Spend time working on the Word Knowledge review in Part 3 of this book.
20	
19	
18	
17	Keep reading and identifying words you don't know.
16	
15	
14	
13	
12	
11	
10	
9	
8	
7	
6	
5	
4	
3	
2	
1	
0	

Part 4. Paragraph Comprehension

Item Number	Correct Answer	Mark X If You Picked the Correct Answer
1	A	
2	A	
3	B	
4	D	
5	D	
6	C	
7	D	
8	C	
9	A	
10	D	
11	C	
12	C	
13	B	
14	D	
15	B	
Total Correct		

Score Interpretation—Total Correct

15	This is pretty good work. Review the explanations for the answers you got incorrect. This test is a part of the AFQT, and you must do well.
14	You are doing pretty well. Review the explanations for the items you got incorrect. This test is a part of the AFQT, and you must do well.
13	You need to keep studying. Pay close attention to the explanations for each item, even for the ones you got correct. This will help you understand why the answer is correct. Spend time reviewing the Paragraph Comprehension and Word Knowledge reviews in Part 3 of this book. Keep reading books and newspapers.
12	
11	
10	
9	
8	
7	
6	
5	
4	
3	
2	
1	
0	

Part 5. Mathematics Knowledge

Item Number	Correct Answer	Mark X If You Picked the Correct Answer
1	A	
2	C	
3	D	
4	B	
5	C	
6	C	
7	D	
8	B	
9	A	
10	C	
11	B	
12	D	
13	A	
14	B	
15	A	
16	D	
17	C	
18	C	
19	D	
20	A	
21	B	
22	B	
23	D	
24	C	
25	D	
Total Correct		

Score Interpretation—Total Correct

25	This is pretty good work. Review the explanations for the answers you got incorrect.
24	
23	
22	You are doing pretty well. Review the explanations for the items you answered incorrectly. If you have time, review the other explanations and you will learn even more.
21	
20	
19	This test is part of the AFQT. You must perform well on this test.
18	
17	
16	You need to keep studying. Pay close attention to the explanations for each item, even for the ones you got correct.
15	
14	
13	
12	Spend time working on the Mathematics Knowledge reviews in Part 3 of this book, and work and rework the problems until you fully understand the processes.
11	
10	
9	
8	
7	
6	
5	
4	
3	
2	
1	
0	

Part 6. Electronics Information

Item Number	Correct Answer	Mark X If You Picked the Correct Answer
1	D	
2	B	
3	C	
4	D	
5	A	
6	C	
7	D	
8	A	
9	A	
10	C	
11	D	
12	B	
13	C	
14	C	
15	A	
16	B	
17	D	
18	A	
19	C	
20	D	
Total Correct		

Score Interpretation—Total Correct

20	This is pretty good work. Review the explanations for the answers you got incorrect.
19	
18	
17	You are doing pretty well. Review the explanations for the items you answered incorrectly. If you have time, review the other explanations and you will learn even more.
16	
15	
14	
13	
12	You need to keep studying. Pay close attention to the explanations for each item, even for the ones you got correct.
11	
10	
9	
8	Spend time working on the Electronics Information review in Part 3 of this book.
7	
6	
5	Your school electronics or physics books may have some helpful information as well.
4	
3	
2	
1	
0	

Part 7. Auto and Shop Information

Item Number	Correct Answer	Mark X If You Picked the Correct Answer
1	C	
2	D	
3	C	
4	A	
5	A	
6	D	
7	C	
8	D	
9	C	
10	D	
11	A	
12	C	
13	B	
14	D	
15	B	
16	C	
17	A	
18	A	
19	C	
20	C	
21	D	
22	C	
23	B	
24	B	
25	D	
Total Correct		

Score Interpretation—Total Correct

Score	Interpretation
25	This is pretty good work. Review the explanations for the answers you got incorrect.
24	
23	
22	
21	
20	You are doing pretty well. Review the explanations for the items you answered incorrectly. If you have time, review the other explanations and you will learn even more.
19	
18	
17	
16	
15	
14	You need to keep studying. Pay close attention to the explanations for each item, even for the ones you got correct.
13	
12	
11	
10	Spend time working on the Auto and Shop Information reviews in Part 3 of this book.
9	
8	
7	
6	
5	
4	
3	
2	
1	
0	

Part 8. Mechanical Comprehension

Item Number	Correct Answer	Mark X If You Picked the Correct Answer
1	A	
2	C	
3	D	
4	C	
5	D	
6	B	
7	C	
8	B	
9	C	
10	A	
11	C	
12	B	
13	C	
14	D	
15	D	
16	C	
17	B	
18	B	
19	A	
20	D	
21	C	
22	A	
23	D	
24	A	
25	D	
Total Correct		

Score Interpretation—Total Correct

Score	Interpretation
25	This is pretty good work. Review the explanations for the answers you got incorrect.
24	
23	
22	
21	
20	You are doing pretty well. Review the explanations for the items you answered incorrectly. If you have time, review the other explanations and you will learn even more.
19	
18	
17	
16	
15	You need to keep studying. Pay close attention to the explanations for each item, even for the ones you got correct.
14	
13	
12	
11	Spend time working on the Mechanical Comprehension review in Part 3 of this book
10	
9	
8	
7	
6	
5	
4	
3	
2	
1	
0	

Part 9. Assembling Objects

Item Number	Correct Answer	Mark X if You Picked the Correct Answer
1	C	
2	A	
3	B	
4	C	
5	B	
6	D	
7	A	
8	C	
9	B	
10	C	
11	C	
12	B	
13	A	
14	D	
15	D	
16	C	
17	B	
18	D	
19	A	
20	D	
21	A	
22	A	
23	D	
24	B	
25	A	
Total Correct		

Score Interpretation–Total Correct

Score	Interpretation
25	This is pretty good work. Review the explanations of the answers you got incorrect.
24	
23	
22	
21	
20	You are doing pretty well. Review the explanations for the items you answered incorrectly. If you have time, review the other explanations and you will learn even more.
19	
18	
17	
16	
15	Keep studying. Pay close attention to the explanations for each item, even for the ones you got correct.
14	
13	
12	
11	Spend time working on the Assembling Objects review in Part 3 of this book.
10	
9	
8	
7	
6	
5	
4	
3	
2	
1	
0	

Answers and Explanations

PART 1. GENERAL SCIENCE

1. **A.** The cell membrane is the part of the cell that determines what enters and exits a cell. The correct answer is choice A.

2. **A.** *Vascular* is the name given to the systems that transport water and nutrients within certain plants, so choice D is not correct. *Annuals* are plants that undergo a full growing cycle in one year, so choice B is not correct. *Deciduous* is a term used for trees that shed their leaves in the winter, so choice C is not correct. Choice A, *angiosperms*, is the term given to describe plants that flower.

3. **A.** The hereditary system (choice C) and the reproductive system (choice B) are clearly incorrect answers. The lymphatic system (choice D) is one of the human organ systems and does not occur in plants. Choice A, the vascular system, is the correct answer. The vascular system takes fluid up from the water and transports it through the stem into the leaves.

4. **B.** The whale is a vertebrate mammal because it has an internal skeletal system and nurses its young with milk. Choice B is the correct answer.

5. **D.** A mammal is an animal that has live births and feeds its young with milk-secreting glands called mammary glands. Fish (choice A), snakes (choice B), and crocodiles (choice C) do not fit this group. Of this group, only apes (choice D) are mammals. Choice D is the correct answer.

6. **B.** Animals are food consumers, while plants are food producers. Frogs (choice A), parrots (choice C), and the manatee (choice D) are all animals, so they are consumers. The tree (choice B) is the only plant on the list and is the food producer.

7. **B.** Bones are held together by fibrous bands called ligaments. Choice B is the correct answer.

8. **A.** The skin is clearly the largest organ of your body, covering your entire skeletal and muscular system. Choice A is the correct answer.

9. **D.** Per gram, fat has much more energy than carbohydrates, proteins and minerals. Fat cells store the most energy. Choice D is the correct answer.

10. **A.** Platelets (choice D), red blood cells (choice C), and white blood cells (choice B) are all part of blood, but the substance that makes up most of the blood's volume is plasma (choice A).

11. **C.** The inner ear contains structures and fluids that move and swirl when you move. These structures send signals to the brain that help you understand your relative position. Choice C is the correct answer.

12. **B.** The basic difference between mitosis and meiosis is in the mechanism of cell division. The result of the division of mitosis is that each cell has the full complement of 46 chromosomes. In sexual reproduction, the process of meiosis produces cells with 23 chromosomes, so that when fertilization takes place between an egg and sperm, the full complement of 46 chromosomes will be present. Choice B is the correct answer.

13. **D.** Looking at the electromagnetic spectrum, ultraviolet radiation is to the right of visible light, which indicates more energy and a higher frequency. Choice D is the correct answer.

14. **C.** It is a fundamental principle that matter cannot be created or destroyed. Although a candle would look smaller, if we would trap

the gases, the total matter would end up the same. The total mass stays the same, so choice C is the correct answer.

15. **A.** The crust is a very thin layer (although very important to our daily lives) and takes up very little of Earth's volume. Choice A, crust, is the right answer.

16. **A.** Oceanic features formed by tectonic plates moving away from one another are called *rifts*. A rift is much like a huge valley across a continent or on the ocean floor.

17. **C.** Warm water is lighter or less dense than cold water. Choice A is not the correct answer. Currents on the surface are not density currents. Choice B is not the correct answer. Water with a high concentration of dissolved gases would be lighter and less dense, so choice D is not the correct answer. Water that is cold and saline or salty would be more dense and would be much more prone to sink, forming density currents. These types of currents form near the cold poles and generally flow slowly along the ocean floor. So choice C is correct.

18. **D.** Tides (choice A) are caused by the gravity of the moon. Day and night (choice B) are caused by the spinning or rotation of Earth as it revolves around the sun. Earth does bulge at the equator (choice C), but Earth's tilt does not cause this. The tilt of Earth's axis as it orbits around the sun causes the sun's rays to fall more directly on the northern hemisphere during the months of June, July, and August, and in the southern hemisphere during the months of December, January, and February. More direct sunlight makes for warmer temperatures and longer days, creating summer. Less direct sunlight and shorter days create winter weather. The tilt causes the seasons, so choice D is the correct answer.

19. **A.** Earth's gravitational pull is so strong that is locks the moon into having revolution and rotation periods that are nearly the same. The moon makes one rotation in about every 27.3 days.

It also revolves around Earth in about that same amount of time. As a result, the moon never shows most of its far side to Earth. We are able to see a small part of the far side of the moon because the rotation and revolution times of the moon are not exactly the same, but most of the far side is never visible by anyone on Earth. Choice A is the correct answer.

20. **A.** Substances can be in a solid, liquid, or gas form, the three states of matter. For matter to change from one form to another, there needs to be a change in thermal energy. At room temperature some substances are naturally gases, some are naturally liquids, and some are naturally solids. Of the options given, the only substance that is naturally a solid at room temperature is sulfur. The other three are gases, so choice A is the correct answer. However, if sulfur is heated to a high enough temperature, it too can be a gas. This temperature, however, is well beyond what we consider room temperature. You usually can smell sulfur gases near volcanic activity and thermal activity such as hot springs.

21. **A.** Earth's weather takes place in the atmospheric layer closest to the ground. That is choice A, the troposphere.

22. **D.** The sun's radiation causes a part of our atmosphere called the *ionosphere* to be electrically charged. AM radio waves from Earth's surface bounce off the ionosphere and are reflected back to ground level. Broadcasters use this property of radio waves to make the waves travel long distances. When solar radiation is overactive, it can cause the ionosphere to become highly charged. When that happens, radio waves can be disturbed, causing static. Choice D is the correct answer.

23. **C.** Erosion is the breaking up and transport of rock. Freezing and thawing (choice A) can cause rocks to break up into smaller pieces. The actions of water in rivers (choice B) break up pieces of rock and can also erode river banks

and create deep valleys and canyons. Lichen and mosses (choice D) use chemical action to break up rock. Lava flows (choice C) are considered to be builders of land rather than erosion agents. Choice C is the correct answer.

24. **C.** The core of the sun is so hot that it promotes the fusion of hydrogen atoms into helium, thereby releasing energy. Choice C is the correct answer.

25. **C.** A charged particle that has either more electrons than protons or fewer electrons than protons is called an *ion*. The process of creating charged particles is called *ionization*. Choice A is not the correct answer. *Refraction* is the bending of light rays. Choice B is not the correct answer. The rate of decay of an atomic nucleus is called its *half-life*. Choice D is not the correct answer. When the nucleus of an atom gives up a particle and its energy in order to become more stable, the process is called *radioactive decay*. Choice C is the correct answer.

PART 2. ARITHMETIC REASONING

1. **C.** This is a simple addition problem. Add the amounts to get the total of $193.69.

2. **C.** This problem has two steps. First you need to add the number of miles driven and then determine how many more miles are left in the trip. Marty has driven a total of 389 miles, so he has 138 to go.

3. **B.** In order to calculate the percent, you need to divide the total number of times at bat into the number of hits. In this case you would divide 72 into 54 to get 0.75. To change that to a percent, move the decimal point two places to the right and add the percent sign to get the correct answer of 75%.

4. **D.** To find the average, add the numbers and divide by the number of numbers. In this problem the total number of calories eaten by Phil is 10,400. Dividing this by the number of days (4) gives the average of 2,600 calories.

5. **D.** For this problem, you need to find out what number is 60% of 450. Change the 60% to 0.60 and multiply that by 450. Doing that calculation results in the number 270, the correct answer.

6. **C.** The basic question is that if 1 inch = 50 miles, how many inches = 450 miles? Set this up as a proportion. $\frac{1}{50} = \frac{x}{450}$. Cross-multiply and solve for x. $50x = 450$. $x = 9$. So the distance on the map between New Town and Old Town is 9 inches.

7. **C.** You need to find either the cost of one burger or the cost of one milk shake. It is possible to find the cost of one burger by subtracting Phil's cost from Janice's cost because the only difference is the cost of one burger. So $14.80 minus $10.30 = $4.50. Therefore, the cost of one burger is $4.50. If Phil's two burgers = $9.00, then one milk shake = $10.30 − $9.00 = $1.30. The problem asks for the cost of two milkshakes, which would be 2($1.30) or $2.60. Therefore the correct answer is $2.60.

8. **C.** Probability = number of favorable outcomes/number of possible outcomes. In this problem, the number of favorable outcomes is a combination of white and black balls or 35 + 45 = 80. The number of possible outcomes is 35 + 75 + 45 = 155. So substituting into the formula, the probability is $\frac{80}{155}$ or $\frac{16}{31}$.

9. **D.** Simple interest problems use the formula $I = prt$, where I is the amount of interest, p is the principal or the amount saved or invested, r is the rate of interest, and t is the amount of time that the interest is accruing. For compounded interest problems, you need to calculate the simple interest for each year, add it to the principal and use that figure as the new principal for the next year. The process is repeated for each year. In this problem, the interest is compounded for 3 years, so you will calculate the interest three times, each time using the new principal.

Year One
Principal = $3,000
Rate = 0.05
Interest = $150
Add the interest to the principal to get $3,150.

Year Two

Principal = $3,150

Rate = 0.05

Interest = $157.50

Add the interest to the principal to get $3,307.50.

Year Three

Principal = $3,307.50

Rate = 0.05

Interest = $165.38

Add the interest to get the principal of $3,472.88, the amount Jose would have after three years.

10. **C.** If Sonya's average over five tests is 89, she has earned a total of 445 points for the five tests. If she received a 95 on the sixth test, that brings her total points to 540. Dividing that by the six tests gives a new average of 90.

11. **D.** In this problem you need to find out how many $\frac{2}{3}$ cups are in 18 cups. So $18 \div \frac{2}{3} = ?$ is the equation. When you divide by a fraction, you invert and multiply, so the equation becomes $18 \times \frac{3}{2} = \frac{18 \times 3}{2} = \frac{54}{2} = 27$. Victor can make 27 batches of lasagna with 18 cups of tomato paste.

12. **D.** Since the final result needs to be in square yards, take the original measurements and convert them to yards. 12 feet = 4 yards, and 24 feet = 8 yards. Since area $= l \times w$, $4 \times 8 = 32$ yd^2. That's how many square yards of carpeting are needed.

13. **A.** Joanne's salary is $3,000 per month. If she pays 28% of that amount on taxes, reduce that amount by 28% by multiplying the total salary by 0.28.

$$\$3,000 \times 0.28 = \$840.00$$

$840.00 represents the amount paid in taxes. To find out how much of Joanne's salary is left, subtract $840.00 from the salary:

$$\$3,000 - \$840.00 = \$2,160.00$$

A faster way to do this (and speed is important on the ASVAB) is to multiply the original cost

by 72% or 0.72 because that is the amount of salary after taxes.

$$\$3,000 \times 0.72 = \$2,160.00$$

14. **D.** Use the following formula:

$$\text{Percent of Change} = \frac{\text{Amount of Change}}{\text{Starting Point}}.$$

In this problem we know that Gene grew from 60 to 69 inches. So the amount of change is the difference between 69 and 60 or 9 inches. The starting point is his original height of 60 inches. Substitute that information into the formula.

$$\text{Percent of Change} = \frac{9}{60} = 0.15.$$

Change that number to a percent by moving the decimal place two places to the right and add the percent sign. $0.15 = 15\%$

15. **A.** If Patrick traveled at 50 mph for 3 hours, the trip was 3(50) or 150 miles. Recall the formula $D = rt$, where $D =$ distance, $r =$ rate, and $t =$ time. Substitute what you know. $D = 150$ miles; $r = 40$. $150 = 40t$. Solve for t. $t = 3.75$ hours.

16. **B.** To calculate the area of the patio, use the formula $A = lw$. In this problem, notice that the dimensions of the patio are given in inches, but the cement bag information is in square feet. Change the inches to feet.

$$360 \text{ inches} = 30 \text{ feet}$$
$$480 \text{ inches} = 40 \text{ feet}$$

Substitute that information into the formula.

$$A = (30)(40)$$
$$A = 1200 \text{ ft}^2$$

If one bag of cement is needed for every 16 square feet, you need to divide that into the total area.

$$\frac{1200 \text{ ft}^2}{16 \text{ ft}^2} = 75 \text{ bags}$$

17. **A.** To calculate the area of a circle, use the formula $A = \pi r^2$. In this problem the radius is 20 feet. Substitute the radius into the formula and solve for A.

$$A = 3.14(20^2)$$
$$A = 3.14(400)$$
$$A = 1,256 \text{ ft}^2$$

18. **C.** Create an equation to solve this problem.

$$\text{Suzie} = 2(\text{Will}) + 4$$

You are told that Will is 9. Substitute that information into the formula. Suzie $= 2(9) + 4$. Solve for Suzie. Suzie $= 22$

19. **B.** If there are four quarters in every dollar, Barry needs to save 4×950 quarters or 3,800 quarters.

20. **C.** Watch the units in this problem. Change the yards to feet.

$$6 \text{ yards} = 18 \text{ feet}$$

To find out how many $1\frac{1}{2}$-foot pieces there are in 18 feet, divide 18 by $1\frac{1}{2}$. Change the mixed number to a fraction. $18 \div \frac{3}{2}$. When dividing by a fraction, invert and multiply.

$$18 \times \frac{2}{3}$$
$$= \frac{18 \times 2}{3} = \frac{36}{3} = 12 \text{ pieces}$$

21. **B.** Treat this like a compound interest problem where you calculate the increase in kilometers each week, using the increased amount as the amount to use in the calculations the next week.

Week One

5 km

Week Two

$5 \text{ km} + 0.20(5) = 6 \text{ km}$

Week Three

$6 \text{ km} + 0.20(6) = 7.2 \text{ km}$

Week Four

$7.2 + 0.20(7.2) = 8.64 \text{ km}$

22. **D.** To solve this problem, use the formula $V = lwh$. First you need to calculate the volume of the box. You have been given the dimensions of $l = 15$ in, $w = 6$ in, and $h = 6$ in. Substitute that information into the formula.

$$V = (15)(6)(6)$$
$$V = 540 \text{ in}^3$$

Now you need to calculate the volume of one brownie. You have been given the dimensions of $l = 3$ inches, $w = 2$ inches, and $h = \frac{1}{2}$ inches. Substitute that information into the formula.

$$V = (3)(2)\left(\frac{1}{2}\right)$$
$$V = 3 \text{ in.}^3$$

The last step is to find out how many brownies of 3 in³ fit into 540 in.³

Divide 540 in³ by 3 in³ to get 180 brownies.

23. **A.** Set this up as a proportion.

$$\frac{1 \text{ lb}}{24 \text{ cups}} = \frac{x}{36 \text{ cups}}$$

Cross-multiply and solve for x.

$$24x = 36$$
$$x = 1.5 \text{ lb of potatoes}$$

24. **C.** To calculate the volume of a cylinder, use the formula $V = \pi r^2 h$. In this problem the diameter is 8 cm, so the radius is 4 cm. The height is given as 10 cm. Substitute that information into the formula.

$$V = (3.14)(4^2)(10)$$
$$V = (3.14)(16)(10)$$
$$V = 502.4 \text{ cm}^3$$

Be sure to pay attention to the information you are given. You could have made an error by using the diameter rather than the radius because the diameter was given in the problem.

25. **B.** To calculate the volume of a sphere, use the formula $V = \frac{4}{3}\pi r^3$. You are given a diameter of 18 inches, so the radius is 9. Substitute that information into the formula.

$$V = \frac{4}{3}\pi(9)^3$$
$$V = \frac{4(3.14)(729)}{3}$$
$$V = \frac{9,156.24}{3} = 3,052.08 \text{ in}^3$$

26. **C.** There are 16 ounces in a pound. Divide 16 by 0.25, the weight of one slice of meat, to get the number of slices.

$$\frac{16}{0.25} = 64 \text{ slices.}$$

27. **A.** Set this up as a proportion.

$$\frac{55 \text{ pages}}{1 \text{ day}} = \frac{880 \text{ pages}}{x \text{ days}}$$

Cross-multiply and solve for x.

$$55x = 880$$
$$x = 16 \text{ days}$$

28. **B.** Use the formula $D = rt$. You are given the distance of 448 miles and the time of 8 hours. Substitute those into the formula. $448 = r8$. Solve for r.

$$r = \frac{448}{8} = 56 \text{ miles per hour}$$

29. **B.** The area of a square is calculated by using the formula $A = s^2$ or $s \times s$. Given the area of 576 ft², you need to find a number that, when multiplied by itself, equals 576. That number is 24. For problems like this, the fastest way to find the correct answer is to multiply each answer choice by itself and see which produces 576 ft².

30. **B.** For this problem, multiply the points by the difficulty and add the scores for each dive.

$$(8.2 \times 1.2) + (9.0 \times 1.4) + (8.3 \times 1.5)$$
$$+ (9.5 \times 1.4) + (9.5 \times 1.2)$$
$$= 9.84 + 12.60 + 12.45 + 13.30 + 11.4$$
$$= 59.59 \text{ pts}$$

PART 3. WORD KNOWLEDGE

1. **C.** *Listless* means "not caring, indifferent, or without energy." *Thirsty* is clearly wrong. The words *active* and *energized* are opposite in meaning. *Limp*, choice C, is the best answer.

2. **B.** *Potent* means "having authority; strong, effective, and forceful." *Colorful* and *movable* do not relate to this definition. *Explosive* certainly conveys the meaning of strength and force, but *powerful*, choice B, is the best answer.

3. **A.** *Compelled* means "forced or coerced." The words *happy*, *honored*, and *free* do not relate to the definition of *compelled*. *Forced*, choice A, is the correct answer.

4. **D.** *Vivid* is based on a root word meaning "full of life or lively." *Dull*, *poor*, and *stagnant* do not share the meaning of the definition. *Colorful*, choice D, is the best answer.

5. **B.** *Futile* means "pointless or incapable of achieving success." *Successful*, *easy*, and *powerful* do not share the meaning of the word *futile*. Thus, choice B, *useless*, is the best answer.

6. **C.** *Solicited* means "asked, begged, or implored." *Ignored*, *rejected*, and *followed* do not share this meaning. Choice C, *requested*, is the best answer.

7. **A.** *Appease* means "to pacify, soothe, or give in to someone else's demands." It does not mean *hurt*, *scare*, or *wonder*. *Satisfy*, choice A, is the correct answer.

8. **C.** To *abhor* means "to feel disgust for or to detest." The words *adore* and *worship* are both opposites of this definition and are clearly wrong. If you detest something you might *reject* it, but the best answer is choice C, *hate*.

9. **B.** To be *prudent* means "to exercise good judgment; to be cautious and not rash." *Reckless* and *wasteful* seem to be near opposites of the definition and cannot be correct. Someone who

is prudent with money might be a little *stingy*, but *careful*, choice B, is the best answer.

10. **A.** To be *staunch* means "to be loyal, solid, dependable, unfaltering, and strong." A staunch supporter cannot be *part time* or *periodic*, so those words are clearly wrong. The word *talkative* does not relate to the meaning of the word, so *steadfast*, choice A, is the correct answer.

11. **D.** To be *zealous* means "to be fervent, obsessive, and extreme." The word *whimsical* does not relate to the definition. A person who is zealous might be *incorrect* and even *unusual*, but the word *passionate*, choice D, is the closest in meaning to *zealous*.

12. **C.** *Volatile* means "unstable, unpredictable, and hot-tempered." It is based on a root word meaning "to fly," as in "fly off the handle." The words *acceptable*, *motivated*, and *humorous* do not relate to the definition. The best answer is choice C, *explosive*.

13. **B.** To be *terse* is to be succinct and not use unneeded words to make a point. *Terse* means "brief and abrupt." The words *expansive* and *wordy* are opposite in meaning to *terse*. Something terse might possibly be a little *confusing*, but the best answer is choice B, *concise*.

14. **C.** To be *austere* means "to be stern and severe; plain and lacking in ornaments." *Austere* means "stark and unadorned." The words *fancy* and *extravagant* are opposite in meaning. *Austere* does not mean *crowded*. Choice C, *simple*, is the best answer.

15. **A.** To be *meticulous* means "to be extremely careful with details, thorough, and precise." *Careless* seems to be the opposite of the definition. The word *doubtful* is not related. One must be *persistent* if one is meticulous, but *painstaking*, choice A, is the best answer.

16. **D.** *Vital* means "essential to life; indispensable, critical, central, or crucial." *Unrelated* and *unimportant* seem almost opposite to the definition.

Harmful does not seem related to the word *vital*. *Essential*, choice D, is the best answer.

17. **B.** *Timid* means "lacking in self-confidence, fearful, and shy." *Talkative* seems to be the opposite in meaning. The words *upset* and *present* do not relate to the definition. Someone who is timid is *hesitant*. Choice B is the correct answer.

18. **A.** The prefix *in-* means "not." *Inaudible* means "not audible." *Audible* means "able to be heard." So *inaudible* means "not able to be heard." The word *loud* seems somewhat opposite in meaning. The words *funny* and *suspicious* are not related to the definition. The best answer is choice A, *unheard*.

19. **B.** *Dormant* means "resting or sleeping." *Growing* seems to be the opposite of that definition. The words *dry* and *seedless* are not related to the definition. *Inactive*, choice B, is the best answer.

20. **C.** *Relinquished* means "gave up, handed over, or let go." The words *saved*, *transferred*, and *enjoyed* do not match this definition. *Surrendered*, choice C, the best answer.

21. **B.** *Delegated* means "transferred or handed over power or responsibility." *Absolved* means "forgiven," and that is clearly wrong. The words *withheld* and *promoted* are also unrelated to the definition. *Assigned*, choice B, is the correct answer.

22. **C.** *Dispensable* means "not important, not necessary, or not needed." The prefix *in-* reverses the meaning, so *indispensable* means the reverse of "not important," which is "important." It is clear that the words *hurtful*, *annoying*, and *energizing* do not match the definition. *Crucial* is the best synonym, which makes choice C the correct answer.

23. **D.** *Plausible* means "possible, probable, and credible." It does not mean *ridiculous*, *lengthy*, or *lofty*. Choice D, *credible*, is the best answer.

24. **A.** To be *advantageous* means "to provide an advantage or a benefit." Something *advantageous* is helpful and useful. The words *harmful* and *useless* are opposite in meaning. The word *compromising* is unrelated. Choice A, *beneficial*, is the best answer.

25. **D.** *Aroused* means "stimulated, provoked, and stirred to action." The word *reduced* seems to be somewhat opposite that concept. The words *increased* and *appeased* are unrelated to the definition. *Awakened* is the best synonym, so choice D is the correct answer.

26. **C.** *Provisional* means "temporary, interim, and conditional." The words *lasting* and *final* are near opposites to that definition. A provisional decision might be *initial*, but choice C, *tentative*, is the best answer.

27. **B.** To be *unparalleled* means "to be unequaled, unmatched, and incomparable." *Equaled* is the opposite of that meaning and is incorrect. The words *appreciated* and *misunderstood* do not relate to the concept. Choice B, *unmatched*, is the correct answer.

28. **A.** *Intermittent* means "starting and stopping at intervals; blinking, alternating, and sporadic." *Constant* seems to be the opposite of that definition. The words *disruptive* and *annoying* are unrelated to the definition. *Periodic*, choice A, is the correct answer.

29. **D.** To be *obstinate* means "to insist on having your own way; to be determined, pigheaded, adamant, and inflexible." The words *positive*, *unsure*, and *hopeful* are unrelated to that definition. *Stubborn*, choice D, is the only clear choice.

30. **C.** *Tactful* means "able to say the right thing in a delicate situation without offending anyone." *Discreet*, *judicious*, *polite*, and *careful* are synonyms. *Thoughtless* seems nearly the opposite. The words *forceful* and *unruly* are somewhat opposite to the definition. *Diplomatic*, choice C, is the best answer.

31. **D.** To be *proficient* means "to be highly competent, talented, and gifted." The word *unschooled* seems unrelated to the definition. It does not necessarily follow that if you are *trained*, then you are competent or talented. *Superior* is close to the definition, but the best answer is *skilled*, choice D.

32. **B.** *Augment* means "make greater, add to, enlarge, or expand." *Reduce* seems to be the opposite of this idea. The words, *invent* and *forget* are unrelated to the meaning. To *supplement* means "to enhance" and is thus a good synonym. Choice B is the correct answer.

33. **D.** *Vindictive* means "revengeful, malicious, and cruel." *Gentle* is the opposite of the definition and cannot be correct. The words *accurate* and *mistaken* are not related in meaning. Choice D, *spiteful*, is the correct answer.

34. **C.** *Obsolete* means "out of use, out of date, or outmoded." The words *vibrant* and *state-of-the-art* are nearly opposite of the definition and cannot be correct. *Broken* is not sufficiently accurate in meaning. The only answer that makes sense is choice C, *outdated*.

35. **B.** *Inundated* means "covered with, deluged, engulfed, or overwhelmed." The words *awakened*, *interrupted*, and *greeted* are not related to that definition. The closest answer is *flooded*, choice B.

PART 4. PARAGRAPH COMPREHENSION

1. **A.** The passage indicates that bombs fall close to the vent, so choice A is the correct answer.

2. **A.** There is no indication in the passage that airlines have gone bankrupt because of volcanoes (choice D) or that planes need to fly around volcanoes even when they are not erupting (choice C). The passage does suggest that crops affected by the ash can be destroyed, but no indication is given that the entire farming

industry has had problems from volcanoes; choice B is not correct. The passage does indicate that areas that are a substantial distance from the volcanoes can be affected by even minor ash falls, so choice A is the correct answer.

3. **B.** The passage states that volcanoes are found in Alaska, Hawaii, California, Oregon, and Washington. These are states in the western part of the United States. Choice B is the correct answer.

4. **D.** The passage directly states that sulfur dioxide mixed with water causes acid rain. Choice D is the correct answer.

5. **D.** The passage indicates that during an explosive eruption, volcanic glass, minerals, and ash rise high into the air, forming a huge, billowing, eruption column. The sentence gives you a sense that the eruption column is growing and expanding. The correct answer is choice D, *swelling*.

6. **C.** There is some truth to all the answers, but the basic thrust of the passage indicates that Hughes started from poor roots to become a praised and successful poet. The title that best represents that is choice C, "From Busboy to Poet."

7. **D.** The passage states that Lindsay was a famous literary critic, so choice D is the correct answer.

8. **C.** The passage indicates that "The Negro Speaks of Rivers" was Hughes's first great poem. Choice D is not the correct answer. There are no overall descriptors of the places Langston Hughes lived in Illinois or Missouri, so choices A and B cannot be correct. The passage indicates that the Harlem Renaissance was the African American artistic movement in the 1920s that celebrated black life and culture. Choice C is the correct answer.

9. **A.** Hughes's poems were praised by Lindsay (choice D), but the passage does not say that Lindsay's praise is the reason Hughes is considered a great poet, so choice D is not correct. It is also true that Hughes came from a humble background to become well known (choice B), but the passage does not suggest that this is what made him a great poet, so choice B is not correct. The passage does not say anything about Hughes's poems being published in many countries, so choice C is not correct. The passage does state that Hughes's literary works helped shape American politics and literature and that he was one of the most important writers and thinkers of his time. Choice A is the correct answer.

10. **D.** There is nothing in the passage to suggest that Hughes did not want to stay in Missouri or that he didn't want to move to Ohio. Choices A and B are not correct. Also there is nothing in the passage that indicates he was not allowed to write poems, so choice C is incorrect. The passage states that his father moved to Mexico and that his mother had to find steady work and was away for long periods. Thus he was raised by his grandmother. Choice D is the correct answer.

11. **C.** Although Wilder's family planted crops, the passage does not suggest that she chose to become a farmer (choice A). Being a daughter is not a profession, so choice B is incorrect. Wilder must have studied to earn a teaching certificate, but she did not remain a student (choice D). The profession she chose was that of teacher (choice C).

12. **C.** The passage does not suggest that Wilder was unoccupied (choice A), that she was too old to become an author (choice B), or that she was driven by a desire for success (choice D). The passage states that she wanted to pass on her experiences to the next generation, so choice C is the correct answer.

13. **B.** The passage indicates that Laura and Almanzo settled on a farm in Missouri called "Rocky Ridge." Choice B, Missouri, is the correct answer.

14. **D.** The passage mentions many hardships that Wilder faced when she was growing up and when she was married. Volcanic eruptions are not one of them. Choice D, volcanic eruptions, is the correct answer.

15. **B.** *Little House in the Big Woods* (choice D) was the title of Wilder's book and is not the correct answer. Although there are descriptions of the hardships of farmers (choice C), that is not the basic intent of the passage. That Wilder was an author (choice A) is also not the major idea in the story. Choice B, "Pioneer Woman and Author," reflects the major aspects of the passage—that Wilder and her family were pioneers and that she developed writing skills for a newspaper and eventually authored a book. Choice B is the correct answer.

PART 5. MATHEMATICS KNOWLEDGE

1. **A.** Isolate the unknown on one side. Add 37 to both sides.

$$k = -10 + 37$$
$$k = 27$$

2. **C.** Perform operations in the parentheses first, then the exponents, and then the remaining operations.

$$-3(4)^2$$
$$= -3(16) = -48$$

3. **D.** $45 = x\%$ of 180. $45 = x180$. Solve for x.

$$x = \frac{45}{180}$$
$$x = \frac{1}{4} \text{ or } 25\%$$

4. **B.** To change a fraction to a percent, first transform the fraction into a decimal. In this problem the decimal equivalent is 0.125. Move the decimal point two places to the right and add the percent sign to obtain the correct answer of 12.5%.

5. **C.** To divide mixed number and fractions, change the mixed number to an improper fraction. As with other division problems, invert and multiply the divisor.

$$\frac{7}{2} \div \frac{3}{4}$$
$$= \frac{7}{2} \times \frac{4}{3}$$

Simplify by canceling.

$$\frac{7}{\cancel{2}} \times \frac{\cancel{4}^2}{3} = \frac{14}{3} = 4\frac{2}{3}$$

6. **C.** In this problem you can easily see that the factors will begin with y. The last terms in the factors need to multiply to 15. The middle term tells you that the numbers you multiply need to add to 8. The factors will have plus signs. $5 \times 3 = 15$ and $5 + 3 = 8$. This gives you the factors $(y + 3)(y + 5)$.

7. **D.** When subtracting, change the sign and add. In this problem, $4x^3 + 5x^2 - 12$ is changed to $-4x^3 - 5x^2 + 12$ and is added to the first term.

$$4x^3 - 2x^2 + 6$$
$$-(4x^3 - 5x^2 + 12)$$

Note that the first term drops out, leaving the correct answer $-7x^2 + 18$.

8. **B.** For this problem, you want to isolate the h on one side of the equals sign. Multiply each side by $\frac{1}{3}$ resulting in $\frac{1}{h} = \frac{1}{33}$. Invert the fractions, which results in $h = 33$. Another way to solve this problem is to cross multiply: $1h = 33$; $h = 33$.

9. **A.** Set each equation to equal zero. Next, arrange the equations so that when one is subtracted from or added to the other, one of the terms results in a zero and drops out of the result. Next, solve for the remaining unknown. Set the equations equal to zero:

$$3m + 3p - 24 = 0$$
$$2m + p - 13 = 0$$

In this problem, notice that if you multiply the second equation by –3 and add the two equations, you can eliminate the p term.

$$3m + 3p - 24 = 0$$
$$(-3)(2m + p - 13) = 0$$

$$3m + 3p - 24 = 0$$
$$-6m - 3p + 39 = 0$$

Add the equations:

$$-3m + 15 = 0$$

Solve for m:

$$-3m = -15$$
$$m = 5$$

Substitute the value of m into one of the original equations.

$$3(5) + 3p - 24 = 0$$
$$15 + 3p - 24 = 0$$
$$-9 + 3p = 0$$

Solve for p.

$$3p = 9$$
$$p = 3$$

The correct answer is $m = 5$, $p = 3$.

10. **C.** To divide numbers with exponents, subtract the exponents. In this problem, there are numbers to divide as well as exponents $\frac{3r^5s^3}{12r^3s^2}$. Note that $\frac{3}{12}$ can be simplified to $\frac{1}{4}$. Next, subtract the 3 from 5 in the r term giving an exponent of 2 and the 2 from 3 in the s term giving an exponent of 1 or plain s. Putting all that together gives:

$$\frac{1}{4}r^2s \text{ or } \frac{r^2s}{4}, \text{ the correct answer.}$$

11. **B.** Factor the equation as follows: $(x - 15)(x - 3)$. Set each factor to equal zero.

$$x - 15 = 0; \ x = 15$$
$$x - 3 = 0; \ x = 3$$

The correct answer is $x = 15$, $x = 3$.

12. **D.** To multiply fractions, multiply the numerators and denominators. Simplify where possible.

$$\frac{6g}{2} \times \frac{3}{4y} = \frac{18g}{8y}$$

Simplify.

$$\frac{9g}{4y}$$

13. **A.** To divide fractions, invert the second term and multiply. Simplify where possible.

$$\frac{x^2}{3y} \div \frac{3x}{2y} \text{ becomes } \frac{x^2}{3y} \times \frac{2y}{3x}.$$

Multiply the numerators and denominators.

$$\frac{2x^2y}{9xy}$$

Simplify.

$$\frac{2x}{9}$$

14. **B.** The cube root is the number that, when multiplied by itself three times, results in the answer. In this instance, $10 \times 10 \times 10 = 1,000$, so the cube root of 1,000 is 10.

15. **A.** In this type of problem, where two fractions are separated by an equals sign, you can cross multiply and then solve for the variable of interest. Cross multiply to get $4g = 1(8)$. In solving for g, $g = 2$.

16. **D.** A quadrilateral has four sides, so choice D is the correct answer.

17. **C.** An isosceles triangle has at least two equal sides. Multiply the length of one of the two equal sides by 2 and add the length of the base. In this problem, the result is $2(24) + 3 = 51$ meters, the correct answer.

18. **C.** Multiply 6.25 by 4.5 to obtain 28.13. When two negatives are multiplied, the result is positive. Thus the answer is 28.13, not -28.13.

19. **D.** If the two angles add up to 75°, the third angle must be 105°.

20. **A.** Adding the measures of any two sides of a triangle gives a result that is greater than the measure of the third side. So in this problem, $AB + BC > AC$.

21. **B.** The right angle is 90°. The other angles have to add up to 90°. If this is an isosceles triangle, those two angles are equal. So 90° ÷ 2 = 45°.

22. **B.** To find the area of a parallelogram, multiply the base times the height. The height of a parallelogram is a line from one angle to the opposite side, making a right angle. In this problem, the area can be determined by multiplying the base 10 by the height 4, giving the correct answer of 40 units^2.

23. **D.** $\angle 2$ and $\angle 4$ are adjacent angles and thus form a straight angle or a straight line. If one angle is 25°, then the other is 180° − 25°, or 155°.

24. **C.** The volume of any rectangular solid is the product of its length, width, and height. For a cube, those measurements are the same, so the volume is the product of three edges. In this problem the edges are each 3 cm, so the volume = 3 × 3 × 3 or 27 cm^3.

25. **D.** The volume of a sphere is found by using the formula $\frac{4}{3}\pi r^3$. You are given the diameter of 10, so the radius is 5. Substituting the information into the formula gives $\frac{4}{3}(3.14)(5^3)$, or 4 × 3.14 × 125 ÷ 3, making the correct answer 523.33 cm^3.

PART 6. ELECTRONICS INFORMATION

1. **D.** Neoprene is an insulator. The other listed materials are all good conductors.

2. **B.** Volts measure the pressure in an electrical circuit (how hard the electrons are "trying" to get around the circuit).

3. **C.** Watts are the unit of electrical power; watts = amperes × volts.

4. **D.** Watts = volts × amperes = 12 × 4 = 48.

5. **A.** Transformers change voltage.

6. **C.** Depending on the chemical treatment, a semiconductor material can work as an insulator or a conductor.

7. **D.** Electric motors create magnetic fields that repel each other (exhibit repulsion).

8. **A.** A generator takes rotating motion and creates electric current.

9. **A.** Without a load, you have a short circuit, which will quickly heat up and burn out. Why are the other answers incorrect? Choices B and C: when a circuit is carrying electricity, it would have both current and voltage, but a "cold" circuit would not. Choice D: a switch is useful but optional.

10. **C.** In a rechargeable battery, the electrochemical reaction goes in one direction during charging and in the opposite direction while discharging.

11. **D.** In a series circuit, add the individual resistances to find the total resistance.

12. **B.** In a parallel circuit like this one, $1/R_{total} = 1/R_1 + 1/R_2 = 1/20 + 1/10 = 3/20$ so $R_{total} = 20/3$ ohms, or $6\frac{2}{3}$ ohms.

13. **C.** A series-parallel circuit has series and parallel sections.

14. **C.** Silicon is a semiconductor and is able to become a conductor or insulator as needed.

15. **A.** Diodes are devices that allow current to flow in one direction only.

16. **B.** The equipment grounding system is a safety, used only when the normal ground fails. Choice C is incorrect because the circuit may work correctly unless the normal ground fails.

17. **D.** A simple circuit tester simply detects whether a circuit is hot (carrying current) or cold (not carrying current).

18. **A.** 3-way switches are used in pairs to control a light.

19. **C.** An electromagnet "throws" a circuit breaker if too much current is present.

20. **D.** Volts = amperes × ohms = 10 × 40 = 400 volts.

PART 7. AUTO AND SHOP INFORMATION

1. **C.** A loose or worn fan belt squeals; the pitch rises along with engine speed.

2. **D.** A spark plug starts the explosion of the gasoline-air mixture.

3. **C.** This is the characteristic smell of leaking coolant.

4. **A.** Without a flywheel, the opposing compression and power strokes would create a jerking motion in the crankshaft.

5. **A.** Two rigid surfaces, like the mating faces of the engine block and the cylinder head, cannot be sealed unless something compressible (like a gasket) is between them.

6. **D.** The ignition coil supplies high-voltage current to the spark plugs.

7. **C.** The piston slides up and down, moving the connecting rod in a linear (straight-line) motion. It connects to the crankshaft, creating the rotary motion.

8. **D.** Brakes are a hydraulic system, where motion created in one place is transferred to another place through hydraulic fluid. The master cylinder pushes brake fluid through the brake lines, expanding the wheel cylinders, which push the brake pads against the disk or drum.

9. **C.** Cylinder heads must be firmly fastened to the engine block, without being warped during tightening. A torque wrench ensures proper tightness, and correct tightening order prevents warping.

10. **D.** Fan belts should be tight enough to grab the pulleys, but if they are too tight, bearings can be damaged.

11. **A.** The tube that supplies a fuel injector is full of high-pressure gasoline. A leak will likely cause a spray of gasoline in the engine compartment.

12. **C.** In a four-stroke engine, only one of the four strokes is a power stroke. Each cylinder fires (explodes) on every other stroke. Each revolution of a 4-cylinder engine has two explosions. Therefore, at 2,000 rpm, there would be 4,000 power strokes, or 4,000 explosions.

13. **B.** Why are the other answers incorrect? Choice A: a carriage bolt is stronger than a lag bolt, which is stronger than a screw. Choice C: a screw is stronger than a nail. Choice D: a carriage bolt is stronger than a nail.

14. **D.** The tool shown is a bar clamp.

15. **B.** Carpenter's glue does not hold unless it is clamped for 30 minutes.

16. **C.** Flux prevents oxidation during heating.

17. **A.** Tin snips shear sheet metal.

18. **A.** Unreinforced concrete is hard to compress, but easy to pull apart. Steel reinforcement adds tensile strength, allowing concrete to be used for beams, bridges, and the like.

19. **C.** The tool shown is a Phillips screwdriver.

20. **C.** Use a center punch to make a starting point when drilling metal. Otherwise, the bit will wander across the surface.

21. **D.** In plywood, actual size is the same as nominal (named) size. Why are the other answers incorrect? Choice A: a 2 × 4 is actually 1½ in × 3½ in. Choice B: a 1 × 4 is actually ¾ in × 3½ in. Choice C: an 8 in concrete block is actually 7⅝ in high (to allow for a ⅜ in mortar joint).

22. **C.** The tool shown is a wood chisel.

23. **B.** A lag-shield anchor must be inserted in a hole drilled in the concrete.

24. **B.** Why are the other answers incorrect? Choice A: a pipe wrench does not have two fixed jaws. Choice C: a pipe wrench can be used on pipe and pipe fittings. Choice D: length varies.

25. **D.** Pipe-joint compound seals a joint and prevents it from seizing up or rusting.

PART 8. MECHANICAL COMPREHENSION

1. **A.** Because 1 pound of pull on the rope produces 1 pound of lift, this pulley system has a mechanical advantage of 1.

2. **C.** When the shaft rotates faster, centrifugal force causes the balls to move outward. This enables a governor to regulate engine speed.

3. **D.** Lubricating the pavement with some sort of grease would reduce friction and cause the block to slide more easily.

4. **C.** In a class 3 lever, the load is between the fulcrum and the force.

5. **D.** When two sheaves are connected by a belt, the larger sheave will rotate more slowly than the smaller one. Sheaves A and B are connected to the same shaft, so they rotate at the same speed. Sheave C is larger than sheave B, so it will rotate more slowly. Sheave D is the largest of all, so it will rotate the slowest.

6. **B.** After ½ hour (30 minutes), the tank will have received 30 gallons. The engine will have used 1.5 gallons (½ hour × 3 gallons/hour = 1.5 gallons). 30 − 1.5 = 28.5.

7. **C.** The mechanical advantage is 2 (two supporting strands). MA = load/effort. 2 = 200/effort. Effort = 100 lb.

8. **B.** MA = load/effort. 400/100 = 4.

9. **C.** MA of an inclined plane = slope/vertical. The correct answer is 13/5.

10. **A.** When gear A rotates 3 times, it will move 72 teeth (3 × 24 = 72 teeth). 72/36 = 2, so gear B will rotate 2 times.

11. **C.** The handles pivot around a pin at the center, making them a lever. And the blades that shear the metal are just wedges.

12. **B.** MA = effort arm/load arm = 6/4 = 1.5.

13. **C.** Because three strands of rope must be shortened to raise the weight, the mechanical advantage is 3. MA = effort distance/load distance.

$$3 = 12/\text{load distance}$$
$$3 \times \text{load distance} = 12$$
$$\text{load distance} = 4$$

14. **D.** Why are the other answers incorrect? Choice A: either gear can drive (smaller drive gears increase the force; larger ones increase speed). Choices B and C: equal sized gears rotate at the same speed, while different sized gears rotate at different speeds.

15. **D.** Calculate the force needed to balance each weight separately, then add them. MA = effort arm/load arm, and MA = load/effort. For the 50 lb weight, the mechanical advantage is 12/6 = 2.

$$2 = \text{load/effort} = 50/\text{effort}$$

Effort = 25 lb. For the 30 lb weight, MA = 12/8 = 1.5. MA = load/effort. 1.5 = 30/effort. Effort = 20.

Total effort = 25 + 20 = 45 lb

16. **C.** The only object that is elastic (springy) is the tire.

17. **B.** Of the choices, only adding a post under the load would help the beam carry a heavier load. Choice D, convert one post into a fulcrum, would make the beam collapse.

18. **B.** Five turns tighter minus three turns looser equals two turns tighter. At 1/8 in per turn, the bolt will tighten by 2/8 in, or ¼ in.

19. **A.** With each turn of the screw, the 12-thread/inch screw will move the load a shorter distance, so it has a greater mechanical advantage. Choices C and D are incorrect because it is not possible to tell from this information whether the screw is stronger or weaker.

20. **D.** Applying the force shown would tip the beam, adding weight to B, but removing it from A.

21. **C.** Water pressure on the bottom depends on the depth of the water, so as water is added, pressure will increase.

22. **A.** MA = driven gear/drive gear. Mechanical advantage is reduced when the driven (rear) gear gets smaller. Therefore, more force is needed on the pedals.

23. **D.** In a closed hydraulic system, pressure must be the same at all points.

24. **A.** When the fulcrum is closer to the load, the effort arm gets longer and the load arm gets shorter. MA = effort arm/load arm. Therefore, the MA increases.

25. **D.** A lock nut and a lock washer are both designed to prevent a nut from moving on a bolt after it is tightened.

PART 9. ASSEMBLING OBJECTS

1. **C.** The original figure has three objects, while choice A has four. Look for the square. The square in choice B is too large, and there are two squares in choice D. Choice C is the correct answer.

2. **A.** The original figure has three objects, while choice C has four and choice D has only two. Look for the arch. Choice B does not have this object. Choice A is the correct answer.

3. **B.** The original figure has three objects, while choice C has four. Look for the five-sided object that looks like a house. Choice D does not have it. Look for the rectangle. Choice A does not have it. Choice B is the correct answer.

4. **C.** The original figure has five objects, while choice A has four and choice B has six. Look for the large rounded object at the top left. Choice D has a circle instead. Choice C is the correct answer.

5. **B.** The original figure has four objects, while choice C has five. The largest piece is the most distinctive. It looks like a rectangle with a corner carved out. Choice C does not have it and in choice A it is a mirror image (choice A also has two triangles). Look for the isosceles right triangle. Choice D does not have it. Choice B is the correct answer.

6. **D.** The original figure has three objects, while choice A has four and choice C has two. Look for the rectangle. Choice B does not have it. Choice D is the correct answer.

7. **A.** The original figure has three objects, while choice B has two and choice C actually only has one object. Look for the object shaped like a plus sign. Choice D has a similar object, but it is shaped like an X rather than a plus sign. Choice A is the correct answer.

8. **C**. The original figure has four objects, while choice A has three and choice D has five. Look for the long object at the top that looks like a rectangle with pointed ends. Choice B does not have this object. Choice C is the correct answer.

9. **B**. The original figure has three objects, while choice C has four. Look for the two identical rhombuses. Choice A has only one Look for the rectangle. Choice D does not have it. Choice B is the correct answer.

10. **C**. The original figure has three objects, while choices A and D have four. Look for the square. Choice B does not have a square. Choice C is the correct answer.

11. **C**. The original figure has three objects, while choice A has four. Look for the big curved object at the lower right. The curved objects in choices B and D are not the same shape. Choice C is the correct answer.

12. **B**. The original figure has four objects, while choice A has only three. Look for the large quad-rilateral at the far right. Choice D does not have it. Choice C has two quadrilaterals, so eliminate it as well. Choice B is the correct answer.

13. **A**. The original figure has three objects, while choice C has four. Look for the triangle. Choice D does not have a triangle. Look for the two identical quadrilaterals. Choice B has rectangles instead. Choice A is the correct answer.

14. **D**. The original figure has four objects, while choice A has five. Look for the five-sided object at the top left that looks like a rectangle with one corner cut off. Choices B and C do not have this object. Choice D is the correct answer.

15. **D**. The original figure has three objects, while choice A has four and choice B has only two. Look for the most distinctive object: the five-sided object at the right that looks like a kite. Choice C does not have this object. Choice D is the correct answer.

16. **C**. The original figure has four objects, while choice D has five. Look for the most distinctive object: the object on the far left that looks like a chair. Choice B does not have this object. Look for the curved object at the upper right. Choice A does not have it. Choice C is the correct answer.

17. **B**. The original figure has four objects, while choice C has five. Look for the object that looks like a triangle with one concave side. Choice D does not have this object. Choice A has a similar object, but it is not the same shape. Choice B is the correct answer.

18. **D**. The second object has a more distinct point, so start with that object. Point B is on the inside corner of the right "leg" of the second object. Choices A and B do not connect there. Choice C connects at the outside corner of that "leg." Choice D is the correct answer.

19. **A**. Point A is at the bottom right corner of the first object in its original orientation. Choice D does not connect the first object at that point. Point B is on the large rounded corner of the second object. Choice B connects at a pointed end. Choice C also connects at a (different) pointed end. Choice A is the correct answer.

20. **D**. Point A is at the bottom right corner of the first object in its original orientation. Choices B and C do not connect the first object at that point. Point B is in the center of the top end of the second object in its original orientation. Choice A does not connect at this spot. Choice D is the correct answer.

21. **A**. For the first object, point A is at the tip of the "leg" on the left (in the object's original orientation). Choice B does not connect the first object at that point. Point B is at the tall point of the second object. Choices C and D do not connect at the pointed end. Choice A is the correct answer.

22. **A.** If you picture the first object sitting on its flat base, then point A is at the lower left corner. All the choices have point A in the correct spot. Point B is at the center of the tip of the teardrop-shaped second object. All the choices have point B in the correct spot as well. Point C is at the indented center of the right side of the third object, in its original orientation. Choices C and D do not connect at that spot. That leaves choices A and B. Since this figure has three objects, check to see if each choice connects the pieces in the same order as the original: A to B and B to C. Choice B connects C to A and A to B. Choice A is the correct answer.

23. **D.** Point A is at middle of the long flat base of the first object in its original orientation. Choices A and B do not connect the first object at that point (and choice B has a mirror image of the object, which would also eliminate it as a possibility). If you picture the second object sitting on its larger flat base, then point B is at the top right corner. Choice C does not connect at this spot. Choice D is the correct answer.

24. **B.** Point A is at center of the concave part of the curve on the first object. Choice A does not connect the first object at that point. If you picture the second object sitting on its larger flat base, then point B is at the upper right corner. Choices C and D do not connect at this spot. Choice B is the correct answer.

25. **A.** In this question, the second object is more distinctive, so start with that one. Point B is on the right "leg" at the lower left corner. Choices B and C do not connect at that point. If you picture the first object—the isosceles triangle—sitting on its base, then point A is at the lower left corner. Choice D connects at the lower right corner. Choice A is the correct answer.

Part 5

JOBS IN TODAY'S MILITARY

Jobs in Today's Military

People in the military do just about every kind of work that exists in civilian life. They may be physical therapists, computer repair technicians, photographers and journalists, management analysts, auto mechanics, life scientists . . . you get the idea. And free job training is provided for every one of the over 400 individual types of military jobs. If a particular type of work interests you, you can most likely find it in the military. The range of job opportunities in today's military is extremely broad.

Military jobs fall into several categories including:

- Accounting, Budget, and Finance
- Aviation
- Combat Operations
- Construction, Building, and Extraction
- Education and Training
- Environmental Health and Safety
- Human Resources Management and Services
- Intelligence
- Law Enforcement, Security, and Protective Services
- Mechanic and Repair Technologists and Technicians
- Naval and Maritime Operations
- Transportation, Supply, and Logistics
- Arts, Communications, Media, and Design
- Business Administration and Operations
- Communications Equipment Technologists and Technicians
- Counseling, Social Work, and Human Services
- Engineering and Scientific Research
- Health Care Practitioners
- Information Technology, Computer Science, and Mathematics
- International Relations, Linguistics, and Other Social Sciences
- Legal Professions and Support Services
- Medical and Clinical Technologists and Technicians
- Personal and Culinary Services

Here you will find many opportunities to serve our country.

High-quality job training is provided right from the start. After Basic Recruit Training, you probably will attend advanced training (AT), where you attend a school that teaches you the skills necessary to do a particular job. AT combines classroom and hands-on learning environments. Well-trained instructors and a low student/teacher ratio are the norm. Over 60 percent of the courses in advanced training are certified for college credit by the American Council on Education.

Can You Choose Your Job If You Enlist?

You *do* have an influence on the job training you receive, but your ASVAB scores and the needs of the military at the time you'd like to enlist also affect your job assignment. Ask your recruiter about all the specialties for which you are eligible based upon your ASVAB scores. If the job you want isn't open at the moment, ask about the Delayed Enlistment Program, or explore other services that may have an equivalent job. Remember that the higher your ASVAB scores, the more job options you have!

Are Jobs in the Military All Open to Women?

About 18 percent of the active duty forces are women. Opportunities for women in the military have never been better. All jobs are open to females who qualify:

At the current time, the percentage of women in each branch of the military is as follows:

Percentage of Female Enlisted Service Members

Army	17%
Marine Corps	11%
Navy	21%
Air Force	19%
Coast Guard	12%

Given that all jobs are now open to women, these number are likely to rise.

What Do All Military Jobs Have in Common?

Responsibility. Excellence. Pride. You're expected to perform your assigned duties with a high level of competence. Others on your team and in your unit need to know that you are dependable, and that they can count on you. More often than not, the military offers a surprising amount of responsibility early in a career. Leading a team or crew of six or seven people at age 20 is common; so is making tactical decisions on the spot—even at junior levels. Most military jobs offer the opportunity to mature quickly . . . through responsibility.

How Many Military Jobs Have Civilian Equivalents?

About 88 percent of military jobs have counterparts in the civilian world, and many military jobs are virtually identical to the "hot" jobs that are forecasted to grow the fastest over the next few years. Virtually all military jobs give you an edge in the civilian world. That's because employers prize the things military veterans have learned—among them dependability, focus on the task, extra effort, reliability, team play, and striving for excellence. Computer and cybersecurity skills are becoming more critical and plentiful in military life.

No matter what your job in the military, there's an opportunity for you to do it well and earn the respect of your peers (and superiors) for your skills. This nearly always leads to greater self-confidence and a sense of pride. Every job in the military is important because each contributes to military readiness and each helps protect the freedoms all Americans enjoy.

INFORMATION ON MILITARY OCCUPATIONS

The following pages provide you with some summary information on 85 enlisted occupations in the

U.S. military. These pages give you brief information on the following characteristics:

- A brief description of the occupation
- What people in the occupation do
- Helpful attributes
- Training provided
- Physical demands
- Work environment
- Civilian counterparts
- Opportunities
- Services that offer this occupation

ADMINISTRATIVE SUPPORT SPECIALISTS

Short Description

The military must keep accurate information for planning and managing its operations. It keeps paper and electronic records on equipment, funds, personnel, supplies, and all other aspects of the military. Administrative support specialists record information, fill out reports, and maintain files to assist in the operation of military offices.

What They Do

Administrative support specialists in the military perform some or all of the following duties:

- Use a computer to type and prepare letters, reports, and other kinds of documents.
- Proofread written material for spelling, punctuation, and grammatical errors.
- Organize and maintain electronic and paper files and publications.
- Order office supplies.
- Greet and direct office visitors.
- Sort and deliver mail to office workers.
- Use office equipment such as fax machines, copiers, and computers.
- Schedule training and leave for unit personnel.
- Answer phones and provide general information.
- Take meeting notes.

Helpful Attributes

Helpful school subjects include English, math, and business administration. Helpful attributes include

- The ability to organize and plan
- Interest in keeping organized and accurate records

- Interest in operating computers and other office machines
- A preference for office work

Training Provided

Job training consists of classroom instruction, including practice in various office functions. Further training occurs on the job. Course content typically includes

- English grammar, spelling, and punctuation
- Keyboard and clerical skills
- Setting up and maintaining filing and publication systems
- Preparing forms and correspondence in military style

Work Environment

Administrative support specialists work in office settings, both on land and aboard ships.

Civilian Counterparts

Civilian administrative support specialists work in most business, government, and legal offices. They perform duties similar to those of military administrative support specialists and are called secretaries, general office clerks, administrative assistants, or office managers.

Opportunities

Each year, the services need new specialists because of changes in personnel and the demands of the field. After job training, administrative support specialists develop their skills under close supervision. As they gain experience, specialists are assigned more difficult tasks and work more independently. In time, they may supervise and eventually manage an office.

Services Offering This Occupation

Army

Navy

Air Force

Marine Corps

Coast Guard

AIRCRAFT MECHANICS

Short Description

Military aircraft are used to fly hundreds of missions each day for transport, patrol, and flight training. They need frequent servicing to remain safe and ready to fly. Aircraft mechanics inspect, service, and repair helicopters and airplanes.

What They Do

Aircraft mechanics in the military perform some or all of the following duties:

- Service and repair helicopter, jet, and propeller aircraft engines.
- Inspect and repair aircraft wings, fuselages, and tail assemblies.
- Service and repair aircraft landing gear.
- Repair or replace starters, lights, wiring, and other electrical parts.

Helpful Attributes

Helpful school subjects include mathematics and shop mechanics. Helpful attributes include

- Ability to use hand and power tools
- Interest in engine mechanics
- Interest in work involving aircraft

Training Provided

Job training consists of classroom instruction, including inspection and repair of aircraft engines and equipment. Training length varies depending upon specialty. Further training occurs on the job and through advanced courses. Course content typically includes

- Engine disassembly and repair
- Repair of hydraulic, fuel, and electrical systems
- Repair of aluminum, steel, and fiberglass airframes and coverings

Physical Demands

Some specialties require moderate to heavy lifting. Normal color vision is required to work with color-coded wiring.

Work Environment

Aircraft mechanics work in aircraft hangars and machine shops located on air bases or aboard aircraft carriers.

Civilian Counterparts

Civilian aircraft mechanics work for aircraft manufacturers, commercial airlines, and government agencies. They perform duties similar to those of military aircraft mechanics. They may also be called airframe or power plant mechanics.

Opportunities

Each year, the services need new mechanics because of changes in personnel and the demands of the field. After job training, mechanics are assigned to an aircraft maintenance unit, where they perform routine maintenance and simple repair jobs. In time, they may perform more difficult repairs and train and supervise new mechanics. Eventually, they may become inspectors, shop supervisors, or maintenance superintendents.

Services Providing This Occupation

Army

Navy

Air Force

Marine Corps

Coast Guard

AIR CREW MEMBERS

Short Description

The military uses aircraft of all types and sizes to conduct combat and intelligence missions, rescue personnel, transport troops and equipment, and perform long-range bombing missions. Air crew members operate equipment on board aircraft during operations. They normally specialize in a particular type of aircraft, such as bomber, intelligence, transport, or search and rescue.

What They Do

Air crew members in the military perform some or all of the following duties:

- Operate aircraft communication and radar equipment.
- Operate and maintain aircraft defensive gunnery systems.
- Operate helicopter hoists to lift equipment and personnel from land and sea.
- Operate and maintain aircraft in-flight refueling systems.

Helpful Attributes

Helpful school subjects include mathematics and mechanics. Helpful attributes include

- The ability to work as a team member
- The ability to work under stress
- Interest in flying

Training Provided

Job training consists of classroom instruction, including practical experience in aircraft systems operation and maintenance. Further training occurs on the job through actual flying time. There are additional courses covering air crew survival, scuba diving, parachuting, aircraft maneuvering, and combat crew training. Course content varies by specialty and may include

- Operation of aircraft gunnery systems
- Operation of aircraft in-flight refueling systems
- Cargo, munitions, and fuel load planning
- Rescue and recovery operations

Physical Demands

Air crew members must be in excellent physical condition and must pass a special physical exam in order to qualify for flight duty. They must be mentally sound and have normal hearing.

Work Environment

Air crew members work inside all sizes and types of aircraft based on land or aboard ships. They fly in all types of weather and in both hot and cold climates.

Civilian Counterparts

There are no direct civilian equivalents to military air crew members. However, some of the skills gained in the military could be useful in civilian government and private agencies that provide emergency medical services. Also, weight and load computation skills are useful for civilian air transport operations.

Opportunities

Each year, the services need new air crew members because of changes in personnel and the demands of the field. After receiving their "air crew qualified" rating, air crew members are assigned to a flying unit. They may work on one of many types of aircraft under the direction of the aircraft commander. With experience, they may supervise and train other enlisted air crew members. They have the opportunity to become air crew chiefs, combat crew chiefs, or supervisors of rescue and recovery units.

Services Offering This Occupation

Army

Navy

Air Force

Marine Corps

Coast Guard

AIR TRAFFIC CONTROLLERS

Short Description

Every day, hundreds of military airplanes and helicopters take off and land all over the world. Their movements are closely controlled in order to prevent accidents. Air traffic controllers direct the movement of aircraft into and out of military airfields. They track aircraft by radar and give voice instructions by radio.

What They Do

Air traffic controllers in the military perform some or all of the following duties:

- Operate radio equipment to issue takeoff, flight, and landing instructions.
- Relay weather reports, airfield conditions, and safety information to pilots.
- Use radar equipment to track aircraft in flight.
- Plot airplane locations on charts and maps.
- Compute the speed, direction, and altitude of aircraft.
- Maintain air traffic control records and communication logs.

Helpful Attributes

Helpful school subjects include general mathematics, English, and typing. Helpful attributes include

- The ability to make quick, decisive judgments
- The ability to work under stress
- Skill in math computation

Training Provided

Job training consists of classroom instruction. Training length varies depending upon specialty. Additional training occurs on the job. Aircraft carrier air traffic controllers receive specialized training. Course content typically includes

- Air traffic control fundamentals
- Visual and instrument flight procedures
- Radar and other landing approach procedures
- Communication procedures

Physical Demands

Normal color vision, normal hearing, and a clear speaking voice are required to enter this occupation. Controllers must pass a special physical exam.

Work Environment

Air traffic controllers work in land-based and shipboard control centers.

Special Requirements

Certification by the Federal Aviation Administration (FAA) normally must be obtained during training.

Civilian Counterparts

Civilian air traffic controllers work for the FAA in airports and control centers around the country. They perform duties similar to those of military air traffic controllers. They may specialize in specific areas, such as aircraft arrivals, departures, ground control, or en route flights.

Opportunities

Each year, the services need new controllers because of changes in personnel and the demands of the field. After job training, new controllers normally perform duties such as ground control or work in airfields with light air traffic. With experience, they perform more difficult controller duties. In time, they may become supervisors of other controllers.

Services Offering This Occupation

Army

Navy

Air Force

Marine Corps

AIRCRAFT LAUNCH AND RECOVERY SPECIALISTS

Short Description

The military operates thousands of aircraft that take off from and land on aircraft carriers all over the world. The successful launch and recovery of aircraft is important to the completion of air missions and the safety of flight crews. Aircraft launch and recovery specialists operate and maintain catapults, arresting gear, and other equipment used in aircraft carrier takeoff and landing operations.

What They Do

Aircraft launch and recovery specialists in the military perform some or all of the following duties:

- Operate consoles to control launch and recovery equipment, including catapults and arresting gear.
- Operate elevators to transfer aircraft between flight and storage decks.
- Install and maintain visual landing aids.
- Test and adjust launch and recovery equipment.
- Install airfield crash barriers and barricades.
- Direct aircraft launch and recovery operations.

Helpful Attributes

Helpful school subjects include shop mechanics. Helpful attributes include

- The ability to use hand tools and test equipment
- Interest in aircraft flight operations
- Interest in working on hydraulic and mechanical equipment

Training Provided

Job training consists of classroom instruction, including practice in maintaining launch and recovery equipment. Course content typically includes

- Operating and maintaining launch and recovery equipment
- Installing crash barriers and barricades

Physical Demands

Normal color vision is required to work with color-coded parts and the wiring of launch and recovery equipment.

Work Environment

Aircraft launch and recovery specialists work outdoors aboard ships while operating and maintaining launch and recovery equipment or holding visual landing aids for incoming aircraft. They are exposed to noise and fumes from jet and helicopter engines.

Civilian Counterparts

There are no direct civilian counterparts to military aircraft launch and recovery specialists. However, many of the skills learned are relevant to jobs performed by ground crews at civilian airports.

Opportunities

Each year, the services need new specialists because of changes in personnel and the demands of the field. After job training, specialists are assigned to an aircraft launch and recovery section aboard an aircraft carrier or at an airfield. Initially, they perform maintenance and repair on equipment, working under close supervision. With experience, they perform more complex activities. In time, they may train and supervise other specialists. Eventually, they may supervise activities on carrier flight and storage decks.

Services Offering This Occupation

Navy

Marine Corps

Coast Guard

ARMORED ASSAULT VEHICLE CREW MEMBERS

Short Description

In peacetime, the role of armored units is to stay ready to defend our country anywhere in the world. In combat, their role is to operate tanks, amphibious assault vehicles, and other types of armored assault vehicles to engage and destroy the enemy. Armored units also conduct scouting missions and support infantry units during combat. Crew members work as a team to operate armored equipment and fire weapons to destroy enemy positions. They normally specialize by type of armor, such as tanks, light armor (cavalry), or amphibious assault vehicles.

What They Do

Armored assault vehicle crew members in the military perform some or all of the following duties:

- Drive armored land or amphibious assault vehicles in combat formations.
- Operate target sighting equipment to aim guns.
- Load and fire guns.
- Operate communications and signaling equipment to receive and relay battle orders.
- Gather and report information about enemy strength and target location.
- Perform preventive maintenance on armored vehicles and mounted guns.
- Read maps and battle plans.

Helpful Attributes

Helpful attributes include

- The ability to follow directions and execute orders quickly and accurately
- The ability to work as a member of a team
- The ability to work well under stress
- Readiness to accept a challenge and face danger

Training Provided

Job training consists of classroom and field training under simulated combat conditions. Further training occurs on the job and through training exercises. Course content typically includes

- Vehicle operations
- Armor offensive and defensive tactics
- Map reading
- Scouting and reconnaissance techniques

Physical Demands

Armored assault vehicle crew members must be in good physical condition and have exceptional stamina.

They must be able to work inside a confined area for long periods of time. Good vision and normal color vision are required in order to read maps, drive vehicles around obstacles, and locate targets.

Work Environment

Armored assault vehicle crew members, like other combat troops, work in all climates and weather conditions. During training exercises, as in real combat conditions, crew members work, eat, and sleep outdoors and in vehicles.

Special Requirements

This occupation is open only to men.

Civilian Counterparts

Although the job of armored assault vehicle crew member has no equivalent in civilian life, the close teamwork, discipline, and leadership experience it provides are helpful in many civilian jobs.

Opportunities

Each year, the services need new crew members because of changes in personnel and the demands of the field. After job training, new crew members help operate weapons and control their armored vehicles. Leadership potential and job performance are the most important factors for advancement in this field.

Services Offering This Occupation

Army

Marine Corps

ARTILLERY AND MISSILE CREW MEMBERS

Short Description

The military uses artillery and missiles to protect infantry and tank units, as well as to secure and protect land and sea positions from enemy attack. The personnel who operate these systems will usually specialize by type of weapon system, such as cannons, howitzers, missiles, or rockets. Artillery and missile crew members position, direct, and fire these weapons to destroy enemy positions and aircraft.

What They Do

Artillery and missile crew members in the military perform some or all of the following duties:

- Operate computerized equipment to determine target locations.
- Prepare ammunition for firing.
- Set up and load weapons.
- Fire artillery and missile systems at enemy targets.
- Clean and maintain weapons.

Helpful Attributes

Helpful attributes include

- The ability to think and remain calm in stressful situations
- The ability to work as part of a team
- Interest in cannon and rocket operations
- Willingness to face danger

Training Provided

Job training consists of classroom instruction and field training under simulated combat situations. Training length varies depending upon specialty. Further training occurs on the job and through advanced courses. Course content typically includes

- Methods of computing target locations
- Ammunition-handling techniques
- Gun, missile, and rocket system operations
- Artillery tactics

Physical Demands

Artillery and missile crew members must have the physical stamina to perform strenuous activities for long periods without rest. They are also required to have normal color vision to identify color-coded ammunition and to read maps and charts.

Work Environment

Artillery and missile crew members work under different conditions depending upon the type of weapon system they use. Some crew members spend a lot of time in field training exercises, where they work, eat, and sleep outdoors and in tents. Others live and work aboard ships or submarines.

Special Requirements

Some specialties in this area are closed to women.

Civilian Counterparts

Although the job of artillery and missile crew member has no equivalent in civilian life, the close teamwork, discipline, and leadership experience it provides are helpful in many civilian jobs.

Opportunities

Each year, the services need new crew members because of changes in personnel and the demands of the field. After job training, new crew members work as part of an artillery or missile team. Leadership ability and job performance are the most important factors for advancement in this field. Those with leadership potential may assume supervisory positions. In time, they may lead artillery or missile crews.

Services Offering This Occupation

Army

Navy

Marine Corps

AUDIOVISUAL AND BROADCAST TECHNICIANS

Short Description

Television and film productions are an important part of military communications. Films are used for training in many military occupations. They are also used to record military operations, ceremonies, and news events. These productions require the teamwork of many technicians. Audiovisual and broadcast technicians perform many specialized tasks, ranging from filming to script editing to operating audio recording devices.

What They Do

Audiovisual and broadcast technicians in the military perform some or all of the following duties:

- Work with writers, producers, and directors in preparing and interpreting scripts.
- Plan and design production scenery, graphics, and special effects.
- Operate media equipment and special effects devices, including cameras, sound recorders, and lighting.
- Follow the script and the instructions of film or TV directors to move cameras, zoom, pan, or adjust focus.

Helpful Attributes

Helpful school subjects include photography, graphics, art, speech, and drama. Helpful attributes include

- Experience in school plays or making home movies
- Interest in creative and artistic work
- A preference for working as part of a team

Training Provided

Training length varies depending upon specialty. Further training occurs on the job and through advanced courses. Course content typically includes

- Motion picture equipment operation
- Audio recording
- Scripting and special effects techniques
- Maintenance of public address sound equipment

Physical Demands

Normal color vision and the ability to speak clearly are required for some specialties in this area.

Work Environment

Audiovisual and broadcast technicians work in studios or outdoors on location. They sometimes work from aircraft or ships. They travel and work in all climates.

Civilian Counterparts

Civilian audiovisual and broadcast technicians work for film production companies, government audiovisual studios, radio and television stations, and advertising agencies. Their duties are similar to those performed by military journalists and newswriters. They may be called motion picture camera operators, audiovisual production specialists, sound mixers, recording engineers, or broadcasting and recording technicians.

Opportunities

Each year, the services need new technicians because of changes in personnel and the demands of the field. After job training, new technicians assist with various production processes. With experience, they work more independently and, in time, may direct audiovisual productions.

Services Offering This Occupation

Army

Navy

Air Force

Marine Corps

AUTOMOTIVE AND HEAVY EQUIPMENT MECHANICS

Short Description

Keeping automotive and heavy equipment in good working condition is vital to the success of military missions. Automotive and heavy equipment mechanics maintain and repair vehicles such as jeeps, cars, trucks, tanks, and other combat vehicles. They also repair bulldozers, power shovels, and other construction equipment.

What They Do

Automotive and heavy equipment mechanics in the military perform some or all of the following duties:

- Troubleshoot problems in vehicle engines, electrical systems, steering, brakes, and suspensions.
- Tune and repair engines.
- Replace or repair damaged body parts, hydraulic arms or shovels, and grader blades.
- Establish and follow schedules for maintaining vehicles.

Helpful Attributes

Helpful school subjects include auto mechanics and industrial arts. Helpful attributes include

- Interest in automotive engines and how they work
- Interest in troubleshooting and repairing mechanical problems
- A preference for physical work

Training Provided

Job training consists of classroom instruction. Training length varies depending upon specialty. Further training occurs on the job and through advanced courses. Course content typically includes

- Engine repair and tune-up
- Troubleshooting mechanical and electrical problems
- Repairing and replacing body panels, fenders, and radiators

Physical Demands

Automotive and heavy equipment mechanics have to lift heavy parts and tools. They sometimes have to work in cramped positions. Normal color vision is required for some specialties to work with color-coded wiring and to read diagrams.

Work Environment

Automotive and heavy equipment mechanics usually work inside large repair garages. They work outdoors when making emergency repairs in the field.

Civilian Counterparts

Civilian automotive and heavy equipment mechanics may work for service stations, auto and construction equipment dealers, farm equipment companies, or state highway agencies. They perform duties similar to those of military automotive and heavy equipment mechanics. They may also be called garage mechanics, transmission mechanics, radiator mechanics, or construction equipment mechanics.

Opportunities

Each year, the services need new mechanics because of changes in personnel and the demands of the field.

After job training, mechanics begin repairing equipment under the direction of a supervisor. In time, they have the opportunity to supervise other workers and possibly manage repair shops, motor pools, or maintenance units.

Services Offering This Occupation

Army

Navy

Air Force

Marine Corps

Coast Guard

AVIONICS TECHNICIANS

Short Description

Airplanes and helicopters have complex electrical and electronic systems for communication, navigation, and radar. Instruments, lights, weapons, landing gear, sensors, and many other aircraft parts are also controlled by electronics. Avionics technicians install, maintain, and repair electronic and electrical systems on all types of aircraft.

What They Do

Avionics technicians in the military perform some or all of the following duties:

- Troubleshoot aircraft electronic and electrical systems using test equipment.
- Repair or replace defective components.
- Inspect and maintain electronic and electrical systems.
- Replace faulty wiring.
- Install electronic components.
- Repair or replace instruments, such as tachometers, temperature gauges, and altimeters.
- Read electronic and electrical diagrams.

Helpful Attributes

Helpful school courses include math and shop mechanics. Helpful attributes include

- The ability to work with tools
- Interest in electronic and electrical equipment
- Interest in solving problems

Training Provided

Job training consists of classroom instruction, including practice in repairing avionics systems. Training length varies depending upon specialty. Further training occurs on the job and through advanced courses. Course content typically includes

- Electronic and electrical theory
- Troubleshooting procedures
- Installation techniques
- Avionics and electrical system maintenance

Physical Demands

Normal color vision is required to work with color-coded wiring.

Work Environment

Avionics technicians usually work indoors, in aircraft hangars, airplanes, and repair shops. They may also work on aircraft parked outdoors.

Civilian Counterparts

Civilian avionics technicians work mainly for airlines and aircraft maintenance firms. They may also work for aircraft manufacturers and other organizations that have fleets of airplanes or helicopters. Their duties are similar to those of military aircraft electricians. They may also be called aircraft electricians.

Opportunities

Each year, the services need new technicians because of changes in personnel and the demands of the field. After job training, avionics technicians perform maintenance and routine repairs under close supervision. With experience, they are assigned more complicated troubleshooting and repairs and may supervise other technicians. In time, they may become supervisors of aircraft maintenance shops.

Services Offering This Occupation

Army

Navy

Air Force

Marine Corps

Coast Guard

BROADCAST JOURNALISTS AND NEWSWRITERS

Short Description

The military publishes newspapers and broadcasts television and radio programs for its personnel and for the public. These services are an important source of general information about people and events in the military. Broadcast journalists and newswriters write and present news programs, music programs, and radio talk shows.

What They Do

Broadcast journalists and newswriters in the military perform some or all of the following duties:

- Gather information for military news programs and publications.
- Write radio and TV scripts.
- Develop ideas for news articles.
- Arrange and conduct interviews.
- Collect information for commercial media use.
- Select photographs and write captions for news articles.
- Write news releases, feature articles, and editorials.

Helpful Attributes

Helpful school subjects include English, journalism, speech, and media communications. Helpful attributes include

- The ability to keep detailed and accurate records
- The ability to write clearly and concisely
- Interest in researching facts and issues for news stories
- A strong, clear speaking voice

Training Provided

Job training consists of classroom instruction. Course content typically includes

- Newswriting and research
- Newspaper format and layout
- Photojournalism (writing news stories featuring pictures)
- Radio and television programming and production

Physical Demands

Normal color vision and the passing of a voice audition are required for some specialties in this area.

Work Environment

Broadcast journalists and newswriters work in broadcasting studios on land or aboard ships, or sometimes outdoors, depending upon the research needed for their articles.

Civilian Counterparts

Broadcast journalists and newswriters work for newspapers, magazines, wire services, and radio and television stations. Their duties are similar to those performed by military journalists and newswriters. They may be employed as newscasters, disc jockeys, writers, directors, producers, or correspondents.

Opportunities

Each year, the services need new journalists and newswriters because of changes in personnel and the demands of the field. After job training, journalists and newswriters research and announce news stories and music programs. Eventually, they may become editors or editorial assistants or managers of broadcasting stations.

Services Offering This Occupation

Army

Navy

Air Force

Marine Corps

Coast Guard

BUILDING ELECTRICIANS

Short Description

The military uses electricity to do many jobs, including lighting hospitals, running power tools, and operating computers. Building electricians install and repair electric wiring systems in offices, repair shops, airplane hangars, and other buildings on military bases.

What They Do

Building electricians in the military perform some or all of the following duties:

- Install and wire transformers, junction boxes, and circuit breakers, using wire cutters, insulation strippers, and other hand tools.
- Read blueprints, wiring plans, and repair orders to determine wiring layouts or repair needs.
- Cut, bend, and string wires and conduits (pipe or tubing).
- Inspect power distribution systems, shorts in wires, and faulty equipment using test meters.
- Repair and replace faulty wiring and lighting fixtures.
- Install lightning rods to protect electrical systems.

Helpful Attributes

Helpful school subjects include science and math. Helpful attributes include

- The ability to use hand tools
- Interest in electricity
- A preference for doing physical work

Training Provided

Job training consists of classroom instruction, including practice in the installation and repair of electric wiring systems. Further training occurs on the job and through advanced courses. Course content typically includes

- Fundamentals of electricity
- Electric circuit troubleshooting
- Safety procedures
- Techniques for wiring switches, outlets, and junction boxes

Physical Demands

Normal color vision is required for working with color-coded wiring and circuits.

Work Environment

Building electricians usually work indoors while installing wiring systems. They work outdoors while installing transformers and lightning rods.

Civilian Counterparts

Civilian building electricians usually work for building and electrical contracting firms. Some work as self-employed electrical contractors. They perform duties similar to those of military building electricians.

Opportunities

Each year, the services need new electricians because of changes in personnel and the demands of the field. After job training, building electricians work under close supervision. As they gain experience, building electricians work more independently. In time, they may be promoted to supervisors of one or more work crews. Eventually, they may become construction superintendents.

Services Offering This Occupation

Army

Navy

Air Force

Marine Corps

Coast Guard

CARDIOPULMONARY AND EEG TECHNICIANS

Short Description

Military health care includes medical treatment for heart, lung, and brain disorders. Physicians need sophisticated tests to help diagnose and treat these problems. Cardiopulmonary and EEG (electroencephalograph) technicians administer a variety of diagnostic tests of the heart, lungs, blood, and brain using complex electronic testing equipment.

What They Do

Cardiopulmonary and EEG technicians in the military perform some or all of the following duties:

- Take patients' blood pressure readings.
- Attach electrodes or other test equipment to patients' bodies.
- Help physicians revive heart attack victims.
- Adjust settings and operate test equipment.
- Monitor graphs and screens during tests.
- Talk to physicians to learn what tests or treatments are needed.
- Keep records of test results and discuss them with medical staff.

- Operate electrocardiographs and other test equipment.

Helpful Attributes

Helpful school subjects include algebra, chemistry, biology, and related courses. Helpful attributes include

- The ability to follow strict standards and procedures
- The ability to keep accurate records
- Interest in electronic equipment
- Interest in learning how the heart, lungs, and blood work together

Training Provided

Job training consists of classroom instruction. Further training occurs on the job and through advanced courses. Course content typically includes

- Diagnostic procedures
- Operation and maintenance of diagnostic equipment
- Preparation of patients for testing
- Methods of resuscitation

Physical Demands

Normal color vision is required for some specialties in order to set up and monitor equipment.

Work Environment

Cardiopulmonary and EEG technicians usually work in hospitals and clinics. In combat situations, they may work in mobile field hospitals.

Civilian Counterparts

Civilian cardiopulmonary and EEG technicians work in hospitals, clinics, and physicians' offices. Their duties are similar to those performed in the military. They may specialize in either cardiovascular (heart), pulmonary (lungs), or electroencephalographic (brain) testing.

Opportunities

The services have about 6,000 cardiopulmonary and EEG technicians. Each year, they need new technicians because of changes in personnel and the demands of the field. After job training, new technicians are assigned to hospitals and clinics, where they work under the supervision of physicians and senior technicians. With experience, they may supervise others and assist in managing clinics.

Services Offering This Occupation

Army

Navy

Air Force

Coast Guard

CARGO SPECIALISTS

Short Description

The military delivers supplies, weapons, equipment, and mail to U.S. forces in many parts of the world. Military cargo travels by ship, truck, or airplane. It must be handled carefully to ensure its safe arrival at the correct destination. Cargo specialists load and unload military supplies and material using equipment such as forklifts and cranes. They also plan and organize loading schedules.

What They Do

Cargo specialists in the military perform some or all of the following duties:

- Load supplies into trucks, transport planes, and railroad cars, using forklifts.
- Load equipment such as jeeps, trucks, and weapons aboard ships, using dockyard cranes.
- Pack and crate boxes of supplies for shipping.
- Inspect cargo for damage.
- Plan and inspect loads for balance and safety.
- Check cargo against invoices to make sure the amount and destination of the material are correct.

Helpful Attributes

Helpful school subjects include general office and business mathematics. Helpful attributes include

- Interest in working with forklifts and cranes
- A preference for physical work

Training Provided

Job training consists of classroom instruction, including practice in loading cargo. Further training occurs on the job. Course content typically includes

- Operation and care of forklifts, power winches, and cranes
- Techniques for loading and storing cargo
- Techniques for planning and scheduling cargo shipments
- Safety procedures for handling potentially dangerous cargo

Physical Demands

Cargo specialists must lift and carry heavy cargo.

Work Environment

Cargo specialists work outdoors on loading docks and indoors in warehouses.

Civilian Counterparts

Civilian cargo specialists work for trucking firms, air cargo companies, and shipping lines. They perform duties similar to those of military cargo specialists. Depending on their specialty, they may also be called industrial truck operators, stevedores, longshoremen, material handlers, or cargo checkers.

Opportunities

Each year, the services need new cargo specialists because of changes in personnel and the demands of the field. After job training, cargo specialists work in teams preparing and loading cargo for shipment under the direction of supervisors. In time, they may advance to become team leaders or supervisors of other cargo specialists. Eventually, they may become warehouse managers.

Services That Offer This Occupation

Army

Navy

Air Force

Coast Guard

CASEWORKERS AND COUNSELORS

Short Description

Just like some civilians, some military personnel need assistance with various problems or concerns, including career decisions, family issues, substance abuse, or emotional problems. Caseworkers and counselors work with military personnel and their families to help them with their particular concerns. They may specialize by the type of counseling that they do, such as career guidance or alcohol and drug abuse prevention. They normally work as part of a team that may include social workers, psychologists, medical officers, chaplains, personnel specialists, and commanders.

What They Do

Caseworkers and counselors in the military perform some or all of the following duties:

- Interview personnel who request help or are referred by their commanders.
- Identify problems and determine the need for professional help.
- Counsel personnel and their families.
- Administer and score psychological tests.
- Help personnel evaluate and explore career opportunities.
- Teach classes on human relations.
- Keep records of counseling sessions.

Helpful Attributes

Helpful school subjects include health, biology, psychology, sociology, social science, and speech. Helpful attributes include

- Interest in working with people
- Patience in dealing with problems that take time and effort to overcome
- Sensitivity to the needs of others

Training Provided

Job training consists of classroom instruction, including practice in counseling. Further training occurs on the job and through advanced courses. Course content typically includes

- Orientation to counseling and social service programs

- Interviewing and counseling methods
- Treatments for drug and alcohol abuse
- Psychological testing techniques

Physical Demands

Caseworkers and counselors need to speak clearly and distinctly in order to teach classes and work with personnel who have problems.

Work Environment

Caseworkers and counselors usually work in offices or clinics.

Civilian Counterparts

Civilian caseworkers and counselors work in rehabilitation centers, hospitals, schools, and public agencies. They are usually required to have a college degree in social work, psychology, or counseling. They may also be called employment counselors, social workers, human services workers, or substance abuse counselors.

Opportunities

Each year, the services need new caseworkers and counselors because of changes in personnel and the demands of the field. After job training, counselors work under close supervision. With experience, they work more independently and may supervise other caseworkers.

Services Offering This Occupation

Army

Navy

Air Force

Marine Corps

Coast Guard

COMMUNICATIONS EQUIPMENT OPERATORS

Short Description

The ability to relay information between air, sea, and ground forces is critical in the military. The military has sophisticated communications systems that use a variety of technologies and telecommunications equipment, such as radios, telephones, antennas, satellites, and complex security and network devices. Communications equipment operators use these systems to transmit, receive, and decode messages at military locations throughout the world.

What They Do

Communications equipment operators in the military perform some or all of the following duties:

- Transmit, receive, and log messages according to military procedures.
- Encode and decode classified messages.
- Operate different types of telephone switchboards, satellite communications terminals, and network switches.
- Set up and operate communications equipment and security equipment.
- Monitor and respond to emergency calls.

Helpful Attributes

Helpful school subjects include English and speech. Helpful attributes include

- The ability to remain calm in an emergency
- Interest in working with codes
- Interest in working with communications equipment

Training Provided

Job training consists of instruction, including practice with equipment. Further training occurs on the job and through advanced courses. Course content typically includes

- Installation and usage of various types of communications equipment
- Communications security
- Message encoding and decoding

Physical Demands

Normal color vision, normal hearing, and the ability to speak clearly and distinctly are required to enter some specialties in this occupation. Operators must often sit for long periods.

Work Environment

Communications equipment operators may work either indoors or outdoors, depending on the specialty. They may be assigned to ships, aircraft, land bases, or mobile field units.

Civilian Counterparts

Civilian communications equipment operators work in airports, harbors, police stations, fire stations, telephone companies, telegraph companies, and many businesses. They may also work aboard ships. Their duties are similar to those of military communications equipment operators. They may be called radio operators, telephone operators, communication center operators, or switchboard operators, depending on their specialty.

Opportunities

Each year, the services need new operators because of changes in personnel and the demands of the field. After job training, operators prepare and send messages under supervision. With experience, they work more independently. In time, they may become supervisors of communications centers.

Services Offering This Occupation

Army

Navy

Air Force

Marine Corps

Coast Guard

COMPUTER SYSTEMS SPECIALISTS
Short Description

The military uses computers to store and process data on personnel, weather, finances, and many other areas, as well as to operate sophisticated equipment during combat and peacetime maneuvers.

What They Do

Computer systems specialists in the military perform some or all of the following duties:

- Install, configure, and monitor local and wide area networks, hardware, and software.
- Collect, enter, and process information using computers.
- Provide customer and network administration services, such as electronic mail accounts, security, virus protection, and troubleshooting.
- Use computer programs to solve problems.
- Determine and analyze computer systems requirements.
- Program information into languages that computers can read.
- Develop, test, and debug computer programs.

Helpful Attributes

Helpful school subjects include computer science, math, and typing. Helpful attributes include

- The ability to communicate effectively
- The ability to understand and apply math concepts
- Interest in solving problems
- Interest in work requiring accuracy and attention to detail

Training Provided

Job training consists of several weeks of classroom instruction, depending upon the specialty area. Further training occurs on the job and through advanced courses in specific computer systems and languages. Course content typically includes

- Use of computers and peripheral equipment
- Computer systems concepts
- Planning, designing, and testing computer systems
- Program structuring, coding, and debugging
- Use of current programming languages
- Computer security issues
- Network management

Physical Demands

Some computer systems specialists may sit at a computer for long periods of time.

Work Environment

Computer systems specialists in the military work in offices or at computer sites on military bases or aboard ships.

Civilian Counterparts

Civilian computer systems specialists work anywhere that computer systems are used. They may be employed as network support technicians for large companies or as data processing technicians in local banks or schools. Those who specialize in computer programming may work as programmers for software developers. The skills learned as a computer systems specialist are highly transferable to the civilian workforce.

Opportunities

Each year, the services need new specialists to meet the changing demands in the field. After training, computer systems specialists work under the direction of experienced computer systems officers. With experience, they may manage other computer systems specialists.

Services Offering This Occupation

Army

Navy

Air Force

Marine Corps

Coast Guard

CONSTRUCTION EQUIPMENT OPERATORS

Short Description

Each year the military completes hundreds of construction projects. Tons of earth and building materials must be moved to build airfields, roads, dams, and buildings. Construction equipment operators use bulldozers, cranes, graders, and other heavy equipment in military construction.

What They Do

Construction equipment operators in the military perform some or all of the following duties:

- Drive bulldozers, road graders, and other heavy equipment to cut and level earth for runways and roadbeds.
- Lift and move steel and other heavy building materials using winches, cranes, and hoists.

- Dig holes and trenches using power shovels.
- Remove ice and snow from runways, roads, and other areas using scrapers and snow blowers.
- Operate mixing plants to make concrete and asphalt.
- Spread asphalt and concrete with paving machines.
- Drill wells using drilling rigs.
- Place and detonate explosives.

Helpful Attributes

Helpful school subjects include shop mechanics. Helpful attributes include

- Interest in operating heavy construction equipment
- A preference for working outdoors

Training Provided

Job training consists of classroom instruction, including practice operating construction equipment. Further training occurs on the job and through advanced courses. Course content typically includes

- Operation of different types of construction equipment
- Maintenance and repair of equipment

Physical Demands

Some specialties require normal hearing, color vision, and heavy lifting.

Work Environment

Construction equipment operators work outdoors in all kinds of weather conditions. They often sit for long periods and are subject to loud noise and vibrations. They may work indoors while repairing equipment.

Civilian Counterparts

Civilian construction equipment operators work for building contractors, state highway agencies, rock quarries, well drillers, and construction firms. Civilian construction equipment operators may also be known as operating engineers, heavy equipment operators, well drillers, or riggers.

Opportunities

Each year, the services need new equipment operators because of changes in personnel and the demands of the field. With time, operators have the opportunity to become construction supervisors or construction superintendents.

Services Offering This Occupation

Army

Navy

Air Force

Marine Corps

Coast Guard

CONSTRUCTION SPECIALISTS

Short Description

The military builds many temporary and permanent structures each year. Lumber, plywood, plasterboard, and concrete and masonry (bricks, stone, and concrete blocks) are the basic building materials for many of these projects. Construction specialists build and repair buildings, bridges, foundations, dams, and bunkers. They work with engineers and other building specialists as part of military construction teams.

What They Do

Construction specialists in the military perform some or all of the following duties:

- Build foundations, floor slabs, and walls with brick, cement block, mortar, or stone.
- Erect wood framing for buildings using hand and power tools, such as hammers, saws, levels, and drills.
- Lay roofing materials, such as asphalt, tile, and wooden shingles.
- Install plasterboard, plaster, and paneling to form interior walls and ceilings.
- Lay wood and ceramic tile floors and build steps, staircases, and porches.
- Build temporary shelters for storing supplies and equipment while on training maneuvers.

Helpful Attributes

Helpful school subjects include math, woodworking, and industrial arts. Helpful attributes include

- The ability to work with blueprints
- Interest in using power tools
- A preference for physical work

Training Provided

Job training consists of instruction, including practice with carpentry and masonry tools. Further training occurs on the job and through advanced courses. Course content typically includes

- Building construction
- Masonry construction methods
- Types and uses of construction joints and braces
- Interpretation of blueprints and drawings
- How to mix and set concrete, mortar, and plaster

Physical Demands

Construction specialists may have to lift and carry heavy building materials, such as lumber, plasterboard, and concrete. Sometimes they climb and work from ladders and scaffolding.

Work Environment

Construction specialists work indoors and outdoors on construction sites.

Civilian Counterparts

Civilian construction specialists usually work for construction or remodeling contractors, government agencies, utility companies, or manufacturing firms. They perform duties similar to those of military construction specialists. They may also be called bricklayers, stonemasons, cement masons, cement finishers, carpenters, or cabinetmakers.

Opportunities

Each year, the services need new specialists because of changes in personnel and the demands of the field. After job training, construction specialists work in teams under close supervision. Initially, they perform simple work, such as form building and rough framing. With experience, they perform more difficult tasks. In time, they may supervise and train other specialists. They may become construction superintendents.

Services Offering This Occupation

Army

Navy

Air Force

Marine Corps

Coast Guard

DENTAL AND OPTICAL LABORATORY TECHNICIANS

Short Description

The military provides dental and optical care as part of its comprehensive health service program. Dental and optical laboratory technicians make and repair dental devices and eyeglasses that are provided for military personnel.

What They Do

Dental and optical laboratory technicians perform some or all of the following duties:

- Make dentures, braces, and other dental or optical devices.
- Construct, assemble, repair, and align dental and optical devices (metal braces and retainers, eyeglass frames and lenses).
- Harden and cure dentures or lenses using high-temperature ovens or other heat-treating equipment.
- Grind, polish, and smooth dentures or lenses using hand or power tools.

Helpful Attributes

Helpful school subjects include biology, chemistry, and industrial arts. Helpful attributes include

- The ability to follow detailed instructions and work procedures
- The ability to use precision tools and instruments
- Interest in work requiring attention to detail
- Interest in working with one's hands

Training Provided

Job training consists of classroom instruction, including practice in making and repairing dental and optical devices. Course content varies depending upon specialty, but typically includes laboratory operating procedures (for the dental or optical specialty). Further training occurs on the job and through advanced courses.

Physical Demands

Normal color vision is required for some specialties to match the color of artificial teeth with natural tooth color.

Work Environment

Dental and optical laboratory technicians normally work in dental or optical laboratories and occasionally in examination and dispensing offices.

Special Requirements

Successful completion of high school algebra is required to enter some specialties in this occupation.

Civilian Counterparts

Civilian dental laboratory technicians normally work for small dental laboratories or large dental offices. Optical laboratory technicians work in optical laboratories or for retail opticians. They perform duties similar to those of military technicians. Civilian optical laboratory technicians may also be called opticians or ophthalmic laboratory technicians.

Opportunities

Each year, the services need new technicians because of changes in personnel and the demands of the field. After job training, technicians work under very close supervision. With experience, they work more independently and perform more challenging tasks. Eventually, they may become supervisors or managers of dental or optical laboratories.

Services Offering This Occupations

Army

Navy

Air Force

Coast Guard

DENTAL SPECIALISTS

Short Description

Dental care is one of the health services provided to all military personnel. It is available in military dental clinics all over the world. Dental specialists assist military dentists in examining and treating patients. They also help manage dental offices.

What They Do

Dental specialists in the military perform some or all of the following duties:

- Help dentists perform oral surgery.
- Prepare for patient examinations by selecting and arranging instruments and medications.
- Help dentists during examinations by preparing dental compounds and operating dental equipment.
- Clean patients' teeth using scaling and polishing instruments and equipment.
- Operate dental x-ray equipment and process x-rays of patients' teeth, gums, and jaws.
- Provide guidance to patients on daily care of their teeth.
- Perform administrative duties, such as scheduling office visits, keeping patient records, and ordering dental supplies.

Helpful Attributes

Helpful school subjects include biology and chemistry. Helpful attributes include

- The ability to follow spoken instructions and detailed procedures
- Good eye-hand coordination
- Interest in working with people

Training Provided

Job training consists of classroom instruction, including practice in dental care tasks. Further training occurs on the job and through advanced courses. Course content typically includes

- Preventive dentistry
- Radiology (x-ray) techniques
- Dental office procedures
- Dental hygiene procedures

Physical Demands

Dental specialists must sometimes stand for long periods.

Work Environment

Dental specialists in the military usually work indoors in dental offices or clinics. Some specialists may be assigned to duty aboard ships.

Civilian Counterparts

Civilian dental specialists work in dental offices or clinics. Their work is similar to work in the military. They typically specialize in assisting dentists to treat patients, providing clerical support (dental assistants), or cleaning teeth (dental hygienists).

Opportunities

Each year, the services need new specialists because of changes in personnel and the demands of the field. After job training, new specialists are assigned to dental offices or clinics, where they work under the supervision of dentists. With experience, dental specialists perform more difficult tasks involving patient care. In time, they may become responsible for assisting dental officers in the management of dental programs.

Services Offering This Occupation

Army

Navy

Air Force

Coast Guard

DIVERS

Short Description

Sometimes, military tasks such as search and rescue, ship repair, construction, and patrolling must be done under water. Divers in the military perform this work. They usually specialize either as scuba divers, who work just below the surface, or as deep sea divers, who may work for long periods of time in depths up to 300 feet.

What They Do

Divers in the military perform some or all of the following duties:

- Perform search and rescue activities.
- Recover sunken equipment.
- Patrol the waters below ships at anchor.
- Inspect, clean, and repair ship propellers and hulls.
- Assist with underwater construction of piers and harbor facilities.
- Survey rivers, beaches, and harbors for underwater obstacles.
- Use explosives to clear underwater obstacles.
- Conduct underwater research.

Helpful Attributes

Helpful school subjects include shop mechanics and building trades. Helpful attributes include

- A high degree of self-reliance
- The ability to stay calm under stress
- Interest in underwater diving

Training Provided

Job training consists of classroom instruction, including practice in diving and repair work. Training length varies depending upon specialty. Further training occurs on the job and through advanced courses. Course content typically includes

- Principles of scuba diving
- Underwater welding and cutting
- Maintenance of diving equipment

Physical Demands

Divers must be good swimmers and physically strong.

Work Environment

Divers work under water. However, they plan and prepare for work on land or aboard ships. Because diving is not usually a full-time job, divers often have another job specialty in which they work.

Civilian Counterparts

Civilian divers work for oil companies, salvage companies, underwater construction firms, and police or fire rescue units. They perform duties similar to those of divers in the military.

Opportunities

Each year, the services need new divers because of changes in personnel and the demands of the field. After job training, divers work in teams headed by experienced divers. Eventually, they may become master divers and supervise diving operations

Services Offering This Occupation

Army

Navy

Marine Corps

Coast Guard

ELECTRICAL PRODUCTS REPAIRERS
Short Description

Much of the military's equipment is electrically powered. Electric motors, electric tools, and medical equipment require careful maintenance and repair. Electrical products repairers maintain and repair electrical equipment. They specialize by type of equipment.

What They Do

Electrical products repairers in the military perform some or all of the following duties:

- Maintain, test, and repair electric motors in many kinds of machines, such as lathes, pumps, office machines, and appliances.
- Inspect and repair electrical, medical, and dental equipment.
- Inspect and repair electric instruments, such as voltmeters.
- Maintain and repair portable electric tools, such as saws and drills.

Helpful Attributes

Helpful school subjects include math, electricity, and shop mechanics. Helpful attributes include

- The ability to use tools
- Interest in electric motors and appliances
- Interest in solving problems

Training Provided

Job training consists of classroom instruction, including practice in repairing electrical products. Training length varies depending upon specialty. Further training occurs on the job and through advanced courses. Course content typically includes

- Maintenance and repair procedures
- Use of electrical test equipment

Physical Demands

Normal color vision is required to work with color-coded wiring.

Work Environment

Electrical products repairers usually work in repair shops on land or aboard ships.

Civilian Counterparts

Civilian electrical products repairers work in many industries, including hospitals, manufacturing firms, and government agencies. They also work in independent repair shops. They perform duties similar to those of military electrical products repairers. They may be called electric tool repairers, electrical instrument repairers, electromedical equipment repairers, or electric motor repairers.

Opportunities

Each year, the services need new repairers because of changes in personnel and the demands of the field. After job training, repairers normally make simple repairs under the direction of more experienced workers. With experience, they perform more complicated repairs. In time, repairers may become electrical repair shop supervisors.

Services Offering This Occupation

Army

Navy

Air Force

Marine Corps

Coast Guard

ELECTRONIC INSTRUMENT AND EQUIPMENT REPAIRS

Short Description

The military uses electronic instruments and equipment in many different areas, including health care, weather forecasting, and combat, to name a few. Electronics repairers maintain and repair instruments and equipment, such as computers, communications equipment, radar and sonar systems, precision measuring equipment, and biomedical instruments. Electronic instrument and equipment repairers normally specialize by type of equipment or instrument being repaired.

What They Do

Electronic instrument and equipment repairers in the military perform some or all of the following duties:

- Maintain, test, adjust, and repair electronic equipment using frequency meters, circuit analyzers, and other specialized test equipment.
- Install and repair circuits and wiring using soldering irons and hand tools.
- Install computers and other data processing equipment.
- Use technical guides and diagrams to locate defective parts and components of equipment.
- String overhead communications and electric cables between utility poles.
- Monitor the operation of air traffic control, missile tracking, air defense, and other radar systems to make sure there are no problems.

Helpful Attributes

Helpful school subjects include math, electrical or electronic repair, shop mechanics, and/or physics. Helpful attributes include

- The ability to apply electronic principles and concepts
- Interest in solving problems
- Interest working with electrical, electronic, and electrochemical equipment

Training Provided

Job training includes classroom instruction, including practice in repairing electronic instruments and equipment. Training length varies depending upon specialty. Course content typically includes

- Mechanical, electronic, and electrical principles
- Maintenance and repair procedures
- Line installation and wiring techniques
- Use of test equipment

Physical Demands

Normal color vision is required to work with color-coded wires. Some repairers may work from ladders or tall utility poles.

Work Environment

Electronic instrument and equipment repairers usually work in repair shops and laboratories on land or aboard ships.

Civilian Counterparts

Civilian electronic instrument and equipment repairers work for a variety of organizations, such as manufacturing firms, communications firms, commercial airlines, and government agencies. They perform the same kind of duties as military electronic instrument and equipment repairers. Depending on their specialty, they may be called electronics mechanics, telecommunications equipment installers and repairers, radio mechanics, or computer technicians.

Opportunities

Each year, the services need new repairers because of changes in personnel and the demands of the field. After job training, repairers are assigned to an operations or equipment maintenance unit, where they perform routine repair jobs. In time, they may perform more difficult repairs and supervise other repair personnel. Eventually, they may become supervisors or managers of electronic equipment maintenance units.

Services Offering This Occupation

Army

Navy

Air Force

Marine Corps

Coast Guard

EMERGENCY MANAGEMENT SPECIALISTS

Short Description

The military prepares for emergencies or natural disasters by developing detailed warning, control, and evacuation plans. Emergency management specialists prepare emergency plans and respond to all types of disasters, such as floods, earthquakes, hurricanes, or enemy attack.

What They Do

Emergency management specialists in the military perform some or all of the following duties:

- Assist in preparing and maintaining disaster operations plans.
- Train military and civilian personnel on what to do in an emergency.
- Operate and maintain nuclear, biological, and chemical detection and decontamination equipment.
- Conduct surveys to determine needs in the event of an emergency.
- Monitor disaster preparedness activities and training operations.
- Serve as members of emergency response teams.

Helpful Attributes

Helpful school subjects include algebra, chemistry, physics, geometry, and trigonometry. Helpful attributes include

- The ability to communicate effectively
- The ability to plan and organize
- The ability to work calmly under stress

Training Provided

Job training consists of classroom instruction, including practice in the use of nuclear, biological, and chemical detection and decontamination equipment. Further training occurs on the job and through advanced courses. Course content typically includes

- Defensive procedures for nuclear, biological, and chemical warfare
- Preparation of emergency plans

Physical Demands

Normal color vision is needed to identify chemical agents.

Work Environment

Emergency management specialists work indoors when conducting training sessions and preparing disaster plans. Sometimes they work outdoors while operating decontamination equipment and monitoring disaster training.

Civilian Counterparts

Civilian emergency management specialists work for federal, state, and local governments, including law enforcement and civil defense agencies. They perform duties similar to those of military emergency management specialists.

Opportunities

Each year, the services need new specialists because of changes in personnel and the demands of the field. After job training, some specialists prepare emergency plans under close supervision. With experience, they work more independently and assist in surveys and inspections. Other specialists conduct inspections and operate decontamination equipment. Eventually, they may become supervisors of emergency management programs.

Services Offering This Occupation

Army

Navy

Air Force

Marine Corps

Coast Guard

ENVIRONMENTAL HEALTH AND SAFETY SPECIALISTS

Short Description

Each military base is a small community. The health and well-being of the residents and surrounding land is a major concern of the services. Keeping military workplaces and living areas sanitary helps to prevent illness. Environmental health and safety specialists inspect military facilities and food supplies for the presence of disease, germs, or other conditions hazardous to health and the environment.

What They Do

Environmental health and safety specialists in the military perform some or all of the following duties:

- Monitor the storage, transportation, and disposal of hazardous waste.
- Analyze food and water samples to ensure quality.
- Conduct health and safety investigations of living quarters and base facilities.
- Provide training on industrial hygiene, environmental health, and occupational health issues.
- Monitor noise and radiation levels at job sites.

Helpful Attributes

Helpful school subjects include algebra, biology, chemistry, and general science. Helpful attributes include

- Interest in gathering information
- Interest in protecting the environment
- A preference for work requiring attention to detail

Training Provided

Job training consists of classroom instruction, including practice in making health and sanitation inspections. Further training occurs on the job and through advanced courses. Training length varies depending upon specialty. Course content typically includes

- Identification of health hazards
- Inspection of food products and food service operations
- Inspection of wastewater and waste disposal facilities

Physical Demands

Normal color vision is required to inspect foods for quality and freshness.

Work Environment

Environmental health specialists work indoors while inspecting food facilities and buildings. They work outdoors while inspecting waste disposal facilities and field camps.

Civilian Counterparts

Most civilian environmental health and safety specialists work for local, state, and federal government agencies. Their duties are similar to the duties of military environmental health specialists. They may be called food and drug inspectors, public health inspectors, health and safety inspectors, or industrial hygienists.

Opportunities

Each year, the services need new specialists because of changes in personnel and the demands of the field. After job training, environmental health and safety specialists help to make inspections. With experience, they work more independently and may supervise other environmental health and safety specialists. Eventually, they may become superintendents of environmental health programs at large military bases.

Services Offering This Occupation

Army

Navy

Air Force

Marine Corps

Coast Guard

FINANCE AND ACCOUNTING SPECIALISTS

Short Description

Millions of paychecks are issued and large amounts of materials are purchased by the services each year. To account for military spending, exact financial records of these transactions must be kept. Finance and accounting specialists organize and keep track of financial records. They also compute payrolls and other allowances, audit accounting records, and prepare payments for military personnel.

What They Do

Finance and accounting specialists in the military perform some or all of the following duties:

- Use computers to perform calculations, record details of financial transactions, and maintain accounting records.
- Review or audit financial records to check the accuracy of figures and calculations.
- Prepare paychecks, earnings statements, bills, and financial accounts and reports.
- Disburse cash, checks, advance pay, and bonds.
- Organize information on past expenses to help plan budgets for future expenses.

Helpful Attributes

Helpful school subjects include mathematics, statistics, bookkeeping, and accounting. Helpful attributes include

- The ability to work with numbers
- Interest in using office machines, such as computers and calculators
- Interest in work requiring accuracy and attention to detail

Training Provided

Job training consists of classroom instruction, including practice in accounting techniques. Course content typically includes

- Accounting principles and procedures
- Preparation and maintenance of financial reports and budgets
- Statistical analyses to interpret financial data
- Computation of pay and deductions

Work Environment

Finance and accounting specialists work in offices on land or aboard ships.

Special Requirements

Depending upon the specialty, entry into this occupation may require courses in mathematics, bookkeeping, or accounting.

Civilian Counterparts

Civilian finance and accounting specialists work for all types of businesses and government agencies. They perform duties similar to those of military finance and accounting specialists. Civilian finance and accounting specialists are also called accounting clerks, audit clerks, bookkeepers, or payroll clerks.

Opportunities

Each year, the services need new specialists because of changes in personnel and the demands of the field. After job training, finance and accounting specialists typically perform routine financial recording activities under the direction of supervisors. With experience, they are given more difficult tasks, such as auditing, and may become responsible for checking the work of others. In time, finance and accounting specialists may become supervisors or managers of accounting units or pay and finance centers.

Services Offering This Occupation

Army

Navy

Air Force

Marine Corps

Coast Guard

FIREFIGHTERS

Short Description

Military bases have their own fire departments. Military firefighting units are responsible for protecting lives and property on bases from fire. Firefighters put out, control, and help prevent fires in buildings, on aircraft, and aboard ships.

What They Do

Firefighters in the military perform some or all of the following duties:

- Operate pumps, hoses, and extinguishers.
- Force entry into aircraft, vehicles, and buildings in order to fight fires and rescue personnel.
- Drive firefighting trucks and emergency rescue vehicles.
- Give first aid to injured personnel.
- Inspect aircraft, buildings, and equipment for fire hazards.

- Teach fire protection procedures.
- Repair firefighting equipment and fill fire extinguishers.

Helpful Attributes

Helpful school subjects include health and general science. Helpful attributes include

- The ability to remain calm under stress
- The ability to think and act decisively
- Willingness to risk injury to help others

Training Provided

Job training consists of classroom training, including practice in fighting fires. Further training occurs on the job. Course content typically includes:

- Types of fires
- Firefighting equipment operations
- Firefighting procedures
- First aid procedures
- Rescue procedures

Physical Demands

Good vision without glasses and a clear speaking voice are required to enter some specialties in this occupation. Firefighters have to climb ladders and stairs. They must also be able to lift and carry injured personnel.

Work Environment

Firefighters work indoors and outdoors while fighting fires. They are exposed to the smoke, heat, and flames of the fires they fight.

Civilian Counterparts

Civilian firefighters work for city and county fire departments, other government agencies, and industrial firms. They perform duties similar to those performed by military firefighters, including rescue and salvage work.

Opportunities

Each year, the services need new firefighters because of changes in personnel and the demands of the field. After training, new firefighters perform work under close supervision. With experience, they work more independently and may supervise others. Eventually, they may become chiefs of base fire departments or similar units.

Services Offering This Occupation

Army

Navy

Air Force

Marine Corps

Coast Guard

FLIGHT ENGINEERS
Short Description

The military operates thousands of airplanes and helicopters. Pilots and air crew members rely upon trained personnel to keep aircraft ready to fly. Flight engineers inspect airplanes and helicopters before, during, and after flights to ensure safe and efficient operations. They also serve as crew members aboard military aircraft.

What They Do

Flight engineers in the military perform some or all of the following duties:

- Inspect aircraft before and after flights.
- Plan and monitor the loading of passengers, cargo, and fuel.
- Assist pilots in engine start-up and shutdown.
- Compute aircraft load weights and fuel distribution and consumption.
- Monitor engine instruments and adjust controls following pilot orders.
- Check fuel, pressure, electrical, and other aircraft systems during flight.
- Inform pilots of aircraft problems and recommend corrective action.

Helpful Attributes

Helpful school subjects include general mathematics and shop mechanics. Helpful attributes include

- The ability to work as a member of a team
- Interest in working with mechanical systems and equipment

- Skill in using wiring diagrams and maintenance manuals
- A strong desire to fly

Training Provided

Job training consists of classroom instruction and practical experience in aircraft inspection. Further training occurs on the job during flight operations. Course content typically includes

- Operation of aircraft systems
- Inspection of aircraft engines, structures, and systems
- Preparation of records and logs

Physical Demands

Flight engineers, like pilots and navigators, have to be mentally alert and physically fit to perform their job. They must pass a special physical exam to qualify for flight duty.

Work Environment

Flight engineers live and work on air bases or aboard ships in all areas of the world. They fly in hot and cold climates and in all types of weather.

Civilian Counterparts

Civilian flight engineers work for passenger and cargo airline companies. They perform the same duties as flight engineers in the military.

Opportunities

Each year, the services need new flight engineers because of changes in personnel and the demands of the field. After receiving their "air crew qualified" rating, flight engineers are assigned to an airplane or helicopter flying unit. With experience, they work more independently and may supervise or train others. They may become flight engineer chiefs or air crew chiefs.

Services Offering This Occupation

Navy

Air Force

Marine Corps

FOOD SERVICE SPECIALISTS

Short Description

Every day, more than one million meals are prepared in military kitchens. Some kitchens prepare thousands of meals at one time, while others prepare food for small groups of people. Food service specialists prepare all types of food according to standard and dietetic recipes. They also order and inspect food supplies and prepare meats for cooking.

What They Do

Food service specialists in the military perform some or all of the following duties:

- Order, receive, and inspect meat, fish, fruit, and vegetables.
- Prepare standard cuts of meat using cleavers, knives, and bandsaws.
- Cook steaks, chops, and roasts.
- Bake or fry chicken, turkey, and fish.
- Prepare gravies and sauces.
- Bake breads, cakes, pies, and pastries.
- Serve food in dining halls, hospitals, or field kitchens or aboard ship.
- Clean ovens, stoves, mixers, pots, and utensils.

Helpful Attributes

Helpful school subjects include home economics, health, mathematics, accounting, and chemistry. Helpful attributes include

- Interest in cooking
- Interest in working with the hands

Training Provided

Job training consists of classroom instruction, including practice in food preparation. Training length varies depending upon specialty. Further training occurs on the job and through advanced courses. Course content typically includes

- Standard and dietetic menus and recipes
- Preparation and cooking of various foodstuffs and bakery products
- Food and supply ordering
- Storage of meats, poultry, and other perishable items

Physical Demands

Food service specialists may have to lift and carry heavy containers of foodstuffs and large cooking utensils.

Work Environment

Food service specialists normally work in clean, sanitary kitchens and dining facilities. They may sometimes work in refrigerated meat lockers. Sometimes they work outdoors in tents while preparing and serving food under field conditions.

Civilian Counterparts

Civilian food service specialists work in cafés, restaurants, and cafeterias. They also work in hotels, hospitals, manufacturing plants, schools, and other organizations that have their own dining facilities. Depending on specialty, food service specialists are called cooks, chefs, bakers, butchers, or meat cutters.

Opportunities

Each year, the services need new specialists because of changes in personnel and the demands of the field. After job training, food service specialists help prepare and serve food under close supervision. Some food service specialists specialize as bakers, cooks, butchers, or meat cutters. With experience, they work more independently and may train new food service specialists. Eventually, they may become head cooks, chefs, or food service supervisors.

Services Offering this Occupation

Army

Navy

Air Force

Marine Corps

Coast Guard

GRAPHIC DESIGNERS AND ILLUSTRATORS

Short Description

The military produces many publications, such as training manuals, newspapers, reports, and promotional materials. Graphic artwork is used in these publications and for signs, charts, posters, and TV and motion picture productions. Graphic designers and illustrators produce graphic artwork, drawings, and other visual displays.

What They Do

Graphic designers and illustrators in the military perform some or all of the following duties:

- Produce computer-generated graphics.
- Draw graphs and charts to represent budgets, numbers of troops, supply levels, and office organization.
- Develop ideas and design posters and signs.
- Help instructors design artwork for training courses.
- Draw illustrations and cartoons for filmstrips and animation for films.
- Make silkscreen prints.
- Work with TV and film producers to design backdrops and props for film sets.

Helpful Attributes

Helpful school subjects include art, drafting, and geometry. Helpful attributes include

- The ability to convert ideas into visual presentations
- Interest in artwork or lettering
- Neatness and an eye for detail

Training Provided

Job training consists of classroom instruction, including practice in preparing graphic designs and illustrations. Further training occurs on the job. Course content typically includes

- Introduction to graphics, lettering, drawing, and layout techniques
- Illustration and television graphic techniques
- Theory and use of color

Physical Demands

Coordination of eyes, hands, and fingers is needed to draw sketches. Normal color vision is required to work with paints and other art materials.

Work Environment

Graphic designers and illustrators usually work in offices on land or aboard ships.

Civilian Counterparts

Civilian graphic designers and illustrators work for government agencies, advertising agencies, print shops, engineering firms, and large organizations that have their own graphics departments. They may be known as graphic arts technicians or commercial artists.

Opportunities

Each year, the services need new designers and illustrators because of changes in personnel and the demands of the field. After job training, graphic designers prepare tables, signs, and graphics under close supervision. With experience, they help formulate and produce more complex designs. In time, they may supervise others and lead large projects. Eventually, they may manage graphics departments.

Services Offering This Occupation

Army

Navy

Air Force

Marine Corps

HEATING AND COOLING MECHANICS
Short Description

Air conditioning and heating equipment is used to maintain comfortable temperatures in military buildings, airplanes, and ships. Refrigeration equipment is used to keep food cold and to keep some missile fuels at subzero storage temperatures. Heating and cooling mechanics install and repair air conditioning, refrigeration, and heating equipment.

What They Do

Heating and cooling mechanics in the military perform some or all of the following duties:

- Install and repair furnaces, boilers, and air conditioners.
- Recharge cooling systems with refrigerant gases.
- Install copper tubing systems that circulate water or cooling gases.

- Replace compressor parts, such as valves, pistons, bearings, and electric motors, on refrigeration units.
- Repair thermostats and electric circuits.

Helpful Attributes

Helpful school subjects include science, math, and shop mechanics. Helpful attributes include

- The ability to use hand and power tools
- Interest in solving problems
- Interest in working on machines

Training Provided

Job training consists of classroom instruction, including practice in repair work. Training length varies depending upon specialty. Additional training is available on the job and in advanced courses. Course content typically includes

- Refrigeration theory
- Installation and repair of refrigeration and air-conditioning units
- Installation and repair of furnaces and boilers
- Use of diagrams and blueprints

Physical Demands

Heating and cooling mechanics may have to lift or move heavy equipment. They are often required to stoop, kneel, and work in cramped positions. Normal color vision is required for locating and repairing color-coded wiring.

Work Environment

Heating and cooling mechanics may work inside repair shops. Frequently, they work wherever equipment is to be installed or repaired.

Civilian Counterparts

Civilian heating and cooling mechanics work for contractors that install home furnaces and air conditioners or for firms that repair refrigerators and freezers in homes, grocery stores, factories, and warehouses. Heating and cooling mechanics in civilian life often specialize more than those in the military. They may be called heating, air-conditioning, refrigeration, or climate control mechanics.

Opportunities

Each year, the services need new mechanics because of changes in personnel and the demands of the field. After job training, mechanics maintain and repair equipment under supervision. With experience, they may learn to diagnose mechanical problems and perform complicated repairs. Eventually, they may become superintendents of utilities for large bases.

Services Offering This Occupation

Army

Navy

Air Force

Marine Corps

Coast Guard

INFANTRY
Short Description

The infantry is the main land combat force of the military. In peacetime, the infantry's role is to stay ready to defend our country. In combat, the role of the infantry is to capture or destroy enemy ground forces and repel enemy attacks. The infantry operates weapons and equipment to engage and destroy enemy ground forces.

What They Do

Infantry perform some or all of the following duties:

- Set up camouflage and other protective barriers.
- Operate, clean, and store automatic weapons, such as rifles and machine guns.
- Parachute from troop transport airplanes while carrying weapons and supplies.
- Carry out scouting missions to spot enemy troop movements and gun locations.
- Operate communications and signal equipment to receive and relay battle orders.
- Drive vehicles mounted with machine guns or small missiles.
- Perform hand-to-hand combat drills that involve martial arts tactics.
- Dig foxholes, trenches, and bunkers for protection against attacks.

Helpful Attributes

Helpful attributes include

- The ability to stay in top physical condition
- Interest in working as a member of a team
- Readiness to accept a challenge and face danger

Training Provided

Infantry training starts with basic training of several weeks. Advanced training in infantry skills lasts for several more weeks. While some of the training is in the classroom, most is in the field under simulated combat conditions. In reality, training for an infantry soldier never stops. Infantry soldiers keep their skills sharp through frequent squad maneuvers, target practice, and war games. War games conducted without live ammunition allow soldiers to practice scouting, troop movement, surprise attack, and capturing techniques.

Physical Demands

The infantry has very demanding physical requirements. Infantry personnel must perform strenuous physical activities, such as marching while carrying equipment, digging foxholes, and climbing over obstacles. They also need good hearing and clear speech to use two-way radios, and good night vision and depth perception to see targets and signals.

Work Environment

Because the infantry must be prepared to go anywhere in the world it is needed, infantry soldiers and marines work and train in all climates and weather conditions. During training exercises, as in real combat, troops work, eat, and sleep outdoors. Most of the time, however, they work on military bases.

Special Requirements

This occupation is open only to men.

Civilian Counterparts

Although the job of infantry soldier or marine has no equivalent in civilian life, the close teamwork, discipline, and leadership experience it provides are helpful in many civilian jobs.

Opportunities

Each year, the services need new infantry soldiers because of changes in personnel and the demands of the field. Leadership ability and job performance are the main factors for advancement in the infantry. Those who have the ability to motivate, train, and supervise others assume greater responsibility.

Services Offering This Occupation

Army

Marine Corps

INTELLIGENCE SPECIALISTS

Short Description

Military intelligence is information needed to plan for our national defense. Knowledge of the number, location, and tactics of enemy forces and potential battle areas is needed to develop military plans. To gather information, the services rely on aerial photographs, electronic monitoring using radar and sensitive radios, and human observation. Intelligence specialists gather and study the information required to design defense plans and tactics.

What They Do

Intelligence specialists in the military perform some or all of the following duties:

- Study aerial photographs of foreign ships, bases, and missile sites.
- Study foreign troop movements.
- Operate sensitive radios to intercept foreign military communications.
- Study land and sea areas that could become battlegrounds in time of war.
- Store and retrieve intelligence data using computers.
- Study foreign military codes.
- Prepare intelligence reports, maps, and charts.

Helpful Attributes

Helpful school subjects include algebra, geometry, trigonometry, and geography. Helpful attributes include

- The ability to organize information
- The ability to think and write clearly
- Interest in gathering information and studying its meaning
- Interest in reading maps and charts

Training Provided

Job training consists of classroom instruction, including practice in intelligence gathering. Training length varies depending upon specialty. Further training occurs on the job and through advanced courses. Course content typically includes

- Planning aerial and satellite observations
- Preparing intelligence reports, maps, and charts
- Analyzing aerial photographs
- Using computer systems

Physical Demands

Normal color vision is required for some specialties in order to work with color-coded maps.

Work Environment

Intelligence specialists work in offices on land and aboard ships, and in tents when in the field.

Civilian Counterparts

Civilian intelligence specialists generally work for federal government agencies such as the Central Intelligence Agency or the National Security Agency. Their duties are similar to those performed by military intelligence specialists. The analytical skills of intelligence specialists are also useful in other fields, such as research or business planning.

Opportunities

Each year, the services need new specialists because of changes in personnel and the demands of the field. After job training, specialists collect information and prepare maps and charts under close supervision. With experience, they are given more responsibility for organizing intelligence data. Eventually, they may become chiefs of intelligence units.

Services Offering This Occupation

Army

Navy

Air Force

Marine Corps

Coast Guard

INTERPRETERS AND TRANSLATORS

Short Description

Some members of the military must be able to read and understand the many languages of the world. Information from foreign-language newspapers, magazines, and radio broadcasts is important to the nation's defense. Interpreters and translators convert written or spoken foreign languages into English or other languages. They usually specialize in a particular foreign language.

What They Do

Interpreters and translators in the military perform some or all of the following duties:

- Translate written and spoken foreign-language material to and from English, making sure to preserve the original meaning.
- Interview prisoners of war, enemy deserters, and civilian informers in their native languages.
- Record foreign radio transmissions using sensitive communications equipment.
- Prepare written reports about the information obtained.
- Translate foreign documents, such as battle plans and personnel records.
- Translate foreign books and articles describing foreign equipment and construction techniques.

Helpful Attributes

Helpful school subjects include speech, communications, and foreign languages. Helpful attributes include

- Interest in reading and writing
- Interest in working with people
- A talent for foreign languages

Training Provided

Job training consists of classroom instruction, including practice in interpretation. Training length varies depending upon specialty. Longer training is necessary for specialties that do not require foreign-language fluency prior to entry. For these specialties, foreign-language training for 6 to 12 months is provided. Further training occurs on the job and through advanced courses. Course content typically includes

- Interrogation (questioning) methods
- Use and care of communications equipment
- Procedures for preparing reports

Physical Demands

Normal hearing and the ability to speak clearly and distinctly are usually required to enter this occupation.

Work Environment

Interpreters and translators normally work on military bases, aboard ships, or in airplanes.

Special Requirements

Fluency in a foreign language is required to enter most specialties within this occupation.

Civilian Counterparts

Civilian interpreters and translators work for government agencies, embassies, universities, and companies that conduct business overseas. Their work is similar to the work of military interpreters and translators.

Opportunities

Each year, the services need new interpreters and translators because of changes in personnel and the demands of the field. After job training, interpreters and translators work under the direction of more experienced workers and supervisors. With experience, they work more independently. In time, interpreters and translators may become directors of translation for large bases.

Services Offering This Occupation

Army

Navy

Air Force

Marine Corps

LAW ENFORCEMENT AND SECURITY SPECIALISTS

Short Description

The military services have their own law enforcement and police forces. These specialists investigate crimes committed on military property or that involve military personnel. Military police do many of the same things as civilian officers: control traffic, prevent crime, and respond to emergencies. They also guard military bases and inmates in military correctional facilities.

What They Do

Law enforcement and security specialists in the military perform some or all of the following duties:

- Investigate criminal activities and activities related to espionage, treason, and terrorism.
- Interview witnesses and arrest suspects.
- Guard correctional facilities and other military installations.
- Patrol areas on foot, by car, or by boat.
- Perform fire and riot control duties.

Helpful Attributes

Helpful school subjects include government and speech. Helpful attributes include

- The ability to remain calm under pressure
- Interest in law enforcement and crime prevention
- Willingness to perform potentially dangerous work

Training Provided

Job training consists of classroom instruction. Training length varies depending upon specialty. Course content typically includes

- Civil and military laws
- Investigation and evidence collection procedures and techniques
- Prisoner control and discipline
- Use of firearms and hand-to-hand defense techniques
- Traffic and crowd control procedures

Physical Demands

Normal color vision is necessary to enter some specialties in this area. Some specialties have minimum age and height requirements.

Work Environment

Law enforcement and security specialists in the military work both indoors and outdoors, depending on their assignment. They may work outdoors while conducting investigations or patrolling facilities.

Civilian Counterparts

Civilian law enforcement and security specialists work for state, county, or city law enforcement agencies. They may also work in prisons, intelligence agencies, and private security companies. They perform duties similar to those performed in the military. They may be called police officers, detectives, private investigators, undercover agents, correction officers, or security guards.

Opportunities

Each year, the services need new specialists because of changes in personnel and the demands of the field. After job training, specialists work under the direction of more experienced specialists. In time, they may supervise and train new workers or lead investigations. Eventually, they may become chiefs of detectives, chiefs of police, or superintendents of correctional facilities.

Services Offering This Occupation

Army

Navy

Air Force

Marine Corps

Coast Guard

LEGAL SPECIALISTS AND COURT REPORTERS

Short Description

The military has its own judicial system for prosecuting lawbreakers and handling disputes. Legal specialists and court reporters assist military lawyers and judges in the performance of legal and judicial work. They perform legal research, prepare legal documents, and record legal proceedings.

What They Do

Legal specialists and court reporters in the military perform some or all of the following duties:

- Research court decisions and military regulations.
- Process legal claims and appeals.
- Interview clients and take statements.
- Prepare trial requests and make arrangements for courtrooms.
- Maintain law libraries and trial case files.
- Use a variety of methods and equipment to record and transcribe court proceedings.
- Prepare records of hearings, investigations, court-martials, and courts of inquiry.

Helpful Attributes

Helpful school subjects include business mathematics, typing, speech, and shorthand. Helpful attributes include

- The ability to keep organized and accurate records
- The ability to listen carefully
- Interest in the law and legal proceedings

Training Provided

Job training consists of several weeks of instruction. Course content typically includes

- Legal terminology and research techniques
- How to prepare legal documents
- High-speed transcription
- Military judicial processes

Physical Demands

Good hearing and clear speech are needed to record and read aloud court proceedings. A clear speaking ability is necessary to interview clients.

Work Environment

Legal specialists and court reporters work in military law offices and courtrooms.

Special Requirements

Some specialties require the ability to type at a rate of 25 to 50 words per minute

Civilian Counterparts

Civilian legal specialists and court reporters work for private law firms, banks, insurance companies, government agencies, and local, state, and federal courts. They perform duties similar to those of military legal specialists and court reporters. Civilian legal specialists and court reporters may also be called legal assistants, law clerks, paralegals, and court reporters.

Opportunities

Each year, the services need new specialists and court reporters because of changes in personnel and the demands of the field. After training, specialists normally work under an attorney or in a legal office. With experience, legal specialists and court reporters perform more demanding activities and may supervise other specialists.

Services Offering This Occupation

Army

Navy

Air Force

Marine Corps

Coast Guard

LOGISTICIANS

Short Description

In order for the military to operate successfully, the proper materials, equipment, and people need to be in the right place at the right time. Logisticians develop, review, and implement plans for coordinating many different variables, such as requirements for and availability of supplies, equipment, personnel, and transportation. In developing their plans, they also take into account maintenance and scheduling considerations, and cost factors. Some logisticians specialize in an area such as aviation logistics.

What They Do

Logisticians in the military perform some or all of the following duties:

- Negotiate and buy goods and services.
- Track inventory levels, process orders, and help determine when to make purchases.
- Distribute and dispose of resources.
- Coordinate with other groups to ensure the continued flow of materials and personnel.
- Coordinate transportation and maintenance schedules for the safe deployment of personnel and materials.
- Use computers and mathematical models to predict and solve logistical problems.

Helpful Attributes

Helpful fields of study include management, operations research, resource allocation, statistics, and business or public administration. Helpful attributes include

- Ability to coordinate the efforts of multiple individuals or groups
- Ability to express ideas clearly and concisely
- Interest in solving problems

Training Provided

Training consists of classroom exercises and practical exercises. Course content typically includes

- Purchasing and contracting
- Resource allocation
- Transportation and personnel coordination

Work Environment

Logisticians normally work in offices, although they may also work in a variety of other locations depending on their assignment.

Civilian Counterparts

Civilian logisticians work in all types of public and private organizations from hospitals to large manufacturing companies. They perform duties similar to those of military logisticians. Civilian logisticians may also be called logistics engineers, logistics analysts, and logistics planners.

Services Offering This Occupation

- Army
- Navy
- Air Force
- Marines Corps

MACHINISTS

Short Description

Sometimes when engines or machines break down, the parts needed to repair them are not available. In these cases, the broken parts must be repaired or new ones made. Machinists make and repair metal parts for engines and all types of machines. They operate lathes, drill presses, grinders, and other machine shop equipment.

What They Do

Machinists in the military perform some or all of the following duties:

- Study blueprints or written plans of the parts to be made.
- Set up and operate lathes to make parts such as shafts and gears.
- Cut metal stock using power hacksaws and bandsaws.
- Bore holes using drill presses.
- Shape and smooth parts using grinders.
- Measure work using micrometers, calipers, and depth gauges.

Helpful Attributes

Helpful school subjects include math, general science, metalworking, and mechanical drawing. Helpful attributes include

- The ability to apply mathematical formulas
- Interest in making things and finding solutions to mechanical problems
- A preference for working with the hands

Training Provided

Job training consists of classroom instruction, including practice in machine operation. Further training occurs on the job and through advanced courses. Course content typically includes

- Machine types and uses
- Machine setup and operation
- Uses of different metals
- Safety procedures

Work Environment

Machinists work in machine shops, which are often noisy.

Civilian Counterparts

Civilian machinists work for factories and repair shops in many industries, including the electrical products, automotive, and heavy machinery industries. They perform duties similar to those of military machinists.

Opportunities

Each year, the services need new machinists because of changes in personnel and the demands of the field. After job training, machinists perform routine repairs under close supervision. In time, they perform more difficult repairs and may train others. Eventually, they may become managers of one or more machine shops.

Services Offering This Occupation

Army

Navy

Air Force

Marine Corps

Coast Guard

MARINE ENGINE MECHANICS

Short Description

The military operates many types of watercraft, from small motor launches to large ships. Many of these vessels are powered by gasoline or diesel engines. Marine engine mechanics repair and maintain gasoline and diesel engines on ships, boats, and other watercraft. They also repair shipboard mechanical and electrical equipment.

What They Do

Marine engine mechanics in the military perform some or all of the following duties:

- Repair and maintain shipboard gasoline and diesel engines.
- Locate and repair machinery parts, including valves and piping systems.
- Repair ship propulsion machinery.
- Repair and service hoisting machinery and ship elevators.
- Repair refrigeration and air conditioning equipment on ships.
- Repair engine-related electrical systems.

Helpful Attributes

Helpful school subjects include shop mechanics. Helpful attributes include

- The ability to use hand and power tools
- Interest in fixing engines and machinery
- A preference for doing physical work

Training Provided

Job training consists of classroom instruction, including practice in marine engine maintenance and repair. Training length varies depending upon specialty. Further training occurs on the job and through advanced courses. Course content typically includes

- Internal combustion engine theory
- Repair of shipboard electronic and electrical machinery systems
- Service and repair of fuel injection systems
- Use and care of hand and power tools

Physical Demands

Normal color vision is required to work with color-coded diagrams and wiring.

Work Environment

Marine engine mechanics work aboard ships, normally in the engine or power rooms. Sometimes they work in repair centers on land bases. Working conditions in engine rooms tend to be noisy and hot.

Civilian Counterparts

Civilian marine engine mechanics work in many industries, including marine transportation, commercial fishing, and oil exploration and drilling. They perform duties similar to those of military marine engine mechanics.

Opportunities

Each year, the services need new mechanics because of changes in personnel and the demands of the field. After job training, mechanics work under close supervision in repair centers or shipboard engine rooms. With experience, they work more independently and may supervise other mechanics. In time, marine engine mechanics may become supervisors of marine engine repair centers or shipboard maintenance sections.

Services Offering This Occupation

Army

Navy

Marine Corps

Coast Guard

MEDICAL CARE TECHNICIANS

Short Description

The military provides medical care to all men and women in the services. Medical care technicians work with teams of physicians, nurses, and other health care professionals to provide treatment to patients. They help give patients the care and treatment required for recovery from illness or injury. They also prepare rooms, equipment, and supplies in hospitals and medical clinics.

What They Do

Medical care technicians in the military perform some or all of the following duties:

- Provide bedside care in hospitals, including taking the body temperature, pulse, and respiration rate of patients.
- Feed, bathe, and dress patients.
- Prepare patients, operating rooms, equipment, and supplies for surgery.
- Make casts, traction devices, and splints according to physicians' instructions.
- Give medication to patients under the direction of physicians and nurses.

Helpful Attributes

Helpful school subjects include general science, biology, and psychology. Helpful attributes include

- The ability to follow directions precisely
- The ability to work under stressful or emergency conditions
- Interest in helping others

Training Provided

Job training consists of several weeks of classroom instruction, including practice in patient care. Training length varies depending upon specialty. Further training occurs on the job and through advanced courses. Course content may include

- Patient care techniques
- Emergency medical techniques
- Methods of sterilizing surgical equipment
- Plaster casting techniques

Physical Demands

Some specialties in this area require sufficient strength to lift and move patients, and some require a normal skin condition to guard against infection.

Work Environment

Medical care technicians work in hospitals and clinics on land or aboard ships. In combat situations, they may work in mobile field hospitals.

Civilian Counterparts

Civilian medical care technicians work in hospitals, nursing homes, rehabilitation centers, psychiatric hospitals, or physicians' offices. They perform duties similar to those performed in the military. They may be called nurse's aides, orderlies, operating room technicians, orthopedic assistants, or practical nurses.

Opportunities

Each year, the services need new technicians because of changes in personnel and the demands of the field. After job training, new technicians are assigned to hospitals or medical units, where they work under close supervision. In time, they may advance to supervisory positions and help train others.

Services Offering This Occupation

Army

Navy

Air Force

Coast Guard

MEDICAL LABORATORY TECHNICIANS

Short Description

Medical laboratories are an important part of the military health care system. The staffs of medical laboratories perform the clinical tests required to detect and identify diseases in patients. Medical laboratory technicians conduct tests on the tissue, blood, and body fluids of medical patients.

What They Do

Medical laboratory technicians in the military perform some or all of the following duties:

- Use lab equipment to analyze specimens (samples) of tissue, blood, and body fluids.
- Examine blood and bone marrow under microscopes.
- Test specimens for bacteria or viruses.
- Draw blood from patients.
- Assist in collecting specimens at autopsies (medical examinations of the dead).
- Record and file the results of laboratory tests.

Helpful Attributes

Helpful school subjects include biology, chemistry, and algebra. Helpful attributes include

- The ability to follow detailed procedures precisely
- Interest in scientific and technical work

Training Provided

Job training consists of classroom and on-the-job instruction, including practice in testing specimens. Training length varies depending upon specialty. Course content typically includes

- Medical laboratory procedures
- Study of human parasites and diseases
- Laboratory administration and record keeping

Physical Demands

Normal color vision is required to work with colored chemicals and dyes.

Work Environment

Medical laboratory technicians work in medical centers, clinics, and hospitals on land or aboard ships.

Civilian Counterparts

Civilian medical laboratory technicians usually work for privately owned laboratories, hospitals, clinics, or research institutions. They perform duties similar to those of military medical laboratory technicians.

Opportunities

Each year, the services need new technicians because of changes in personnel and the demands of the field. After job training, technicians perform routine laboratory tests under close supervision. With experience, they do more complex testing and analysis and work more independently. After demonstrating job proficiency, medical laboratory technicians help train new technicians and supervise laboratory personnel. In time, they may advance to laboratory management positions.

Services Offering This Occupation

Army

Navy

Air Force

Coast Guard

MEDICAL RECORD TECHNICIANS
Short Description

Medical records are important for health care delivery. To provide proper treatment, physicians need complete and accurate information about patients' symptoms, test results, illnesses, and prior treatments. Medical record technicians prepare and maintain patient records, reports, and correspondence.

What They Do

Medical record technicians in the military perform some or all of the following duties:

- Fill out admission and discharge records for patients entering and leaving military hospitals.
- Assign patients to hospital rooms.
- Prepare daily reports about patients admitted and discharged.
- Organize, file, and maintain medical records.
- Prepare reports about physical examinations, illnesses, and treatments.
- Prepare tables of medical statistics.
- Maintain libraries of medical publications.

Helpful Attributes

Helpful school subjects include general science and business administration. Helpful attributes include

- The ability to communicate well
- Interest in using computers and other office machines
- Interest in work requiring accuracy and attention to detail

Training Provided

Job training consists of classroom instruction. Training length varies depending upon specialty. Course content typically includes

- Basic computer skills
- Medical terminology
- Medical records preparation and maintenance
- Maintenance of medical libraries

Work Environment

Medical record technicians work in admissions or medical records sections of hospitals and clinics. They work in land-based facilities and aboard ships.

Civilian Counterparts

Civilian medical record technicians usually work for hospitals, clinics, and government health agencies. They perform duties similar to those of military medical record technicians. However, civilian medical record technicians tend to specialize in areas such as admissions, ward, or outpatient records. Those working in admission or discharge units are called admitting or discharge clerks.

Opportunities

Each year, the services need new technicians because of changes in personnel and the demands of the field. After training, new technicians are assigned to hospitals or clinics, where they work under close supervision. With experience, they may assume supervisory positions and may manage medical record units or admission or discharge units.

Services Offering This Occupation

Army

Navy

Air Force

Coast Guard

MEDICAL SERVICE TECHNICIANS

Short Description

In emergencies or in combat, physicians are not always immediately available to treat the injured or wounded. When a physician is not available, medical service technicians provide basic and emergency medical treatment. They also assist medical officers in caring for sick and injured patients.

What They Do

Medical service technicians in the military perform some or all of the following duties:

- Examine and treat emergency or battlefield patients.
- Interview patients and record their medical histories.
- Take patients' temperature, pulse, and blood pressure.
- Prepare blood samples for laboratory analysis.
- Keep health records and clinical files up to date.
- Give shots and medicines to patients.

Helpful Attributes

Helpful school subjects include chemistry, biology, psychology, general science, and algebra. Helpful attributes include

- The ability to communicate effectively
- The ability to work under stressful conditions
- Interest in helping others

Training Provided

Job training consists of many weeks of classroom instruction, depending upon specialty. Further training occurs on the job and through advanced courses. Course content typically includes

- Emergency medical treatment
- Basic nursing care
- Study of the human body
- Minor surgical procedures
- Clinical laboratory procedures
- Methods for diagnosing diseases

Physical Demands

Medical service technicians may have to lift and carry wounded or injured personnel during emergency situations. Air medical evacuation specialists must pass a flight physical exam.

Work Environment

Medical service technicians usually work in hospitals and clinics on land or aboard ships. Medical service technicians may give emergency medical treatment in the field.

Civilian Counterparts

Civilian medical service technicians work in hospitals, clinics, nursing homes, and rehabilitation centers. They perform duties similar to those performed by medical service technicians in the military. Civilian medical service technicians are known by the type of work they do: emergency medical technicians treat victims of accidents, fire, or heart attacks; medical assistants work for physicians and perform routine medical and clerical tasks; medication aides give shots and medicine under the close supervision of physicians; and physician assistants perform routine examinations and treatment for physicians.

Opportunities

Each year, the services need new technicians because of changes in personnel and the demands of the field. After job training, technicians are assigned to serve in their medical specialty. They work under the direction and supervision of medical officers and experienced medical service technicians. Eventually, they may advance to supervisory positions and help manage a medical facility.

Services Offering This Occupation

Army

Navy

Air Force

Coast Guard

METEOROLOGICAL SPECIALISTS

Short Description

Weather information is important for planning military operations. Accurate weather forecasts are needed to plan troop movements, airplane flights, and ship traffic. Meteorological specialists collect information about weather and sea conditions for use by meteorologists. They make visual observations and take readings from weather equipment, radar scans, and satellite photographs.

What They Do

Meteorological specialists in the military perform some or all of the following duties:

- Launch weather balloons to record wind speed and direction.
- Identify the types of clouds present and estimate cloud height and amount of cloud cover.
- Take readings of barometric pressure, temperature, humidity, and sea conditions.
- Operate radio equipment to receive information from satellites.
- Plot weather information on maps and charts.
- Forecast weather based on readings and observations.

Helpful Attributes

Helpful school subjects include geography, mathematics, and physical science. Helpful attributes include

- The ability to communicate effectively
- Interest in gathering and organizing information
- Interest in learning how weather changes
- Interest in working with formulas, tables, and graphs

Training Provided

Job training consists of classroom instruction. Training length varies depending upon specialty. Advanced training in weather forecasting is available for some specialties. Course content typically includes

- Basic meteorology (study of weather) and oceanography (study of the ocean)
- Methods for plotting weather data
- Analyzing radar and satellite weather information
- Preparation of weather reports

Physical Demands

Normal color vision is required to use color-coded maps and weather charts. Some specialties may involve heavy lifting.

Work Environment

Meteorological specialists usually work in offices, either on land or aboard ships. They work outdoors when making visual weather observations and launching weather balloons.

Civilian Counterparts

Civilian meteorological specialists work for government agencies (such as the U.S. Weather Service), commercial airlines, radio and television stations, and private weather forecasting firms. They perform duties similar to those of military meteorological specialists. Civilian meteorological specialists may also be called oceanographer assistants and weather clerks.

Opportunities

Each year, the services need new specialists because of changes in personnel and the demands of the field. After job training, new specialists collect weather information under the supervision of experienced workers. With experience, they perform more complex collection and analysis tasks and may become weather forecasters. Eventually, they may become managers of weather observation units.

Services Offering This Occupation

Army

Navy

Air Force

Marine Corps

Coast Guard

MUSICIANS

Short Description

Music is an important part of military life. Service bands and vocal groups have a strong tradition of performing at ceremonies, parades, concerts, festivals, and dances. Musicians and singers perform in service bands, orchestras, and small groups. They perform many types of music, including marches, classics, jazz, and popular music.

What They Do

Musicians in the military perform some or all of the following duties:

- Play in or lead bands, orchestras, combos, and jazz groups.
- Sing in choral groups or as soloists.
- Perform for ceremonies, parades, concerts, festivals, and dances.
- Rehearse and learn new music when not performing.
- Play brass, percussion, woodwind, or string instruments.

Helpful Attributes

Helpful school subjects include band, music theory, harmony, and other music courses. Helpful attributes include

- The ability to play more than one instrument
- The ability to sing
- Poise when performing in public

Training Provided

Although musicians must be musically proficient to enter the service, music training is given to new band members. Job training consists of several weeks of classroom instruction, including practice playing instruments. Training length varies depending upon musical specialty. Further training occurs on the job through regular rehearsals and individual practice. Course content typically includes

- Music theory
- Group instrumental techniques
- Sight-reading musical scores
- Dance band techniques

Work Environment

Musicians play indoors in theaters, concert halls, and at dances; outdoors at parades and open-air concerts. They also travel regularly.

Special Requirements

To qualify for a service band, applicants must pass one or more auditions. They must be fairly accomplished musicians and be able to sight-read musical notations.

Civilian Counterparts

Civilian musicians work for many types of employers, including professional orchestras, bands, and choral groups. They work in nightclubs, concert halls, theaters, and recording studios.

Opportunities

Each year, the services need new musicians because of changes in personnel and the demands of the field. After job training, musicians are assigned to band units located with U.S. forces around the world. They perform as members of bands and vocal groups. In time, they may become heads of their instrument sections and, possibly, bandleaders or orchestra conductors. The most outstanding performers are selected for the official service bands or orchestras of their service.

Services Offering This Occupation

Army

Navy

Air Force

Marine Corps

Coast Guard

NONDESTRUCTIVE TESTERS

Short Description

Military equipment is often placed under heavy stress. An airplane's landing gear absorbs heavy runway impact. Submarine hulls withstand tremendous pressure in the ocean depths. In time, stress may cause structural weakening or damage. Nondestructive testers examine metal parts for stress damage. They use x-rays, ultrasonics, and other testing methods that do not damage (are nondestructive to) the parts tested.

What They Do

Nondestructive testers in the military perform some or all of the following duties:

- Inspect metal parts and joints for wear and damage.
- Take x-rays of aircraft and ship parts.
- Examine x-ray film to detect cracks and flaws in metal parts and welds.
- Operate ultrasonic, atomic absorption, and other kinds of test equipment.
- Conduct oil analysis and heat damage tests to detect engine wear.
- Prepare inspection reports.

Helpful Attributes

Helpful school subjects include math and metal shop. Helpful attributes include

- Interest in machines and how they work
- Interest in operating test equipment
- Thoroughness and dependability

Training Provided

Job training consists of classroom instruction, including practice in testing metal parts. Course content typically includes

- Methods for inspecting parts and welds
- Operation of x-ray and film processing equipment
- Operation of ultrasonic test equipment
- Preparation of test reports

Physical Demands

Normal color vision is required to read color-coded diagrams.

Work Environment

Nondestructive testers work indoors in laboratories and aircraft hangars. They also work outdoors in shipyards and in the field.

Civilian Counterparts

Civilian nondestructive testers work for commercial testing laboratories, airlines, aircraft maintenance companies, and industrial plants. They perform duties similar to those of military nondestructive testers and may be called radiographers.

Opportunities

Each year, the services need new testers because of changes in personnel and the demands of the field. After job training, testers are assigned to testing units, where they perform tests under supervision. With experience, they work more independently. In time, nondestructive testers may become supervisors of testing laboratories or maintenance units.

Services Offering This Occupation

Navy

Air Force

Marine Corps

Coast Guard

OPTOMETRIC TECHNICIANS

Short Description

Optometry, or vision care, is one of the many health benefits available to military personnel. The military operates its own clinics to examine eyes and fit glasses or contact lenses. Optometric technicians assist optometrists in providing vision care. They work with patients and manage clinic offices.

What They Do

Optometric technicians in the military perform some or all of the following duties:

- Use and maintain ophthalmic instruments and equipment.
- Perform screening tests.
- Order eyeglasses and contact lenses from prescriptions.
- Fit eyeglasses to patients.
- Make minor repairs to glasses.
- Place eyedrops and ointment into patients' eyes.
- Keep records in optometry offices.

Helpful Attributes

Helpful school subjects include algebra, geometry, biology, and related courses. Helpful attributes include

- The ability to communicate effectively
- Interest in work requiring accuracy and attention to detail

Training Provided

Job training consists of classroom instruction, including practice in optometric procedures. Further training occurs on the job. Course content typically includes

- Preparing and fitting glasses and contact lenses
- Vision testing
- Maintenance of optometric instruments

Physical Demands

Normal color vision is required for some specialties to use optometric instruments.

Work Environment

Optometric technicians normally work in optometric clinics.

Civilian Counterparts

Civilian optometric technicians work in private optometry offices, clinics, and government health agencies. They perform duties similar to those performed by military optometric technicians. Optometric technicians are also called optometric assistants.

Opportunities

Each year, the services need new technicians because of changes in personnel and the demands of the field. After training, new technicians give simple vision tests under close supervision and perform office duties. As they gain experience, they work with less supervision and perform more difficult tasks. In time, they may help to manage optometric clinics.

Services Offering This Occupation

Navy

Air Force

ORDNANCE SPECIALISTS

Short Description

Ordnance is a military term for ammunition and weapons. Ordnance includes all types of ammunition, missiles, toxic chemicals, and nuclear weapons. Ammunition and weapons must be handled carefully and stored properly. Ordnance specialists transport, store, inspect, prepare, and dispose of weapons and ammunition.

What They Do

Ordnance specialists in the military perform some or all of the following duties:

- Load nuclear and conventional explosives and ammunition on aircraft, ships, and submarines.
- Inspect mounted guns, bomb release systems, and missile launchers.
- Assemble and load explosives.
- Defuse unexploded bombs.
- Locate, identify, and dispose of chemical munitions.

Helpful Attributes

Helpful school subjects include general science and shop mechanics. Helpful attributes include

- The ability to remain calm under stress
- Interest in working with guns and explosives

Training Provided

Job training consists of classroom instruction, including practice in ordnance maintenance. Training length varies depending upon specialty. Further training occurs on the job and through advanced courses. Course content typically includes

- Maintenance of nuclear weapons
- Handling, testing, and maintenance of missiles and rockets

Physical Demands

Ordnance specialists may have to lift and carry artillery shells and other heavy ordnance.

Work Environment

Ordnance specialists work indoors and outdoors. They work in repair shops while assembling explosives and repairing weapons. They work outdoors while repairing equipment in the field and loading weapons on tanks, ships, or aircraft.

Civilian Counterparts

There are no direct civilian counterparts for many of the military ordnance specialties. However, there are many occupations that are related. For example, civilians work for government agencies and private industry doing research and development. Others work for police or fire departments as bomb-disposal experts. Some also work for munitions manufacturers and firearms makers. Ordnance specialists may also be called bomb-disposal experts.

Opportunities

Each year, the services need new ordnance specialists because of changes in personnel and the demands of the field. After job training, ordnance

specialists work under close supervision. With experience, they perform more complex duties. In time, they may become trainers or supervisors. Eventually, they may become managers of weapons maintenance units.

Services Offering This Occupation

Army

Navy

Air Force

Marine Corps

Coast Guard

PERSONNEL SPECIALISTS
Short Description

Personnel management helps individuals develop their military careers. It also serves the military's need to fill jobs with qualified workers. Personnel specialists collect and store information about the people in the military, such as training, job assignment, promotion, and health information. They work directly with service personnel and their families.

What They Do

Personnel specialists in the military perform some or all of the following duties:

- Organize, maintain, and review personnel records.
- Enter and retrieve personnel information using computer terminals.
- Assign personnel to jobs.
- Prepare correspondence, organizational charts, and reports.
- Provide career guidance.
- Assist personnel and their families who have special needs.

Helpful Attributes

Helpful school subjects include English, speech, and business administration. Helpful attributes include

- The ability to compose clear instructions or correspondence
- The ability to follow detailed procedures and instructions
- Interest in working closely with others

Training Provided

Job training consists of classroom instruction. Further training occurs on the job and through advanced courses. Course content typically includes

- Preparation of military correspondence and forms
- Personnel records management
- Computer update and retrieval procedures

Work Environment

Personnel specialists normally work in office settings on land or aboard ships.

Civilian Counterparts

Civilian personnel specialists work for all types of organizations, including industrial firms, retail establishments, and government agencies. They perform duties similar to those of military personnel clerks. However, specific jobs vary from company to company.

Opportunities

Each year, the services need new specialists because of changes in personnel and the demands of the field. After job training, specialists process personnel actions and add information to records. In time, they may supervise other personnel specialists and eventually may manage personnel offices.

Services Offering This Occupation

Army

Navy

Air Force

Marine Corps

Coast Guard

PETROLEUM SUPPLY SPECIALISTS

Short Description

Ships, airplanes, trucks, tanks, and other military vehicles require large amounts of fuel and lubricants. These and other petroleum products require special storage and handling. Petroleum supply specialists store, handle, and ship petroleum products, such as oil, fuel, compressed gas, and lubricants.

What They Do

Petroleum supply specialists in the military perform some or all of the following duties:

- Connect hoses and valves and operate pumps to load petroleum products into tanker trucks, airplanes, ships, and railroad cars.
- Test oils and fuels for pollutants.
- Repair pipeline systems, hoses, valves, and pumps.
- Check the volume and temperature of petroleum and gases in tankers, barges, and storage tanks.
- Prepare storage and shipping records.
- Store and move packaged petroleum products using forklifts.

Helpful Attributes

Helpful school subjects include shop mechanics and business math. Helpful attributes include

- The ability to follow spoken instructions
- Interest in working with machines and equipment
- A preference for physical work

Training Provided

Job training consists of classroom instruction, including practice in using petroleum pumping equipment. Further training occurs on the job and through advanced courses. Course content typically includes

- Testing oil and fuels
- Operating airplane refueling systems and equipment
- Operating pumps, pipelines, and tanker equipment
- Planning and scheduling petroleum transport
- Safety regulations and procedures for handling dangerous materials

Physical Demands

Petroleum supply specialists may have to perform moderate to heavy lifting.

Work Environment

Petroleum supply specialists work outdoors in all types of weather while filling storage tanks and refueling airplanes, ships, and tankers.

Civilian Counterparts

Civilian petroleum supply specialists work for oil refineries, pipeline companies, and tanker truck and ship lines. They may also refuel airplanes at large airports. They perform many of the same duties as military petroleum supply specialists.

Opportunities

Each year, the services need new specialists because of changes in personnel and the demands of the field. After training, specialists work in teams while performing oil and fuel pumping operations. Each team works under the direction of a supervisor. With experience, petroleum supply specialists may become team leaders, pipeline or pump station supervisors, or petroleum storage supervisors.

Services Offering This Occupation

Army

Navy

Air Force

Marine Corps

Coast Guard

PHARMACISTS

Short Description

Drugs and medicines are sometimes prescribed by doctors when treating patients in military hospitals and clinics. Pharmacists manage the purchasing, storing, and dispensing of drugs and medicines.

What They Do

Pharmacists in the military perform some or all of the following duties:

- Manage pharmacy technicians who prepare, label, and dispense orders for drugs and medicines.
- Advise doctors and patients on the proper use and side effects of drugs and medicines.
- Train medical, nursing, and pharmacy staffs on the use of drugs.
- Consult on drug and medicine research programs.
- Check drug and medicine supplies and reorder when necessary.
- Direct pharmacy record keeping.

Helpful Attributes

Helpful attributes include

- Interest in chemical formulas
- Interest in understanding the effects of drugs and medicines
- Interest in work requiring accuracy and attention to detail

Training Provided

No initial job training is provided to officers in this occupation.

Work Environment

Pharmacists work in hospitals and clinics on land and aboard ships.

Civilian Counterparts

Civilian pharmacists work for pharmacies, drug stores, and drug departments of stores and supermarkets. They also work for hospitals, nursing homes, and clinics. They perform duties similar to those performed by military pharmacists. Civilian pharmacists who specialize in radioactive drugs (radioisotopes) are known as radiopharmacists.

Services Offering This Occupation

Army

Air Force

Marine Corps

Coast Guard

PHARMACY TECHNICIANS

Short Description

Prescription drugs and medicines are important to medical treatment. Patients and physicians depend on military pharmacies to fill their prescriptions accurately. Pharmacy technicians prepare and dispense prescribed drugs and medicines under the supervision of pharmacists or physicians. They also maintain pharmacy supplies and records.

What They Do

Pharmacy technicians in the military perform some or all of the following duties:

- Read physicians' prescriptions to determine the types and amount of drugs to prepare.
- Weigh and measure drugs and chemicals.
- Mix ingredients in order to produce prescription medications.
- Prepare labels for prescriptions.
- Dispense medications to patients.
- Store shipments of drugs and medications.

Helpful Attributes

Helpful school subjects include algebra, chemistry, biology, physiology, and anatomy. Helpful attributes include

- The ability to follow strict procedures and directions
- The ability to work using precise measurements and standards
- Interest in body chemistry

Training Provided

Job training consists of classroom instruction. Course content typically includes

- Pharmacy laws and regulations
- Drug types and uses
- Mixing and dispensing drugs

Physical Demands

Normal color vision is required, as is the ability to speak clearly. Some specialties may involve heavy lifting.

Work Environment

Pharmacy technicians usually work in hospitals and clinics on land or aboard ships. They may also work in field hospitals.

Civilian Counterparts

Civilian pharmacy technicians work in pharmacies, drugstores, hospitals, and clinics under the direction of pharmacists. They are usually known as pharmacy helpers and generally do not have responsibility for the compounding and dispensing of drugs. They perform simple tasks, such as storing supplies, cleaning equipment, and delivering prescriptions. While military pharmacy technicians generally have more job responsibilities than civilian pharmacy helpers, they do not have the qualifications needed to become civilian pharmacists. Pharmacists must complete a college pharmacy degree program, pass a state board exam, and serve in a pharmacy internship.

Opportunities

Each year, the services need new technicians because of changes in personnel and the demands of the field. After job training, new technicians work under the supervision of experienced pharmacy technicians and pharmacists. With experience, they work more independently. Eventually, they may supervise other technicians and may manage military pharmacies.

Services Offering This Occupation

Army

Navy

Air Force

Coast Guard

PHOTOGRAPHIC SPECIALISTS

Short Description

The military uses photographs for many purposes, such as intelligence gathering and news reporting. The services operate photographic laboratories to develop the numerous photos taken by the military. Photographic specialists take and develop still color or black-and-white or digital photographs.

What They Do

Photographic specialists in the military perform some or all of the following duties:

- Select camera, film, and other equipment needed for assignments.
- Determine camera angles, lighting, and any special effects needed.
- Take still photos of people, events, military equipment, land areas, and other subjects.
- Develop, duplicate, or retouch film negatives, photos, or slides.
- Maintain photographic equipment.

Helpful Attributes

Helpful school subjects include photography, chemistry, art, and mathematics. Helpful attributes include

- The ability to recognize and arrange interesting photo subjects
- Accuracy and attention to detail

Training Provided

Job training consists of classroom instruction, including practice in taking and developing photographs. Length of training varies depending upon the specialty. Further training occurs on the job and through advanced courses. Course content typically includes

- Photographic processing and reproduction
- Principles of photojournalism
- Operation and maintenance of photographic equipment

Physical Demands

Normal color vision is required to produce accurate color prints.

Work Environment

Photographic specialists work both indoors and outdoors while photographing their subjects. They may take photos from aircraft or ships. They process photographs in photographic laboratories on bases or aboard ships.

Civilian Counterparts

Civilian photographic specialists work for photography studios, newspapers, magazines, advertising agencies, commercial photograph developers, and large businesses. They perform duties similar to those of military specialists. Depending on the specialty, they may be known as photojournalists, aerial or still photographers, film developers, automatic print developers, or print controllers.

Opportunities

Each year, the services need new specialists because of changes in personnel and the demands of the field. After job training, specialists work under supervision. With experience, they are given more responsibility and, eventually, may supervise other photographic specialists.

Services Offering This Occupation

Army

Navy

Air Force

Marine Corps

Coast Guard

PHYSICAL AND OCCUPATIONAL THERAPY SPECIALISTS

Short Description

Physical and occupational therapy consists of treatment and exercise for patients disabled by illness or injury. Physical and occupational therapy specialists assist in administering treatment aimed at helping disabled patients regain strength and mobility and preparing them to return to work.

What They Do

Physical and occupational therapy specialists in the military perform some or all of the following duties:

- Test and interview patients to determine their physical and mental abilities.
- Assist physical and occupational therapists in planning therapy programs and exercise schedules.
- Fit artificial limbs (prostheses) and train patients in their use.
- Provide massages and heat treatments to patients.
- Teach patients new mobility skills.
- Set up and maintain therapeutic equipment, such as exercise machines and whirlpools.

Helpful Attributes

Helpful school subjects include general science, biology, physiology, and psychology. Helpful attributes include

- The ability to communicate effectively
- Interest in working with and helping people

- The patience to work with people whose injuries heal slowly

Training Provided

Job training consists of classroom instruction, including practice in applying therapy techniques. Further training occurs on the job and through advanced courses. Course content typically includes

- Anatomy, physiology, and psychology (the study of the body, body functions, and the mind)
- Methods of therapy, including massage, electric therapy, and radiation therapy
- Handling and positioning of patients
- Principles of rehabilitation

Physical Demands

Therapy specialists may have to lift and support patients during exercises and treatments.

Work Environment

Therapy specialists work in hospitals, clinics, and rehabilitation centers.

Civilian Counterparts

Civilian therapy specialists work in hospitals, rehabilitation centers, nursing homes, schools, and community health centers. They perform duties similar to those of military therapy specialists. Civilian therapy specialists often specialize in treating a particular type of patient, such as children, the severely disabled, the elderly, or those who have lost arms or legs (amputees).

Opportunities

Each year, the services need new specialists because of changes in personnel and the demands of the field. After job training, therapy specialists provide routine therapy care under the direction of supervisors. With experience, they work with patients with more serious problems. Eventually they may advance to supervisory positions.

Services Offering This Occupation

Army

Navy

Air Force

Coast Guard

PHYSICIAN ASSISTANTS

Short Description

Physician assistants provide routine health care for patients, freeing physicians to concentrate on more serious health problems. Physician assistants examine, diagnose, and treat patients under the supervision of medical doctors.

What They Do

Physician assistants in the military perform some or all of the following duties:

- Record medical histories, examine patients, and make initial diagnoses.
- Treat common illnesses or injuries, calling in supervising physicians for serious health problems.
- Perform routine physical examinations and collect specimens for laboratory tests.
- Order laboratory studies, such as blood tests, urinalysis, and X-rays.
- Provide information to patients about diet, family planning, use of drugs, and the effect of treatments.
- Provide emergency care in situations where doctors are not available.

Helpful Attributes

Helpful attributes include

- Ability to express ideas clearly and concisely
- Desire to help others
- Patience with others, especially those in pain or stress
- Self-confidence and the ability to remain calm in stressful situations

Training Provided

Job training, when available from the services, consists of classroom instruction, including practice in providing patient health care. Course content typically includes

- Fundamental medical care procedures
- Principles of behavioral and dental science
- Health care administration techniques

Work Environment

Physician assistants work in hospitals and clinics on land and aboard ships.

Civilian Counterparts

Civilian physician assistants work in hospitals, clinics, doctor's offices, and nursing homes. They perform duties similar to those performed by military physician assistants.

Services Offering This Occupation

Army

Navy

Air Force

Coast Guard

PLUMBERS AND PIPE FITTERS
Short Description

Military buildings and equipment require pipe systems for water, steam, gas, and waste. Pipe systems are also needed on aircraft, missiles, and ships for hydraulic (fluid pressure) and pneumatic (air pressure) systems. Plumbers and pipe fitters install and repair plumbing and pipe systems.

What They Do

Plumbers and pipe fitters in the military perform some or all of the following duties:

- Plan layouts of pipe systems using blueprints and drawings.
- Bend, cut, and thread pipes made of lead, copper, and plastic.
- Install connectors, fittings, and joints.
- Solder or braze pipe and tubing to join them.
- Install sinks, toilets, and other plumbing fixtures.
- Troubleshoot, test, and calibrate hydraulic and pneumatic systems.

Helpful Attributes

Helpful school subjects include math and shop mechanics. Helpful attributes include

- The ability to work with detailed plans
- A preference for doing physical work

Training Provided

Job training consists of classroom instruction, including practice in repairing plumbing systems. Course content typically includes

- Installation, operation, and repair of pipe systems
- Installation and repair of plumbing fixtures and boiler controls
- Maintenance and repair of hydraulic and pneumatic systems
- Methods of soldering, welding, silver brazing, and cutting

Physical Demands

Plumbers and pipe fitters have to lift and carry heavy pipes and tubes.

Work Environment

Plumbers and pipe fitters work both indoors and outdoors on land and aboard ships.

Civilian Counterparts

Civilian plumbers and pipe fitters usually work for mechanical or plumbing contractors or as self-employed contractors. Some plumbers and pipe fitters work for public utilities. Civilian plumbers and pipe fitters perform duties similar to those performed in the military.

Opportunities

Each year, the services need new plumbers and pipe fitters because of changes in personnel and the demands of the field. After job training, plumbers and pipe fitters work under close supervision. With experience, they work more independently and may supervise others. Eventually, they may advance to become managers of utilities departments, construction units, or missile maintenance units.

Services Offering This Occupation

Army

Navy

Marine Corps

Coast Guard

POWER PLANT ELECTRICIANS

Short Description

Each military base—anywhere in the world—must have its own electricity. Power plant electricians maintain and repair electricity generating equipment in mobile and stationary power plants.

What They Do

Power plant electricians perform some or all of the following duties:

- Maintain and repair motors, generators, switchboards, and control equipment.
- Maintain and repair power and lighting circuits, electrical fixtures, and other electrical equipment.
- Detect and locate grounds, open circuits, and short circuits in power distribution cables.
- Read technical guides and diagrams to locate damaged parts of generators and control equipment.

Helpful Attributes

Helpful school subjects include electrical and electronic theory, math, and technical drawing. Helpful attributes include

- The ability to use hand and power tools
- Interest in electricity
- Interest in working with machinery

Training Provided

Job training consists of classroom instruction, including practice in maintaining electric power systems. Course length varies depending upon specialty. Further training occurs on the job and through advanced courses. Course content typically includes

- Generator and power plant operations
- Electrical generation and distribution
- Diesel generator operation, disassembly, inspection, and maintenance
- Principles of electric and electronic circuitry

Physical Demands

Normal color vision is required to work with color-coded wiring.

Work Environment

Power plant electricians work in repair shops on land, aboard ships, or wherever generating equipment needing repair is located.

Civilian Counterparts

Civilian power plant electricians often work for construction companies, manufacturers, and utility companies. They perform duties similar to those of military power plant electricians.

Opportunities

Each year, the services need new electricians because of changes in personnel and the demands of the field. After job training, power plant electricians perform routine maintenance and repairs under supervision. In time, they perform more complex tasks and may help train others. Eventually, they may become supervisors of power plant operations.

Services Offering This Occupation

Army

Navy

Air Force

Marine Corps

Coast Guard

POWER PLANT OPERATORS

Short Description

Power plants generate electricity for ships, submarines, and military bases. The military uses many different types of power plants. Many ships and submarines have nuclear power plants. Power plant operators control power-generating plants on land and aboard ships and submarines. They operate boilers, turbines, nuclear reactors, and portable generators.

What They Do

Power plant operators in the military perform some or all of the following duties:

- Monitor and operate control boards to regulate power plants.
- Operate and maintain diesel generating units.

- Monitor and control nuclear reactors that produce electricity and power ships and submarines.
- Operate and maintain stationary engines, such as steam engines, air compressors, and generators.
- Operate and maintain auxiliary equipment.
- Inspect equipment for malfunctions.
- Operate the steam turbines that generate power for ships.

Helpful Attributes

Helpful school subjects include math and shop mechanics. Helpful attributes include

- Interest in nuclear power
- Interest in working with large machinery

Training Provided

Job training consists of classroom instruction, including practice in operating power plants. Nuclear specialties have training programs that last 1 year or more, covering all aspects of nuclear power plant operations. Course content typically includes

- Operation of pressure boilers
- Operation and maintenance of reactor control systems
- Operation and maintenance of mechanical systems on nuclear-powered ships and submarines

Physical Demands

Power plant operators lift heavy parts or tools when maintaining power plants. They may also have to stoop and kneel and work in awkward positions while repairing.

Work Environment

Power plant operators usually work indoors. They are subject to high temperatures and noise.

Civilian Counterparts

Civilian power plant operators work for power companies, factories, schools, and hospitals. They perform duties similar to those of military power plant operators. Depending on the specialty, they may also be called boiler operators, stationary engineers, nuclear reactor operators, or diesel plant operators.

Opportunities

Each year, the services need new power plant operators because of changes in personnel and the demands of the field. After job training, power plant operators work under the close direction of supervisors. With experience, they may gain greater responsibility for plant operations and supervise other operators. Eventually, they may become superintendents of utilities for large bases or chiefs of ships' engineering departments.

Services Offering This Occupation

Army

Navy

Marine Corps

Coast Guard

POWERHOUSE MECHANICS

Short Description

Power-generating stations (powerhouses) provide electric power for military bases, ships, and field camps. There are many types of powerhouses, from small gas generators to large nuclear reactors. Powerhouse mechanics install, maintain, and repair electrical and mechanical equipment in power-generating stations.

What They Do

Powerhouse mechanics in the military perform some or all of the following duties:

- Install generating equipment, such as gasoline and diesel engines, turbines, and air compressors.
- Repair and maintain nuclear power plants.
- Inspect and service pumps, generators, batteries, and cables.
- Tune engines using hand tools, timing lights, and combustion pressure gauges.
- Diagnose (troubleshoot) engine and electrical system problems.
- Replace damaged parts, such as fuel injectors, valves, and pistons.

Helpful Attributes

Helpful school subjects include shop mechanics and math. Helpful attributes include

- Interest in nuclear power
- Interest in repairing machines and equipment
- A preference for doing physical work

Training Provided

Job training for nonnuclear specialties consists of classroom instruction, including practice in repairing power-generating equipment. Nuclear specialties have training programs that last 1 year or more, covering all aspects of nuclear power plant operations. Further training occurs on the job and through advanced courses. Training length varies depending upon the specialty. Course content typically includes

- Principles of electricity
- Gas and diesel engine theories
- Hydraulic (fluid pressure) and pneumatic (air pressure) system maintenance

Physical Demands

Powerhouse mechanics may have to lift and move heavy electric generators or batteries. Normal color vision is required to work with color-coded wiring and cables.

Work Environment

Powerhouse mechanics work in equipment repair shops, power plant stations, or power-generating rooms aboard ships. Sometimes they work outdoors while repairing substation generating equipment.

Civilian Counterparts

Civilian powerhouse mechanics work for a wide variety of employers, such as utility and power companies, manufacturing companies, and other organizations that operate their own power plants. They perform duties similar to those of military powerhouse mechanics.

Opportunities

Each year, the services need new mechanics because of changes in personnel and the demands of the field.

After job training, mechanics perform routine maintenance tasks under close supervision. With experience, they perform more complex repair work. In time, they may become powerhouse repair crew supervisors or power plant operations managers.

Services Offering This Occupation

Army

Navy

Air Force

Marine Corps

Coast Guard

PRECISION INSTRUMENT AND EQUIPMENT REPAIRERS
Short Description

The military uses precision instruments and equipment to perform a variety of functions. Some precision instruments are used to measure distance, pressure, altitude, temperature, underwater depth, and other physical properties. Other types of precision equipment include photographic and imaging equipment, such as cameras, projectors, and film processing equipment. All of these items have many sensitive mechanisms that require regular attention to stay in good working order. Precision instrument and equipment repairers maintain and adjust these delicate items. They may specialize by the type of equipment that they work on.

What They Do

Precision instrument and equipment repairers in the military perform some or all of the following duties:

- Calibrate and repair instruments used in aircraft.
- Calibrate measuring instruments, such as barometers, thermometers, and telemeters.
- Adjust and repair weapon aiming devices, such as range finders, telescopes, and periscopes.
- Diagnose and repair problems in all types of cameras and photo processing equipment.
- Repair watches, clocks, and timers.
- Calibrate electrical test instruments.

Helpful Attributes

Helpful school subjects include math, science, electronics, and shop mechanics. Helpful attributes include

- The ability to solve mechanical problems
- The ability to use repair tools

Training Provided

Job training consists of classroom instruction, including practice in repairing precision instruments and equipment. Training length varies depending upon specialty. Further training occurs on the job and through advanced courses. Course content typically includes

- Calibration and repair of precision measuring instruments
- Use of blueprints and schematics
- Test and repair of cameras and darkroom equipment
- Test and repair of aerial sensor equipment

Physical Demands

Normal color vision is required to work with color-coded wiring.

Work Environment

Precision instrument and equipment repairers usually work in repair shops on land or aboard ships.

Civilian Counterparts

Civilian precision instrument and equipment repairers work in a variety of industries that use precision instruments and equipment. They may work for manufacturing firms, airlines, machinery repair shops, photographic labs, or engineering firms. Civilian precision instrument and equipment repairers perform duties similar to those of military repairers. Depending on their specialty, they may also be called instrument mechanics, calibration specialists, camera repairers, or photographic equipment technicians.

Opportunities

Each year, the services need new repairers because of changes in personnel and the demands of the field. After job training, precision instrument and equipment repairers make routine adjustments and simple repairs under close supervision. With experience, they perform more complicated repairs and may supervise others. They may eventually become managers of repair shops.

Services Offering This Occupation

Army

Navy

Air Force

Marine Corps

PREVENTIVE MAINTENANCE ANALYSTS

Short Description

Regular maintenance extends the time that aircraft, vehicles, and machinery can be used. To make sure that military equipment is well maintained, the services prepare detailed maintenance schedules. Preventive maintenance analysts promote equipment maintenance. They watch schedules and notify mechanics about upcoming maintenance needs.

What They Do

Preventive maintenance analysts in the military perform some or all of the following duties:

- Review maintenance schedules and notify mechanics about the types of service needed.
- Compare schedules to records of maintenance work actually performed.
- Prepare charts and reports on maintenance activities.
- Calculate how many mechanics and spare parts are needed to maintain equipment.
- Operate computers and calculators to enter or retrieve maintenance data.

Helpful Attributes

Helpful school subjects include general mathematics and algebra. Helpful attributes include

- The ability to use mathematical formulas
- Interest in working with computers
- Interest in working with numbers and statistics
- A preference for work requiring attention to detail

Training Provided

Job training consists of classroom instruction. Training length varies depending upon specialty. Course content typically includes

- Equipment maintenance management concepts
- Accounting procedures
- Statistical reporting methods
- Parts and supply inventory control procedures

Physical Demands

Normal color vision is required to read and interpret maintenance charts and graphs in some specialties. Some specialties require the ability to speak clearly.

Work Environment

Preventive maintenance analysts usually work in office settings.

Civilian Counterparts

Civilian preventive maintenance analysts work for government agencies, airlines, and large transportation firms. They also work for firms with large numbers of machines. They perform duties similar to those of military preventive maintenance analysts.

Opportunities

Each year, the services need new analysts because of changes in personnel and the demands of the field. After job training, new analysts work under close supervision. As they gain experience, they are given more responsibility and more difficult work assignments. Eventually, they may become supervisors of maintenance control units.

Services Offering This Occupation

Army

Navy

Air Force

Marine Corps

Coast Guard

PRINTING SPECIALISTS
Short Description

The military produces many printed publications each year, including newspapers, booklets, training manuals, maps, and charts. Printing specialists operate printing presses and binding machines to make finished copies of printed material.

What They Do

Printing specialists in the military perform some or all of the following duties:

- Reproduce printed matter using offset lithographic printing processes.
- Prepare photographic negatives and transfer them to printing plates using copy cameras and enlargers.
- Prepare layouts of artwork, photographs, and text for lithographic plates.
- Produce brochures, newspapers, maps, and charts.
- Bind printed material into hardback or paperback books using binding machines.
- Maintain printing presses.

Helpful Attributes

Helpful school subjects include shop mechanics and photography. Helpful attributes include

- Interest in learning about printing
- A preference for doing physical work

Training Provided

Job training consists of classroom instruction, including practice in operating printing presses. Training length varies by specialty. Further training occurs on the job and through advanced courses. Course content typically includes

- Photolithography techniques
- Operation of offset presses
- Techniques for making printing plates
- Binding techniques

Physical Demands

Normal color vision is required to enter some specialties in this occupation.

Work Environment

Printing specialists work indoors in print shops and offices located on land or aboard ships.

Civilian Counterparts

Civilian printing specialists work for commercial print shops, newspapers, insurance companies, government offices, or businesses that do their own printing. They perform duties similar to those of military printing specialists. They may be called offset printing press operators, lithograph press operators, offset duplicating machine operators, lithograph photographers, or bindery workers.

Opportunities

Each year, the services need new specialists because of changes in personnel and the demands of the field. After job training, specialists normally operate printing and binding machines under direct supervision. With experience, they work more independently, setting up and operating machines. In time, printing specialists may become supervisors of printing plants.

Services Offering This Occupation

Army

Navy

Marine Corps

PURCHASING AND CONTRACTING MANAGERS

Short Description

The military buys billions of dollars' worth of equipment, supplies, and services from private industry each year. The services must make sure their purchases meet military specifications and are made at a fair price. Purchasing and contracting managers negotiate, write, and monitor contracts for purchasing equipment, materials, and services.

What They Do

Purchasing and contracting managers in the military perform some or all of the following duties:

- Review requests for supplies and services to make sure they are complete and accurate.
- Prepare bid invitations or requests for proposals for contracts with civilian firms.
- Review bids or proposals and award contracts.
- Prepare formal contracts, specifying all terms and conditions.
- Review work to make sure that it meets the requirements of contracts.

Helpful Attributes

Helpful fields of study include management and business or public administration. Helpful attributes include

- Ability to develop detailed plans
- Interest in negotiating

- Interest in work requiring accuracy and attention to detail

Training Provided

Job training consists of classroom instruction. Training length varies depending on specialty. Further training occurs through advanced courses. Course content typically includes

- Purchasing and accounting procedures
- Use of computers in contract administration
- Supply and financial management

Work Environment

Purchasing and contracting managers work in offices.

Civilian Counterparts

Civilian purchasing and contracting managers work for a wide variety of employers, including engineering, manufacturing, and construction firms. They perform duties similar to those performed by military purchasing and contract managers. They may also be called procurement services managers, purchasing directors, contracts administrators, or material control managers.

Services Offering This Occupation

Army

Navy

Air Force

Marine Corps

Coast Guard

QUARTERMASTERS AND BOAT OPERATORS

Short Description

The military operates many small boats for amphibious troop landings, harbor patrols, and transportation over short distances. Quartermasters and boat operators navigate and pilot many types of small watercraft, including tugboats, gunboats, and barges.

What They Do

Quartermasters and boat operators in the military perform some or all of the following duties:

- Direct the course and speed of boats.
- Consult maps, charts, weather reports, and navigation equipment.
- Pilot tugboats when towing and docking barges and large ships.
- Operate amphibious craft during troop landings.
- Maintain boats and deck equipment.
- Operate ship-to-shore radios.
- Keep ship logs.

Helpful Attributes

Helpful school subjects include mathematics. Helpful attributes include

- Ability to follow detailed instructions and read maps
- Ability to work with mathematical formulas
- Interest in sailing and navigation

Training Provided

Job training consists of classroom instruction including practice in boat operations. Course content typically includes

- Boat handling procedures
- Log and message-handling procedures
- Use of compasses, radar, charts, and other navigational aids
- Navigational mathematics

Work Environment

Quartermasters and boat operators work aboard all types of boats and in all types of weather conditions. When not piloting boats, they may work on or below deck repairing boats and equipment or overseeing cargo storage. When ashore, they may work in offices that make nautical maps or in harbor management offices. Some boats are operated in combat situations.

Civilian Counterparts

Civilian quartermasters and boat operators may work for shipping and cruise lines, piloting tugboats, ferries, and other small vessels. Depending upon specialty, they may also be called tugboat captains, motorboat operators, navigators, or pilots.

Services Offering This Occupation

Army

Marine Corps

Coast Guard

RADAR AND SONAR OPERATORS

Short Description

Radar and sonar devices work by bouncing radio or sound waves off objects to determine their location and measure their distance. They have many uses, such as tracking aircraft and missiles, determining positions of ships and submarines, directing artillery fire, forecasting weather, and aiding navigation. Radar and sonar operators monitor sophisticated equipment. They normally specialize in either radar or sonar.

What They Do

Radar and sonar operators in the military perform some or all of the following duties:

- Detect and track the position, direction, and speed of aircraft, ships, submarines, and missiles.
- Plot and record data on status charts and plotting boards.
- Set up and operate radar equipment to direct artillery fire.
- Monitor early warning air defense systems.
- Send and receive messages using electronic communication systems.

Helpful Attributes

Helpful school subjects include geometry, algebra, and science. Helpful attributes include

- The ability to concentrate for long periods
- Interest in working with electronic equipment

Training Provided

Job training consists of classroom instruction and practice operating radar or sonar equipment. Training length varies by specialty. Further training occurs on the job and through advanced courses. Course content typically includes

- Operation and maintenance of radar and sonar equipment
- Identification of ships, submarines, aircraft, and missiles
- Computation of aircraft or missile speed, direction, and altitude

Physical Demands

Normal color vision is required to enter this occupation. Specialties involving flying require passing a special physical exam.

Work Environment

Radar and sonar operators in the military primarily work indoors in security-controlled areas. They work in operations centers and command posts, either on land or aboard aircraft, ships, or submarines. Some may work in a mobile field radar unit.

Civilian Counterparts

There are no direct civilian counterparts to military radar and sonar operators. However, workers in civilian occupations that use radar and sonar equipment in their jobs include weather service technicians, air traffic controllers, ship navigators, and ocean salvage specialists.

Opportunities

Each year, the services need new operators because of changes in personnel and the demands of the field. After job training, new operators use radar or sonar equipment under close supervision. With experience, they work more independently and may eventually become supervisors of ground, airborne, or shipboard radar or sonar units.

Services Offering This Occupation

Army

Navy

Air Force

Marine Corps

Coast Guard

RADIOLOGIC (X-RAY) TECHNICIANS

Short Description

Radiology (the use of x-rays) is important in the diagnosis and treatment of medical conditions. X-rays and other diagnostic techniques, such as ultrasound and magnetic resonance imaging (MRI), help physicians detect injuries and illnesses. Radiology is also used to treat some diseases, such as cancer. Radiologic technicians operate x-ray and other imaging-related equipment used in diagnosing and treating injuries and diseases. They work as part of a medical team of physicians and specialists to provide health care to patients. Radiologic technicians may specialize by the type of equipment they operate.

What They Do

Radiologic technicians in the military perform some or all of the following duties:

- Read requests or instructions from physicians to determine each patient's x-ray or imaging needs.
- Position patients under radiologic equipment.
- Operate imaging equipment.
- Adjust equipment to the correct time and power of exposure.
- Process x-ray pictures.
- Prepare radioactive solutions and administer them to patients.
- Keep records of patient treatment.

Helpful Attributes

Helpful school subjects include algebra, biology, and other science courses. Helpful attributes include

- The ability to follow strict standards and procedures
- Interest in activities requiring accuracy and attention to detail
- Interest in helping others

Training Provided

Job training consists of classroom instruction, including practice with radiologic equipment. Extensive on-the-job training is also provided. Additional training occurs through advanced courses. Training length varies depending upon specialty. Course content typically includes

- Operation of diagnostic imaging equipment
- Radioactive isotope therapy
- X-ray film processing
- Anatomy and physiology

Work Environment

Radiologic technicians work in hospitals and clinics. In combat situations, they may work in mobile field hospitals. They follow strict safety procedures to minimize their exposure to radiation.

Civilian Counterparts

Civilian radiologic technicians work in hospitals, diagnostic clinics, and medical laboratories. They perform duties similar to those of military radiologic technicians. They may specialize in various areas of radiology and may be called x-ray technologists, radiographers, sonographers, radiation therapy technologists, or nuclear medicine technologists.

Opportunities

Each year, the services need new technicians because of changes in personnel and the demands of the field. After job training, technicians start operating routine imaging equipment. With experience, they may specialize in nuclear medicine and administer radiation and radioisotopic treatment and therapy. In time, they may advance to become supervisors of radiologic units.

Services Offering This Occupation

Army

Navy

Air Force

Coast Guard

RECREATION, WELFARE, AND MORALE SPECIALISTS

Short Description

The military has an obligation to provide for the overall well-being of its Service members and their families, not only in peacetime, but especially during times of war or crisis. In peacetime, programs are designed to maintain mission readiness, promote fitness and esprit de corps, and create a strong sense of military community that enhances the quality of life. During conflict, high morale is critical for those personnel who are deployed, as well as for the families that remain behind. In order to withstand the physical and emotional stresses endured, particularly during deployment situations, the military community depends upon a strong support system. This system is comprised of programs designed to encourage positive individual values; aid in recruitment and retention of personnel; provide for physical, mental, cultural, and social needs, and the general well-being of Service members and their families; and establish a core sense of community for its transient population. Without providing these kinds of support services, including physical fitness facilities, libraries, youth and outdoor recreation activities, arts and crafts, and unit-level sports, the military would have difficulty accomplishing its basic missions.

What They Do

Recreation, welfare, and morale specialists in the military perform some or all of the following duties:

- Plan, prepare, and direct social functions, meetings, or recreational activities.
- Prepare daily activity reports.
- Track inventory, purchasing, receiving, and storage of equipment and goods for club and entertainment services.
- Direct operation of clubs, open messes, recreational buildings, and libraries.
- Arrange publicity for social or recreational events, such as plays, concerts, and tournaments.
- Issue and maintain recreation gear and resources, such as sports equipment and movies.
- Conduct surveys to determine interests and attitudes of the military population and their dependents.
- Schedule facility or property maintenance.

Helpful Attributes

Helpful school subjects include psychology, speech communications, business, and physical education. Helpful attributes include

- Interest in working with people
- Interest in physical fitness, athletics, arts and crafts, and other recreational activities
- Ability to plan and organize group and individual events, programs, and activities
- Enjoy helping, teaching, and caring for others
- Ability to coordinate and prioritize the work and activities of others
- Ability to work with minimal supervision

Work Environment

These specialists typically work indoors when planning and organizing events or maintaining facilities, or outdoors when conducting recreational activities.

Civilian Counterparts

Civilian recreation, welfare, and morale specialists may work in state and local government agencies or private industry, such as departments of parks and recreation, vocational rehabilitation, social services, nursing homes, fitness centers, schools, libraries, and community or recreation centers.

Services Offering This Occupation

Navy

Air Force

Marine Corps

RECRUITING SPECIALISTS

Short Description

Attracting young people with the kinds of talent needed to succeed in today's military is a large task. Recruiting specialists provide information about military careers to young people, parents, schools, and local communities. They explain service employment and training opportunities, pay and benefits, and service life.

What They Do

Recruiting specialists in the military perform some or all of the following duties:

- Interview civilians interested in military careers.
- Describe military careers to groups of high school students.
- Explain the purpose of the ASVAB (Armed Services Vocational Aptitude Battery) and test results to students and counselors.
- Participate in local job fairs and career day programs.
- Talk about the military to community groups.
- Counsel military personnel about career opportunities and benefits.

Helpful Attributes

Helpful school subjects include the social sciences, speech, psychology, and English. Helpful attributes include

- The ability to speak before groups
- The ability to work independently
- Interest in working with youths

Training Provided

Job training consists of classroom instruction. Further training occurs on the job and through advanced courses. Course content typically includes

- Recruiting procedures
- Interviewing techniques
- Public speaking techniques
- Community relations practices

Work Environment

Recruiting specialists work in local recruiting offices, on high school campuses and career centers, and in local communities. They may have to travel often.

Civilian Counterparts

Civilian recruiting specialists work for businesses of all kinds that are searching for talented people to hire. Recruiters also work for colleges that are seeking to attract and enroll talented high school students.

Opportunities

Normally, personnel must have been in the service for several years before they are eligible to become recruiters. Each year, the services need new recruiters, since some specialists spend only a few years in recruiting before returning to their primary occupational area. Those who choose to make a career of recruiting may, in time, supervise one or more recruiting offices.

Services Offering This Occupation

Army

Navy

Air Force

Marine Corps

Coast Guard

RELIGIOUS PROGRAM SPECIALISTS

Short Description

The military has personnel from many religions and faiths. The military provides chaplains and religious program specialists to help meet the spiritual needs of its personnel. Religious program specialists assist chaplains with religious services, religious education programs, and related administrative duties.

What They Do

Religious program specialists in the military perform some or all of the following duties:

- Assist chaplains in planning and religious programs and activities.
- Assist chaplains in conducting religious services.
- Prepare religious, educational, and devotional materials.
- Organize charitable and public service volunteer programs.
- Maintain relations with religious communities and public service organizations.
- Perform administrative duties for chaplains.

Helpful Attributes

Helpful school subjects include English, public speaking, accounting, and typing. Helpful attributes include

- The ability to express ideas clearly
- Interest in administrative work
- Interest in religious guidance
- Knowledge of various religious customs and beliefs
- Sensitivity to the needs of others

Training Provided

Job training consists of classroom instruction. Course content typically includes

- Principles of religious support programs
- Guidance and counseling techniques
- Leadership skills
- Office procedures

Physical Demands

The ability to speak clearly and distinctly is required to enter this occupation.

Work Environment

Religious program specialists in the military usually work indoors. They also serve aboard ships or with land and air units in the field.

Civilian Counterparts

Civilian religious program specialists help manage churches and religious schools. Their duties are similar to those performed by military religious program specialists, including planning religious programs and preparing religious educational materials. They are also called directors of religious activities.

Opportunities

Each year, the services need new specialists because of changes in personnel and the demands of the field. After job training, religious program specialists help chaplains and supervisors with administrative matters. With experience, they gain more responsibility for organizing activities and working in the local community. In time, they may supervise other specialists.

Services Offering This Occupation

Army

Navy

Air Force

SALES AND STOCK SPECIALISTS

Short Description

The military operates retail stores that sell food and merchandise to make it easier for personnel to obtain whatever they need at the locations where they are stationed. Sales and stock specialists perform a variety of duties to support the operation of these stores, whether working aboard a ship or overseas in a remote location.

What They Do

Sales and stock specialists in the military perform some or all of the following duties:

- Order and receive merchandise and food for retail sale.
- Inspect food and merchandise for spoilage or damage.
- Price retail sales items, using stamping machines.
- Stock shelves and racks for the display of products.
- Count merchandise and supplies during inventory checks.
- Operate cash registers.
- Record money received and prepare bank deposits.

Helpful Attributes

Helpful school subjects include bookkeeping and mathematics. Helpful attributes include

- The ability to use cash registers and calculators
- Interest in working with people

Training Provided

Job training consists of classroom instruction for some specialties. For others, training occurs on the job. Further training occurs on the job. Course content includes

- Stock procedures
- Record keeping and bookkeeping procedures

Physical Demands

The ability to speak clearly is required. Sales and stock specialists may have to lift and carry heavy objects.

Work Environment

Sales and stock specialists work on land and aboard ships in retail stores and storerooms.

Civilian Counterparts

Civilian sales and stock specialists work in many kinds of retail businesses, such as grocery stores and department stores. They perform duties similar to those of military sales and stock specialists. They may also be called sales clerks or stock clerks.

Opportunities

Each year, the services need new specialists because of changes in personnel and the demands of the field. After job training, sales and stock specialists are assigned to retail stores and storerooms. Initially, they work under close supervision. With experience, they work more independently, train new workers, and assume more responsibility for sales and stock activities.

Services Offering This Occupation

Navy
Air Force
Marine Corps
Coast Guard

SEAMEN

Short Description

All ships must have teams of individuals with "jack-of-all-trades" skills who make things run smoothly above deck. Seamen perform many duties to help operate and maintain military ships, boats, and submarines.

What They Do

Seamen in the military perform some or all of the following duties:

- Operate hoists, cranes, and winches to load cargo or set gangplanks.
- Operate and maintain on-deck equipment and ship rigging.
- Supervise firefighting and damage control exercises.
- Handle lines to secure vessels to wharves or other ships.
- Stand watch for security, navigation, or communications.
- Supervise crews painting and maintaining decks and sides of ships.

Helpful Attributes

Helpful school subjects include mathematics and shop mechanics. Helpful attributes include

- The ability to work closely with others
- Interest in sailing and being at sea
- A preference for physical work

Training Provided

Although classroom training is provided to seamen, most training occurs on the job. Training programs vary depending upon service and specialty.

Physical Demands

Seamen may have to climb ships' rigging and perform work at heights. Their work often involves moderate to heavy lifting.

Work Environment

Seamen and deckhands work aboard all types of ships and submarines. On ships, they often work outdoors on deck while servicing shipboard equipment.

Civilian Counterparts

Civilian seamen work primarily for shipping companies, sometimes called the Merchant Marine. They also work for cruise ship lines. They perform many duties similar to those of military seamen. They are called able seamen, deckhands, or boatswains.

Opportunities

Each year, the services need new seamen because of changes in personnel and the demands of the field. New seamen work together on teams led by experienced supervisors. Through practice, they learn the many tasks they must perform. In time, seamen supervise one or more teams. Eventually, they may become managers responsible for planning and directing the work of many seamen. Often, seamen receive additional training that prepares them for other occupations in their service.

Services Offering This Occupation

Navy

Coast Guard

SHIP ELECTRICIANS
Short Description

Electrical systems supply power to operate ships and submarines. Lights, radar, weapons, and machinery all need electricity. Ship electricians operate and repair electrical systems on ships. They keep electric power plants, wiring, and machinery in working order.

What They Do

Ship electricians in the military perform some or all of the following duties:

- Install wiring for lights and equipment.
- Troubleshoot electric wiring and electrical equipment using test meters.
- Inspect and maintain devices that distribute electricity throughout ships, such as circuits, transformers, and regulators.

- Monitor and maintain electrical devices connected to the ship's main engines or nuclear reactors.

Helpful Attributes

Helpful school courses include math and shop mechanics. Helpful attributes include

- The ability to use tools
- Interest in electricity and how electrical machines work
- Interest in solving problems

Training Provided

Job training consists of classroom instruction, including practice repairing electrical systems. Further training occurs on the job and through advanced courses. Course content typically includes

- Electrical theory
- Troubleshooting procedures
- Maintenance and repair procedures
- Reading diagrams and calculating amperage, voltage, and resistance levels

Physical Demands

Normal color vision is required to work with color-coded wiring.

Work Environment

Ship electricians usually work indoors, aboard ships or submarines. They also work in ship repair shops on land.

Civilian Counterparts

Civilian ship electricians work for shipbuilding and drydock firms and shipping lines. They perform duties similar to those of military ship electricians. Other civilian electricians, such as building electricians and electrical products repairers, also perform similar work.

Opportunities

Each year, the services need new ship electricians because of changes in personnel and the demands of the field. After job training, ship electricians perform maintenance work and repair electrical problems.

Eventually, they may become superintendents of electrical repair shops or of ship electrical systems.

Services Offering This Occupation

Navy

Coast Guard

SPACE OPERATIONS SPECIALISTS
Short Description

Orbiting satellites and other space vehicles are used for communications, weather forecasting, and collecting intelligence data. In the future, more and more military operations will involve space systems. Space operations specialists use and repair spacecraft ground control command equipment, including the electronic systems that track spacecraft location and operation.

What They Do

Space operations specialists in the military perform some or all of the following duties:

- Transmit and verify spacecraft commands using aerospace ground equipment.
- Monitor computers and telemetry display systems.
- Analyze data to determine spacecraft operational status.
- Repair ground and spacecraft communication equipment.
- Assist in preparing spacecraft commands to meet mission objectives.
- Operate data-handling equipment to track spacecraft.

Helpful Attributes

Helpful school subjects include physics, geometry, algebra, and trigonometry. Helpful attributes include

- The ability to work with formulas to solve math problems
- Interest in operating electronic equipment and systems
- Interest in space exploration
- Interest in working as part of a team

Training Provided

Job training consists of classroom instruction, including practice in spacecraft command and control operations. Course content typically includes

- Operation of electronic transmitting, receiving, and computing equipment
- Analysis of data that indicate spacecraft operational status
- Application of electronic and satellite system principles
- Alignment of ground and spacecraft communications systems
- Space command and control system operational procedures

Physical Demands

Normal color vision is required to enter this occupation.

Work Environment

Space operations specialists work in space operations centers.

Civilian Counterparts

Civilian space operations specialists work for the National Aeronautics and Space Administration, the U.S. Weather Service, and private satellite communications firms. They perform duties similar to those of military space operations specialists.

Opportunities

Each year, the services need new specialists because of changes in personnel and the demands of the field. After job training, space operations specialists are assigned to space operations centers, where they use and repair equipment under close supervision. After gaining experience, they work more independently and may help train new workers. Eventually, space operations specialists may become supervisors of space operations centers.

Services Offering This Occupation

Navy

Air Force

SPECIAL FORCES
Short Description

When the military has difficult and dangerous missions to perform, it calls upon special forces teams.

These elite combat forces stay in a constant state of readiness to strike anywhere in the world on a moment's notice. Special forces team members conduct offensive raids, demolitions, intelligence, search and rescue, and other missions from aboard aircraft, helicopters, ships, or submarines. Because of the wide variety of missions, special forces team members are trained swimmers, parachutists, and survival experts, in addition to being combat trained.

What They Do

Special forces team members in the military perform some or all of the following duties:

- Carry out demolition raids against enemy military targets, such as bridges, railroads, and fuel depots.
- Clear minefields, both underwater and on land.
- Conduct missions to gather intelligence information on enemy military forces.
- Conduct offensive raids or invasions of enemy territories.
- Destroy enemy ships in coastal areas, using underwater explosives.

Helpful Attributes

Helpful attributes include

- The ability to remain calm in stressful situations
- The ability to work as a team member
- Readiness to accept a challenge and face danger

Training Provided

Job training consists of many weeks of formal classroom training and practice exercises. Additional training occurs on the job. Basic skills are kept sharp through frequent practice exercises under simulated mission conditions. Course content typically includes:

- Physical conditioning, parachuting, swimming, and scuba diving
- Using land warfare weapons and communications devices
- Explosives handling and disposal

Physical Demands

The special forces have very demanding physical requirements. Good eyesight, night vision, and physical conditioning are required to reach mission objectives by parachute, overland, or underwater. In most instances, special forces team members are required to be qualified divers, parachutists, and endurance runners.

Work Environment

Because special forces team members must be prepared to go anywhere in the world, they train and work in all climates, weather conditions, and settings. They may dive from submarines or small underwater craft. Special forces team members may also be exposed to harsh temperatures, often without protection, during missions in enemy-controlled areas. Most of the time, however, they work and train on military bases, ships, or submarines.

Special Requirements

This occupation is open only to men.

Civilian Counterparts

Although the job of special forces team members has no equivalent in civilian life, training in explosives, bomb disposal, scuba diving, and swimming may be helpful in such civilian jobs as blaster, police bomb disposal specialist, diver, or swimming instructor. The discipline and dependability of special forces are assets in many civilian occupations.

Opportunities

Each year, the services need new team members because of changes in personnel and the demands of the field. After training, team members practice their skills under close supervision. With experience, they may supervise and train other team members. They may also work alone on certain missions. Eventually, they may become team leaders.

Services Offering This Occupation

Army

Navy

Air Force

Marine Corps

SURVEYING, MAPPING, AND DRAFTING TECHNICIANS

Short Description

The military builds and repairs many airstrips, docks, barracks, roads, and other projects each year. Surveying, mapping, and drafting technicians conduct land surveys, make maps, and prepare detailed plans and drawings for construction projects. Surveys and maps are also used to locate military targets and plot troop movements.

What They Do

Surveying, mapping, and drafting technicians in the military perform some or all of the following duties:

- Draw maps and charts using drafting tools and computers.
- Make scale drawings of roads, airfields, buildings, and other military projects.
- Conduct land surveys and compute survey results.
- Draw diagrams for wiring and plumbing of structures.
- Build scale models of land areas that show hills, lakes, roads, and buildings.
- Piece together aerial photographs to form large photomaps.
- Use global positioning systems to collect location information from satellites.

Helpful Attributes

Helpful school subjects include algebra, geometry, and trigonometry. Helpful attributes include

- The ability to convert ideas into drawings
- Interest in maps and charts
- Interest in working with drafting equipment and computers

Training Provided

Job training consists of several weeks of classroom instruction, depending on specialty. Further training occurs on the job and through advanced courses. Course content typically includes

- Surveying and drafting techniques
- Aerial photo interpretation
- Architectural and structural drawing

Physical Demands

Good depth perception is required to study aerial photos through stereoscopes. Normal color vision is required to work with color-coded maps and drawings.

Work Environment

Surveying, mapping, and drafting technicians work both indoors and outdoors in all climates and weather conditions. Those assigned to engineering units sometimes work outdoors with survey teams. Those assigned to intelligence units may work on ships as well as on land.

Civilian Counterparts

Civilian surveying, mapping, and drafting technicians work for construction, engineering, and architectural firms and government agencies such as the highway department. Their work is used for planning construction projects such as highways, airport runways, dams, and drainage systems. They are also called cartographic technicians and photogrammetrists.

Opportunities

Each year, the services need new technicians because of changes in personnel and the demands of the field. After job training, technicians make simple drawings, trace photos, perform basic survey duties, or help make maps under close supervision. With experience, they work more independently. Eventually, they may supervise mapmaking facilities, surveying teams, or construction units.

Services Offering This Occupation

Army

Navy

Air Force

Marine Corps

Coast Guard

SURVIVAL EQUIPMENT SPECIALISTS

Short Description

Military personnel often have hazardous assignments. They depend on survival equipment to protect their lives in case of emergencies. Survival equipment specialists inspect, maintain, and repair survival equipment, such as parachutes, aircraft life support equipment, and air-sea rescue equipment.

What They Do

Survival equipment specialists in the military perform some or all of the following duties:

- Inspect parachutes for rips and tangled lines.
- Pack parachutes for safe operation.
- Repair life rafts and load them with emergency provisions.
- Test emergency oxygen regulators on aircraft.
- Stock aircraft with fire extinguishers, flares, and survival provisions.
- Train crews in the use of survival equipment.

Helpful Attributes

Helpful school subjects include shop mechanics and science. Helpful attributes include

- The ability to do work requiring accuracy and attention to detail
- Interest in working for the safety of others

Training Provided

Job training consists of classroom instruction, including practice in working with survival equipment. Further training occurs on the job and through additional courses. Course content typically includes

- Parachute rigging techniques
- Repair of inflatable rafts and other survival equipment
- Maintenance of oxygen equipment
- Maintenance of air-sea rescue equipment

Physical Demands

Normal color vision is required to work with color-coded wiring and repair charts.

Work Environment

Survival equipment specialists in the military work in repair shops on land or aboard ships.

Civilian Counterparts

Civilian survival equipment specialists work for commercial airlines, parachute rigging and supply companies, survival equipment manufacturing firms, and some government agencies. They perform duties similar to those of military survival equipment specialists. Those who specialize in parachutes are called parachute riggers.

Opportunities

Each year, the services need new specialists because of changes in personnel and the demands of the field. After job training, survival equipment specialists work on survival equipment under the close direction of supervisors. With experience, they work with less supervision and perform more challenging tasks. In time, survival equipment specialists may become supervisors, assisting in the management of survival equipment repair facilities.

Services Offering This Occupation

Army

Navy

Air Force

Marine Corps

Coast Guard

TRAINING SPECIALISTS AND INSTRUCTORS

Short Description

The military trains new personnel in the job skills needed to begin their careers in the service. The military also offers advanced training and retraining to nearly all personnel. Instruction in electronics, health care, computer sciences, and aviation are just a few of the many vocational and technical areas for which the military has training programs. Training specialists and instructors teach classes and give demonstrations to provide military personnel with the knowledge they need to perform their jobs.

What They Do

Training specialists and instructors in the military perform some or all of the following duties:

- Prepare course outlines and materials to present during training.
- Select training materials, such as textbooks and films.

- Teach classes and give lectures in person, over closed-circuit TV, or on videotape.
- Work with students individually when necessary.
- Test and evaluate student progress.

Helpful Attributes

Helpful school subjects include public speaking and English. Helpful attributes include

- The ability to communicate effectively, both in writing and in speaking
- Interest in counseling and promoting human relations
- Interest in teaching

Training Provided

Training consists of classroom instruction, including practice teaching. Length of training varies depending on specialty. Course content typically includes

- Lesson planning
- Instructional methods
- Communications skills

Physical Demands

Training specialists and instructors must be able to speak clearly and distinctly.

Work Environment

Training specialists and instructors in the military work either indoors or outdoors, depending on the type of training they provide and their specialty area.

Civilian Counterparts

Civilian training specialists and instructors work for vocational and technical schools, high schools, colleges, businesses, and government agencies. Their duties are similar to those performed by military training specialists and instructors. Civilian training specialists and instructors may be called teachers, trainers, or training representatives.

Opportunities

Each year, the services need new specialists and instructors because of changes in personnel and the demands of the field. Because training specialists

and instructors must have an in-depth knowledge of a subject to be effective, only experienced personnel may become training specialists and instructors. Normally, training specialists and instructors are selected from those workers in each occupation who both are good at their work and have shown an ability to teach. Often, they divide their time between regular work and training duties.

Services Offering This Occupation

Navy

Air Force

Marine Corps

Coast Guard

TRANSPORTATION SPECIALISTS

Short Description

The military constantly moves passengers and cargo. Personnel often travel to meetings, training sessions, and new assignments. Supplies and equipment to support troops must be shipped regularly. Transportation specialists plan and assist in air, sea, and land transportation for people and cargo. Some assist passenger travel as gate agents and flight attendants.

What They Do

Transportation specialists in the military perform some or all of the following duties:

- Arrange for passenger travel via plane, bus, train, or boat.
- Arrange for shipment and delivery of household goods.
- Determine which vehicles to use based on freight or passenger movement requirements.
- Determine transportation and shipping routes.
- Prepare transportation requests and shipping documents.
- Check in passengers and baggage for military transport flights.
- Serve as military airplane flight attendants.
- Inspect cargo for proper packing, loading, and marking.

Helpful Attributes

Helpful school subjects include mathematics and English. Helpful attributes include

- Interest in arranging travel schedules
- Interest in serving people
- Interest in using computers

Training Provided

Job training consists of classroom instruction, including practice in making transportation arrangements. Further training occurs on the job and through advanced courses. Course content typically includes

- Planning transportation for personnel and cargo
- Proper cargo handling, shipping, and storing methods
- Analysis of transportation documents

Work Environment

Transportation specialists usually work in offices. They may work outdoors when escorting passengers or processing shipments. Flight attendants work on land and in airplanes.

Civilian Counterparts

Civilian transportation specialists work for airlines, shipping firms, and commercial freight lines. They perform duties similar to those of military transportation specialists. Civilian transportation specialists may also be called travel clerks, reservation clerks, or transportation agents.

Opportunities

Each year, the services need new specialists because of changes in personnel and the demands of the field. After job training, the specialists make travel and shipping arrangements under direct supervision. Some may specialize as flight attendants and gate agents. With experience, they may become supervisors of other transportation specialists. In time, they may manage transportation offices.

Services Offering This Occupation

Army

Navy

Air Force

Marine Corps

UAV OPERATIONS SPECIALISTS

Short Description

The military uses remotely piloted unmanned vehicles for a variety of purposes, such as deep sea exploration, intelligence gathering, remote surveillance, and target applications. These vehicles are used in the air, on land, and at sea in operations or missions that could be dangerous for human operators on board the vehicle. The military requires skilled operators and technicians to maintain and control these vehicles. Personnel normally specialize by the type of vehicle they operate, such as unmanned aerial vehicles, ground vehicles, surface vehicles, and undersea vehicles.

What They Do

Unmanned vehicle operations specialists in the military perform some or all of the following duties:

- Prepare and install equipment on or within the unmanned vehicle.
- Operate, navigate, launch, track, and recover unmanned vehicles.
- Operate equipment in remote receiving stations and ground control stations.
- Coordinate with other personnel to complete the designated mission.
- Inspect and maintain components in unmanned vehicles.

Helpful Attributes

Helpful attributes include

- Enjoying working with tools
- Knowledge of electronic theory and schematic drawing
- Superior adaptability to three-dimensional spatial relationships

Training Provided

The length of job training varies depending upon the position. Course content typically includes

- Unmanned vehicle concepts and capabilities
- Operation of unmanned vehicles
- Basic preventive maintenance

Physical Demands

Normal color vision is required for some specialties.

Work Environment

Unmanned vehicle operations specialists work under a variety of conditions, depending upon the type of vehicle and the mission. Some specialists work in control stations or receiving stations on land, while others work aboard ships.

Civilian Counterparts

Unmanned vehicles are used in several civilian areas, such as mining, petroleum exploration, environmental research, and manufacturing. Civilian unmanned vehicle operations specialists perform duties similar to those of their military counterparts.

Opportunities

Each year, the services need new specialists because of changes in personnel and the growing use of this kind of technology. After job training, new unmanned vehicle operations specialists normally work under close supervision to prepare unmanned vehicles for their missions. With experience, they may perform more difficult duties, such as piloting, navigating, and recovering unmanned vehicles. In time, some operations specialists may plan and oversee unmanned vehicle missions.

Services Offering This Occupation

Army

Navy

Air Force

Marine Corps

VEHICLE DRIVERS

Short Description

The military uses numerous vehicles to transport its troops, equipment, and supplies. Together, the services own and operate about 50,000 heavy trucks and buses. Vehicle drivers operate all types of heavy military vehicles. They drive fuel or water tank trucks, tractor-trailers, heavy troop transports, and passenger buses.

What They Do

Vehicle drivers in the military perform some or all of the following duties:

- Read travel instructions to determine travel routes, arrival dates, and types of cargo.
- Make sure vehicles are loaded properly.
- Check oil, fuel, and other fluid levels and tire pressure.
- Drive vehicles over all types of roads, traveling alone or in convoys.
- Keep records of mileage driven and fuel and oil used.
- Wash vehicles and perform routine maintenance and repairs.

Helpful Attributes

Helpful school courses include driver education. Helpful attributes include

- Interest in driving
- Interest in mechanics

Training Provided

Job training consists of classroom instruction, including practice in driving heavy military vehicles. Course content typically includes

- Accident prevention
- Safety check procedures
- International road signs
- Basic vehicle maintenance

Physical Demands

Normal color vision is required to read road maps. Drivers sometimes must change heavy tires.

Work Environment

Vehicle driving involves long periods of sitting.

Civilian Counterparts

Civilian vehicle drivers work for trucking companies, moving companies, bus companies, and businesses with their own delivery fleets. They perform duties similar to those of military vehicle drivers. They may specialize as tractor-trailer truck drivers, tank truck drivers, heavy truck drivers, or bus drivers.

Opportunities

Each year, the services need new vehicle drivers because of changes in personnel and the demands of the field. After job training, vehicle drivers are assigned to motor pools or motor transport units. They generally work without close supervision. In time, vehicle drivers may advance to supervisory positions assisting in the management of motor transport units.

Services Offering This Occupation

Army

Navy

Air Force

Marine Corps

Coast Guard

WAREHOUSING AND DISTRIBUTION SPECIALISTS

Short Description

The military maintains a large inventory of food, medicines, ammunition, spare parts, and other supplies. Keeping the military's supply system operating smoothly is an important job. The lives of combat troops in the field may depend on receiving the right supplies on time. Warehousing and distribution specialists receive, store, record, and issue military supplies.

What They Do

Warehousing and distribution specialists in the military perform some or all of the following duties:

- Perform inventory and financial management procedures, including ordering, receiving, and storing supplies.
- Locate and catalog stock.
- Give special handling to medicine, ammunition, and other delicate supplies.
- Select the correct stock for issue.
- Load, unload, and move stock, using equipment such as forklifts and hand trucks.
- Keep records on incoming and outgoing stock.

Helpful Attributes

Helpful school subjects include math, bookkeeping, accounting, and business administration. Helpful attributes include

- The ability to keep accurate records
- Interest in operating forklifts and other warehouse equipment

- A preference for physical work
- A preference for work requiring attention to detail

Training Provided

Job training consists of classroom instruction, including practice in handling and storing stock. Further training occurs on the job and through advanced courses. Course content typically includes

- Stock control and accounting procedures
- Procedures for shipping, receiving, storing, and issuing stock
- Procedures for handling medical and food supplies
- Movement, storage, and maintenance of ammunition

Physical Demands

Warehousing and distribution specialists may have to lift and carry heavy boxes of ammunition and other supplies. Normal color vision is required for specialties that handle color-coded parts, supplies, and ammunition.

Work Environment

Warehousing and distribution specialists work in large general supply centers, small specialized supply rooms, or ship storerooms.

Civilian Counterparts

Civilian warehousing and distribution specialists work for factories, parts departments in repair shops, department stores, and government warehouses and stockrooms. They perform duties similar to those of military warehousing and distribution specialists. Civilian warehousing and distribution specialists may also be called stock control clerks, parts clerks, or storekeepers.

Opportunities

Each year, the services need new specialists because of changes in personnel and the demands of the field. After job training, specialists stock shelves, learn about different parts and supplies, and fill supply requests. In time, they also estimate needs, order stock, and supervise others. Eventually, they may become superintendents of supply centers.

Services Offering This Occupation

Army

Navy

Air Force

Marine Corps

Coast Guard

WATER AND SEWAGE TREATMENT PLANT OPERATORS

Short Description

Military bases operate their own water treatment plants when public facilities cannot be used. These plants provide drinking water and safely dispose of sewage. Water and sewage treatment plant operators maintain the systems that purify water and treat sewage.

What They Do

Water and sewage treatment plant operators in the military perform some or all of the following duties:

- Operate pumps to transfer water from reservoirs and storage tanks to treatment plants.
- Add chemicals and operate machinery that purifies water for drinking or cleans it for safe disposal.
- Test water for chlorine content, acidity, oxygen demand, and impurities.
- Regulate the flow of drinking water to meet demand.
- Clean and maintain water treatment machinery.
- Keep records of chemical treatments, water pressure, and maintenance.

Helpful Attributes

Helpful school subjects include chemistry, math, and shop mechanics. Helpful attributes include

- Interest in chemistry and pollution control
- Interest in working with mechanical equipment

Training Provided

Job training consists of classroom instruction, including practice operating water and sewage treatment equipment. Further training occurs on the job and through advanced courses. Course content typically includes

- Operation of treatment systems
- Water testing and analysis

- Maintenance and repair of pumps, compressors, and other equipment

Physical Demands

Normal color vision is needed to examine water for acidity and impurities.

Work Environment

Water and sewage treatment plant operators work indoors and outdoors. They may be exposed to strong odors.

Civilian Counterparts

Civilian water and sewage treatment plant operators work for municipal public works and industrial plants. Their work is similar to that of military water and sewage treatment plant operators. Civilian plant operators usually specialize as water treatment plant operators, waterworks pump station operators, or wastewater treatment plant operators.

Opportunities

Each year, the services need new plant operators because of changes in personnel and the demands of the field. After job training, new operators work under close supervision in water or sewage treatment plants. With experience, they may supervise plant operations. Eventually, they may become base utilities superintendents.

Services Offering This Occupation

Army

Navy

Air Force

Marine Corps

Coast Guard

WEAPONS MAINTENANCE TECHNICIANS

Short Description

Combat forces use many different types of weapons, from small field artillery to large ballistic missiles. Weapons may be fired from ships, planes, and ground stations. Most modern weapons have electronic components and systems that assist in locating targets, aiming weapons, and firing them. Weapons maintenance technicians maintain and repair weapons used by combat forces.

What They Do

Weapons maintenance technicians in the military perform some or all of the following duties:

- Repair and maintain artillery, naval gun systems, and infantry weapons.
- Clean and lubricate gyroscopes, sights, and other electro-optical fire control components.
- Repair and maintain missile mounts, platforms, and launch mechanisms.
- Test and adjust weapons firing, guidance, and launch systems.

Helpful Attributes

Helpful school subjects include science and math. Helpful attributes include

- The ability to do work requiring accuracy and attention to detail
- Interest in working with electronic or electrical equipment
- Interest in working with weapons

Training Provided

Job training consists of classroom instruction and practical experience. Training length varies depending upon specialty. Further training occurs on the job and through advanced courses. Course content typically includes

- Electronic and mechanical principles and concepts
- Use of schematics, drawings, blueprints, and wiring diagrams
- Operation, testing, and maintenance of weapons systems and fire control systems

Physical Demands

Some specialties involve moderate to heavy lifting. Normal color vision is required to read color-coded charts and diagrams.

Work Environment

Weapons maintenance technicians work in workshops when testing and repairing electronic components. They may work outdoors while inspecting and repairing combat vehicles, ships, artillery, aircraft, and missile silos.

Civilian Counterparts

Civilian weapons maintenance technicians work for firms that design, build, and test weapons systems for the military. They perform duties similar to those of military weapons maintenance technicians. They may also be called avionics technicians, electronic mechanics, or missile facilities repairers.

Opportunities

Each year, the services need new technicians because of changes in personnel and the demands of the field. After job training, technicians are assigned to weapons operations or maintenance units. They perform routine maintenance and work under close supervision. With experience, they may work more independently and train new personnel. Eventually, they may become managers of missile facilities, avionics, or electronics maintenance units or shops.

Services Offering This Occupation

Army

Navy

Air Force

Marine Corps

Coast Guard

WELDERS AND METALWORKERS
Short Description

Sheet metal is used as a building material in many military construction projects. Ships, tanks, and aircraft are made of heavy metal armor. Welders and metalworkers make and install sheet metal products, such as roofs, air ducts, gutters, and vents. They also make custom parts to repair the structural parts of ships, submarines, landing craft, buildings, and equipment.

What They Do

Welders and metalworkers in the military perform some or all of the following duties:

- Weld, braze, or solder metal parts together.
- Repair automotive and ship parts using welding equipment.
- Measure work with calipers, micrometers, and rulers.

Helpful Attributes

Helpful school subjects include auto mechanics and industrial arts. Helpful attributes include

- Interest in working with repair tools
- A preference for physical work

Training Provided

Job training consists of classroom instruction. Training length varies depending upon specialty. Further training occurs on the job and through advanced courses. Course content typically includes

- Sheet metal layout and duct work
- Procedures for cutting, brazing, and heat treating
- Operation and care of welding, soldering, and brazing equipment

Physical Demands

Welders and metalworkers may have to lift heavy metal parts and work in crouching or kneeling positions. Good color vision is required for locating and marking reference points, setting and adjusting welding equipment, and matching paints.

Work Environment

Welders and metalworkers work indoors in metalworking shops and aircraft hangars. They also work outdoors at construction sites, on ships, and in the field.

Civilian Counterparts

Civilian welders and metalworkers may work for metal repair shops, auto repair shops, construction companies, pipeline companies, aircraft manufacturing plants, shipyards, and marine servicing companies. They perform duties similar to those of military welders and metal workers.

Opportunities

Each year, the services need new welders and metalworkers because of changes in personnel and the demands of the field. After job training, welders and metal workers begin to make and repair metal equipment under the direction of a supervisor. With experience, they may become managers of repair shops, maintenance depots, or shipyards.

Services Offering This Occupation

Army
Navy
Air Force
Marine Corps
Coast Guard